EFFICIENT DECISION SUPPORT SYSTEMS – PRACTICE AND CHALLENGES IN BIOMEDICAL RELATED DOMAIN

Edited by **Chiang S. Jao**

Efficient Decision Support Systems – Practice and Challenges in Biomedical Related Domain
Edited by Chiang S. Jao

Published by InTech
Janeza Trdine 9, 51000 Rijeka, Croatia

Publishing Process Manager Petra Zobic

Technical Editor Teodora Smiljanic

Cover Designer InTech Design Team

Additional hard copies can be obtained from orders@intechopen.com

Efficient Decision Support Systems – Practice and Challenges in Biomedical Related Domain, Edited by Chiang S. Jao
p. cm.
ISBN 978-953-307-258-6

For EU product safety concerns:
IN TECH d.o.o., Prolaz Marije Krucifikse Kozulić 3, 51000 Rijeka, Croatia, info@intechopen.com or visit our website at intechopen.com.

Meet the editor

Chiang S. Jao, Ph.D., is chief biomedical informaticist with Tranformation Inc. based in Maryland. He has been involved medical informatics since coming to University of Illinois at Chicago in 1992 to work on clinical decision support systems. His research was awarded the grant from National Patient Safety Foundation in investigating the matching of prescribing medications and clinical problems in electronic heath records. He was the visiting scholar in the Lister Hill National Center for Biomedical Communications, National Library of Medicine and built a standard drug-problem database based on authoritative information from approved drug package inserts. He has extensive experience as a software consultant to healthcare institutions. He is a senior member of the Institute of Electrical and Electronic Engineers (IEEE) and the American Medical Informatics Association (AMIA).

Contents

Preface XI

Part 1 Barriers, Challenges, Impacts, and Success Factors of System Adoption 1

Chapter 1 **Challenges in Developing Effective Clinical Decision Support Systems 3**
Kamran Sartipi, Norman P. Archer and Mohammad H. Yarmand

Chapter 2 **Impacts and Risks of Adopting Clinical Decision Support Systems 21**
Wilfred Bonney

Chapter 3 **Success Factors and Barriers for Implementation of Advanced Clinical Decision Support Systems 31**
Anne-Marie J.W. Scheepers-Hoeks, Rene J. Grouls, Cees Neef, Eric W. Ackerman and Erik H. Korsten

Part 2 Guideline-Based Clinical Decision Support System 45

Chapter 4 **Information Extraction Approach for Clinical Practice Guidelines Representation in a Medical Decision Support System 47**
Fernando Pech-May, Ivan Lopez-Arevalo and Victor J. Sosa-Sosa

Chapter 5 **Guideline-Based Decision Support Systems for Prevention and Management of Chronic Diseases 67**
Niels Peek

Part 3 Applications for Disease Management 87

Chapter 6 **Emerging Information Technologies to Provide Improved Decision Support for Surveillance, Prevention, and Control of Vector-Borne Diseases 89**
Saul Lozano-Fuentes, Christopher M. Barker, Marlize Coleman, Michael Coleman, Bborie Park, William K. Reisen and Lars Eisen

Chapter 7 **Optimization Models, Statistical and DSS Tools for Prevention and Combat of Dengue Disease 115**
Marcos Negreiros, Adilson E. Xavier, Airton F. S. Xavier, Nelson Maculan, Philippe Michelon, José Wellington O. Lima and Luis Odorico M. Andrade

Chapter 8 **A Decision Support System Based on Artificial Neural Networks for Pulmonary Tuberculosis Diagnosis 151**
Carmen Maidantchik, José Manoel de Seixas, Felipe F. Grael, Rodrigo C. Torres, Fernando G. Ferreira, Andressa S. Gomes, José Márcio Faier, Jose Roberto Lapa e Silva, Fernanda C. de Q Mello, Afrânio Kritski and João Baptista de Oliveira e Souza Filho

Part 4 Applications for Medical Procedures 167

Chapter 9 **Temporal Knowledge Generation for Medical Procedures 179**
Aida Kamišalić, David Riaño and Tatjana Welzer

Chapter 10 **Predicting Pathology in Medical Decision Support Systems in Endoscopy of the Gastrointestinal Tract 195**
Michael Liedlgruber and Andreas Uhl

Chapter 11 **Workflow and Clinical Decision Support for Radiation Oncology 215**
Daniel L McShan

Chapter 12 **Computerized Decision Support Systems for Mechanical Ventilation 227**
Fleur T. Tehrani

Chapter 13 **Decision Support Systems in Anesthesia, Emergency Medicine and Intensive Care Medicine 239**
Thomas M. Hemmerling

Chapter 14 **Decision Support by Visual Incidence Anamneses for Increased Patient Safety 263**
Kerstin Ådahl and Rune Gustavsson

Part 5 Miscellaneous Case Studies 287

Chapter 15 **Pharmacoepidemiological Studies Using the Veterans Affairs Decision Support System 289**
Benjamin Wolozin, Austin Lee, Nien-Chen Li and Lewis E. Kazis

Chapter 16 **Decision Support Systems in Animal Health 299**
Nguyen Van Long, Mark Stevenson and Bryan O'Leary

Chapter 17 **Development of an Image Retrieval Model for Biomedical Image Databases 311**
Achimugu Philip, Babajide Afolabi,
Adeniran Oluwaranti and Oluwagbemi Oluwatolani

Preface

Series Preface

This series is directed to diverse managerial professionals who are leading the transformation of individual domains by using expert information and domain knowledge to drive decision support systems (DSSs). The series offers a broad range of subjects addressed in specific areas such as health care, business management, banking, agriculture, environmental improvement, natural resource and spatial management, aviation administration, and hybrid applications of information technology aimed to interdisciplinary issues.

This book series is composed of three volumes: Volume 1 consists of general concepts and methodology of DSSs; Volume 2 consists of applications of DSSs in the biomedical domain; Volume 3 consists of hybrid applications of DSSs in multidisciplinary domains. The book is shaped decision support strategies in the new infrastructure that assists the readers in full use of the creative technology to manipulate input data and to transform information into useful decisions for decision makers. This book series is dedicated to support professionals and series readers in the emerging field of DSS.

Preface

Clinical decision support systems (CDSSs) are computer-based applications that can effectively assist clinical practitioners and healthcare providers in decision making to improve their clinical practice skills and reduce preventable medical errors. A popular example of CDSSs is computerized physician order entry (CPOE) systems that provide patient-specific recommendations, collaborate active problems on the problem list with prescribed medications on the medication list, attach care reminders and alerts to the charts of patients in electronic health records, link laboratory test data to alert physicians while atypical values are detected.

Patient safety was once an emerging field when the Institute of Medicine's (IOM) report ("To Err is Human: Building a Safer Health System") was first released and captured the attention of the healthcare community in late 1999. Many of the errors in the biomedical domain result from a culture and a fragmented system. Evidences from research studies indicated that mistakes were not due to clinicians not trying hard enough; they resulted from inherent shortcomings in the health caring system. Appropriate design of CDSSs assists in reducing such kinds of mistakes and promoting patient safety.

Book Volume 2 extends the concepts and methodology of decision support systems (DSS) mentioned in Book Volume 1 to the applications of CDSS in the biomedical-related domain. This book collects a variety of topics that cover design and development of CDSS applications. It can be used as a textbook in formal courses or a reference book for practitioners. The readers will gain in-depth knowledge about the applications of CDSSs to detect/prevent specific diseases, to facilitate medical procedures during operations, and to collaborate the knowledge of biomedical domain experts for making better decisions.

Section 1, including Chapter 1 through 3, illustrates challenges, impacts, risks and success factors in developing and adopting a DSS in the clinical domain. Chapter 1 and 2 explore challenges, impacts and risks in developing and adopting effective CDSS. Chapter 3 presents potential success factors and barriers of implementing advanced CDSS. These findings assist decision makers in identifying potential bottlenecks about the development and assessment of a useful CDSS. It is evident that the appropriate use of CDSSs with emerging technologies could enhance the adoption and acceptance rate of CDSS in clinical practice.

Section 2, including Chapter 4 and 5, illustrates the applications of CDSS based on clinical practice guidelines (CPG). Chapter 4 highlights the importance of CPG in documenting the clinical diagnosis, prognosis, and treatment of specific diseases. The information extraction approach can connect relevant information in the clinical documents and is critical in enhancing the knowledge acquisition on CPG in CDSS. An experiment was conducted to obtain an intermediate representation of actions from a textual CPG in XML format by means of an information extraction module. Chapter 5 presents a guideline-based CDSS for prevention and management of chronic diseases. The example of an evidence-based conceptual CDSS framework is illustrated how to identify that CDSS can improve CPG implementation by reducing guideline complexity.

Section 3 and 4, including Chapter 6 throughout 14, present extensive applications of CDSS developing to diagnose/treat specific diseases (such as vector-borne diseases and pulmonary tuberculosis) or to operate medical procedures (such as endoscopy and radiation oncology) effectively. In each chapter, the readers are able to identify the use of appropriate CDSS models in individual specialty frameworks. It is noteworthy that Chapter 14 presents the visual incidence anamneses (VIA) tool to improve decision support and process transparency in diagnosing patients using the DSS so as to improve patient safety. The readers are able to recognize the deficiencies of patient safety in health care due to the invisibility of potential causes of incidents, injuries and deaths. The VIA can be supportive to screen out unnecessary alternatives and identify the cause of vulnerable events.

Section 5, including Chapter 15 through 17, present three case studies of CDSS Applications in the field of pharmaco-epidemiology, animal health, and image data retrieval. Chapter 15 introduces the design and execution of pharmaco-epidemiological databases using the Veterans Affairs DSS. The authors employ data mining strategies applied to the DSS database. This study generates the DSS database that led to the outcomes of reducing incidents of given clinical problems related to the use of medications. It is significant that the DSS data can be cross-referenced to Medicare in USA, which can capture some off-plan elements such as nursing home utilization and use of health systems outside the system.

Chapter 16 presents the infrastructure and implementation of an animal health DSS. This chapter covers the current situation of the animal health DSS in developing countries and discusses the issues when the DSS is used to detect emerging diseases in an animal population. Future directions in developing an animal health DSS are also suggested to reduce the cost and alleviate the obstacles for widespread update of this technology.

This book concludes in Chapter 17 that presents an interesting topic about image retrieval for biomedical image databases that support communication among healthcare decision makers and communities at large. A neural network model with backward propagation algorithm is applied to generate expert rules and to improve predictive accuracy. The proposed methodology for image indexing can facilitate efficient retrieval of time-oriented medical images that have direct reliance on medical diagnosis and intervention.

Chiang S. Jao
Transformation, Inc. Rockville
Maryland University of Illinois (Retired) Chicago
Illinois

Part 1

Barriers, Challenges, Impacts, and Success Factors of System Adoption

1

Challenges in Developing Effective Clinical Decision Support Systems

Kamran Sartipi, Norman P. Archer and Mohammad H. Yarmand
McMaster University
Canada

1. Introduction to CDSS

Decision making is one of the most important and frequent aspects of our daily activities. Personal decisions display our characteristics, behavior, successes, failures, and the nature of our personalities. These decisions affect us in different ways, such as reasoning style, relationships, education, purchasing, careers, investments, health, and entertainment. The effectiveness of such decisions is affected by our age, knowledge, environment, economic status, and regulations. Our business related decisions are influenced by our knowledge, experience, and the availability of supporting systems in terms of employed processes, standards and techniques. Due to the importance of decision making, different technologies have been developed to help humans make effective decisions in the shortest time. Current advances in Information and Communication Technology (ICT) have revolutionized the way people communicate, share information, and make effective decisions.

Decision making is a complex intellectual task that uses assistance from different resources. In the past, such resources were restricted to personal knowledge, experience, logic, and human mentors. However, the norms of current society and existing technologies have enhanced critical decision making. Educational systems are not restricted to physical classrooms any more; on-line education is gradually taking over. Knowledge about a technical domain can be obtained easily using Internet search engines and free on-line scientific articles. Mentorship has expanded from colleagues and friends to a large community of domain experts through subject-specific social networking facilities. Moreover, due to ubiquitous wireless communication technologies, such facilities are also accessible from small and remote communities. As a result, technology and different web-based tools (browse and search, document sharing, data mining, maps, data bases, web services) can be utilized as computing support for people, to help them make more knowledgeable and effective decisions.

The healthcare domain has recently embraced new information and communication technologies to improve the quality of healthcare delivery and medical services. This long overdue opportunity is expected to reduce high costs and medical errors in patient diagnosis and treatment; enhance the way healthcare providers interact; increase personal health knowledge of the public; improve the availability and quality of health services; and promote collaborative and patient-centric healthcare services. To meet demands arising from these improved services, new tools, methods, and business models must emerge.

Clinical Decision Support Systems (CDSS) are defined as computer applications that assist practitioners and healthcare providers in decision making, through timely access to electronically stored medical knowledge, in order to improve their medical practices. For example, with the recent increased focus on the prevention of medical errors, Computer-based Physician Order Entry (CPOE) systems enhanced by CDSS have been proposed as a key element in improving patient safety (Berner, 2007).

An "effective" CDSS must also take into consideration the working environment of the practitioners and care providers. Hence such a CDSS should: not interfere with professional authority; recognize the context of the user and adapt itself accordingly; manage different types of information and interruptions that may affect the physician; save operating cost and time; be easy to use; adhere to medical guidelines provided by evidence-based research and practice; and support a patient-centric and collaborative decision making environment.

Clinical Decision Support Systems (CDSS) are specialized forms of general Decision Support Systems (DSS) that have been applied in many other domains. Research in decision support systems for organizational decision making began in the late 1950s, and research in the more technical aspects started in the 1960s (Keen & Morton, 1978). Scott Morton (1971) was one of the first researchers to coin the term decision support systems (Eom & Kim, 2006). Since then, major advances in computer technology have contributed to the application of DSS in many different disciplines and problem domains. In particular, advances in information technology infrastructure, data processing, microcomputers, networks, and human computer interactions have influenced DSS developments. Use of the Internet has enhanced DSS in terms of efficiency, widespread usage, and the employment of typical web browsers as user interface components. Recent advances in wireless communication technology and mobile devices have resulted in many new applications for decision support systems in daily activities (Shim et al., 2002).

The structure of this chapter is as follows. Section 2 provides an overview of different techniques and standards for representing clinical knowledge and information, with an emphasis on international standards such as HL7. Section 3 explores the nature of data mining techniques in assisting clinicians to diagnose illnesses and communicating the results of data mining. Section 4 discusses the influence of modern technologies and ad hoc web-application integration techniques to make collaborative decisions. Section 5 discusses the importance of user context and customizable software agents at the client platform. Section 6 provides a set of approaches to evaluate the success or failure of existing techniques, with a focus on business aspects and user adoption. In Section 7 the authors propose some research ideas that might contribute to the future development of more effective and acceptable clinical decision support systems. Section 8 provides several models and techniques from different fields that are used to support CDSS. Finally, Section 9 summarizes conclusions from this chapter.

2. Clinical knowledge and information representation

In a nutshell, a decision support system consists of the following components: i) knowledge base to store, maintain and retrieve knowledge from the relevant domain; ii) inference engine to retrieve the relevant knowledge from the knowledge base and interpret the knowledge to infer a decision; and iii) user support to interact with the user in a meaningful and natural way, with operations for data entry, representation, and result output. Such a system can also be improved by adding a history of the previous decisions, which is dynamically updated when new decisions are made.

We will discuss knowledge representation in this section. The inference engine is represented by different models and techniques that will be discussed in Section 8. The user support component is mostly designed with web-based Graphical User Interfaces (GUI); however since this component has a major impact on the effectiveness of a CDSS, it requires particular attention from the research community.

Knowledge should be represented formally so that it can be efficiently processed. Such representation should be: human and machine readable; accurate in specifying domain knowledge; and portable and reusable among organizations (Verlaene et al., 2007). In general, knowledge representation methods can be categorized as *declarative* (using propositions and sentences), and *procedural* (explicitly defining the actions to be taken) (Aleksovska-Stojkovska & Loskovska, 2010).

According to (Kong et al., 2008) four categories of knowledge representation are: i) *Logical conditions*: where variables and their valid ranges are provided and variable values are verified against their ranges; Boolean operators are used to specify more complicated cases. ii) *Rules*: expressed by if-then-else statements which emulate human reasoning processes; nesting statements are used for more complex cases. iii) *Graphs*: including decision trees and artificial neural networks. iv) *Structures*: high level categorization of relevant knowledge that allows focused observation of each of the healthcare sub-domains.

A major source of medical knowledge for decision making in a diagnosis or treatment process is the *medical or clinical guidelines* which have been used throughout the history of medicine. Modern clinical guidelines are developed based on rigorous studies of the medical literature and are based on consensus and evidence in medical research and practice. Such guidelines are represented as rules or flow charts and may include the computation algorithms to be followed. Guideline engines are used to execute the clinical guidelines in the context of Electronic Medical Record (EMR) systems. The GuideLine Interchange Format (GLIF) (Collaboratory, 2004) is a computer representation format for clinical guidelines that can be used for developing interoperable flow-based guidelines to be executed by such engines.

Another source of medical knowledge is the *clinical terminology systems* which allow healthcare professionals to use widely agreed sets of terms and concepts for communicating clinical information among healthcare professionals around the world for the purposes of diagnosis, prognosis, and treatment of diseases. A clinical terminology system facilitates identifying and accessing information pertaining to the healthcare process and hence improves the provision of healthcare services by care providers. The (*Systematized Nomenclature of Medicine Clinical Terminology (SNOMED CT)*, 2011) is a comprehensive clinical terminology system that provides clinical content and expressiveness for clinical documentation and reporting. It can be used to code, retrieve, and analyze clinical data. The terminology is comprised of concepts, terms and relationships with the objective of precisely representing clinical information across the scope of healthcare. SNOMED CT uses healthcare software applications that focus on the collection of clinical data, linking to clinical knowledge bases and information retrieval, as well as data aggregation and exchange.

A number of tools exist that support knowledge construction during the CDSS development process. Four important tools are introduced here. **UMLS** - Unified Medical Language System is a repository of biomedical vocabularies which integrates over 2 million names for some 900 000 concepts from more than 60 families of biomedical vocabularies, as well as 12 million relations among these concepts (Bodenreider, 2004). **Protege** is an ontology editor and knowledge-base framework that provides a suite of tools to construct domain models using frames and the Web Ontology Language (OWL) (*Protege website*, 2011). **GLARE** is used to acquire, represent, and execute clinical guidelines. It provides consistency checking and temporal and hypothetical reasoning (Anselma et al., 2011). **PROforma** is a formal knowledge representation language for specifying clinical guidelines in a machine executable format.

Each guideline is expressed as a set of tasks, where a task can be of type: *plan* - contains any number of tasks; *decision* - taken at a point where options are presented; *action*: medical procedure; or *inquiry* - request for further information (*Open Clinical: PROforma website*, 2011).

2.1 HL7 v3 reference information modeling

Health Level Seven (HL7) (*Health Level Seven official website*, 2011) is an international community of healthcare experts and information scientists collaborating to create standards for the exchange, management and integration of electronic healthcare information. HL7 also refers to internationally accepted standards for healthcare information. Over the two decades since its inception, HL7 has undergone an evolutionary process starting from version 2.1 to its current version 3 (v3). HL7 v3 was a complete overhaul of its predecessor and was designed with consistency and comprehensive coverage in mind. It supports a wide range of areas such as patient care, patient administration, laboratory, pharmacy, diagnostic imaging, surgical procedures, insurance, accounting and clinical decision support systems. While all these topics are related, each of them has unique features and information requirements that need to be addressed by the standard. Furthermore, HL7 v3 uses several standard clinical terminology systems such as SNOMED and LOINC to represent information content. HL7 v3 uses Reference Information Model (RIM), a large class diagram representation of the clinical data. HL7 v3 applies object-oriented development methodology to RIM and its extensions to create standard message content.

The HL7 refinement process uses RIM class diagrams, HL7-specified vocabulary domains, and data type specifications, and applies refinement rules to these base standards to generate information structures for HL7 v3 messages. The message development process consists of applying constraints to a pair of base specifications, i.e., *HL7 RIM* and *HL7 Vocabulary Domains*, and the extension of those specifications to create representations constrained to address a specific healthcare requirement.

We now refer to the artifacts generated in the refinement process. The Domain Message Information Model (D-MIM) is a subset of RIM that includes a fully expanded set of class clones, attributes and relationships that are used to create messages for any particular domain. The Refined Message Information Model (R-MIM) is used to express the information content for one or more messages within a domain. Each R-MIM is a subset of the D-MIM and contains only those classes, attributes and associations required to compose the set of messages. Hierarchical Message Description (HMD) is a tabular representation of the sequence of elements (i.e., classes, attributes and associations) represented in an R-MIM. Each HMD produces a single base message template from which the specific HL7 v3 message types are drawn (*Health Level Seven Ballot*, 2011; HL7, 1999).

3. Data mining and interoperability in CDSS

In this section, we describe a set of related techniques that demonstrate the role of data mining in discovering important hidden patterns among clinical data. In this case, association mining using *concept lattice analysis* discovers groups of diseases, symptoms, and signs that are highly associated. These groups assist the physician in disease diagnosis process. We further discuss how such important patterns of relationships (we call them *mined-knowledge*) can be transported to the point of use, where such knowledge can be incorporated into decision support systems to enhance physician decision making activity. We also present the supporting standards and infrastructure that allow such collaboration among heterogeneous systems. *Data mining* is the process of analyzing data from different perspectives to extract information and hidden patterns that are useful for planning and configuration purposes. Technologies from various domains such as statistics, data warehousing, and artificial intelligence support data mining activities. Chapter 3 in the book by (Berner, 2007) discusses the applications of data mining in CDSS.

3.1 Concept lattice analysis in diagnostic process

The following discussion is based on (Yousefi et al., 2009). The exploration nature of the association based data mining techniques (e.g., concept lattice analysis) in a diagnostic process simulates the normal process that a practitioner follows in clinical practice. On a daily basis, physicians encounter complex clinical scenarios where they compare a set of clinical observations in the form of symptoms and signs, with those they know based on their medical knowledge and experience, in order to make accurate disease diagnoses. In this context, the patient history from the EMR is also used as complementary information to clinical observations. The approach takes advantage of the automatic extraction of patterns from a patient EMR system using concept lattice analysis and uses a ranking mechanism to indicate the degree of relevancy of the clinical observation to each member of the identified group of diseases. *Syndrome* is a set of signs and symptoms which tend to occur together and reflect the presence of a particular disease. There are a large number of major clinical syndromes that can be modeled according to this technique. As a case study, the authors modeled a syndromic approach to *Fever of Unknown Origin* (FUO) due to its importance and complexity in the medical domain. There are a large number of cases with FUO which are undiagnosed despite hospitalization, costly paraclinic requests and invasive procedures. The authors have modeled FUO as an example of a major clinical syndrome. The case study modeled 45 diseases and 64 common symptoms and signs associated with FUO from a heavily cited medical reference by (Mandell et al., 2004). In this approach, a Concept Explorer tool (*Formal concept analysis toolkit version 1.3*, 2009) was used to illustrate the *context table* and *concept lattice* which present the relations among the diseases and their associated symptoms and signs in a large lattice consisting of 499 concept nodes. The concept lattice can be used as follows. During a patient visit, the physician observes and records the patient symptoms and signs, and consults the patient EMR to obtain other possible symptoms that may be relevant to the current visit. The tool then compares this set of symptoms and signs with those of different concepts in the concept lattice. The concepts with the highest overlap of symptoms and signs are then retrieved and a ranked list of the diseases within the concepts is presented to the physician. The physician uses his/her discretion to identify which disease within the provided concepts would be the best match with the patient's situation. The authors discuss a case of an elderly female patient who had a fever for four days with other symptoms such as anorexia, malaise, non productive cough, night sweats, and chill. Using the approach described, four diseases were suggested to the physician: Tuberculosis, Sarcoidosis, Lymphoma, and Recurrent Pulmonary Emboli, where the latter was found to have the highest overlap with the patient's symptoms.

3.2 Interoperability of mined-knowledge for CDSS

The details of this technique were presented in (Sherafat & K. Sartipi, 2010). Currently, decision making knowledge within most guideline modeling languages are represented by basic logical expressions. However, the results of data mining analyses from healthcare data can be employed as a source of knowledge to improve decision making. A CDSS can interact with practitioners and electronic medical records systems to receive patient data as input and provide reminders, alerts, or recommendations for patient diagnosis, treatment, long-term care planning, and the like. A CDSS requires access to healthcare data and knowledge that are stored in data and knowledge bases. Since these repositories normally have diverse internal representations, data and knowledge interoperability are major issues. To achieve data interoperability, two systems that participate in data communication must use the same vocabulary set, data model, and data interpretation mechanism. On the other hand, knowledge interoperability refers to the ability of healthcare information systems to incorporate and interpret the knowledge that is produced in other systems. Here, we focus on encoding, sharing, and using the results of data mining analyses for clinical decision making at the point of care.

The proposed approach relies on adoption of standards to encode healthcare data and knowledge. In an off-line operation, existing healthcare databases (i.e., EMRs) are mined using different mining techniques to extract and store clinical mined-knowledge. In order to make this knowledge portable it is encoded in the form of a data mining model using a specialized XML-based standard, namely Predictive Model Markup Language (PMML) (DMG, 2010). Also, it is necessary for the patient data that are stored in EMR systems to be encoded using a specialized XML-based standard, namely Clinical Data Architecture (CDA) (HL7, 2005) so the data can be ported between heterogeneous systems. At the point of care, a decision module accesses and operates on both data and knowledge in order to make patient-specific interpretations of the knowledge available to the healthcare practitioner. Within the CDSS we adopt a flow-oriented clinical guideline modeling language GLIF3 (Collaboratory, 2004) to specify the overall decision making process. In this context, at different states of the flow-oriented guideline the CDSS accesses patient data by querying the EMR. Moreover, to perform knowledge-based decision making, the CDSS supplies patient data to the decision modules and receives the results of applying mined-knowledge to the patient data. Finally, healthcare personnel receive comments, recommendations, or alerts through interaction with the CDSS system, allowing them to make more knowledgeable decisions based on system-provided information.

3.3 Interoperability of clinical information and concept

The details of this technique were presented in (Jayaratna & Sartipi, 2009). A key objective of effective healthcare delivery is to facilitate seamless integration among heterogeneous applications, to provide a unified view of information to health practitioners and other stakeholders. Achieving such flawless integration requires interoperability among data sources serving the applications. This can only be achieved through standardization of information exchange and representation. The HL7 Reference Information Model (RIM) was introduced in Section 2.1. HL7 v3 based integration of systems requires an expert in medical domain who is also familiar with HL7 v3 standards and documentation. Hence, such an integration process is expensive, slow, and expert-based. In the following, we present a framework to support HL7 v3 message extraction for standard compliant integration projects, based on Semantic Web (SW) technologies.

We have observed that the existing HL7 domain model does not facilitate efficient discovery of HL7 v3 messages due to overlaps and disconnects among the domains. Therefore, we developed a more intuitive and finer categorization for HL7 domains, namely *contexts*, which consist of 50 contexts to represent areas of healthcare that superimpose well with actual healthcare transactions. Each HL7 v3 message was associated with a single context. Context acts as a key piece of metadata in the search tool. Next, we classified HL7 messages into a hierarchy of classes based on the purpose of the messages they convey. This classification has been designed to be intuitive and general enough so that it could also be used to formally express a clinical transaction. In the following, the steps for the message extraction process are discussed.

- *Step 1: Integration Requirements Analysis.* This step consists of: i) Storyboards which are a set of scenarios in the health domain written by health professionals in their own terminology. ii) *Context extraction*, where the tool searches storyboard text to create possible semantic maps between the Contexts and the words and phrases in the text. Within the tool, each Context has been annotated with Cognitive Synonyms that describe it. WordNet and SNOMED vocabularies were used to incorporate as many cognitive synonyms and phrases needed to describe each Context. iii) *Identify transaction initiators*, where each initiator starts a message in a sequence of messages that complete a transaction. Transaction initiators can be easily identified manually from storyboard text, while adhering to the obtained Contexts.
- *Step 2: Structured transaction generation.* Each transaction initiator is then structured according to the proposed transaction schema so it is in machine readable format.
- *Step 3: Mapping.* This step consists of: i) *Message mapping*, where structured transactions are entered into the tool, and the tool's advanced semantic search feature searches the main artifact repository to find a matching message. ii) *Vocabulary mapping*, which converts local terms into standard terminology codes for transmission. The tool integrates with terminology systems SNOMED and LOINC to search for the most appropriate code for a particular legacy clinical term. Data fields extracted during Step 1 are used as search criteria.

4. Collaborative decision making

In this section, we discuss the influence of modern technologies in social networks and ad hoc web application integration techniques to form focused groups of specialists to make collaborative decisions about a critically ill patient. Such an environment integrates different facilities for collecting patient records from the Electronic Health Record (EHR) system according to the case at hand and allows clinicians, nurses, and other support staff to communicate asynchronously through email, text messaging, and video conferencing. The platform will support conversations, collaborative decisions, etc. in a secure data center and will issue reminders and follow-ups to the group and the patient.

In current healthcare systems, patients are often not active participants in their treatment; instead they rely on the practitioner who guides the diagnosis and treatment process. This process is not particularly effective as the patient may not be interested in the process, but just in a favorable outcome, i.e., a successful treatment. With the advent and popularity of social networking, people tend to form groups with special interests and share information and knowledge. This allows different patients with the same health related subject of interest to form small communities to share their experiences, augment their knowledge, and mutually encourage themselves to be more involved in their treatment process (Bos et al., 2008). Current Personal Health Record (PHR) systems help patients to be more aware of their treatment processes and to obtain information about their health. However, future PHR systems will allow more patient involvement through improved user interfaces to access their own healthcare data and sophisticated services through new features empowered by Web 2.0 technologies (*Oreilly Web 2.0 Books*, 2011).

A Mashup (Abiteboul et al., 2008) is a Web 2.0 technology which is gaining popularity for developing complex applications by combining data, presentations, and applications from different sources to create a new web application. The approach is new and is still being enhanced. However, the need for fast and easy development of ad hoc web based applications has caused a large number of Mashups to be developed that are organized into different categories (*ProgrammableWeb Web site*, 2011). Such characteristics make Mashups an ideal tool for non-critical web-based data management applications, since they can be developed in a short time, with very little programming skill. The goal of a Mashup is to provide a means to utilize a large number of web based applications and heterogeneous data sources in a unified representation. However, Mashups do not meet the hard constraints imposed by application domains that incorporate sensitive data, real-time operations, or mission critical tasks.
An example of a Mashup, namely MedickIT, is presented by (Abiteboul et al., 2008), and it consists of six components (or Mashlets). These Mashlets can be GUI-based components (i.e., widgets) or web services. The MedickIT consists of six Mashlets: an Electronic Health Record viewer, a map widget, a calendar, a medical search engine, an SMS, and a medical data analyzer. Such a Mashup allows a patient to access his/her medical data through the EMR; retrieve a doctor appointment from the calendar and drag it into the map to see the location of the doctor's office, or drag it into the SMS widget so that a phone call is initiated to remind the patient about forthcoming doctor appointments. Such a Mashup will allow the patient to gain more control over his/her health information. Depending on the needs of the patient, other combinations of Mashlets are feasible.
The (*IBM Mash up Center*, 2011) is an end-to-end enterprise Mashup platform that supports rapid assembly of dynamic web applications with management, security, and governance capabilities. It allows both nontechnical users and IT personnel to develop complex applications. In the case of collaborative healthcare delivery, an ad hoc case-specific team of local and remote professionals can be formed which consists of doctors, nurses, administrative and support staff. The team can communicate and brainstorm through the e-conferencing widget, access the patient's EMR record, obtain reports of the patient's risk factors by consulting with a CDSS tool, and make collaborative diagnostic decisions for the patient.

5. Challenges in future CDSS

In this section, we discuss some challenges that designers of future clinical decision support systems face. Such challenges include better interactions with users to understand their work context, and utilizing customizable computer agents in the client platform. In general, user-centric and collaborative features of CDSS systems impose higher levels of abstraction and more intelligent service-based computing at both the application and middle-ware layers.

5.1 Customizable and context-based CDSS

The current state of CDSS web applications is represented by the services that require extra knowledge and expertise from a normal user to take advantage of the available features and operations of these services. Given the large variety of web applications as Mashups and the tight time schedules of users, they will have to limit themselves to a minimum set of available service features. This is also the case in using other types of computerized systems such as automobile gadgets, home appliances and entertainment centers. In other words, the proper and efficient use of computerized systems (embedded or software based) requires an extended level of knowledge in different application domains. The user interaction capabilities of these systems tend to be sophisticated and hence these systems act as effective *user assistants* by providing different types of information to assist users in performing their tasks. However, domain knowledge and expertise are still needed by users.

The next generation of CDSS systems will become even more sophisticated when the required expertise is incorporated as part of the system's functionality. For example, instead of expecting users of a collaborative CDSS that uses a Mashup service to understand the details and the operational steps needed to use the specialized web application, the web service itself should act as an expert. This expert would consult with the user to provide an effective and customized use of operations according to the user's specific context information. This would provide an opportunity for the user to employ an expert software agent for managing web assets and performing the desired tasks with minimum effort and time. Such a software agent would support smart interactions with the system by the user. Such customizable software agents are resident at the client platform (as opposed to mobile agents that can move among different platforms) with a customizable architecture that receives a set of well-defined tasks in order to become expert and serve the user. The proposed customizable software agents would add to current traditional services, which receive a client's request for a service, perform the service at the provider's platform, and return the results to the user. In the following, the steps for using such a client-based customizable expert agent are presented:

- **Step 1: identifying user context**. Context refers to any information that can be used to characterize the situation of a service requester or provider. We define a context as a tuple: <User, Role, User Location, Server Location, Time of Day, Team, Delegation, Requested Profile Status, Service Invocation Type, Requested Data Type, Login/Logout Event>. This context information is monitored dynamically to feed a database of context logs which will be used during the service selection.
- **Step 2: selecting the required task**. The user (e.g., a physician) asks for a specific task and the required expertise needed for assistance. By mining the context logs (Step 1) and consulting with a web registry, a client proxy obtains a list of relevant services to perform the task, and generates a list that ranks them according to their capabilities and any associated charges. The user then selects an appropriate service, which best matches with the situation. In this context, the web registry must possess a list of application domains such as: banking, insurance, healthcare, telephone, airline, government, etc.; as well as a list of tasks within each domain, such as: PHR viewer, medication administrator, medical data analyzer, and medical search engine, within the healthcare domain.
- **Step 3: delegating expertise to the client**. After selecting the required task, the client proxy retrieves the service descriptions of the selected service and invokes the service from the provider's platform. Instead of performing the requested task for the client, the provider will send a set of instructions to the client where the customizable expert agent will customize itself to serve the physician in an interactive clinical decision activity.

We have already applied the above architecture in several projects, including a customizable virtual remote nurse (Najafi et al., 2011), web service composition (Najafi & Sartipi, 2010), and web service selection tasks.

6. Evaluation of techniques, adoption, and success of CDSS

The four key functions of CDSS were outlined by (Perreault & Metzger, 1999), as follows: i) *Administrative*: supporting clinical coding and documentation, authorization of procedures, and referrals; ii) *Managing clinical complexity and details*: keeping patients on chemotherapy protocols, tracking orders, referrals follow-up, and preventive care; iii) *Cost control*: monitoring medication orders, avoiding duplicate or unnecessary tests; and iv) *Decision support*: supporting clinical diagnosis and treatment plan processes and promoting use of best practices, condition-specific guidelines, and population-based management. These functions are not necessarily logically separable, so they are addressed in a relatively all-inclusive manner in this section.

In some cases, a CDSS may not need to be justified through improved patient outcomes because these systems are designed to influence healthcare providers and it is necessary only to demonstrate changes in clinician performance (Balas & Boren, 2007). But in many cases relationships between process and outcome is unclear (such as personal electronic medical records used by patients for self-management of certain chronic illnesses). However, in order to compete for scarce resources in the healthcare environment, developers must demonstrate the relevance of their systems to healthcare quality improvement and cost control. This requires evaluation approaches that are convincing to potential users, and focused on differences in the process or care outcomes involving the use of the CDSS (Balas & Boren, 2007).

CDSS vendors often claim that their systems can directly improve clinical decisions. A wide variety of approaches and methodologies are available to assess these claims, ranging from controlled clinical trials to use of questionnaires and interviews with users. Techniques that are used should be based on fundamental principles and methods from cognitive science and usability engineering, where human computer interaction and usability in both laboratory and natural environments are examined. Methods can and should include the formative evaluation of systems during iterative development, and can also complement traditional summative assessment methods for completed systems (Kushniruk & Patel, 2004). CDSS designers may prefer to use benchmark tests, surveys, and historical control comparisons (before-after studies) to indicate improvements in quality due to the use of a new system. But benchmark tests only measure a system's technical performance, and do not indicate the system's impact on processes or outcomes of care. User opinion surveys can only provide indirect information about system impact. Before-after studies may provide useful information, but analysis of databases or historical control groups of patients cannot replace planned clinical experimentation. Randomized Controlled clinical Trials (RCTs) are generally recognized as the gold standard for determining the efficacy of computerized information systems in patient care. There are many types of randomized clinical trials but the basic principles are the same: prospective and contemporaneous monitoring of the effect of a randomly allocated intervention (Balas & Boren, 2007).

One dissenter is (Kaplan, 2001) who suggests that Randomized Controlled clinical Trials (RCTs) are not suited to determining whether and/or how systems will be used. In particular, since CDSS are not yet widely used, it is important to develop evaluation techniques that will determine why this is the case, even for systems that seem to offer a great deal of promise for clinical support. Kaplan proposes a 4C approach that focuses on communication, control, care, and context, an approach that can be used for evaluating other types of clinical systems. For a fuller understanding of system operations, it is important to investigate social, cultural, organizational, cognitive, and other contextual concerns that can increase the understanding of other influences that affect systems application development and deployment.

In a systematic review of controlled clinical trials of CDSS systems on physician performance and patient outcomes in 1998, (Johnston et al., 1994) studied 68 controlled trials, and found that 43 of the 65 that evaluated physician performance showed a benefit, and six of 14 studies assessing patient outcomes found an improvement. Their basic conclusions were that CDSS can enhance physician clinical performance for drug dosing, preventive care, and other aspects of medical care, but not convincingly for diagnosis and that there was not yet sufficient evidence to determine the effects of CDSS on patient outcomes. In a 2005 followup review of 100 studies, (Garg et al., 2005) found that improved practitioner performance was associated with CDSS that automatically prompted users to activate the system, or when the study authors actually developed the CDSS. However, there were still not enough studies of patient outcomes available, so the impact on patient outcomes was not clear. RCTs do have limitations, since they can test only hypotheses about certain aspects of computer systems. RCT studies need to identify the conditions to be treated, interventions to be tested, and outcome variables to be measured. The results can then be regarded as specific, interpretable, and useful for practical purposes (Balas & Boren, 2007).

Measuring and managing user attitudes toward various aspects of information systems is important in showing that computer systems are successful, since success is not possible without gaining the support of practitioners. Questionnaires can be used to measure user attitudes to the system. A critical success criterion for the usefulness of a system is how users react to various system aspects. Overall high satisfaction levels usually result in users adapting their activities to take advantage of the system. If satisfaction levels are low, users may actually become antagonistic and sabotage the system, or develop workarounds that avoid using the system.

Randomized controlled trials have shown that there are four generic information interventions that can make a significant difference in patient care (patient education, treatment planning, physician and patient reminders) (Balas et al., 1996). It is therefore important to incorporate these information services into any CDSS that will be used for primary care, in order to improve its effectiveness.

Following are three examples that demonstrate the diversity of methods for implementing and evaluating CDSS that all include the modern approach of using some form of a parallel development and evaluation process.

- (Trafton et al., 2010) developed and implemented a CDSS using iterative evaluation throughout system analysis, design, development, implementation, including simulation and in-clinic assessments of usability for providers followed by targeted system revisions. Volunteers that evaluated the system at particular times provided detailed feedback that was used to guide improvements in the graphical user interface, system content, and design changes that increased clinical usefulness, understandability, clinical workflow fit, and ease of completing recommended practices according to specific guidelines. These revisions led to improved CDSS usability ratings over time, including attention to other practice concerns outside the scope of the CDSS.
- One of the anticipated benefits from Computerized Physician Order Entry (CPOE) systems is the reduction of medication errors, but only a minority of hospitals have successfully implemented such systems. Physician resistance and frustration with such systems have been barriers to their use. An innovative approach to improve adoption and to realize the full benefits of such systems is to involve nurses in the order entry process in order to reduce physician data entry workload and resistance. (Kazemi et al., 2010) investigated whether a collaborative order entry method consisting of Nurse Order Entry (NOE) followed by physician verification and countersignature was as effective as a strictly Physician Order Entry (POE) method in reducing dose and frequency medication errors in a neonatal ward. They found a significant reduction in medication errors during the NOE

period compared to the POE approach. The additional benefit to using such an approach is that physicians no longer have to participate in data entry, helping to overcome this barrier to CPOE use.

- A good example of modern CDSS development is provided in a paper by (Leslie et al., 2005). This work focused on the development and evaluation of a CDSS to assist physicians in treating patients with chronic heart failure, and provides definitive support for the concept of iterative evaluation during CDSS development (Trafton et al., 2010) combined with a multidisciplinary approach to organizational and social aspects of the system environment (Kaplan, 2001). The CDSS was developed after discussions with a multidisciplinary panel, and evaluation took place during three stages over a 6 month period that involved an editorial check, interviews with potential users, and educational meetings with users. The process resulted in several changes to the CDSS at different stages of evaluation and development. Trends were found when comparing the CDSS with paper guidelines. GPs scored less well but junior doctors and medical students appeared to improve their scores. 70% of the users indicated that the CDSS was more useful than written guidelines. Implementation barriers included lower computer literacy among GPs, a lack of complexity within the CDSS that could address non-medical needs of patients, and medical staff reluctance to consult guidelines during patient consultations.

7. Research challenges in CDSS

In this section, the authors propose some research ideas that they believe would contribute to the development of more effective and acceptable clinical decision support systems in future. Due to several limitations imposed by current economic and environmental situations world-wide, both the public and industry have raised their expectations in terms of the quality, performance and cost of future systems and equipment in different fields. Healthcare is no exception. In fact, given the recent increased adoption of IT by healthcare professionals we envision that promising changes in terms of efficiency and effectiveness of healthcare service delivery will happen in the near future. As suggested in this chapter, clinical decision support systems have already taken advantage of existing techniques and models from the computer science and information systems fields. However, the following research avenues need more exploration:

- *Human Computer Interaction* (HCI): current computer interfaces seem to be restrictive and less flexible than expected for seamless and natural interactions that clinicians might expect to use in daily practice when using clinical decision support. Therefore, HCI research plays a key role in making CDSS systems more effective and acceptable. HCI involves inter-disciplinary research covering computer vision, machine learning, network security, database design, artificial intelligence, multimedia technology, embedded computation, ergonomics and cognitive psychology. It includes the design, implementation and evaluation of interactive computing systems for human use (*ACM SIGCHI Curricula for Human-Computer Interaction*, 2011). The goal of HCI is to achieve natural interaction between humans and computers. Actions of users can be captured as inputs, including vision (e.g., body movement and hand gestures), audio (e.g., speech), smell, touch, and taste. Advances in context awareness and context mining technologies have made it possible to extract and analyze implicit inputs. These implicit outputs can be integrated with the user environment instead of interrupting the user, allowing users to concentrate on their work (Schmidt, 2002).

- *Security and privacy*: healthcare systems that operate with sensitive clinical data require particular attention and procedures to ensure authorized access in order to prevent privacy and security breaches of clinical data residing in the CDSS. There has been a dramatic increase in reports of security breaches. In particular, since most healthcare systems (including CDSS) are web and service-based (e.g., Mashups), preserving the integrity, security and privacy of patient data has utmost importance. Therefore, a research challenge is to target security and privacy issues. As an example of such research, (Sandell, 2007) secures personal health data by proposing a framework which breaks CDSS into data gathering, data management, and data delivery functions. It then provides vulnerability factors and the required measures to protect data.
- *Mobile CDSS*: uses mobile devices or smart phones as the mediator between the healthcare provider (clinician, pharmacist, emergency staff) and the patient, so that the provider sends specific instructions and guidelines to the mediator. The mobile device then interacts with the patient to control his/her health condition according to the received instructions and guidelines. New advances in mobile communications allow remote areas and homecare to use a variety of remote health services. This opportunity has aroused much attention in the research and development of mobile healthcare (mHealth) and related services, such as Mobile CDSS (Tsumoto et al., 2005).

8. Related techniques in CDSS

Several models and approaches have been proposed for decision support systems. In particular, management science and operations research models have been used frequently. In this section, we briefly present the techniques that have been applied in health and medical domains (Berner & Lande, 2007; Eom & Kim, 2006; Shim et al., 2002). These techniques can be categorized as follows.

Deterministic models

- *Linear programming*: a method for finding the best solution for a given mathematical model satisfying certain constraints by maximizing or minimizing an objective function, subject to linear equality and inequality constraints. (Hershey, 1991) uses linear programming to find optimal clinical strategies when event probabilities are not known but their value ranges are available. Linear programming has also been used for an operating room planning problem which employs 0-1 linear programming (Testi & Tànfani, 2009).
- *Inventory models*: designed to minimize inventory costs by setting optimal values for time to place an order and order quantity. Placing an order can be performed either at fixed time spots or decisions can be based on the condition or level of the inventory (Oh & Hwang, 2005).
- *Integer programming*: a mathematical optimization problem and a special form of linear programming problems where variables are restricted to be integer. In (Eben-Chaime & Pliskin, 1992) a mixed integer programming model is used to decide on the size and location of beds required in a given region, incorporating travel times into dialysis planning.
- *Nonlinear programming*: used to maximize or minimize an objective function subject to a system of equality and inequality constraints where either the objective function or some of the constraints are nonlinear. (Aspden et al., 1981) use a non-linear programming model

to study the problem of distributing available healthcare resources (such as hospital beds or nurses) to assist health services planing.

- *Dynamic programming*: a problem solving method similar to divide-and-conquer with overlapping sub-problems that have optimal sub-structures. (Hall, 2010) uses dynamic programming models to investigate individual behaviors and their economic implications. This approach has been applied to healthcare spending, long-term care insurance, employment, entrepreneurial risk taking, and consumer debt.

Stochastic models

- *Queuing*: a technique for representing different types of queues to study their behavior. Certain performance measures are extracted as the result of queueing analysis. (Patrick & Puterman, 2006) use a queueing model to increase the utilization of Computed Tomography (CT) scanning devices and reduce waiting times of patients with several priority levels.
- *Markov*: a stochastic model that is suitable for problems where the Markov assumption holds, i.e., problems that have memoryless properties. Problems may become intractable without this assumption. (Sonnenberg & Beck, 1993) discuss applications of Markov models in CDSS. They introduce the generic class of problems suitable for modeling with Markov models and different evaluation methods such as matrix algebra, cohort simulation, or Monte Carlo simulation.

Artificial Intelligence

- *Artificial neural networks*: an information processing paradigm that is inspired by the structure and functional aspects of biological neural networks and the way they process information. A neural network consists of an interconnected group of processing elements (artificial neurons). Adaptive learning, self-organizations, and fault tolerance are among dominant features of this paradigm. (Mangalampalli et al., 2006) used the concept of neural networks to develop a decision-support system, that suggests medications for a gynecological disease, based on the primary and secondary symptoms of the disease.
- *Genetic algorithms*: an adaptive heuristic search algorithm that relies on the concept and process of natural evolution, selection, and genetics. This method is used in search spaces where little knowledge exists about the domain, the existing knowledge is difficult to encode, or mathematical models are not available. (Zellner et al., 2004) employed genetic algorithms to improve the performance of a logistic regression model in predicting the presence of brain neoplasia with magnetic resonance spectroscopy data.
- *Game theory*: mathematical modeling for games in which a player attempts to achieve a certain goal which is dependent on the choices of other players. Game theory offers strategies for increasing the probability of success. Solutions can be extended to cases where several players seek goals with multiple criteria (Parsons et al., 2002).
- *Decision trees*: visual and analytical tools that consist of three types of nodes: decision nodes, chance nodes, and end nodes. Decision trees are usually used for guidelines and are extensively used in CDSS. Examples can be found in (Critchfield & Willard, 1986; Hazen et al., 1998; Sonnenberg & Beck, 1993).

Practical

- *Simulation*: a generic term that encompasses approaches using simulation for decision making. (Critchfield & Willard, 1986) use Monte Carlo simulation techniques to model the uncertainty in the specification of decision tree probabilities. They apply their method to the clinical problem of anti-coagulation versus observation in combatting deep vein thrombosis during the first trimester of pregnancy. Their method provides decision analysts with tools to quantitatively evaluate the problem. In another work, simulation was used to determine the utilization of a cancer agency ambulatory care unit. This work analyzed the impact of operations, scheduling, and resource allocation on patient wait time, clinic overtime, and resource utilization (Santibanez et al., 2009).
- *Visual interactive modeling*: provides animated graphics for target applications. This model offers interaction facilities so users can explore the dynamics of an application in order to gain an understanding of its features (Au & Paul, 1996).

9. Conclusion

The healthcare system is witnessing major changes, in terms of reengineering healthcare processes and policies which will affect all stakeholders, ranging from healthcare providers to policy makers to consumers. These changes will bring technologists and medical experts closer together and will provide a more homogeneous environment for effective collaboration of these two groups. Effective and efficient decision making processes are the most critical aspect of any application domain but particularly in healthcare, as the costs of erroneous decisions are huge in terms of human quality of life, and the resulting damage in most cases is irreversible. In this chapter, we outlined different aspects and challenges in providing effective clinical decision support systems, mostly from a technical view point. We discussed different models and approaches, information and knowledge representations, using data mining techniques to provide patterns and trends as additional type of clinical knowledge, challenges in future systems through customization of expert agents, and evaluation and acceptance of CDSS by users. However, as clinical decision systems are heavily user-oriented systems and clinicians are in general less technically oriented and overwhelmed by different types of information and workplace interruptions, user acceptance and adoption is very important to the success of such systems. We have included a section to overview the challenges in system evaluation, user adoption, and other related topics that consider the impact of human factors in the success of clinical decision support systems.

10. References

Abiteboul, S., Greenshpan, O. & Milo, T. (2008). Modeling the mashup space, *Information and Data Management*, pp. 87–94.

ACM SIGCHI Curricula for Human-Computer Interaction (2011). http://sigchi.org/cdg/.

Aleksovska-Stojkovska, L. & Loskovska, S. (2010). Clinical decision support systems: Medical knowledge acquisition and representation methods, *IEEE International Conference on Electro/Information Technology (EIT)*, pp. 1–6.

Anselma, L., Bottrighi, A., Molino, G. Montani, S., Terenziani, P. & Torchio, M. (2011). Supporting knowledge-based decision making in the medical context: the GLARE approach, *International Journal of Knowledge-Based Organizations*. 1: 42–60.

Aspden, P., Mayhew, L. & Rusnak, M. (1981). Dram: a model of health care resource allocation in czechoslovakia, *omega - the international journal of management science* 9(5): 509–518.

Au, G. & Paul, R. J. (1996). Visual interactive modelling: A pictorial simulation specification system, *European Journal of Operational Research* 91(1): 14–26.

Balas, E. A., Austin, S. M., Mitchell, J. A., Ewigman, B. G., Bopp, K. D. & Brown, G. D. (1996). The clinical value of computerized information services: A review of 98 randomized clinical trials, *Arch Fam Med* 5(5): 271–278.

Balas, E. A. & Boren, S. A. (2007). Clinical trials of information interventions, *in* E. S. Berner (ed.), *Clinical Decision Support Systems*, Health Informatics, Springer New York, pp. 140–155.

Berner, E. S. (2007). *Clinical Decision Support Systems - Theory and Practice*, Springer.

Berner, E. S. & Lande, T. J. (2007). Overview of clinical decision support systems, *in* E. S. Berner (ed.), *Clinical Decision Support Systems*, Health Informatics, Springer New York, pp. 3–22.

Bodenreider, O. (2004). The Unified Medical Language System (UMLS): integrating biomedical terminology, *Nucleic Acids Research* 32(1): 267–270.

Bos, L., Marsh, A., Carroll, D., Gupta, S. & Rees, M. (2008). Patient 2.0 empowerment, *International Conference on Semantic Web and Web Services*, pp. 164–167.

Collaboratory, I. (2004). Guideline interchange format (GLIF) 3.5 - technical specification.

Critchfield, G. & Willard, K. (1986). Probabilistic analysis of decision trees using monte carlo simulation, *Medical Decision Making* 6: 85–92.

DMG (2010). Predictive model markup language (PMML) version 4.x specification. http://www.dmg.org/pmml-v4-0-1.html.

Eben-Chaime, M. & Pliskin, J. (1992). Incorporating patient travel times in decisions about size and location of dialysis facilities, *Medical Decision Making* 12: 44–51.

Eom, S. & Kim, E. (2006). A survey of decision support system applications, *Journal of the Operational Research Society* 57: 1264–1278(15).

Formal concept analysis toolkit version 1.3 (2009). http://sourceforge.net/projects/conexp.

Garg, A. X., Adhikari, N. K. J., McDonald, H., Rosas-Arellano, M. P., Devereaux, P. J., Beyene, J., Sam, J. & Haynes, R. B. (2005). Effects of Computerized Clinical Decision Support Systems on Practitioner Performance and Patient Outcomes, *JAMA: The Journal of the American Medical Association* 293(10): 1223–1238.

Hall, R. E. (2010). *Forward-Looking Decision Making: Dynamic Programming Models Applied to Health, Risk, Employment, and Financial Stability*, Princeton University Press.

Hazen, G. B., Pellissier, J. M. & Sounderpandian, J. (1998). Stochastic-tree models in medical decision making, *Medical Decision Making* 28: 64–80.

Health Level Seven Ballot (2011). http://www.hl7.org/v3ballot/html/welcome/environment/index.htm.

Health Level Seven official website (2011). http://www.hl7.org.

Hershey, J. (1991). Sensitivity analysis in medical decision making: a direct line to linear programming, *Medical Decision Making* 11: 57–60.

HL7 (1999). Message development framework. version 3.3.

HL7 (2005). The clinical document architecture (CDA) standard specification. version 2.0.

IBM Mash up Center (2011). http://www-01.ibm.com/software/info/mashup-center/.

Jayaratna, P. & Sartipi, K. (2009). Tool-assisted Healthcare Knowledge to HL7 Message Translation, *International Conference on Complex Medical Engineering*, pp. 1–7.

Johnston, M. E., Langton, K. B., Haynes, R. B. & Mathieu, A. (1994). Effects of Computer-based Clinical Decision Support Systems on Clinician Performance and Patient Outcome: A Critical Appraisal of Research, *Annals of Internal Medicine* 120(2): 135–142.

Kaplan, B. (2001). Evaluating informatics applications - some alternative approaches: Theory, social interactionism, and call for methodological pluralism, *International Journal of Medical Informatics* 64: 39–56.

Kazemi, A., Fors, U. G., Tofighi, S., Tessma, M. & Ellenius, J. (2010). Physician order entry or nurse order entry? comparison of two implementation strategies for a computerized order entry system aimed at reducing dosing medication errors, *Journal of Medical Internet Research* 12(1): e5.

Keen, P. & Morton, M. S. (1978). *Decision Support Systems: An Organizational Perspective*, Addison-Wesley.

Kong, G., Xu, D.-L. & Yang, J.-B. (2008). Clinical decision support systems: A review on knowledge representation and inference under uncertainties, *International Journal of Computational Intelligence Systems* 1: 159–167.

Kushniruk, A. W. & Patel, V. L. (2004). Cognitive and usability engineering methods for the evaluation of clinical information systems, *Journal of Biomedical Informatics* 37: 56–76.

Leslie, S. J., Hartswood, M., Meurig, C., McKee, S. P., Slack, R., Procter, R. & Denvir, M. A. (2005). Clinical decision support software for management of chronic heart failure: Development and evaluation, *Computers in Biology and Medicine* 36: 495–506.

Mandell, G., Bennett, J. & Dolin, R. (2004). *Principles and Practice of Infectious Diseases: 2-Volume*, Churchill Livingstone.

Mangalampalli, A., Mangalampalli, S. M., Chakravarthy, R. & Jain, A. K. (2006). A neural network based clinical decision-support system for efficient diagnosis and fuzzy-based prescription of gynecological diseases using homoeopathic medicinal system, *Expert Systems with Applications* 30: 109–116.

Najafi, M., Aghtar, S., Sartipi, K. & Archer, N. (2011). Virtual remote nursing system, *IEEE International Workshop on Consumer eHealth Platforms, Services and Applications*, pp. 1–5.

Najafi, M. & Sartipi, K. (2010). Client-side service composition using generic service representative, *Proceedings of the 2010 Conference of the Center for Advanced Studies on Collaborative Research*, pp. 238–252.

Oh, Y. H. & Hwang, H. (2005). Deterministic inventory models for recycling system, *Intelligent Manufacturing* 17(4): 423–428.

Open Clinical: PROforma website (2011). http://www.openclinical.org/gmm-proforma.html.

Oreilly Web 2.0 Books (2011). http://oreilly.com/web2/.

Parsons, S., Gymtrasiewicz, P. & Wooldridge, M. (eds) (2002). *Game Theory and Decision Theory in Agent-Based Systems*, Springer. Collection of papers.

Patrick, J. & Puterman, M. L. (2006). Improving resource utilization for diagnostic services through flexible inpatient scheduling: A method for improving resource utilization, *Journal of Operational Research Society* 58(2): 235–245.

Perreault, L. & Metzger, J. (1999). A pragmatic framework for understanding clinical decision support, *Journal of Healthcare Information Management* 13: 5–21.

ProgrammableWeb Web site (2011). http://www.programmableweb.com/.

Protege website (2011). http://protege.stanford.edu/.

Sandell, P. (2007). Framework for securing personal health data in clinical decision support systems, *Journal of Healthcare Information Management* 21(3): 34–40.

Santibanez, P., Chow, V., French, J., Puterman, M. & Tyldesley, S. (2009). Reducing patient wait times and improving resource utilization at british columbia cancer agency's ambulatory care unit through simulation, *Journal of Health Care Management Science* 12(4): 392–407.

Schmidt, A. (2002). Ubiquitous computing-computing in context. PhD Thesis. Lancaster University, U.K.

Sherafat, R. & K. Sartipi, P. J. (2010). A framework for data and mined-knowledge interoperability in clinical decision support systems, *International Journal of Healthcare Information Systems and Informatics* 5(1): 37 – 60.

Shim, J. P., Warkentin, M., Courtney, J. F., Power, D. J., Sharda, R. & Carlsson, C. (2002). Past, present, and future of decision support technology, *Decision Support Systems* 33(2): 111 – 126.

Sonnenberg, F. & Beck, J. (1993). Markov models in medical decision making: A practical guide, *Medical Decision Making* 13: 322–38.

Systematized Nomenclature of Medicine Clinical Terminology (SNOMED CT) (2011). http://www.snomed.org/snomedct/index.html.

Testi, A. & Tànfani, E. (2009). Tactical and operational decisions for operating room planning: Efficiency and welfare implications, *Health Care Management Science* 12: 363–373.

Trafton, J., Martins, S., Michel, M., Lewis, E., Wang, D., Combs, A., Scates, N., Tu, S. & Goldstein, M. K. (2010). Evaluation of the acceptability and usability of a decision support system to encourage safe and effective use of opioid therapy for chronic, noncancer pain by primary care providers, *Pain Medicine* 11: 575–585.

Tsumoto, S., Hirano, S., Abe, H., Nakakuni, H. & Hanada, E. (2005). Clinical decision support based on mobile telecommunication systems, *Web Intelligence, IEEE / WIC / ACM International Conference on* 0: 700–703.

Verlaene, K., Joosen, W. & Verbaeten, P. (2007). Arriclides: An architecture integrating clinical decision support models, *Proceedings of the 40th Annual Hawaii International Conference on System Sciences*, pp. 1–10.

Yousefi, A., Mastouri, N. & Sartipi, K. (2009). Scenario-oriented information extraction from electronic health records, *IEEE International Symposium on Computer-Based Medical Systems*, pp. 1 –5.

Zellner, B., Rand, S., Prost, R., Krouwer, H. & Chetty, V. (2004). A cost-minimizing diagnostic methodology for discrimination between neoplastic and non-neoplastic brain lesions: utilizing a genetic algorithm, *Academic Radiology* 11(2): 169–177.

2

Impacts and Risks of Adopting Clinical Decision Support Systems

Wilfred Bonney
Capella University/ HL7 International
Canada

1. Background

The development of interoperable Healthcare Information Systems such as Electronic Health Record (EHR), Electronic Medical Record (EMR), and Personal Health Record (PHR) has created a platform environment whereby massive data is collected, stored, shared, and analyzed at the point of care to support patient outcomes and efficient healthcare delivery. However, the analysis of structured and unstructured clinical datasets to support the decision-making process of healthcare providers is proving to be difficult in the healthcare industry as data is being captured in different and/or multiple formats. Clinical Decision Support Systems (CDSS) have emerged as toolkits for efficiently managing and analyzing the clinical datasets stored in the repositories of EHR, EMR, and PHR. In this book chapter, a literature review is used to explore and answer the following questions:

- What are clinical decision support systems (CDSS)?
- How does CDSS influence the decision-making process of clinicians in medical practice?
- What are the significant impacts and risks associated with the use and adoption of CDSS?

2. Introduction

Increasing in computing power has provided a platform for developers to build numerous computing applications that "would have been impossible just a few years ago" (Seltzer, 2005, p. 50). Clinical Decision Support Systems (CDSS) are computer-based healthcare applications used to integrate clinical and patient information to provide support for decision-making in patient care as well as to generate case-specific advices (Bonney, 2009; Kotze & Brdaroska, 2004). CDSS aid in clinical decision-making not only by providing physicians and other healthcare stakeholders with computerized advice regarding drug doses, medications, laboratory results and diagnosis but also by enhancing a clinician's ability to process data and information (Bonney, 2009; Kaushal, Shojania, & Bates, 2003; K. Kawamoto, Houlihan, Balas, & Lobach, 2005). However, there is growing evidence that when poorly designed, deployed and/or used, CDSS may lead to more harm than good (Coiera, Westbrook, & Wyatt, 2006; Kotze & Brdaroska, 2004; Toth-Pal, Wårdh, Strender, & Nilsson, 2008).

This paper aims to explore the significant impacts and risks of adopting CDSS in clinical practice. Whereas the impact factors will explore how the use of CDSS has impacted clinical decision-making, clinical practice guidelines, efficiency of healthcare delivery, and patient safety and outcomes; the risk factors will focus on the CDSS dependence on repositories, knowledge management, misinterpretation of clinical datasets, and failure to fit routine works of clinicians.

3. Methodology

A literature review is used to highlight the relevant impacts and risks of adopting CDSS in clinical practice. The methodology involves a systematic review of relevant publications, found and accessed with the help of ProQuest (with multiple databases option) and EBSCOhost databases. Additional sources were retrieved using the ScienceDirect, PubMed and ACM digital libraries. Whereas the impact factors explore how the use of CDSS has impacted clinical decision-making, clinical practice guidelines, efficiency of healthcare delivery, and patient outcomes and safety; the risk factors focus on the CDSS dependence on repositories, knowledge management, misinterpretation of clinical datasets, and failure to fit routine works of clinicians.

4. Overview of Clinical Decision Support Systems (CDSS)

CDSS have been recognized as promising tools for influencing healthcare provider performance to improve and streamline the quality of healthcare delivery (Bassa et al., 2005; Pearson et al., 2009). CDSS originated from Decision Support Systems (DSS). According to Donzelli (2006), DSS simply "combine individuals' and computers' capabilities to improve the quality of decisions" (p. 67). These functionalities and capabilities of DSS have contributed to its popularity and use in the healthcare domain. Hwang, Chang, Hung, Sung, and Yen (2004) asserted that a "DSS that supports physicians with the potential to minimize practice variation and improve patient care" (p. 240) is known as CDSS.

Throughout their inception in the medical arena in the early 1970s, CDSS have evolved immensely to support the workflow of clinicians and improved the effectiveness of decision outcomes (Bassa et al., 2005; Hwang et al., 2004; Pearson et al., 2009). Although several challenges are facing the use and adoption of CDSS in the healthcare setting, the technology still remains promising when it comes to its ability to support evidence-based practice and enhancing the clinical decision-making process of healthcare providers. It is in this regard that Kawamoto et al. (2005) noted that CDSS provide "clinicians with patient-specific assessments or recommendations to aid clinical decision making" (p. 765). Examples of CDSS include technologies such as Computerized Physician Order Entry (CPOE) systems that provide patient-specific recommendations as part of the order entry process; outpatient systems that attach care reminders to the charts of patients in need of specific preventive care services; and laboratory alerting systems that page physicians when critical laboratory values are detected (Kawamoto & Esler, 2006).

The architecture components of CDSS consist of knowledge base, inference/reasoning engine, and user communication/interaction (Kola, n.d.; O'Kane et al., 2010). Figure 1 shows the architecture components of CDSS. Whereas the knowledge base is made up guidelines, rules, and probabilistic models, the inference/reasoning engine combines the data in the knowledge base with that of the patient data. The user communication component of the architecture consists of a simple way of getting data into the system and getting results to the user (O'Kane et al., 2010; Berner & La Lande, 2007). The fact that the architecture of the

CDSS depends on knowledge bases means that inappropriate representation of data, information, and knowledge present enormous threats to the adoption of CDSS in clinical practice.

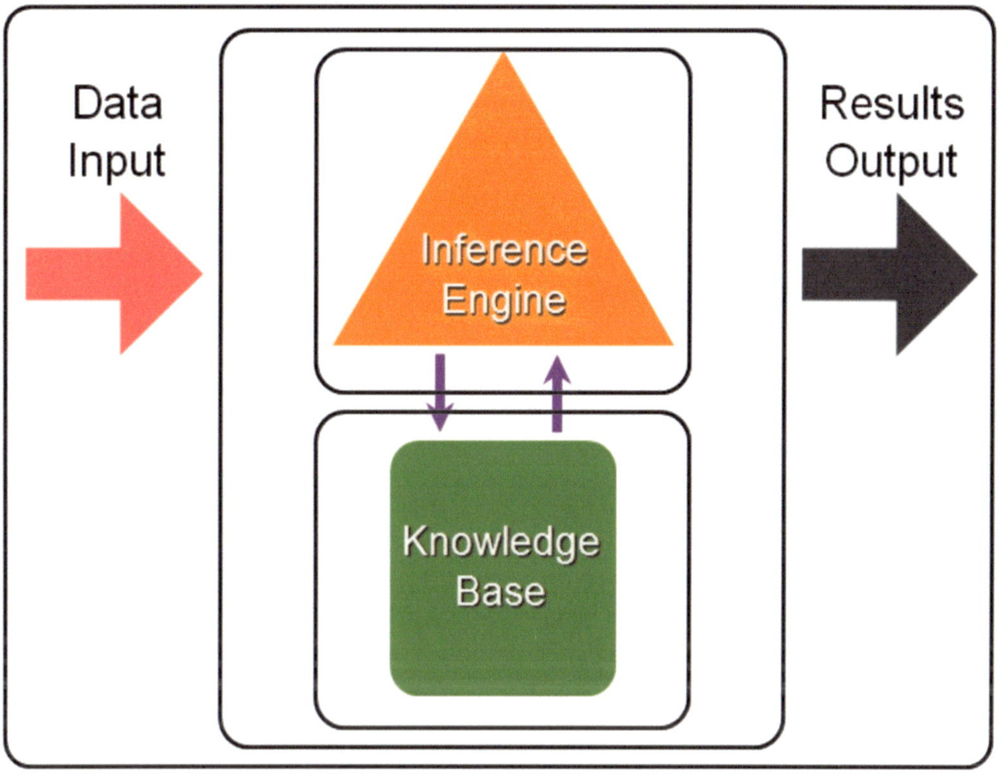

Fig. 1. Architecture components of CDSS (Kola, n.d.)

5. Impact factors

The impact factors associated with the use and adoption of CDSS could be categorized under five broad themes: clinical decision-making, clinical practice guidelines, efficiency of healthcare delivery, and patient safety and outcomes.

5.1 Clinical decision-making

CDSS has a significant impact on the quality of decision making by healthcare providers. According to Kawamoto et al. (2005), CDSS provide "clinicians with patient-specific assessments or recommendations to aid clinical decision making" (p. 765). However, this goal of achieving quality decision making is not an easy endeavour. Clinical decision-making is a "complex task requiring a knowledgeable practitioner, reliable informational inputs, and a supportive environment" (O'Neill, Dluhy, & Chin, 2005, p. 69). According to Buckingham (2002), clinical decision-making consists of classification tasks "where cues are used to assign patients to one of a number of potential categories" (p. 238). This complexity of achieving quality clinical decision making by healthcare providers is often facilitated with the use of CDSS as a supportive tool.

In an attempt to improve the use of CDSS to support quality decision making in clinical practice, Buckingham (2002) proposed a *gelatean* model with the goal of linking "intuitive explanations of clinical expertise with empirical data analysis to enhance judgement accuracy" (p. 250). Buckingham (2002) identified this relation as a symbiotic relationship between clinicians and computers. Whereas the clinicians are responsible for using their psychological validity, the computers' side of the symbiosis comes with its powers of data storage and analysis (Buckingham, 2002, p. 249). Enhancing judgement accuracy of clinicians is critical in ensuring that information emanating from the CDSS are interpreted well by the attending clinicians and not misinterpreted. Physicians can enhance their clinical judgement accuracy by combining their experiential knowledge with the use of CDSS so that a symbiotic relationship can be established.

5.2 Clinical practice guideline

Many healthcare providers depend on clinical practice guidelines for quality and evidence-based healthcare delivery. Clinical practice guidelines are "systematically developed statements to assist practitioners and patient decisions about appropriate health care for specific clinical circumstances" (Kotze & Brdaroska, 2004, p. 361). According to Kotze and Brdaroska (2004), clinical practice guidelines have "little influence upon clinician practice and patient outcomes unless they are effectively implemented and integrated into the clinical setting" (p. 362).

One approach for effectively integrating clinical practice guidelines into medical practice is the use of CDSS. The use of CDSS has facilitated clinicians' adherence to clinical practice guidelines, thereby improving patient outcomes (Kotze & Brdaroska, 2004; Kwok, Dinh, Dinh, & Chu, 2009). Kotze and Brdaroska (2004) noted that the "ability of computers to store, search and sort large volumes of data rapidly, as well as the everexpanding knowledge, access and use of computers, have paved the way for the incorporation of clinical practice guidelines into computer-based decision support systems" (p. 362). This is because not only does the use of CDSS demand clinical practice guidelines but it also makes it easier for programmers to develop rule-based and/or case-based reasoning to support the advices emanating from the CDSS.

The encoded rules in the clinical practice guidelines provide the framework in which programming rules are encoded and used in the development of CDSS. For example, Kwok et al. (2009) found that the use of an integrated and dynamic electronic decision support system (EDSS) at a single emergency department promoted strict adherence to asthma clinical guidelines and improved clinical documentation and discharge management plans for asthma management. It is in this regard that Kotze and Brdaroska (2004) indicated that CDSS are "crucial elements in long-term strategies for promoting the use of clinical practice guidelines" (p. 362).

5.3 Efficiency of healthcare delivery

In a study conducted to assess the impact of CDSS on the management of patients with Hypercholesterolemia, Bassa et al. (2005) found that "it is possible to optimize the efficiency of the management of hypercholesterolemia in standard practice by the implementation of a CDSS" (p. 71). In a similar study, Cobos et al. (2005) found that the use and adoption of CDSS in clinical practice "was as effective as usual care and induced important savings in the management of hypercholesterolemia" (p. 431). The above two studies contribute to our understanding about the need to implement CDSS in clinical practice so as to support the efficiency of healthcare delivery.

Healthcare providers stand to gain enormously and streamline the workflow of physicians by adopting CDSS. For example, Pomerleau (2008) noted that the use of CDSS allow "nurses to have information and unit policies at their fingertips, which help them adhere to standards while at the bedside" (p. 154). Successful implementation of CDSS in clinical settings will reduce waiting times, minimize the length of stay in hospitals, and enhance the efficiency of healthcare delivery.

5.4 Patient safety and outcomes

Improving patient outcomes requires the use of efficient decision-making process and evidence-based practice that can only be best achieved through the utilization of CDSS. One of the ultimate uses of CDSS is to improve patient safety and outcomes. CDSS have consistently shown great promise for reducing medical errors and improving patient care, safety, and outcomes (K. Kawamoto et al., 2005; Mahoney, Berard-Collins, Coleman, Amaral, & Cotter, 2007; Pomerleau, 2008; Sintchenko, Coiera, Iredell, & Gilbert, 2004; Subramanian et al., 2007). When it comes to the use of medications and diagnostic testing in clinical settings, CDSS has emerged as a technology to reduce medication errors, "improve diagnostic accuracy, provide easier and more rapid access to patient information and more complete medical records" (Courtney, Alexander, & Demiris, 2008, p. 692).

According to Mahoney et al. (2007), medication errors are deleterious, prevalence and costly. Hence the need to use robust healthcare information systems to monitor, track, and manage medications administered to patients is of prime concern to many healthcare providers. Mahoney et al. (2007) found that the use of integrated clinical information system technology "decreased selected types of medication errors throughout the medication-use process in a health care system and improved therapeutic drug monitoring in patients" (p. 1969). In the context of identifying the potential adverse drug events (ADEs) at the medication ordering stage, Roberts et al. (2010) noted that successful implementation of CPOE and other advanced CDSS tools "significantly increased the number of potential ADE alerts for pharmacist review and the number of true-positive ADE alerts identified per 1000 admissions" (p. 1845).

Moreover, in a randomized control trial conducted to evaluate the effectiveness of CDSS in reducing potentially inappropriate prescribing to older adults, Terrell et al. (2009) found that CPOE with decision support "significantly reduced prescribing of potentially inappropriate medications for seniors" (p. 1389). In another study, Subramanian et al. (2007) found that the increasing use of CPOE has facilitated the "elimination of handwriting identification problems, reductions in error associated with similar drug names, faster delivery of orders to the pharmacy" (p. 1451). These studies and others from the literature affirm the significant impact of CDSS in reducing medical errors in clinical practice, thereby, improving the quality of care, patient safety, and patient outcomes (Pearson et al., 2009).

6. Risk factors

The risk factors focus on the CDSS dependence on repositories, knowledge management, misinterpretation of clinical datasets, and failure to fit routine works of clinicians.

6.1 Dependence on repositories

One of the critical architecture components of all CDSS is the knowledge base. The knowledge base depends on a centralized clinical data repository (K. Kawamoto, Lobach, Willard, & Ginsburg, 2009; Roberts et al., 2010). The fact that CDSS depends on good quality clinical data repository reinforces the need for standardized data representation, storage, and retrieval that can be centrally managed in the knowledge base repositories. Lack of good clinical data warehouse could have significant impact on the quality of advices emanating from CDSS. Data mining algorithms require good quality clinical data repositories to be able to extract knowledge to support clinical decision-making.

CDSS also depend profoundly on large volumes of readily-accessible, existing clinical datasets (Bonney, 2009). These large volumes of data are usually extracted from the repository content of EHR, EMR and PHR. Lack of standardized data capture by these systems will lead to corrupt datasets. When the entries in these data repository are not coded appropriately, there is tendency that the resulting datasets will not be a good representative of the patient population (Bonney, 2009). It is therefore essential that standardized data representation are used for leveraging the knowledge base repositories contained in the CDSS so as to facilitate the generation of patient-specific care recommendations at the point of care (K. Kawamoto et al., 2009).

6.2 Knowledge management

CDSS depend on appropriate implementation of knowledge management. According to Kalkan (2008), the whole concepts of data, information and knowledge are generally misunderstood. Acknowledging the fact that information results from replacing data within some meaningful content, Kalkan (2008) noted that knowledge is an "organized and transformed combination of information, assimilated with a set of rules, procedures and operations learnt through experience and practice" (p. 391). This definition of knowledge emphasizes the need to manage knowledge appropriately. Without proper set of rules, guidelines and operations, knowledge cannot be assimilated. Thus the need for knowledge management in CDSS cannot be ignored.

Knowledge management is defined as a "systematic management of knowledge-related activities, practices, programs and policies within the enterprise" (Kalkan, 2008, p. 392). Knowledge management has gain popularity in the IT industry because of its emphasis on how to articulate, capture and distribute explicit and tacit knowledge in different formats (Herschel & Jones, 2005; Kalkan, 2008). Knowledge management activities aim to "effectively apply an organization's knowledge to create new knowledge to achieve and maintain competitive advantage" (Kalkan, 2008, p. 392). Creating new knowledge in the medical field is crucial in helping healthcare providers in combating new diseases and symptoms. However, when the newly created knowledge is based on poor quality data, the resulting outcome could be very devastating in clinical settings.

The fact that CDSS have "become increasingly sophisticated by matching patient characteristics with computerised knowledge bases and using algorithms to generate patient-specific assessments or treatment recommendations" (Pearson et al., 2009, p. 155) demand that appropriate management of knowledge is implemented in the CDSS to ensure that the patient-specific assessments and/or treatment recommendations are not based on poor quality data. It is therefore important that narrative information emanating from the CDSS is further processed and analyzed by healthcare providers before clinical decisions are made (Pearson et al., 2009).

6.3 Misinterpretation of clinical datasets

Clinical information stored in the CDSS are often misrepresented and misinterpreted. This is partly due to the inconsistencies in data coding and extraction of poor quality data. According to Coiera et al. (2006), the use of CDSS can "improve the overall safety and quality of health care delivery, but may also introduce machine-related errors" (p. 20). Coiera et al. (2006) noted that the use of poor quality data could lead to wrong medications and misdiagnosis. Coiera et al. (2006) also noted that automation biases and using evidence-retrieval systems may generate decision errors that might not necessarily correlates with the experiential knowledge of the physicians.

Acknowledging the fact that inference rules forms the basic building blocks of any given CDSS and are usually extracted by data mining existing clinical datasets, Bonney (2009) noted that the "trustworthy of CDSS is based on how effective the extracted inference rules correlates with the experiential knowledge of domain experts" (p. 116). Chaudhry (2008) also emphasized the misrepresentation of clinical datasets by noting that, "real clinical data from patient interviews or medical records are far less structured and would likely alter the performance of the system considerably" (p. 86), if not extracted appropriately. This has a significant effect on the quality of data used in developing CDSS. Poor quality data will lead to misinterpretation of clinical datasets. The use of health information standards such as ICD-10, SNOMED, LOINC and UMLS will ensure uniformity and consistency of the health datasets, used in generating the inference rules (Bonney, 2009).

6.4 Failure to fit routine works of clinicians

According to Hwang et al. (2004), accessing CDSS in a computer by medical practitioners is not a smooth process for actual usage/implementation. Hwang et al. (2004) attributed the complexity of the process to the fact that in actual clinical settings, integrating CDSS with the routine work of clinicians will demand that the physicians "run back and forth from point of care to computer station to complete their diagnosis" (p. 240). This approach could be daunting considering the workload of average physicians. Moreover, the routine use of CDSS during consultation could alienate patients from the direct contact with their physicians.

When it comes to the use and adoption of technology, medical practitioners with experiential knowledge are more likely to override the decisions and advices presented by CDSS. For example, Dowding et al. (2009) noted that nurses are "less likely to use CDSS for telephone triage decisions that they feel they have experience in making" (p. 1160). These attitudes of medical practitioners towards CDSS often impede their overall acceptance and adoption in clinical practice.

Acknowledging the fact that perceived usefulness of medical information is a function of its relevance, validity, and the effort involved in searching for it, Sintchenko et al. (2004) noted that physicians often "choose not to use available evidence at the time of decision making but rely on what they know and choose the strategy requiring least effort" (p. 75). Hence clinicians' attitudes and the environment in which decisions are made influence the overall acceptance and adoption of decision support tools (Sintchenko et al., 2004; Toth-Pal et al., 2008). It is therefore recommended that the development and deployment of the CDSS should fit the workflow of clinicians so as to ensure that the system is enabling without constraining (Ash, Gorman, Lavelle, & Payne, 2003; Bonney, 2009).

7. Discussion and conclusion

In a qualitative study conducted to explore general practitioners' (GPs) handling of a CDSS during the implementation process, Toth-Pal et al. (2008) found that despite their benefits in medicine, CDSS are rarely used in clinical practice. Toth-Pal et al. (2008) attributed CDSS barriers to "limited computer skills, shortage of time during consultation, problems with interpreting the recommendations given, and the GPs' concerns about patient reactions" (p. 40).

Moreover, in an analysis of 70 randomized controlled trial, Kawamoto et al. (2005) found that successful implementation of CDSS should "(*a*) provide decision support automatically as part of clinician workflow, (*b*) deliver decision support at the time and location of decision making, (*c*) provide actionable recommendations, and (*d*) use a computer to generate the decision support" (p. 771). These four recommendations seem to support the overall use of CDSS in improving the quality of clinical care. They also make it easier for clinicians to use CDSS thereby minimising the effort required by clinicians to receive and act on system recommendations (Kawamoto et al., 2005). The development of CDSS should also utilize health information standards so as to ensure its interoperability with other legacy systems and support distributed computing (Bonney, 2009).

This research has the potential to benefit healthcare providers and stakeholders in determining the significant impacts and risks of adopting CDSS in medical practice. With the impacts and risks presented in the paper, it is evident that the appropriate use CDSS with emerging technologies could enhance the adoption and acceptance rate of CDSS in clinical practice. Future research should therefore focus on how to integrate Business Intelligence (BI) into CDSS. This is because BI is emerging as the new frontier in data mining that will facilitate the extraction of both structured and unstructured datasets. It is also important that future research promote the rigorous testing of CDSS to provide high quality evidence about their clinical and economic impacts on healthcare delivery (Pearson et al., 2009).

8. References

Ash, J. S., Gorman, P. N., Lavelle, M., & Payne, T. H. (2003). A cross-site qualitative study of physician order entry. *Journal of the American Medical Informatics Association, 10*(2), 188-200.

Bassa, A., Miguel, d. V., Cobos, A., Torremadé, E., Bergoñón, S., Crespo, C., Espinosa, C. (2005). Impact of a clinical decision support system on the management of patients with hypercholesterolemia in the primary healthcare setting. *Disease Management & Health Outcomes, 13*(1), 65-72.

Berner, E. S., & La Lande, T. J. (2007). Overview of clinical decision support systems. In *Clinical decision support systems – theory and practice,* (2nd ed.)., Berner E.S (ed.), Springer: New York.

Bonney, W. (2009). Is it appropriate, or ethical, to use health data collected for the purpose of direct patient care to develop computerized predictive decision support tools? *Studies in Health Technology and Informatics, 143,* 115-121.

Buckingham, C. (2002). Psychological cue use and implications for a clinical decision support system. *Medical Informatics & the Internet in Medicine, 27*(4), 237-251.

Chaudhry, B. (2008). *Computerized clinical decision support: Will it transform healthcare?* doi:10.1007/s11606-007-0432-9

Cobos, A., Vilaseca, J., Asenjo, C., Pedro-Botet, J., Sáonchez, E., Val, A., Bergoñón, S. (2005). Cost effectiveness of a clinical decision support system based on the recommendations of the european society of cardiology and other societies for the management of hypercholesterolemia: Report of a cluster-randomized trial. *Disease Management & Health Outcomes, 13*(6), 421-432.

Coiera, E., Westbrook, J. I., & Wyatt, J. C. (2006). The safety and quality of decision support systems. *Methods of Information in Medicine, 45*(Suppl. 1), 20-25.

Courtney, K. L., Alexander, G. L., & Demiris, G. (2008). Information technology from novice to expert: Implementation implications. *Journal of Nursing Management, 16*(6), 692-699.

Donzelli, P. (2006). A decision support system for software project management. *IEEE Software, 23*(4), 67-75.

Dowding, D., Mitchell, N., Randell, R., Foster, R., Lattimer, V., & Thompson, C. (2009). Nurses' use of computerised clinical decision support systems: A case site analysis. *Journal of Clinical Nursing, 18*(8), 1159-1167.

Herschel, R. T., & Jones, N. E. (2005). Knowledge management and business intelligence: The importance of integration. *Journal of Knowledge Management, 9*(4), 45-55.

Hwang, H., Chang, I., Hung, W., Sung, M., & Yen, D. (2004). The design and evaluation of clinical decision support systems in the area of pharmacokinetics. *Medical Informatics & the Internet in Medicine, 29*(3), 239-251. doi:10.1080/14639230400009158

Kalkan, V. D. (2008). An overall view of knowledge management challenges for global business. *Business Process Management Journal, 14*(3), 390-400.

Kaushal, R., Shojania, K. G., & Bates, D. W. (2003). Effects of computerized physician order entry and clinical decision support systems on medication safety: A systematic review. *Archives of Internal Medicine, 163*(12), 1409-1416.

Kawamoto, K., & Esler, B. (2006). *HL7 service functional model specification - decision support services (DSS)*. Retrieved December 2, 2005, from http://www.hl7.org/documentcenter/ballots/2006SEP/support/AUDIT_SDO_CDS_DSS_R1_D1_2006SEP_20070129061919.pdf

Kawamoto, K., Houlihan, C. A., Balas, E. A., & Lobach, D. F. (2005). Improving clinical practice using clinical decision support systems: A systematic review of trials to identify features critical to success. *British Medical Journal, 330*(7494), 765-772.

Kawamoto, K., Lobach, D. F., Willard, H. F., & Ginsburg, G. S. (2009). A national clinical decision support infrastructure to enable the widespread and consistent practice of genomic and personalized medicine. *BMC Medical Informatics & Decision Making, 9*(1), 17-30. doi:10.1186/1472-6947-9-17

Kola, J. (n.d.). *Clinical decision support systems: Approach and use*. Retrieved November, 21, 2010, from https://www.nibhi.org.uk/Health%20Informatics/Decision%20Support%20Systems%20Export.ppt

Kotze, B., & Brdaroska, B. (2004). Clinical decision support systems in psychiatry in the information age. *Australasian Psychiatry, 12*(4), 361-364. doi:10.1111/j.1440-1665.2004.02127.x

Kwok, R., Dinh, M., Dinh, D., & Chu, M. (2009). Improving adherence to asthma clinical guidelines and discharge documentation from emergency departments: Implementation of a dynamic and integrated electronic decision support system. *Emergency Medicine Australasia, 21*(1), 31-37.

Mahoney, C. D., Berard-Collins, C., Coleman, R., Amaral, J. F., & Cotter, C. M. (2007). Effects of an integrated clinical information system on medication safety in a multi-hospital setting. *American Journal of Health-System Pharmacy, 64*(18), 1969-1977.

O'Kane, T., O'Donoghue, J., Gallagher, J., Aftab, A., Casey, A., Angove, P., Courtney, G. (2010). MEWS to e-MEWS: From a paper-based to an electronic clinical decision support system. *Proceedings of the European Conference on Information Management & Evaluation,* , 301-311.

O'Neill, E., Dluhy, N. M., & Chin, E. (2005). Modelling novice clinical reasoning for a computerized decision support system. *Journal of Advanced Nursing, 49*(1), 68-77.

Pearson, S., Moxey, A., Robertson, J., Hains, I., Williamson, M., Reeve, J., & Newby, D. (2009). Do computerised clinical decision support systems for prescribing change practice? A systematic review of the literature (1990-2007). *BMC Health Services Research, 9*, 154-167.

Pomerleau, M. (2008). Electronic health record: Are you ready for the next step? *Nursing for Women's Health, 12*(2), 151-156.

Roberts, L. L., Ward, M. M., Brokel, J. M., Wakefield, D. S., Crandall, D. K., & Conlon, P. (2010). Impact of health information technology on detection of potential adverse drug events at the ordering stage. *American Journal of Health-System Pharmacy, 67*(21), 1838-1846. doi:10.2146/ajhp090637

Seltzer, M. (2005). Beyond relational databases. *Queue, 3*(3), 50-58.

Sintchenko, V., Coiera, E., Iredell, J. R., & Gilbert, G. L. (2004). Comparative impact of guidelines, clinical data, and decision support on prescribing decisions: An interactive web experiment with simulated cases. *Journal of the American Medical Informatics Association, 11*(1), 71-77.

Subramanian, S., Hoover, S., Gilman, B., Field, T. S., Mutter, R., & Gurwitz, J. H. (2007). Computerized physician order entry with clinical decision support in long-term care facilities: Costs and benefits to stakeholders. *Journal of the American Geriatrics Society, 55*(9), 1451-1457.

Terrell, K. M., Perkins, A. J., Dexter, P. R., Hui, S. L., Callahan, C. M., & Miller, D. K. (2009). Computerized decision support to reduce potentially inappropriate prescribing to older emergency department patients: A randomized, controlled trial. *Journal of the American Geriatrics Society, 57*(8), 1388-1394.

Toth-Pal, E., Wårdh, I., Strender, L., & Nilsson, G. (2008). Implementing a clinical decision-support system in practice: A qualitative analysis of influencing attitudes and characteristics among general practitioners. *Informatics for Health & Social Care, 33*(1), 39-54. doi:10.1080/17538150801956754

3

Success Factors and Barriers for Implementation of Advanced Clinical Decision Support Systems

Anne-Marie J.W. Scheepers-Hoeks, Rene J. Grouls, Cees Neef, Eric W. Ackerman and Erik H. Korsten
Catharina-hospital Eindhoven / University of Technology Eindhoven
The Netherlands

1. Introduction

Ten years ago, the US Institute of Medicine (IOM) called for a massive redesign of the healthcare delivery system.(Committee on Quality of Health Care in America, 2001) Today it is clear that one of the goals, the nationwide use of an electronic medical record (EMR) by 2010, has failed to be reached as the process of adoption has been slow. Some may consider an EMR as a final destination, although in fact it is only the start point of a revolution in healthcare: the implementation of clinical decision support systems (CDSS) that 'make it easy to do it right'.(James, 2001) These systems are able to address the large, potential additional value of the implementation of an EMR. When an EMR is available, this is already a step in the right direction, to have an easy and structured access to all patient data available for all healthcare professionals that need them. However, this is still a huge amount of data, but one should also have the ability to integrate all these data and use these data in making the right choices in therapy. Practice has shown that despite the availability of an EMR, still many medication errors are made. Therefore, CDSS are designed to aid clinical decision-making by matching patient characteristics to a computerized knowledge or rule base to generate patient-specific recommendations.(Kawamoto et al., 2005) In the trendsetting IOM reports 'To Err is Human' (2000) and 'Crossing the quality chasm' (2001), a CDSS was endorsed as one of the most powerful tools available for improving patient safety and healthcare quality.(Kohn et al., 2000;Committee on Quality of Health Care in America, 2001)

It is difficult to accept that despite multiple opportunities and promising results, these systems instead of being common practice, still remain 'next-generation'.(James, 2001)

During the last five years, research gave more insight in the success factors that could accelerate the idle process of CDSS adoption. (Kawamoto et al., 2005; Garg et al., 2005;Nies et al., 2006) The conclusions however are not univocal because the reviews included a wide variety of systems ranging from computerised to non-computerised CDSS as well as from basic to advanced systems. Basic decision support includes checking on drug-drug interactions, duplicate therapy, drug-allergies and generalized drug dosing. Advanced CDSS, used in addition to basic CDSS, includes for example checking on contra-indications (disease and drugs), individualized dosing support during renal impairment or guidance for medication-related laboratory testing.(Kuperman et al., 2007) Basic decision support is nowadays commonly available. In the Netherlands, this provision is used nationwide since 1980, integrated in a drug database (G-standaard, Royal Dutch Association for the Advancement of Pharmacy). Despite this support that is available for every physician and pharmacy, medication errors occur frequently which emphasizes the urge for advanced solutions.(Leendertse et al., 2008)

In our 600-bed university-affiliated hospital, we have implemented an advanced CDSS in practice on a few departments already and are on the eve of hospital-wide expansion. A critical examination of the literature made clear which prerequisites are needed for optimal implementation of advanced CDSS. To accelerate the process of CDSS adoption, we present an overview of success factors and barriers for implementation of advanced CDSS in hospital practice. Subsequently, we present our own experienced success factors and barriers after implementing an advanced decision support system in 2008 in daily hospital practice and compare these results with literature findings.

2. Background

Medication errors occur distressingly frequent due to deficiencies in the overall system of healthcare delivery despite use of current medication safety systems.(Kohn et al., 2000;Committee on Quality of Health Care in America, 2001;Schiff et al., 2003) Many reports call attention to the gaps between optimal and actual practice. (Kohn et al., 2000;Committee on Quality of Health Care in America, 2001;Aspden et al., 2006) The report 'To Err is human' indicated that 44.000 to 98.000 patients die in hospitals each year due to medical errors.(Kohn et al., 2000) The recent IOM report 'Preventing Medication Errors'(Aspden et al., 2006) showed that in the USA medications harm at least 1.5 million people per year of which at least 400,000 preventable adverse drug events (ADE's) in hospitals.

The number of patients, dying from medical errors is probably a low estimate and the situation in Europe is not expected to be different. The Dutch statistics are, for example, not encouraging either. From the patients that died in Dutch hospitals in 2007, 10.7% experienced preventable medical complications; resulting in the death of 1735 patients (4.1%). Even more discouraging is the fact that the number of unnecessary deaths tends to increase. For the Netherlands these were 1745 deaths in 2004 and 1960 in 2008; an increase of 11.5%, despite advances in knowledge and IT-systems (Langelaan, 2010) The HARM-report (2006, NL) showed 19.000 preventable drug related admissions a year in Dutch hospitals; 5.6 % of all acute admissions, associated with a total cost of 86 million euros.(Leendertse et al., 2008)

Medication errors occur due to the rapidly increasing complexity of evidence based medicine and error sensitivity of healthcare.(James, 2002) Physicians need to take many drug- and patient specific characteristics into account and literature shows that this is often omitted or not recognized in time.(Levy et al., 1999;Schiff et al., 2003;Denekamp, 2007) Beyond reminders, CDSS can integrate clinical data to support professionals managing an increasingly complex practice environment.(James, 2001) Integration of these specific parameters is necessary to guide patients through the complete clinical pathway from anamnesis to evaluation and fine-tuning of the therapy.

Reviews of Kawamoto and Garg have shown that a CDSS is effective in decreasing medication errors and improving efficiency and quality of care.(Kawamoto et al., 2005;Garg et al., 2005) These reviews found that 64% respectively 68% of the decision support systems significantly improve clinical practice.(Kawamoto et al., 2005;Garg et al., 2005)
In literature, basic and advanced decision support are both called CDSS and exact descriptions of the systems used are scarce, which makes these systems difficult to compare. This review will only include advanced CDSS, defined as a multi-purpose rule based expert system which contains complex electronic guidelines that can integrate data from different domains.(Sucher et al., 2008) Goals of implementing advanced CDSS are to decrease errors and improve patient safety, improve quality through adoption of best practices, increase cost-effectiveness and optimize the management of chronic diseases.(Greenes, 2007) In our hospital, research is performed with clinical decision support since 1998, in which we found that these goals can be achieved though structured development, validation and implementation. The objective of this chapter is to extend a practical overview of success factors and barriers of advanced CDSS found in literature and practice, before widespread hospital implementation, concentrating on these central aspects.

3. Success factors

Right message	Accurate content
	Reliable messages
	Easy and actionable messages
	Inclusion of references in the message
Right time	Save time
	Integration in workflow
	High system's speed
Right place	Deliver message at the point of care
	Active alerting mechanism
Right system	Electronic availability of data in the EMR
	Integration with other systems
	Maintenance of the system and content

Table 1. Overview of success factors for implementation of advanced CDSS (see text for references)

3.1 The right message

3.1.1 Accurate content

To facilitate the adoption of evidence based medicine in practice, paper guidelines have to be translated into a computer-interpretable format, called *clinical rules*. This is a challenging task, because evidence based recommendations are often non-specific, multi-interpretable and either too complex to recall or too general to apply specifically.(Trivedi et al., 2002;Denekamp, 2007;Kuperman et al., 2007;Sucher et al., 2008) For example, according to guidelines, leukocyte counts should be measured frequent during lithium therapy, but the exact frequency, cut-off values and relevance is lacking.(Wessels-Basten et al., 2007) This problem can be solved by involving a multidisciplinary expert team to review and optimize the clinical rules.(Dexter et al., 2001;Trivedi et al., 2002;Osheroff et al., 2005;Leslie and Denvir, 2007;Wessels-Basten et al., 2007) One should compose the expert team carefully, being a reflection of end users and recognised experts in the particular field, as this determines the strength of the clinical rule developed. In fact, this is generally alike to the development of a new guideline. Benefits of this approach are that the specific subject gains renewed attention from the experts which may already increase compliance to these guidelines and user commitment is gained as the experts will be end-users of the system and motivate other users once implemented in practice.(de Clercq and Hasman, 2004;Osheroff et al., 2005;Wessels-Basten et al., 2007)

3.1.2 Reliable messages

Current medication safety systems generate masses of irrelevant alerts leading to alert fatigue as a result of the often low specificity and clinical relevance.(van der Sijs et al., 2006) This is especially the case with basic, drug-oriented decision support, as we know in the Netherlands for about 30 years. Many alerts are generated, and the research of van der Sijs showed that more than 90% of alerts are overridden, without the physician even looking at the alert. The underlying conditions are: low alert specificity, information content unclear, low sensitivity, handling was insufficient and unsafe and the workflow was unnecessary disrupted. Also, physicians were not trained on the alerts and trusted the pharmacy in checking their medication orders. In summary, there are many failures of the systems used today, that can be solved with these new advanced decision support systems. Even, these current systems can be dangerous, which pleads for a rapid response. These basic systems increases the risk of overriding a potentially harmful alert.(Bates et al., 2003;van der Sijs et al., 2006;Denekamp, 2007) Even pharmacists have been found to override a third of life-threatening drug-drug interactions.(Bates et al., 2003) Therefore, it is vitally important to validate the clinical rules extensively before bringing these into practice to ensure reliable recommendations.(Dexter et al., 2001;Wetter, 2002;Wessels-Basten et al., 2007;Sucher et al., 2008;Varonen et al., 2008) The above mentioned obstacles need to be taken into account when designing en implementing these newer systems. Also, validation of the alerts is fundamental for success. Scheepers et al (2009) has described a strategy that can be used in various settings to create clinical rules of a high reliability. By measuring the positive and negative predictive value during the development process and afterwards, one can easily monitor if the quality of the clinical rules is high enough before implementation in practice. Since few studies have focused on validation of clinical rules, more research is needed. There is a need for other successful strategies to be described, to help others with these fundamental questions. Also, research may answer the question which minimal notification threshold is needed for effective alerting before bringing the alert into practice.(Osheroff et al., 2005)

3.1.3 Easy and actionable messages

A CDSS is effective when it minimizes the effort required by physicians to receive and act on system recommendations.(Kawamoto et al., 2005;Varonen et al., 2008) This can be accomplished by giving clear advice and a straightforward way to perform the action indicated. (Bates et al., 2003;Osheroff et al., 2005;Varonen et al., 2008;Mollon et al., 2009) Besides that, applications must anticipate physicians needs for gathering and translating data into actionable recommendations.(Bates et al., 2003;Kawamoto et al., 2005;Mollon et al., 2009) For example, a clinical rule is developed to check if a patient needs a gastro-protective drug when using a NSAID or dosage adjustment because of renal insufficiency.

(Field et al., 2008) If necessary, an automatic medication order pops-up and only one click on the 'authorize' button is needed to prevent the patient from having adverse drug events. This is all in line with the words of James (2001) to 'Make it easy to do it right' and emphasises the need of an expert/end users team that is well involved in the development process.

3.1.4 Inclusion of references in the message

A valuable addition to the message is to present the source of the information and the explanation of the rationale for the guideline.(Maviglia et al., 2003;Kawamoto et al., 2005; Goud et al., 2008;Mollon et al., 2009) Many guidelines exist and these are continuously renewed, which makes it difficult to keep up with all recommendations. Although it appears that not all users use this option(Bates et al., 2003), it is a valuable addition that literature citations and web-based evidence are available when desired. (Bates et al., 2003)

3.2 The right time

3.2.1 Save time

Physicians encounter a barrier to invest time in another computer system. All health professionals face time pressure and increasing data overload. The number of therapies is so large that physicians cannot effectively keep track of them all.(Bates et al., 2003) A CDSS can save time by making associations between different data domains, which physicians might miss because of the large amount of data. Time saving can be achieved by making it easy to do it right and is therefore a highly valued success factor.(Wetter, 2002; Mollon et al., 2009) It is important to find the right balance between over- and under reporting in accordance with the wishes of the end-users of the system and to convince users that the added value of the system compensates for the time required to learn and use the system.(Goud et al., 2008)

3.2.2 Integration in clinical workflow

The most important success factor of CDSS is that the system is integrated in the clinical workflow.(Kawamoto et al., 2005;Osheroff et al., 2005;Mollon et al., 2009) A CDSS will otherwise have no beneficial effect and will not be used. Messages should be presented at the moment of decision making, though with as less disturbance for the physician as possible. Therefore different alert mechanisms (pop-up, automatic lab order, prescription order, email, etc) should be developed, suitable for different alerting priorities.(Osheroff et al., 2005) In this particular field, the research is very limited and needs to be expanded soon. Understanding the clinical workflow and user's wishes thoroughly strongly increases the probability for success.(Bates et al., 2003)

3.2.3 High system's speed

As with every computer system, speed is a very important parameter for user's acceptance. (Mollon et al., 2009) As explained above, recommendations should appear exactly at the right time of decision making. When the speed of an application is slow, user satisfaction declines markedly. Bates et al found that this parameter is valued most by users and therefore it should be a priority factor of the CDSS.(Bates et al., 2003)

3.3 The right place

3.3.1 Point of care

An important quality of advanced CDSS is the ability to deliver recommendations at the point of care.(Mollon et al., 2009) The question is who should receive the message. The point of care may vary, as patients therapy is guided by various health professionals in the process. The multidisciplinary expert team can identify the receiver of the recommendations (e.g. physician, pharmacist, nurse etc).(Wessels-Basten et al., 2007)

3.3.2 Active alert mechanism

The performance of systems in which users are automatically prompted to use the system is significantly more effective, compared with studies in which users were required to actively initiate the system.(Dexter et al., 2001; Kawamoto et al., 2005; Garg et al., 2005; van Wyk et al., 2008) Also a larger positive impact is seen when a recommendation is prompting for an action and not ignorable.(Dexter et al., 2001; Bates et al., 2003) Dexter found that relatively small changes in the presentation of alerts made the difference between a significantly increase in preventive measurement rates and no effect at all.(Dexter et al., 2001) So it is important to select the alert mechanism carefully, as the type of alert will greatly affect the impact of the clinical rule.

3.4 The right system

3.4.1 Electronic availability of data

A CDSS acts on electronically available patient data in the EMR (clinical data, pharmacy, laboratory, diagnoses, complications, microbiology etc).(Soman et al., 2008) Progress of implementation and adoption of EMR is slow, which inhibits adoption of CDSS. The most specific and advanced clinical rules can be developed if a CDSS is able to gather all mentioned data from the EMR, but at least a pharmacy-laboratory link is needed. (Schiff et al., 2003; Maviglia et al., 2003; Jha et al., 2008) The ability to integrate outpatient data in the CDSS can give additional improvements for more specific clinical rules.(Goud et al., 2008)

3.4.2 Integration with other systems

Integrated systems (e.g. in CPOE) are significantly more likely to succeed than stand alone systems.(Kawamoto et al., 2005;Garg et al., 2005;Mollon et al., 2009) This provides relevant information to physicians at key times in decision making, enabling to prompt alerts during drug prescription or chart review.(Denekamp, 2007;Varonen et al., 2008)

3.4.3 Maintenance of system and content

Once a CDSS is implemented it is essential for long term success that the system and content remains up-to-date.(Trivedi et al., 2009) Technical maintenance is important to guarantee a flawless link between the CDSS and the EMR. Maintenance concerning content is needed to ensure that the clinical rules remain applicable regarding the latest evidence-based guidelines.(Osheroff et al., 2005) Sometimes corrections are required after implementation when it turns out that the impact or physician's satisfaction is not as expected.(Trivedi et al., 2002;Bates et al., 2003) Therefore Bates et al(Bates et al., 2003) assigned each area of decision support to an individual. For example, a cardiologist has to evaluate the clinical rules regarding his specialism periodically. Regarding the novelty of complex CDSS, maintenance of the system and content is hardly studied yet.

4. Barriers

Certain barriers found in literature may hamper implementation of advanced CDSS. Besides the lack of the described success factors, an often mentioned barrier to implementation is low computer skills among physicians.(Garg et al., 2005;Leslie and Denvir, 2007;Trivedi et al., 2009) This must be carefully taken into account within the design of the alerts. New-generation physicians, like medical students and junior doctors, may bring a higher level of computer literacy to clinical practice and stimulate implementation of a CDSS in practice. (Leslie and Denvir, 2007)

Another barrier, brought forward by Bates(Bates et al., 2003), is the loss of physician's autonomy with the use of CDSS. However, CDSS are able to present the best evidence-based practice automatically, without requiring extra thought or work. This allows the health professionals to focus on those areas of special need and adjust care to each individual patient.(James, 2002) This not only increases patient safety, but also physician's safety by reducing the risk on malpractice claims. Even, the system may improve clinical skills through a learn effect of the corrective messages.(Varonen et al., 2008)

5. Own experienced success factors and barriers

In our years of research we evolved a development and validation strategy for clinical rules. This three-step strategy (retrospective technical, retrospective therapeutic and prospective validation step), following a Plan-do-check-act-cycle in combination with an expert team, has led to high success rates.(Wessels-Basten et al., 2007;Helmons et al., 2009) We found that a well considered strategy, that creates rules with a high positive predictive value (PPV) is essential for accurate content and reliable messages. Application of this strategy has led to clinical rules with a reliability (PPV) of at least 94%, which indicates that more than 94% of the alerts are technically correct and clinically relevant as indicated by the expert team and end-users.(Wessels-Basten et al., 2007)

This strategy mentioned is described in detail in another publication (Scheepers, 2009) and tries to solve important barriers described earlier, especially the ones regarding content and reliability. In our hospital we use the advanced CDSS Gaston, a commercially available system described in many publications. (de Clercq, 2004). Gaston is a software system - you could also call it an intelligent agent - that consists of two parts. The first part - the guideline-editor (Fig. 1) - allows the user to build the guidelines as flowcharts in a user-friendly environment. The steps in the flowchart contain the selection definitions based on the parameters that are available in the EHR. The second part, the decision support module (DCS) is the guideline execution engine. This engine translates the guideline from the guideline-editor into a routine that can be executed.

As the expert team is the key quality of the strategy developed in our previous research, we experienced some specific factors that need to be taken into account. These aspects may help others to compose the right team in order to optimised outcomes:

- Define the objective clearly. The context of the clinical rule and how it will be applied in practice should be clear for all participants.
- Start by making a clear structure in which the clinical rule is developed. Some content covers only one drug, some covers a certain drug class, while others concern a complete (contra-)indication. One should try to classify the content correctly.

- Develop the clinical rule in a way that is clear for all participants before start and in a structured way with a pre-defined strategy.
- Compose the team of experts with experts from different departments and specialisms. Also, compose the team with people that can be trusted to have an active role in the discussion and reflect the opinion of others well.
- Communicate to the experts what effort is expected form them and how much time it will cost them. How will they be rewarded for their input.
- Communicate clearly how feedback will be given, in meetings or digital communication.
- Determine how decisions are made when not all experts agree. Which experts are identified as having the last word or should there be a majority with the same opinion.
- When opinions differ, stay objective as being the chairman of the session. Try to make a clear overview of all pro- and contra arguments and try to literature to create an agreement.

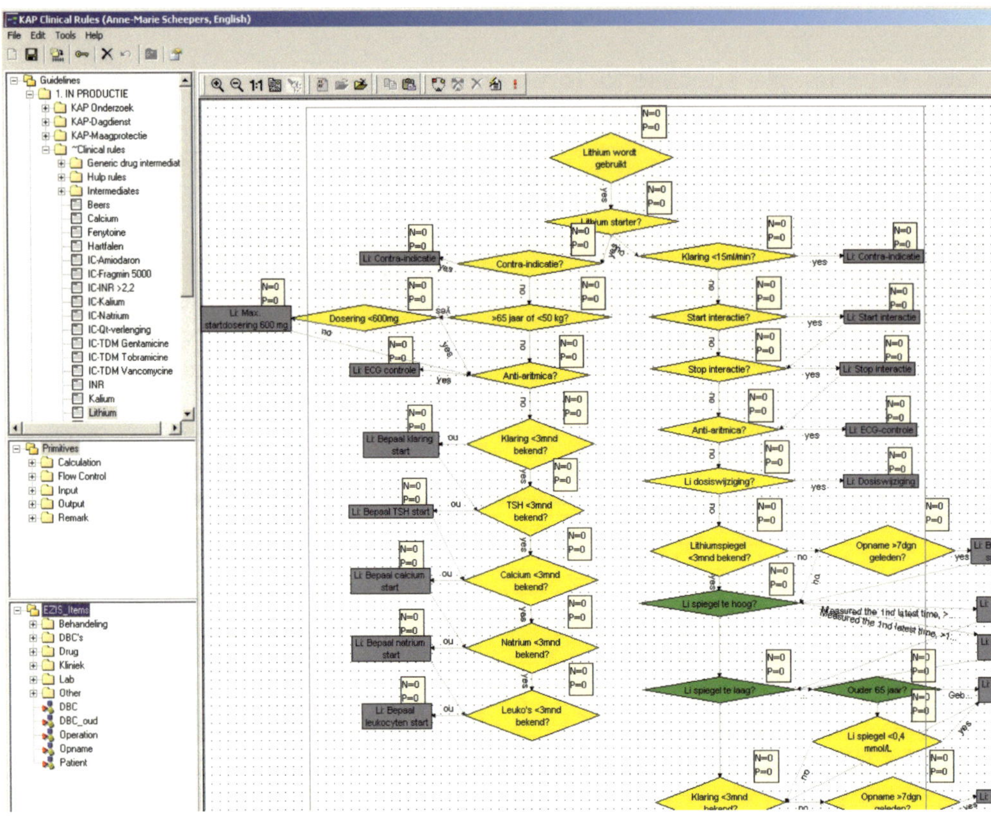

Fig. 1. Screenshot of the Gaston Guideline Editor, with an example of a clinical rule, build as a flowchart to cover the complete therapy of lithium.

Integration of all computer systems in one environment is also found to be important to ease implementation. In our hospital, CPOE is integrated in the EMR. Only one link is needed between CDSS and EMR/CPOE which facilitates technical implementation, maintenance and costs.(de Clercq and Hasman, 2004) An example: we found that every time the EMR was upgraded to a new version, also adaptations in de CDSS were needed. Besides these two factors, we experienced that the success factors as described above are important for an effective foundation before widespread hospital implementation.

5.1 Barriers experienced in practice

When the dependence on a CDSS is growing for the checking of guidelines in a more consistent and reliable way, it is necessary that the well-functioning of the CDSS is guaranteed in the hospital. During our research we experienced a lot of barriers. For the guarantee of well-functioning, the following 'commandments' need to be addressed:

1. **Stability and performance of the CDSS**: When the CDSS is increasingly used, it may impact the performance of the system itself as well as other systems. It is important that the position of the CDSS is well known amongst all and that these performance problems are known, controlled and monitored continuously by the ICT-department.
2. **Maintenance of the CDSS**: Maintenance can be divided in functional and technical maintenance, with different responsibilities. It should be indicated clearly who is responsible for the content of the system and all the parameters used in these clinical rules (functional). This is usually a task for the medical professional, who builds, tests and releases these clinical guidelines. Between function and technical maintenance is the maintenance of the data and parameters used (data dictionary). When a parameter, location or database structure are changed for the information systems that feed the CDSS with data (e.g. the EHR or laboratory information system), the data dictionary of the CDSS should be changed accordingly. The use of so-called 'free-text' in the data feeding information systems should be minimized for as much as possible. Typo-errors or different use of text for the same concept makes it impossible to guarantee the correct functioning of the CDSS. Technical maintenance includes the maintenance of the CDSS application, installing updates and new releases of the CDSS (and EHR) and testing the technical correct functioning of the CDSS. Because a CDSS uses data from other information systems like the EHR, it is important that technical testing of the CDSS is also performed after installing updates or new releases of other information systems like the EHR. This is usually done by the ICT-department. In addition, advanced reporting systems should be able for signalling and solving errors of the CDSS. When one is not aware of an error or malfunctioning of the CDSS, the patient safety could be at risk without anybody noticing it. The responsibility of the functional and technical maintenance of the CDSS should be clearly defined and time and budget should be available for medical professionals and the hospital IT -department.
3. **Skills and knowledge of personnel**: When there are errors concerning the CDSS, one should be able to estimate the possible risks on patient safety and immediately act upon it. This requires effort from all personnel, medical as well as IT personnel. Documentation on the guidelines, possible errors and their risks and an emergency procedure, in case of malfunctioning of the CDSS is an important aspect of the safe use of a CDSS.
4. **A generalised format**: Agreements should be made between the hospital departments about the layout, priority and content of warnings of the CDSS, the way they should respond to them and the content of guidelines. The presence of a wide variety of warnings could cause that medical professionals lose interest for them. In that case the warnings of the CDSS are not used and their additional value declines.

5. **Continuity and support of the CDSS vendor**: This support is essential for continued technical quality of the system and the validated manner of application in practice. In every setting local adaptations are needed to fulfil the demands of the CDSS customer.
6. **Comprehensive testing protocols:** These should be available for the testing of guidelines before implementation and for the testing of guidelines after new releases and updates. Also testing protocols should be available for the technical testing of the CDSS. When the number of guidelines increases in a hospital, it will cost an increasing amount of time to test all the guidelines after a new release or update. One should develop testing strategies, which allow adequate testing within a limited amount of time.

This list is not a complete list and not a completely new list: Most of the issues are also applicable for other information systems like the EHR itself. It is important that the issues on this list are addressed because downtime and malfunctioning of the EHR or the CDSS have severe implications for the hospital and its patients. One should be aware that malfunctioning of the CDSS is not immediately visible for the medical professional because it generally results in the absence of warnings. Warnings are, however, not always present, only in case of treatment differing from guidelines. The absence of warnings will therefore not automatically alarm a medical professional. Continuously monitoring of the CDSS by the IT department is therefore important, to prevent unreported malfunctioning CDSS, which is a potential risk for patient safety.

6. Discussion

The primary finding in this chapter is that many factors determine the successful implementation of advanced decision support. Although several publications have addressed the need of detailed description of system design and implementation features, these are continuously poorly reported.(Kawamoto et al., 2005;Garg et al., 2005;Mollon et al., 2009) Also the definition of a CDSS is used confusingly, as they include a wide variety of computerized and non-computerized systems that apply basic and advanced decision support. This complicates to conclude which factors really contribute to success of advanced decision support and seriously hampers widespread implementation of these systems that are so urgently needed.

The implementation of effective clinical decision support is a challenging task and in this complex process there are no easy solutions to guarantee success or to avoid failure. When starting with a CDSS, first certain prerequisites must be met. First, nationwide adoption of an EMR must be accelerated, as this is a prerequisite for CDSS adoption. Secondly, it is important to gather the right data and create a clinical rule with high reliability with technically correct and clinically relevant messages. Essential is that an effective system must minimize the effort required by clinicians to receive and act on systems recommendations.(Kawamoto et al., 2005) Last but not least, the commitment and participation of physicians as most frequent end-users is crucial for success.(Bates et al., 2003) It is important to identify stakeholders that support the implementation and a multidisciplinary team to achieve realisation, distribution and continuation.(Osheroff et al., 2005) When these people address the value and possibilities of these systems, time and money can be made available. It is very time consuming to add knowledge to a CDSS, continuously test and validate the clinical rules and recommendations. Consequently, high

costs are associated with the development of clinical rules and the cost-effectiveness of CDSS has rarely been studied yet.(Field et al., 2008)
Nevertheless, a CDSS is a powerful tool that can even fulfil 'latent needs'. These needs, that are present but not yet realized, can be fulfilled by detecting errors that need prevention but are too time-consuming with current possibilities. An example is the clinical rule for renal function Helmons et al developed.(Helmons et al., 2009) This clinical rule checks when a patient has a decreased renal function and dose adjustments of the medication are necessary. Compared to chart review, this clinical rule decreases time needed for checking and intervention by 80%. This example illustrates that today many gaps exist between optimal and actual practice. Although a pharmacist should check all patients on the combination of drug dosing and decreased renal function, in the current situation it is impossible as time is limited. Our research shows that with every developed clinical rule, remarkable differences between guidelines and practice were found, even though guidelines are well known.(Wessels-Basten et al., 2007;Helmons et al., 2009) Prospective research must demonstrate the effect of these clinical rules in practice.

7. Conclusion and further recommendations

This chapter demonstrates a practical overview of success factors which are crucial for successful implementation of advanced CDSS to facilitate widespread implementation in hospital practice. These success factors are focused on presenting the right message, at the right time, in the right place with the right system. More adequate descriptions of system design features and implementation are needed to translate these factors to effects on patient outcomes.
CDSS are expected to unchain a revolution in healthcare and fill the existing information gap by bringing relevant data and knowledge to the point of care.(Bates et al., 2003) Despite the consciousness that change is indispensable and the years of research and effort worldwide, this has only led to slow adoption of EMR and CDSS. We believe it is now the time to bring these identified success factors in practice to accelerate the adoption of these systems and reap the benefits of this promising next-generation in medication safety.
More research is needed in most areas concerning CDSS (Kuperman et al., 2007;van Wyk et al., 2008) The focus of this research should be which alerting mechanism (list, pop-ups, e-mail, SMS, dedicated quality persons) results in the best adherence of physicians to previously agreed standards of care and how do these methods effect patient outcomes? Eventually this will give an answer to the question: how to optimally implement a CDSS in clinical practice in order to reduce errors and omissions so frequently noted.

8. References

Aspden, P., J. Wolcott, J. Bootman, and L. Cronenwett, 2006,Aspden, P., J. Wolcott, J. Bootman, and L. Cronenwett Preventing Medication Errors: Quality Chasm Series: Washington, DC, National Academy Press.

Bates, D. W. et al., 2003, Ten commandments for effective clinical decision support: making the practice of evidence-based medicine a reality: J.Am.Med.Inform.Assoc., v. 10, no. 6, p. 523-530.

Committee on Quality of Health Care in America, 2001,Committee on Quality of Health Care in America Crossing the quality chasm: a new health system for the 21st century: Washington, D.C, National Academy Press.

de Clercq, P., and A. Hasman, 2004, Experiences with the development, implementation and evaluation of automated decision support systems: Stud.Health Technol.Inform, v. 107, no. Pt 2, p. 1033-1037.

Denekamp, Y., 2007, Clinical decision support systems for addressing information needs of physicians: Isr.Med.Assoc.J., v. 9, no. 11, p. 771-776.

Dexter, P. R., S. Perkins, J. M. Overhage, K. Maharry, R. B. Kohler, and C. J. McDonald, 2001, A computerized reminder system to increase the use of preventive care for hospitalized patients: The New England Journal of Medicine, v. 345, no. 13, p. 965-970.

Field, T. S., P. Rochon, M. Lee, L. Gavendo, S. Subramanian, S. Hoover, J. Baril, and J. Gurwitz, 2008, Costs Associated with Developing and Implementing a Computerized Clinical Decision Support System for Medication Dosing for Patients with Renal Insufficiency in the Long-term Care Setting: Journal of the American Medical Informatics Association, v. 15, no. 4, p. 466-472.

Garg, A. X., N. K. J. Adhikari, H. McDonald, M. P. Rosas-Arellano, P. J. Devereaux, J. Beyene, J. Sam, and R. B. Haynes, 2005, Effects of Computerized Clinical Decision Support Systems on Practitioner Performance and Patient Outcomes: A Systematic Review: JAMA: The Journal of the American Medical Association, v. 293, no. 10, p. 1223-1238.

Goud, R., A. Hasman, and N. Peek, 2008, Development of a guideline-based decision support system with explanation facilities for outpatient therapy: Computer Methods and Programs in Biomedicine, v. 91, no. 2, p. 145-153.

Greenes, RA., 2007,Greenes, RA. Clinical Decision Support. The Road Ahead: Boston, Elsevier Academic Press.

Helmons, P., R. Grouls, A. Roos, A. Bindels, P. De Clercq, S. Wessels-Basten, E. Ackerman, and H. Korsten, 2009, The potential value on medication safety of a clinical decision support system in intensive care patients with renal insufficiency: QSHC, in press.

James, B., 2001, Making It Easy to Do It Right: The New England Journal of Medicine, v. 345, no. 13, p. 991-993.

James, B., 2002, Quality improvement opportunities in health care - Making it easy to do it right: J Manag.Care Pharm., v. 8, no. 5, p. 394-399.

Jha, A. K., J. Laguette, A. Seger, and D. W. Bates, 2008, Can Surveillance Systems Identify and Avert Adverse Drug Events? A Prospective Evaluation of a Commercial Application: Journal of the American Medical Informatics Association, v. 15, no. 5, p. 647-653.

Kawamoto, K., C. A. Houlihan, E. A. Balas, and D. F. Lobach, 2005, Improving clinical practice using clinical decision support systems: a systematic review of trials to identify features critical to success: BMJ, v. 330, no. 7494, p. 765.

Kohn, L., J. Corrigan, and M. Donaldson, 2000,Kohn, L., J. Corrigan, and M. Donaldson To Err Is Human: Building a Safer Health System: Washington, DC, National Academy Press.

Kuperman, G. J., A. Bobb, T. H. Payne, A. J. Avery, T. K. Gandhi, G. Burns, D. C. Classen, and D. W. Bates, 2007, Medication-related Clinical Decision Support in

Computerized Provider Order Entry Systems: A Review: Journal of the American Medical Informatics Association, v. 14, no. 1, p. 29-40.

Leendertse, A. J., A. C. G. Egberts, L. J. Stoker, P. M. L. A. van den Bemt, and for the HARM Study Group, 2008, Frequency of and Risk Factors for Preventable Medication-Related Hospital Admissions in the Netherlands: Archives of Internal Medicine, v. 168, no. 17, p. 1890-1896.

Leslie, S. J., and M. A. Denvir, 2007, Clinical decision support software for chronic heart failure: Crit Pathw.Cardiol., v. 6, no. 3, p. 121-126.

Levy, M., T. Azaz-Livshits, B. Sadan, M. Shalit, G. Geisslinger, and K. Brune, 1999, Computerized surveillance of adverse drug reactions in hospital: implementation: Eur J Clin Pharmacol, v. 54, no. 11, p. 887-892.

Maviglia, S. M., R. D. Zielstorff, M. Paterno, J. M. Teich, D. W. Bates, and G. J. Kuperman, 2003, Automating Complex Guidelines for Chronic Disease: Lessons Learned: Journal of the American Medical Informatics Association, v. 10, no. 2, p. 154-165.

Mollon, B., J. Chong, A. Holbrook, M. Sung, L. Thabane, and G. Foster, 2009, Features predicting the success of computerized decision support for prescribing: a systematic review of randomized controlled trials: BMC Medical Informatics and Decision Making, v. 9, no. 1, p. 11.

Nies, J., I. Colombet, P. Degoulet, and P. Durieux, 2006, Determinants of success for computerized clinical decision support systems integrated in CPOE systems: a systematic review: AMIA Annu Symp Proc, p. 594-598.

Osheroff, J., E. Pifer, J. Teich, D. Sittig, and R. Jenders, 2005,Osheroff, J., E. Pifer, J. Teich, D. Sittig, and R. Jenders Improving outcomes with clinical decision support: an implementer's guide.: Health Information Management and Systems Society.

Schiff, G. D., D. Klass, J. Peterson, G. Shah, and D. W. Bates, 2003, Linking Laboratory and Pharmacy: Opportunities for Reducing Errors and Improving Care: Archives of Internal Medicine, v. 163, no. 8, p. 893-900.

Soman, S., G. Zasuwa, and J. Yee, 2008, Automation, Decision Support, and Expert Systems in Nephrology: Advances in Chronic Kidney Disease, v. 15, no. 1, p. 42-55.

Sucher, J. F., F. A. Moore, S. R. Todd, R. M. Sailors, and B. A. McKinley, 2008, Computerized clinical decision support: a technology to implement and validate evidence based guidelines: J.Trauma, v. 64, no. 2, p. 520-537.

Trivedi, M. H., J. K. Kern, A. Marcee, B. Grannemann, B. Kleiber, T. Bettinger, K. Z. Altshuler, and A. McClelland, 2002, Development and implementation of computerized clinical guidelines: barriers and solutions: Methods Inf.Med, v. 41, no. 5, p. 435-442.

Trivedi, M., E. Daly, J. Kern, B. Grannemann, P. Sunderajan, and C. Claassen, 2009, Barriers to implementation of a computerized decision support system for depression: an observational report on lessons learned in "real world" clinical settings: BMC Medical Informatics and Decision Making, v. 9, no. 1, p. 6.

van der Sijs, H., J. Aarts, A. Vulto, and M. Berg, 2006, Overriding of Drug Safety Alerts in Computerized Physician Order Entry: Journal of the American Medical Informatics Association, v. 13, no. 2, p. 138-147.

van Wyk, J. T., M. A. M. van Wijk, M. C. J. M. Sturkenboom, M. Mosseveld, P. W. Moorman, and J. van der Lei, 2008, Electronic Alerts Versus On-Demand Decision Support to

Improve Dyslipidemia Treatment: A Cluster Randomized Controlled Trial: Circulation, v. 117, no. 3, p. 371-378.

Varonen, H., T. Kortteisto, M. Kaila, and for the EBMeDS Study Group, 2008, What may help or hinder the implementation of computerized decision support systems (CDSSs): a focus group study with physicians: Family Practice, v. 25, no. 3, p. 162-167.

Wessels-Basten, S., A. Hoeks, R. Grouls, P. Helmons, E. Ackerman, and H. Korsten, 2007, Development strategy and potential impact on medication safety for clinical rules: the lithium case: Br J Clin Pharmacol, v. 63, no. 4, p. 507-508.

Wetter, T., 2002, Lessons learnt from bringing knowledge-based decision support into routine use: Artificial Intelligence in Medicine, v. 24, no. 3, p. 195-203.

Part 2

Guideline-Based Clinical Decision Support System

4

Information Extraction Approach for Clinical Practice Guidelines Representation in a Medical Decision Support System

Fernando Pech-May[1], Ivan Lopez-Arevalo[2] and Victor J. Sosa-Sosa[2]
[1]*Instituto Tecnológico Superior de los Ríos*
Balancan, Tabasco
[2]*Information Technology Laboratory, Cinvestav – Tamaulipas*
Victoria, Tamaulipas
Mexico

1. Introduction

Errors in healthcare are a leading cause of death and injury. Kohn et al. (Kohn et al., 2000) mention that, for example, preventable adverse events are a leading cause of death in the United States. In their studies they state that at least 44,000 and perhaps as many as 98,000 americans die in hospitals each year as result of medical errors. Similar scenarios are for other countries. This situation has motivated the usage of Clinical Practice Guidelines (CPGs) to reduce the uncertainty of the clinical professional (nurses and physicians) when making decisions about the patient illness.

Clinical Practice Guidelines (CPGs) are documents containing guidelines and structured recommendations that are defined by domain experts based on medical and scientific evidence (Teije et al., 2006; Twaddle, 2005). Thus CPGs provide guides and scientific evidence to clinical professional to make flexible recommendations about specific health circumstances (Field & Lohr, 1990).

The main objective of CPGs is to offer to clinical staff a set of recommendations that are focused on helping in the diagnosis, prognosis, and treatment of specific illness. The goal is to enhance the medical attention to patients. Furthermore, a CPG is an important support for the patient itself and his/her family on understanding the efficiency of a treatment and an important tool to improve the quality in medical care. Because CPGs are largely documents in narrative form, sometimes are ambiguous and lack of a defined structure and internal consistency, which make them too complicated for being understood directly by a computer. The information usually contained in a CPG is plain texts, lists, diagrams, tables, and annotations in HTML, XHTML or PDF format. To make this information understandable for a computer, it is required the usage of CPGs formal representation languages (Clercq et al., 2004; Votruba et al., 2004). In this sense, many researchers have proposed different frameworks, approaches, representation languages, and tools for CPGs modelling, which can be interpreted by computers (Hripcsak et al., 2005; Isern & Moreno, 2008). Some of these tools and approaches provide orientation for a specific representation of CPGs, others are intended for a more general use in several representation languages.

However, nowadays the formalization process is still carried out manually. Although there exist several formal languages, their usage represents a complex and time-consuming work for a manual formalization of CPGs. The usage of tools for the formalization of CPGs requires not only knowledge about formal methods, but also about the medical domain.
This paper describes a basic Information Extraction (IE) approach to enhance the knowledge acquisition on Clinical Practice Guidelines. The aim is to support the CPG modeller during the formalization process facilitating the CPG interpretation by computers, becoming an important module in every Medical Decision Support System. The output of this approach can be used for a better understanding by non-clinical medical people of CPGs. The starting point of this work was motivated for a preliminary effort wherein a CPG interpreter was developed (Pech-May, 2010).
The paper is organised as follows. In section 2 the contextualisation background about Clinical Practice Guidelines and Information Extraction is given. Section 3 describes the proposed Information Extraction approach. Section 4 shows the experiments carried out and the obtained results of a first prototype for the proposed approach. Finally, the section 5 presents some conclusions, remarks, and further work.

2. Background

2.1 Clinical Practice Guidelines

For interpretation issues, the medical procedures within a CPG are translated into algorithms that describe such procedures for diagnosis, prognosis, and treatment. The representation of a CPG as algorithms allows the organization of the relevant information in a directly applicable manner. In consequence this representation can enhance and support the decisions making process (Patel et al., 2001; Lyng et al., 2008).
Several languages for CPGs representation have been developed for different purposes, users, and applications. Shiffman et al. (Shifman et al., 2000) described the requirements for modelling the knowledge of CPGs taking into account issues as completeness, expressivity, usability, and reuse.
Most of the representation languages use the XML format as readable-machine language. Some of the most used languages for representing CPGs are:

- **Asbru** (Young et al., 2007) is a task-specific and intention-based plan representation language. It was designed specifically for a set of management-task plans. Some tools that help the formalization of GPCs in Asbru are AsbruView[1] and DELT/A[2].
- **GLIF** (Wang et al., 2004) (the Guideline Interchange Format) defines an ontology for the representation of CPGs, as well as a medical ontology for representing medical data and concepts. GLIF (on its third version) includes a formal expression language for specifying decision criteria and patient state. A tool that allows modeling CPGs in GLIF is Protégé[3].
- **GEM** (Ciccarese et al., 2004) (the Guideline Elements Model) is an XML-based guideline document model that can store and organize the heterogeneous information contained in practice guideline documents. A tool that supports the formalization of CPGs in GEM is GEM Cutter[4].

[1] http://www.asgaard.tuwien.ac.at/asbruview/
[2] http://gem.med.yale.edu/default.htm
[3] http://protege.stanford.edu
[4] http://gem.med.yale.edu/default.htm

- **EON** (Tu et al., 2001) is a guideline modeling and execution system that is part of the EON architecture, a component-based suite of models and software components for the creation of guideline-based applications.
- **PROforma** (Sutton and Fox, 2003) allows the guideline to be modeled as a set of tasks and data items, it is designed to support the management of medical procedures and clinical decision making at the point of care. The PROforma task model divides a generic task (keystone) into four types: plans, decisions, actions, and enquiries.

The following list includes some remarkable aspects that are considered in the most typical formal languages such as Asbru, PROforma, and GLIF.

- **Organization of plans:** Asbru as well PROforma use an isolate generic object class for modelling plans: *the plan object*. GLIF uses two types of plans: *guides and macros*. The guides cover the direction and flow control decisions. The macros are used to specify in a declarative way the procedure patterns for specific purposes by means of a set of implementation steps, which appear as a one block in the CPGs.
- **Specification of goals/intentions:** GLIF specifies goals as strings; Asbru represents the intentions of plans as temporal patterns depending on the context.
- **Action model:** Actions are the primitives for the modeling used to represent tasks in a CPG (for instance, prescription, clinical research). All the languages allow specifying medical actions, but just GLIF has special structured classes to do it. This modeling method has an efficient mechanism to map instances of medical actions to terms of a restricted vocabulary. Regarding to the effect of actions, Asbru and PROforma, unlike GLIF, support express effects allowing to reason about actions based on its effects. In Asbru the effects of a plan can be used to select between different alternative plans and express causal relations. In turn in PROforma the effect of actions are modelled as postconditions, which are semantically different to the effects on Asbru because they represent assertions when an action is completed.
- **Representation of medical knowledge and patient data:** PROforma model medical knowledge by means of relations between concepts (indications, conindications, interaction between drugs, etc.). Such relations are included as arguments in alternative decisions. In GLIF the medical knowledge is represented as instances of concept-relation. Asbru has not a explicit representation for this kind of knowledge as part of the CPG model; nevertheless, this knowledge can be accessed by means of functions calls.

The use of any of the formal languages involves several additional tasks that depend on the particular language. To tackle this issue, several assistant tools have been developed to support the formalization process. They range from markup-based tools, such as DELT/A, Stepper, and GEM-Cutter, to graphical tools using symbols to model diagrams, such as Protégé or the plan body wizard of the DeGel framework. A brief description of these tools is given below.

- **Stepper** (Růzicka and Svatek, 2004) is a markup tool for the formalization of narrative CPGs. The formalization of the CPGs is done through user-defined stages and each stage transformed to XML.
- **GEM Cutter** (Karras et al., 2000) transforms CPGs into GEM format. The GEM Cutter interface shows the textual CPG and its XML representation, thereby facilitating the user interaction in the transformation of the CPG.
- **DELT/A** (Votruba et al., 2004) support the translation of HTML documents to XML. DELT/A provides two main features: (1) linking between a textual guideline and its formal representation, and (2) applying design patterns as macros forms.

- **Uruz** is part of the Degel framework (Shalom et al., 2003), it uses a markup mechanism that allows the user to introduce medical terms in the CPG. Such terms can come from some vocabulary as ICD-9-CM (ICD-9-CM, 2010)[5].
- **Protégé** (Gennari et al., 2002) is a general purpose tool for knowledge acquisition. It is broadly used in several knowledge domain fields. This tool allows modelling CPGs in different representation formal languages.
- **AsbruView** (Kosara et al., 2002) is a graphical user interface for Asbru to support the development of CPGs and medical protocols. AsbruView is focused on visualising data and plans during the design and execution.

According to the specialized literature, important work has been done trying to translate CPG documents into a readable-machine presentation (Pech-May, 2010). Dart et al. (Dart et al., 2001) proposed a generic model to represent any CPG in XML format. Moreover, they proved that CPGs can be modeled in a generic XML file. Bosse (Bosse, 2001) developed an interpreter capable of simulating CPGs written in Asbru language for one CPG. Geldof (Geldof, 2002) presented a methodology to formalize CPGs in several languages, from his understanding until computerizing in XML. Aguirre-Junco et al. (Aguirre-Junco, et al., 2004) described a knowledge specification method based on a structured and systematic analysis of text allowing a detailed specification of a decision tree for CPGs. Fuchsberger and Miksch (Fuchsberger & Miksch, 2002) presented an execution unit tailored for a particular CPG representation in Asbru plans.

The main aim for all the above work is the reasoning with the extracted medical knowledge. A reasoning process over such knowledge is desirable by nurses and physicians. Following this tendency, some efforts have been done to develop Medical Decision Support Systems (Kaiser & Miksch, 2005). But, like in similar works about Decision Support Systems, the knowledge acquisition becomes a bottleneck, which is the main limitation for this kind of systems. In this sense, we are introducing an approach to extract knowledge from textual CPGs that integrates an innovative Information Extraction module that facilitates knowledge acquisition.

2.2 Information Extraction

The Information Extraction (IE) is responsible for structuring information contained in plain texts, which can be relevant for a particular domain (called extraction domain) (Karras, et al., 2000; Lehnert et al., 1994). The IE is a research subject that covers many areas. The goal of an IE system is finding and linking relevant information while ignoring the strange and irrelevant information. Peshkin and Pfeffer (Peshkin & Pfeffer, 2003) define the Information Extraction as the task of filling template information from previously unseen text which belongs to a pre-defined domain.

One of the main reasons to use IE is its role in the evaluation and comparison of different Natural Language Processing technologies in domains highly influenced by human interactions, like the medical domain.

The IE systems can be classified based on two approaches:

---

[5]International Classification of Diseases. This is a classification of diseases and procedures used in the coding of clinical information derived from medical assistance, mainly in the hospital environment and specialized medical care centers.

- **Knowledge Engineering (KE):** This is focused on an empiric method or based on a domain corpus to develop efficient and robust Natural Language Processing systems (Kasabov 2006).
- **Machine Learning (ML):** This has a well-known set of documents and outputs and uses a set of patterns to extract knowledge by means of Machine Learning techniques (Ethem, 2004).

Based on the ML approach, the IE can be seen as useful technique to extract information from Clinical Practice Guidelines (CPGs) with the aim of enhancing its formalization. Particularly one of the tools used in the medical domain is the Badger system (Soderland, et al., 1995), which is a text analysis tool to summarize medical patient records by extracting diagnoses, symptoms, physical findings, test results, and therapeutic treatments based on linguistic concepts.

There are other IE systems based on Machine Learning techniques such as SRV -Sequence Rules with Validation- (Freitag, 1998), which transforms the patterns learning problem into a classification problem; RAPIER (Califf, 1998) that uses pairs of test documents and fills templates; and WHISK (Sonderland, 1999) that uses learning rules to extract a set of text styles. These tools can be adapted to several domains.

Some authors consider the Information Extraction (IE) as a later stage in the Information Retrieval (IR) process (Marie-Francine, 2006), the main difference between both is that IE provides the exactly desired information, while IR is in charge of finding the documents wherein the desired information should appear. Some new technologies try to merge advantages from both, such as some web wrappers (XWRAP (Liu et al, 2000) or (Baumgartner et al., 2001)) that extract information from HTML documents and search answers (automatic response over punctual queries). In this sense, a wrapper is a program that retrieves information from different repositories, merging, and unifying them. The aim of a wrapper is to locate relevant information in a semi-structured data and put it into a self-described representation for further processing (Kushmerick et al., 1997).

3. Approach

Most representation languages for CPG are very powerful and complex. They can contain many different types of information and data. The main goal for the application of Information Extraction on CPG documents is to obtain the relevant text by means of natural language patterns which can be used in the formalization of the CPG. This approach is illustrated in Figure 1.

The approach facilitates the formalization process by using several intermediate representations that are obtained by stepwise procedures. The idea is to obtain an intermediate representation of a CPG in XML format for reasoning. Such intermediate representation takes into account all the most important pieces from the CPG (such as actions, processes, sequences, etc.). The final output is a XML representation. This approach is an extension and adaptation of the work carried out by Cem Akkaya (Akkaya, 2005), which is a basic method for IE. The initial idea is to enhance the performance of a preliminary prototype to match patient data against CPGs (Pech-May et al., 2009) within a more general Medical Decision Support System.

To make the extraction, some specific templates have been generated, which are filled by the desired information. To detect such information, a heuristic method is applied. The filled templates are later processed.

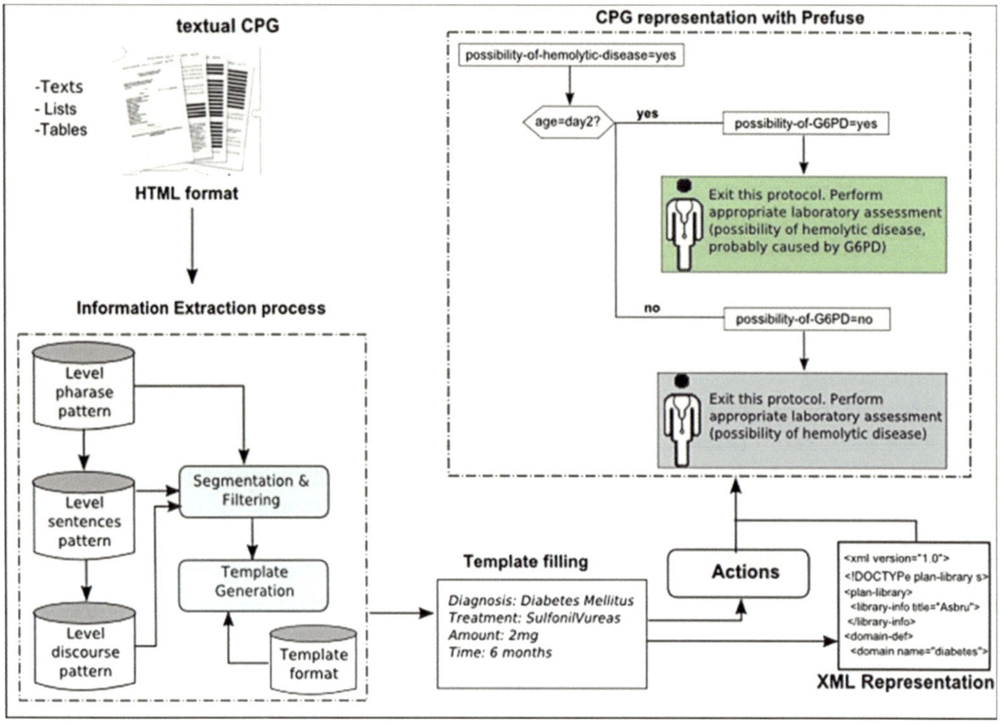

Fig. 1. Proposed IE approach.

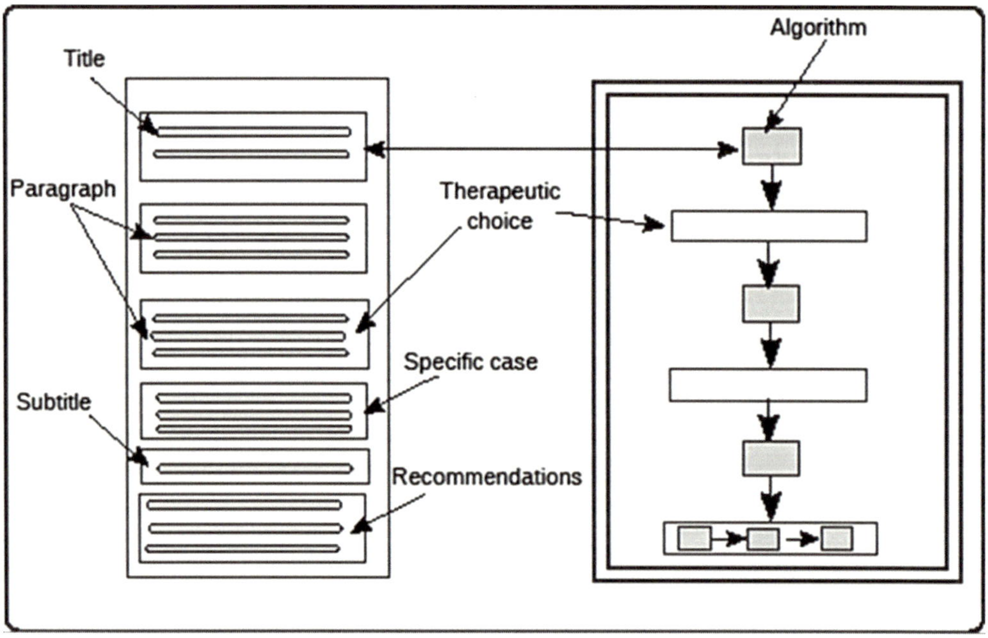

Fig. 2. General structure for CPGs.

The input CPGs are chosen from the National Guideline Clearinghouse[6] (NGC) repository in XHTML format. Then, XHTML documents are analyzed to extract relevant information, and subsequently to obtain the intermediate representation. Such representation is displayed through templates in form of views by means of the Prefuse[7] tool (Jeffrey et al., 2005). The approach considers that tested CPGs follow the structure of the NGC repository since these CPGs have a predefined structure. This approach works only for textual CPGs because in graphical or chart representation few text is included, relevant text (from medical experts) is mandatory for the approach. In general, a GPC has a structure consisting of separated sections for the treatment of a disease. For example, Figure 2 shows the general sections for diagnosis and treatment of a disease.

A general flowchart for a CPG is depicted in Figure 3, based on the general structure of a CPG. In order to obtain information from CPGs, this approach is based on the transformation of multiple processes following three heuristic patterns for Information Extraction:

a. Phrase pattern level (lexical level)
b. Sentence pattern level (syntactic level)
c. Speech pattern level (semantic level)

It is necessary a parsing process to obtain the extraction rules. This is based on a knowledge engineering approach considering syntactic and semantic restrictions, and taking into account delimiters.

In order for processing a large amount of documents and information, it is necessary specific heuristics for each type of information required, for example:

a. Different types of information, in which each type of information needs specific methods for its processing (e.g. processes, parameters).
b. Different representations of information, in which it should be taken into account that the information could be represented in different ways (structured, semi-structured, or plain text).
c. Different types of guidelines, in which there may be CPGs for different diseases, diverse user groups, and several organizations that may contain similar CPGs.

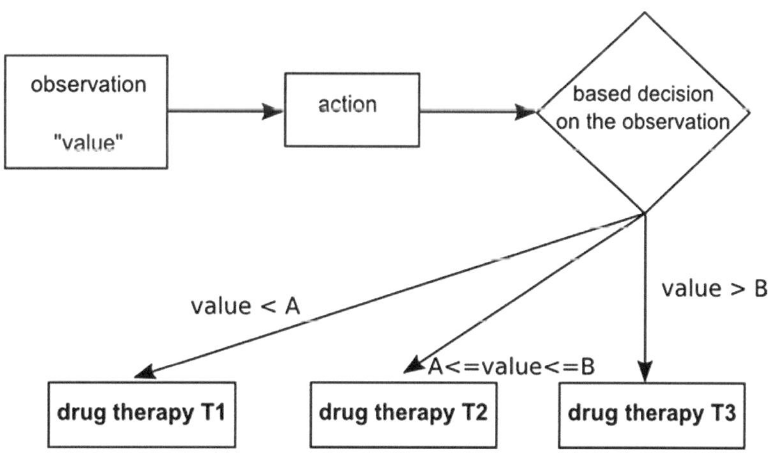

Fig. 3. General flowchart for CPGs

[6]www.guideline.gov

[7]The Prefuse toolkit is a set of software tools for creating interactive data visualizations for Java language.

The core of the approach is based on the atomic approach (Appelt & Israel, 1999), which basic idea is to assume that every noun phrase and verb of the right type, independently of the syntactic relations obtained among them, indicate an event/relationship of interest. It does not take into account the accuracy of the data extraction. Subsequently to the extracted data, a segmentation and filtering process is performed for its depuration. In this way, only the data concerning to the information of interest (diagnosis, treatment, drugs, etc.) is obtained. These data is stored in specific templates for further processing. The medical terms used in our prototype come from the Medical Subject Headings (MeSH)[8] of the National Library of Medicine from United States. Next, each heuristic pattern is briefly described.

3.1 Phrase pattern level

In this stage a lexical parser is used. It has the responsibility of splitting the text in paragraphs, tokens, and identifies important phrases in the CPG (e.g. administration of a drug, surgical procedures, dose of a drug, etc.). The lexical analyzer function is to identify the relevant information and then extract important data from the CPG. The lexical analyzer is in charge of filtering, for the second level of IE (sentence pattern level), the information that can be used by the syntactic level. They are defined by regular expressions as:

- Action terms (mainly verbs; e.g., "activate", "perform", "prescribe", "treat", "integrate", "receive", etc).
- Condition terms (regular expressions describing a condition, such as "if [, : \.]+", "in case(s)? [, : \.]+", "if [_,2 weeks]+", etc.).
- Time Annotations (e.g. [ESS, LSS], [EFS, LFS], [MinDu, MaxDu], REFERENCE)
- Dose unit terms (e.g. "(m | d | c)?(l | g)(/kg/day)?", "drop(s)?", "teaspoon(s)?", "tsp").

3.2 Sentence pattern level

In this level (syntactic level), the entire document is parsed and split into sentences. Then every sentence is processed with regard to its context within the document and its group affiliation. Thereby, the context is obtained by captions (e.g. "Acute Pharyngitis in children Algorithm Annotations | Treatment | Recommendations:") and a group contains sentences from the same paragraph or the same list, if there are no sublists. Thus, each sentence is now checked for relevance. Useful medical terms and keywords to identify medical actions can be found. The words or groups of words are mainly verbs indicating the application of a therapy, administration of a drug or a surgical procedure. This level considers two groups of patterns:

- **Free text pattern**. It is used to identify paragraphs from a list of items. The pattern indicates therapy instruments (surgical procedures) combined with key terms (e.g. prescribe, indicate, execute, etc).
- **Concise text pattern**. It is used to detect specific defined patterns such as lists of items with incorrect grammar. In general, it denotes the right therapy to apply, instruments for the therapy or drugs. These can be merged with other detected labels in the sentence or phrase pattern level.

Detecting relevant sentences is a challenging task, which is undertaken in two steps:

1. detecting irrelevant sentences to exclude them from further processing, and
2. detecting relevant sentences.

---

[8] http://www.nlm.nih.gov/mesh/

In both steps, special keywords are used to detect whether a sentence is irrelevant or relevant. Keywords describing irrelevant sentences are "history", "diagnosis", "criteria", "symptom", "clinical assessment", "risk factor", "complicating factor", "etiology", and so on. These terms point out that the following paragraph does not describe treatment processes, but that it describes symptoms, demonstration of diagnoses, and so on. If such a term appears within a caption the corresponding section is removed.

3.3 Speech pattern level

In this level semantic aspects are solved and the design and the structure of the final document XML are improved. In addition, this level is used to categorize sentences, actions, and to find their relationships. To accomplish the later task the following processes in the CPG are identified:

a. processes with temporal dependencies (processes at some point depending on another process),
b. sequential processes (the processes that are required to run with the authorization of other),
c. processes containing a thread,
d. selection process, and
e. recurring processes.

The application of the extraction rules gives as a result a well-structured XML document which can be represented by using specific templates or graphical forms (by using the Prefuse tool):

- **Templates**. It is the final representation of the Information Extraction module; these can be filled with specific CPG data. After collected all the relevant phrases from the CPG, the document is generated by using the representation of sentences, actions, relationships, and hierarchical structure. The representation is done through a document markup listing all relevant sentences and an identification of MeSH terms. Thus the document contains information for a dose, duration, actions, administration of a disease, etc.
- **Graphical representation**. The generated document is represented visually using Prefuse. In this way, it provides data to optimize table structures, tree graph design, visual encoding techniques, dynamic queries, integrated search, and database connectivity.

4. Experiments

A first implementation of this approach was developed by using Java language. For a performance analysis, different CPGs corresponding to different specific diseases were employed, which are:

- Diagnosis and treatment of otitis media in children
- Diagnosis and treatment of diabetes-mellitus (type 2)
- Acute pharyngitis in children
- Diagnostics and treatment of jaundice
- Management and treatment of dengue hemorrhagic fever at first and second attention level
- Treatment of breast cancer
- Chronic cough in a child

The CPGs were divided into two groups:

1. Clinical guidelines to develop and improve the heuristics
2. Clinical guidelines to test the obtained heuristics

The choice of these groups is not a trivial task because the organizations that develop CPGs do not regularly take care of following the same hierarchical structure. In this experiment, complex hierarchical structures were used as selection criteria, and distributed evenly to each group. Before applying the heuristics, some pre treatment was carried out (to verify that XHTML documents satisfy the structuring elements). This is achieved through the conversion of paragraphs/sections from the CPG and their corresponding items (according to the three pattern levels). Our test considered the following two tasks:

- **Task 1**: detection of relevant sentences, and
- **Task 2**: summarization of the detection types of sentence and the relationship between processes.

The performance of the prototype was evaluated by using the precision and recall measures. The recall score measures the ratio of correct information extracted from the texts against all the available information present in the text. The precision score measures the ratio of correct information that was extracted against all the information that was extracted (Lehnert et al., 1994). The following summarizes the obtained results by task:

- **Task 1:** It obtains promising results (Table 1), even if it means lowering the precision punctuation. The lower recall score implies that detecting relevant sentences has to be improved. The high accuracy on precision score shows that irrelevant sentences were classified as relevant.
- **Task 2**: The entry for task 2 (Table 2) consists of sentences identified with very high punctuation in the previous task. The recall score is very high, which means that only few sentences were falsely not detected. The precision score implies that some slots were filled out incorrectly. The reason for this is that they do not always detect the correct type of sentence and specially when assigning annotations to their particular actions, situation that has to be improved.

Table 3 presents an overall evaluation. For all the tables, the nomenclature for columns is:

COR -Number of correct slots that were identified by our IE system
MAT -Total number of slots that match a CPG template in the CPGs group
IDE -Total number of slots that were identified by our IE system
REC: Represents our system recall that is given by COR/IDE
PRE: Represents our system precision that is given by COR/MAT

At the phrase pattern level several regular expressions were necessary. Figure 4 shows a fragment for a pattern in this level. At the sentence pattern level the text free patterns were identified, such as <p> and </p> (to identify de paragraphs), <li> and </li> (to identify lists of items), and some additional labels. These labels are combined with the labels from de phrase pattern level like <dosage> or </dosage>, <dose> or </dose>, etc.

After each CPG was processed in the three analysis stages (phrase level, sentence level, and speech level), an intermediate representation was obtained. For this, two files were generated, the first one containing the list of relevant sentences (see Table 5) and a second one which is a mark-up document (see Table 6).

The intermediate representation shown in Table 6 contains a set of actions and relations. An action contains sentences describing the action and annotation assigned by means of the DELT/A tool. It also contains the instrument for the treatment and an identifier within the MeSH dictionary. If the information is about a dose, duration of treatment or drug management, then a corresponding MeSH identifier is assigned to it. Table 7 partially shows the actions and its assigned MeSH identifiers for the CPG "Diagnosis and treatment of otitis media in children".

CPG	COR	MAT	IDE	REC	PRE
Diagnosis and treatment of otitis media in children	23	24	26	0.958	0.884
Diagnosis and treatment of diabetes-mellitus (type 2)	45	57	53	0.789	0.849
Acute pharyngitis in children	9	12	10	0.75	0.9
Diagnostics and treatment of jaundice	53	56	53	0.946	1
Management and treatment of dengue hemorrhagic fever at first and second attention level	65	68	75	0.955	0.866
Treatment of breast cancer	56	59	74	0.946	0.756
Chronic cough in a child	23	31	26	0.741	0.884

Table 1. Evaluation of Task 1 for each CPG.

CPG	COR	MAT	IDE	REC	PRE
Diagnosis and treatment of otitis media in children	27	32	27	0.843	1
Diagnosis and treatment of diabetes-mellitus (type 2)	32	34	40	0.941	0.8
Acute pharyngitis in children	56	58	67	0.965	0.835
Diagnostics and treatment of jaundice	36	42	45	0.857	0.8
Management and treatment of dengue hemorrhagic fever at first and second attention level	73	75	75	0.973	0.973
Treatment of breast cancer	86	116	98	0.741	0.877
Chronic cough in a child	14	18	20	0.777	0.7

Table 2. Evaluation of Task 2 for each CPG.

Task	COR	MAT	IDE	REC	PRE
Task 1	355	443	432	0.801	0.821
Task 2	849	865	978	0.981	0.868

Table 3. Overall evaluation results

<table>
<tr><td><number></td><td>([\d]+(([\.]([\d]+)) | ((\s*[\d]+)?/[\d]+))?)</td></tr>
<tr><td><numberOrRange></td><td><number>(((_to_) | (\s*-\s*))<number>)?</td></tr>
<tr><td><time-unit></td><td>m(illi)?)?sec(ond)?(s)? | min(ute)?(s)? | hour(s)? |
day(s)? | week(s)? ...</td></tr>
<tr><td><dose-unit></td><td>(m | c | d)?(l | g)(/kg(/<time-unit>)?)? | drop(s)? | tab(s)? ...</td></tr>
<tr><td><dosage></td><td><numberOrRange>[\s]*<dose-unit></td></tr>
<tr><td><time></td><td><numberOrRange>[\s]*<time-unit></td></tr>
<tr><td><iteration></td><td>TID | BID | QD | (Q | every) <time> |
<numberOrRange> _(times | doses)_(per | a)_<time-unit></td></tr>
<tr><td><person></td><td>those | patient(s)? | person(s)? | child(ren)? ...</td></tr>
<tr><td><condition></td><td>(in_(case(s)? | areas) | if | unless | who(m)?)_[^,:]+ |
In_.*allergic [^,\.:]+ | (for | in)_(a_)?(<person>) [^,\.:]+</td></tr>
</table>

Table 4. Examples of phrase level patterns.

```
<sentence>
  <delta-link link-id="8"/>
  <description>In children with risk factors for Streptococcus pneumoniae,
          it is recommended that Amoxicillin, high dose (80 to 90
          mg/kg/day) or Augmenting (with high dose amoxicillin component)
          be utilized as first-line therapy (Nash and Wald, 2001 [S];
          Wald, Chiponis, and Ledesma-Medina, 1986 [B]; Nelson, Mason,
          and Kaplan, 1994 [C]; Dowell et al., 1999 [E]; Dowell, 1-1998
          [E]; Friedland and McCracken, 1994 [E]; Local Expert Consensus
          [E]).
  </description>
</sentence>
<sentence>
  <delta-link link-id="9"/>
  <description>Note: Failure with amoxicillin is likely to be due to resistant
               Streptococcus pneumoniae, Haemophilus influenzae, or Moraxella
               catarrhalis.
  </description>
</sentence>
<sentence>
  <delta-link link-id="10"/>
  <description>High dose amoxicillin will overcome Streptococcus pneumoniae
               resistance (changes in penicillin-binding proteins)
               (Dowell et al., 1999 [E]; Whitney et al., 2000 [D]).
  </description>
</sentence>
```

Table 5. Fragment of the relevant sentence file corresponding to the GPC "Diagnosis and treatment of otitis media in children".

```
<li>
  <a id="delta:8">In children with risk factors for  Streptococcus
            pneumoniae, it is recommended that Amoxicillin, high dose
            (80 to 90  mg/kg/day) or Augmenting (with high dose
            amoxicillin component) be utilized as first-line therapy
            (Nash and Wald, 2001 [S]; Wald, Chiponis, and Ledesma-
            Medina, 1986 [B]; Nelson, Mason, and Kaplan, 1994 [C];
            Dowell et al., 1999 [E]; Dowell, 1 -1998 [E]; Friedland
            and McCracken, 1994 [E]; Local Expert Consensus [E]).
  </a>
  <ul type="disc">
    <li>
      <a id="delta:9">Note: Failure with amoxicillin is likely to be due
            to resistant <Streptococcus pneumoniae, Haemophilus
            influenzae, or Moraxella catarrhalis.
      </a>
      <a id="delta:10">High dose amoxicillin will overcome Streptococcus
            pneumoniae resistance (changes in penicillin-
            binding proteins) (Dowell et al., 1999 [E]; Whitney
            et al., 2000 [D]).
      </a>
      The clavulanic acid component of Augmentin is active against
      Resistant Haemophilus influenzae and Moraxella catarrhalis (B-
      lactamase enzyme) (Wald, Chiponis, and Ledesma-Medina, 1986 [B];
      Dagan et al., 2000 [A]).
    </li>
  </ul>
</li>
```

Table 6. Fragment of the mark-up document file corresponding to the GPC "Diagnosis and treatment of otitis media in children".

With the obtained actions from a CPG, it is possible transform the CPG into an Asbru document. At this moment this step is carried out manually.
In Asbru, a plan is represented by means of plans definitions. A plan contains a *plan name, arguments, knowledge role,* and a *plan body*. Table 8 shows an example for a fictitious plan following the Asbru specification. In Table 9 can be seen fragment of sentences, actions and plans for the CPG *Diagnosis and treatment of otitis media in children* in Asbru.

```
<action id="8" parent="5" group="18" selection="0">
  <delta-link link-id="8"/>
  <description>In the child with no risk factors for penicillin-resistant Streptococcus
            pneumoniae standard dose amoxicillin or Augmentin (with standard
            dose Amoxicillin component) may be considered as initial therapy.
  </description>
  <agents>
```

```
    <agent MeSH="D000658" name="amoxicillin"/>
    <agent MeSH="D019980" name="Augmentin"/>
  </agents>
  <condition>
    <item>In the child with no risk factors for penicillin-resistant Streptococcus
            pneumoniae
    </item>
  </condition>
  <annotations>
    <annotation>Note: Forty-six percent of isolates at Children's Hospital Medical
                Center of Cincinnati, Ohio have intermediate or high
                 Penicillin-resistant Streptococcus pneumoniae and local data
                supports that 15% of children locally may fail initial therapy
                with standard dose amoxicillin.
      <delta-link link-id="9"/>
    </annotation>
  </annotations>
  <context>
    <item>Antibiotic Treatment</item>
  </context>
</action>
```


Table 7. Partial actions corresponding to the GPC "Diagnosis and treatment of otitis media in children"

Plan	Plan-1
TIME ANNOTATION	([,], [,24 hours], [,], *NOW*)
PREFERENCES	Select-method: exact-fit
INTENTIONS	Avoid intermediate state: (glucose-level = high)
CONDITIONS	Abort-condition: (glucose-level = high) Filter-condition: ((patient-age > 60) AND (patient-age < 80))
EFFECTS	Plan-effect: Parameter="glucose-level" Relationship="decrement" Likelihood 0.65
PLAN_BODY	Parallel subplans: Continuation spaci_cation: (treatment-1 OR treatment-2) Diagnosis Treatment-1 Treatment-2

Table 8. Example of a fictitious plan in Asbru

<**treatment** title="Diagnosis and treatment of otitis media in children."> <**sentences**> <**sentence**> ... <**sentence**> <**sentence**> <**delta-link link-id**="14"/> <**description**>Therapeutic (10 day) course of antibiotics.</**description**> </**sentence**> <**sentence**> <**delta-link link-id**="15"/> <**description**>Consideration may be given to **a** shortened course of antibiotics (5 days) for children who are at low risk (i.e., age > 2 years, no history of chronic or recurrent otitis media and intact tympanic membranes).</**description**> </**sentence**> <**sentence**> <**delta-link link-id**="16"/> <**description**>First-Line Medications</**description**> </**sentence**> <**sentence**> <**delta-link link-id**="17"/> <**description**>amoxicillin (40 mg/kg/day) if low risk (> 2 years, no day care, and no antibiotics for the past three months).</**description**> </**sentence**> <**sentence**> <**delta-link link-id**="18"/> <**description**>80 mg/kg/day if not low risk or for resistant AOM if the lower dose was used initially .</**description**> </**sentence**> <**sentence**> ... <**sentences**>	<**treatment** title="Diagnosis and treatment of otitis media in children."> <**actions**> <**action group**="3" **id**="1" **parent**="0"> ... </**action**> <**action group**="9" **id**="14" **parent**="12"> <**delta-link link-id**="14"/> <**description**>Therapeutic (10 day) course of antibiotics.</**description**> <**agents**> <**agent MeSH**="D000900" **name**="antibiotic"> <**duration** term="10 day"/> </**agent**> <**agent MeSH**="D000900" **name**="antibiotic"> <**duration** term="5 days"/> </**agent**> </**agents**> <**annotations**> <**annotation**>Consideration may be given to **a** shortened course of antibiotics (5 days) for children who are at low risk (i.e., age & > 2 years, no history of chronic or recurrent otitis media and intact tympanic membranes). <**delta-link link-id**="15"/> </**annotation**> <**annotation**>The use of nasal decongestants and corticosteroids is not supported in the literature. <**delta-link link-id**="34"/> </**annotation**> </**annotations**> <**context**> ... </**context**> </**action**>
a) SENTENCES	**b) ACTIONS**

Table 9. Fragments for the GPC " Diagnosis and treatment of otitis media in children"; a) fragment of sentences, b) fragment of extracted actions; *continue in the Table 10.*

```
<plan name="PLAN_PARENT_2"
   title="Therapeutic (10 day) course of antibiotics.">
  <conditions>
   <setup-precondition confirmation- required="yes"> <none/>
   </setup-precondition>
  </conditions>
  <plan-body>
    <plan-activation>  <plan-schema name="PLAN_PARENT_1">
                          <delta-link link-id="1"/>
                       </plan-schema>
    </plan-activation>
   </plan-body>
</plan>
<plan name="PLAN_14" title="Therapeutic (10 day) course of antibiotics.">
  <delta-link link-id="14"/>  <delta-link link-id="15"/>
  <delta-link link-id="34"/>
  <explanation text="Consideration may be given to a shortened  course of antibiotics (5 days) for
children who are at low risk (i.e., age & > 2 years,  no history of chronic or recurrent otitis media and
intact tympanic membranes). The use of nasal  decongestants and corticosteroids is not supported in
the literature."/>
  <conditions/>
   <plan-body>
    <subplans type="unordered"> <wait-for> <all/> </wait-for>
      <plan-activation> <plan-schema name="PLAN_16">
                           <delta-link link-id="16"/>
                        </plan-schema>
      </plan-activation>
      <plan-activation>
       ...
      <plan-activation>
   ...
</plan>
```

c) ASBRU PLANS

Table 10. Continuation from Table 9, c) fragment from the transformation of actions to the Asbru format.

The above actions can be seen graphically as a tree graph by using the Prefuse tool. This view enhance the support to the clinical staff about identifying, in a easy way, what are the symptoms in the patient to decide a dose for a drug or the right therapy. Figure 4 shows a small fragment for a visual plan of the CPG *Diagnosis and treatment of otitis media in children.*

5. Conclusions

This paper describes a basic Information Extracting approach applied to obtain knowledge from Clinical Practice Guidelines. The final objective of this work is to obtain an intermediate representation of actions from a textual CPG in XML format by means of an

Information Extraction module. The approach applies three heuristics using specific expression patterns over the structure of CPG documents. Through the application of generic Information Extraction heuristic rules, a single formatted document is obtained, which contain the lists, sub-lists, and paragraphs from the original CPG. This document is an intermediate knowledge representation in XML format. The result of the extracted information is used to fill individual slots templates, which represent processes and their relationships in a CPG document. It can be translated into two formal representations: 1) Asbru language (although other languages can be used) and 2) A graph representation by using the Prefuse tool. The aim of the second option is to show the hierarchical structure of the CPG; thus a physician can see in a graphical view the symptoms and routes on the CPG where the patient can be directed for an action or therapy.

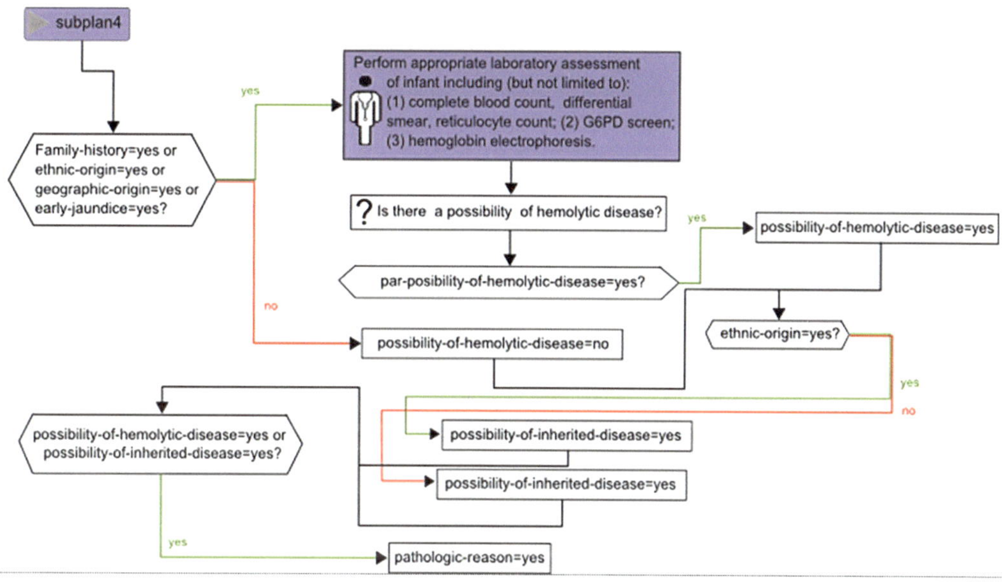

Fig. 4. Example of a visual plan for the CPG Diagnosis and treatment of otitis media in children.

To obtain the actions for a CPG, three stages are necessary for phrases (lexical), sentences (syntactic) and semantic. The first stage is the phrase pattern level wherein a CPG document is lexically analysed; the document is tokenised, relevant phrases are identified and important data is detected. This level filters, to the sentence pattern level, only information used within the syntactic level. The second stage is basically a syntactic analyser, it uses the relevant phrases or identified tokens in the lexical level. At this level medical terms and keywords, to identify medical actions, are identified. The set of terms consist mainly of verbs denoting the application of a therapy, administration of drugs or surgical procedure. This level is divided in two groups of patterns: text free pattern and concise text pattern. The third stage is the speech pattern level where the design and structure of the document is enhanced. It categorises sentences and finds their relations. The approach has been implemented in a first prototype. The experiments show that the proposed heuristic-based approach can achieve good results, especially for CPG with a major portion of semi-structured text. The obtained intermediate representation may be used in a next stage for a better formalisation of the CPG.

As a future work the rules for processing CPGs containing complex information will be improved. Another goal is to create a support model with the ability for evaluating plans that are contained in CPGs.

6. Acknowledges

This research was partially funded by project number 153880 from "Fondo Mixto Conacyt-Gobierno del Estado de Tamaulipas" and project number TAB-2010-C19-144199 from "Fondo Mixto Conacyt-Gobierno del Estado de Tabasco".

7. References

Aguirre-Junco, A.R., Colombet I., Zunino, S., Jaulent, M.C., Leneveut, L. & Chatellier G. (2004). Computerization of guidelines: A knowledge specification method to convert text to detailed decision tree for electronic implementation, *Stud Health Technol Inform.*107(1):115-9.

Akkaya, C. (2005). Extracting process information from clinical practice guidelines. Master's thesis, Vienna University of Technology.

Appelt, D. E. and Israel D. J. (1999). Introduction to information extraction technology, A tutorial prepared for IJCAI-99, Stockholm,scheweden.

Baumgartner, R., Flesca, S. & Gottlob G. (2001). VisualWeb Information Extraction with Lixto, *Proceedings of the 27th International Conference on Very Large Data Bases*, Morgan Kaufmann Publishers Inc., San Francisco, CA, USA, pp 119-128.

Bosse, T. (2001). An interpreter for clinical guidelines in asbru. Master's thesis, Department of Artificial Intelligence, Faculty of Sciences. Vrije Universiteit Amsterdam. Amsterdam, The Netherlands.

Califf, M. (1998). Relational Learning Techniques for Natural Language Information extraction. Ph.D. thesis, Department of Computer Sciences, University of Texas, Austin, TX, USA

Ciccarese, P., Caffi, E., Boiocchi, L., Quaglini, S. & Stefanelli, M. (2004). A guideline management system, *Proceedings of 11th World Congress of the International Medical Informatics Association*, IOS Press, San Francisco, USA, pp. 28–32.

CIE-9-CM (2010) International Classification of Diseases, Ninth Revision, Clinical Modification. National Center for Health Statistics of USA. USA.

Clercq, P. A., Blom, J.A., Korsten, H.H. & Hasman, A. (2004). Approaches for creating computer-interpretable guidelines that facilitate decision support, *Artificial Intelligence in Medicine,* 31(1):1–27.

Dart, T., Xu, Y., Chatellier, G. & Degoulet, P. (2001). Computerization of guidelines: Towards a "guideline markup language", pp 186-190.

URL: http://www.metapress.com/content/mhd4p271n0653xx2

Ethem, A. (2004). *Introduction to Machine Learning (Adaptive Computation and Machine Learning)*, The MIT Press.

Field, M. J. & Lohr, K. (1992). *Guidelines for Clinical Practice: From development to use, Institute of Medicine*, National Academy Press.

Freitag, D. (1998). Machine Learning for Information Extraction in Informal Domains. Ph.D. thesis, Computer Science Department, Carnegie Mellon University. Pittsburgh, PA, USA

Fuchsberger, C. & Miksch, S. (2002). Asbru's execution engine: Utilizing guidelines for artificial ventilation of newborn infants. *Technical report,* Vienna University of Technology, Institute of Software Technology and Interactive Systems.

Geldof, M. (2002). The formalization of medical protocols: easier said than done. Master's thesis, Department of Artificial Intelligence, Faculty of Sciences. Vrije Universiteit Amsterdam. Amsterdam, The Netherlands.

Gennari, J. H., Musen, M. A., Fergerson, R. W., Grosso, W. E., Crubézy, M., Eriksson, H., Noy, N. F. & Samson, W.T. (2002). The evolution of protégé: An environment for knowledge-based systems development, *International Journal of Human Computer Studies*, 58(1):89-123.

Hripcsak, G., Clayton, P. B., Pryor, T. A., Haug, P. & Wigertz, O. B. (2005). The arden syntax for medical logic modules, *International Journal of Clinical Monitoring and Computing,* 10(4): 215–224.

Isern, D. & Moreno, A. (2008). Computer-based execution of clinical guidelines: A review, *International Journal Medical Informatics*, 77(12):787-808.

Jeffrey, H., Stuart, K. C. & James, A. L. (2005). Prefuse: a toolkit for interactive information visualization, *Proceedings of the SIGCHI conference on Human factors in computing systems*, ACM, Portland, Oregon, USA, pp. 421-430.

Kaiser, K. & Miksch, S. (2005). Modeling computer-supported clinical guidelines and protocols. Technical report, Vienna University of Technology, Institute of Software Technology and Interactive Systems, Vienna.

Karras, B., Deshpande, A., Polvani, K., Agrawal, A. & Shiffman, R.N. (2000). *Gem cutter manual*. Yale Center for Medical Informatics.

Kasabov, N. (2006). *Evolving Connectionist Systems: The Knowledge Engineering Approach,* Springer-Verlag New York, Inc.

Kohn, L. T., Corrigan, J. M. & Molla, S. (2000). *To Err Is Human: Building a Safer Health System*, National Academy Press, Washington, D.C.

Kosara, R., Miksch, S., Seyfang, A. & Votruba. P. (2002). Tools for acquiring clinical guidelines in asbru, *Proceedings of the 6th World Conference on Integrate Design and Process Technology (IDPT'02),* Society for Design and Process Science, New York, pp. 22-27.

Kushmerick, N. (1997). Wrapper induction for information extraction, Ph.D. thesis, Department of Computer Science and Engineering, University of Washington.

Lehnert, W. & Cowie, J. (1994). Evaluating an information extraction system, *Commun.* ACM, 39(1):80-91.

Liu, L., Pu, C. & Han, W. (2000). XWRAP: An XML-enabled Wrapper Construction System for Web Information Sources, *Proceedings 16th International Conference on Data Engineering (ICDE),* IEEE Computer Society, Washington, DC, USA, pp. 611–621.

Lyng, K. M., Hildebrandt, T. & Mukkamala, R. R. (2008). From paper based clinical practice guidelines to declarative workflow management, *Business Process Management Workshops*, Springer, Milano, Italy, pp. 336-347.

Marie-Francine, M. (2006). *Information Extraction: Algorithms and Prospects in a Retrieval Context (The Information Retrieval Series)*. Springer-Verlag.

Patward, S. & Riloff E. (2006). Learning Domain-Specific Information Extraction Patterns from the Web, *Proceedings of the ACL 2006 Workshop on Information Extraction Beyond the Document,* Association for Computational Linguistics, Stroudsburg, PA, USA, pp. 66-73.

Pech-May, F., Lopez-Arevalo, I. & Sosa-Sosa, V. (2009) Toward the validation of patient data for clinical practice guidelines. In Proceeding of the 6th International Conference on Electrical Engineering, Computing Science and Automatic Control. Toluca, Mexico, pp. 467-472.

Pech-May F. Validator for Clinical Practice Guidelines in Patients. (2010). Master's Thesis, Laboratory of Information Technology, Cinvestav, Tamaulipas, Mexico.

Peshkin, L. & Pfeffer, A. (2003). Bayesian information extraction network, *Proceedings Of the 18th International Joint Conference on Artificial Intelligence (IJCAI), Morgan Kaufmann Publishers Inc.*, Acapulco, Mexico, pp. 421-426.

Patel, V. L., Arocha J., Diermeier, M., How, J. & Mottur-Pilson C. (2001). Cognitive psychological studies of representation and use of clinical practice guidelines, *International Journal of Medical Informatics,* 63(3):147–167.

Růzicka, M. & Svatek V. (2004). Mark-up based analysis of narrative guidelines with the stepper tool, *Journal of Studies in health technology and informatics,* 101(1):132–136.

Soderland, S., Aronow, D., Fisher, D., Aseltine, J. & Lehnert, W. (1995). Machine learning of text analysis rules for clinical records, Tr 39, Center for Intelligent Information Retrieval.

Sonderland, S. (1999). Learning information extraction rules for semi-structured and free text. Machine Learning, *Kluwer Academic Publishers,* 34(1):233-272.

Sutton, D. R. & Fox, J. (2003). The syntax and semantics of the proforma guideline modeling language, Journal *of the American Medical Informatics Association (JAMIA),* 10(5):433-443.

Teije, A. T., Marcos, M., Balser, J., Croonenborg, V., Duelli C., Harmelen, F. V., Lucas, P. J., Miksch, S., Reif, W., Rosenbrand, K. & Seyfang, A. (2006). Improving medical protocols by formal methods, *Artificial Intelligence in Medicine,* 36(1):193-209.

Terenziani, P., Montani, S., Bottrighi, A., Molino, G. & Torchio, M. (2005). Clinical guidelines adaptation: managing authoring and versioning issues, in: S. Miksch, J. Hunter, E. Keravnou (Eds.), *Proceedings of 10th Conference on Artificial Intelligence in Medicine (AIME 2005),* Springer-Verlag, Aberdeen, Scotland, pp. 151–155.

Tu S. W. & Musen, M. (2001). Modeling data and knowledge in the EON guideline architecture, *Proceedings of 10th Triennial Congress of the International Medical Informatics Association (MEDINFO 2001),* Studies in Health Technology and Informatics, IOS Press, London, UK, pp. 280–284.

Twaddle, S. (2005). Clinical practice guidelines, *Singapore Medical Journal* 46(12):681-687.

Votruba, P., Miksch, S. & Kosara, R. (2004). Facilitating knowledge maintenance of clinical guidelinesand protocols, *Proceeding of 11th World Congress Of Medical Informatics,* Studies in health technology and informatics, IOS Press, Amsterdam, Netherlands pp. 57–61.

Wang, D., Peleg, M., Tu, S.W., Boxwala, A.A., Ogunyemi, O., Zeng, Q., Greenes, R. A., Patel, V. L. & Shortliffe, E.H. (2004). Design and implementation of the GLIF3 guideline execution engine, *Journal of Biomedical Informatics,* 37(1):305–318.

Young, O., Shahar, Y., Liel, Y, Lunenfeld, E., Bar, G., Shalom, E., Martins, S. B., Vaszar, L. T., Marom, T. & Goldstein, M. K. (2007). Runtime application of Hybrid-Asbru clinical guidelines, *Journal of Biomedical Informatics,* 40(1):507–526.

5

Guideline-Based Decision Support Systems for Prevention and Management of Chronic Diseases

Niels Peek
Dept. of Medical Informatics, Academic Medical Center, University of Amsterdam
The Netherlands

1. Introduction

One of the greatest challenges in today's health care is closing the gap between scientific evidence and medical practice. Keeping up with information in health care has never been easy, but with 500,000 clinical trials currently listed in the Cochrane Controlled Trials Register, and 75 clinical trials and 11 systematic reviews published daily (Bastian, 2010), physicians face unmanageable information processing tasks. It has been estimated that clinicians would have to read 20 papers a day to keep abreast of advances in biomedical knowledge (Shaneyfelt, 2001), and that it may take up to 20 years before findings from scientific studies are implemented in medical practice (Institute of Medicine [IOM], 2001). Medicine is not reaping the full benefits of research efforts, and much of the knowledge that is acquired in scientific studies is lost in translation.

The lack of success in translating research findings into medical practice is particularly prevalent in the prevention and management of chronic diseases (Lenfant, 2003). For instance, the protective benefits of beta-blockers for patients who are recovering from myocardial infarction were established in 1981 (β-Blocker Heart Attack Study Group, 1981), and confirmed by several later studies. Yet in 1996, beta-blockers were being prescribed for only 62.5 percent of patients who had had a myocardial infarction in the U.S. (National Committee for Quality Assurance, 1997). Similarly, in 1983 it was shown that aspirin is a highly effective therapy in patients with acute myocardial infarction and unstable angina, and as long-term, secondary preventive therapy in patients with established cardiovascular disease (Awtry & Loscalzo, 2000). Nonetheless, in the year 2000 aspirin was being prescribed for at most one third of patients with coronary artery disease for whom there were no contraindications to its use (Stafford & Radley, 2003).

Clinical practice guidelines are considered essential instruments to increase the application of scientific evidence to routine care (IOM, 2001). Guidelines summarize the available evidence for specific medical conditions, and provide cut-and-dried recommendations for common medical tasks such as screening, diagnosis, triage, treatment selection, and long-term management of patients. However, guidelines are often not followed in clinical practice. Implementing clinical practice guidelines in routine care has proved to be a challenging problem of its own. Computerised decision support is an effective means to solve this problem, as computers can provide, concurrent with care, reminders and advice that are based on practice guidelines and tailored to the needs of individual patients. Decision support is also one of the central elements of the Chronic Care Model (Bodenheimer et al., 2002), an evidence-based conceptual framework that describes changes to the healthcare system that help practices to improve outcomes among patients with chronic illness.

This chapter presents an overview of guideline-based decision support systems for prevention and management of chronic diseases. Running example throughout the chapter will be the prevention and management of cardiovascular disease (CVD), which is discussed in Section 2. In Section 3, we review the literature on guideline implementation strategies. Section 4 discusses guideline-based decision support systems, and Section 5 presents an example in the field of cardiac rehabilitation. Section 6 summarizes the chapter and presents an outlook to future developments.

2. Prevention and management of cardiovascular diseases

Cardiovascular disease (CVD) is a family of chronic and highly prevalent conditions in Western countries that lead to life-threatening events (such as myocardial infarctions and strokes), multi-morbidity, disabilities, and death. All cardiovascular diseases are caused by atherosclerosis, an excess build-up of plaque on the inner wall of blood vessels, which restricts the flow of blood. Atherosclerosis may lead to coronary heart disease, cerebrovascular disease, abdominal aortic aneurysms, and peripheral arterial disease. As a result, CVD is the main cause of disease burden (illness and death) in the Western world (Murray & Lopez, 1997).

The lion's share of recent gains in life expectancy in the Western countries has come from reductions in mortality from myocardial infarction and stroke. In the U.S., life expectancy increased by six years between 1970 and 2000, and nearly two thirds of that increase can be attributed to reductions in mortality due to CVD. These reductions were due largely to improvements in pharmaceutical treatment, surgical techniques, and angioplasty. At the same time, demographic trends and unhealthy lifestyles have led to quickly increasing numbers of people with CVD, and it is estimated that the prevalence of CVD will increase by more than 40% over the decade (Murray & Lopez, 1997). So, while the disease has become less threatening in its acute phases due to technological developments, there exist major challenges for our health care system in preventing that more people get diseased and in managing CVD patients in the chronic phases of their illness.

In 2004 the Interheart study showed that 90% of myocardial infarctions can be attributed to a set of nine modifiable risk factors: abnormal lipids, smoking, hypertension, diabetes, abdominal obesity, psychosocial factors, low consumption of fruits and vegetables, alcohol intake, and lack of regular physical activity (Yusuf et al., 2004). Patients with atherosclerosis have an increased risk of a new vascular event in the same or different arterial beds. Several lifestyle measures (healthy diet, exercise, quit smoking) and treatment of risk factors with medication (antiplatelet agents, blood pressure-, and lipid-lowering agents, beta-blockers, and ACE-inhibitors) can strongly reduce the risks of future cardiovascular events. This knowledge provides important opportunities for improving CVD prevention and cardiovascular risk management, and procedures for optimal controlling these risk factors are nowadays described in all the prevailing guidelines. Unfortunately, these guidelines are poorly implemented in clinical practice

(Beaglehole et al., 2007). Many patients with coronary heart disease, cerebrovascular disease, abdominal aortic aneurysm, and vascular disease in general do not reach treatment goals (EUROASPIRE Study Group, 2001a, 2001b).

Insights into the risk factors of CVD and the growing number of patients have increased the importance of managing the non-acute phases of the disease. Patient-centred counseling and team-driven care, multidisciplinary collaboration, and continuity of care (follow-up arrangements) are required in these phases. These tasks are usually carried out by specialized nurses and other paramedical personnel. For instance, cardiac rehabilitation is a multidisciplinary therapy for outpatient recovery after hospitalization for cardiac incidents (such as myocardial infarctions) and cardiac interventions (such as heart surgery) (Ades, 2001). A typical cardiac rehabilitation programme lasts for 6-12 weeks, and may consist of exercise training, relaxation and stress management training, education about the disease and its consequences, lifestyle change interventions, and psychosocial counseling, mostly provided in group therapy. The aim of cardiac rehabilitation is to ensure that patients are in the best possible physical and psychosocial condition to return to and maintain their normal place in society and to reduce their future cardiovascular risk (World Health Organisation, 1993). To this end, cardiac rehabilitation teams usually include specialized nurses, physical therapists, psychologists, dietitians, social workers, rehabilitation physicians, and cardiologists.

3. Implementation of clinical practice guidelines

Clinical practice guidelines are systematically developed statements to assist medical practitioners in making decisions about appropriate care (Field & Lohr, 1990). They are designed to promote effective care and discourage the use of ineffective treatments, to reduce variations in care practice, and to make more effective use of health care resources. Guidelines are nowadays an intrinsic component of disease management programmes, increasingly applied to improve outcomes for patients with chronic illnesses such as cardiovascular disease (Ellrodt et al, 1997). Guidelines should provide clinicians with scientific knowledge in a readily digestible form without requiring that they search through large volumes of published material (Woolf, 1990). Increasingly, adherence to guidelines is considered a measure of quality of care (Epstein, 1995). While there may be debate about whether or not guidelines result in improved medical care (Brook, 1989), there is little question that they are a well-established and increasingly important part of medical practice.

Over the last two decades, it is increasingly recognized that dissemination of paper-based guidelines alone does not lead to the change in care practice. Instead, carefully designed methods for change are required for effective implementation of guidelines (Grimshaw et al., 2004).

3.1 Why clinical practice guidelines are not always followed in practice

Based on an extensive review of the literature, Cabana and colleagues (1999) developed a conceptual framework for barriers to physician adherence to practice guidelines. Starting from Woolf's (1993) distinction between knowledge, attitudes, and behaviour, the framework identifies *internal* (cognitive and affective) and *external* barriers to behavioural change. Cognitive barriers may consist of a lack of awareness that specific guidelines exist and a lack of familiarity with their details. Both may be caused by the overload of information that is presented to health care professionals, a lack of time to keep up with new guidelines, and poor accessibility of the guidelines in question. Most guidelines are issued either as published articles, as specialized monographs or both (Woolf et al., 1999). In either case, such guidelines often have little impact on clinical practice either because clinicians are unaware of them or because the guideline is not accessible during the provision of care (Grimshaw & Russell, 1993; Lomas et al., 1989). Tunis and colleagues (1994) showed that physicians were poorly informed about the details of several well-established guidelines yet claimed knowledge of a non-existent guideline presented in the study as a control.

Affective barriers may consist of a lack of agreement with specific guidelines or guidelines in general, believing that one cannot perform the guideline recommendation, not believing that following the guideline recommendation will lead to the desired outcome, and a lack of motivation or inertia of previous practice due to habit and routines. When professionals do not agree with specific guidelines, this may due to a different interpretation of the underlying evidence, because they believe that the guideline is not applicable for a specific patient, that it is not cost-beneficial, or because of a lack of confidence in the guideline developers. A general aversion against guidelines is typically motivated by stating that guidelines are "too cookbook", too rigid to apply, present a biased synthesis, challenge professional autonomy, or are not practical.

External barriers may be related to patients, to the environment, or to the guidelines themselves. Patient-related barriers include poor compliance with prescribed drugs, lack of time, financial constraints, and lack of motivation to make lifestyle changes (e.g., quit smoking). For instance, in a study examining the patterns and predictors of compliance with concomitant antihypertensive and lipid-lowering agents, only one third of the patients fully adhered to both medication prescriptions (Whelton et al., 1998). Environmental barriers, finally, may consist of organisational constraints, lack of resources, lack of reimbursement, or (perceived) legal constraints.

3.2 Strategies for improving the implementation of guidelines

Following Davis & Taylor-Vaisey (1997), we will use the term *diffusion* for the distribution of information and the unaided adoption of recommendations, *dissemination* for more active communication of information to improve knowledge or skills, and *implementation* for active dissemination, involving strategies to overcome barriers. It is broadly agreed that diffusion of clinical practice guidelines is generally ineffective and, at best, results only in small changes in practice (Grimshaw & Russell, 1993; Oxman et al., 1995; Bero et al., 1998; Grimshaw et al., 2004). Nevertheless, it is probably the most common approach adopted by researchers, professional bodies, and health care organisations. The use of specific interventions to disseminate and implement clinical practice guidelines is less common, but many studies have pointed out that such interventions are necessary to ensure that practices change, and evidence suggests that more intensive efforts to alter practice are generally more successful (Bero et al., 1998; Grimshaw et al., 2004).

A wide variety of change interventions have been described in the literature. Roughly speaking, we can distinguish interventions orientated toward health care professionals, interventions orientated toward health care organisations, and those orientated toward health care consumers (Thorsen & Mäkelä, 1999). Here, we will focus on interventions directed at health care professionals. These interventions generally attempt to change professional behaviour by influencing the knowledge of professionals from preferred practice, changing their attitude toward preferred practice, or both (Bero et al., 1998). They can be classified into the following categories:

- educational interventions (distribution of educational materials, regional or national conferences, and/or small-group conference with active participation),
- outreach visits (use of a trained person who meets with professionals in their practice settings to provide information on preferred practice advocated by the guidelines),
- audit and feedback (providing summaries of recent clinical performance, obtained from medical records, computerised databases, observation, or from patients),
- assignment of local opinion leaders, nominated by their colleagues as 'educationally influential', to influence professional behaviour,
- local consensus processes (inclusion of care professionals in discussions on guideline recommendations and preferred practice),
- patient-mediated interventions, where information concerning professional behaviour is sought from patients or information about preferred practice given to patients,
- financial and regulatory incentives (fee-for-service, professional penalties; changes in medical liability, accreditation, or licensure),
- patient-specific reminders to physicians to perform a certain action, based on eligibility criteria described in the guidelines, and
- patient-specific, computerised decision support at the point of care.

Little or no effect was usually obtained with large-scale educational interventions. Audit and feedback interventions, assignment of local opinion leaders, local consensus processes, and patient mediated interventions have yielded variable results. Patient-mediated interventions do seem to improve the provision of preventive care, where baseline performance is often very low (Oxman et al., 1995). Small-group educational interventions, outreach visits, patient-specific reminders, and computerised decision support have consistently been shown to be effective implementation strategies across different studies. We note that patient-specific reminders can be either paper-based (i.e., consisting of memos, stickers, or slips of paper within the patient charts to remind physicians of preferred actions) or computer-based (i.e., consisting of automatic identification of eligible patients for specific actions, and provisions of prompts when the electronic clinical information system is accessed by the treating physician) (Dexheimer et al., 2008) The boundary between computer-based reminders and computerised decision support is not always clear-cut, and some authors consider them to belong to the same category.

Grilli and Lomas (1994) concluded that the choice of intervention should be guided by the characteristics of the guideline in question. Oxman and colleagues (1995) and Grol (1992) stated that it is important to identify local barriers to change before the actual intervention is started. Multifaceted interventions, i.e., combinations of two or more interventions such as participation in audit and a local consensus process, are more effective than single interventions (Wensing & Grol, 1994; Oxman et al., 1995). Grimshaw & Russell (1993; 2004) concluded that guideline-implementation interventions are most likely to be effective if they deliver patient-specific advice at the time and place of a medical consultation. Typically, this can be accomplished by computer applications. They can provide, concurrent with care, reminders and advice that are based on practice guidelines and tailored to the needs of individual patients. This insight has led to a broad consensus that clinical practice guidelines should be made available during clinical encounters through clinical information systems. During the last 15 years, the literature on the effects of deploying clinical guidelines has focused on computer based interventions (e.g., Rossi & Every, 1997; Ornstein, 2001; Subramanian et al., 2004). While many of these focus on simple reminder systems, many others represent increasingly complete presentations of entire clinical guidelines.

4. Guideline-based decision support systems

Since the invention of the digital computer, people have considered the application of computerized advice to improve the quality of medical decisions. In 1970s this led to the development of the first computer systems advising doctors in their clinical choices. Since that time, a large number of systems have been developed for a variety of clinical tasks and for a large number of clinical settings. Many of these have involved simple types of support like recognizing that a laboratory test result is out of normal range, or that a medication being ordered has a dangerous interaction with another one that a patient is taking, or determining that a patient is now due for an influenza vaccination. But also more complex systems have been developed, advising in advanced tasks such as diagnostic reasoning, diagnostic test selection, choice and planning of therapeutic actions, and prognostic assessment.

4.1 Computerized decision support

Based on Wyatt & Spiegelhalter (1991), we define computerized decision support (CDS) systems as knowledge-based reasoning systems which use two or more items of patient data to generate case-specific advice. This definition excludes systems that only retrieve patient information or medical knowledge without performing reasoning steps with these data, and systems that merely help to focus attention by performing range checks (e.g. alarm systems in anaesthesia and intensive care) or by warning for potential drug-drug interactions. This is not to say that these tools are not useful or effective - they simply form belong to different classes of systems.

Two types of CDS system were developed and thoroughly evaluated in the 1970s en 1980s: *Bayesian diagnostic systems* and *expert systems* (Shortliffe et al., 2003, Ch. 20). In Bayesian diagnostic systems, the knowledge base typically consisted of statistical associations between clinical parameters and medical disorders, and (pseudo-)Bayesian probabilistic inference was used to calculate posterior probabilities for each of the disorders included in the system, given a set of clinical observations. Cognitive psychological studies had shown that people, including experienced physicians, tend to make systematic errors in this type of reasoning (Kahneman et al., 1982). Bayesian diagnostic systems assisted physicians in proper reasoning with probabilities when establishing a diagnosis. A disadvantage of these systems was the fact that the results were sometimes counter-intuitive, and that these systems could not provide an explanation of their reasoning. Expert systems, in contrast, aimed to capture the nuances of human expertise and reasoning, by building a heuristic model of the knowledge from clinical experts. Reasoning in these systems was primarily symbolic (e.g., based on IF-THEN rules), and would aim to follow the line of thinking of human experts. Expert systems often had extensive facilities for justifying their advice to the user.

Several authors have defined characterizing features of CDS systems (Shortliffe et al., 2003, Ch. 20; Kawamoto et al., 2005; Garg et al., 2005). Table 1 lists 10 features that have been investigated in the scientific literature and are often associated with effectiveness. We note that these are not independent features. For instance, active systems have more effects on decision making behaviour than passive systems, which require users to recognize situations when advice would be useful and then must make an explicit effort to access the CDS system. It is only possible, however, to create an active CDS system when it is integrated with the electronic clinical information infrastructure. The same holds for the requirement that no additional data entry is needed from the user. Consultation and critiqueing are generally considered to be complementary models. System integration, advice at the point of care, active system, and absence of the need for additional data entry all point in the same direction: At best, the decision-support element should be embedded within the users' professional routine—thus making decision support a by-product of the practitioners' ordinary workflow.

system feature	explanation
system integration	CDS system is integrated with the clinical information infrastructure, e.g. the system is connected the electronic patient record system, laboratory system, and CPOE system.
advice at point of care	Decision support is provided at time and location where decisions are actually made, e.g. during clinical encounters with patients or during multidisciplinary team meetings.
active system	CDS system does not wait for its users to ask for assistance but automatically provides advice as part of clinician workflow.
actionability of advice	CDS system advices in what to do for the patient (e.g., What test should be ordered?, Which treatment should be initiated?) instead of in what is true about a patient (e.g., What is the correct diagnosis? or What is the risk of developing specific disorders in the future?).
consultation model	CDS system serves as an advisor, accepting patient-specific data, possibly asking questions, and generating advice for the user about diagnosis or management.
critiqueing model	The clinician has a preconceived idea of what is happening with a patient or which therapy would be appropriate, and the system acts as a sounding board, expressing agreement or suggesting alternatives.
no need for additional data entry	All information that is necessary to generate advice is automatically extracted from patient records.
justification of advice	Advice is justified to user by explaining the reasoning steps or by provision of underlying research evidence
ease of use	The system has a clear and intuitive user interface with prominent display of advice; the system is fast, saves clinicians time or requires minimal time to use.
additional change interventions	CDS is accompanied by educational interventions, periodic performance feedback, active involvement of local opinion leaders or other change strategies.

Table 1. Characterising features of CDS systems, based on Shortliffe et al. (2003; Ch. 20), Kawamoto et al. (2005), and Garg et al. (2005).

Another characterizing feature, not included in the table, it the system's underlying reasoning process, i.e. the logic or algorithms that are used to generate advice. A wide variety of techniques has been used to do this, predominantly stemming from Bayesian probability, decision analysis, and artificial intelligence. After evaluations showed a poor uptake of expert systems (Miller & Masarie, 1990) and modest benefit of diagnostic systems

(Berner et al., 1994), emphasis has shifted towards the implementation of clinical practice guidelines and protocols. These systems generally build on computer-interpretable models of the guidelines or protocols in question, and are described in Section 4.2.

Kawamoto and colleagues (2005) conducted a systematic review and meta-analysis of randomised clinical trials that assessed efficacy of decision support systems in improving clinical practice. They included both computerized and non-computerized systems, e.g., manual systems for attaching care reminders to the charts of patients needing specific preventive care services. From 70 studies that were included in the review, 48 (68%) significantly improved clinical practice. Four features were identified as independent predictors of improved practice, from which "active system" was by far the strongest. The other features were computerized (vs. manual) decision support, advice at point of care, actionability of advice. In another systematic review of the literature, Garg and colleagues (2005) summarized findings from 100 studies evaluating the effects of CDS systems, in both randomised and non-randomised controlled trials. From 97 studies that assessed improvement in clinical practice, 62 (64%) found statistically significant effects. Garg et al. also found that active systems are more effective than passive systems. In addition, studies in which the evaluators developed the CDS system themselves more often found positive effects than studies where the evaluators were not the developers. CDS was particularly effective for provision of preventive care (reminder systems), drug dosing and drug prescribing, and chronic disease management, but not for diagnosis. The success of CDS in prevention and chronic disease management is probably explained by the fact that in these areas, CDS is an effective means to transfer tasks from busy physicians to nurse practitioners and other paramedics (Jones & Peterson, 2008).

4.2 Computer interpretable guideline models

A variety of approaches has been used to computerize guidelines (Sonnenberg & Hagerty, 2006). At the most rudimentary level, these are merely electronically readable versions of text guidelines (e.g., in PDF), made available through hospital intranets or through the Internet. Computerized reasoning with documents in natural language is not feasible. So, to provide genuine guideline-based CDS, it is imperative to translate guidelines to a format in which they can be reasoned with by computer algorithms. These translated guidelines are called computer interpretable guideline models.

One of the earliest attempts to translate clinical practice guidelines into a computer interpretable format was used in systems for raising context-sensitive alerts and reminders, with so-called *situation–action rules*. The most widely used format for specifying such rules is the Arden Syntax (Hripcsak, 1994), an Health Level Seven (HL7) and ANSI standard, an example of which is given in Fig. 1. A rule interpreter processes the rules, scanning the patient database for relevant situations that trigger rules and evaluating whether the condition part of the rule holds. If so, the CDS executes the action part of the rule, which often consists of displaying an alert or reminder to the user.

Situation-action rules are suited for systems that need to issue simple, one-time reminders and alerts, such as reminder systems. Investigators have demonstrated significant enhancement of adherence to preventive-care guidelines, such as those for the administration of pneumococcal and influenza vaccinations, by integrating simple reminders with clinical information systems (Dexheimer et al., 2008). The success of these systems is probably explained by the fact that they provide actionable advice at the point of care, they are easy to use, well integrated with other systems, and there is no need for additional data entry.

```
CHD_discharge := event {discharge
                      where dx = myocardial_infarction or
                            treatment = CABG or
                            treatment = PTCA}

NYHA_class := read_last {HF_NYHA_class}

;;

evoke: CHD_discharge ;;

logic:

if exist(NYHA_class) and (NYHA_class > 2) then conclude false
else conclude true;

endif;

;;

action:

write
"Patient should be referred to cardiac rehabilitation"

;;
```

Fig. 1. Example of a situation-action rule expressed in the Arden syntax. This rule prints a warning whenever a patient is discharged after hospitalization for myocardial infarction, coronary artery bypass grafting (CABG) surgery, or percutaneous transluminal coronary angioplasty and the patient does not have severe heart failure (NYHA class III or IV), that this patient should be referred to outpatient cardiac rehabilitation.

Situation-action rules are however not suitable to model more complex guidelines (Peleg et al., 2001). Development and maintenance of large rule bases can be difficult because interactions among rules may have unanticipated side effects. Rule-based models also do not support the application of elaborate procedures with multiple steps and procedures that extend over long periods of time, as is necessary for the support of the care of patients with chronic diseases. A final limitation of the Arden Syntax is the fact that it mixes representation of decision logic with specification of connections to other information systems (exemplified by the "event { ... }" and "read_last { ... }" statements in Fig. 1). Situation-action rules that are written in Arden Syntax therefore cannot be shared between institutions, as specifications of connections to other information systems depend on the local situation. This is often called the "curly braces" problem in the literature (Shortliffe et al., 2003, Ch. 20). For these reasons, the Arden Syntax is no longer in use to build guideline-based CDS systems.

Since the late 1990s, a number of more expressive guideline representation formats have been developed. Examples are GLIF (Ohno-Machado et al., 1998), PROforma (Fox et al.,

1998), ASBRU (Shahar et al, 1998), GASTON (De Clercq et al., 2001), GUIDE (Quaglini et al., 2001), and SAGE (Tu et al., 2007). Most of these representation schemes share a number of elements that solve the limitations of the Arden Syntax (Peleg et al., 2003, De Clercq et al., 2004). To describe multi-step procedures and procedures that extend over long periods of time, they represent guidelines in graphical flowcharts called task-network models. Each node in such a network model represents a single step and is either targeted at data input, performing calculations, flow control, executing a subguideline, or data output; examples are given in Table 2. Furthermore, a medical concept model (ontology) and virtual medical record are used to separate decision logic with the specification of connections to other information systems, rendering guideline models sharable between institutions. For most representation schemes, toolsets exist to create computer-interpretable guideline models and verify their consistency and completeness. In addition, execution engines have been developed for building decision support systems that are linked to clinical information systems and use these models to provide patient-specific advice to care professionals (Isern & Moreno, 2008).

type of step	examples
data input	• reading the latest serum cholesterol values from the laboratory information system • prompting the user whether or not the patient smokes
calculation	• computing the patient's cholesterol ratio from total cholesterol and high-density lipiprotein cholesterol values
flow control	• choosing the next node to execute, based on whether the cholesterol ratio is above the threshold for initiating medical treatment • iterating over all patient records in the laboratory information system
execute subguideline	• determine the correct dosage of cholesterol lowering drugs, based on the patient's age, body weight, and kidney function
output	• setting a warning flag in the electronic patient record • writing the drug dose determined to the electronic patient record • displaying a message on the computer screen

Table 2. Typical steps of task-network models.

Clinical practice guidelines often contain ambiguities, inconsistencies, and logical errors that hamper their translation to computer interpretable guideline models. The models are often more precise than the original guidelines, with crisp thresholds where the guidelines tended to be vague and recommendations for situations that were originally overlooked. These discrepancies are unintended side effects of the translation, and may lead users of the CDS system to become suspicious of its advice. Goud and colleagues (2009a) have proposed a strategy where development of the paper guideline and development of the computer interpretable guideline model take place concurrently, exchanging information at crucial steps. With this strategy, it is possible to ensure perfect consistency between the paper guideline and the CDS model.

4.3 Using CDS for guideline implementation

In 1999, Shiffman and colleagues (1999) performed a systematic review of 25 studies of guideline-based CDS systems. Adherence to guidelines was improved in 14 of 18 studies that evaluated it. Shiffman et al. also identified a set of eight information management services that foster uptake of such systems. However, not all guideline-based CDS systems have been successful. In a later study by Tierney and colleagues (2003), primary care physicians and pharmacists used a sophisticated electronic health record system with evidence-based cardiac care suggestions. The intervention had no effect on physicians' adherence to the care suggestions (23% for intervention patients vs. 22% for controls), and there were no improvements in quality of life, medication compliance, health care utilization, costs, or satisfaction with care. Physicians viewed guidelines as providing helpful information but constraining their practice and not helpful in making decisions for individual patients. Ansari and colleagues (2003) found no benefit from computerized physician reminders to use beta blockers in patients with heart failure. Montgomery and colleagues (2000), finally, investigated the prescription of blood pressure lowering medication in primary care when physicians received patient-specific cardiovascular risk charts and guideline-based CDS. Unaided physicians poorly assessed cardiovascular risks and this was significantly improved by risk charts. CDS did however not provide additional benefit.

5. Example: The CARDSS project

This section describes the development and evaluation of CARDSS, a guideline-based decision support system for cardiac rehabilitation and secondary prevention of cardiovascular disease. CARDSS (acronym for CArdiac Rehabilitation Decision Support System) was developed by the University of Amsterdam in collaboration with the Netherlands Heart Foundation and the Netherlands Society of Cardiology, with the aim to stimulate implementation of the Dutch national guidelines for cardiac rehabilitation. The system was used in approximately 40 Dutch outpatient rehabilitation clinics. Section 5.1 gives a brief overview of the Dutch guidelines for cardiac rehabilitation and the development of CARDSS, and Section 5.2 describes the results of two evaluation studies.

5.1 Development of the CARDSS system

To improve the quality of care in cardiac rehabilitation and secondary cardiovascular prevention, national guidelines were published in the Netherlands in 2004 (Rehabilitation Committee, 2004). These guidelines state that all patients with established coronary artery disease should be offered an individualised rehabilitation programme, built up from four possible group-based therapies (exercise training, relaxation and stress management training, education therapy, and lifestyle change therapy) and if needed, different forms of individual counseling (e.g. by physical therapists, psychotherapists, or dietitians). Patients should only receive therapies and forms of counseling that they really need, and not others. For instance, to decide whether a patient should receive exercise training, the patient's desired level of exercise capacity should be compared with the results of a maximal exercise capacity test.

The guidelines' recommendations with respect to assessing patient needs and selecting the appropriate therapies for individual patients were summarized by a clinical algorithm. In total, the needs procedure requires 15 to 40 data items concerning the patient's physical, emotional, and social condition and lifestyle to be gathered. It generally takes place two weeks after discharge from the hospital, after which, during weekly meetings, the multidisciplinary team formally decides on the content of the patient's rehabilitation programme. The clinical algorithm consists of nine decision trees. When following the decision trees, each of their branches leads to one or more therapeutic goals and indications. To stimulate implementation of the guidelines, it was decided to develop a CDS system that would assist cardiac rehabilitation professionals in conducting the needs assessment and therapy selection procedure as described by the clinical algorithm (Goud et al., 2008). CARDSS consists of an EPR for outpatient CR, a structured dialogue module for gathering the information that is required to assess patient needs, a decision support module that generates guideline-based therapy recommendations, and several information management services. The EPR and information management functionalities were developed in Microsoft's .NET framework with an SQL server database that is accessible to multiple CARDSS clients within the same clinic. The structured dialogue and decision support modules were developed in GASTON (De Clercq et al., 2001). The system facilitates a genuine multidisciplinary needs assessment, where different clinical users can start, interrupt, and continue the structured dialogue at any time. Fig. 2 displays a sample CARDSS screen with therapy recommendations.

5.2 System evaluation

There exist several potential sources of bias when empirical studies are carried out with CDS systems (Friedman & Wyatt, 2006):

- "Hawthorne effect": human performance may improve as a result of attention from investigators, a psychological phenomenon;
- "carry-over effect": clinical decisions may be influenced by earlier system advice given to the same professional or to a colleague from the same clinic;
- "checklist effect": the structuring of information (e.g. dialogue structure) by an information system may improve the quality of decision making of its users;
- registration bias: information entered into the system may reflect socially desirable behaviour and not actual clinical practice; and
- "clustering effect": observations on decision making that were made within the same clinic may be correlated.

In contrast to uncontrolled studies and before-after studies, randomised controlled studies do not suffer from the "Hawthorne effect" because this will cancel out when the study groups are contrasted. It was therefore decided to evaluate the effect of CARDSS on concordance to the Dutch cardiac rehabilitation guidelines in a randomised trial (Goud et al., 2009b). To avoid "carry-over effects" resulting from professionals or teams learning from CARDSS, a cluster randomised design was chosen (Donner & Klar, 2000). Participating clinics worked with either of two versions of the system: an intervention version (having full functionality) or a control version which comprised the EPR, needs assessment dialogue, and information management services but did not provide therapeutic recommendations. This design controlled for the "checklist effect", because the structuring of information was equal for both groups. During the trial, one or more members of the multidisciplinary rehabilitation team, usually a specialised nurse or therapist, recorded needs assessment data into CARDSS during a 30-60 minute meeting with the patient. The data were subsequently used as input for the weekly multidisciplinary team meeting, where all decisions about the patient's rehabilitation programme were made. In intervention clinics also the guideline-based therapy recommendations from CARDSS were available during such meetings. Teams recorded their final therapeutic decisions in CARDSS at the end of the meetings.

Fig. 2. Screen from the CARDSS system in which the rehabilitation programme is formulated based on therapy recommendations by the guidelines. The pop-up window displays the explanation why the system recommends giving exercise training for this particular patient.

From 44 Dutch clinics that used CARDSS, 31 clinics agreed to participate in the trial. Fifteen clinics were allocated to work with the control version of CARDSS, from which four discontinued participation. After the trial, data audits were conducted in all participating clinics to assess the quality and completeness of record keeping in CARDSS. The results of these audits were used to correct for registration bias. Four intervention clinics were excluded from the analysis because of discrepancies between the information recorded in CARDSS and the information recorded in an independent source. In addition, three intervention clinics had not recorded all their clinical decisions properly into CARDSS, and one clinic had too much missing data. These clinics were also excluded from the analysis. One control clinic, finally, accidentally erased its database and was also excluded.

The resulting data set from 21 centres (12 intervention, 9 control) comprised 2787 patients (1655 intervention, 1132 control). The numbers of patients enrolled per clinic ranged from 78 to 171; the median number of patient per month per clinic was 14. The mean (SD) age of patients was 60.8 (11.4), and the number of male patients was 2060 (73.9%). The main reasons for referral to cardiac rehabilitation were heart surgery (n=1104, 39.6%), acute coronary syndrome (n=1086, 39.0%), and hospitalisation and treatment for stable angina pectoris, including percutaneous coronary intervention (n=454, 16.3%). Table 3 lists the results of the trial in terms of concordance to the guideline recommendations.

Therapy	Concordance (intervention)	Concordance (control)	Crude difference	Adjusted difference [95% CI]
Exercise training	92.6	84.7	7.9	3.5 [0.1 to 5.2]
Education	87.6	63.9	23.7	23.7 [15.5 to 29.4]
Relaxation	59.6	34.1	25.5	41.6 [25.2 to 51.3]
Lifestyle change	57.4	54.1	3.3	7.1 [-2.9 to 18.3]

Table 3. Results of trial: differences in concordance with guideline recommendations between intervention and control clinics. Values are percentages.

Concordance was generally high for exercise training and education therapy, and low for relaxation therapy and lifestyle change interventions. To control for "clustering effects", the differences between intervention and control groups were statistically analysed with generalised estimation equations (Zeger & Liang, 1986). CDS increased guideline concordance for exercise training, education therapy, and relaxation therapy, but not for lifestyle change interventions. Both cases of over- and undertreatment were reduced by CDS, but reduction in undertreatment (i.e., not receiving guideline-recommended therapy) occurred more often. Concordance with recommendations for lifestyle change interventions was poor across both study arms: only 26% of the patients for which it was recommended actually received it. Similarly, despite the positive effect of the CDS, there remained still considerable undertreatment for relaxation therapy. In addition, there was a large variation between clinics in their levels of guideline concordance for all four therapies, in both intervention and control groups.

While randomised clinical trials can be used to study the magnitude of change in decision making behaviour, they do not provide insight into the reasons why professional behaviour changes. For this reason, it was decided to also study the effect of CARDSS on factors that hamper guideline implementation with qualitative research methods (Goud et al., 2010). This study consisted of in-depth, semi-structured interviews with end-users of the system, focusing on reasons for improved concordance or persistent non-concordance to the guidelines after successful adoption of CARDSS. Interviews were transcribed verbatim, and all remarks regarding guideline implementation were extracted, and classified using the conceptual framework from Cabana and colleagues (1999) that was described in Section 3.1.

Twenty-nine rehabilitation nurses and physiotherapists from 21 Dutch clinics were interviewed, resulting in the identification of eighteen barriers. Seven barriers had vanished since the introduction of CARDSS. Table 4 lists five examples, including the barrier type, whether or not the barrier was removed by CARDSS, and a sample comment.

Interviewees reported that CARDSS increased their familiarity with the guidelines' recommendations and decision logic, stimulated them to abandon their conventional way of reasoning, and helped them to apply the guideline in practice, for example by calculating and interpreting of quality-of-life scores. If the system's recommendations were shared with patients, these were more often willing to participate in psychosocial therapies. Interestingly, none of the participants reported that their decision making for exercise training and education therapy had changed because of the introduction of CARDSS. However, these were two of the three therapies for which the trial had shown that the CDS increased concordance to guideline recommendations. Many clinics lacked the facilities and resources to offer all patients all recommended therapies. This fact explained the considerable undertreatment of patients with lifestyle change interventions and relaxation therapy. Similar problems existed with lacking reimbursements and difficult collaboration with other departments. CARDSS was not effective in solving these organisational barriers.

Barrier	Type	Effect	Sample comment
Guideline complexity	External	r	"We now use the quality-of-life questionnaire with every patient."
Lack of familiarity	Internal	r	"Since CARDSS we focus more on [lifestyle related] questions."
Inertia to previous practice	Internal	p	"We don't offer lifestyle change interventions in this clinic. We haven't thought about it yet. I think that is just because of a lack of time."
Lack of resources	External	p	"[Exercise training] is currently full due to a lack of accommodation. The physiotherapist says he just wants five patients in his group, because otherwise the hall is too small for sports activities."
Lack of reimbursement	External	p	"The insurance companies do not reimburse relaxation therapy."

Table 4. Examples of reported barriers to following the cardiac rehabilitation guidelines, with barrier type, effect of CARDSS (r = reduced, p = persistent), and sample comment from interviews.

6. Summary and conclusions

Clinical practice guidelines are well-established instruments to bridge the gap between scientific knowledge and clinical reality. This is crucial in many medical areas, but especially in the prevention and management of patients with chronic illnesses, such as cardiovascular disorders. These disorders are the main cause of disease burden in the Western world and responsible for quick increases in care consumption. Substantial changes in the provision of medical care are needed to anticipate this problem. Many important insights into the factors that are responsible for the development and progression of CVD have been laid down in practice guidelines, urging physicians to initiate preventive therapies in early phases of the disease and provide proper management in later phases. However, guidelines are often not followed in practice, and during the last decade attention has therefore shifted towards implementation of guidelines in clinical practice.

Barriers to guideline adherence vary from knowledge and attitude of individual clinicians to environmental factors which reside in the organisation of care, lack of resources or reimbursement, legal constraints, and in patients that refuse to make the necessary changes to their lifestyles. Different strategies for improving the implementation of guidelines have been used to address these barriers, with variable success. CDS has proven to be among the most effective among these strategies, but is limited to tackling cognitive and affective barriers. In the CARDSS project, for instance, CDS improved guideline implementation by increasing the knowledge of guideline recommendations, by reducing inertia to previous practice, and by reducing guideline complexity. However, CARDSS was not effective when organisational or procedural changes were required that users considered to be beyond their tasks and responsibilities. It has therefore become clear that in many situations CDS must be combined with other strategies into a multi-faceted intervention, to tackle all the existing barriers.

7. Acknowledgment

The author wishes to thank Rick Goud, Nicolette de Keizer, Gerben ter Riet, Jeremy Wyatt, Irene Hellemans, Arie Hasman, and Mariëtte van Engen for their contributions to the CARDSS project. This project was funded by ZonMW, the Netherlands Organisation for Health Research and Development under project nos. 945-14-205 and 17088.3002.

8. References

Ades, P.A. (2001). Cardiac rehabilitation and secondary prevention of coronary heart disease, *New England Journal of Medicine*, Vol.345, pp. 892-902.

Ansari, M.; Shlipak, M.G.; Heidenreich, P.A.; Van Ostaeyen, D.; Pohl, E.C.; Browner, W.S. & Massie, B.M. (2003). Improving guideline adherence: a randomized trial evaluating strategies to increase beta-blocker use in heart failure, *Circulation*, Vol.107, No.22, pp. 2799-2804.

Awtry, E.H. & Loscalzo, J. (2000). Aspirin, *Circulation*, Vol.101, pp. 1206-1218.

Bastian, H.; Glasziou, P. & Chalmers, I. (2010). Seventy-five trials and eleven systematic reviews a day: how will we ever keep up? *PLoS Medicine*, Vol.7, No.9, e1000326.

β-Blocker Heart Attack Study Group (1981). The β-blocker heart attack trial, *Journal of the American Medical Association*, Vol.246, pp. 2073-4.

Beaglehole, R.; Ebrahim, S.; Reddy, S.; Voûte, J.; Leeder, S. & Chronic Disease Action Group. (2007). Prevention of chronic diseases: a call to action, *Lancet*, Vol.370, No.9605, pp. 2152-2157.

Berner, E.S.; Webster, G.D.; Shugerman, A.A.; Jackson, J.R.; Algina J.; Baker, A.L.; Ball, E.V.; Cobbs, C.G.; Dennis, V.W.; Frenkel, E.P.; Hudson, L.D.; Mancall, E.L.; Rackley, C.E. & Taunton, O.D. (1994). Performance of four computer-based diagnostic systems, *New England Journal of Medicine*, Vol.330, No.25, pp. 1792-1796.

Bero, L.A.; Grilli, R.; Grimshaw, J.M.; Harvey, E.; Oxman, A.D. & Thomson, M.A. (1998). Closing the gap between research and practice: an overview of systematic reviews of interventions to promote the implementation of research findings. *British Medical Journal*, Vol.317, No.7156, pp. 465-468.

Bodenheimer, T.; Wagner, E.H. & Grumbach, K. (2002). Improving primary care for patients with chronic illness. The Chronic Care Model, Part 2, *Journal of the American Medical Association*, Vol.288, pp. 1909-1914.

Brook, R.H. (1989). Practice guidelines and practicing medicine. Are they compatible?, *Journal of the American Medical Association*, Vol.262, No.21, p. 3027.

Cabana, M.D.; Rand, C.S. ; Powe, N.R.; Wu, A.W.; Wilson, M.H.; Abboud, P.A. & Rubin, H.R. (1999). Why don't physicians follow clinical practice guidelines? A framework for improvement, *Journal of the American Medical Association*, Vol.282, pp. 1458-1465

Davis, D.A. & Taylor-Vaisey, A. (1997). Translating guidelines into practice: a systematic review of theoretic concepts, practical experience and research evidence in the adoption of clinical practice guidelines, *Canadian Medical Association Journal*, Vol.157, pp. 408-416.

De Clercq, P.A.; Hasman, A.; Blom, J.A. & Korsten, H.H. (2001). Design and implementation of a framework to support the development of clinical guidelines, *International Journal of Medical Informatics*, Vol. 64, pp. 285–318.

De Clercq, P.A.; Blom, J.A.; Korsten, H.H. & Hasman, A. (2004). Approaches for creating computer-interpretable guidelines that facilitate decision support, *Artificial Intelligence in Medicine*, Vol.31, No.1, pp. 1–27.

Dexheimer, J.W.; Talbot, T.R.; Sanders D.L.; Rosenbloom S.T. & Aronsky D. (2008). Prompting clinicians about preventive care measures: a systematic review of randomized controlled trials, *Journal of the American Medical Informatics Association*, Vol.15, No.3, pp. 311-320.

Donner, A. & Klar, N. (2000). *Design and Analysis of Cluster Randomization Trials in Health Research*. Arnold, London, UK.

Ellrodt, G.; Cook, D.J.; Lee, J.; Cho, M.; Hunt, D. & Weingarten, S. (1997). Evidence-based disease management, *Journal of the American Medical Association*, Vol.278, No.20, pp. 1687-1692.

Epstein, A. (1995). Performance reports on quality—prototypes, problems, and prospects, *New England Journal of Medicine*, Vol.333, No.1, p. 57.

EUROASPIRE Study Group (2001a). Lifestyle and risk factor management and use of drug therapies in coronary patients from 15 countries; principal results from EUROASPIRE II Euro Heart Survey Programme, *European Heart Journal*, Vol.22, pp. 554-572.

EUROASPIRE Study Group (2001b). Clinical reality of coronary prevention guidelines: a comparison of EUROASPIRE I and II in nine countries. EUROASPIRE I and II Group, *Lancet*, Vol.357, pp. 995-1001.

Field, M.J. & Lohr, K.N. (Eds.) (1990). *Clinical practice guidelines: Directions for a new program*. National Academy Press, Institute of Medicine, Washington D.C., U.S.A.

Fox, J.; Johns, N.; Rahmanzadeh, A. & Thomson, R. (1998). Disseminating medical knowledge: the PROforma approach, *Artificial Intelligence in Medicine*, Vol. 14, pp. 157-181.

Friedman, C.P. & Wyatt, J.C. (2006). *Evaluation Methods in Medical Informatics*. 2nd ed. Springer, New York.

Garg, A.X.; Adhikari, N.K.; McDonald, H.; Rosas-Arellano, M.P.; Devereaux, P.J.; Beyene, J.; Sam, J. & Haynes, R.B. (2005). Effects of computerized clinical decision support systems on practitioner performance and patient outcomes: a systematic review. *Journal of the American Medical Association*, Vol.293, pp. 1223-1238.

Goud, R.; Hasman, A. & Peek, N. (2008). Development of a guideline-based decision support system with explanation facilities for outpatient therapy, *Computer Methods and Programs in Biomedicine*, Vol.91, No.2, pp.145-153.

Goud, R.; Hasman, A.; Strijbis, A.M. & Peek, N. (2009a). A parallel guideline development and formalization strategy to improve the quality of clinical practice guidelines, *International Journal of Medical Informatics*, Vol.78, No.8, pp. 513-520.

Goud, R.; de Keizer, N.F.; ter Riet, G.; Wyatt, J.C.; Hasman, A.; Hellemans, I.M. & Peek, N. (2009b). Effect of guideline based computerised decision support on decision making of multidisciplinary teams: cluster randomised trial in cardiac rehabilitation, *British Medical Journal*, Vol.338, b1440.

Goud, R.; Van Engen-Verheul, M.M.; De Keizer, N.F.; Bal, R.; Hasman, A.; Hellemans, I.M. & Peek, N. (2010). The effect of computerized decision support on barriers to guideline implementation: a qualitative study in outpatient cardiac rehabilitation, *International Journal of Medical Informatics*, Vol.79, No.6, pp. 430-437.

Grilli, R. & Lomas, J. (1994). Evaluating the message: the relationship between compliance rate and the subject of a practice guideline, *Medical Care*, Vol.32, pp. 202-213.

Grimshaw, J.M. & Russell, I.T. (1993). Effect of clinical guidelines on medical practice: a systematic review of rigorous evaluations, *Lancet*, Vol.342, pp. 1317-1222.

Grimshaw, J.M.; Thomas, R.E.; MacLennan, G. ; Fraser, C.; Ramsay, C.R.; Vale, L.; Whitty, P.; Eccles, M.P.; Matowe, L.; Shirran, L.; Wensing, M.; Dijkstra, R.; Donaldson, C. (2004). Effectiveness and efficiency of guideline dissemination and implementation strategies, *Health Technol Assess*, Vol.8, No.6, pp. 1-72.

Grol, R. (1992). Implementing guidelines in general practice care, *Quality in Health Care*, Vol. 1, pp. 184-191.

Grol, R. & Grimshaw, J. (2003). From best evidence to best practice: effective implementation of change in patients' care, *Lancet*, Vol.362, pp. 1225-1230.

Hripcsak, G. (1994). Writing Arden Syntax Medical Logic Modules, *Computers in Biology and Medicine*, Vol.24, No.5, pp. 331-363.

Institute of Medicine (2001). *Crossing the Quality Chasm: A New Health System for the 21st Century*. National Academy Press, Washington, DC, USA.

Isern, D. & Moreno, A. (2008). Computer-based execution of clinical guidelines: a review, *International Journal of Medical Informatics*, Vol.77, No.12, pp. 787-808.

Jones, D.W. & Peterson, E.D. (2008). Improving hypertension control rates: Technology, people, or systems?, *Journal of the American Medical Association*, Vol.299, No.24, pp. 2896-2898.

Kahneman, D.; Slovic, P. & Tversky, A. (eds.) (1982). *Judgment under Uncertainty: Heuristics and Biases*, Cambridge University Press, Cambridge, UK.

Kawamoto, K.; Houlihan, C.A.; Balas, E.A. & Lobach, D.F. (2005). Improving clinical practice using clinical decision support systems: a systematic review of trials to identify features critical to success, *British Medical Journal*, Vol.330, No.7494, pp. 765.

Lenfant, C. (2003). Clinical research to clinical practice - Lost in translation?, *New England Journal of Medicine*, Vol.349, No.9, pp. 868-874.

Lomas, J.; Anderson, G.M.; Domnick-Pierre, K.; Vayda, E.; Enkin, M.W. & Hannah, W.J. (1989). Do practice guidelines guide practice? The effect of a consensus statement on the practice of physicians, *New England Journal of Medicine*, Vol.321, No.19, pp. 1306-1311.

Miller, R.A. & Masarie, F.E. Jr. (1990). The demise of the "Greek Oracle" model for medical diagnostic systems, *Methods of Information in Medicine*, Vol.29, No.1, pp. 1-2.

Montgomery, A.A.; Fahey, T. ; Peters, T.J.; MacIntosh, C. & Sharp, D.J. (2000). Evaluation of computer based clinical decision support system and risk chart for management of hypertension in primary care: randomised controlled trial, *British Medical Journal*, Vol.320, No.7236, pp. 686-690.

Murray, C.J. & Lopez, A.D. (1997). Alternative projections of mortality and disability by cause 1990-2020 : Global Burden of Disease Study, *Lancet*, Vol.349, pp. 1498-1504.

National Committee for Quality Assurance (1997). *The State of Managed Care Quality*, National Center for Quality Assurance, Washington, DC, USA.

Ohno-Machado, L.; Gennari, J.H.; Murphy S.N.; Jain, N.L.; Tu, S.W.; Oliver, D.E.; Pattison-Gordon, E.; Greenes, R.A.; Shortliffe, E.H. & Barnett, G.O. (1998). The Guideline Interchange Format: A model for representing guidelines, *Journal of the American Medical Informatics Association*, Vol.5, No.4, pp. 357-372.

Ornstein, S.M. (2001). Translating research into practice using electronic medical records the PPRNet-TRIP project: primary and secondary prevention of coronary heart disease and stroke, *Topics in Health Information Management*, Vol.22, No.2, pp. 52-58.

Oxman, A.D.; Thomson, M.A.; Davis, D.A. & Haynes R.B. (1995). No magic bullets: a systematic review of 102 trials of interventions to help health care professionals deliver services more effectively or efficiently, *Canadian Medical Association Journal*, Vol.153, pp. 1423-1431.

Peleg, M.; Boxwala, A.A.; Bernstam, E.; Tu, S.; Greenes, R.A. & Shortliffe, E.H. (2001). Sharable representation of clinical guidelines in GLIF: relationship to the Arden Syntax, *Journal of Biomedical Informatics*, Vol.34, No.3, pp. 170-181.

Peleg, M.; Tu, S.; Bury, J.; Ciccarese, P.; Fox, J.; Greenes, R.A.; Hall, R.; Johnson, P.D.; Jones, N.; Kumar, A.; Miksch, S.; Quaglini, S.; Seyfang, A.; Shortliffe, E.H. & Stefanelli, M. (2003). Comparing computer-interpretable guideline models: a case-study approach, *Journal of the American Medical Informatics Association*, Vol.10, No.1, pp. 52–68.

Quaglini, S.; Stefanelli, M.; Lanzola, G.; Caporusso, V. & Panzarasa, S. (2001). Flexible guideline-based patient careflow systems, *Artificial Intelligence in Medicine*, Vol. 22, pp. 65–80.

Rossi, R.A. & Every, N.R. (1997). A computerized intervention to decrease the use of calcium channel blockers in hypertension, *Journal of General Internal Medicine*, Vol.12, No.11, pp. 672-678.

Shahar, Y.; Miksch, S. & Johnson, P. (1998). The Asgaard Project: a task-specific framework for the application and critiquing of time-oriented clinical guidelines, *Artificial Intelligence in Medicine*, Vol.14, pp. 29-51.

Shaneyfelt, T.M. (2001). Building bridges to quality, *Journal of the Americam Medical Association*, Vol.286, No.20, pp. 2600-2601.

Shekelle, P.G.; Woolf, S.H.; Eccles, M. & Grimshaw, J. (1999). Clinical guidelines: developing guidelines, *British Medical Journal*, Vol.318, No.7183, pp. 593–596.

Shiffman, R.N.; Liaw, Y.; Brandt, C.A. & Corb, G.J. (1999). Computer-based guideline implementation systems: a systematic review of functionality and effectiveness, *Journal of the American Medical Informatics Association*, Vol. 6, pp. 104-114.

Shortliffe, E.H.; Perreault, L.E.; Wiederholt, G. & Fagan, L.M. (2003). *Medical Informatics: Computer Applications in Health Care and Biomedicine*. New York: Springer.

Sonnenberg, F.A. & Hagerty, C.G. (2006). Computer-interpretable clinical practice guidelines. Where are we and where are we going? In : *IMIA Yearbook of Medical Informatics 2006*, Schattauer, Stuttgart, Germany, pp. 145-158.

Stafford, R.S. & Radley, D.C. (2003). The underutilization of cardiac medications of proven benefit, 1990 to 2002, *Journal of the American College of Cardiologists*, Vol.41, pp. 56-61.

Subramanian, U.; Fihn, S.D.; Weinberger, M.; Plue, L.; Smith, F.E.; Udris, E.M.; McDonell, M.B.; Eckert, G.J.; Temkit, M.; Zhou, X.H.; Chen, L. & Tierney, W.M. (2004). A controlled trial of including symptom data in computer-based care suggestions for managing patients with chronic heart failure, *American Journal of Medicine*, Vol.116, No.6, pp. 375-384.

Thorsen, T. & Mäkelä, M. (1999). *Changing professional practice. Theory and practice of Clinical Guidelines Implementation.* Danish Institute for Health Services, Copenhagen, Denmark.

Tierney, W.M.; Overhage, J.M.; Murray, M.D.; Harris, L.E.; Zhou, X.H.; Eckert, G.J.; Smith, F.E.; Nienaber, N.; McDonald, C.J. & Wolinsky, F.D. (2003). Effects of computerized guidelines for managing heart disease in primary care, *Journal of General Internal Medicine*, Vol.18, No.12, pp. 967-976.

Tu, S.W.; Campbell, J.R.; Glasgow, J. ; Nyman, M.A.; McClure, R.; McClay, J.; Parker, C.; Hrabak, K.M.; Berg, D.; Weida, T.; Mansfield, J.G.; Musen, M.A. & Abarbanel, R.M. (2007). The SAGE Guideline Model: achievements and overview, *Journal of the American Medical Informatics Association*, Vol.14, No.5, pp. 589-598.

Tunis, S.R.; Hayward, R.S.; Wilson, M.C.; Rubin, H.R.; Bass, E.B.; Johnston, M. & Steinberg, E.P. (1994). Internists' attitudes about clinical practice guidelines, *Annals of Internal Medicine*, Vol.120, No.11, pp. 956-963.

Wensing, M. & Grol, R. (1994). Single and combined strategies for implementing changes in primary care: a literature review, *International Journal of Quality in Health Care*, Vol. 6, pp. 115-132.

Whelton, P.K.; Appel, L.J.; Espeland M.A.; Applegate W.B.; Ettinger, W.H., Jr.; Kostis, J.B.; Kumanyika, S.; Lacy, C.R.; Johnson, K.C.; Folmar, S. & Cutler, J.A. (1998). Sodium reduction and weight loss in the treatment of hypertension in older persons: a randomized controlled trial of nonpharmacologic interventions in the elderly (TONE), *Journal of the American Medical Association*, Vol.279, pp. 839-846.

Woolf, S.H. (1990). Practice guidelines: a new reality in medicine. I. Recent developments, *Archives of Internal Medicine*, Vol.150, No.9, p. 1811-1818.

Woolf, S.H. (1993). Practice guidelines: a new reality in medicine. III. Impact on patient care, *Archives of Internal Medicine*, Vol.153, No.23, pp. 2646-2655.

Woolf, S.H.; Grol, R.; Hutchinson, A.; Eccles, M. & Grimshaw, J. (1999). Clinical guidelines: potential benefits, limitations, and harms of clinical guidelines, *British Medical Journal*, Vol.318, No.7182, pp. 527-30.

World Health Organization (1993). *Needs and Action Priorities in Cardiac Rehabilitation and Secondary Prevention in Patients with Coronary Heart Disease*, WHO Regional Office for Europe, Geneva, Switzerland.

Wyatt, J. & Spiegelhalter, D. (1991). Field trials of medical decision-aids: potential problems and solutions, *Proceedings of the Annual Symposium on Computer Application in Medical Care*, pp. 3-7.

Yusuf, S.; Hawken, S.; Ounpuu, S.; Dans, T.; Avezum, A.; Lanas, F.; McQueen, M.; Budaj, A.; Pais, P.; Varigos, J.; Lisheng, L. & INTERHEART Study Investigators. (2004). Effect of potentially modifiable risk factors associated with myocardial infarction in 52 countries (the INTERHEART study): case-control study, *Lancet*, Vol.364, No.9438, pp. 937-952.

Zeger, S.L. & Liang, K.Y. (1986). Longitudinal data analysis for discrete and continuous outcomes, *Biometrics*, Vol.42, pp. 121-130.

Part 3

Applications for Disease Management

6

Emerging Information Technologies to Provide Improved Decision Support for Surveillance, Prevention, and Control of Vector-Borne Diseases

Saul Lozano-Fuentes[1], Christopher M. Barker[2,3], Marlize Coleman[1,4], Michael Coleman[4], Bborie Park[2], William K. Reisen[2,3] and Lars Eisen[1]

[1]*Colorado State University, Fort Collins, Colorado*
[2]*University of California, Davis, California*
[3]*Fogarty International Center, National Institutes of Health, Bethesda, Maryland*
[4]*Liverpool School of Tropical Medicine, Liverpool*
[1,2,3]*United States of America*
[4]*United Kingdom*

1. Introduction

Vector-borne diseases, caused by pathogens transmitted by arthropods, result in significant morbidity and mortality of humans, especially in the developing world (Gratz, 1999). Malaria caused an estimated 247 million cases and nearly a million deaths in 2008, and up to 50 million dengue infections and 500,000 cases of severe dengue hemorrhagic fever are estimated to occur each year (World Health Organization, 2008, 2009). Furthermore, new vector-borne diseases have emerged and become established in developed parts of the world in recent decades. Vector-borne diseases that now are a fact of life in such areas, and unlikely to be eliminated, include West Nile virus disease in North America and Lyme borreliosis in Asia, Europe, and North America (Sonenshine, 1993; Kramer et al., 2008).

Surveillance and control of a vector-borne disease is a complex undertaking because it involves arthropod vectors, pathogens, and vertebrate amplification/reservoir hosts, each of which may be represented by one or more species. Humans may be amplification/reservoir hosts for the pathogens (e.g., dengue and malaria) or dead-end hosts (e.g., Lyme borreliosis and West Nile virus disease). Vector/disease control programs are thus faced with the challenge of handling a wide range of information including entomological surveillance data (vector collection details, vector abundance, and insecticide resistance) and pathogen-related surveillance data (infection of vectors, enzootic amplification/reservoir hosts or sentinel animals, and passively or actively acquired data on infection in humans). They also need to manage data relating to the control of the vector and/or the pathogen, potentially including the coverage in space and time of a wide range of prevention or control activities (e.g., vaccination, education campaigns, and different interventions targeting arthropod vectors or vertebrate amplification/reservoir hosts) as well as the time and amount of stock materials (e.g., vaccines or insecticides) expended in the effort. In an ideal scenario, this is complemented by the determination of entomological and epidemiological outcome measures to assess control program performance.

Without adequate capacity for data management and analysis, a control program stands little chance of being able to assess and improve its performance. This can lead to poor decision making, including the continued use of ineffective surveillance or control methods and a failure to target available resources to areas and time periods where they would have the greatest impact. Emerging information technologies present new opportunities to reduce the burden of vector-borne diseases through improved decision support for surveillance, prevention, and control of vectors and their associated pathogens (reviewed by L. Eisen & R.J. Eisen, 2011). This ranges from improved basic capacity for data management and analysis to development of integrated systems with decision support functionalities such as custom calculations for important surveillance or control parameters, automated alerts when thresholds for key entomological or epidemiological risk measures are reached, and capacity for map-based data visualization. The flow scheme in Figure 1 illustrates how such a system can be incorporated into control program operations.

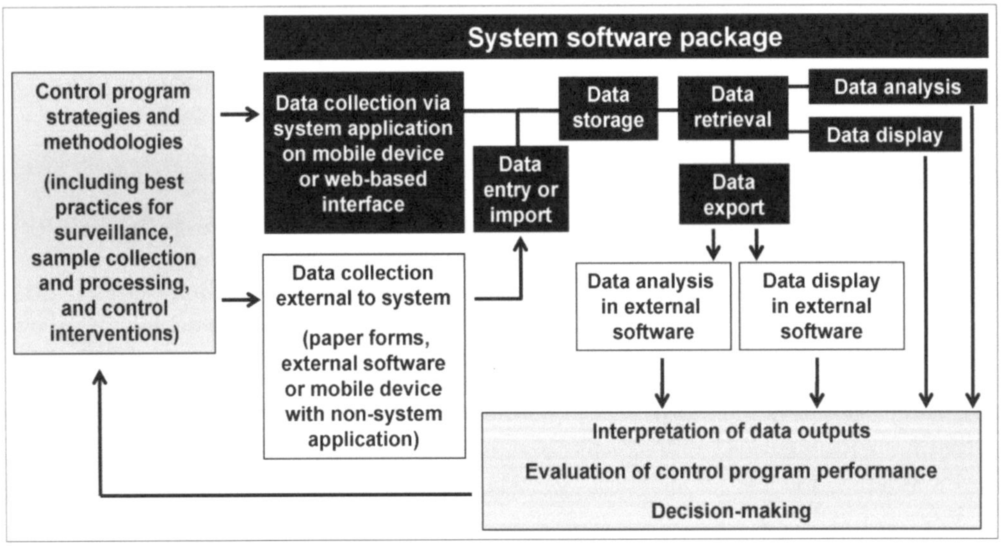

Fig. 1. Flow scheme illustrating how a data management system or decision support system can be incorporated into vector and disease control program operations.

This chapter provides a brief overview of information technologies with the potential for application to vector-borne disease surveillance, prevention, and control (section 2), and provides examples of novel decision support tools for vector-borne diseases (sections 3-4). Special emphasis is placed on information technologies that can be implemented in the resource-constrained environments that suffer the greatest burden of vector-borne diseases. Here, we use the terminology "data management system/decision support system" to avoid issues related to the definition of a decision support system and to recognize that system packages may have different levels of built-in decision support functionalites regardless of whether they are labeled data management systems or decision support systems.

2. Information technologies with the potential for application in data management systems/decision support systems for vector-borne diseases

Data management and analysis are facilitated by use of database, reporting, and mapping/ Geographic Information System (GIS) software, especially when multiple applications are combined in an integrated system. For example, the recent introduction of mosquito-borne West Nile virus into North America resulted in the development of novel systems that include GIS to provide enhanced capacity for data display and to support decision-making: the Integrated System for Public Health Monitoring of West Nile Virus in Canada (Gosselin et al., 2005) and the California Vectorborne Disease Surveillance Gateway (section 4).

Many systems include software components with high acquisition and/or licensing costs, thus preventing implementation in resource-constrained environments and limiting the potential for using the systems to address vector-borne diseases in developing countries. One way of overcoming this problem is to harness the explosion of software products that can be distributed and used without licensing costs, e.g., open source products, and to develop an integrated system based on such components (Yi et al., 2008). Both systems described below (sections 3-4) make extensive use of open source products. The infectious disease community is now starting to use freely available software, especially in resource-constrained environments where software with high licensing costs are not sustainable. Below, the mapping tool Google Earth (http://www.google.com/earth/index.html) is used as an example of a stand-alone application with a freely available version which now is being used as a decision support tool in public health, including vector-borne diseases (Lozano-Fuentes et al., 2008; Stensgaard et al., 2009).

Google Earth provides free access to satellite imagery and includes tools allowing for production and customization of polygons, lines, and points overlaid on the image. These features can be saved, with their spatial references, as Keyhole Markup Language (KML) files and distributed to other parties, for example as e-mail attachments. The other parties can then view the created features in Google Earth, overlaid on the same satellite image from which they were created based on the spatial reference of the features. The application also can generate dynamic time-series maps that show, in a far more intuitive way than a series of static map images, how the spatial distribution of disease cases, or other data of interest, changes over time. The features included in these dynamic time-series maps can be saved as KML files and viewed by other parties, similar to the features in a static map.

One basic use of this type of mapping tool in public health is to produce "electronic pin maps" that show the locations of disease cases overlaid on an image showing the physical environment. This reveals case clustering and may provide insights into risk factors for pathogen exposure such as aquatic mosquito habitat adjacent to urban areas. To enhance the value of a disease case pin map produced in a mapping software, it can be augmented with data for locations of health facilities or transport routes, and thus provide additional information useful to guide public health actions (Kamadjeu, 2009). Other uses for Google Earth include display of malaria parasite rates in the Malaria Atlas Project (Hay & Snow, 2006) and collection locations for insecticide-resistant vector mosquitoes (Dialynas et al., 2009).

Mapping software that provides access to high-quality imagery of the physical environment can complement GIS software in settings where spatial data layers are unavailable but imagery that can be accessed through the mapping software is of high quality. Lozano-Fuentes et al. (2008) demonstrated how an image available through Google Earth, combined with the basic editing tools included in the application, can be used to first develop a basic city infrastructure representation and then use this representation to display disease case locations, in this instance for dengue. Because KML files can be converted into shapefiles for use in GIS software, and vice versa, there is great potential for combined use of GIS and Google Earth. Kamadjeu (2009) imported district boundaries originally developed in a GIS into Google Earth and then developed a chloropleth map for polio vaccination coverage by district which was overlaid by the location of polio cases. In Nicaragua, a base map for town infrastructure developed in Google Earth was imported into a GIS and used, together with data for dengue case locations and development sites for the mosquito vector, to support dengue control operations (Chang et al., 2009). These examples highlight the potential for creative use of emerging information technologies as stand-alone decision support tools.

Mobile data capture is an emerging information technology with potential for incorporation into a data management system/decision support system. It provides the opportunity, through mobile computers (laptops or netbooks), personal digital assistants (PDAs; also known as palmtop computers), remote sensors, or even cell phones, to move the stage of electronic data capture all the way down to the initial data capturing session in the field or laboratory. Mobile computing has been potentiated with the advent of faster, cheaper low-power processors and more robust wireless data tranmission technologies. The technical limitations of mobile devices are constantly changing and mobile internet access is now achieved in most large urban areas of the world, including those in developing countries.

The basic workflow for mobile data capture involves initial capture of data on the mobile electronic device followed by upload into a central data repository. Uploading data can be done by direct connection or by transmission of data over wireless networks (Wi-Fi or cell phone networks). In an ideal scenario, the data-capturing device also has capacity to act as a Global Positioning System receiver and thus generate data for the spatial location where data were entered (Vanden Eng et al., 2007). When a software application on the mobile device is directly compatible with a data management system/decision support system, the mobile device essentially becomes part of the system and the data collection excecuted on the device becomes part of the work flow where the user interfaces directly with the system (Figure 1). Additional relevant data, e.g., from subsequent laboratory diagnostic tests, visualizations, or analyses, later can be entered into the system through other means.

There is strong interest in using mobile data capture in public health including vector-borne disease surveillance; recent studies have evaluated the use of PDAs for data collection during household surveys for malaria or bed net use (Vanden Eng et al., 2007; Ahmed & Zerihun, 2010) and collection of data for suspected dengue patients in clinical studies in Nicaragua (Aviles et al., 2008). The potential for use of cell phones as mobile data capturing devices was evaluated for infectious disease surveillance in Peru (Johnson & Blazes, 2007) and for malaria surveillance and monitoring in Thailand (Meankaew et al., 2010).

3. A multi-disease data management system/decision support system for tropical vector-borne diseases

The Innovative Vector Control Consortium (IVCC) recognized the potential for using information technologies to improve vector and disease control program performance and ultimately reduce the burden of tropical vector-borne diseases such as dengue and malaria (Hemingway et al., 2006). This resulted in an initiative that led to the development of the software package described herein: a multi-disease data management system/decision support system (hereafter, the system) with current capacity for dengue and malaria, and with potential for addition of other important tropical vector-borne diseases such as Chagas disease, human African trypanosomiasis, leishmaniasis, lymphatic filariasis, and onchocerciasis (L. Eisen et al., 2011). To some extent, the system builds upon previous experience with development and implementation of data management systems for malaria in southern Africa (Booman et al., 2000, 2003; Martin et al., 2002; Marlize Coleman et al., 2008). Key goals for the system include: (1) ensuring that it can be distributed without the user incurring licensing costs, (2) producing a flexible system that can be adapted to local circumstances by the user with no or minimal involvement of software developers, (3) achieving a user-friendly system with capacity to support data entry, storage, and querying, and production of maps and reports, as well as including decision support functionalities such as custom calculations and automated alerts, and (4) delivering a system capable of enhancing the user's ability to carry out surveillance, engage in evidence-based decision making, monitor interventions, and evaluate control program performance.

3.1 System development, architecture, requirements, installation, and licensing

The system was developed in an iterative process with close contact between developers and subject matter experts including operational field input from Malawi, Mexico, Mozambique, South Africa, and Zambia public health partners. System functionalities were assessed by positive and negative testing by an internal testing team. Additional testing needs to include pilot implementations in different operational settings with naïve users.

The system was developed with a 3-tiered architecture (data tier–application/business logic tier–presentation tier) and is comprised exclusively of software components which can be distributed without licensing costs. The data tier includes a PostgreSQL database (http://www.postgresql.org/) enhanced with PostGIS (http://postgis.refractions.net/) to support spatial data. The business logic tier includes Java (http://www.java.com/en/) and Apache Tomcat (http://tomcat.apache.org/). The presentation tier uses Firefox (http://www.mozilla.com/en-US/firefox/ie.html), and is augmented by applications to support production of reports, BIRT (http://www.eclipse.org/birt/phoenix/), and maps, GeoServer (http://geoserver.org/display/GEOS/Welcome) and OpenLayers (http://openlayers.org/). To link the tiers, and to allow the user to make changes that automatically are reflected across the 3-tiered architecture, the system includes TerraFrame's Runway SDK application (http://www.terraframe.com/products/runwaysdk).

The system requires a minimum of 2 GB RAM, 100 GB storage, and 2.0 GHz CPU to operate on a stand-alone machine (projected cost of $500-600 per stand-alone desktop in 2011). The target operating system is Microsoft Windows XP (Microsoft Corporation, Redmond, Washington, U.S.A.) but the system has been informally tested on and shown to function also for Windows Vista, Windows 7, Apple Mac OSX (Apple Inc., Cupertino, California, U.S.A.), and Ubuntu Desktop (http://www.ubuntu.com/). The system can be implemented on a single stand-alone computer, in a client/server environment where the client (user) logs in remotely to the system, or as a pool of installations with one master and one or multiple dependent installations (the system includes synchronization functionality).

The system installation package includes the system itself, the system manual, and stand-alone versions of OpenOffice (http://www.openoffice.org/), the reporting tool BIRT, to allow the user to create customized report templates which then can be imported into the system, FWtools (http://fwtools.maptools.org/) to assist the user in transforming spatial data into well known text (WKT) format, and QCal which calculates dose/time response curves for insecticide resistance bioassays (http://sourceforge.net/projects/irmaproj/). Distribution and licensing is currently executed through the IVCC (http://www.ivcc.com/). There is no cost associated with the license (the system is a royalty free, licensed software).

3.2 Adaptability of the system

One key goal was to produce a flexible system that can be adapted to local circumstances by the user with no or minimal involvement of software developers. Key points of system adaptability are described below.

The system currently handles dengue and malaria. Selection of the disease in which to work is done through a menu item called Disease. Selecting a disease of interest in the Disease menu results in the user being presented with a default menu for the selected disease. This default menu can be re-configured by the user, including: (1) incorporation of functionalities that are present in the system but not as a default for the disease of interest and (2) changes to menu label names. This provides an economy of scope as new diseases downstream can be added to the system at decreased cost through re-use of already existing functionalities.

The system also includes the capacity to customize user roles and their permissions. It is delivered with a set of default roles but these are completely configurable in that the user can change the names of existing roles, create new roles, and, importantly, define separate permissions for each role to access or work with different system functionalities (Write, Read, or None/No access). The permissions can be further refined by generating individual log-in names and passwords for each person using the system and then assigning one or multiple roles to a given individual. This helps to restrict access to sensitive information such as data for individual patients. Furthermore, the system allows the user to define, by disease of interest, the status of many data entry fields, i.e., whether they are mandatory or non-mandatory, and also to select, by disease of interest and role, whether to show or hide a given data entry field (Figure 2). Exceptions are fields which are system mandatory and thus cannot be made non-mandatory or hidden. A data entry field also may be given different display label names in the different disease menus. This is accomplished with a localization functionality which also can be used to develop display labels, by disease, for a language other than the default English (i.e., languages or dialects based on the Latin character set).

The system includes three user-configurable information trees: (1) a controlled vocabulary term tree, (2) a universal tree for key spatial concepts, and (3) a geographical entity tree, where each entity is an instance of a universal (e.g., the geo entity United States is an instance of the universal Country).

The term tree, based on ontological principles following the Open Biomedical Ontologies (Smith et al., 2007), is used in the system to define options in pop-up select lists for data entry fields and for pre-configured entries for rows and/or columns in data entry tables (Figure 3B). An ontology is a set of standardized and logically defined terms (controlled vocabulary) and their inter-relationships. The controlled vocabulary term tree is built on a single ontological relationship, is_a; for example virus isolation is_a laboratory test for dengue virus (Figure 3A).

The system is delivered with a default term tree and each data entry field or row/column configuration in a data entry table that is populated from the term tree has a pre-configured root term (Figure 2) that defines what is included in the select list for the data entry field or which terms that are used to define table rows/columns. Both the term tree itself and the selection of root terms are completely configurable by the user, including the ability to make terms active or inactive by disease (Figure 3A). The term tree has multiple benefits including

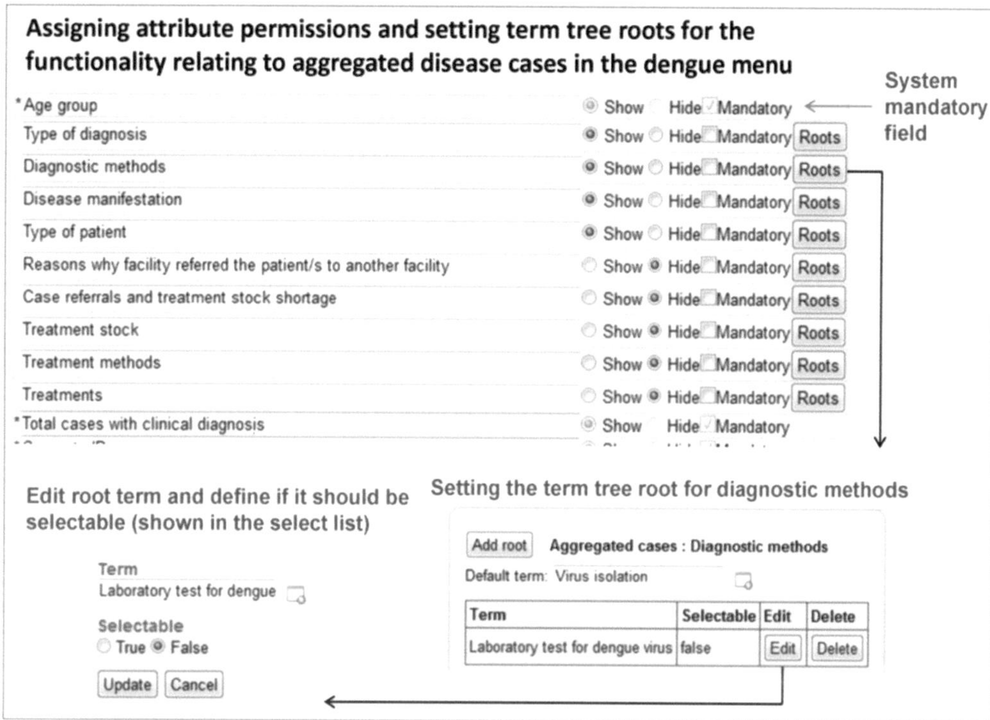

Fig. 2. Administration functionality to assign attribute permissions and set term tree roots. Adapted from a figure presented previously by L. Eisen et al. (2011).

the use of standardized terms. Each term is given a name, display label, and ID, and the user also can provide a definition for the term (Figure 3A). Use of standardized terms provides potential for sharing of data with related database or ontology initiatives. The system's term tree includes terms related to insecticide resistance that were derived from the Mosquito Insecticide Resistance Ontology and are used in the IRbase global database for insecticide resistance in mosquito vectors (Dialynas et al., 2009). It also includes terms drawn from the malaria ontology IDOMAL (Topalis et al., 2010). The term tree provides capacity to dynamically change both the number of rows/columns that appear in a data entry table and their respective header labels (Figure 3B) simply by making changes to the term tree content under the root term that is used to populate that specific data entry table. This type of dynamic data entry table provides exceptional potential for system adaptation to local conditions without the involvement of software developers. Finally, based on the is_a ontological relationship of the term tree, data can be aggregated to higher levels of the term tree in the system's internal data querying tools.

Universals, as used in this system, are key spatial concepts that can be defined with regards to how they are used to support system functionalities. A small set of universals are required for specific system functionalities (health facility, collection site, sentinel site, spray zone, stock depot, and surface) and these typically will be complemented in the system by a set of user-created universals, such as country, state, county, settlement, etc.

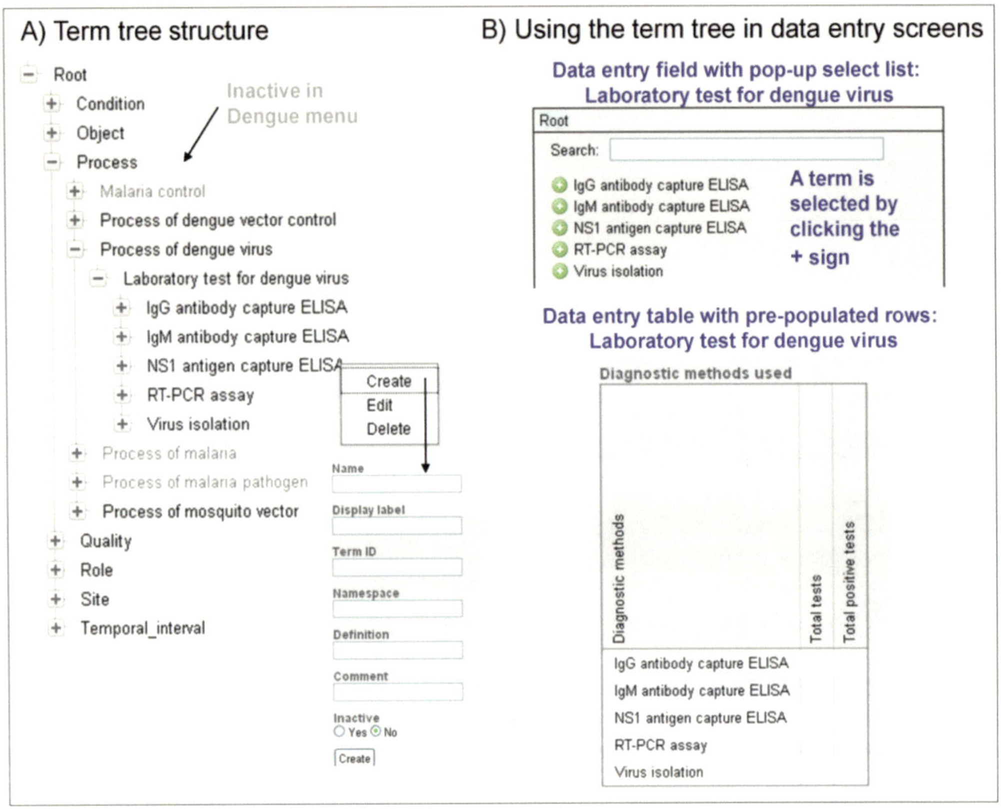

Fig. 3. Partially opened term tree structure for dengue menu and use of configurable term tree lists in data entry screens. A) Example of term tree section leading to laboratory tests for dengue virus. B) Using the term tree section for laboratory tests for dengue virus in data entry fields and tables. Adapted from a figure presented previously by L. Eisen et al. (2011).

The geographical entity tree provides a representation of the area in which the system is implemented and, for geo entities in the system which have spatial data associated with them, can be used for mapping. Geo entities have the properties of universal type, entity status (active/inactive), name and ID, type of geometry (point, polygon, etc.), and spatial data (in WKT format). Each entity is related to other entities by means of a located_in relationship defined by the total inclusion of one entity inside another: for example Colorado is located in the United States. The system default is a single root entity called Earth under which the user can build a locally relevant geographical entity tree. Once this is configured, the user can add or delete geo entities and edit the information for existing ones. One benefit of the geographical entity tree, derived from its located_in relationship structure, is the potential for aggregating data to coarser spatial resolutions in the system's internal data querying tools.

3.3 Data entry, data query, and reporting/mapping

To minimize data entry error, data entry fields make extensive use of hard-coded select lists or radio buttons, geo entities selected from the geographical entity tree, dates selected from pop-up calendars, and terms selected from pop-up select lists from the term tree. Data querying is done through a set of unique system tools referred to as query builders, linked to specific data input screens, where the user can define a specific data query (Figure 4).

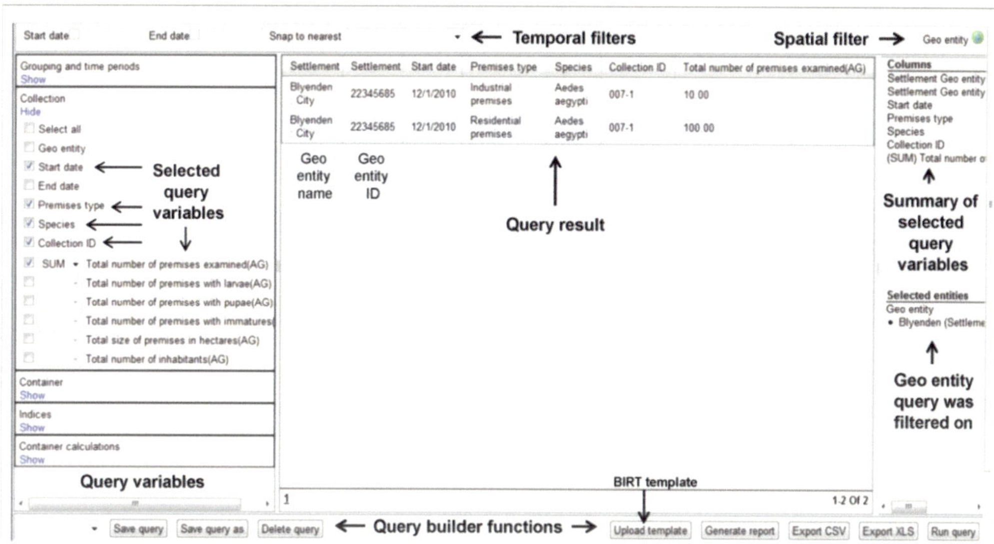

Fig. 4. Example of query builder screen. Adapted from a figure presented previously by L. Eisen et al. (2011).

All query builders include the capacity to filter a query on start and end dates and geo entities from the geographical entity tree (top pane in query builder; Figure 4). Additional filtering of a query can be done on specific variable fields (left pane in query builder, Figure 4) corresponding to the data entry fields in the relevant data input screens; this can include terms from a term tree root, values from hard-coded select lists or numerical values or ranges. Many of the query builders also include pre-defined custom calculations (section 3.4.1). The query builders also include options to export query results as .csv or .xls files, to save and re-use specific querying field combinations that are executed on a regular basis, and to upload pre-configured report templates (from BIRT) and use these to produce standardized reports (bottom pane of query builder; Figure 4). Mapping is directly linked to the query builders as the system's map generation process makes use of information that is saved in the query builders as specific named query results. Maps can combine data that are generated through different query builders, e.g., for intervention coverages and disease case locations or disease incidence, and overlaid on a map base layer showing locations of households, administrative boundaries, etc. (Figure 5).

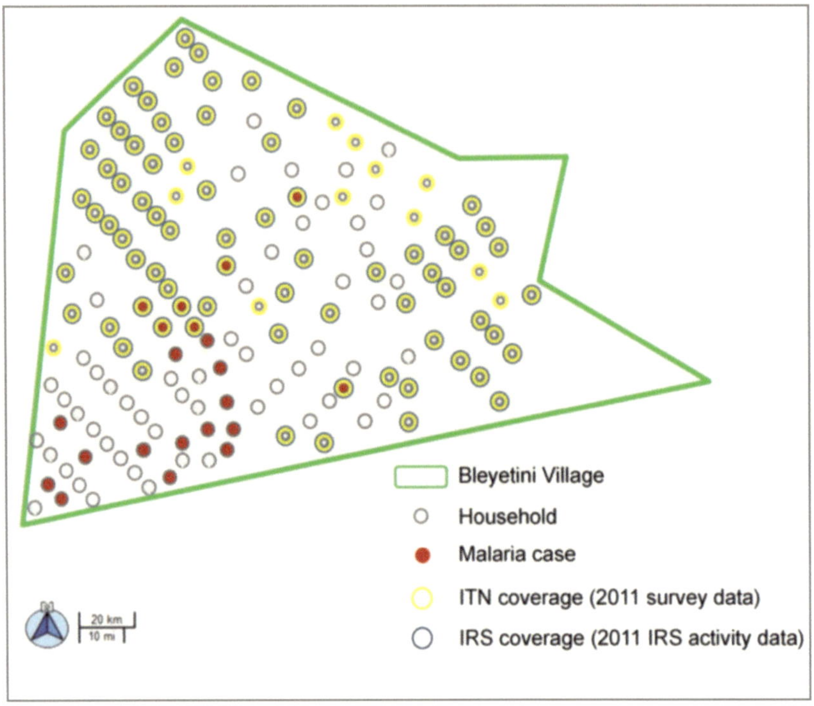

Fig. 5. Example of map output. The base layer shows locations of households within a village and this is overlaid with data for disease cases and coverage by control interventions including insecticide-treated nets (ITN) and indoor residual spraying (IRS).

3.4 Examples of system decision support functionalities

One key goal was to produce a system capable of enhancing the user's ability to carry out continuous surveillance, engage in evidence-based decision making, monitor interventions, and evaluate control program performance. The following sections provide examples relevant to dengue control programs of system decision support functionalities, including pre-defined custom calculations relating to specific surveillance or control parameters and automated alerts when system thresholds for key entomological or epidemiological risk measures are reached.

3.4.1 Custom calculations in query builders

The system provides decision support through pre-defined custom calculations that are included in query builders and address issues of operational relevance for a vector/disease control program. Examples of custom calculations relevant to dengue are provided below.

Entomological surveillance relating to dengue is peculiar in that the immature stages (larvae and pupae) of key dengue virus vectors, especially *Aedes aegypti*, exploit a wide range of containers (e.g., water storage containers, tires, bottles, cans, etc.) that accumulate in the peridomestic environment as development sites (Focks, 2003). This has led to a strong focus in vector and dengue control on reducing availability of containers, especially the container types that locally are most productive for immatures, through environmental sanitation to remove trash containers and treatment of necessary containers with biological or chemical control agents to kill immatures (World Health Organization, 2009). The system therefore includes specific functionalities for collection of data on immatures from containers. Local variability of important container types is addressed by user definition of a locally relevant set of container types in the term tree for use in data entry screens (as term tree-driven pop-up select lists or prepopulated rows in data entry tables) and corresponding query builders. To enhance the capacity of the system to support decisions regarding the need for vector control actions, the specific query builder which handles immatures by container type includes pre-defined custom calculations for commonly used immature abundance indices that are used in operational settings to determine whether or not control actions should be executed. Additional custom calculations are included to help the user determine which container types contribute the most to production of mosquito vector immatures and thus are especially important to target for control.

Other examples of pre-defined custom calculations in query builders in the system's dengue menu that provide information directly useful for making operational decisions regarding surveillance and control activities include: (1) incidence of disease cases and case fatality rate in the case surveillance query builders and (2) percentages of available and visited premises within a given geographical area and time period for which prevention or control activities were carried out (this can also be broken down by prevention/control method, as defined by the user in the term tree), and percentage of visited premises that were not treated (this can also be broken down by reason for non-treatment, as defined by the user in the term tree), in the intervention monitoring query builder. The intervention monitoring query builder also illustrates the value of the term tree in the system. The user can specify, through the section of the term tree that is used to dynamically create the columns (and their labels) in the data entry table for prevention or control activities that data are to be collected against, any combination of different prevention or control methods and then use the intervention monitoring query builder to produce a breakdown by method for their spatial coverages in a given area during a specific time period.

3.4.2 Automated alerts

Automated alerts that are triggered when threshold values are reached are perhaps the clearest examples of decision support in the system. Alerts are currently included for: (1) abundance indices for container-inhabiting mosquito immatures and (2) disease cases. In both cases thresholds can be configured by the user to suit local conditions so that alerts are not excessive to the point of being meaningless due to lack of resources to respond to them. The system can provide alerts as on-screen pop-ups (Figure 6B) and/or e-mail notifications.

Thresholds for abundance indices for container-inhabiting mosquito immatures are set as fixed numbers and up to 13 different indices can be activated by entering threshold values against them in a configuration screen (Figure 6A). An alert that the threshold value was reached for a given index is triggered on entry of a data record for immatures by container type (defined by geo entity, time period, premises type, and mosquito species). When the user saves a data record, the system automatically calculates the 13 abundance indices and compares the results to the configured threshold values. Alerts are then provided for the indices where the threshold values were reached (Figure 6B).

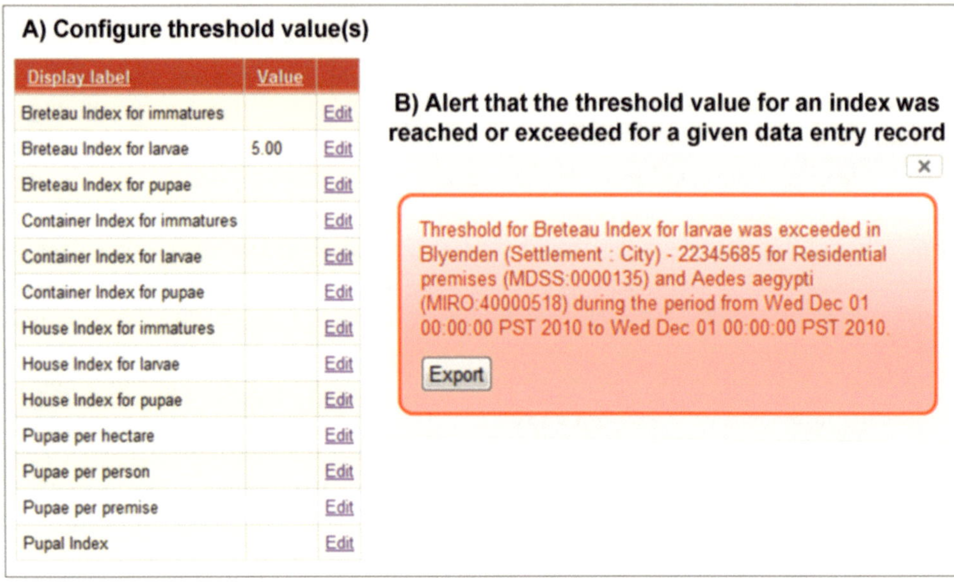

Fig. 6. Thresholds and automated alerts for abundance indices for container-inhabiting mosquito immatures. A) Threshold value configuration screen. B) Example of automated on-screen pop-up alert that the threshold value for a given index was broken for a given data entry record (defined by geo entity, time period, premises type, and mosquito species).

Setting alert threshold values for disease cases, which is done by disease and presumed source of infection (a geo entity representing an administrative boundary unit) or health facility (where the case was reported), is more complicated because there are several options for the user to configure the threshold value calculation. Thresholds can be calculated using different algorithms including mean + 1.5 SD, mean + 2 SD, modified binomial 95%, modified binomial 99%, and the upper third quartile (Marlize Coleman et al., 2008), and two of these can be included as separate threshold alert levels 1 and 2. Based on what type of historical data have been entered into the system, the threshold values can be calculated from data for aggregated cases, individual cases, or individual and aggregated cases combined. The system also allows the user to: (1) define the number of weeks preceding and following an epidemiological week that are included in the threshold value calculation for epidemiological week, (2) define the number of previous pathogen transmission seasons, which can be contained within a single year or span two years, for which to include data for the threshold value calculation, and (3) provide a weight for each pathogen transmission season to address the effect of outliers with unusually low or high disease case loads. To address scenarios where an initial clinical diagnosis often may prove incorrect and many clinically diagnosed patients do not return to provide convalescent samples for confirmatory tests of pathogen exposure, the system automatically calculates which percentage of clinically diagnosed cases should be included in the threshold value calculation based on historical data in the system for confirmed positive cases (for dengue; cases where laboratory tests for dengue virus or dengue virus exposure were positive) versus confirmed negative cases (for dengue; cases where laboratory tests for dengue virus and dengue virus exposure were negative). Finally, the system provides the option to manually enter or edit threshold values, by geo entity, transmission season, and epidemiological week, for thresholds alert levels 1 and 2.

The system tracks a current case count, by disease, which is updated every time a new individual case is entered into the system. An alert is triggered on the case entry for which the threshold value is reached for a given disease in a given geo entity or health facility for a given time period (the system allows for selection of standard epidemiological week or a sliding week that includes cases occurring from six days prior to the date of onset of symptoms for the case that is entered into the system). If disease cases are entered into the system on a timely basis, these alerts can be used to facilitate outbreak response. To address the scenario outlined above where an initial clinical diagnosis often may prove incorrect (and laboratory confirmation is slow or often lacking), the alert functionality can be modified by the user defining which percentage of clinically diagnosed cases that should be used for calculation of the current case count. Because the percentage is set manually, it can be changed temporarily in response to extraordinary events such as outbreaks of other diseases resulting in increased levels of clinical misdiagnosis.

Notably, the development of tools for rapid detection of outbreaks/epidemics supports the long-term goal of global malaria eradication and the current drive for elimination in countries and regions of low malaria endemnicity. Scaling up control efforts and improving surveillance practices are critical objectives for these undertakings to succeed. Sensitive tools to timely identify an unusual increase in disease cases followed by prompt outbreak response will support such efforts.

3.5 Range of the information handled in the system's dengue menu

In addition to the generic system modules for administration and GIS, the latter of which includes the geographical entity tree and the functionality for map generation, the system's dengue menu includes modules dealing with case surveillance, entomological surveillance, intervention planning, intervention monitoring , and stock control. Case surveillance includes separate functional components for: (1) aggregated disease case data and (2) data for individual disease cases. Aggregated disease case data are captured by time period, geo entity or health facility, and age group. The core of the data entry functionality is comprised of entries for numbers of cases with clinical diagnosis, confirmed positive diagnosis, and confirmed negative diagnosis together with a series of data entry tables relating to type of diagnosis, disease manifestation, and type of patient where both the rows (e.g., specific disease manifestations such as dengue fever and dengue hemorrhagic fever) and the columns (e.g., providing breakdowns by gender, dengue virus serotype, and locally acquired versus imported cases) are generated dynamically from the term tree and thus can be readily configured by the user to be relevant in the local setting. Data entry for individual disease cases include basic patient data as well as symptomology, laboratory diagnostic data, and administrative information such as whether a case was detected through passive or active surveillance and, in the case of passively detected cases, data for the health facility and attending physician.

The module for entomological surveillance includes functional components which can handle data relating to non-container based collections of mosquito vectors, for example collection of adults by traps or active collection with aspirators, as well as container-based surveillance data for immatures which was mentioned previously. In the latter case, the system includes separate data entry screens for data collected by individual container versus data collapsed to user-defined container types. This is complemented by functionalities relating to capture of data for assays conducted on mosquito collections, including assays for pathogen detection, assays to determine killing efficacy of insecticides, and insecticide resistance bioassays, biochemical assays, and molecular genetic assays.

Intervention planning is restricted to a planning calculator tool which helps the user determine the man-power or amount of insecticide product needed to complete an intervention. Intervention monitoring deals with coverage, in space and time, of different types of control interventions. This includes functionalities to handle data relating to person-days and amount of insecticide product used for the intervention as well as data for intervention coverage, by user-configured control methods, collected on a premises-to-premises basis or aggregated to larger spatial units such as blocks or neighborhoods. Finally, the system's stock control module helps the user to track stock levels in different storage locations and also to track cost of stock. Locally relevant stock items are configured by the user in the term tree.

3.6 System limitations and plans for future improvements

The system's potential for adaptation by the user to local circumstances without the involvement of software developers results in increased complexity of the system, most notably for the system administrator when it is first installed and configured. The system includes extensive capacity for data import, including import spreadsheets that are tailored to specific functionalities. However, the import process is, for data quality purposes, unforgiving when it comes to poor quality data. Furthermore, because the system lacks capacity for mass-deletion of data, import of large amounts of data must be considered very carefully to avoid time-consuming data deletion exercises. The system was developed to support operational control programs and therefore has very limited statistical and spatial analysis capacity. Statistical operations that are directly supported are restricted to: (1) query builder calculations of sums, averages, and minimum and maximum values and (2) pre-defined query builder custom calculations that relate to specific system functionalities, such as disease case incidence or vector abundance indices. Other statistical operations require the user to export data for subsequent import into a statistical software package. Finally, the system supports basic mapping functions but essentially lacks spatial analysis capacity. To achieve this, the user needs to export a shapefile from the system for subsequent import into GIS software with spatial analysis capacity.

Plans for future system improvements include: (1) making the system directly compatible with hand-held mobile data capturing devices, especially PDAs and smart phones, (2) developing an over-arching query builder to make it easier to combine data from different parts of the system, (3) developing additional user-configurable functionalities such as configurable surveys, and (4) expanding the system to include other important vector-borne diseases in addition to dengue and malaria.

4. The California Vectorborne Disease Surveillance Gateway: A data management system/decision support system for vector control programs and public health agencies

California's arbovirus surveillance program is a collaborative project between the network of vector control agencies that make up the Mosquito and Vector Control Association of

California, the California Department of Public Health, and the University of California at Davis (UC Davis). These agencies are autonomous but are linked by a cooperative agreement that defines their respective roles in vector-borne disease surveillance, and together, they are charged with surveillance and control of mosquitoes and arboviruses to protect the health of California's human population of more than 38 million (~12% of U.S. population).

In recent decades, record-keeping has graduated from paper-only systems to electronic data storage, initially weekly spreadsheets -- essentially electronic versions of paper forms -- and presently relational databases that link data over long time periods and permit efficient data storage, data analysis, and reporting. The transition was facilitated by National Oceanic and Atmospheric Administration-funded projects that supported the conversion of California's paper-based surveillance records from the last 50 years to electronic form, now stored in databases maintained at UC Davis. Once this centralized data repository was established, there was a need to provide participating agencies with access to the data and to provide mechanisms for ongoing data input and retrieval. In 2006, the first step was taken toward these goals with the launch of the first version of the California Vectorborne Disease Surveillance Gateway (hereafter, the Gateway). The Gateway was designed for three overarching purposes: (1) to provide a user-friendly system for the storage of surveillance data, (2) to facilitate more efficient data exchange among the collaborating agencies, including the diagnostic laboratories, and (3) to provide tools for analysis and visualization of surveillance results and the calculation of risk estimates to support control decisions.

Vector control in California is conducted within local districts, and each agency is independently operated and funded by local property taxes. Budgets vary widely, from a single salary and control supplies in rural areas to multi-million dollar budgets in urban areas with more complex control needs. These differences in budgets, work forces, and control strategies result in a diverse array of data management solutions among agencies, and because of the autonomy of the agencies, implementation of a centralized software solution for statewide data management hinges on its ability to accommodate their needs and provide tools that enhance their surveillance and control activities. The system described below has been in place as the software decision support tool used for mosquito control in California since 2006 and has combined large-scale monitoring of encephalitis virus enzootic amplification with immediate reporting, analysis, and visualization.

4.1 System architecture, requirements, and licensing

The Gateway is designed for use by local vector control agencies to store, manage, and analyze data collected through their surveillance activities. Agencies are the primary administrative units, and the Gateway was designed to scale from an individual agency to groups of collaborating local agencies and to accommodate the needs of a hierarchy of agencies at many levels. Here, we focus on California's implementation of the system, where it is used to coordinate and streamline surveillance activities and provide summaries and calculations to be utilized by the local agencies, as well as other state and national public health agencies, such as the California Department of Public Health and the United States Centers for Disease Control and Prevention.

The system was written using a modified Model-View-Controller (MVC) architecture to facilitate rapid development and customization by the local user. All components of the system are readily available at no cost, can be adapted for specific use, and nearly all are open-source. Data are stored in a PostGIS-enabled PostgreSQL database while server-side code is written in PHP (http://www.php.net/). HTML templates using jQuery (http://jquery.com/) and Google Maps (http://maps.google.com/) comprise the client code and are accessible through standard web browsers. Use of Google Maps requires compliance with the Google Maps Terms of Service.

The minimum hardware requirements for running the system on a single computer are 1 GB RAM, 40 GB storage, and 1.4 GHz CPU. Though the system can be installed and operated on a single computer, it is strongly recommended that the system be installed in a client-server environment with the database and server running in a UNIX-like environment, although installation on Windows is possible. On the client side, access to the Gateway occurs through a web-based interface. Software installation is not required, and any operating system can be used, as long as the internet browser is current and supports established web development standards. Operating systems tested include Microsoft Windows XP and 7, Apple Mac OSX, and Ubuntu Desktop. Web browsers tested include Microsoft Internet Explorer 8 (http://www.microsoft.com/windows/internet-explorer/default.aspx), Mozilla Firefox 3.6, Apple Safari 5 (http://www.apple.com/safari/), and Google Chrome 8 (http://www.google.com/chrome/).

The Gateway system is available as a compressed file archive and can be obtained by contacting the administrator of the CalSurv website (http://www.calsurv.org) or the UC Davis Center for Vectorborne Diseases' website (http://cvec.ucdavis.edu). The system is licensed under the GNU General Public License version 3 and has no costs associated with distribution and use of the software.

4.2 System security and extensibility

Data integrity is ensured in the Gateway by having all records include identifying information of the user who created or modified the information. A background audit log tracks every record added or changed in the system. To eliminate the possibility of accidentally deleting important data, the Gateway has no ability to completely remove information but can remove a record from view, which also excludes the record from reporting and analysis. With the identification information stored with each Gateway record, end users are restricted to only the records of their agency, thereby ensuring an agency's privacy. For California's instance of the Gateway, the system is housed at the UC Davis Center for Vectorborne Diseases in a climate-controlled, locked server room protected by several layered firewalls that regulate network traffic and, in addition to the university network structure, prevent unwanted access. Temperature and humidity are monitored remotely, with thresholds set to trigger notification e-mails to a system administrator if conditions exceed allowable tolerances. A back-up server with a RAID 5 drive array and a LTO5 tape drive provides short- and long-term storage for all Gateway data. Back-ups occur hourly, daily, weekly, monthly, and yearly to the RAID 5 array and tapes. Monthly and yearly tapes are stored offsite.

Agencies are the principal administrative unit for managing users' access to the Gateway, and each agency assigns permissions to its users that regulate their ability to view, add, or modify data. Each agency designates at least one agency manager, which is a senior person who manages privileges for all other users within the agency. Users receive permission to access the agency's data from their manager, and privileges are based on the user's category, which is one of the following: view-only, diagnostic, user, or agency manager.

The Gateway's architecture (i.e., code and database schema) is not confined to a particular structure, and the system is designed to be broadly applicable for vector surveillance and control programs in any location. Users of the system can be assigned to one or more agencies, with no limits on the number of agencies or assigned users. Agencies also may share data with other agencies (e.g., their neighbors) by providing them with a "user" or "view-only" account. Other extensible features include arthropod names that are structured according to taxonomic rank from phylum through species levels, and the system is extensible to include new taxa as required. Spatial data are stored using a consistent, global spatial reference system (WGS 1984), and these data can be transformed using PostGIS into any other spatial reference system as needed for individual applications.

4.3 Data input and output

Two mechanisms are provided for entering data into the Gateway -- direct record-by-record entry through a web-based front-end, or bulk import of record sets after entry into a local data management system. The first and most common method for entering data is direct input using the Gateway's data entry forms. Forms are provided for field data (surveillance site locations, arthropod collections, sentinel chicken samples, and dead bird reports) and results of laboratory testing for arboviruses (mosquitoes, sentinel chickens, and dead birds). Accuracy of entry is maximized by the use of drop-down menus, pop-up calendars, and messages or mouse-over tips clarifying the meanings of individual fields.

Keyboard-only data entry is also supported, and the Gateway suggests possible values as the user types part of a field's value, with the range of possibilities narrowing with each keystroke. Once the desired value has been identified, the user can tab to the next field. Samples of mosquitoes (i.e., mosquito pools) to be submitted for virus testing can be entered directly below the collection data, which links the pools with the collection information and avoids redundant entry (Figure 7). Later, diagnostic test results for mosquito pools and sentinel chickens can be added directly without re-entry of collection information. Many of California's vector control agencies use the Gateway as their primary means for data management, but a number of other agencies also maintain in-house data solutions that range from generic spreadsheet or database software to fully customized programs. To avoid redundant data entry, the Gateway provides mechanisms for bulk data import from these systems. Data that can be imported include surveillance site locations, field data on sentinel animals and arthropod collections or pools, and laboratory test results. Structures and plain-text formats are specified for each data type, along with a sample data set. Once the data are in the appropriate format, the user simply selects the type of data and the file to be imported, and a preview of the data is shown before they are uploaded into the Gateway.

For users who prefer storing a copy of their data locally or want to import data back into their local data management systems, the Gateway offers the ability to export any data set for download. Before export, the data may be filtered by criteria relevant for the data type, such as agency, date range, site list, mosquito trap type, or mosquito species. Several formats can be selected for the export file, such as OpenDocument spreadsheet (http://opendocument.xml.org/), Microsoft Excel, plain text, or HTML.

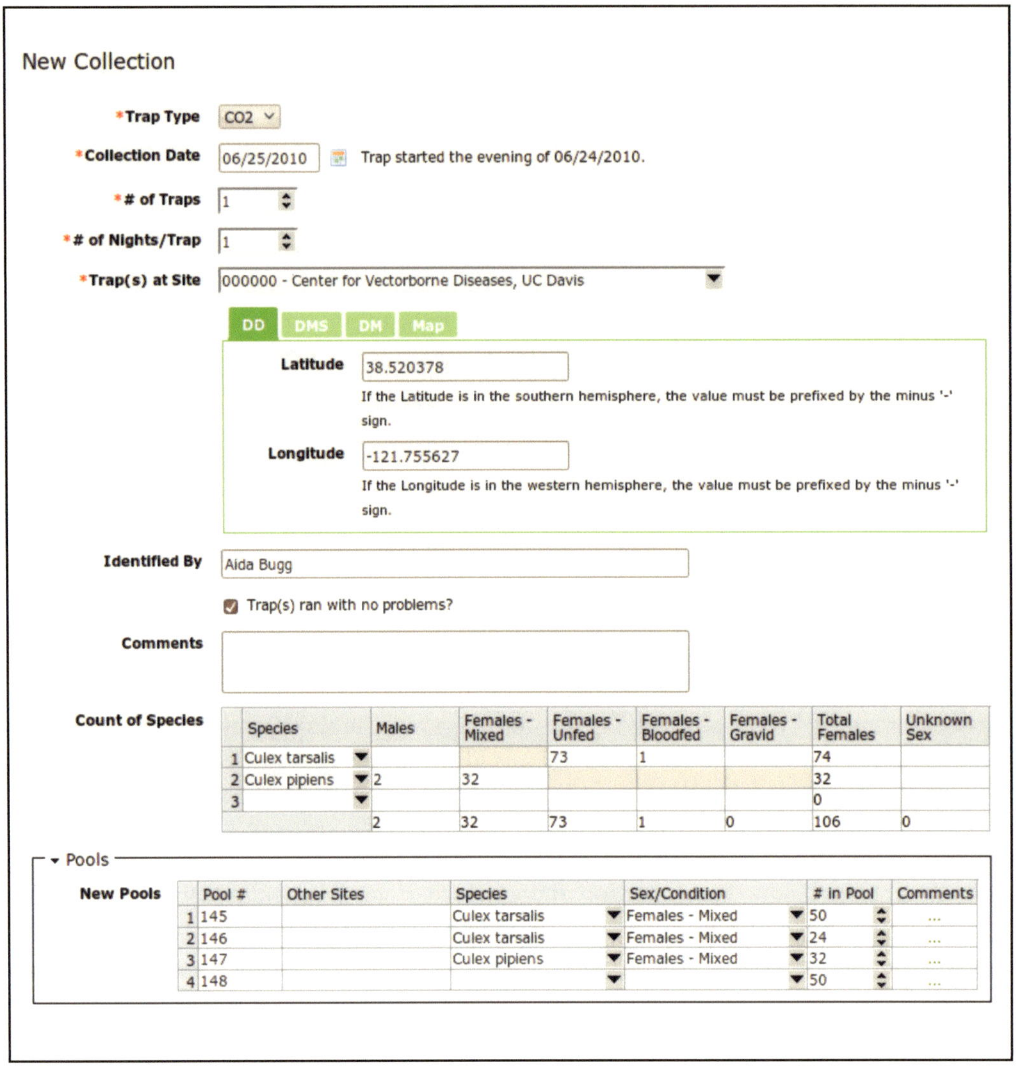

Fig. 7. Example showing the Gateway's data input screen for mosquito collections, including entry of mosquito pools associated with the collection that are to be tested for arboviruses in the lower pane.

4.4 Examples of Gateway functionality

In the following sections, we describe several of the Gateway's features that add value to the underlying data sets and provide decision support for vector control agencies.

4.4.1 Calculators for mosquito abundance and arboviral prevalence

The Gateway provides two calculators that are used to assess the current year's (or any other selected year's) mosquito abundance and virus activity (Figure 8). Each calculator has filtering options for agency, time interval, and site groupings, including the spatial features discussed below in section 4.4.3. Other choices include mosquito species and sex, mosquito trap type, and virus, depending on the calculator. If multiple selections are made for the filters, users are provided an option to treat each of the choices individually in the calculations, which makes calculations for several species or spatial features quite easy. In addition to the requested time period, averages are calculated for comparison of mosquito abundance to the prior 5-year period. Mosquito infection prevalence and 95% confidence intervals are estimated using maximum likelihood estimate methods (Biggerstaff, 2006). After running any of the calculations, the results can be downloaded to the user's computer or graphed as shown in Figure 8.

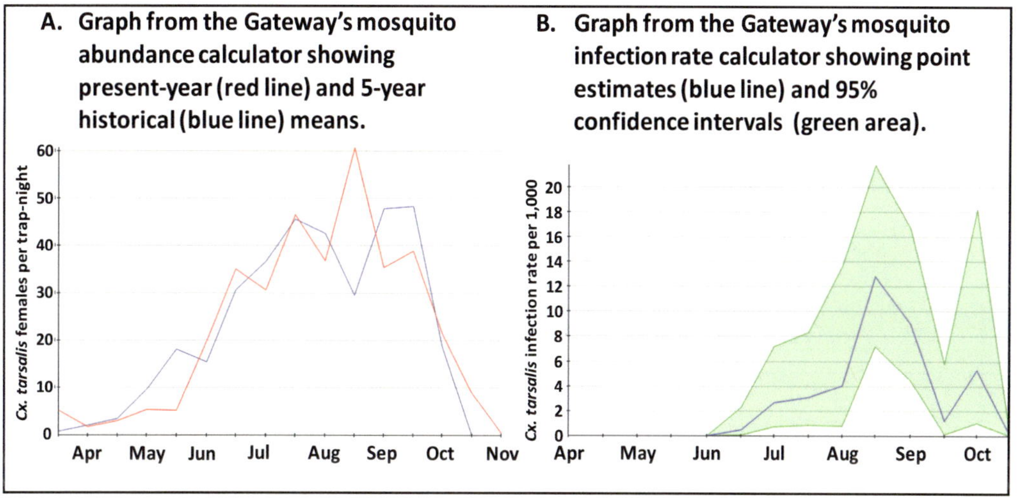

Fig. 8. Output graphs, aggregated by half-month, from the Gateway's calculators. A) Female mosquitoes per trap-night. B) Infection rate per 1,000 tested mosquitoes.

4.4.2 Risk of West Nile virus (WNV) transmission to humans

The California Department of Public Health publishes the California Mosquito-borne Virus Surveillance and Response Plan (California Department of Public Health et al., 2010) to provide guidance for vector control and public health agencies and to specify appropriate interventions if the risk for transmission of WNV to humans escalates. The plan includes an assessment of arboviral transmission risk based on climate and the components of enzootic surveillance systems, including mosquito abundance, WNV infection prevalence, avian serology, and diagnostic testing of dead birds (Barker et al., 2010). Each factor is assigned a risk value from 1-5 and all available factors are averaged to obtain an overall risk level.

The Gateway automates these risk calculations, taking advantage of the stored historical surveillance data for estimation of baseline mosquito abundance and temperature data from the NASA Terrestrial Observation and Prediction System (TOPS) (Jolly et al., 2005; Nemani et al., 2007) available through a collaboration with Ames Research Center. Calculations are scripted to run automatically at the conclusion of each half-month during the surveillance season and graphs are automatically e-mailed as PDF files to agency managers throughout California showing risk estimates overall and for individual surveillance factors (Figure 9).

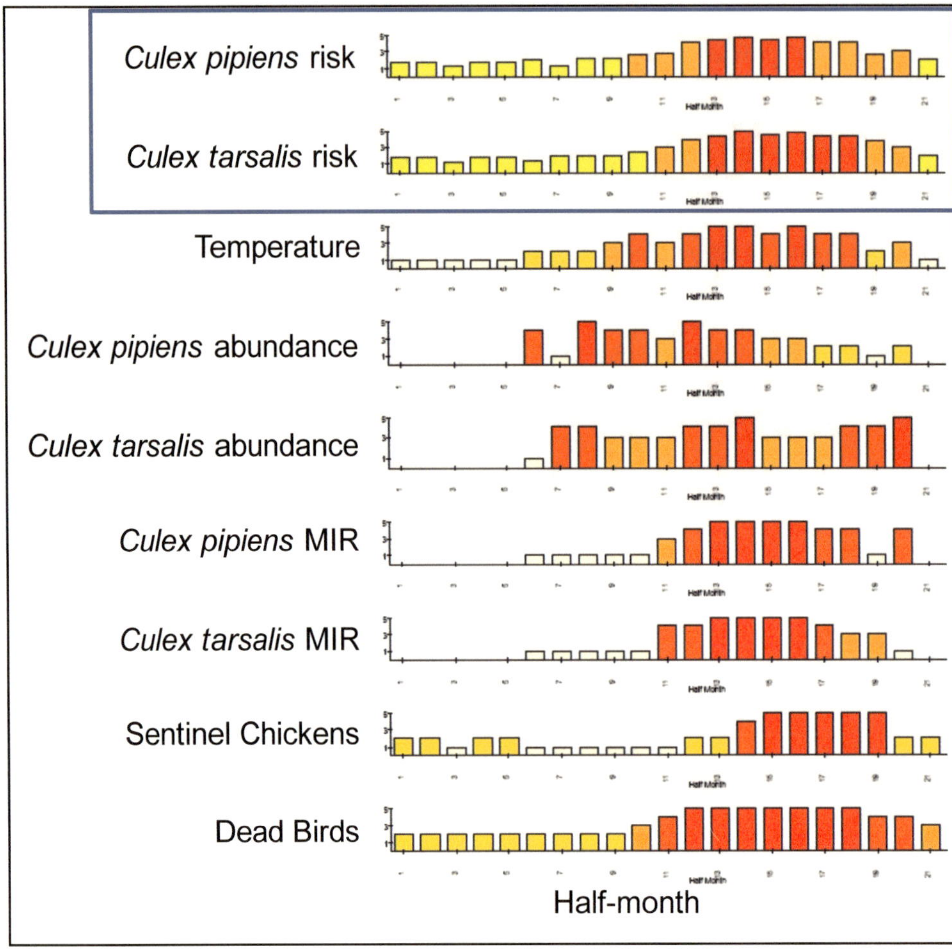

Fig. 9. Example from a PDF file showing an agency's calculated risk for each half-month. The top two graphs indicate overall risk based on the two key mosquito vectors in California, and remaining graphs show calculated risk for individual surveillance factors.

4.4.3 Spatial features

Perhaps the most exciting new capability of Gateway 2.0 (launched in early 2010) has been the addition of spatial features. Most aspects of surveillance are inherently spatial, and calculations (section 4.4.1) are frequently aggregated over spatial units. In previous versions of the Gateway, calculations at the sub-agency level had been limited to the use of site groups, which required tedious assignment of surveillance site codes to groups that could be used for calculations. Site groups remain a flexible option, but new spatial features make this process easier by capturing sites that fall within a user-defined area without identifying the site codes a priori.

Spatial features are collections of one or more polygons of any shape that are defined by a user and shared (or not) with other users in the agency. The features are created through a graphical interface that allows users to point and click with the mouse to define one or more polygons for each feature (Figure 10) or by import of an ESRI (Redlands, California, U.S.A.)

shapefile that defines the features. After features have been created and saved, they appear along with individual sites, site groups, and agencies as choices for spatial filtering in all of the Gateway's calculators. Each agency's boundary is provided as a spatial feature by default.

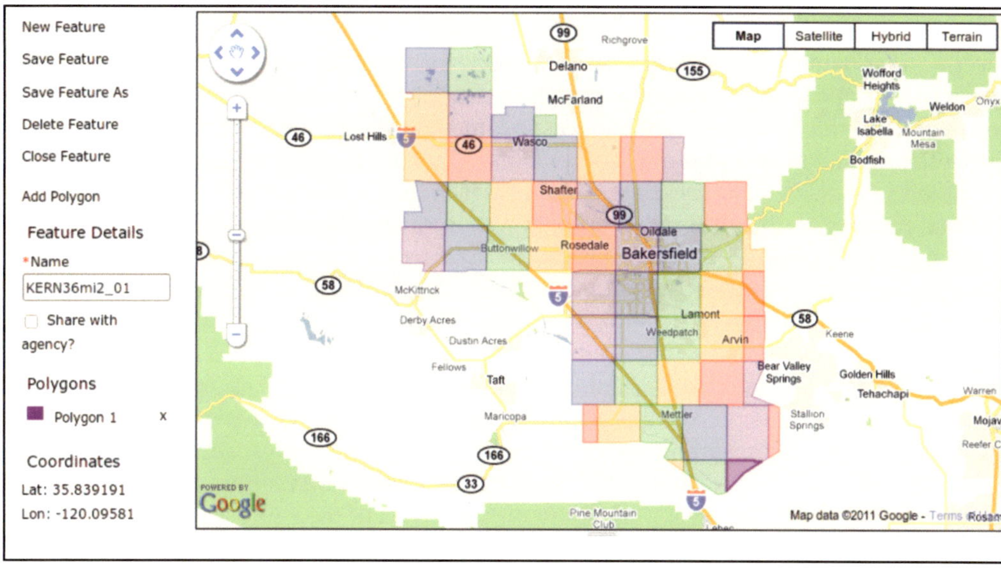

Fig. 10. Gateway editor showing spatial features that correspond to townships defined by the Public Land Survey System within the Kern Mosquito and Vector Control District.

4.5 System limitations

The Gateway is designed primarily for use by one or more agencies in an environment where the software and underlying database would reside on a central server with clients utilizing web-based interfaces through an internet browser. This results in a requirement for a reliable network connection, which can be a limitation in some environments. Benefits of this centralization are that corrections can be made or new features added quickly, without the need for periodic distribution and installation of software by the system's users. Also, operating system compatibility is maximized by the web-based interface. However, this centralization also limits the tools available for data input, output, and analysis to those created by the developer(s) with access to the central server, and there is no facility available for development of tools by end users. As a result, the success of the system for a particular implementation and its value to users will rely on developers being responsive to users' needs for a given system. The Gateway's data export mechanisms also allow users to download their agency's data for additional analysis using other software.

The Gateway's calculators of mosquito abundance and arbovirus prevalence are highly flexible in terms of their options for aggregating and filtering data according to space, time, or other attributes, such as mosquito species or sex. Each filtering option also typically allows for selecting multiple choices and treating each choice individually for calculations. If several of these grouping variables are applied simultaneously, this can result in an extreme number of dimensions for calculations, which would require a large amount of compute time. To address this potential problem, Gateway calculators have hard-coded limits on the number of dimensions for calculations, and if calculations exceed a pre-specified threshold for total compute time, an error message is returned on the user's screen, and a message is sent to the system administrator. Hard-coded limits and notification triggers may be set by the system administrator as needed for a particular implementation of the Gateway.

4.6 Future of the Gateway

Several important improvements are planned for the Gateway, including enhanced interactive mapping, management of pesticide use and resistance data, and development of an interactive risk calculator and forecasting module to complement the existing tools. Currently, the Gateway provides interactive maps that are updated in real-time as new data are added to the Gateway. These are run on ArcIMS (ESRI) and Geocortex IMF (Geocortex, Victoria, British Columbia, Canada), but this system is being transitioned to a Google Maps-based system later in 2011. The key advantages to the new system will be: (1) free software that eliminates licensing costs, (2) automatically updated base layers maintained by Google, and (3) increased freedom to customize the user interface for queries and other interactions with the underlying PostgreSQL/PostGIS databases.

In addition to surveillance, vector control agencies must carefully track and report their use of pesticides. This aspect of control programs is receiving increased emphasis due to new regulations aimed at preventing pollutant discharge into waterways, and user surveys are currently underway to assess the data management needs of California's vector control agencies in this important area. Depending on the results of the surveys, new modules will be added to the Gateway to collect information on pesticide use and resistance that is consistent with the requirements of the United States Environmental Protection Agency and state or county-level agencies, such as the California Department of Pesticide Regulation.

The existing tools on the Gateway support vector control decisions by adding value to California's surveillance data. To improve assessments of concurrent arboviral transmission risk (section 4.4.2) as the surveillance season progresses, a new calculator will be added to utilize the aggregation and filtering options from existing calculators and provide finer-grained calculation of arboviral transmission risk at user-specified spatial and temporal scales. Better lead-time is also needed for planning interventions, and we are currently working to extend historical datasets using hierarchical Bayesian models for forecasting mosquito abundance and arbovirus transmission. These models explicitly account for spatial and temporal structure in the data, and climate and land cover predictors have been evaluated for the varied ecological regions of California. Once validation is complete, these will be used to provide seasons-in-advance regional forecasts via the Gateway.

5. Conclusions

Emerging information technologies present new opportunities to reduce the burden of vector-borne diseases through improved decision support for surveillance and control of vectors and their associated pathogens. Such technologies range from stand-alone mapping applications, for example Google Earth, to integrated data management system/decision support system software packages, such as those described in sections 3-4, and mobile data capturing devices. Incorporation of novel technology solutions into operational control programs will lead to improved data management and analysis capacity and thus provide knowledge to support evidence-based decision-making that enhances the control program's ability to carry out surveillance, monitor interventions, and improve program performance including the targeting of limited intervention resources where they would have the biggest impact. The rapid growth in software applications which can be used without licensing costs is now setting the stage for development of integrated data management system/decision support system software packages that can be readily distributed to resource-poor environments and used to reduce the terrible burden of tropical vector-borne diseases.

6. Acknowledgments

Funding for the multi-disease system for tropical vector-borne diseases was provided (to LE, MC, MC, and SLF) by the Innovative Vector Control Consortium and the United States National Institutes of Allergy and Infectious Diseases (1R03AI083254-01). Personnel from many organizations contributed, including the system development and testing teams at Colorado State University, the Innovative Vector Control Consortium/Liverpool School of Tropical Medicine, the Medical Research Council of South Africa, Akros Research, and TerraFrame, Inc. We also thank field site partners in Mexico and Africa for their invaluable support: Universidad Autónoma de Yucatán, México, Servicios de Salud de Yucatán, México, the Malaria Alert Centre, Malawi, the National Malaria Control Programme, Mozambique, and the National Malaria Control Centre, Zambia.
Funding for the Gateway was provided (to CMB, BP, and WKR) by NASA Decision Support through Earth-Sun Science Research Results (RM08-6044 for NNA06CN02A) and the United States Centers for Disease Control and Prevention's program on Climate Change: Environmental Impact on Human Health (5U01EH000418). CMB and WKR also acknowledge financial support from the Research and Policy for Infectious Disease Dynamics (RAPIDD) program of the Science and Technology Directorate, United States Department of Homeland Security, and the Fogarty International Center, United States National Institutes of Health. Important contributions were made by the member agencies of the Mosquito and Vector Control Association of California and the Vector-borne Disease Section of the California Department of Public Health, and by Forrest Melton and Andrew Michaelis at California State University, Monterey Bay and NASA Ames Research Center.

7. References

Ahmed, S.M. & Zerihun, A. (2010). Possession and Usage of Insecticidal Bed Nets Among the People of Uganda: Is BRAC Uganda Health Programme Pursuing a Pro-Poor Path? *PLoS One*, Vol. 5, e12660.

Aviles, W.; Ortega, O.; Kuan, G.; Coloma, J. & Harris, E. (2008). Quantitative Assessment of the Benefits of Specific Information Technologies Applied to Clinical Studies in Developing Countries. *American Journal of Tropical Medicine and Hygiene*, Vol. 78 , pp. 311-315.

Barker, C.M.; Kramer, V.L. & Reisen, W.K. (2010). Decision Support System for Mosquito and Arbovirus Control in California. Available from http://www.earthzine.org/2010/09/24/decision-support-system-for-mosquito-and-arbovirus-control-in-california/

Biggerstaff, B.J. (2006). *PooledInfRate, Version 3.0: A Microsoft Excel Add-In to Compute Prevalence Estimates from Pooled Samples.* United States Centers for Disease Control and Prevention, Fort Collins, Colorado, United States of America.

Booman, M.; Durrheim, D.N.; La Grange, K.; Martin, C.; Mabuza, A.M.; Zitha, A.; Mbokazi, F.M.; Fraser, C. & Sharp, B.L. (2000). Using a Geographical Information System to Plan a Malaria Control Programme in South Africa. *Bulletin of the World Health Organization* Vol 78, pp. 1438-1444.

Booman, M.; Sharp, B.L.; Martin, C.L.; Manjate, B.; La Grange, J.J. & Durrheim, D.N. (2003). Enhancing Malaria Control Using a Computerised Management System in Southern Africa. *Malaria Journal* Vol. 2, 13.

California Department of Public Health, Mosquito and Vector Control Association of California, and University of California. (2010). *California Mosquito-Borne Virus Surveillance and Response Plan.* California Department of Public Health, Sacramento, California, United States of America.

Chang, A.Y.; Parrales, M.E.; Jimenez, J.; Sobieszczyk, M.E.; Hammer, S.M.; Copenhaver, D.J. & Kulkarni, R.P. (2009). Combining Google Earth and GIS Mapping Technologies in a Dengue Surveillance System for Developing Countries. *International Journal of Health Geographics* Vol. 8, 49.

Coleman, M.; Coleman, M.; Mabuza, A.M.; Kok, G.; Coetzee, M. & Durrheim, D.N.D. (2008). Evaluation of an Operational Malaria Outbreak Identification and Response System in Mpumalanga Province, South Africa. *Malaria Journal*, Vol 7, 69.

Dialynas, E.; Topalis, P.; Vontas, J. & Louis, C. (2009). MIRO and IRbase: IT Tools for the Epidemiological Monitoring of Insecticide Resistance in Mosquito Disease Vectors. *PLoS Neglected Tropical Diseases*, Vol. 3, e465.

Eisen, L. & Eisen, R.J. (2011). Using Geographic Information Systems and Decision Support Systems for the Prediction, Prevention, and Control of Vector-Borne Diseases. *Annual Review of Entomology*, Vol. 56, pp. 41-61.

Eisen, L.; Coleman, M.; Lozano-Fuentes, S.; McEachen, N.; Orlans, M. & Coleman, M. (2011). Multi-Disease Data Management System Platform for Vector-Borne Diseases. *PLoS* Neglected Tropical Diseases Vol 5 (3), e1016. doi:10.1371/journal.pntd.0001016.

Focks, D.A. (2003). *A Review of Entomological Sampling Methods and Indicators for Dengue Vectors,* World Health Organization Special Programme for Research and Training in Tropical Diseases, Geneva, Switzerland.

Gosselin, P.; Lebel, G.; Rivest, S. & Douville-Fradet, M. (2005). The Integrated System for Public Health Monitoring of West Nile Virus (ISPHM-WNV): A Real-Time GIS for Surveillance and Decision-Making. *International Journal of Health Geographics* Vol. 4, 21.

Gratz, N.G. (1999). Emerging and Resurging Vector-Borne Diseases. *Annual Review of Entomology*, Vol. 44, pp. 51-75.

Hay, S.I. & Snow, R.W. (2006). The Malaria Atlas Project: Developing Global Maps of Malaria Risk. *PLoS Medicine*, Vol. 3, e473.

Hemingway, J.; Beaty, B.J.; Rowland, M.; Scott, T.W. & Sharp, B.L. (2006). The Innovative Vector Control Consortium: Improved Control of Mosquito-Borne Diseases. *Parasitology Today*, Vol. 22, pp. 308-312.

Johnson, P.R. & Blazes, D.L. (2007). Using Cell Phone Technology for Infectious Disease Surveillance in Low-Resource Environments: A Case Study from Peru. In *Global Infectious Disease Surveillance and Detection: Assessing the Challenges – Finding Solutions. Institute of Medicine Workshop Summary*, S.M. Lemon, M.A. Hamburg, P.F.

Sparling, E.R. Choffnes & A. Mack, (Eds.), pp. 136-157, The National Academies Press, ISBN 9780309111140, Washington, D.C., United States of America.

Jolly, W.M.; Graham, J.M.; Michaelis, A.; Nemani, R. & Running, S.W. (2005). A Flexible, Integrated System for Generating Meteorological Surfaces Derived from Point Sources Across Multiple Geographic Scales. *Environmental Modelling and Software* Vol. 20, pp. 873-882.

Kamadjeu, R. (2009). Tracking the Polio Virus Down the Congo River: A Case Study on the Use of Google Earth in Public Health Planning and Mapping. *International Journal of Health Geographics* Vol. 8, 4.

Kramer, L.D.; Styer, L.M. & Ebel, G.D. (2008). A Global Perspective on the Epidemiology of West Nile Virus. *Annual Review of Entomology*, Vol. 53, pp. 61-81.

Lozano-Fuentes, S.; Elizondo-Quiroga, D.; Farfan-Ale, J.A.; Loroño-Pino, M.A.; Garcia-Rejon, J.; Gomez-Carro, S.; Lira-Zumbardo, V.; Najera-Vazquez, R.; Fernandez-Salas, I.; Calderon-Martinez, J.; Dominguez-Galera, M.; Mis-Avila, P.; Coleman, M.; Morris, N.; Moore, C.G.; Beaty, B.J. &. Eisen, L. (2008). Use of Google Earth to Strengthen Public Health Capacity and Facilitate Management of Vector-Borne Diseases in Resource-Poor Environments. *Bulletin of the World Health Organization*, Vol. 86, pp. 718-725.

Martin, C.; Curtis, B.; Fraser, C. & Sharp, B. (2002). The Use of a GIS-Based Malaria Information System for Malaria Research and Control in South Africa. *Health & Place* Vol. 8, pp. 227-236.

Meankaew, P.; Kaewkungwal, J.; Khamsiriwatchara, A.; Khunthong, P.; Singhasivanon, P. & Satimai, W. (2010). Application of Mobile-Technology for Disease and Treatment Monitoring of Malaria in the "Better Border Healthcare Programme". *Malaria Journal*, Vol. 9, 237.

Nemani, R.; Votava, P.; Michaelis, A.; White, M.; Melton, R.; Milesi, C.; Pierce, L.; Golden, K.; Hashimoto, H.; Ichii, K.; Johnson, L.; Jolly, M.; Myneni, R.; Tague, C.; Coughlan, J. & Running, S. (2007). Remote Sensing Methodologies for Ecosystem Management. In: *Food and Water Security*, U. Aswathanarayana, (Ed.), pp. 3-19, Taylor & Francis, ISBN 9780415440189, Oxford, United Kingdom.

Smith, B.; Ashburner, M.; Rosse, C.; Bard, J.; Bug, W.; Ceusters, W.; Goldberg, L.J.; Eilbeck, K.; Ireland, A.; Mungall, C.J.; Leontis, N.; Rocca-Serra, P.; Ruttenberg, A.; Sansone S.-A.; Scheuermann, R.H.; Shah, N.; Whetzel, P.L. & Lewis, S. (2007). The OBO Foundry: Coordinated Evolution of Ontologies to Support Biomedical Data Integration. *Nature Biotechnology* Vol. 25, pp. 1251-1255.

Sonenshine, D.E. (1993). *Biology of Ticks. Volume 2.* Oxford University Press, ISBN 9780195084313, Oxford, United Kingdom.

Stensgaard, A.S.; Saarnak, C.F.L.; Utzinger, J.; Vounatsou, P.; Simoonga, C.; Mushinge, G.; Rahbek, C.; Mohlenberg, F. & Kristensen, T.K. (2009). Virtual Globes and Geospatial Health: The Potential of New Tools in the Management and Control of Vector-Borne Diseases. *Geospatial Health*, Vol. 3, pp. 127-141.

Topalis, P.; Mitraka, E.; Bujila, I.; Deligianni, E.; Dialynas E.; Siden-Kiamos, I.; Troye-Blomberg, M. & Louis, C. (2010). IDOMAL: An Ontology for Malaria. *Malaria Journal*, Vol. 9, 230.

Vanden Eng, J.L.; Wolkon, A.; Frolov, A.S.; Terlouw, D.J.; Eliades, M.J.; Morgah, K.; Takpa, V.; Dare, A.; Sodahlon, Y.K.; Doumanou, Y.; Hawley, W.A. & and Hightower, A.W.

(2007). Use of Handheld Computers with Global Positioning Systems for Probability Sampling and Data Entry in Household Surveys. *American Journal of Tropical Medicine and Hygiene*, Vol 77, pp. 393-399.

World Health Organization. (2008). *World Malaria Report 2008*, World Health Organization, ISBN 9789241563697, Geneva, Switzerland.

World Health Organization. (2009). *Dengue: Guidelines for Diagnosis, Treatment, Prevention and Control*, World Health Organization, ISBN 9789241545006, Geneva, Switzerland.

Yi, Q.; Hoskins, R.E.; Hillringhouse, E.A.; Sorensen, S.S.; Oberle, M.W.; Fuller, S.S.; & Wallace, J.C. (2008). Integrating Open-Source Technologies to Build Low-Cost Information Systems for Improved Access to Public Health Data. *International Journal of Health Geographics* Vol. 7, 29.

7

Optimization Models, Statistical and DSS Tools for Prevention and Combat of Dengue Disease

Marcos Negreiros et al.[1]
Universidade Estadual Do Ceará, Mestrado Profissional Em Computação – Uece/Ifce-Ce, Mestrado Em Saúde Pública
Brazil

1. Introduction

The objective of this study is to illustrate how **operational research** techniques can be used in the organization and resolution of logistic operations for combat of dengue in Sobral, Fortaleza and Rio de Janeiro, middle and large-sized Brazilian cities located in the states of Ceará and Rio de Janeiro, Brazil.

Considering that the activities to combat dengue are similar to those used to combat other zoonoses, we have the expectation and the insight that this methodology has a much larger scope, be it for diseases that are similar to dengue or for other countries with economical and social development similar to Brazil.

In this study, we basically describe the utilization of a selected set of operational research methodologies used in planning the activities of combat and control of dengue in middle and large-sized Brazilian cities, supported by a complex information system. The objective is to speed up the process of information coming from the field concerning the growth of the disease, and improve in quality and effectiveness the decision making by the municipality health managers.

Some of the logistical models related to districting here are well known and have been regularly used in applications associated with various economic and health care sectors, (Bourjolly et al 1981), (Menhotra et al 1998), (Bozkaya et al 2003), (Blais et al 2003), (Zhong et al 2007). The innovative character of the current study is the articulation of these techniques, using others to support them, for solving a public health problem, therefore consisting of an application of great social and economical importance in a sector where the use of such tools has not generally yet received much attention in developing countries.

The study is organized in the following sequence. In Section 2, we describe the characteristics of the dengue disease, the standard control procedures and its presence in the world, with a special focus on Brazil. In Section 3, we present the operational plan in the

---

[1] Adilson E. Xavier[2], Airton F. S. Xavier[1], Nelson Maculan[2], Philippe Michelon[3], José Wellington O. Lima[1] and Luis Odorico M. Andrade[4]

[1]*Universidade Estadual Do Ceará, Mestrado Profissional Em Computação – Uece/Ifce-Ce, Mestrado Em Saúde Pública, Brazil*

[2] *Universidade Federal Do Rio De Janeiro, Department Of Systems Engineering And Computer Science, Brazil*

[3] *Université D'avignon Et Des Pays De Vaucluse, Lia – Ceri, France*

[4]*Universidade Federal Do Ceará, Faculdade de Medicina - Campus Sobral. ,Brazil,*

cities of Sobral, Fortaleza and Rio de Janeiro, for the activities of control and combat of the disease. Concurrently, we make an initial description of the information system proposed to support such information, which is basically grounded on geoprocessing combined with database systems for the Web and the acquisition of remote data. In Section 4, we present briefly a set of logistic optimization models considering the planning of the sanitary agents' services to combat dengue, as well as some formulations of mathematical programming models, related solution methodologies used by the state-of-the-art heuristics and their respective counterparts in the information system. In Section 5, we consider the prevention aspects by using statistical tools for forecasting the disease and tracking the *Aedes* by spatial clustering techniques (natural group detection). In section 6, we do a discussion of our Web base Spatial Decision Support System and consider its applicability nationwide. Finally, Section 7 sets out the preliminary conclusions.

2. General considerations on dengue

The fast demographical changes resulting from non-planned migration from rural to urban areas and from the population growth in the urban areas with low infrastructure lead to an increased incidence of the disease transmission and the dissemination of pathologies in areas that have not yet been affected. However, in respect to the emergence of diseases transmitted by mosquitoes, even a population that lives in a risk area may register low infection rates, if preventive measures are taken, such as: operations for closing ditches, the placement of nets in cisterns and water-tanks, the use of repellents and, whenever possible, educational and vaccination campaigns.

The migration process facilitates the introduction and the dissemination of new infection agents, with no previous immunity measures. On the other hand, isolated populations might not have access to a constant treatment, increasing, thus, the morbidity/mortality rates associated to a certain specific disease, (Keating 2001).

The temperature increase associated with the pluviometric precipitations also favor, in a meaningful way the introduction and the dissemination of pathologies that are harmful to people's health. Temperature changes affect the birth of disease transmitting mosquitoes (vectors) as well as the epidemic potential, since it alters the reproduction rate or the quantity of bites in humans, it transfers the geographical boundaries of the vector or its distribution, it alters the extrinsic incubation of the pathogen and it increases or decreases the vector-pathogen-host interaction, affecting, therefore, the susceptibility of the host. Rainfall increase leads to an increase of reproduction sites and, consequently, to an increased number of mosquitoes. With an increased number of female mosquitoes there is also an increased chance that a mosquito may acquire a pathogen and transmit it to a second susceptible host, (Keating 1991), (Wu et al 2007).

In Figure 1 we see three successive curves, in blue, green (vert) and red. They refer to events in Regional II - Fortaleza, concerning to the period January-October 1995; being considered: (i) the accumulated percentage of the rainfall (varying from 0 to 100%); (ii) the accumulated percentage of the number of larvae (focus); and (iii) the accumulated percentage of human cases.

Then if we fix some percentage p, let be: (i) $t_1 = t_1(p)$ the time for the rain may reach that value p; (ii) $t_2 = t_2(p)$ an analogue time for the focus; (iii) $t_3 = t_3(p)$ an analogue time for the human cases. Let also $\alpha(p) = \alpha = t_2 - t_1$ that is the time elapsed in sort that the percent of focus reaches the same value of the rainfall; and $\beta(p) = \beta = t_3 - t_2$ for the percent of focus reaching

the same value of the percent of cases. Thus α and β are "waiting times". In general, as in the figure, we have that $t_1 < t_2 < t_3$. We can also consider $\gamma(p) = \gamma = \alpha + \beta = t_3 - t_1$.
We argue that the increasing of α , β and γ is the result of a good prevention and/or combat process of dengue (Negreiros et al 2007). Unhappily we do not have all the data necessary to observe the occurrences in other years. But we can test to see what is occurring with γ from 1998 just to 2005, that is, considering the two curves, for the rainfall and the cases, Figure 2.

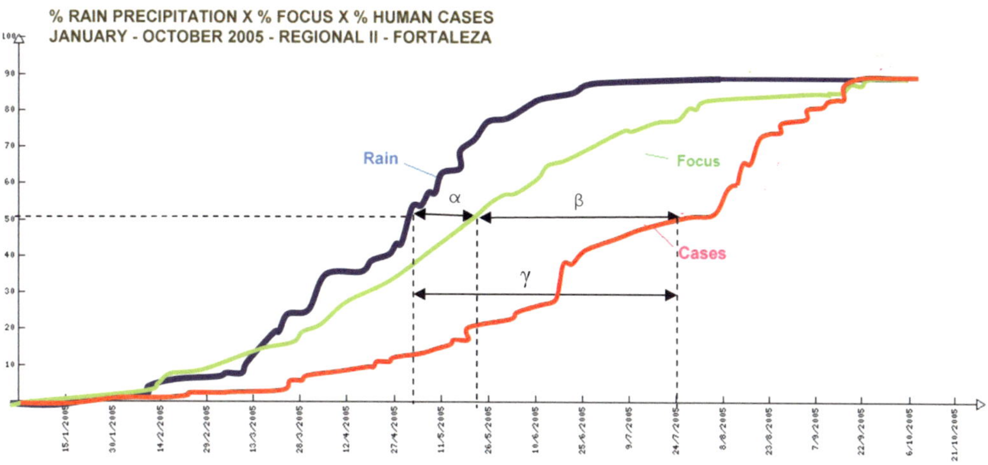

Fig. 1. Accumulated Percentages of the Rainfall, Number of Focus (Focus) and Cases (from 0% to 100%) per day in Regional II – Fortaleza/BR, along the period January-October 2005. *Graph produced by Webdengue, Data source: FUNCEME and SMS/PMF-CVS.*

With respect to the Figure 2 the following considerations are pertinent: 1) 1998, also 1999 and 2005 are "typical years", since the "lags" or "waiting-times" were present along all the epidemic year (in general taken from January to October); 2) In the years 2000 and 2002 the "lags" were viewed only later, that is, with $p \geq 50\%$ approximately; 3) In the year 2004 there were practically inexistent "lags" or "waiting times", and also within 2001. We must interrogate if with these two years the combat to dengue was neglected or developed in a wrong way. For the year 2003 the data are incomplete but it is still possible to verify the "lag" between rain and the number of human cases for the same period of that year.
Similar graphics were obtained with respect to intervals of five days, or "pêntadas", but showing exactly the same behavior. In fact, references found in other articles in this direction are somewhat limited in nature, restricting themselves to one or two annual epidemics periods and considering trivial correlation techniques. But a technique also recommended, and found in DePradine & Lovell (2004), refers to the determination of cross-correlations.
An issue in terms of climatic influence refers to the possible effect of ENSO (El Niño/LaNiña-Southern Oscillation). Some items surveyed are not clear enough because they suggest that an El Niño episode would itself be a trigger for dengue, malaria, etc. This is not true in a strict manner because the impacts of ENSO vary widely geographically and are modulated by several other interconnections and also by epidemiologic factors.
For instance, in the septentrional northeastern Brazil, and particularly in Ceará, a strong El Niño points with very high probability to scarce rainfall and hence to a limited cases of dengue cases along the rain months, unless the appearance of new or very older (as DEN-1)

viruses strains. Otherwise, with "neutral years" in northern of northeastern-Brazil, are more common or usual "extreme" occurrences, this is, with very scarce or with very high rainfall from February to June, as referred in Xavier (2005) and Xavier et al (2007).

Dengue fever and/or hemorrhagic dengue fever are systems of endemic diseases that occur in many tropical and subtropical regions, highly influenced by the environmental conditions, by climatic instability and demographic changes, in areas that conceal the vectors of the primary mosquitoes: *Aedes aegypti* and *Aedes albopictus*. As far as morbidity and mortality are concerned, dengue fever, hemorrhagic dengue fever (HDF) and the the dengue shock syndrome (DSS) are considered to be the most important viral diseases transmitted by arthropods.

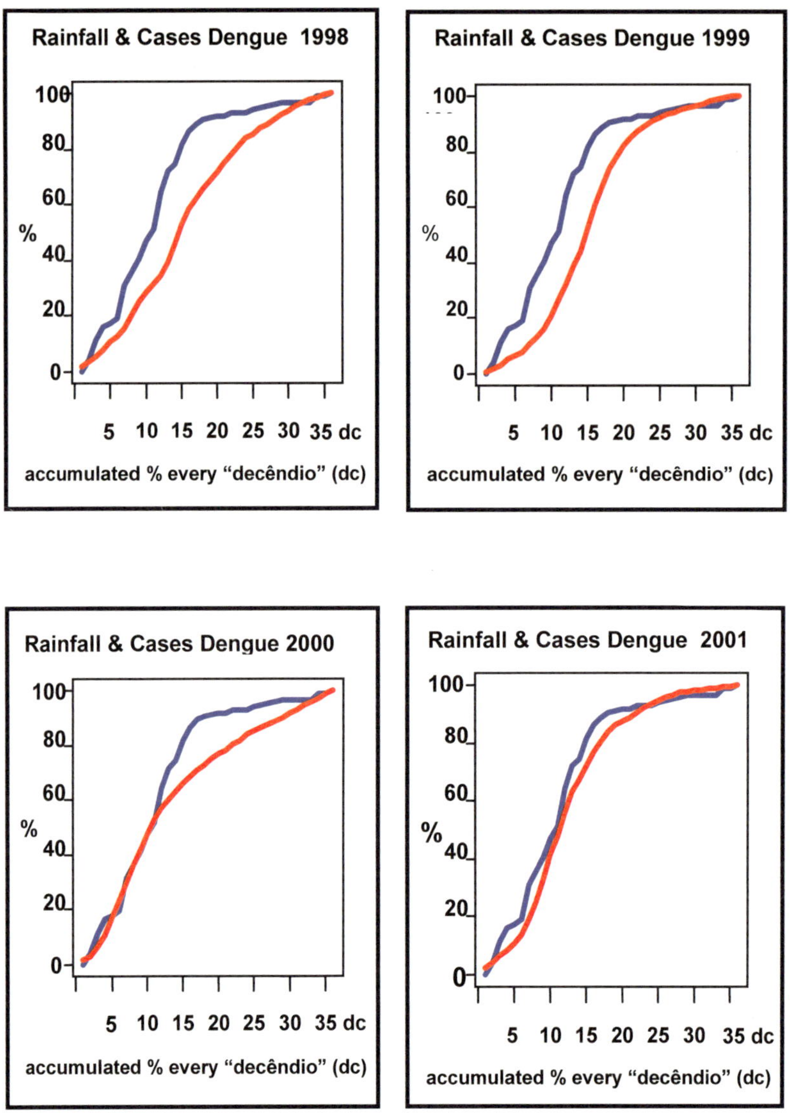

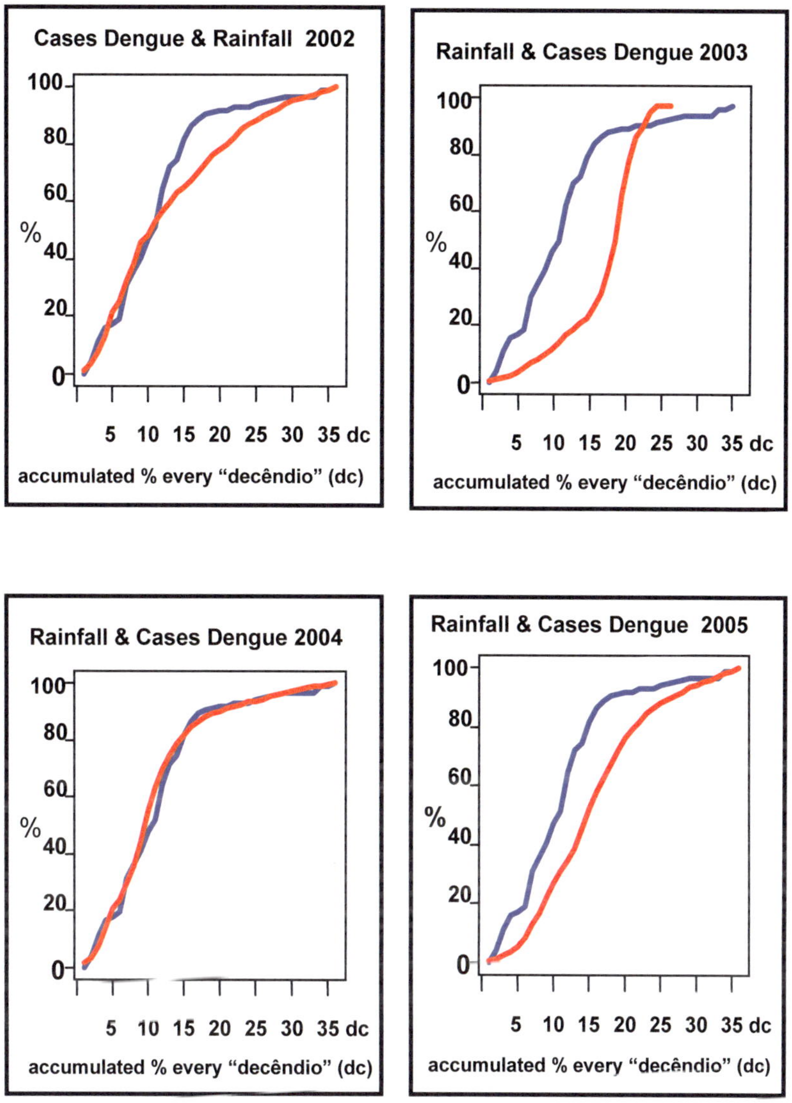

Fig. 2. Rainfall & Cases of Dengue accumulated (0 to 100%) in the period 1998-2005 by intervals of ten days = "decêndios" = dc , Fortaleza-Ceará, Xavier *et al* (2008)

The World Health Organization (WHO) estimates that approximately two-thirds of the world population live in areas that are infected by the vectors of dengue, mainly, *Aedes aegypti* and *Aedes albopictus*. These populations are running the risk of contracting one of the four varieties of dengue serotypes that currently circulate in the world. An outbreak of dengue fever or of hemorrhagic dengue fever may affect between 70-80% of the population, drastically reducing the productive capability of an urban environment or of a rural economic sector. Figure 3 shows a picture of the disease dissemination in the world, presenting a detailed division of the areas at risk by dengue fever and by hemorrhagic dengue fever, for the year 2008.

The global impact of dengue has drastically increased in the last decades, and today it is classified as an infectious disease that emerges and re-emerges. Nowadays, dengue fever and hemorrhagic dengue fever (HDF) occur in more than 100 countries, with more than 2.5 billion people at risk annually, and it is estimated that there are 20 million cases of dengue infection, resulting in approximately 24,000 deaths. It's important to emphasize that the most of the cases refer to children. The WHO considers that it's *necessary to make a global coordinated effort to bring the resources of modern science to bear on the control of ten major tropical diseases* in the world, (TDR, 2004). Most recently, their position turn to: *To foster an effective global research effort on infectious diseases of poverty in which disease endemic countries play a pivotal role*, (TDR, 2007).

Fig. 3. Countries at risk of dengue fever, as occurred until in November 2008 (TDR, 2009).

Dengue appears as the second major important tropical disease worldwide where malaria comes in the first position. Considering the number of people who are infected annually by viral dengue, with more than 500,000 hospitalizations per year, there is a growth tendency, as the control measures of the dengue mosquito either fail or are not effectively implemented or regulated from a global scale point of view. For the eradication of dengue to succeed, the target populations must be quickly identified, so that large scale educational and biological control programs can be implemented immediately (WHO 1999), (KEATING 2001), (TDR 2004/2007/2009).

Alarmed with the resurgent situation of the disease, the WHO estimated that the number of individuals infected with viral dengue might exceed 100 million annual cases around the year 2001. The sub-notification of human cases is a real problem in the major third world countries (those last years' estimative of 5 to 7 sub-notifications per 1 correct). The real situation is actually far worse most recently.

Understanding the relationships between human behavior, environment and the disease systems, is crucial to reduce the morbidity and mortality rates associated to the epidemic and endemic dengue transmission. In order to avoid the introduction of the dengue fever in new areas and to reduce the re-incidence of epidemic dengue in endemic areas, studies must be carried out so as to identify the correlation between climatic varieties, demographic changes and the increase of the incidence of dengue, to have better forecasts of the disease growth based on more appropriate models, and to define logistical criteria for attack operations through agents and vehicles, that may facilitate and guarantee, in a broad manner, the coverage of the affected regions. All this is necessary in order to define an organization of how, when and where to control the efforts that will be implemented. Since effective dengue vaccines are not foreseen for the immediate future, the government, health insurance companies and researchers must continue their efforts to understand the transmission dynamics associated with dengue.

The number of dengue cases in Fortaleza 2001-2006 (a), Sobral 2006 (b), Brazilian Regions (c-d) and Brazil from 1989-2010 (e), can be seen in Figure 4. The rapid growth and the resurgent behavior of the disease in Fortaleza, Sobral, Rio de Janeiro and Brazilian regions is one of the major worries of the health authorities.

Today, Brazil spends approximately US$ 1.0 billion dollars annually with the prevention and combat of dengue. From that volume, approximately 80% is used to maintain the infrastructure of direct prevention in the real estate units and the rest is spent in management and education. Despite that, it is estimated that US$ 5.5 billion dollars are lost annually due to local epidemic situations like the one that occurred in 2002, (SVS, 2004-2007).

3. The computational framework for dengue management

Dengue is endemic in Brazil, but it often appears in epidemic outbreaks, as we have seen in the previous section. The control of dengue requires managing a huge volume of information on the presence of breeding sites, the presence of the vector in the different real estate unit breeding sites, the occurrence of human cases, the realization of interventions in the larva and adult forms of the vector, and on educational interventions to reduce and eliminate breeding sites. These information changes in time and space. The actual decision making as to when and where to intervene is based on computational systems with outdated technologies that take into account only a small part of that information, such as: occurrence of human cases for urgent interventions and presence of the vector for medium term interventions.

In the city of Sobral, in the state of Ceará, the work to combat dengue is being developed by the Center for the Control of Zoonoses as in Regional II for the city of Fortaleza. The information on vector focuses, collected by approximately 200 sanitary agents is registered daily in Sobral and 300 agents for Regional II in Fortaleza.

By mastering and making use of Information technologies combined with Geoprocessing and Database Systems for the Web and Remote Data Collection, we identify the possibility to dispose the information gathering (through databases) available directly on the field, through *palmtops* or *pocket PCs (Hand-Held)*, or turning available a network of equipment, through which the print forms are transcribed directly into the network by the sanitary agents themselves, who are trained to do that. The database manager treats the relevant information, which is immediately published on the web, in such a way that the health officials can follow what happens in terms of the expansion of the focuses and cases, with a dynamic vision of their evolution in time. Such an accompanying process is done through a

Manager system, installed on the desktop of the center of Zoonoses or through the Webdengue system, available on an Internet website (www.webdengue.com).
The framework is thus made up of a set of five computational systems: Webdengue, Manager, Geographvs, a geographical editor to keep actual major urban occupation information, "Hand-Held" Agent and "Hand-Held" Supervisor, that exchange information so as to provide the managing person the necessary resources for making decisions on "what to do" in case of an endemic or epidemic situation of such disease.

Brazil

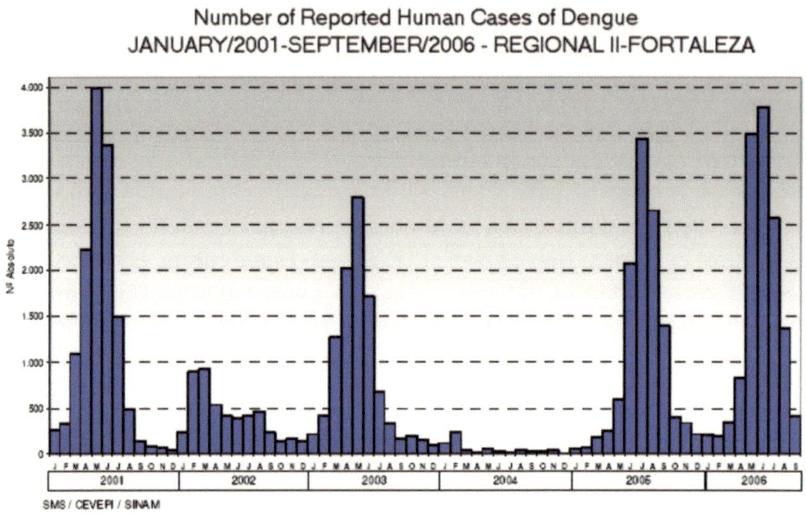

(a)

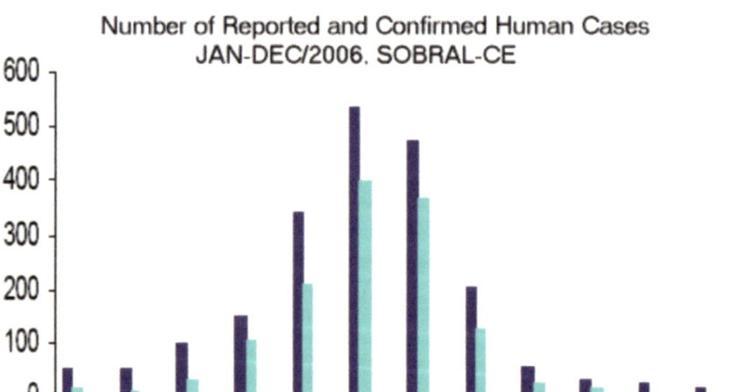

	Jan	Fev	Mar	Abr	Mai	Jun	Jul	Ago	Set	Out	Nov	Dez
No Reported	48	52	101	151	342	532	475	205	53	35	30	17
No Confirmed	19	13	33	105	208	395	368	126	28	16	5	5

SINAN

(b)

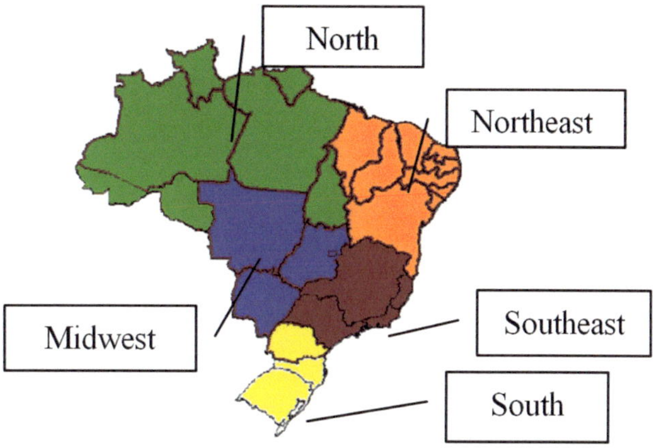
North
Northeast
Midwest
Southeast
South

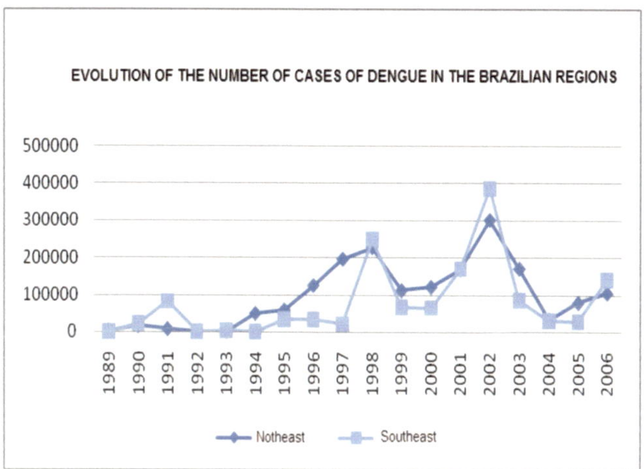
EVOLUTION OF THE NUMBER OF CASES OF DENGUE IN THE BRAZILIAN REGIONS
500000
400000
300000
200000
100000
0
1989
1990
1991
1992
1993
1994
1995
1996
1997
1998
1999
2000
2001
2002
2003
2004
2005
2006
Notheast
Southeast

(c)

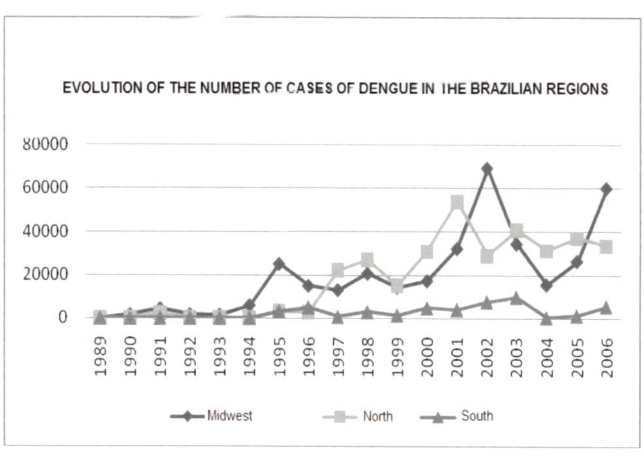
EVOLUTION OF THE NUMBER OF CASES OF DENGUE IN THE BRAZILIAN REGIONS
80000
60000
40000
20000
0
1989
1990
1991
1992
1993
1994
1995
1996
1997
1998
1999
2000
2001
2002
2003
2004
2005
2006
Midwest
North
South

(d)

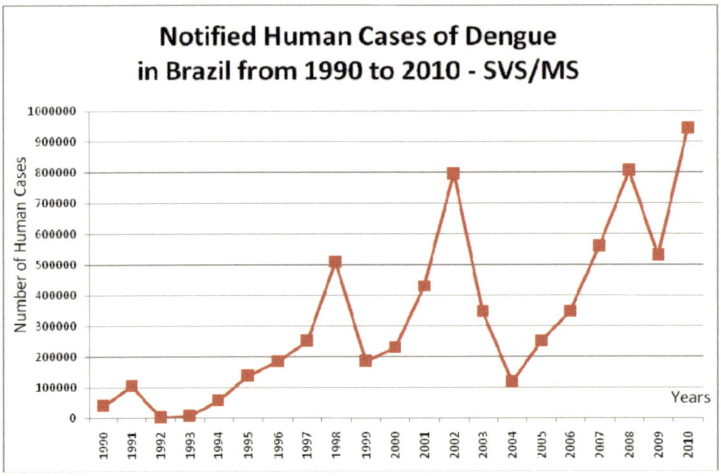

(e)

Fig. 4. Disaese evolution in number of cases: (a) Fortaleza, Jan/2001-Sep/2006; (b) Sobral, Jan-Dec/2006; (c) Brazilian Northeast and Southeast regions; (d) Brazilian North, Midwest and South regions; (e) dengue re-emerging in Brazil. (*) Source: Ministry of Health (SVS/MS).

The system Webdengue is basically used to increase the speed of information gathering on the evolution of the disease through human cases, and to cross that information in regard to focuses within a certain period of time. This procedure usually takes about 15-30 days, and may take much longer. When the information comes from the web by the medical and laboratories staff, it comes within seconds. Furthermore, decision-making support tools based on optimization models have been included - the Manager System -, as a differential so as to help supervisors of zoonoses centers to optimize the coverage of sanitary agents, besides scheduling the services, and other resources.

Since it is necessary to disseminate the information about the presence of focuses from "real estate unit to real estate unit" in Sobral or by block in Fortaleza, our work extends itself as advantageous in the sense of the georeference of the residences, the businesses and others, resulting in direct gains to both the municipal and the health administration (via the system Geographvs).

As for the "Hand-helds", the systems for palms or pockets, "Hand-Held" Agent and Supervisor, speed up the process of writing down the field data and the consolidation of the results, pending visits, as well as sporadic surveys of habits, personnel pets survey, educational level and behavior of the citizens who live in the urban regions.

Once they are integrated, the systems can quickly present to the officials the table of the evolution of the diseases, and they can also help analyze other aspects that are not directly related to the diseases. The national information systems on such diseases (SINAN[2], National System for Accompanying the Cases of Dengue and FAD[3], National System for Accompanying the Focuses of Yellow Fever and Dengue) are automatically fed by the

[2] SINAN - Sistema de Informação de Agravos de Notificação (Aggravation of Notification Information System)

[3] FAD - Sistema de Notificação de Febre Amarela e Dengue (Yellow Fever and Dengue Notification System)

system. Therefore the exact place, period and day of the presence of the *Aedes aegypti* mosquito is stored in a space-temporal georeferenced database.

Figure 5 presents our framework. It is possible to notice the modeling concept of the information management to appreciate the technological content added for minimizing the temporal distances in processing the information and making pertinent decisions on prevention and combat.

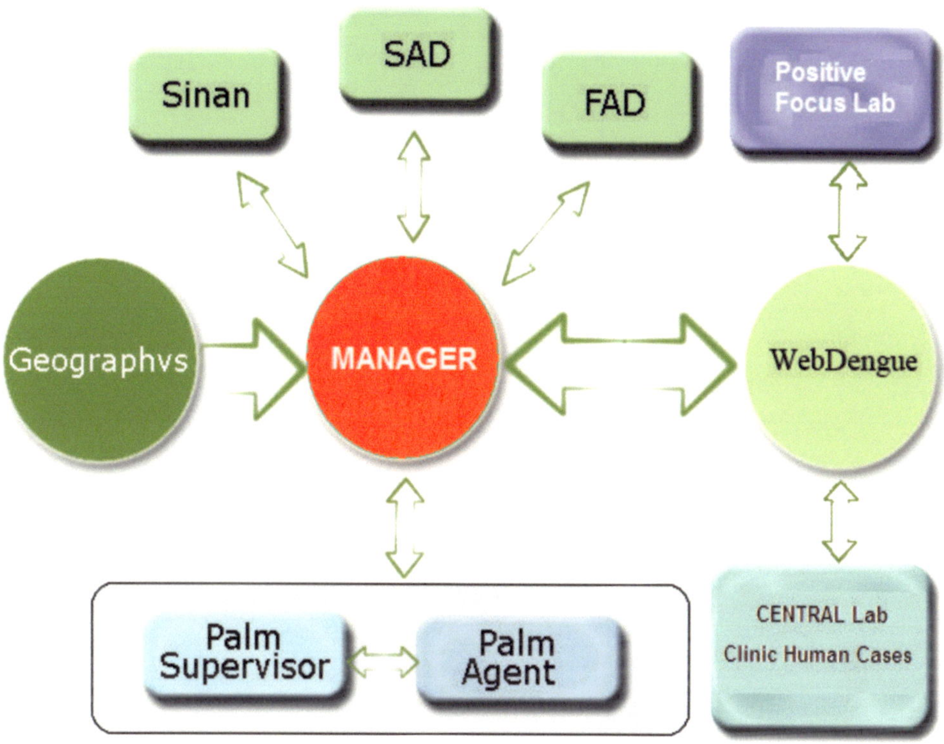

Fig. 5. The proposed computational Framework for the management of dengue

Thus, once the information is available at the necessary speed and precision level (now possibly right after each agent's working day), statistical models for a climatic tracing × forecast of case occurrence, clustering of focuses and cases in significant sizes, as well as infection models were also developed to better estimate the expansionist influences and to indicate the inhibitors for the epidemic advance in a Decision-Making Support process. Such tools are timely and useful to health officials, providing them with a contextual and temporal vision of the expansion of the disease.

This technology was evaluated in Regional II - Fortaleza/CE, with the support of CVS[4]/PMF[5], to the control of strategic points (real estates with control of every 15 days: tire-repair places, buildings in construction, old-car deposits, cemeteries, etc.), having reached excellent results, with "zero focus" in 20 of its 21 boroughs, or more precisely, from 5443

[4] CVS - Célula de Vigilância Sanitária

[5] PMF - Prefeitura Municipal de Fortaleza

visits in special real estate units done by 13 agents during June to November 2005 only one focus with *Aedes* remained in a build in construction. Also in Sobral, the framework was partially developed, where we built the city thematic maps, and evaluate some results considering the evolution of focus that were investigated for the years of 2004 and 2005. In Figure 6, we show the thematic maps used in the software for managing the evolution of the disease in different cities (Sobral, Fortaleza and Rio de Janeiro).

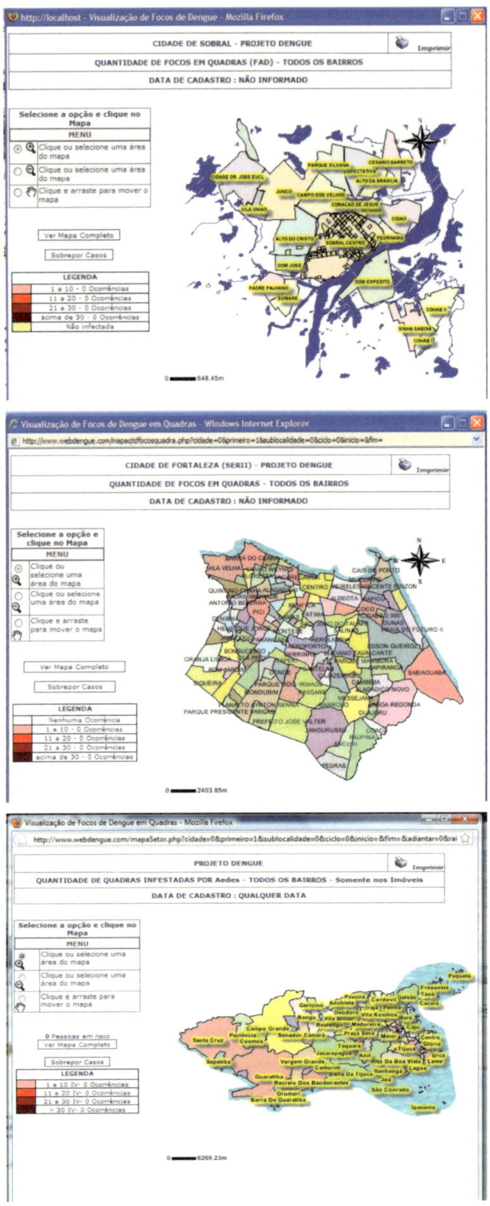

Fig. 6. Areas where the computational framework was prepared to run, Sobral and Fortaleza in the state of Ceará, and Rio de Janeiro in the state of Rio de Janeiro, Brazil.

4. Combinatorial models for the logistic of prevention and combat

As it can be identified in the above-described researches on dengue, the prevention logistics in place is characterized by the extended use of spraying vehicles and sanitary agents within the regions affected by the mosquito, generally with an inefficient planning which does not take the process of servicing into consideration from the Operational Research point of view. The use of spraying vehicles as a preventive measure is adopted in Brazil; nevertheless, as we have seen, its effectiveness is questioned in some places.

In 1999, we witnessed both phases of preparation for the massive combat of dengue, namely, planning for attacking the infection sectors and the infrastructure of the spraying-vehicle system. We observed that the organization of the system uses, in a precarious manner, a set of computational modules that register thematic maps, distributed according to the need for action. The distribution of the agents and of the vehicles does not optimize the efforts, but it demonstrates a lot of good will in attacking the problem, (Negreiros, 1996).

The spraying vehicles task can be in fact largely improved by better designing their itineraries, in creating service areas according to risk sectors, or in minimizing the effort undertaken to meet the itineraries of the vehicle, considering its work periodicity.

As for the sanitary agents, practical experience demonstrates that they account for a significant portion of the operational cost and the effectiveness of the combat process. Groups of agents are formed to act in a certain area and, during the visiting cycle, which often consist of 35-45 working days (3 to 4 months cycle), for the focal agent, the entire city must be covered, real estate unit by real estate unit. Work distribution among agents is done superficially, although the managers keep a record of all blocks and places that are difficult to reach by manually drawn maps. SVS indicators are relevant for the teams in respect to coverage of real estate units, and those real estate unit pending (real estate units that have not been visited because they are closed or because the occupant, for any reason, didn't allow the agent to visit it) must be covered within the cycle, since this is a major indicator for work quality within a period.

The work of the agents is our greatest preliminary concern. The task of assigning them and distributing them among the real estate units is acknowledged as being a difficult task for the Manager of the Center. Next, we report three models that are pertinent to the distribution of the daily service load of the sanitary agent, and one model related to the assignment of the spraying vehicles to service areas.

4.1 The planning process for the sanitary agents' task

For planning the coverage of the sanitary agents task, districting models were used by extending clustering methods as in classical districting approaches, (Garfinkel & Nemhauser, 1970), (Blais et al, 2003), (Zhong et al 2007). The clustering methods can be treated in the following way:

Let S be the set of real estate units or city blocks to be visited, $S = \{ s_1, \ldots, s_m \}$, where $s_j \in \Re^2, j = 1,\ldots,m$. The objective of this first model is to partition S into no empty q disjointed subsets S_i, $i = 1,\ldots, q$, [1], in such a way as to divide the operations of planning and control of the activities to combat dengue,

$$S = \bigcup_{i=1}^{q} S_i, \quad S_i \bigcap S_k = \varnothing, \quad i = 1,\ldots,q, k \neq i \tag{1}$$

It is, therefore, a classical clustering problem treated by several publications in the bibliography, for example (Hartingan 75), (Spath 85), (Hansen & Jaumard, 1997), (Kaufmann & Rousseauw, 1990) and more recently (Everitt et al 2001), (Theodorides and Koutrambas, 2003).
Each subset S_i can be represented by its centroid or center of gravity,

$$x_i = \frac{1}{|S_i|} \sum_{j \in S_i} s_j , \tag{2}$$

where $|S_i|$ is the cardinality of subset S_i, $i = 1, ..., q$.
The most traditional formulation of the clustering problem can be represented by the following optimization problem,

$$\textit{(Min-sum Clustering)} \qquad \text{minimize} \sum_{i=1}^{q} \sum_{j \in S_i} \| s_j - x_i \|^2 \tag{3}$$

such that $X = \{ x_1, ..., x_q \}$ and $x_i \in \Re^2$, $i = 1, ..., q$.
The problem [3] above is known as the clustering one, according to the criterion of the minimum sum of squares. This problem is often presented in the following alternative format,

$$\underset{x}{\text{minimize}} \sum_{j=1}^{m} d_j^2 (x) \tag{4}$$

such that $d_j(x) = \min_i \| s_j - x_i \|$

It is thus a non-linear problem, with a set of constraints that are intrinsically non-differentiable. Within the scope of the project, a new method was developed for the solution that turns it into the solution of a sequence of problems that are completely differentiable, (Xavier, 2005), the so-called Hyperbolic Smoothing Method (HSM), which found out high quality solutions for the clustering over the set of blocks' centroid of the city of Sobral.
Figure 7 shows the result for a set of 11 distinct groups from 13280 city blocks (Sobral), (Xavier, 2005).
Other clustering methods exist, between the exact and heuristic ones, the most used are the heuristics as: Forgy, *k*-Means, *j*-Means, *c*-Means, and many other variations, (Forgy 1965), (Hansen & Mladenovic, 2001), (Theodoridis & Koutroumbas, 2003), (Negreiros & Palhano, 2006). To have an idea about the performance of the HSM, table 1 shows the *clustering* results obtained for different number of groups (q=8,..,11), over the Sobral instance. In the table, we have:
f_{HSC}, is the cost of the objective function for the HSM ;
$f_{j\text{-means}}$, is the cost obtained by the *j*-means method, (Hansen & Mladenovic, 2001);
$Time_{HSC}$, is the time (in seconds) for the HSM;
$Time_{j\text{-means}}$, is the time (in seconds) for the *j*-means method.
$E = \dfrac{100(f_{HSC} - f_{j-means})}{f_{j-means}}$, is the gap to the method *j*-means, and

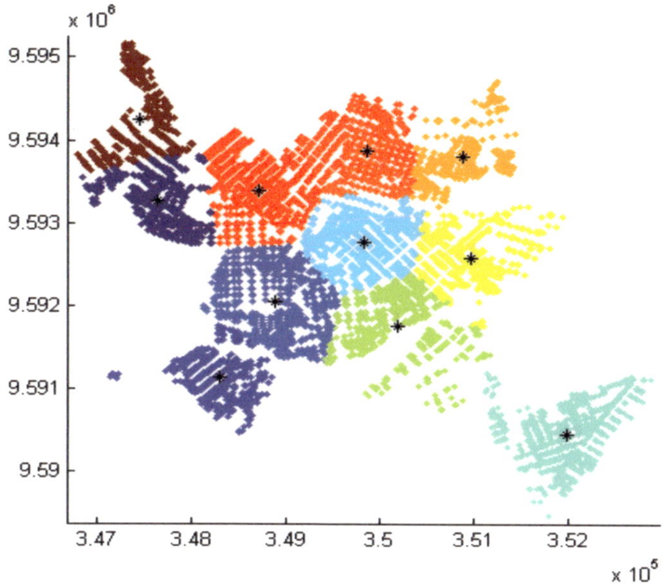

Fig. 7. Result from a clustering of 13260 centroides of blocks, of the city of Sobral/CE, after applying the HSM.

$Ratio = \dfrac{Time_{HSC}}{Time_{j-means}}$, is the computational time between the HSM and j-means, in a PC-Atlhon 0.5GHz, 0.5Gb RAM.

The results on Table 1 reveal the superior quality of the HSM in consideration to one of the state of the art OR methodologies reported, (Xavier, 2010), (Xavier & Xavier, 2011).

Q	f_{HSC}	$Time_{HSC}$ (s)	$f_{j-means}$	$Time_{j-means}$ (s)	E	Ratio
8	0.40663×10^{10}	95.55	0.40671×10^{10}	2220.61	-0.03	0.0430
9	0.35783×10^{10}	78.11	0.38988×10^{10}	18.08	-8.22	4.3202
10	0.31477×10^{10}	127.89	0.56343×10^{10}	2259.02	-44.13	0.0566
11	0.27637×10^{10}	107.08	0.27637×10^{10}	26142.94	0.00	0.0041

Table 1. Results for the instance of the city of Sobral/CE

Among the alternative approaches directly related to covering planning problem of sanitary agents, two are directly extracted from solutions to clustering problems with capacity constraints: traps placement and coverage division of city by group of agents.

4.1.1 Traps placement

The increase of *Aedes aegypti* mosquitoes on the urban space constitutes an important hole for the dengue propagation. The permanent estimation of mosquito population densities is fundamental information for prevention of the disease.

Different types of traps were developed by Brazilian biologists, which are used in the context of prevention the *Aedes aegypti* expansion. There are traps whose types are to capture the adult mosquito (female) - Mosquitrap, others to capture grubs and eggs (Ovitraps) and others the female mosquito, and its grubs and eggs, Figure 8.

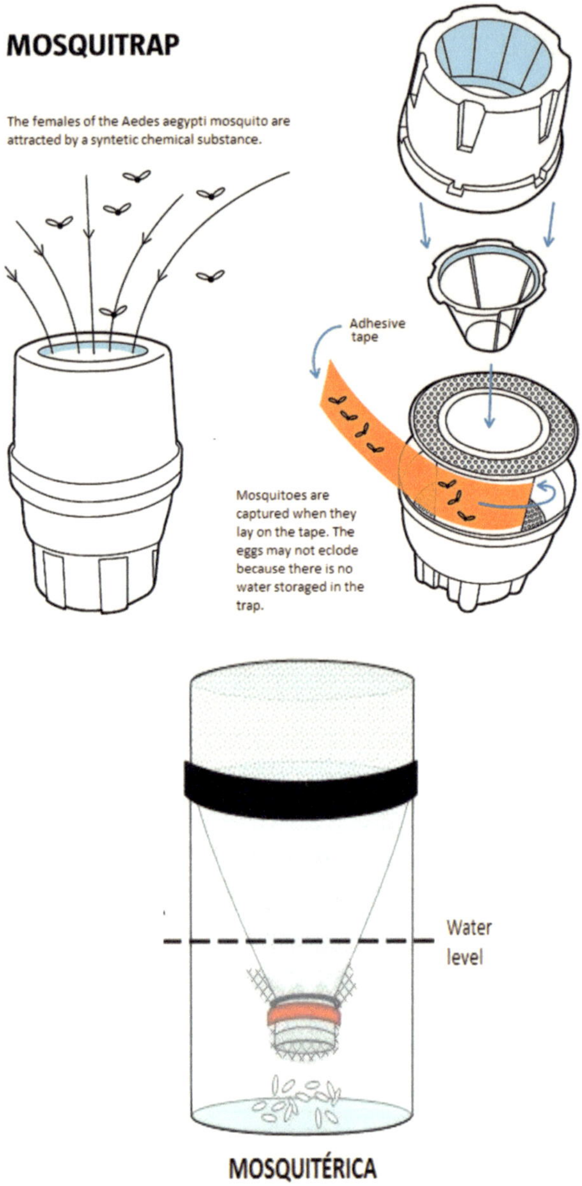

Fig. 8. Different types of traps developed by Brazilian biologists, Mosquitrap (left) - to capture adult female, by Álvaro Eiras and Mosquitérica (right) - to capture grubs and eggs, by Maulori Cabral.

The use of traps for capturing dengue vectors is a universal strategy for such proposes, therefore the traps placement problem appears, once the cost of some of these apparatus are related to the number installed in square area of the field. Three major approaches that may appear: the first can define the placement of the traps considering its coverage in a given radius throughout the blocks of the boroughs, and one wishes to cover all the area by using the least number of traps; a second approach consider the placement of the traps by introducing the spatial distribution (position) of the buildings and it is desired to obtain the least number of sets of buildings where in each set the trap will be located at the center of the group; and finally a third approach the placement of the traps must be positioned in one building of each set of buildings defined.

To equate the first strategy it was adopted a formulation considering a plane region covering by equal circles, since the mosquitoes have a limited circular range, (Xavier & Oliveira, 2005), (Brito & Xavier, 2006).

Let S be a finite region in a plane. A set of q circles, C_i, i=1,…,q, constitutes a covering of S, if each point in S belongs to at least one circle. The core focus of the adopted approach is the smoothing of the min-max-min problem engendered by the modeling of the covering problem.

Let x_i, i=1,…,q be the centers of the circles. The set of these centers coordinates is represented by $X \subset \Re^{2q}$. Given a point $s \in S$, we initially calculate the distance from s to the center in X that is the nearest. This is given by:

$$d(s,X) = \min_{x_i \in X} \|s - x_i\|_2 \tag{5}$$

A measurement of the quality of a covering of domain S by the q circles is, of course, provided by the largest distance $d(s,X)$, which corresponds exactly to the most critical covering of a point. The optimal position of the centers must provide the best-quality covering for the region S, that is, it must minimize the most critical covering. If X^* denotes an optimal placement, then we have the problem:

$$X^* = \underset{X \in \Re^{2q}}{\operatorname{argmin}} \; \max_{s \in S} \; \min_{x_i \in X} \|s - x_i\|_2 \tag{6}$$

In order to solve the above problem numerically, we first discretize the domain S into a finite set of m points, s_j, j=1,…,m thus obtaining the following model (TPP1):

(TPP1) minimize z

subject to

$$z_j = \min_{i=1,\dots,q} \|s_j - x_i\|_2, \quad j = 1,\dots,m, \tag{7}$$

$$z \geq z_j, \; j = 1,\dots,m. \tag{8}$$

Let $\varphi(y)$ denote max(0,y). By using a ε perturbation, it is derived the problem (TPP2):

(TPP2) minimize z

subject to

$$\sum_{i=1}^{q} \varphi(z_j - \|s_j - x_i\|_2) \geq \varepsilon, \quad j = 1,\dots,m, \tag{9}$$

$$z \geq z_j, \; j = 1, \ldots, m. \tag{10}$$

For overcoming the extremely rigid non-differentiable structure, the function $\varphi(y)$ is replaced by the hyperbolic function $\phi(y,\tau)=(y+(y^2+\tau^2)^{1/2})/2$ approximation, which can be replaced in the model (TPP2) by (TPP3) as:

(TPP3) minimize z

subject to

$$\sum_{i=1}^{q} \phi(z_j - \|s_j - x_i\|_2, \tau) \geq \varepsilon, \quad j = 1, \ldots, m, \tag{11}$$

$$z \geq z_j, \; j = 1, \ldots, m. \tag{12}$$

The solution to the equivalent covering problem (TPP3) is obtained by resolving an infinite sequence of the last problems obtained by a gradual decreasing of both parameters ε and τ. Figure 9a shows the process of placing the traps for a coverage of approximately 150m in the boroughs of Dionísio Torres (64 traps) and Praia de Iracema (64 traps) and it indicates the shortest expanses for this type of trap placement.

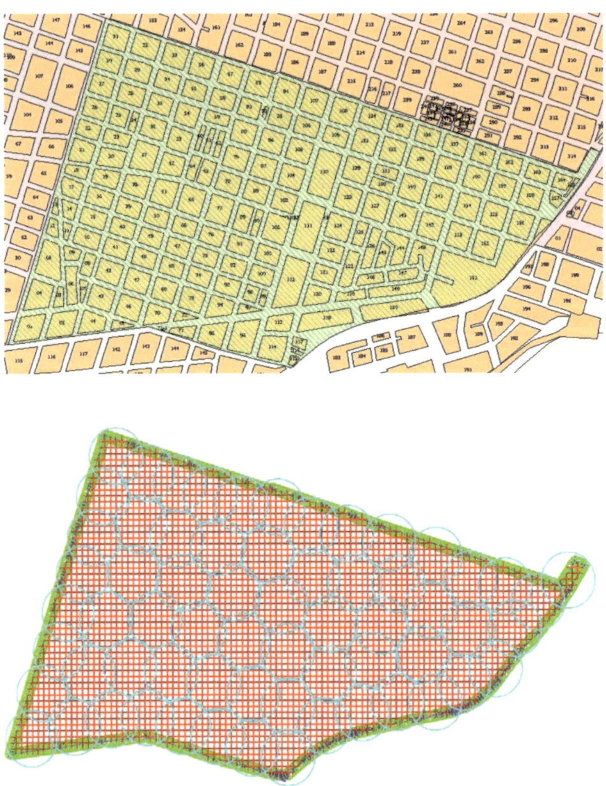

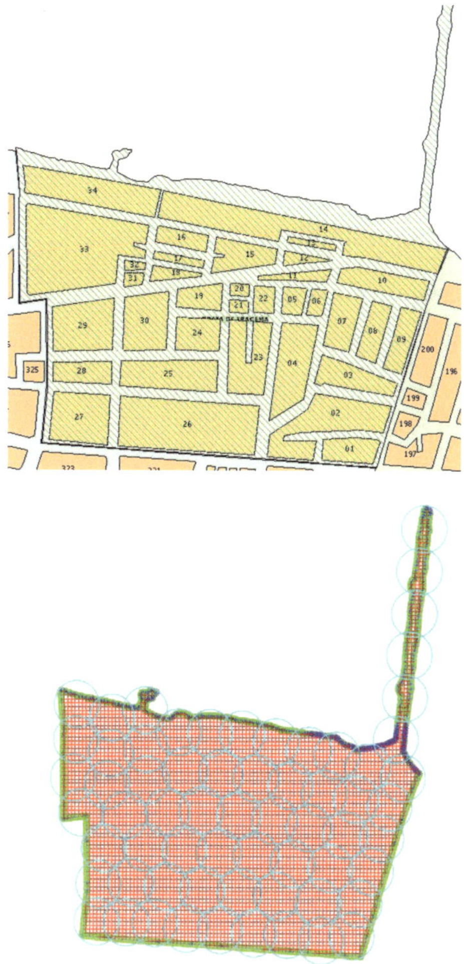

Fig. 9. a. Placement of traps for the boroughs of Dionísio Torres (64 traps) – above, and Praia de Iracema (64 traps) – below, by using the hyperbolic smoothing technique.

The trap placement problem can also be solved by min-sum-of-square clustering problem (second strategy), if the placement must be introduced in the center of sets of buildings, for a defined maximum number of traps. In this case it is an input the position of the real estate units which are the items to be clustered. As third strategy one can use the classical Euclidean p-medians problem to precede the coverage. In this case, the median will be the place (building/real estate) where the trap must be located. The classical p-median model can be stated as follows, (Daskin, 1995). Consider:

Sets:

$$V \text{ - is the set of real estate unit, } ||V|| = n$$

$$J \text{ - is the set centers, } 1 \leq ||J|| \leq p;$$

$$p - \text{ is the number of medians or centers.}$$

Parameter:

d_{ij} – is the distance between real estate i and j in the euclidean space $\Re^2$;

Variables:

x_j – is the vertex center of median j;

$$y_{ij} = \begin{cases} 1, \text{ if a real estate unit } i \text{ is assingned to median } j, \\ 0, \text{ otherwise;} \end{cases}$$

$$(p-\text{Median}) \text{ minimize } \sum_i \sum_j d_{ij} y_{ij} \quad (13)$$

$$\text{subject to } \sum_j y_{ij} = 1 \quad \forall i \in V \quad (14)$$

$$\sum_j x_j = p \quad (15)$$

$$y_{ij} \le x_j \quad \forall i \in V, \forall j \in V \quad (16)$$

$$y_{ij} \in \{0,1\} \quad \forall i \in V, \forall j \in V \quad (17)$$

$$x_j \in \{0,1\} \quad \forall j \in V \quad (18)$$

In the classic *p*-median model, [13] defines the minimum cost to assign medians of real estate's to their real estates, [14] indicates the assignment of only one median to a real estate, [15] defines the number of medians to be assigned, [16] indicates that if an assignment of a real estate to its related median is used it must be at most equal to the fixed median, [17] and [18] indicates the used binary variables, (Daskin, 1995).

Figures 9b and 9c show the two techniques (clustering in Figure 9b, and *p*-median for Figure 9c) employed for the same set of points for the city of Fortaleza in the boroughs of Dionísio Torres and São João do Tauape, both considering an area of a large number or real estates. A set of methods from Xavier (2009) for the min-sum-clustering and also for the *p*-median as described in Daskin (1995), Taillard (2003) and others could be used to solve instances of that size within 15 seconds in a PC.

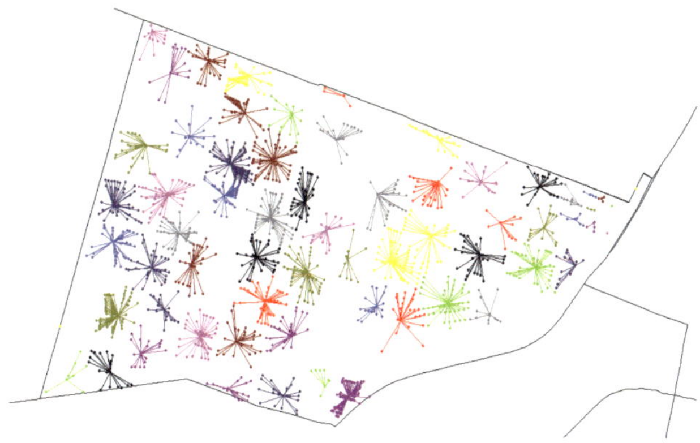

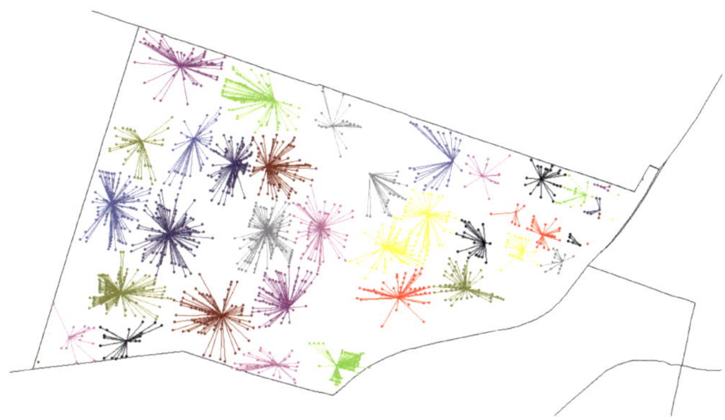

Fig. 9. b. Placement of traps in a borough of Dionisio Torres described by its limits and the spatial distribution of the 3947 real estate units (top), by using a min-sum-of-square clustering method (middle, Error=14,707,808.02) or an Euclidean p-median method (bottom, Error: 16,444,592.42) for placing 64 traps each.

4.1.2 Coverage division of the city by the groups of agents with capacity constraints

Such a vision must be done in such a manner that each partition be covered by the same group throughout the visiting cycle. Here there is a problem of Constrained Clustering, which can be solved by means of the Capacitated Centred Clustering Problem. The division of work among the agents will be done according to the quantity of real estate units per agent per cycle, and also taking into account a lower and an upper limit of service within the area (18-22 real estate units per agent per day, groups with 4 agents, and a calendar with 42 working days in the cycle, for example, would thus mean regions with 3024-3696 real estate units for this cycle). Figure 9 shows a solution to the problem - the process of distributing the area coverage among the agents is done with an adaptation of the technique proposed by Negreiros & Palhano (2006), which is already incorporated into the Manager system.
Sets:

I - is the set of real estate unit, $||I|| = n$

J - is the set of possible clusters, $1 \leq ||J|| \leq n$;

$F-$ is the fixed cost to open a cluster.

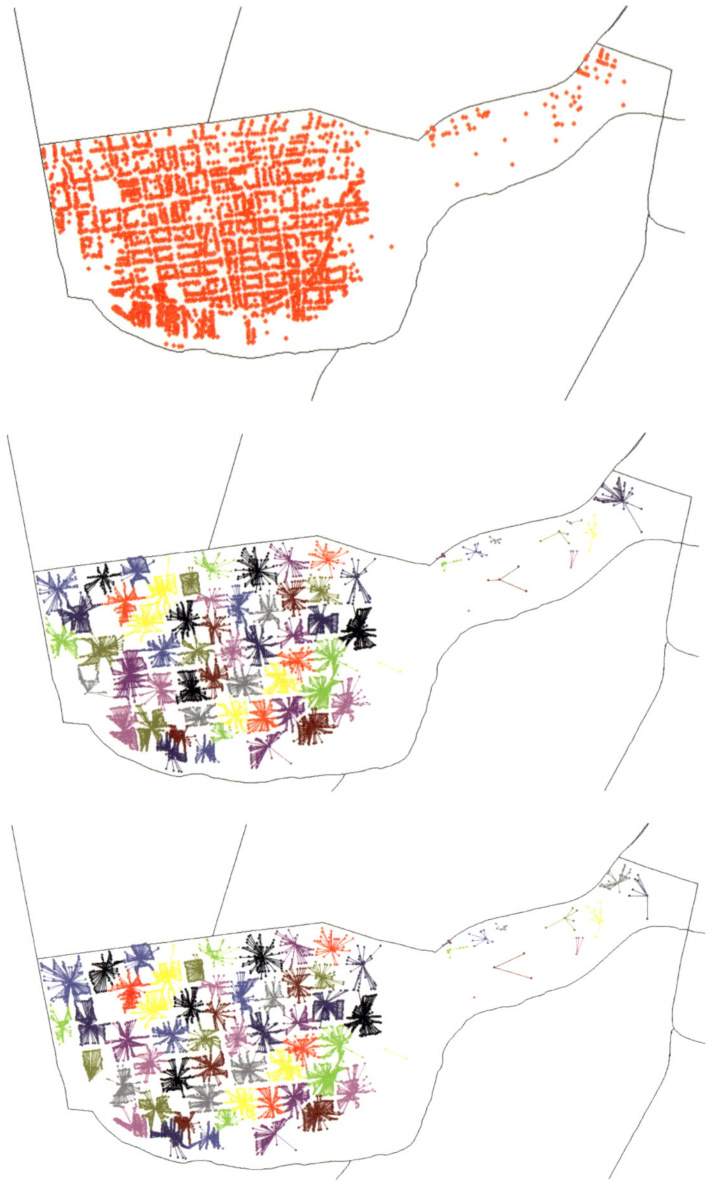

Fig. 9. c. Placement of traps in a borough Sao Joao do Tauape described by its limits and the spatial distribution of the 6950 real estate units (top), by using a min-sum-of-square clustering method (middle) or an Euclidean *p*-median method (bottom) for placing 64 traps each.

Parameters:

s_i – is the position of the real estate unit i in the euclidean space $\Re^2$;

$\underline{Q}_j$ – is the minimum capacity of cluster j;

$\overline{Q}_j$ – is the maximum capacity of cluster j;

Variables:

$$z_j = \begin{cases} 1, \text{ if a cluster } j \text{ is open,} \\ 0, \text{ otherwise;} \end{cases}$$

$\bar{x}_j$ – is the geometric center of cluster j;

$$y_{ij} = \begin{cases} 1, \text{ if a real estate unit } i \text{ is assingned to cluster } j, \\ 0, \text{ otherwise;} \end{cases}$$

Model of the General Capacitated Centred Clustering Problem:

$$\text{(g- PACCG) Minimize } (F \sum_{j \in J} z_j) + \sum_{j \in J} (\sum_{i \in I} | \, | s_i - \bar{x}_j | \, |^2 \, y_{ij}) \quad (19)$$

Such that,

$$\sum_{j \in J} y_{ij} = 1, \; \forall i \in I \quad (20)$$

$$\sum_{i \in I} s_i y_{ij} = \bar{x}_j \left(\sum_{i \in I} y_{ij} \right), \quad \forall j \in J \quad (21)$$

$$\underline{Q}_j z_j \le \sum_{i \in I} y_{ij} \le \bar{Q}_j z_j, \quad \forall j \in J \quad (22)$$

$$\bar{x}_j \in \Re^2, \, z_j, y_{ij} \in \{0,1\}, \quad \forall i \in I, \; \forall j \in J \quad (23)$$

In the model (g-PACCG), the objective function aims to minimize the number of real estate unit groups to be visited and the sum of the dissimilarities of each of these clusters, [19]. A real estate unit can only be assigned to a single cluster, in the set of constraints [20]. In the constraints [21], we have the guarantee of the location of the center of each cluster at its geometrical center. The constraints [22] take into account the maintenance of the demand of individuals limited to the capacity of each specific cluster, and the constraints [23] specify the decision.

This is called the General Capacitated Centered Clustering Problem. The formulation above shows that it can only be reduced to a NP-Complete equivalent problem, which is the *Min-Sum Clustering* (MSCP) problem itself, (Garey & Johnson 1979).

The set of methodologies used for this problem consider a GRASP based type framework, where a multi-start greedy constrained (capacitated) clustering method followed by the improvement procedure (VNS), is used to find the solutions, (Mladenovic & Hansen 2002), (Feo & Resende, 1995).

The method has an unconstrained (static) phase and a constrained (multi-start, greedy). In the first step we develop the unconstrained clustering by HMS method. The second, actually the GRASP phase, we perform evaluations to hold the capacity constraints by different constructive strategies, differing in some sense from the original methodologies proposed by (Negreiros & Palhano, 2006). These methodologies consider the shape of the clusters built

and also their capacity limits, exploring constructive Euclidean minimum spanning tree and Delaunay triangulation proximities, as the convex hull of the groups formed, to treat feasibility. The best configuration is then selected to be the solution, after a VNS improvement step, (Preparata & Shamos 85).
The quality of the meta-heuristic proposed is suited to performance ratio and shape of the clusters, otherwise if the solution does not convince the manager, he/she can interfere directly in the result (as it is a spatial DSS), moving a set of real estate units or blocks from one cluster to another, and see the effect of the movement.

Fig. 10. Formation of real estate unit block *clusters* in the city of Sobral/CE, first phase of allocation and service division, using a proposed solution for the problem of Capacitated Centred Clustering Problem.

In order to solve the problem of territorial coverage division for the focal sanitary agent, we first run a method of generic restricted *clustering*, for the creation of the coverage areas of the agent groups (for example areas with 3024-3696 real estate units), and then for each area we generate the daily clusters (18-22 real estate units). The contrary can also be done. For each daily group we then generate a visiting list within the real estate units of the group, taking a traveling salesman`s path between two extremes of the group. Also, the same can be done if the travel is considered between street blocks. Figure 11 presents this methodological reality.

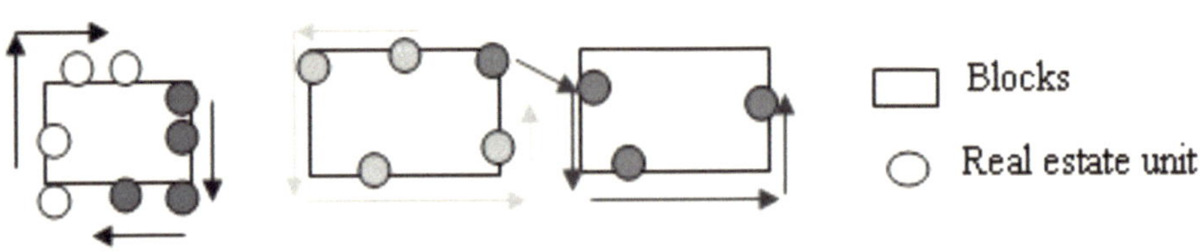

Fig. 11. Itinerary of a sanitary agent in subsequent days, among real estate units of a certain coverage area (cluster) after the restrictive clustering process in a certain area (generating sub-clusters).

This same methodology was used to design coverage areas and routes for the SP (special points) sanitary agents. The SPs are distributed into (Regional II), and first we cluster a number of agents and than make the routes between the SP's. An agent that travels between different boroughs has to complete one borough at a time, as in the Clustered Travelling Salesman Problem, (Prunner, 2003). Figure 12, shows the results of this application in the city of Fortaleza.

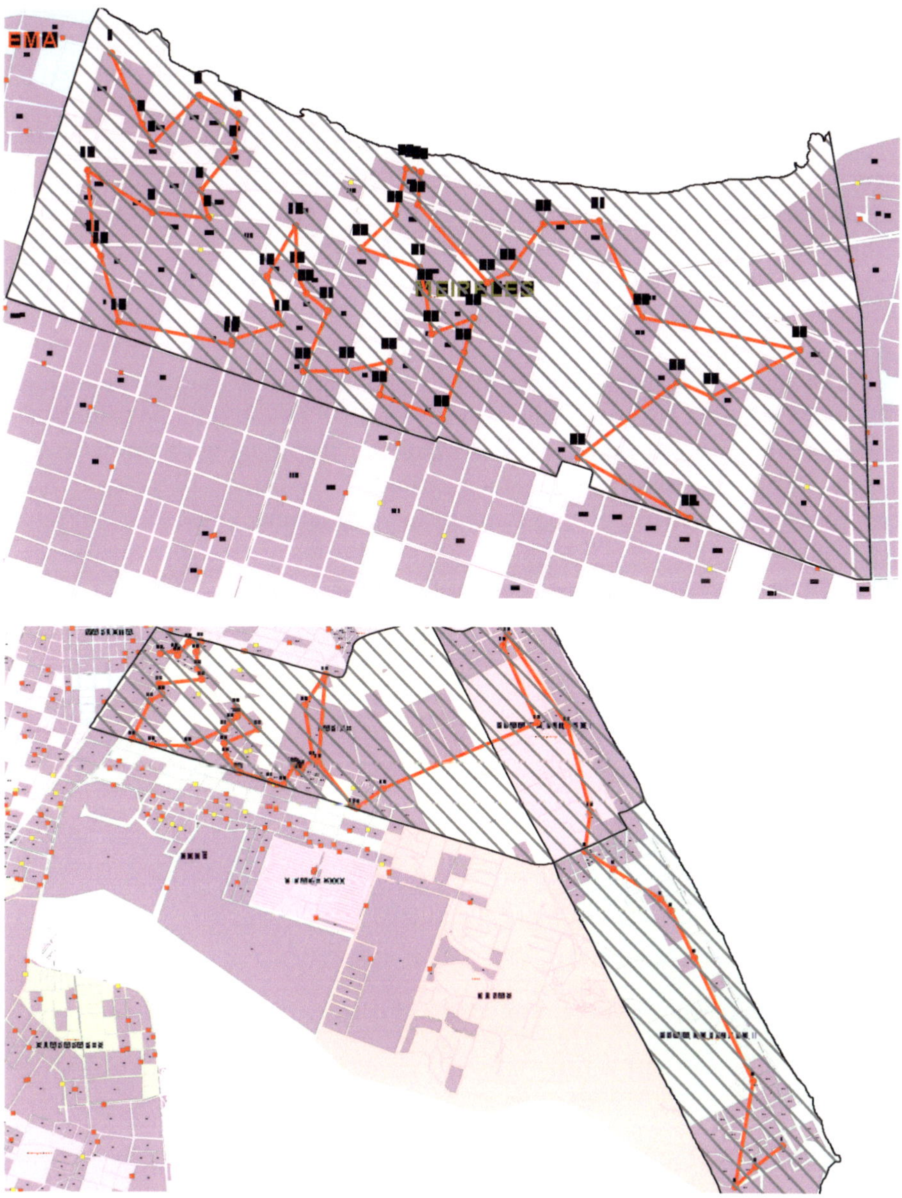

Fig. 12. Itinerary of a Sanitary SP's agent for a cycle of 15 working days in one borough (up) and 3 between boroughs (down), (Manager System)

4.1.3 Division of the agents work in the coverage areas

In this phase, using the previous example, since the agents have 42 working days within the area which is defined for their group, only 72-88 real estate units are visited per day, and the coverage of the entire city is slow and arduous. In this case, our interest is to distribute the agents by "macro-region" (clusters), in such a way that the (ideally) a representative sample of the total coverage of the city is explored each day. That is, the daily samples (sub-clusters) will present the picture of the city in regard to focuses. In this case, for our approach we consider that the agents must be closer to one another among distinct cluster while being as far apart as possible within the same cluster, though in the following days they must take real estate units that are the closest to the ones visited in the previous day.

This problem is related to a situation which seems to be multi-objective, with a dynamic coverage component. The expected model takes into account a process of dynamic localization that has been studied by many researchers and that has been reported in a recent *survey* about strategic location, (Owen & Drezner 1997).

To better illustrate how this may be done, Figures 13 presents a division of the agents' work for the city of Sobral/CE, real estate unit by real estate unit, for a defined area (cluster), though it must be taken into account that the work of the agents acting in this area could be the most disperse among them, at the same time that the following day it would be undertaken in groups of real estate units (18-22) located in the neighborhood of those that the agent visited on the previous day. For that neighborhood to be obtained, one can use Delaunay triangulation methods, in which the centers of the daily real estate unit groups would be taken as being those of the displacement assessment (Preparata & Shamos 1985).

We will call this problem the Sanitary Agent Coverage Assignment Problem (SACAP). A preliminary {0,1} formulation for this problem may be considered as follows:

Sets:

a_c - each cluster c has a set of a_c sub-clusters;

C - is the set of Clusters (areas to be covered);

$N(i)$ – are neighbour sub-clusters of sub-cluster i;

Parameters:

d_{ij} – is the distance between two agents i and j;

H – is the horizon in working days;

M – is a great number;

Variables:

t_k – is the minimum distance between two agents in day k;

$$x_{lj}^k = \begin{cases} 1, \text{if the agent } l \text{ visits the sub-cluster } j \text{ in day } k; \\ 0, \text{otherwise.} \end{cases}$$

Model of Sanitary Agent Coverage Assignment Problem (SACAP):

$$\text{(SACAP) Maximize } \left(\sum_{k=1}^{H} t_k\right) \tag{24}$$

Such that,

$$t_k \leq d_{ij} + M\max(1 - x_{li}^k, 1 - x_{l'j}^k), \forall k, \forall i, \forall j, \forall l, \forall l'; \tag{25}$$

$$\sum_{l \in a_c} \sum_{k=1}^{H} x_{lj}^k = 1, \forall j \in C, \forall c \in C \tag{26}$$

$$\sum_{j \in C} x_{lj}^k \leq 1, \forall k, \forall l = 1, \ldots, a_c, \forall c \in C \tag{27}$$

$$x_{lj}^k + \sum_{j \notin N(i)} x_{lj}^{k+1} \leq 1, \forall k, \forall l, \forall j \tag{28}$$

$$t_k \geq 0, \quad x_{lj}^k \in \{0,1\}, \forall k, \forall l, \forall j \tag{29}$$

In the model (SACAP), the objective function [24] searches to maximize the sum of the minimum displacement distances between two days in a row of the coverage period undertaken by the sanitary agents. The constraints [25] consider t_k as the shortest distance that separates two visited sub-clusters (real estate units of a visiting day). In the constraints [26], each sub-cluster of each cluster must be visited by an agent of the cluster. In [27] the constraints indicate that each agent of cluster c can only visit a sub-cluster from c. The constraints [28] consider that within a visiting period the visit to neighbor sub-clusters is only permitted on the following day. The constraints [29] consider the decision variables of the model, being the one that expresses the real distance and the binary allocation distance. Other objective functions can be considered, such as in equations [30] and [31] below:

$$\text{(SACAP-1)} \quad \text{Maximize} \sum_{k=1}^{H} (t_k)^{\frac{1}{2}} \tag{30}$$

or in the same way,

$$\text{(SACAP-2)} \quad \text{Maximize Min } t_k \tag{31}$$

The SACAP model although designed to real estate units, a group of real state units belonging to the same block can define a block to be covered by an agent. The same model can be stated taking into account the blocks of the cities, since each block can be covered in less than a day of visit.

For this problem, by addressing blocks, a set of greedy heuristics were implemented based on clustering and routing, in dynamic context. The means of the heuristic developed is to keep track of the groups while the agents are as far as possible and moving in a route between neighbor blocks at his assigned area. The triangulation phase defines the neighbor of the blocks, and it is done by the Delaunay triangulation and an extension for treating the shape and elongated blocks, that the triangulation (algorithm for points) does not match as real neighbor of polygons in plane. In the second phase, we design the clusters and then the dynamic routes, (Serghine, 2006).

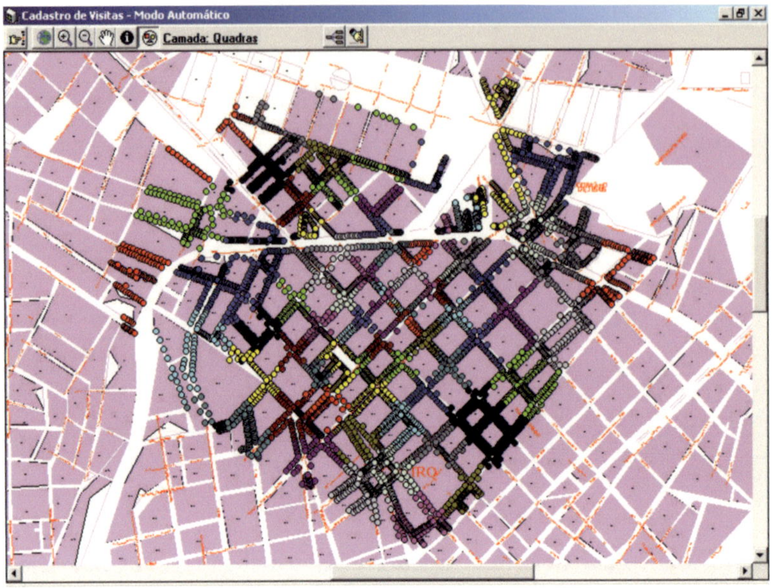

Fig. 13. a. Division of the visits made by a group of agents in a defined service area for the group.

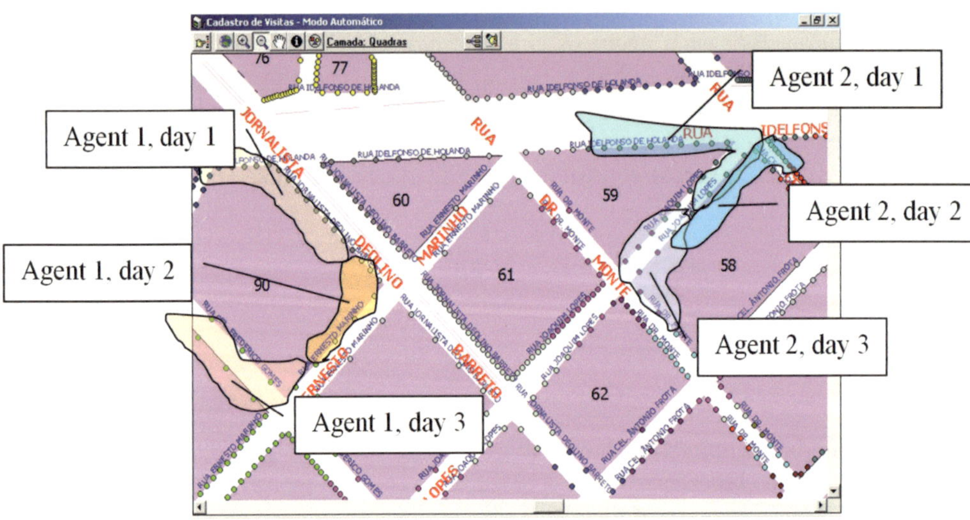

Fig. 13. b. Accurate visualization of the coverage of the agents and of the visits of a group in the area defined in Figure 13(a).

Fig. 13. Division of the labor using the Manager system, by means of the SACAP model.

A test for a number of 10 boroughs for the Regional II- Fortaleza/CE, was done. Figure 14 shows the result of one of these instances considered. Although Figure 15 is a static view of the final solution, it can be seen that the neighborhood of the blocks was avoided in the routes by the heuristic, once it can not find feasible solutions for this instance of the SACAP. In fact, as the supervisor of Regional II considered, "it is not so important that this constraint may be fully satisfied". Although, considering the related districting solution found, "gerrymandering" (*elongated* clusters) is not avoided, and for him "must be" avoided, the use of other criteria in the objective function as shape of the cluster, as overlapping of the shapes, and others, can be also addressed here as in districting problems, (Garfinkel & Nemhauser, 1970), (Blais et al 2003). Much research work must be done here, for this interesting problem.

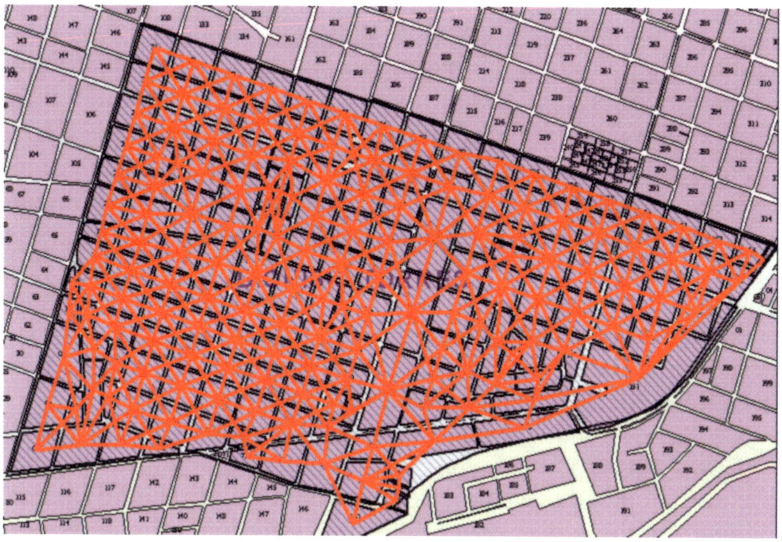

Fig. 14. Neighbor graph associated to the blocks of the borough Dionísio Torres/Fortaleza-CE.

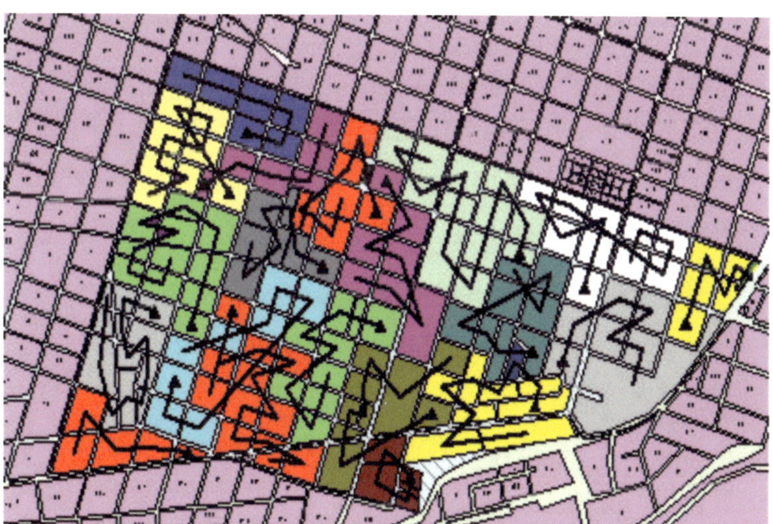

Fig. 15. A dynamic path and clustering for the borough of Dionísio Torres/Fortaleza-CE, instance with 20 agents in 12 working days

4.2 The planning process of spraying vehicles

Two models can be considered for scheduling spraying vehicles, periodical task scheduling and routing. The routing model over street networks is not considered once it was not applied in the field, although one can report to the Mixed Capacitated Arc Routing literature, for this approach. These models are related to situations where it is necessary to combat the mosquitoes in their adult phase, (Eiselt et al 1995), (Belenguer et al, 2006).

The problem of designing periodical visit to areas by spraying vehicles is inserted in a dynamic planning of the risk areas coverage, starting from the identified or the reported cases, or from a statistical knowledge of the expansionist behavior of the mosquito in the region. This methodology is often used when we are dealing with the problem of division of service among spraying vehicles that undertake the task during periods of epidemic outbreaks. Since the fleet of such equipment is limited, they are critically needed in this important moment. Moreover, in order to cover urban regions within metropolis or even in medium-sized cities, many coverage areas are necessary, as well as many vehicles to deal with the problem.

The phase of dimensioning the service sectors, either for the agents, or for the spraying vehicles, is undertaken before the scheduling phase, according to the following model. In that model, there is a guarantee that the service is dimensioned for a certain time period or a total service load (number of blocks to be served per day).

The planning problem is inserted within a context of problems for scheduling of periodical tasks, where there is a set of tasks to be undertaken in certain defined areas, at certain times (in the dengue case, for the spraying vehicle, from 5:00 A.M. to 7:00 A.M. and from 5:00 P.M. to 7:00 P.M., and for the agents directly in the residences and businesses, during the morning and the afternoon) and in a certain minimum and maximum service periodicity (intervals between two services). The periodical scheduling of tasks problem is NP-Hard, and it is a problem with few related studies, (Verhaegh et al 1998), (Baptist et al 2001). For the specific case, we can use a mathematical formulation, in the following way:

Premises: 1 area / 1 vehicle / 1 day, or one vehicle serves one area totally in one day

We want to undertake the scheduling task so as to minimize the fleet used, which must cover all areas over the minimum and the maximum stipulated periodicity need.

Sets:

H - is the planning horizon in subsequent days;

A - the set of areas to be covered;

Parameters:

LI(a) – inferior range over the number of days between two visits in area a ;

LS(a) – superior range over the number of days between two visits in area a;

Variables:

$$x_{ia}^{k} = \begin{cases} 1, \text{if vehicle } i \text{ visits an area } a \text{ in day } k; \\ 0, \text{ otherwise} \end{cases}$$

$$z_{a}^{k} = \begin{cases} 1, \text{if an area } a \text{ is visited in day } k; \\ 0, \text{ otherwise} \end{cases}$$

$$y_i = \begin{cases} 1, \text{if vehicle } i \text{ is used;} \\ 0, \text{otherwise.} \end{cases}$$

Periodical Scheduling of Vehicles in Areas Model (PSVA):

$$\text{(PSVA) Minimize } (\sum_{i=1}^{K} y_i) \tag{32}$$

Such that,

$$\sum_{i=1}^{LS(a)} z_a^k \geq 1, \forall a; \tag{33}$$

$$z_a^k = \sum_{i=1}^{K} x_{ia}^k, \forall a, \forall k \tag{34}$$

$$z_a^k \leq \sum_{s=LI(a)}^{LS(a)} z_a^{k+s}, \forall a, \forall k = 1, \dots, H - LS(a) \tag{35}$$

$$\sum_{a=1}^{A} x_{ia}^k \leq y_i, \forall i, \forall k \tag{36}$$

$$y_i, z_a^k, x_{ia}^k \in \{0,1\}, \forall i, a, k \tag{37}$$

In the model of Periodical Scheduling of Vehicles in Areas (PSVA), the objective function [32] searches to minimize the number of vehicles of the allocated fleet in the period. The constraints [33] consider that each area must be visited within the first LS(a) days. The constraints [34] establish a link between variables z and x. The constraints [35] consider that one must go back to each area, between LI(a) and LS(a) days after a visit. The constraints [36] consider that only one vehicle visits no more than one area per day. And finally, the constraints [37] present the decision variables of the Periodical Scheduling model.

We evaluated short instances of this problem using CPLEX. For the framework, we implemented a multi-start greedy heuristic to find solutions for real large instances. The heuristic contains a greedy construction phase which orders the major areas and also the minimum periodicity in a list of candidates. After that, for each randomly selected area from the list (or part of it), a feasible path is built. If a feasible path cannot be built, the process starts again. A number of tests were made with the multi-start greedy solution that returns good quality in comparison to optimal results for the situation where the areas have the same limits between two visits, (Negreiros et al 2001), (Coutinho 2003).

Most recently, Michelon et al (2008) present some general properties of the problem, an integer programming formulation for which they give the optimal solution of the linear relaxation, a trivial lower bound which is compared to the linear relaxation bound and a new greedy heuristic, (Michelon, Quadri, Negreiros, 2008).

4.3 Design the itinerary of spraying vehicles

Once the service areas are defined and the service of scheduling the agents is done, there is also the phase of establishing the service itinerary of the spraying vehicles, in such a way as to facilitate the work of the manager in the task of serving the population in epidemic situations. In this phase, we use models that are based on the Rural Postman Problem (RPP), in which it is guaranteed that the service will be accomplished with the passing of the spraying vehicle by all the blocks where its service has been requested, with the lowest cost in the itinerary, (Eiselt el al 95), (Negreiros 1996), (Corberán et al 2000).

This problem actually relates to the minimization of the spending of insecticides and with the duration of the itinerary, besides the guarantee as to the complete coverage of the affected areas, since the spraying vehicles turn on the pulverizing pumps as soon as they enter the service areas, turning them off only when the task in each sector is concluded. The expense reduction would be reasonable, starting with a better elaboration of the itineraries, and, furthermore, the defined sectors would have a quicker service, (Negreiros 1996).

Since the itinerary of the rural postman is limited beyond the specific area, as well as to the quantity of insecticide present in the environment, there is the Constrained Itinerary using the Capacitated Arc Routing problem (CARP), initially proposed by Golden & Wong (1981) though taking into account, furthermore, the specific orientation in the routes for the passing of the spraying vehicle, considering that the pulverizing nozzle of the insecticide is fixed and is located at the right side. Once the network is mixed, it is worth to consider the techniques for the Mixed Capacitated Arc Routing Problem (MCARP), or the General Routing Problem (GRP), as in (Negreiros 1996), (Belenguer et al 2006).

For this problem, the basic ideas from the algorithm produced proposed by Negreiros (1996) are used, in a GRASP variation of a multi-start greedy mixed capacitated general routing heuristic and an improvement procedure for each route using a mixed rural postman problem approach, designed by Coutinho (2003). These procedures are before used for the garbage collection, and obtain high quality solutions also for the case of dengue combat. This problem fortunately was not evaluated on field, since there was no epidemic situation in the evaluation time.

Figures from 16 to 18 below show some of the visualizations of the output results of this model, to adequately organize the work of planning the logistics for the dengue prevention. Figure 16 shows a division process, for example, of region 02 in 4 sub-areas, with a capacity limited to 2000 liters of poison. In Figure 17, the service schedules of the area presume a fixed working program, in established days, with maximum service periodicity within the mosquito cycle and the thematic itinerary for servicing the area, where we can visualize a resulting multi-graph, with the possible itinerary that can be made by the spraying vehicle or by the health agent. Finally, in Figure 18, there is the problem of movement of the spraying vehicle, considering that the pulverizing nozzle will always be oriented towards the front of the residences, (Negreiros et al 2001).

The strong integration between the problems of coverage by the sanitary agents and by the spraying vehicles of the regions infested with larvae of the *Aedes aegypti* mosquito, their scheduling into periods and the distribution of the door-to-door service requires specific studies about the effectiveness of optimization methods that serve well he desires of the manager - optimization of costs, serving its needs in a rational way. We have been applying methodologies that we have developed that have been able to approach the problem of prevention and combat of dengue with a high level of reliability for the manager of the Zoonoses center, (Negreiros, 1996), (Negreiros et al 2001), (Coutinho, 2003), (Negreiros & Palhano, 2006).

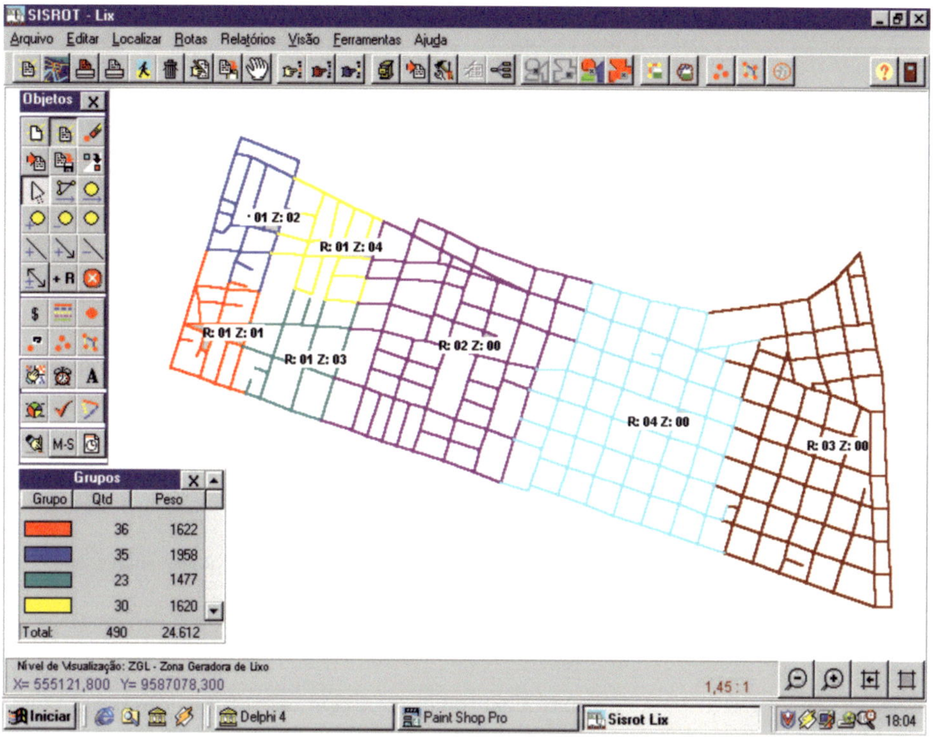

Fig. 16. Division of areas and sub-areas where the spraying vehicles work per day.

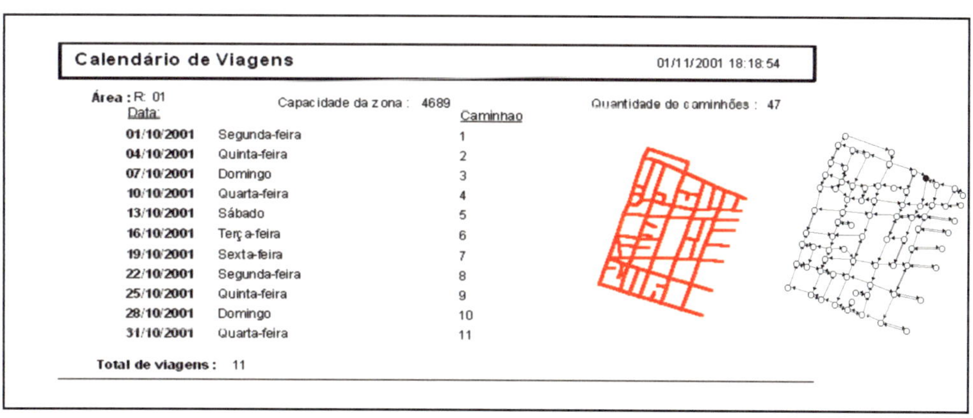

Fig. 17. Proposed form for service calendar in a given area and corresponding multi-graph itinerary.

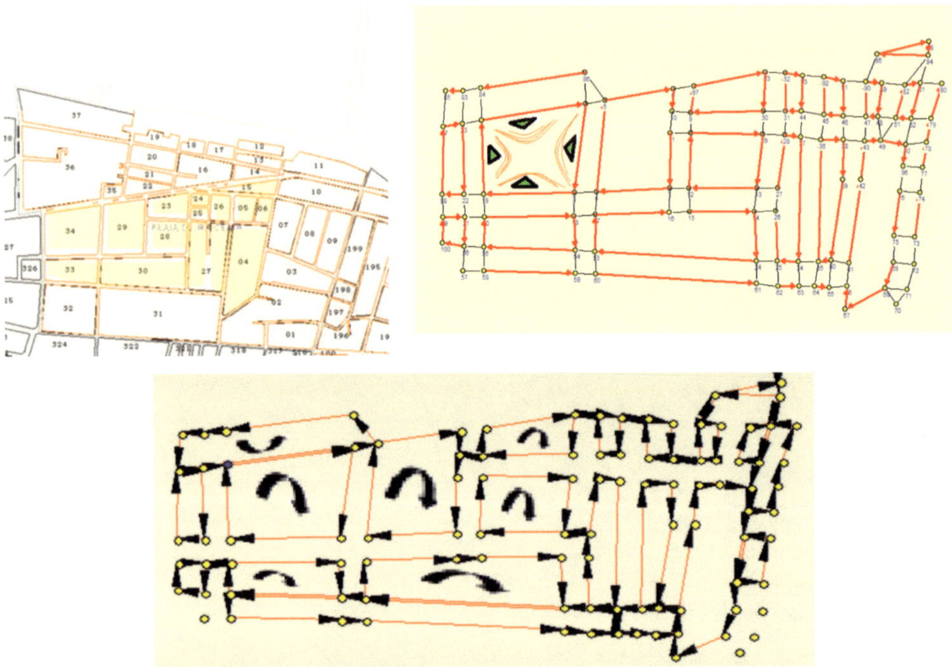

Fig. 18. View of the orientation graph of the spraying vehicle itinerary in an area (Praia de Iracema, Fortaleza) and its related RPP multi-graph solution where the tour of spraying is always pointing to the inner-center of the block or the right side of the vehicle (opposite side of the driver sit).

5. Statistical models for the prevention and combat of dengue

The use of statistical models for tracking the evolution of dengue is very frequent by the municipalities in Brazil and worldwide. General forecasts are considered in advance for prevention proposes but mostly in Brazilian cities they are disaggregated and processed by different institutions. Tracking the evolution of the disease is another important tool, but mostly not used. The integration of the forecasts and tracking methodologies to follow the disease is crucial. Decision makers may use these tools in an integrated environment to help focusing in the directions of the process.

In the following subsections we consider these problems, and ways to forecast and track the evolution of dengue for prevention proposes.

5.1 Forecasting *Aedes aegypti* presence

A usual technique for prevention is following dengue expansion by forecasting techniques over the evolution of the number of human cases. It is well known by health managers that the cycles of dengue in tropical areas have periodical meanings. The resurgence of the disease was followed by researchers. In Rio de Janeiro, the impact of the cyclic causes pandemics in periods of 5 to 7 years, as can be seen in the plots studied by Amaral, Voughon, Duarte (2009), Figure 19.

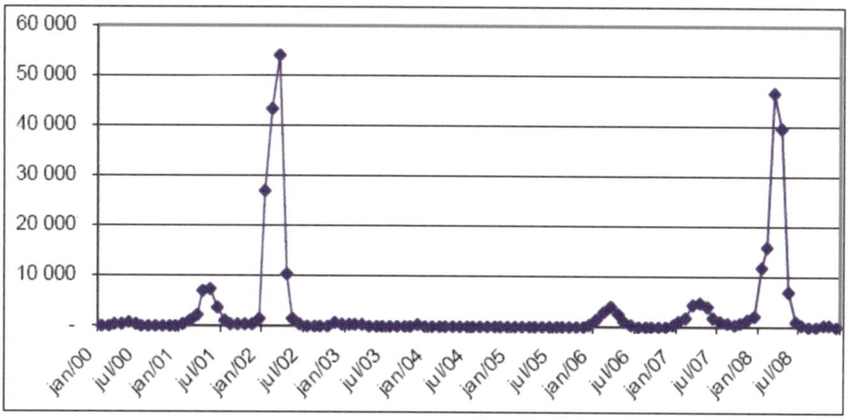

Fonte: Informação Epidemiológica: S / SUBASS / SVS / GERÊNCIA DE VIGILÂNCIA EPIDEMIOLÓGICA - SMS/RJ

Fig. 19. Pandemias of Dengue in Rio de Janeiro (2002 and 2008)

Using the actual Data Bases as SQL-Server, PostGre or Oracle, the data can be stored conveniently by territory and periods. A number of techniques may be used for that, although there are many forecast methods, the selection of the most adequate to ensure and help the health manager is an important result. Freire, Xavier and Negreiros (2007) developed a procedure to automatic detect the best forecast from four classical forecasting methods: Random Walk, ARIMA, Holt-Winters and Neural Nets, and selecting the best of them by using a Kohonen Neural Net score classifier (Table 2). In Figure 20 it is shown the forecasts plotted by using the statistical software R, and the minimum-square-error (score) obtained for each forecast, in relation to the real result obtained for the period of the forecast. The data used were obtained from the information given by the municipality of Fortaleza from the years of 2002-2005.

Method	Recommended	Suggested KHNN
Random Walk	4	4
ARIMA	3	2
Holt-Winters	2	3
Neural Net	1	1

Table 2. Visualization of the forecasts by neural net vs desirable selection

This methodology was implemented in the system Webdengue, for forecasting boroughs, regions and city. This tool considers the information obtained from previous years which are stored in its data base. The best score obtained by the KHNN is then plotted to the user for evaluation and decision.

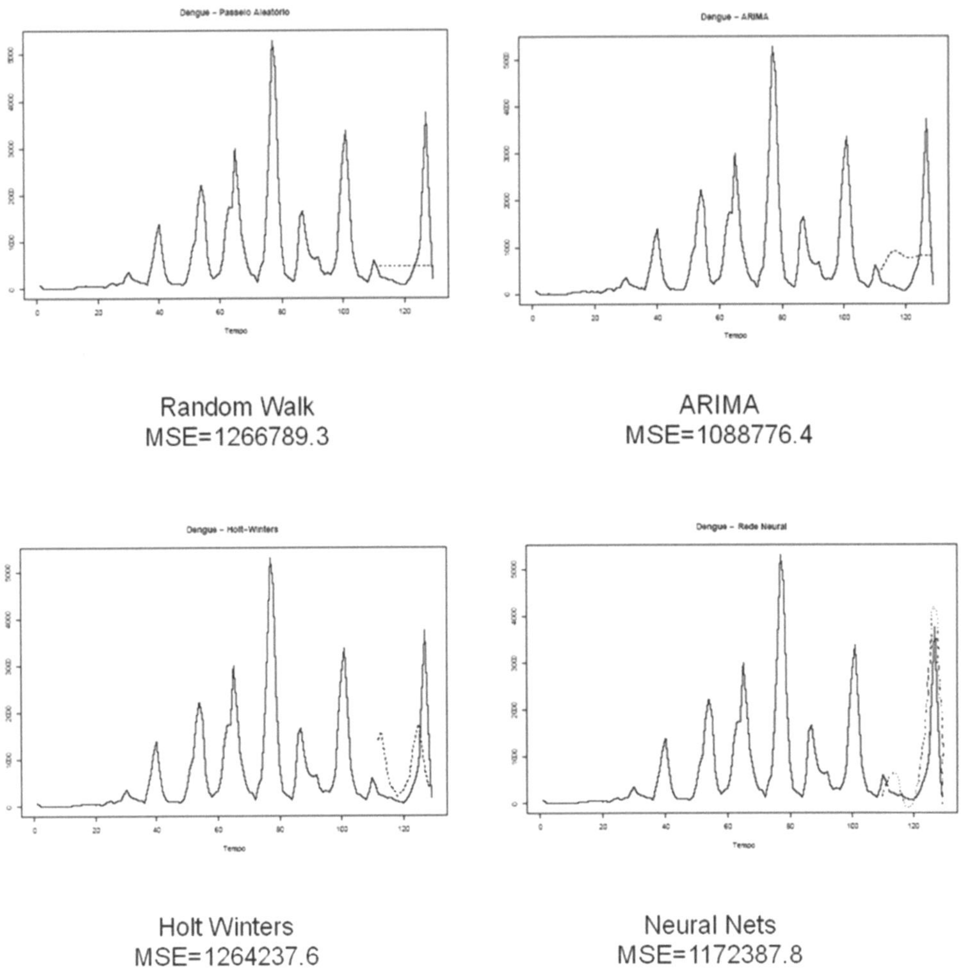

Fig. 20. MSE results obtained by evaluating the ranks (scores) using Kohonen Neural Net of different classical forecasting methods.

5.2 Tracking colony of *Aedes aegypti* or human cases by natural clusters methods

A number of works recently developing for dengue prevention, in Mexico and Singapore, are using internet to show where the human cases are for a specified period of evaluation. In Mexico, the project considers the use of the Google Earth™ technology to track the *Aedes* presence, also including Decision Support System designed to follow data warehouse where management tools, plots, statistics and mapping visualization are delivered to detect in block the *Aedes* presence. In Singapore, thematic digital maps are generated which are more emphatic in delivering to the user precise information of places where the human cases occur to the population thought web maps and charts of evolution. Both technologies have their impact, in visualization and decision support, joining both are very useful and we consider in the **Webdengue** project the join of these processes tools to help health managers to track dengue, (Lozano-Fuentes et al 2008), (Eisen & Beaty 2008), (Lozano-Fuentes & Eisen 2009).

The city of Singapore, considers the importance of advising people by internet where the cases of dengue are in the last week. They publish weekly the principal groups formed by at least 3 human cases and define the center of the group as the potential area where dengue exists, and where the population have to take care of being infected by *Aedes*. Figure 21a shows the basic follow up in Singapore by internet, and Figure 21b shows both ideas integrated in the Webdengue environment also in the web.

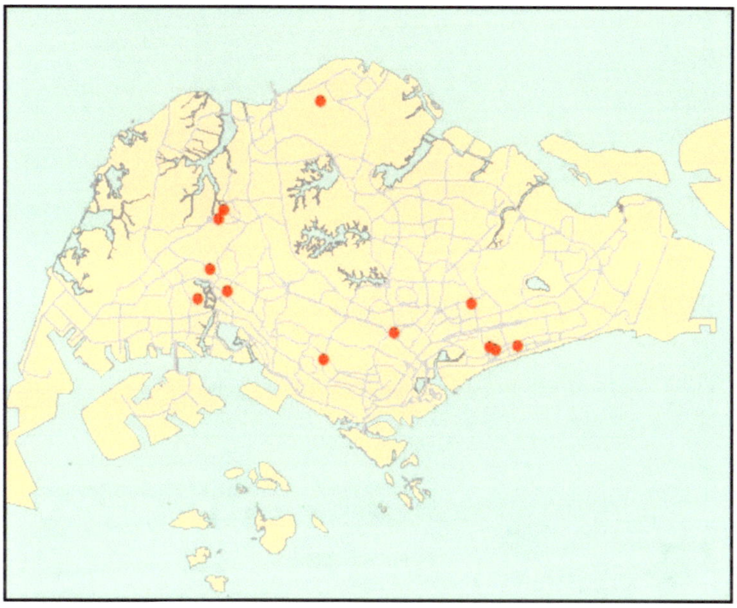

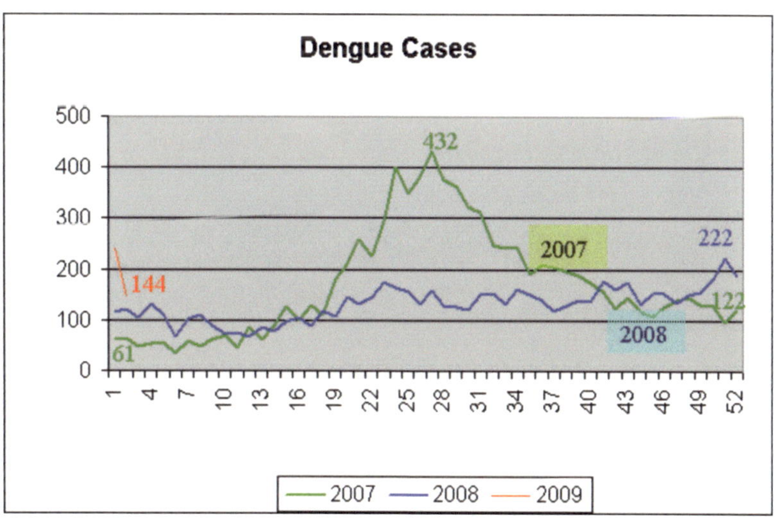

Fig. 21. a. Last week clusters of human cases in Singapore and evolution of the number of human cases published by the city of Singapore in the web.

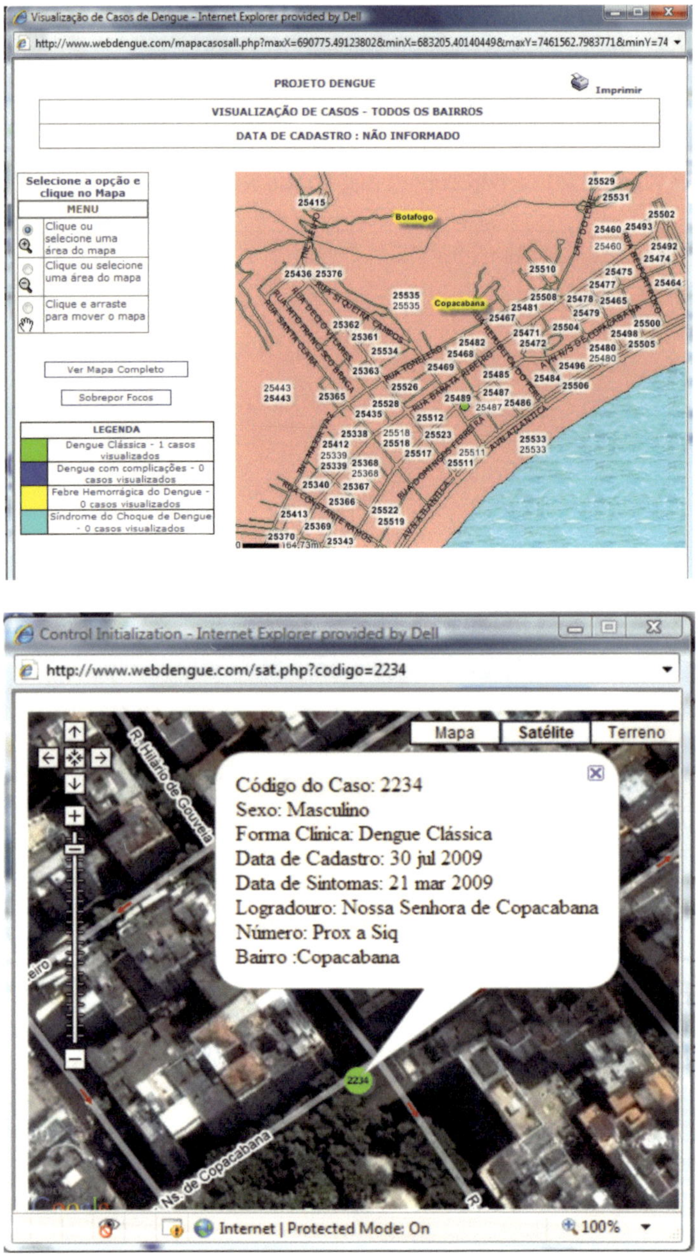

Fig. 21. b. Integrating visualizations between digital thematic mapping and Google Earth mapping systems in Webdengue for the city of Rio de Janeiro.

To model the Singapore strategy of defining these clusters, let be $\mathbf{G}$ a symmetric weighted graph $\mathbf{G}(\mathbf{V},\mathbf{E})$ generated from the vertices (points) defined by the set of spatial coordinates focus of *Aedes* or human cases identified in a certain period of time. Let define $G(V,E)$ as a neighbor graph, where the set of edges are defined by $e_{ij} \in \mathbf{E}$, $\forall\ i,j \in \mathbf{V}$, then equation define the neighbor graph:

$$e_{ij} = \begin{cases} 1, d_{ij} < Max\{d_{ik}, d_{kj}\}, \forall i,j,k \in V \\ 0, \text{ otherwise} \end{cases} \tag{31}$$

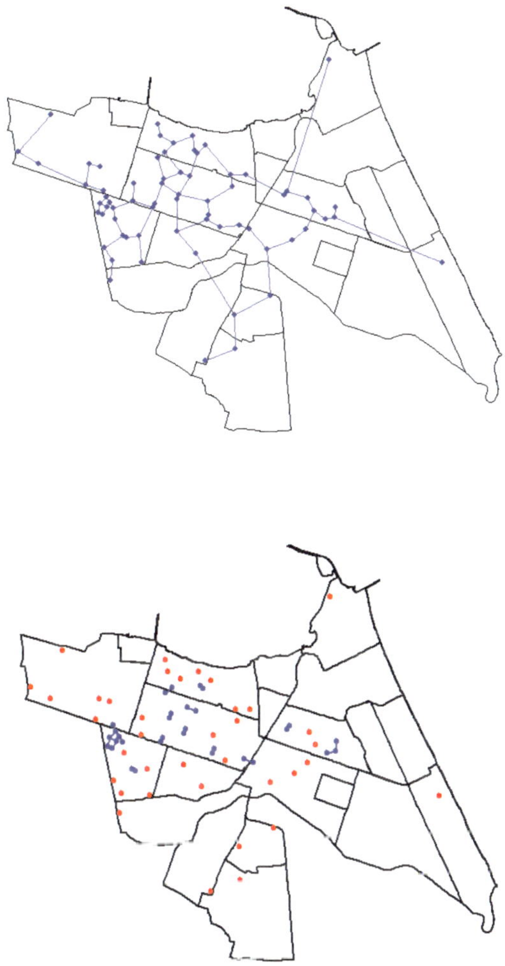

Fig. 22. Formation of clusters by defined distance (p.ex. 250m between human cases), Singapure strategy, the aggregation is considered if $d_{ij} \leq 250$ and the resulting components of G(V,E) are of more than 3 vertices.

Figure 22 illustrates the use of neighbor graph to find groups of human cases. Although the technique used by the city of Singapore is very useful, it may obtain results that cannot incorporate to the set of clusters of vertices that are a bit far than the specified parameter, or even groups that are formed with distance between vertices a bit more far from the specified greater distance. To define the natural clusters, without distance parameter, but by an aggregation parameter (minimum number of elements that defines a cluster) we used the

IGN method, by Negreiros, Xavier and Roldan (2005), that considers by hierarchical clustering the formation of the clusters using horizontal and or vertical cuts automatically processed in the related dendrogram, Figure 23.

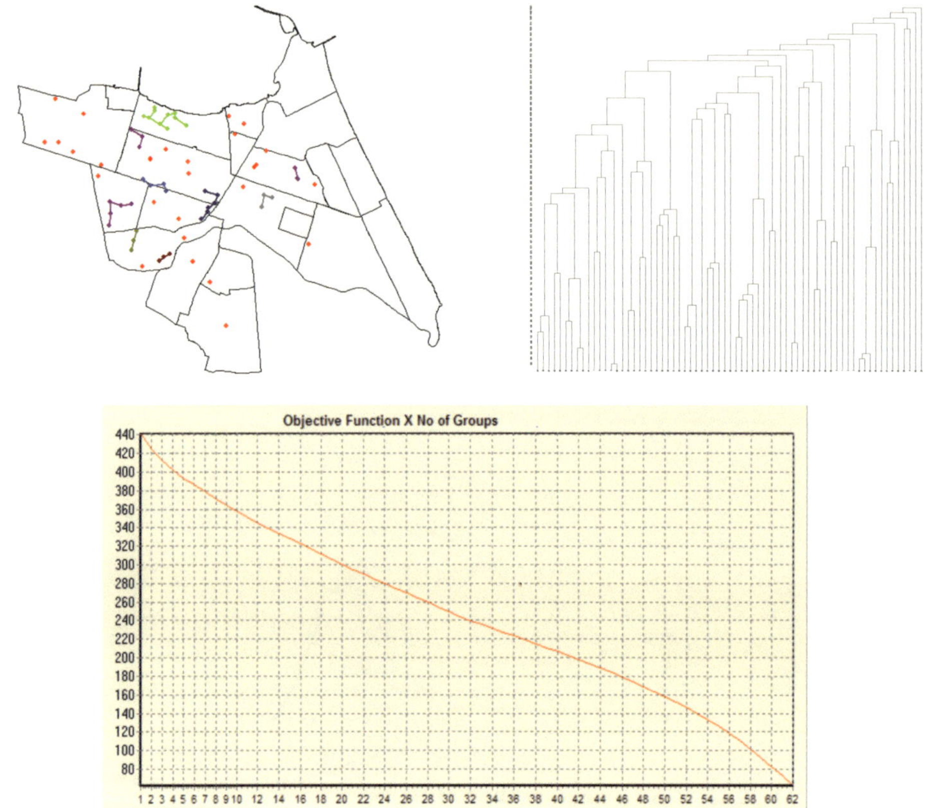

Fig. 23. Dendrogram of the Euclidean graph at left, and the cutting curve for automatic selection of the aggregation of individuals (focus or human cases).

IGN can find easily the number of clusters without parameters, if the aggregations are well defined. If not, one may consider the use of neighbor graph to accomplish the disease.

6. Discussion

Decision Support Systems have been designed to epidemic and entomological control of dengue disease. Groups of researchers perform an important issue in this direction, but it is considerably difficult to implement management decision tools once the control operation of the *Aedes* varies widely from country to country.

This work shows the situation in Brazil, where there are two important forces that work for dengue. A preliminary force works in the direction of the mosquito hunting, by using vehicles and human force (agents) to verify real estate by real estate units the Aedes' eggs, grubs and the adult mosquito. The second force uses the health system to attend the disease in humans, in its variety of forms and complications. The health manager is not a unique person it is formed of a number of persons all responsible to manage both sides of the process.

This work shows a framework of computational systems (Webdengue) that was tested and/or evaluated in three different Brazilian cities: Sobral, Fortaleza and Rio de Janeiro. Each test, revealed the necessity of including a number of tools (graphs, maps, charts, data base management system, GPS, hand-helds, statistics and optimization models) which consider state-of-the-art as classical methods for supporting the decision makers in many different directions. The tools include visualization in the web and cross data from *Aedes* presence and human cases for better decision making, Figure 24.

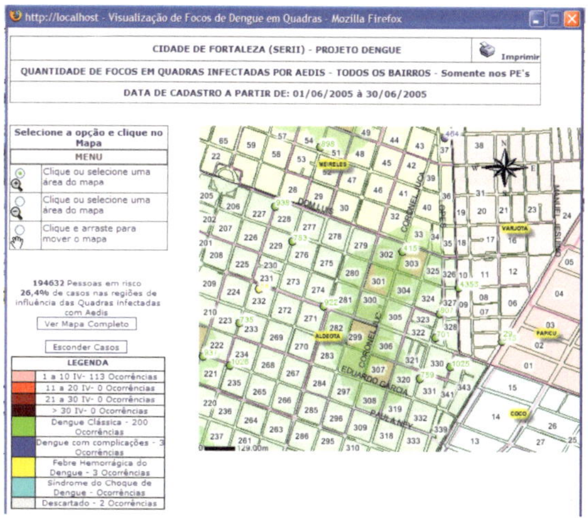

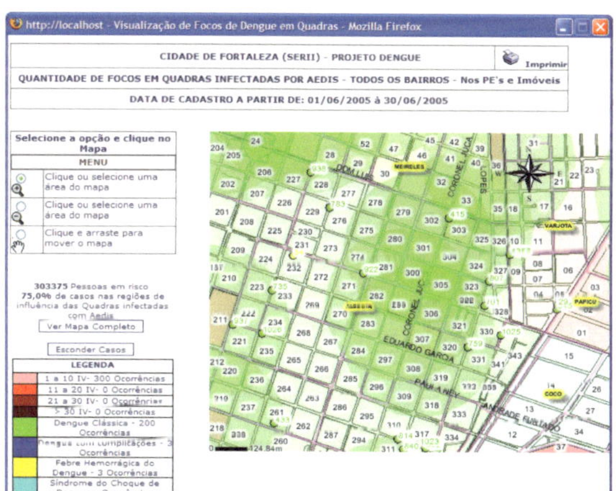

Fig. 24. Confronting human cases (circles) with the region of influence of Aedes focus (blocks in cyan) in Fortaleza/CE. By enlarging the influence zone of Aedes in 100m means for this case an increasing of 50% in the risk of dengue in the area, for the same period of time.

The tools need to be used mainly to shorten the time needed to process the information from the field or from health units to rapidly respond to managers where to allocate resources with optimal cost/benefit to the municipalities, and stop dengue increase. The systems may only be included if the changing factor does not eliminate previous effort in the organization of the forces, in fact they have to sum, although it will became another computational system in an increasingly set of software that are used to solve just parts of the hole problem.

The computational infrastructure needed for control and prevention of dengue, are mainly reported here, as in the Brazilian cities reality. The framework has been in development since 2002, and it is supported by a number of Brazilian research agencies and a private firm until today. The main step-forward of our system is the inclusion of the logistic models to organize the phase of *Aedes* increase. The other phase is also considered by a short number of research works worldwide. Our success in organizing the logistic of the agents were obtained in Fortaleza/CE, in 2005, when we maintain a region populated by approximately 300,000 habitants free of *Aedes* in the great majority of the places of control.

In Figure 25 we show the region that was tested showing the position of the following special points, and the situation in the end of November/2005 when we finish our test and in December/2005 when we follow the results without monitoring the evolution of the visits by the agents.

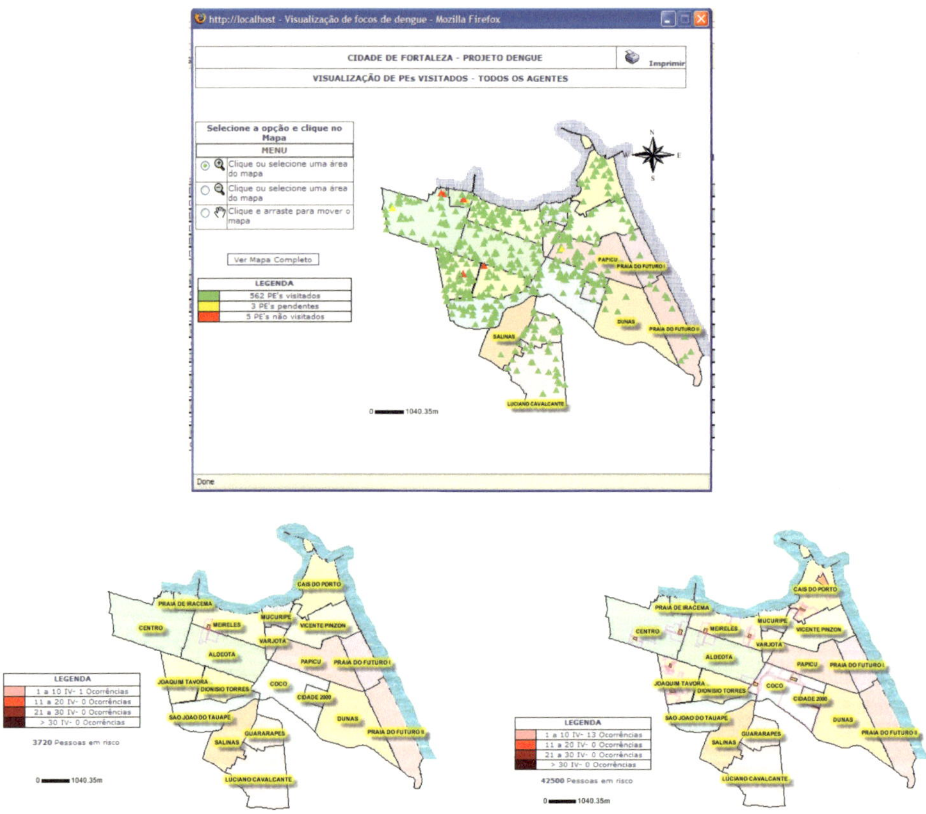

Fig. 25. Region of Fortaleza/CE where the text of the system was made in 550 SP. The following pictures show the situation of blocks in November/2005 (1 SP with Aedes) after following the agents and in December/2005 (13 SP with Aedes) when we stopped the use the Framework by the agents.

The difficulties in implementing the system in the field, is a great barrier to be transposed. Our experience with public health municipalities in Brazil was laborious. Main difficulty is the belief in spending money with control by software. In fact, once Dengue is re-emerging disease, Brazilian health managers only consider the problem "when it comes". Once the agents are working day-by-day, they think they are doing the prevention, but careless with its quality. As can be seen in Figure 4, Brazilian indices reveal that this posture has to be change soon.

7. Conclusions

This study described, in general lines, the problem of Dengue in the tropical regions of the world, highlighting the World Health Organization's concern in making the peculiarities of this disease accessible to researchers and public health officials, so that better and more effective methods of combating the disease can be made available.

A computational framework (WEBDENGUE) has been presented to support the activities of prevention and control of dengue. Furthermore, practical operational situations of problems related to the logistics for prevention and combat of dengue have been described, which consist of problems to be equated. With these problems in mind, a set of mathematical models for the logistical control of the sanitary agents visits and the spraying vehicles have been developed. Most of those models have already been incorporated.

The complexity of the problems involved demands the use of both the traditional and the latest optimization tools in order to find solutions to such problems. Such models are being solved by heuristics and incorporated in a SDSS to meet, in a timely manner, the needs of health officials in the assignment of the services of prevention and combat of dengue.

This Computational Framework was prepared for the cities of Sobral (Geographvs and Webdengue), in most total features for the city of Fortaleza (Geographvs, Hand-Held Agent and Supervisor, Webdengue, Manager) and more recently for the state of Rio de Janeiro (Integration with SINAN).

During the period of tests in Fortaleza, the framework was adapted to the reality of the service and helped 13 agents to follow their routine in Regional II, by June to November/2005. The success of the pilot project in Fortaleza came after the coverage of approximately 550 SP units during 14 cycles of 15 days (5443 visits), where just one SP (a building in construction) was found with *Aedes* grubs. Also, the municipality health managers evaluated with our team the tools and methodology used to manage the information and the organization of the work done in the field. They were very impressed by its impact with the agents and supervisors quality of work, also the information treatment flexibility and visibility to manage the disease, by crossing human cases and the *Aedes* presence in the field.

Most recently we use GeoGRAPHVS to prepare all the city of Fortaleza to track dengue. The project used the parallel version of the system where 7 people georreferenced in five months 48 thousand street segments and 18 thousand blocks, for the Fortaleza's Municipality Secretary of Health. They are using the results of the work to follow the disease growth since 2009. Expectations of professional use of the Computational Framework are still great.

8. Acknowledgements

We would like to thank the Secretary of Social Development and Health of Sobral/CE and Fortaleza/CE, the Town Hall and Center of Zoonoses and Epidemiology of Sobral and Fortaleza/CE, for the support to this project in the field. We like to thank the

CAPES/COFECUB project 0467/04, CNPq project PQ 202457 (pos-doctorate), and program ALFA-EUROPEAID project ALFA II-0457-FA-FCD-F1-FC, FUNCAP-FINEP/CE Empresas Competitivas, CNPq-RHAE Inovação projeto 505594/2004-8, and to GRAPHVS Ltda, to the financial support. We would also like to thank the GRAPHVS system development team for their commitment to making this work come true. We finally thank the State Secretary of Health (SESDC-RJ) and COPPETEC/RJ, for the support on Rio de Janeiro evaluation project 492/2008 process E-08/10471/2008.

9. References

Amaral,J.R.S. Vaughon,A.P., Duarte,K.S. (2009) "Modelo Econométrico para Previsão da Incidência de Dengue no Município do Rio de Janeiro", *Anais do XLI SBPO 2009* - Pesquisa Operacional na Gestão do Conhecimento, pgs 1435-1447

Baptiste, P., Le Pape, C. & Nuijten, W. 2001 Constraint-Based Scheduling: Applying Constraint Programming to Scheduling Problems. Kluwer Academic Publishers

Blais, M, Lapierre, SD, Laporte, G., 2003, "Solving a home-care districting problem in a urban setting", *Journal of the Operations Research Society*, vol 54, pp 1141-1147.

Belenguer, J-M., Benavent, E., Lacomme, P. , Prins, C., 2006, "Lower and upper-bounds for the mixed capacitated arc routing problem", *Computers & Operations Research*, vol 33 pp 3363–3383

Brito, J. ; Xavier, AE (2006) "Modelagens min-max-min para o problema de localização de estações de rádio base", Pesquisa Operacional 26 (2), pp. 295-319

Bourjolly, J-M, Laporte, G., Rousseau J-M., 1981, "Découpage electoral automatisé: application à l'Île de Montreal", *INFOR* vol 19 pp 113-124

Bozkaya, B Erkut, E Laporte, G., 2003. "A tabu search heuristic and adaptative memory procedure for political districting", *European Journal of Operations Research* vol 144 pp 12-26

Coutinho, EF. 2003. Algoritmos de escala e roteamento de veículos para aplicação em serviços sistemáticos de regiões urbanas, MSc Dissertation (MPCOMP-UECE/CEFET-CE), Jul/2003

CPLEX Optimization,Inc.,Suite 279,930 Tahoe Blvd. Bldg. 802. Incline Village. NV 89451-9436,e-mail: cplex.com

Daskin, M.S. 1995. Network and Discrete Location: Models, Algorithms and Applications, ED. John Wiley

Depradine, C.A. & Lovell, E.H. 2004. "Climatological Variables and the Incidence of Dengue Fever in Barbados", *International Journal of Environmental Health Research*, Vol. 14, No.. 6, pp 429-441.

Eiselt, H. A, Gendreau, M., Laporte. G., 1995. "Arc Routing Problems, Part II: The Rural Postman Problem" - *Operations Research*, vol. 43(3) pgs. 399-414.

Eisen, L. & Beaty, B,J., 2008, "Innovative decision support and vector control approaches to control dengue ." In *Institute of Medicine report on "Vector-Borne Diseases - Understanding the environmental Human Health, & Ecological Connections"*, pgs 150-161.

Eisen, L. & Lozano-Fuentes, S., 2009, "Use of mapping and spatial and space-time modeling approaches in operational control of Aedes aegypti" PLOS Neglected Tropical Diseases, pgs vol 3(4) e411.

Everitt, BS, Landau, S, Leese, M. 2001. Cluster Analysis, Arnold, Ed and Oxford University Press

Garey, MR Jonhson, DS., 1979. Computers and Intractability: A guide to the theory of the NP-Completeness, Ed Freeman, San Francisco

Garfinkel, RS, Nemhauser, GL 1970. "Optimal political districting by implicit enumeration techniques", *Management Science*, vol 16 pp 495-508

Feo, T , Resende, M 1995. "Greedy Randomised Adaptative Search Procedures", *Journal of Global Optimisation Algorithms,* vol 6 pp 109-133, Kluwer Academic Press.

Forgy EW. 1965 "Cluster analysis of multivariate data: efficiency versus interpretability of classifications". *Biometrics* vol 21(3) pg 768.

Hartingan,J., 1975. Clustering algorithms. New York : Wiley Interscience.

Hansen P, Jaumard B. 1997. "Cluster analysis and mathematical programming". *Mathematical Programming* vol 79, pp 191–215.

Hansen,P., Mladenovic, N. 2001. "J-Means: A New Heuristic for Minimum Sum-of-Squares Clustering", *Pattern Recognition,* Vol. 34 pp 405-413.

Kaufmann, L., Rousseauw, P. J. 1990. Finding groups in data: an introduction to cluster analysis. New York : John Wiley & Sons, 1990.

Keating,J. 2001. "An Investigation of Cyclical Incidence of Dengue Fever", *Social Science & Medicine,* vol. 53 p. 1587-1597.

Lozano-Fuentes, S., Elizondo-Quiroga, D., Farfan-Ale, J.A., Loroño-Pino, M.A., Garcia-Rejon, J., Gomez-Carro, S., Lira-Zumbardo, V., Najera-Vazquez, R., Fernandez-Martinez, J., Dominguez-Galera,M., Mis-Avila, P., Morris, N., Coleman, M., Moore, C.G., Beaty, B,J., Eisen, L. 2008, "Use of Google Earth™ to strengthen public health capacity and facilitate management of vector-borne diseases in resource-poor environments." *Bulletin of the World Health Organization,* vol 86(9) pgs 718-725.

Mehrotra, A, Johnson, EL , Nemhauser, GL. 1998. "An optimization based heuristic for political districting", *Management Science* vol 44 pp 1100-1114

Michelon, P., Quadri, D., Negreiros, MJ. 2008 "On a class of Periodic Scheduling Problems", *XXI European Chapter in Combinatorial Optimisation (ECCO), Dubrovnik, Croatia May/2008*

Mladenovic ,N., Hansen, P., 1997. "Variable neighborhood search", *Computers and Operations Resesearch,* vol 24 pp 1097-1100.

Negreiros, MJ. 1996, "Contribuições para Otimização em Grafos e Problemas de Percursos de Veículos: Sistema SisGRAFO", *D.Sc. Thesis, UFRJ-COPPE, Eng. Sistemas e Computação.*

Negreiros, MJ, Palhano, AWC (2006), "The Capacitated Centred Clustering Problem", *Computers & Operations Research* vol 33 pg.1639-1663

Negreiros, MJ, Lima, JWO, Xavier, AE, Maculan, N, Xavier, AFS, Michelon, P., 2006, "The Prevention and Combat of the Dengue Disease by a Computational DSS WEB Based System. Application Results to Fortaleza and Sobral/CE - Brazil", *Euronewsletter#9,* Electronic Publication on www.euro-online.org.

Negreiros, MJ, Coutinho, EF, Palhano, AWC, Oliveira, JGB., 2001, "Agrupamento Capacitado Espacial e Escalonamento de Áreas de Serviço Sistemático através do Sistema SisRot LIX", *XXXIII SBPO'2001 – Campos do Jordão/SP, Anais.*

Owen, S.H. , Drezner, Z. 1998. "Strategic Facility location: A Review", *European Journal of Operational Research* vol 111 pp 423-447.

Prunnen, AP (2002) "The traveling salesman problem: Applications, formulations and variations", *Combinatortial Optimization, The Traveling Salesman Problem and Its Variations,* Ed Gregory Gutin and Abraham P Punnen, Kluwer Academic Press

Preparata, F. P. , Shamos, M.I., 1985. Computational Geometry: An Introduction, Springer-Verlag Ed.

Serghine, N. 2006. Système de Prévention et de Combat de la Dengue à Fortaleza - Brésil: Planification d'emploi du temps d'agent sanitaires., *MSc Dissertation*, Universitè de Avignon, IMOD Master 2

Späth, H., 1985. Cluster Dissection and Analysis (Theory, Fortran Programs, Examples), Ellis Horwood, Chichester.

SVS 2004, 2005, 2006, 2007. "DENGUE - Distribuição de casos confirmados, por Unidade Federada. Brasil, 1980 - 2007", Boletim das semanas epidemiológicas. Electronic Publication - Secretaria de Vigilância da Saúde.

Thaillard, ED. (2003) "Heuristic methods for large centroid clustering problems" , *Journal of Heuristics*, vol. 9 pgs 51–73

Theodoridis, S., Koutroumbas, K.., 2003. Pattern Recognition, 2nd Ed. Elsevier Academic Press

TDR 2004, 2007, 2011. *Tropical Disease Research Center* – WHO – http://www.who.int/tdr/index.html

TDR 2009. Dengue: guidelines for diagnosis, treatment, prevention and control. WHO Library Cataloguing-in-Publication Data, World Health Organization

Verhaegh, WFJ, PER Lippens, ERL Aarts, JL van Meerbergen, A. van der Werf, 1998. "The Complexity of Multidimentional Periodic Scheduling", *Discrete Applied Mathematics*, vol. 89, pp. 213-242.

World Health Organization (WHO) (1998-1999), "The world Health Report", Geneva, 1999.

Wu, PC., Guo, HR., Lung, SC., Lin, CY., Su, HJ. (2007) "Weather as an Effective Predictor for Occurrence of Dengue Fever in Taiwan", *Acta Tropica*, vol 103(1) pgs 50-57.

Xavier, A.E., Oliveira, A.A.F. "Optimal covering of plane domains by circles via hyperbolic smoothing technique", *Journal of Global Optimization*, vol 31, pgs 493-504

Xavier, A.E. (2010) "The hyperbolic smoothing clustering method", *Pattern Recognition*, 43 (3), pp. 731-737

Xavier, A.E. , Xavier, V.L. (2011) "Solving the min-sum-of-squares clustering problem by hyperbolic smoothing and partition into boundary and gravitational regions", *Pattern Recognition*, 44 (1), pp. 70-77

Xavier, T.de Ma.B.S. (2005). "Chuvas Intensas em Janeiro/Fevereiro de 2004 e a Previsão em Anos de Neutralidade no Pacífico", *BSBMET-Boletim da Sociedade Brasileira de Meteorologia*, Vol. 28/29, pp. 17-26.

Xavier, T.de Ma.B.S., Xavier, A.F.S. & Alves, J.Ma.B. (2007). Quantis & Eventos Extremos - Aplicações das Ciências da Terra & Ambientais, RDS Ed. / Livrarias Livro Técnico, Fortaleza-Ceará-Brazil, 278pp.

Xavier, A.F.S, Negreiros, MJ, Xavier, TMBS, Andrade, LO M, Freire, LAM, "Climatologic interferente in Dengue Human Cases and Aedes Growth in Fortaleza/CE: Pluviometry", *CLAIO 2008 – XIV Congreso Latino- Americano de Investigación de Operaciones*, Cartagena, 9-12 sept 2008., Cartagena-Colombia.

Zhong, H, Hall, R W, Dessouky, M. 2007. "Territory Planning and Vehicle Dispatching with Driver Learning", *Transportation Science* Vol. 41, No. 1, pp. 74–89

8

A Decision Support System Based on Artificial Neural Networks for Pulmonary Tuberculosis Diagnosis

Carmen Maidantchik et al.*
Signal Processing Lab, COPPE/POLI, Federal University of Rio de Janeiro
Brazil

1. Introduction

In 2005 the Faculty of Medicine, the Electronic and Computing Engineering Department of the Federal University of Rio de Janeiro (UFRJ) and the Electrical Engineering Department of the Federal Center of Technological Education (CEFET-RJ) started a collaborative research project to develop a Decision Support System for Smear Negative Pulmonary Tuberculosis (SNPT). The motivation was to develop, through a multi-disciplinary, multi-institutional, innovative and cost-effective approach, new paradigms to prevent the disease progression and support the rapid evaluation of new therapies. The project also aims at increasing the scientific and technological capacity in the country for the progress of new technologies incorporation in the public and private system as well revising public policies to control tuberculosis.
The conception of the initiative was based on previous experiences of all participants and innovative proposals applied to known restrictions. The initial step was the merging of mathematical modeling and information management through the Web. Paper forms to acquire patient's information were substituted by digital ones. In this way, all data could rapidly be accessed and available online. TB experts defined the data inputs and were responsible to validate the system and its outputs. Data quality methods were used to guarantee the accuracy of records, avoiding uncertain information and improving the value of the final result. Finally, portability was a mandatory requirement in order to guarantee the use of the system in different regions of the Country. The use of symptomatic information to feed a neural network model in order to build the decision support system would guarantee a reliable proposal, constructed with low cost resources.

2. Challenges in TB diagnosis

The increasing number of TB cases encourages the elaboration of modern, competent and economical feasible diagnosis methods. The diagnosis of SNPT is still a challenge

* José Manoel de Seixas[1], Felipe F. Grael[1], Rodrigo C. Torres[1], Fernando G. Ferreira[1], Andressa S. Gomes[1], José Márcio Faier[1], Jose Roberto Lapa e Silva[2], Fernanda C. de Q Mello[2], Afrânio Kritski[2] and João Baptista de Oliveira e Souza Filho[3]
[1]*Signal Processing Lab, COPPE/POLI, Federal University of Rio de Janeiro, Brazil*
[2]*Faculty of Medicine, Federal University of Rio de Janeiro, Brazil*
[3]*Federal Center of Technological Education Celso Suckow da Fonseca, Brazil*

although the availability of effective and suitable diagnosis tests. For the last 15 years, global tuberculosis (TB) control efforts have led to impressive results. However, despite these important achievements, the absolute numbers of TB cases continue to rise. In 2008, 9.4 million TB cases were estimated and 1.7 million individuals die globally (WHO, 2009). Highly effective and widely accessible diagnostics, drugs and vaccines are needed to address this problematic situation. Beside that, however, there are technical and structural challenges that impede optimal detection and treatment of all forms of TB cases in TB control programmes in different countries (Marais, 2010). TB control in most endemic countries relies heavily upon direct sputum smear microscopy, as this is most often the only simple test that can be used below reference laboratory level. Currently, however, only about 60% of all infectious TB cases are being detected with this test, and a proportion of those detected (i.e. listed in the laboratory registers as having at least one positive smear) do not come back to the clinic after submitting the first specimen, so do not receive appropriate treatment (Guillerm, 2006). Since direct smear microscopy is less sensitive in HIV-associated TB, further testing using complex technologies in sophisticated laboratories has been evaluated to reliably diagnose HIV/TB, in SNPT cases (Perkins, 2007). New simple inexpensive tools are needed to identify the various forms of TB (including drug-resistant and HIV-associated TB) at the lower levels of health services. Current assessment of the present diagnostics pipeline suggests that new tools will soon be available (Pai, 2010).

Since 2007, WHO has endorsed the use of at least 10 new diagnostic tools (technologies or approaches) that, if used wisely, could facilitate considerably TB control, and very recently endorsed a new automated real-time nucleic acid amplification technology (NAAT) for rapid and simultaneous detection of TB and Rifampicin resistance (Xpert MTB/RIF system) that offers drastically new prospects for the diagnostics of active and drug-resistant TB. Nevertheless, in a recent survey, 16 high-burden TB countries evaluated, about 50% of them are using TB diagnostic tools recommended by WHO from 2007-2009, NTP managers reported diverse challenges to the implementation of new diagnostics, but no impact assessment of its introduction on TB control was carried out (Van Kampen, 2010).

Therefore, there is insufficient evidence available to determine which package of current and newly developed diagnostic tests would work best in a given set of circumstances, and there is as yet little guidance available to countries on what new diagnostic tools, or combinations of tools, should be implemented in particular epidemiological/health system settings, with high prevalence of SNPT cases, and at what level of the health service it should be done. Recently, to address this issue, an impact assessment framework (IAF) was proposed and endorsed by WHO (Mann, 2010).

The decision support system corresponds to an innovative approach for SNPT diagnosis using statistical models, which might be useful in guiding health care workers in estimating the risk of SNPT, optimizing the use of more expensive tests for TB diagnosis.

3. Neural networks

Among statistical models that have been used to assist medical procedures, one can enumerate Bayesian networks, multivariate logistic regression, neural networks (El-Solh et al., 1999) and classification trees (Mello, 2006). Artificial Neural Network (ANN) is a biological inspired intelligence model, capable to learn through examples and to generalize, i.e. to produce coherent results to data not explored during learning process (Haykin, 2008).

This technique is attractive to a large scale of problems belonging to different domains, since it does not presume any statistical assumption about data variables or the problem itself and explores non-linear relationships between data variables to produce effective models, even in complex applications with a small number of available events in the dataset (Bishop, 2007), as typically occurs in medical applications.

The neural network mathematical problem modeling may provide extremely efficient and helpful tool in distinctive areas, mainly in diagnosis, prognosis and therapy, especially if models are properly formulated and data that is used to feed the neural network has good quality, reliability and represent a certain reality. When formulated in a systematic way and implemented with qualified data, statistical models can be representative of the clinical problem under evaluation and could be useful for physicians in their clinical routine, as well as for public health policy administration (Castelo et at, 2004).

Neural networks are made of a basic processing element known as neuron. Neurons are interconnected though synaptic weights forming the network. Roughly speaking, in the network learning process, knowledge is extracted from data and stored in these synaptic weights (Haykin, 2008). Different neurons models, network architectures and algorithms for training are available (Theodoridis, 2008). Basically, with respect to the learning process, neural models may be classified in supervised and non-supervised methods. Supervised training models are applicable to problems for which a desirable output network value (target vector) is available for each incoming data, i.e. tasks as function approximation and data classification. Non-supervised models, otherwise, identify groups which share similar statistical characteristics (clustering procedure) or extract specific features from data.

In order to produce realistic and accurate models, during the neural network development, one should focus on the selection of the variables which are problem representative, especially in the case of small datasets, which usually lacks of enough statistics to a better problem description as well as possesses class imbalance problems (Hastie, 2009). In this case, the selection of the training algorithm, the choice of the parameters involved in the algorithm, the complexity of the network structure adopted, the mechanism selected to control training, when applicable, are critical to obtain models with good generalization properties (Sahiner, 2008). Medical application usually also involves different kinds of variables, which should be properly coded to do not impact on network learning.

The decision support system here discussed explores both supervised as non-supervised neural models. Based on variables collected from triage, which were chosen by expert physicians on TB diagnosis, a multi-layer perceptron network - MLP- (Haykin, 2008), which is a supervised model, identifies the probability of a patient has TB. Additionally, a self-organizing network inspired on ART-2 algorithm (Vassali, 2002) assigns the patient to one of the following risk groups: low, medium or high. These methods provide independent and complementary information about the patient that is useful to support the decision taking process. In the sequence, these methods will be discussed in more details.

3.1 MLP neural network

The feedforward MLP architecture has neurons distributed into layers. The neuron model consists on a weighted sum of its inputs and applies this summing value to a non-linear function, usually hyperbolic tangent, which is referred as the activation function (Haykin, 2008). Each layer has a defined number of neurons with forward connections to neurons that belong to the next layer. Usually, due to universal approximation theorem (Haykin, 2008), just three layers (input, hidden and output) are used in most of the problems. An arbitrary three-layer feedforward MLP network is shown in figure 1.

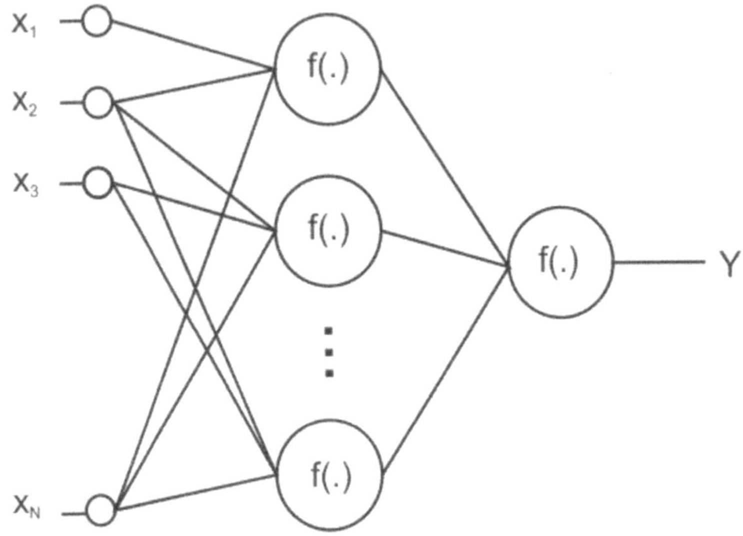

Fig. 1. Three-layer feedforward MLP network.

Considering three-layer feedforward networks, the number of hidden neurons has to be established, since the input nodes and output neurons are defined according to the quantity of input variables and to the desired network response, respectively. This choice should be according to the parsimonious principle (Medeiros, 2006), i.e. must follow a compromise between minimal complexity (few neurons) and maximum efficiency, otherwise the network generalization may be poor, especially for small datasets (Sahiner, 2008).

Another factor that may also jeopardize network generalization is the overtraining, which must be avoided through an appropriate training control mechanism control. A common adopted procedure is the early stop (Haykin, 2008), which consists on interrupting the training when the generalization error starts to increase. This procedure demands the construction of two disjoint sets: training and test, the first used during network learning phase and the last to evaluate generalization error. In applications with statistical restrictions, as the TB diagnosis modeling, training and test sets must be carefully chosen; otherwise learning may not occur properly. An inappropriate split may result in poor problem representation for training or non-realistic evaluation of network generalization, both prejudicial to model performance.

3.2 Self-organized ART-2 inspired network

This neural network explores a competitive learning algorithm which identifies groups of events that share similar statistical characteristics (Vassali, 2002). Each neuron responds to a one identified group and defines a hypersphere in the input data space. The algorithm automatically determines neurons number and network connections needed to enclosure the data. Groups are described in terms of their center coordinates and radius, the last commonly referred as vigilance radius. Typically, all neurons share a same vigilance radius. In figure 2, clusters identified for arbitrary data by ART-2 inspired network are illustrated.

During network learning process, events should be presented to the network in a random order. Given an input event, the Euclidean distance from this event to the already identified group centers is determined. If this distance is lower than the vigilance radius, it means the event is inside at least one neuron coverage space. In this case, the neuron which shows lower distance (higher similarity) is declared the winner and has its center coordinates adjusted itself. If the event does not belong to any group, a new neuron (group) is created having the own event as its center. This process is stopped when: (i) no more neurons are created during training process or (ii) the center coordinates vary below a threshold between two consecutive iterations.

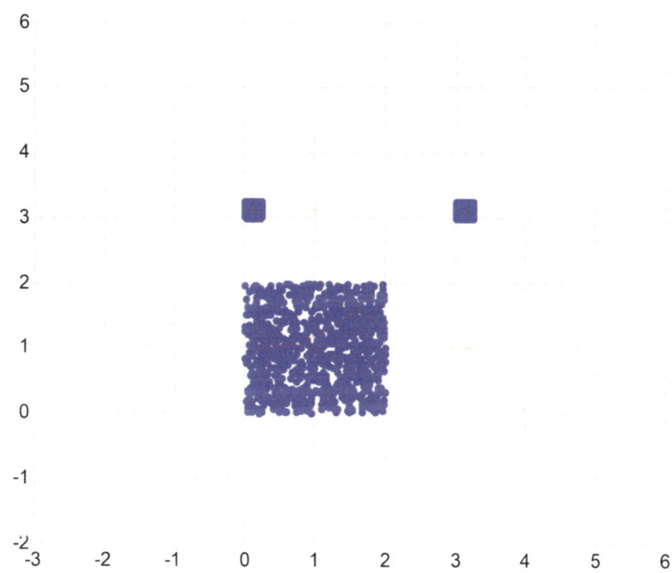

Fig. 2. Data clusters identified by ART-2 inspired network.

3.3 Pilot neural network models

Our feasibility studies to produce and apply neural models in supporting TB diagnosis started considering patients from the Clementino Fraga Filho University Hospital. In order to determine the set of symptoms and characteristics that would indicate the disease, one hundred and thirty-six patients agreed to participate. They were referred to the University Hospital from March, 2001 to September, 2002, with clinical-radiological suspicion of SNPT. The input data set for the neural networks model corresponds to information from clinical interview integrated to demographic and risk factors typically associated with tuberculosis diagnosis. All patients that took part in our research project were under suspicion of active pulmonary tuberculosis, presenting smear negative results. Forty three per cent of these patients actually showed to have active TB. Initially, twenty-six clinical variables were considered: age, coughs, spit, sweat, fever, weight loss, chest pain, shiver, dyspnea, diabetes, alcoholism, and others. Later, the data set was described with twelve and eight clinical variables, selected by experts on tuberculosis research.

The dichotomy variables were codified as -1 and 1, representing the absence and presence of a symptom, respectively. Qualitative variables with three categories were implemented as -1 (lack of an indication), 1 (presence of the symptom) and 0 (ignored). Hyperbolic tangent was used as the activation function of all neurons from both hidden and output layers. All networks were trained using RPROP algorithm (Riedmiller, 1993) and the mean square error (MSE) between target vectors and network outputs was used as the objective function (Haykin, 2008). Networks having from 1 to 15 hidden neurons were produced. Due to local minima problem (Haykin, 2008), each network was trained using fifty different initialization parameters, being selected the training which showed high accuracy. Early stop was used as the learning mechanism control. Two approaches were considered to define the training and test sets used in early stop procedure. The first considered random splits of data. The second explored the partition of data on three clusters identified through the ART-2 inspired network. Seventy-five percent of the events belonging to each identified group formed the training set as the twenty-five remaining ones the test set.

The performance evaluation of the trained networks was based on the correct classification rate (accuracy over all patients), sensitivity and specificity. The best performance was obtained by the model having fifteen neurons and twelve variables (age, cough, fever, hemoptysis, anorexic, loss of weight, AIDS, night sweat, dyspnea, smokes actually, extra-pulmonary TB and ward hospital admission), which achieved 100% of sensitivity and 80% of specificity. This model was based on training and test sets selected by the clustering procedure. For the risk group identification, the vigilance radius of ART-2 inspired network was adjusted to produce three clusters. These groups were ranked in low, medium and high risk according their TB prevalence. The most frequent symptoms verified for each risk group were validated by TB experts.

4. The NeuralTB system

The NeuralTB, a decision support system for smear negative pulmonary tuberculosis, could be used by health care workers to sustain the diagnosis of SNPT under routine conditions in the hospitals and primary health care units. The purpose of using the system is not to replace physicians or other heath care workers, but to support them in decision taking. The proposed model suggests that mathematical modeling for classifying SNPT cases could be a useful tool for optimizing the utilization of expensive tests and to avoid costs of unnecessary anti-PT treatment, as may also permit an earlier diagnosis. The diagnosis corresponds to an ongoing process that requires accurate investigation and, therefore, the system output should be analyzed together with clinical interviewing, physical examination, and evaluation of laboratory results. One main concern for system design was to be suitable for areas of limited resources. Therefore, the requirements of low cost, easy access, and user-friendliness were considered. Since the disease in question is geographically spread among different places, the system is implemented using the Web technology, guaranteeing its access. To places where the Internet is not available, the system can be easily installed in a portable computer. NeuralTB makes use of open source software, which makes the proposed system free of licensing costs, which comes to an inexpensive tool to support the identification of the various forms of TB and to be employed in different health services.

4.1 Main goals

The first step to develop the system to support the diagnosis of SNPT was to define its requirements. The NeuralTB system operates over symptoms and social characteristics of patients, which are used to feed the neural network model. SNPT specialists defined a set of symptoms and characteristics that would be presented in the first anamnesis procedure to be useful in a triage sector, usually the nurse attendant. The system also supports the registration of clinical procedures and laboratory exams to help physicians to start or not the anti-TB treatment and to make regimen changes furthermore, when indicated. The objective is to support the whole treatment from the arrival of a patient supposed to have TB, exams, drugs monitoring, till the medical discharge.

Electronic engineers designed, implemented, and trained neural networks, so that the system indicates the probability that a patient have SNPT or not and the risk group (low, medium or high) that this patient would belong to. The neural models were developed using data from patients with different TB modalities and associated co-morbidities. Software experts specified and developed the Web system to register the input information, execute the neural network processing, store the result, monitor the patients' data, and manage data files. The whole process is integrated with features that analyze, standardize, associate, clean and extract information according to data quality criteria: accuracy, completeness, updating, interpretability, security, access, privacy, consistency, etc. Professionals from the medical area supported the whole development process of the system design, validating each step to guarantee that the resulting system would achieve the predefined goals.

Another important requirement was to allow the use of the system in wireless devices. The software could be easily installed in a netbook allowing mobility and patient's treatment independently of his/her location. This approach is extremely useful to avoid treatment dropout since health agents may reach a patient at his/her residence and guarantee the continuation of the therapy. The whole system development was based on open source concepts, avoiding costs on acquiring software during either the implementation phase or implanting, using, and maintaining the product. The web system is installed in a central server that is accessed through the Internet. Nevertheless, in case a hospital or health care unit does not have Internet access, the computer can be connected to the main server through the 3rd generation of standards for mobile telecommunications services (3G). At last, in case the location does not have a good quality of mobile network coverage, the system can be installed in a local server. The interface was designed to be intuitive and user friendly, as normal site in the Web, which would prevent exhaustive training or any kind of assistance. To use the system, the only requirement for the end-users is a browser that usually is provided together with the operational system of the computer. The system is platform independent, it means that it does not require specific technological issues.

The central database manages the data of each hospital or health care separately. A location will access only the information that comes from itself and all other records are protected. For overall system management, fast and efficient retrieval mechanisms are provided for an administrator who will have full data access. The central system allows concurrent access of several locations. The data stored are certificated through intelligent computing methods in order to confirm certain characteristics of the information and avoid that distortions are recorded. The database design also considered the use of data profiling, i.e., analytical techniques used to examine existing data for completeness and accuracy. Data profiling is the first step towards data quality and would benefit the investigation of the disease, supporting the definition of policies to control tuberculosis.

4.2 Hardware and software requirements

The NeuralTB Web System runs over the Apache HTTP Server for both UNIX and Windows operating systems. The system provides a shell executable of setup programs that automatically install a directory structure and respective files in the computer of the health care unit or hospital. The minimum hardware requirements are: PC computers with a USB driver for file transfer (in case of local version) or an Internet connection, and having 128 MB, or preferentially, 256 MB RAM.

The system operations were implemented as CGI (Common Gateway Interface) programs, using the C language. The Javascript language is used to write functions that are embedded in or included from HTML pages and interact with the Document Object Model (DOM) of the page to perform tasks not possible in HTML alone. The Cascading Style Sheets (CSS) language is used to style the web pages written in HTML and format the XML documents. In order to draw the risk group representation, the GD graphics library was used. GD is an open source code library for the dynamic creation of images, allowing programmers to easily generate PNG, JPEG, GIF (among other images formats) from many different programming languages.

The central repository was implemented using MySQL, an open source relational database management system (RDBMS) that uses Structured Query Language (SQL). The choice of these technologies also facilitates the portability of the system to diverse platforms.

4.3 The web forms

The Web system forms allow users to enter data that are sent to the main server for processing and storage. Electronic forms facilitate not only the validation of input data but also the information access through the search of different fields of a document. It is also easy to make backups of the entire set of records and it does not spoil as easy as a paper form.

The web forms were implemented according to the paper form format and to the order of the questions, which minimizes the impact of introducing a new technology in the hospital or health care units. Users fill out the forms using checkboxes, radio buttons or text fields. Therefore, the web forms offer several advantages when compared to paper forms. They provide guidance, it means, the interface presents all possible choices and the user has just to select one. As an example, the marital status, the sex, the state where the patient lives, among other questions. Another type of guidance refers to conditional queries, for example, the date of a previous TB treatment will be asked to the patient only if the previous answer to the question "previous TB treatment" is yes.

Another benefit of electronic forms is that they avoid submitting wrong data. Invalid entries are not allowed and an alert immediately pops up to notify the user that is filling the form. As an example, the user cannot insert a date where the month is greater than 12 or type letters of the alphabet to inform a zip code. Therefore, the system avoids typing errors. The forms were implemented to avoid submitting it if any question is not answered. The system automatically calculates one field according to the values of previous ones. As an example, the body mass index is determined after providing the weight and the height of the patient.

Together with the patient's data, the system records the date of the triage and name of the healthcare assistant or nurse that filled out the form. The information is retrieved from the login of the Web system and from the operating system. In case the patient does not know the answer of a question, there is an option to inform that this information is ignored. After saving the form, any further modification is completed together with additional information, such as the name of the user that modified the data, the reason for the change, the date when the alteration was performed and the previous value.

Figure 3 illustrates the anamnesis web form, where the patients' data are inserted. The forms were implemented to support the insertion of data related to the anamnesis interview, medical consultation, medical monitoring, exams and cost (that is split into two forms). The system informs in case a questionnaire was not properly filled out. The red color indicates that the form is complete while the black color points out forms that should be concluded.

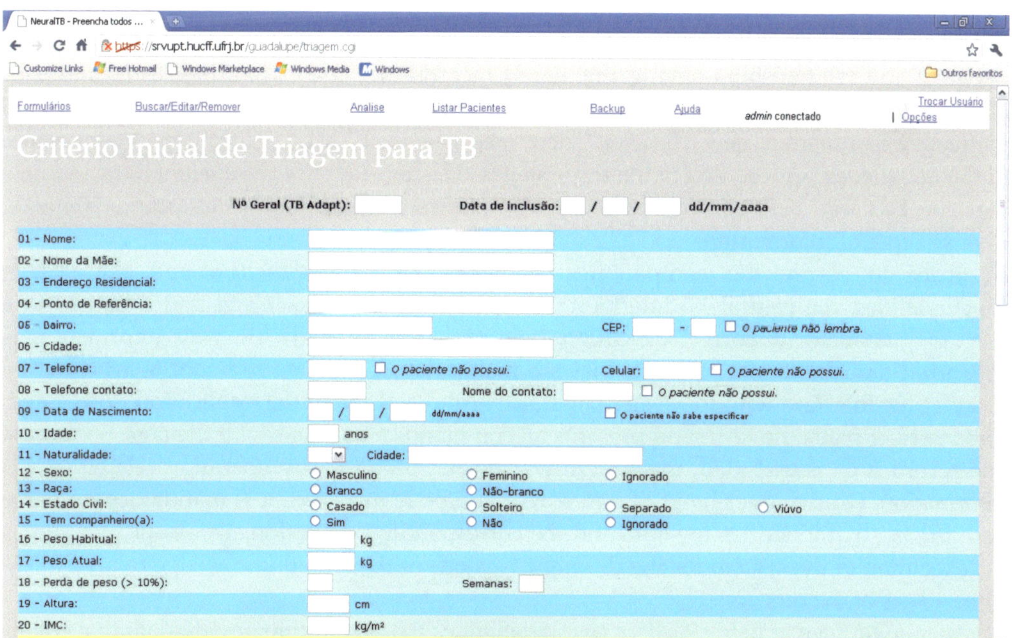

Fig. 3. Anamnesis web form. Fields are in Portuguese.

The system also provides several functions, such as, the search for a specific patient and the editing of patient data. The removal of a patient, for security reasons, corresponds to the absence of the patient data in the list but all the data continues to be stored in the database. The function analysis provides the percentage of a certain symptom or characteristic that can be combined by logical operators. It is also possible to list the name of all patients and then access the corresponding data. The user can export all records to an external program that would help building statistical graphics and can make a local backup. At last, the system provides a help that presents some explanation about how to fill out the forms.

4.4 Representing and assuring the data

Each item presented in the input data form is associated with the knowledge required to perform the anamnesis interview. Even facilitating the patients' data access, their analyses and interpretation is a laborious task and, in addition, records may contain redundant or incomplete information. Therefore, the plan was to represent the knowledge, patients' data, and other related details in a proper way. The data representation format is an important aspect that was considered to efficiently manage the whole information. Markup languages, as XML, can be used to describe knowledge structures and to support institutional memory development (Rabarijaona, 2000, Cook, 2000). XML may provide a standard structure to communicate and interchange data and knowledge among diverse systems. The language allows the creation of multiple visions of the same item and also provides an easy mechanism to capture, store, present and recover information. Considering these benefits, a XML-based approach was developed to describe the different types of knowledge and information manipulated during the whole process of the SNPT diagnosis.

There are three stages where data had to be properly represented: during the anamnesis interview, for describing the patient data, and to extract statistical information within research activities. TB specialists warned that risk factors, the questions made to the patients, and relationships among the stored records may vary according to locations or other factors, such as multidrug resistance (MDR), which is one of the main causes of ineffective treatment of new TB cases. Therefore, the use of XML facilitates the maintenance of the knowledge represented in the three stages. The tags identify the current data and new tags can be easily defined. The language also allows the definition of associations among diverse types of information.

In order to assure the compatibility between the data structure and the system functionalities, the Neural-TB interface and operations were conceived and designed in a way to guarantee its correct execution independently on both the way information is organized and the kind of records that are manipulated. This requirement is achieved by creating the interface with the system operations in the moment the application is executed. The interface reads the XML and presents all commands associated with the tags. So, in case one record type is excluded, the system will do not perform any operation related to this information. On the other hand, if a new record type is included, it is mandatory to define both the tag that identifies the data and the corresponding operation. This approach allows the execution of the system for the different versions of the stored knowledge related to the three stages of the process.

Another advantage of using XML is that it facilitates the integration among data that comes from different health care units and hospitals. Markup languages make easy the combination of heterogeneous records. The use of XML also allows uniform systems interoperability and offers efficient mechanisms for information recovery. The interface between the knowledge and the neural networks model is also defined through a XML file. This archive describes the name of the application, the parameters used by the neural network, and the output. This approach facilitates when users want to execute a different neural network system or update the network parameters.

Data Quality refers to the adequacy of information to the needs, it means, the data have to be correct, do not duplicated, complete, reliable, consistent, standardized, updated, accessible, understandable to all category of users, such as patients, nurses, physicians, researches, etc. Increasing the quality of the data, the quality of the results produced by all processes that depends on this data is also enhanced.

The data quality monitoring is performed online to avoid error propagation and offline to improve the analysis of the data quality. The database is certified since all data is validated and corrected. This study can also come out with the measurement of the data quality, determining the magnitude of distortions and, therefore, identifying faults in the process that can be later corrected.

4.5 The pilot system

In order to demonstrate the feasibility of the proposal, a pilot system was designed. The main objective was to verify whether all requirements were accomplished and all necessities mapped. The chosen place was the Augusto Amaral Peixoto Policlinic, situated in Guadalupe neighborhood, Rio de Janeiro City, because the acquisition of patients' data had already started there using paper forms. The connection to the Internet in that site has a firewall that would prevent any link to the main server. In addition, the location does not have a good quality of mobile network coverage. In this case, our group had to install a proper server in the Policlinic. There, one room is dedicated to the triage and the second room is used to fill out the exam results and to the medical monitoring. A third room is used to the anamnesis interview. Since there were not other rooms available, the cost-effectiveness form could be filled out through a mobile device, such as a personal digital assistant (PDA), in any place of the Policlinic.

The infrastructure was organized to respect this arrangement. Three low-cost PCs with Windows operating system were installed in the three rooms. There was no need to install a special configuration since the only software requirement is the availability of a browser. The local server has a Linux operating system and a wireless network was established to provide connection to the PDA. Electrical secure systems were settled down there. Electric grounds were installed in each plug. High autonomy uninterruptible power source (UPS) were plugged to each computer where in case of lack of energy, the user's computer would run still one hour and the server computer would run still 6 hours. In order to guarantee that no data is lost, the server has redundant hard disk and power supply. The chosen operating system is Ubuntu since it is free, fast and secure. The access to the server is restricted to the administrators and protected with passwords. In case of faults, a spare PC, mouse, computer monitor, keyboard were available. The group made a set of studies to identify the robustness of the proposal and, consequently, the probability of failure of the architecture. Table 1 summarizes the performed analysis.

One copy of the system was installed in the local server while another copy was placed in the main server to allow the input of patient data previously registered in paper. For security reasons, the paper forms could not leave the Policlinic in order to avoid lost of information. So, all paper forms were digitalized and a printed copy was sent to the typist. Another aspect that our team noticed was the fact that since the paper form had no guidance and no automatic error detection during the filling out procedure, the system version placed in the main server had to be modified in order to accept empty or not completely filled fields. Data conflicts had to be marked and later discussed with the physicians. The next step corresponds to the data validation by nursery technicians, who compared the original paper forms with the digital ones. A system to monitor the whole process of registering previously acquired data was also implemented. Therefore, one could check whether a paper form was digitalized, typed into the system and, finally, validated, guaranteeing the management of the information and its quality.

Component	Failure probability in the first year (%)	Recovery action	Recovery estimated time
PC (server)	0.017	Maintenance	2 days
PC (user)	16.0	Spare PC	30 minutes
Keyboard, mouse, monitor	34.35	Spare piece	15 minutes

Table 1. Failure probability, recovery action and recovery estimated time.

An additional feature had to be implemented since some data acquired during the medical monitoring was recorded into spreadsheet and data analysis proprietary software. The import functionality allowed the integration of data placed outside the system with the central database. The association is done using the identification number, patient's name and date of the interview.

Our group developed an automatic backup system to avoid data loss. All data is periodically sent to another server placed in the University Hospital and to external devices. Another web system gathers information of all backup files and monitors the number of patients and status of each form.

In order to support the activities in the health care unit, a control management system was also developed. It controls the versions of the forms, the data status and the access to the web system. Each time a new version of a form is created, the control system saves the previous version that are retrieved each time the user access data that was acquired through the earlier form. It is also necessary to keep track of the data origin, whether it was inserted directly to the NeuralTB system in a specific form or the information was written in paper and afterwards included in the system by the typist. In case of inconsistencies, a user can review the paper to check whether it was a typing mistake. Moreover, all data that was previously written in paper have to be verified after its insertion in the system. Without this validation, the data cannot be used for analysis. Therefore, the control system also administrates the two project repositories: one that contains data from the health care unit and other which data was entered by the typist.

The system access control is based on the users groups and their privileges, the system functionalities and the data itself. Within the system, there are three categories of users: administrator, physician and attendant. Administrators can insert new users, modify users attributes and perform several actions related to the data files and system installation. Attendants may include a patient, symptoms, and edit registered data. Physicians is the user category that have all rights related to the patient's data and are the only ones that can see the artificial neural networks output, it means, whether the patient has SNPT or not and the risk group that the patient belongs.

4.6 System scalability

The pilot system demonstrated that each place can have its own requirements and the automation of routine cannot bring difficulties to the professionals who work in the hospital and health care units. Our group learned that is more efficient to adapt the software to each place than require each location to adapt to the system. So, in order to respect this requirement, an environment was build where different forms are defined and they can be combined to deliver a specific system for a certain hospital or health care unit. In this second part of the development, forms were implemented with Python language, an interpreted, interactive, object-oriented and extensible programming language. In order to merge the forms, our group used an open source web application framework, which follows the model-view-controller architectural pattern, thus facilitating the creation of database-driven web systems. The patient's data of each place is organized in local databases that use SQLite relational database management system. The source code for SQLite is in the public domain and implements most of the SQL standard.

Using 3G technology, it was not necessary to build a data transmission network among hospitals and health care units. Laboratories can connect to the system in order to insert the results of the exams, guaranteeing a high connectivity among different locations and the central database.

5. Impacts

The main objectives of the NeuralTB system are to increase the precision of an early TB diagnostic and to introduce a wireless triage associated with the neural networks. Therefore, this model avoids that patients are obliged to go to health care units, reducing queues and medical care delays. The benefits are extended to those patients who are unable to walk or have no resources to pay the transport. This technology will bring a cost-effective hospitalization approach since just patients with a high TB risk are placed in the respiratory isolation rooms or emergency health care units, resulting into a more efficient use of the government resources. So, for both patient and health care units, the proposal will bring a significant reduction of TB diagnosis and treatment costs. The research group also looks forward to enhance the TB control by reducing the number of new cases, with direct benefits to the whole population.

6. Conclusions

More than 4,000 patient forms are already registered in the main database. From this amount of records, 1,100 new patients were inserted directly through the system in the Policlinic of Guadalupe with the advantage that the system validates input data and alerts possible mistakes during the form filling process. Data quality techniques avoided recurrent problems during input data, such as duplicated records, typing errors, lack of information, non-standardized or not validated registers, incoherence data, inconsistencies, etc. In addition, concerning information previously acquired, the data quality module assures the correctness and certification of the central database.

The repository gathers patient information from diverse regions and provides functionalities to easily handle a huge amount of data. The database contents can be migrated to other proprietary programs that provide specific features to analyze the data. Therefore, TB research groups can make use of the main database. Information privacy and secure data access are guaranteed by the system that encompasses functions to manage users and their permissions. Consequently, the system can keep track of modifications and register when and who carried out any data adjustment.

The use of markup language facilitates changes in the digital forms, which contributes to the continuously enhancement of not only the forms but also the whole process. Laboratories can connect to the system to directly insert exam results in the system. The complete patient treatment can be monitored wherever and the mobility allows home care by transmitting the data to the central repository. The system can incorporate specificities according to certain locations or contexts. The use of open source code assures the low cost of the software, which facilitates its installation and use in different environments. As a result, the solution corresponds to an economical feasible diagnosis method suitable to face the increasing number of TB cases

The decision support system can be considered as another element that helps physicians on the smear negative pulmonary tuberculosis diagnosis. The neural network model with fifteen neurons and twelve variables (age, cough, fever, hemoptysis, anorexic, loss of weight, AIDS, night sweat, dyspnea, smokes actually, extra-pulmonary TB and ward hospital admission) achieved 100% of sensitivity and 80% of specificity.

To incorporate this diagnostic test in the public systems, further investigation using the IAF proposed by Mann et al (2010) could be carried out in order to present important evidence on the costs and other resources required for the decision support system in the SNPT diagnosis implementation and optimized scale-up, along with the effects on patients and their clinical management, and TB transmission patterns in a variety of epidemiological settings. Additionally, through the policy transfer analysis, evidence about the processes that facilitates innovation uptake and policy transfer should be provided.

7. References

Bishop, C. M. (2007). *Pattern Recognition and Machine Learning,* Springer, ISBN 978-0387310732, New York, USA.

Castelo A., Kritski A.L., Werneck A., Lemos A.C., Ruffino Netto A., et al. (2004). Diretrizes Brasileiras para Tuberculose. *Jornal Brasileiro de Pneumologia,* Vol.30, suppl.1, (June 2004), pp. 1-86, ISSN1806-3713

El-Solh, A.A., Hsiao, C.-B., Goodnough, S., Serghani, J., Grant, B.J.B. (1999). Predicting Active Pulmonary Tuberculosis using an Artificial Neural Network. *Chest,* Vol.116, No.4, pp.968–973, ISSN: 0012-3692

Guillerm, M. (October 2006). Tuberculosis Diagnosis and Drug Sensitivity Testing: an Overview of the Current Diagnostics Pipeline. Campaign for Access to Essential Medicines. MSF, Paris.

Hastie T., Tibshirani R., Friedman J. (2009). *The Elements of Statistical Learning: Data Mining, Inference and Prediction,* Springer, ISBN 978-0387952840, New York, USA.

Haykin S. (2008). *Neural Networks and Learning Machines*, Prentice Hall, ISBN 978-0131471399, New Jersey, USA.

Mann G, Squire S. B., Bissell K., Elisee v P., Du Toit E., Hesseling A., et al. (2010). Beyond accuracy: creating a comprehensive evidence base for TB diagnostic tools. *Int J Tuberc Lung Dis*, Vol.14, No.12, pp.1518–1524, ISSN 1027-3719.

Marais B. J., Raviglione M. C., Donald P.R., Harries A.D., Kritski A.L., et al. (2010). Scale-up of services and research priorities for diagnosis, management, and control of tuberculosis: a call to action. *The Lancet*, Vol. 375, No.9732, pp. 2179 - 2191, Published Online, DOI:10.1016/S0140-6736(10)60554-5

Medeiros M. C., Terävirta T., Rech G. (2006). Building Neural Network Models for Time Series: A Statistical Approach, *Journal of Forecasting*, Vol.25, No.1, pp.49-75, ISSN: 0277-6693.

Mello F. C., Bastos L. G., Soares S. L., Rezende V. M., Conde M.B., Chaisson R.E., Kritski A. L., Ruffino-Netto A., Werneck G. L. (2006). Predicting Smear Negative Pulmonary Tuberculosis with Classification Trees and Logistic Regression: a cross-sectional Study. *BMC Public Health*, Vo.6, No.43, Published Online 2006, DOI:10.1186/1471-2458-6-43

Pai M., Minion J., Steingart K., Ramsay A. (2010). New and improved tuberculosis diagnostics: evidence, policy, practice, and impact. *Curr Opin Pulm Med.*, Vol.16, No.3, pp.271-284, ISSN 1070-5287.

Perkins M. D., Kritski A. L. (2002). Perspectives. Diagnostic Testing in the Control of Tuberculosis. *Bulletin of the WHO*, Vol.80, No.6, pp.512-513. ISSN 0042-9686

Cook J. (2000). XML Sets Stage for Efficient Knowledge Management, *IT professional*, Vol.2, No.3, pp.55-57, ISSN: 1520-9202

Rabarijaona A., Dieng R., Olivier C., Quaddari R. (2000). Building and Searching an XML-Based Corporate Memory, *IEEE Intelligent Systems*, Vol.15, No.3 pp.56-63. ISSN 0884-8173

Riedmiller M., Braun H. (1993). A Direct Adaptive Method for Faster Backpropagation Learning: the RPROP Algorithm, *Proceedings of the IEEE Conference on Neural Networks*, pp.586-591, ISBN 0-7803-0999-5, San Francisco, California, USA, 28 March 28 - April 01, 1993

Sahiner B., Chan H.-P., Hadjiiski L. (2008). Classifier performance estimation under the constraint of a finite sample size: Resampling schemes applied to neural network classifiers, *Neural Networks*, Vol.21, No2-3, pp.476-483, ISSN 0893-6080

Theodoridis S., Koutroumbas K. (2008). *Pattern Recognition*, Academic Press, ISBN 978-0126858754, Amsterdam, Netherlands

van Kampen S. C., Ramsay A. R., Anthony R. M., Klatser P.R. (2010). Retooling national TB control programmes (NTPs) with new diagnostics: the NTP perspective. *PLoS One*. Vol.5, No.7, p.e11649, ISSN 1932-6203

Vassali M.R., Seixas J.M., Calôba L.P. (2002). A Neural Particle Discriminator based on a Modified ART Architecture, *Proceedings of the IEEE International Symposium on Circuits and Systems*, Vol.II, pp.121-124, ISBN 0-7803-7448-7, Phoenix-Scottsdale, Arizona, USA.

WHO - World Health Organization. (2009). *Global tuberculosis control: a short update to the 2009 report*. WHO/HTM/TB/2009.426. ISBN 978 92 4 159886, Geneva.

Part 4

Applications for Medical Procedures

9

Temporal Knowledge Generation for Medical Procedures

Aida Kamišalić[1], David Riaño[2] and TatjanaWelzer[1]
[1]University of Maribor
[2]Rovira i Virgili University
[1]Slovenia
[2]Spain

1. Introduction

Decision support systems (DSSs) in medicine are designed to aid medical professionals on making clinical decisions about prevention, diagnosis and corresponding treatment. When DSSs are applied to medical procedures, two sorts of predictions are possible: procedural (i.e. indications on what to do), and temporal (i.e. indications on what are the time restrictions). Clinical Practice Guidelines (CPGs) are statements that assist physicians making appropriate medical decisions during patient encounters. They are a set of assertions used to manage patients with a particular disease to improve quality of care, decrease unjustified practice variations and save costs. Clinical algorithms (CAs) obtained from CPGs are introduced to make the procedural knowledge explicit and formal. It is important to enable the latest clinical knowledge to be accessible and usable at the point of care, and therefore make significant contributions to safety and quality in medicine. Medical knowledge is used to assist patients suffering from one or several diseases. CAs could be explicitly given, or obtained with a knowledge management mechanisms. Among these mechanisms, there are some that aim at generating CAs from existing patients' data for a particular disease. However, either explicitly given or generated CAs are atemporal, which means that there is no an explicit time labelling of the elements in the CA. Time plays a major role in medicine and therefore also in medical information systems. It is an important concept of the real world, which needs to be managed in different ways (events occur at some time points, facts hold during time periods, temporal relationships exist between facts and events) (Combi et al., 2010). If we want to overcome the gap of atemporal CAs it is necessary to define a time dimension and make also temporal knowledge (the indications on what are the time restrictions) explicit and formal. It has been proved that obtaining explicit temporal knowledge from physicians is often a difficult and time-consuming task regardless of the knowledge engineering mechanisms or tools employed to simplify the process. As data saved in hospital databases are primarily time dependent, they can be used to obtain temporal constraints to define the time dimension of CAs. We have propose generation of temporal constraints considering patients' data of a particular disease for atemporal CAs. We have defined two types of temporal constraints: macro-temporality and micro-temporality. Macro-temporality is defined as a constraint $[t_{min}, t_{max}]$ on the time required to cross a particular edge of a CA, where t_{min} and t_{max} are the lower and the upper

bounds of the time-lag, respectively (Kamišalić et al., 2007). Macro-temporality denotes time delays which have to be fulfilled before the treatment of the patient proceeds. For example, [1*d*, 4*d*] assigned to the edge between two actions, would mean that after applying the first action the treatment should wait a minimum of one day and a maximum of four days before proceeding with the next action (Kamišalić et al., 2007). The concept of micro-temporality is defined as a constraint $[s_t, e_t, f_t]$ on the start time s_t, the end time e_t, and the frequency of occurrence f_t of some medical action (Kamišalić et al., 2007). For example, the term 'prehypertension' can be considered as a state term, where [1*w*, 3*d*, 6*h*] constraint means that 'prehypertension' was part of the patient condition since one week ago (1*w*), till three days ago (3*d*), and it was observed every six hours (6*h*). In the case of action term, micro-temporality means that the action must start after time st, that should last till et, and that the application of the action has a frequency of ft (for example, take beta-blocker agent for two weeks every six hours $[-, 2w, 6h]$).
There are several formalisms which can be used to represent CAs. Some of them are very complete from a medical point of view and therefore difficult to manage by untrained physicians (e.g. Asbru (Seyfang et al., 2002) or EON (Musen et al., 1996)), some are oriented to the description of medical activities as processes rather than as an explicit representation of the treatment as a procedure (e.g. Asbru), and some others are limited in the representation of time constraints (e.g. PROforma (Fox et al., 1998)). Whenever CAs comprise the concept of state as a description of a medical situation, they can be represented with State Transition Diagrams (STD's) (see Fig. 1) where each possible individual transition between two states is represented. As the levels of simplicity, intuitiveness, and time representation of the SDA* formalism (Riaño, 2007) (see Fig. 2) were close to our requirements, this one has been the chosen formalism for representing macro- (Kamišalić et al., 2007) and micro-temporalities (Kamišalić et al., 2009) in CAs. We have also used Timed-transition diagrams (TTD's) (see Fig. 4, Fig. 5, Fig. 6) as representation formalism for macro-temporality constraints (Kamišalić et al., 2008).
The rest of the chapter is divided into 4 main sections. Section 2 provides an overview and examples of used representation formalisms - SDA*s and TTDs. They are used for representation of time dimension in CAs. The process of generation of macro-temporalities from clinical data is described in the section 3. Section 4 describes a methodology for generation of micro-temporalities. Finaly, section 5 gathers some conclusions.

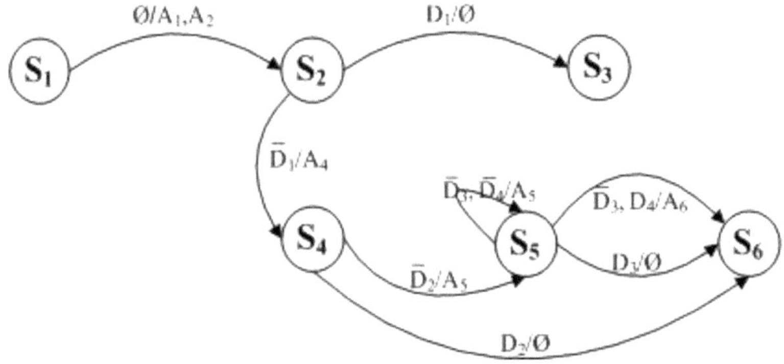

Fig. 1. Clinical algorithm for Hypertension in STD representation

2. Representation formalisms

As we have mentioned above, there are different formalisms which can be used to represent CAs. STDs can be used for representation of timeless CAs. As our goal is to introduce temporal constraints to CAs, the representation formalism have to permit representation of temporal restrictions for CAs. TTDs are used to represent CAs with generated macro-temporality constraints. These diagrams permit the integration of several sequences in a single structure, each sequence representing the individual treatment of one patient (Kamišalić et al., 2008). (Sections 3 and 4 introduce processes of macro- and micro-temporality generation, respectively.) SDA* formalism is not convenient for representation of individual sequences. It can be used for representation of macro- and micro-temporality restrictions, but not for representation of all possible transitions from one to another state. When it is important to represent all possible transitions (sequences) from which generation of macro-temporality restriction is done, TTDs are used for CAs representation. Finally, obtained macro-temporality constraints as well as micro-temporality constraints can be introduced to SDA* diagrams as it results more simple and intuitive for interpretation. To represent time dimension in CAs we are using TTD's and SDA* formalism.

2.1 SDA* formalism

SDA stands for state-decision-action notation and it is used to represent CAs as SDA* diagrams, where each diagram is a directed graph that contains state, decision and action nodes (see Fig. 2). Each state node contains the set of terms which represent the signs and symptoms of a particular patient at the moment of making observations. In the diagram, state nodes are indicated as circles, which bring the feasible patient medical conditions. Decision nodes provide criteria to derive the treatment in one or other direction according to the patient's features and current condition. These branching points are represented as diamonds that deploy all the alternative clinical treatments at this point, each one attached to a condition that the patient must fully satisfy in order to follow this treatment. Action nodes represent the activities which should be taken as a result of an earlier made decision. It is represented as a square, which gives recommendations about medical orders considering medication and clinical procedures.

For each disease D, $T_D = \{t_1, t_2, , t_n\}$ represents a set of terms related to D. These terms can be state, decision or action terms depending on whether they are able to be involved in the description of a SDA* state, decision or action, respectively. $SV \subset T_D$ is the set of state terms that are used to determine the condition of a patient considering some disease. $DV \subset T_D$ is the set of decision terms that can be used to derive the treatment to some or some other medical actions. $AV \subset T_D$ is the set of action terms representing the individual medical actions a physician may prescribe in the treatment of the disease the SDA* diagram represents. In a SDA* diagram the meaning of node connectors can vary according to the sort of nodes the connectors have as starting and ending elements. So, C_{SS}, C_{SD}, and C_{SA} are the names given to connectors going from a state node to a state node, to a decision node or to an action node, respectively; C_{DS}, C_{DD}, and C_{DA} are the names of the nodes going from decision nodes to other nodes, and C_{AS}, C_{AD}, C_{AA} the names of the connectors that start at an action node.

Macro-temporality constraints in the form of $[t_{\min}, t_{\max}]$ intervals affect to some of the above sort of connectors: C_{SS}, C_{AS}, C_{AD}, and C_{AA}; but not to the rest, for which they are defined as the constant [0, 0] (i.e. lack of delay or instantaneous transition).

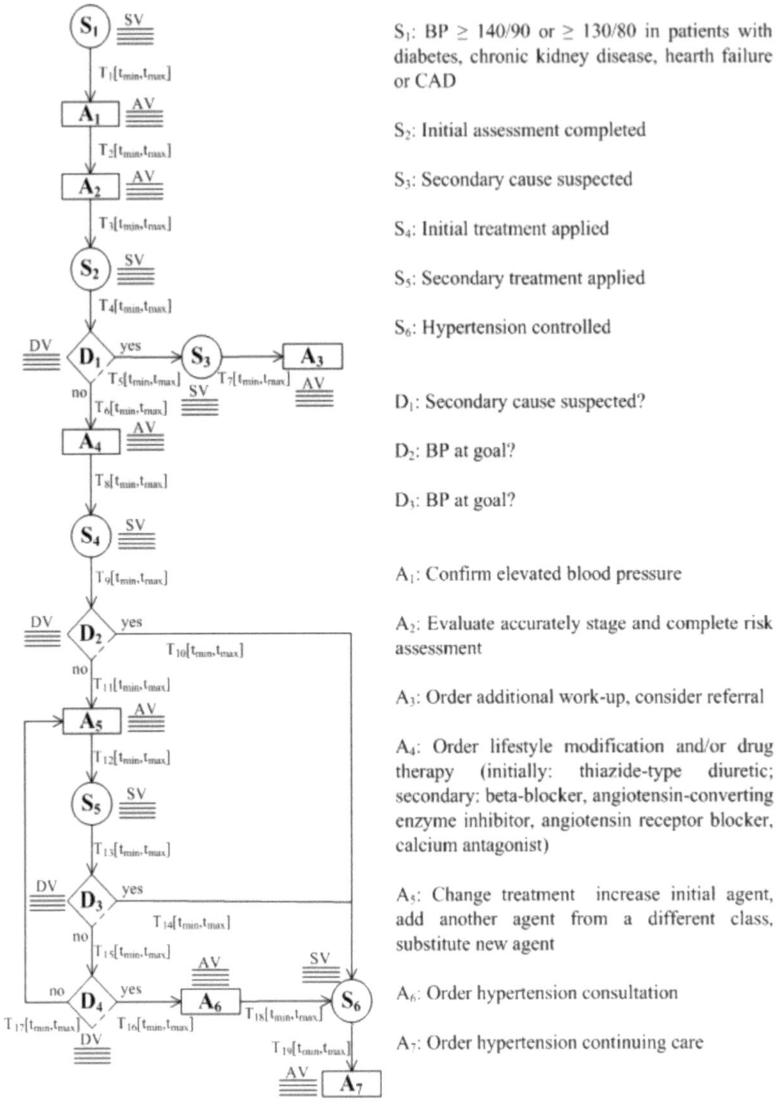

Fig. 2. Clinical algorithm for Hypertension in SDA* representation

In C_{SS} connectors, macro-temporality is obtained from the times between consecutive encounters in which the patient has not received any treatment as a consequence of the first encounter. In C_{AS} connectors, macro-temporality is calculated from the times between consecutive encounters in which, during the first encounter the physician ordered the actions A, and in the second encounter the patient had evolved to state S. Finally in C_{AD} and C_{AA} connectors, macro-temporality is a combination of the times between consecutive encounters in which a treatment was proposed during the first visit and the state of the patient in the second visit is implicit, i.e. lacking of medical interest. The difference in the macro-temporalities of C_{AD} and C_{AA} connectors is in the fact that the first one is applied when not all the patients in encounters with the same implicit state receive the same state-caused treatment. On the contrary, if all the patients that show sequences of state transitions in which the same implicit state (i.e. the state description of the patient during the encounter) is always followed by the same state-caused treatments, then a decision node will not be needed in the SDA* diagram that will connect two consecutive action nodes.

Micro-temporality is assigned to the terms in T_D and it affects states, actions and decisions. Terms that represent the signs and symptoms of a particular patient at the moment of making an observation are called state terms. Decision terms in a CA are building decision criteria which lead the treatment in a specific direction considering the patient's current signs and symptoms, while action terms represent medical activities which should be performed as a result of an earlier analysis of the medical context (e.g., patient condition or hospital resources). Micro-temporality constraints is represented as a triplet $[s_t, e_t, f_t]$ on the term $t \in T_D$; where s_t stands for the start time of t, e_t for the ending time, and f_t for the frequency. A term is atemporal if [-,-,-] micro-temporality is assigned, as presented in the Fig. 3. From temporal point of view it means that term t is present now. Considering temporal aspects, state and decision terms are past-to-present terms, while action terms are present-to-future terms. It means that state and decision terms have start time constraint s_t in the past, while end time constraint e_t can be in the past or in the present. Action terms have start time constraint s_t in the present or in the future, while the end time constraint e_t is in the future. Considering possible combinations of time constraints (s_t, e_t and f_t) existence in a micro-temporality, there are detected different modes of micro-temporalities, as presented in the Fig. 3. The first micro-temporality mode $[s_t,-,-]$ includes start time constraint s_t, but excludes end time e_t and frequency f_t constraints, as shown in the Fig. 3. In the case of state or decision terms it means that specific term was present since start time s_t till now, without having information about the frequency of occurance f_t. In the case of action terms it means that specific term will be present from start time s_t, but there is no information till when (e_t) and with which frequency (f_t) this term will be present. The second micro-temporality mode $[-,e_t,-]$ includes end time constraint e_t, but excludes start time s_t and frequency f_t constraints, as shown in the Fig. 3. In the case of state or decision terms it means that specific term was present till end time e_t, without having information when it started (s_t) and with which frequency f_t it occured. In the case of action terms it means that specific term is present from now till end time e_t, without having information about the frequency constraint f_t. The third micro-temporality mode $[-,-,f_t]$ includes frequency constraint f_t, but excludes start time s_t and end time e_t constraints, as shown in the Fig. 3. In the case of state or decision terms it means that specific term was present till now with frequency f_t, without having information when it started (s_t). In the case of action terms it means that specific term is present from now with frequency f_t, without having information when it will end (e_t).

The fourth micro-temporality mode $[s_t,e_t,-]$ includes start time s_t and end time e_t constraints but excludes frequency f_t constraint, as shown in the Fig. 3. In the case of state or decision terms it means that specific term was present since start time s_t till end time e_t, without having information about the frequency of occurance f_t. In the case of action terms it means that specific term will be present from start time s_t till end time e_t, without information about frequency f_t. The fifth micro-temporality mode $[s_t,-,f_t]$ includes start time s_t and frequency f_t constraints, but excludes end time e_t constraint, as shown in the Fig. 3. In the case of state or decision terms it means that specific term was present from start time s_t till now with the frequency f_t. In the case of action terms it means that specific term will be present from start time s_t with the frequency f_t, without having information about the end time e_t. The sixth micro-temporality mode $[-,e_t,f_t]$ includes end time e_t and frequency f_t constraints, but

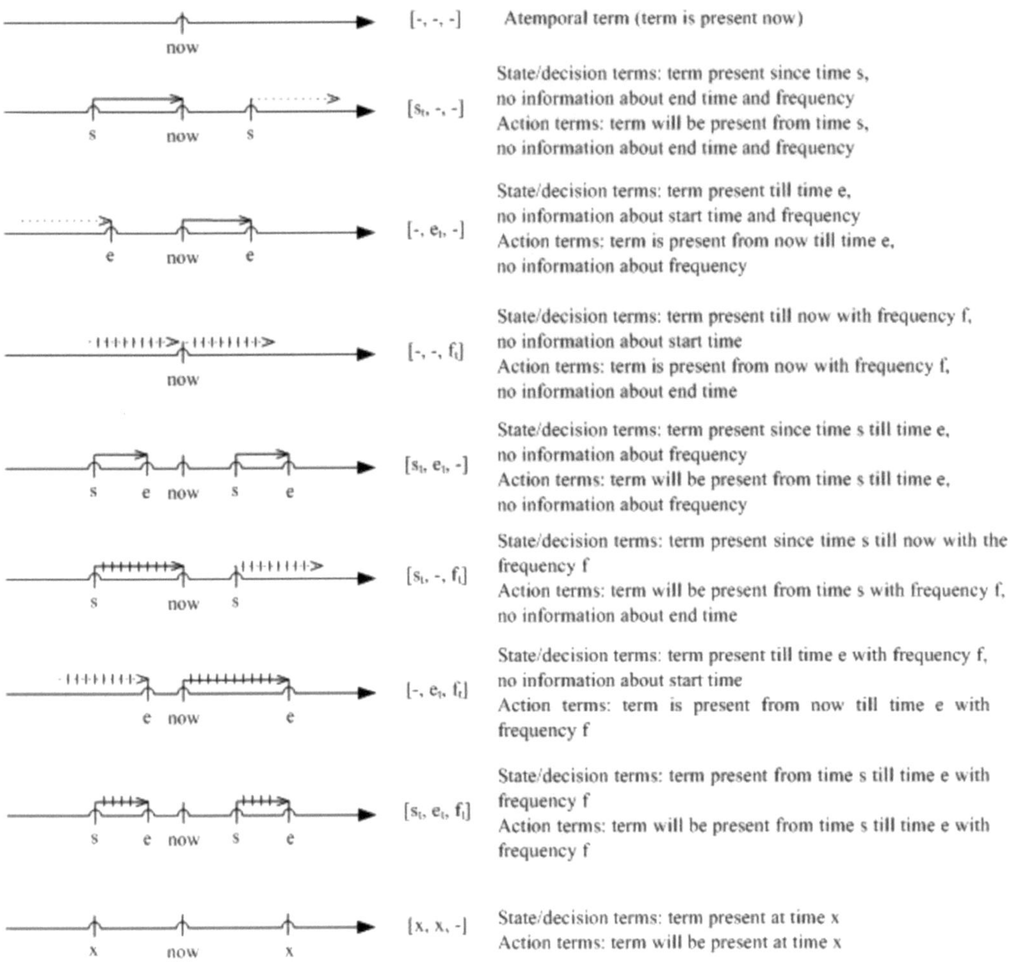

Fig. 3. Different micro-temporality modes

excludes start time s_t constraint, as shown in the Fig. 3. In the case of state or decision terms it means that specific term was present till end time e_t with frequency f_t, without having information when it started (s_t). In the case of action terms it means that specific term is present from now till end time e_t with frequency f_t. The seventh micro-temporality mode [s_t,e_t,f_t] includes start time s_t, end time e_t and frequency f_t constraints, as shown in the Fig. 3. In the case of state or decision terms it means that specific term was present since start time s_t till end time e_t with the frequency of occurance f_t. In the case of action terms it means that specific term will be present from start time s_t till end time e_t with the frequency f_t. The ninth micro-temporality mode [x,x,-] is specific as its start and end constraints are the same and there is no frequency constraint included, as shown in the Fig. 3. It means that term occured at certain point in time. In the case of state or decision terms it means that term was present at time x. In the case of action terms it means that term will be present at time x.

2.2 Timed-transition diagrams

A Timed Transition System (TTS) (Herzinger et al., 1992) is a quintuple $\langle V, \sum, T, l, u \rangle$ where V is a finite set of terms $V = \{v_1, v_2, ..., v_n\}$; $\sum$ is a set of states $\sum = \sigma_1, \sigma_2, ..., \sigma_n$ where every state $\sigma_i \in \sum$ is a subset of terms (i.e.$\sum \subseteq 2^V$); T is a finite set of transitions where every transition $t \in T$ is a binary relation on $\sum$; $l : T \rightarrow IN$ is the minimal delay function, and $u : T \rightarrow IN \cup \{\infty\}$ is the maximal delay function such that for any $t \in T$, $l(t) \leq u(t)$. For every state $\sigma_i \in \sum$, a set of t-successors $t(\sigma) \subseteq \sum$ is defined. TTSs use to be represented as timed-transition diagrams (TTDs)(see Fig. 4, Fig. 5, Fig. 6). In (Kamišalić et al., 2008) we have used TTDs to represent macro-temporality constraints in CAs.

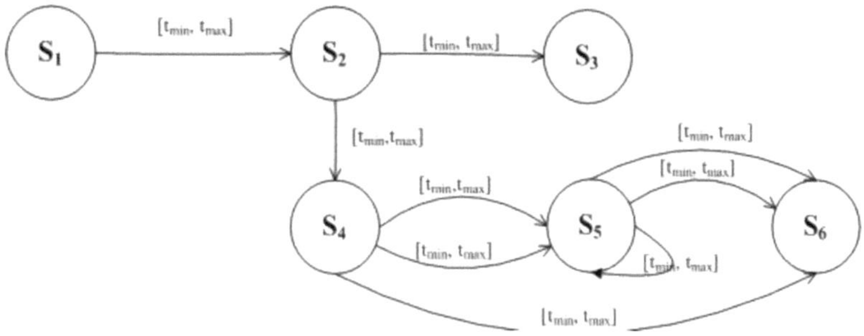

Fig. 4. Clinical algorithm for Hypertension (level 0 data) in TTD representation

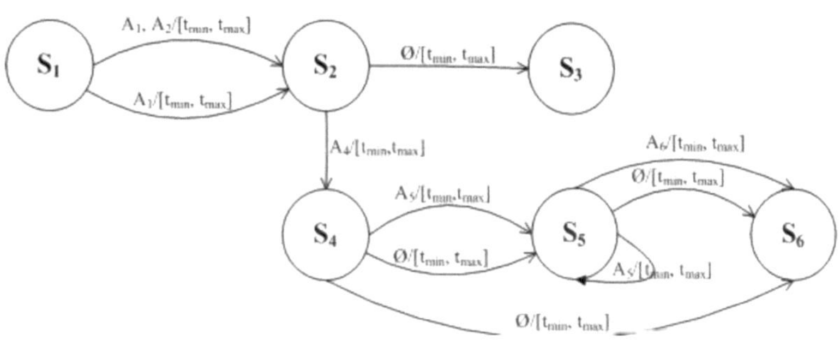

Fig. 5. Clinical algorithm for Hypertension (level 1 data) in TTD representation

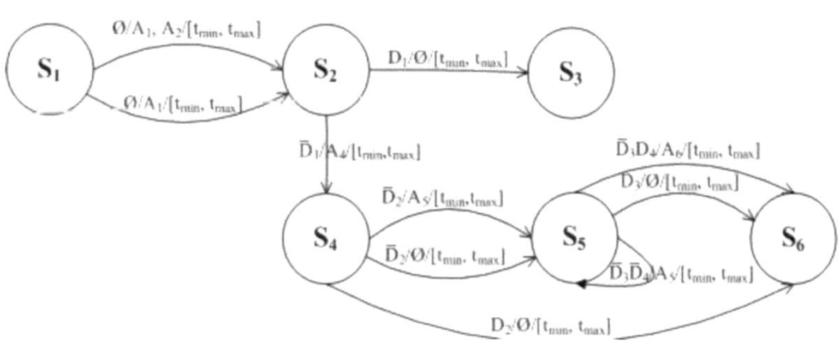

Fig. 6. Clinical algorithm for Hypertension (level 2 data) in TTD representation

3. Generation of macro-temporalities

3.1 Data model

Input data for generation of macro-temporalities represent the evolution of patients through a medical treatment as sequences of state transitions. These data are based on the concept of encounter. An encounter is defined as a meeting between a medical professional and a patient in order to assess patient's condition and to determine the best medical course of action (Kamišalić et al., 2007). For each encounter some data about the patient condition (e.g. signs and symptoms) and the actions of the patient treatment (e.g. prescriptions or medical orders) are saved. Patient's evolution is seen as a sequence of state transitions through different consecutive encounters. In the i-th encounter, a patient P_k is in state S_i^k (described by the observed state terms) and, optionally, receives a state-caused treatment A_i (described by the action terms the physician orders). The time between this encounter and the next one is $t_{i,i+1}$. The sequences of state transitions of all the patients affected by and treated of a particular disease define a data model that describes the input data. For a particular disease, if the states in the data model are the same that the states in the CA describing the treatment of that disease, then each state-to-state transition of a sequence represents an instance of the sort of patient evolving between two consecutive states in the CA representation diagram (SDA* or TTD).

There were identified different data levels in hospital databases. The description of the treatment of a particular patient is defined at level 0 when only the states the patient passes through and the times passing between consecutive states are provided. These structures are called level 0 sequences (Kamišalić et al., 2008)(see representation of level 0 sequences in Fig. 4). Level 1 data describe individual treatments of concrete patients as level 0 sequences of states together with the medical actions performed between each pair of consecutive states, and the time that each change of state takes. These are called level 1 sequences (Kamišalić et al., 2008)(see representation of level 1 sequences in Fig. 5). Level 2 data extends level 1 data with decisions representing the reasons that justify the actions. These are level 2 sequences (Kamišalić et al., 2008)(see representation of level 2 sequences in Fig. 6).

3.2 Macro-temporality generalization

Considering different data levels introduced, there are also defined different procedures for generation of macro-temporalities. In some cases the input data can follow some of the known distributions, such as normal distribution, while in others not. For generation of macro-temporalities in both cases there were defined two different approaches considering distribution of input data. In the case of known distribution there can be used known statistical methods to generate macro-temporality. In this case it is obtained more adjusted macro-temporality interval and there can be reached a higher confidence in the obtained interval. In the case where the distribution function of the data is unknown, for generation of macro-temporality there are used quantiles, which give a first approximation about the interval with less confidence. Both approaches are described in the next subsections. In the case of level 0 data, for each pair of consecutive states S_i, S_j, it is applied process of macro-temporality constraint generation from all the tij times of all the sequences available. Each time a patient takes to evolve directly from S_i to S_j is taken in the calculation of macro-temporality interval, whether using one of the known statistical models or using quantiles. In the case of level 1 data, first there is applied process of actions classification, where all the actions of the sort A_{ij} are used to obtain a group of action classes in which each action class contains A_{ij} actions that are mutually similar and dissimilar to the actions in other actions classes (see Fig. 9 and Section 4.2 for more details about similarity criterion) (see an example of 10 evolutions of level 1 sequence in Fig. 7; considering these evolutions there is made a classification of all the evolutions with the same actions, shown in Fig. 8).

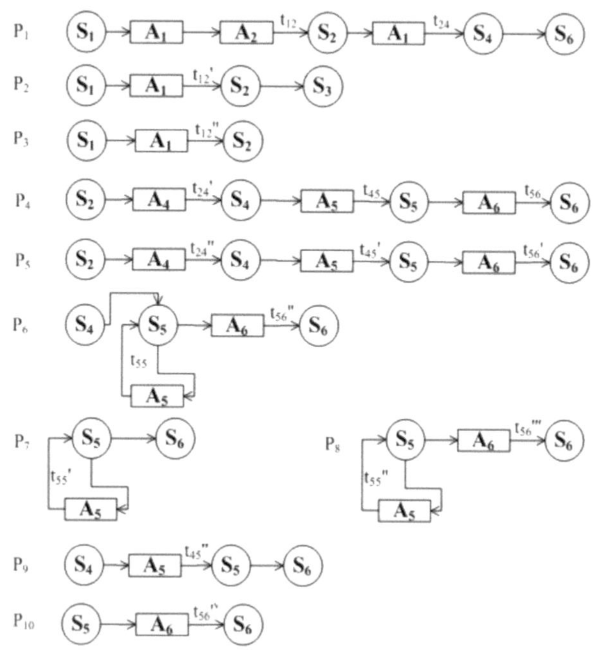

Fig. 7. Example of 10 evolutions of level 1 sequence for Hypertension

The t_{ij} times related to evolutions in which the actions applied belong to a concrete action class are used to calculate a macro-temporality constraint (see Fig. 8).

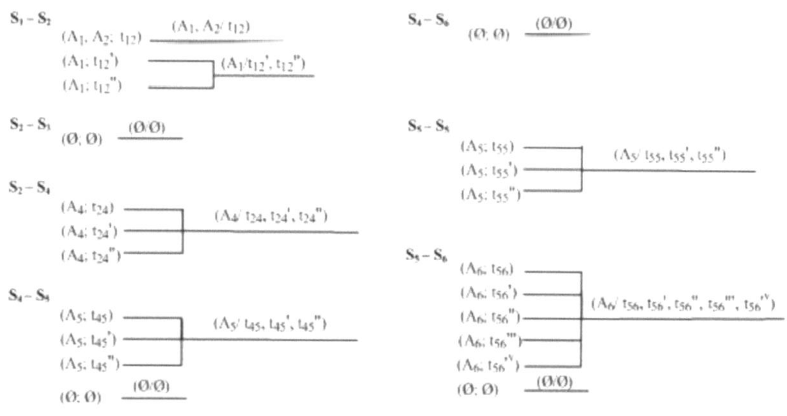

Fig. 8. Actions classification for Fig. 7 example

Finally for level 2 data, there is applied not only the process of actions classification (as in the case of level 1 data) but also the process of decisions classification (the same procedure as in the case of actions classification for level 1 data) (see Fig. 9 and Section 4.2 for more details about similarity criterion). The next step consists of calculating the time t_{ij} between states from all of the times t_{ij} of all the classified transitions from S_i to S_j taken from all the sequences available (Kamišalić et al., 2008).

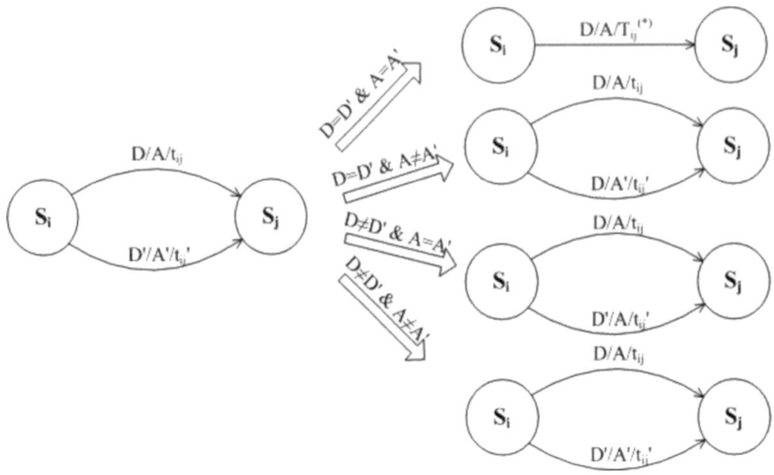

Fig. 9. Macro-temporality generalization considering decisions and actions similarity

3.2.1 The statistical model

If we assume that for each pair of consecutive states S_i, S_j and time between them t_{ij}, the sample of t_{ij} times of all the transitions from S_i to S_j taken from patient sequences approach one of the known distributions then we can use statistical methods for macro-temporality constraints generation. Here it is presented the statistical model for the sample approaching a *t*-student distribution. In this case, $\bar{t_{ij}}$ represents the mean of all t_{ij} values in the sample of patients evolving from S_i to S_j. $S_{t_{ij}}$ is the standard deviation of that same sample. Equation 1 is used to calculate the macro-temporality, where t_n is the *z*-value of *t*-student distribution (Kamišalić et al., 2007).

$$t = \bar{t_{ij}} \pm t_n \cdot S_{t_{ij}} \quad (1)$$

The calculated macro-temporalities between consecutive states S_i and S_j can be assigned to the SDA* connectors ending in S_j. The connectors could be of the sort C_{SS}, C_{AS} or C_{DS}.

3.2.2 Quantiles

Quantiles are more useful than other statistical methods if the distribution function of the data we are analysing is unknown. For each pair of consecutive states (S_i, S_j) there is an assigned time t_{ij} between them. The t_{ij} times of all transitions from S_i to S_j taken over all the patient sequences available defines a sample that is used to generate a macro-temporality constraint on tij times. Quantiles of q-quantiles are the data values that divide an ordered list of data into q essentially equal-sized data subsets. Quantiles are data values which mark the boundaries between consecutive subsets. For example, percentiles are 100-quantiles. Using the precentile is a way of providing estimation of proportions of the data that should fall above and below a given value.The 1st percentile cuts off the lowest 1% of data and the 99th percentile cuts off the highest 1% of data. Considering the confidence we aim to reach for the generated interval we can decide which lowest and highest percentiles we will cut off. For example, if we decide to keep 90% of confidence in generated interval, we would cut off till 5th and from 95th percentile. In this case, macro-temporality interval would consist of tmin as a value of 5th percentile and tmax as a value of 95th percentile (Kamišalić et al., 2008). If the input data follow some of the known distributions, such as normal distribution, then we could use other statistical methods to generate macro-temporality which would give us a more adjusted interval and a higher confidence in the obtained interval.

3.3 Incorporation of macro-temporalities in representation diagrams

Transitions (connectors) in temporal CAs can be extended with macro-temporalities with the help of the instances of treatment in the medical databases under the data model described in section 3.1. SDA* diagrams or TTDs are choosen as representation formalism for temporal CAs (representation of macro-temporality constraints). Each encounter in the database represents the medical actions taken for a patient in a particular state. Identifying the state of the patient S_E among all the states in the SDA* is made with the operation of similarity $S_E \approx S_{SDA}$ defined in subsection 4.2. Identifying the medical action of the encounter A_E in the SDA is made as well with the operation of similarity $A_E \approx A$, where A is each one of the actions in $Actions(S_{SDA}, S_E)$, and $Actions(S_{SDA}, S_E)$ the set of alternative actions in the SDA that patients in condition S_E may follow after the SDA state S_{SDA}.

After this identification of the encounter in the states, decisions and actions of the CA, the macro-temporalities of the encounter are attached to the corresponding connectors between identified states, decisions and actions in the SDA* or TTD. This process is repeated for all the encounters in the database. At the end, all the macro-temporalities attached to each one of the connectors in the SDA* or TTD are combined with the procedure of macro-temporality generalization (using statistical model or quantiles), described in subsection 3.2. The final SDA* or TTD has several macro-temporalities attached to each one of its connectors. If all the micro-temporalities of the terms are close (i.e., temporalities in similar cases are similar) then the connectors in the SDA* or in TTD are related a single macro-temporality (see example of attached macro-temporalities in Fig. 2 for SDA* representation or Fig. 5 for TTD representation).

3.4 Case study

For the connector C_{AS} between the action A_4 and the state S_4, shown in Fig. 2, we consider times t_{ij} between consecutive encounters in which, during the first encounter the physician ordered the action A_4, and in the second encounter the patient had evolved to state S_4. Assume we have different patients who evolved through the same transition with different times (*2d*, *14h*, *4d*, *3d*, *5d*, *20h*, *1w*, *14h*, *1d*, *6d*, *18h*, *2d*, *20h*, *1w*, *4d*, *10h*, *2d*, *4d*, *14h*, *3d*). We assume that the distribution function of the given data is unknown, so we calculate quantiles of the times in the list, to obtain macro-temporality $[t_{\min}, t_{\max}]$ for given transition. First step consists of deviding the times in an ordered list. In this example we will use deciles (10-quantiles). It means that the list of times will be divided into 10 equal-sized subsets. Depending on the confidence we aim to reach for generated interval, we decide which lowest and highest deciles we cut of. Say that we want to keep 60% of confidence in the interval, then we cut the first 2 and the last 2 deciles. As a result we obtain the macro-temporality interval T_8=[*18h*, *4d*].

4. Generation of micro-temporalities

4.1 Data model

The data model is based on the concept of encounter. For each encounter all the relevant data about the patient condition and the treatment actions are saved. These data use state, decision and action terms to describe both the condition in which the professional finds the patient at the particular moment of the encounter, and the decision which that professional took for the patient. That is to say, the actions which were proposed in the encounter as part of the treatment.

In the data model, all state, decision and action terms are attached a micro-temporality constraint that is not necessarily complete (as presented in Section 2.1, Fig. 3).

4.2 Micro-temporality generalization

In order to be able to generate micro-temporality from data, we have to know how to compare states, decisions and actions. Two states, two decisions or two actions can be considered the same, if they are similar enough to be accepted as the same. That is to say, they are atemporarily the same (represented as $\approx$) if each term of the states, decisions or actions corresponds to some of the terms of the other state, decision or action; or if they differ in some terms that have no major signification (i.e., their effects do not change the essence of a particular state, decision or action). Our method uses the similarity criterion (Kamišalić et al., 2009):

$$S \approx S' \Leftrightarrow \frac{(S \cap S')}{(S \cup S')} > \alpha$$

for some predefined parameter $\alpha \in [0,1]$, where 0 determines total difference (no single term matching in compared states, decisions or actions) and 1 determines total equality (all terms matching) of compared states, decisions or actions.

If we come to the conclusion that several states, several decisions or several actions are atemporarily the same, then we also consider the micro-temporalities of the corresponding terms in the states, decisions or actions as it is depicted in Fig. 10 in order to evaluate if they are also the same at the level of time.

For all the micro-temporalities $[s_t, e_t, f_t]$ corresponding to the same term, it is necessary to measure the distance between these temporal constraints. The distance is measured for all constraints s_t, e_t and f_t, separately. This approach is called S-time-distance (Sicherl, 2005). The distance between temporal constraints $s_t^{'}$ and $s_t^{''}$ is calculated with Equation 2, between $e_t^{'}$ and $e_t^{''}$ with Equation 3, and between $f_t^{'}$ and $f_t^{''}$ with Equation 4.

$$d_s(s_t^{'}, s_t^{''}) = \Delta s_t = | s_t^{'} - s_t^{''} | \tag{2}$$

$$d_t(e_t^{'}, e_t^{''}) = \Delta e_t = | e_t^{'} - e_t^{''} | \tag{3}$$

$$d_f(f_t^{'}, f_t^{''}) = \Delta f_t = | f_t^{'} - f_t^{''} | \tag{4}$$

The result of calculating the distances of temporal constraints are three values which have to be compared to some predefined parameter β. When all three distances are lower than or equal to a predefined parameter β, we say the terms with such micro-temporalities are the

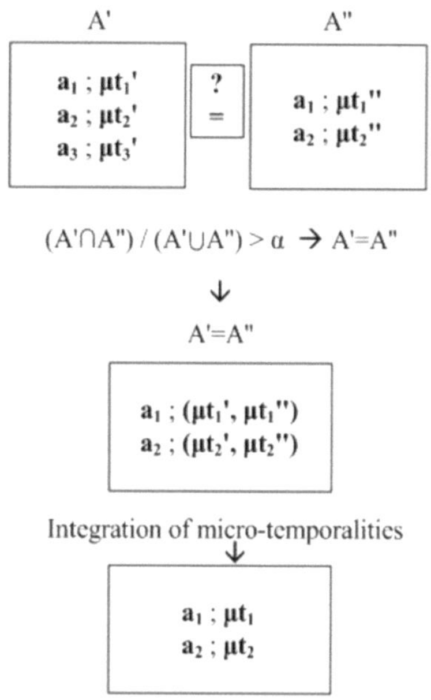

Fig. 10. Comparing action terms and providing integration of micro-temporalities

same as far as time is concerned. Formally speaking, we define two micro-temporalities $\mu t'$ and $\mu t''$ are the same (represented as $\mu t' \approx \mu t''$) if:

$$\mu t' \approx \mu t'' \Leftrightarrow d_s(s_t', s_t'') \leq \beta, \text{ and}$$
$$d_e(e_t', e_t'') \leq \beta, \text{ and}$$
$$d_f(f_t', f_t'') \leq \beta.$$

When there are several micro-temporalities related to a same term, these micro-temporalities may be combined with a clustering algorithm that employs the distance functions d_s, d_e, and d_f defined above. Hierarchical taxonomy clustering algorithms (Sneath & Sokal, 1973) are numerical approaches to the construction of dendrograms on a set of numerical data. Given a set of micro-temporalities $[s_i, e_i, f_i]$, $i = 1, ..., n$ that we want to combine, our method constructs a dendrogram for each one of the square matrices $\{d_s(s_i, s_j)\}_{i,j=1,...,n}$, $\{d_e(e_i, e_j)\}_{i,j=1,...,n}$, and $\{d_f(f_i, f_j)\}_{i,j=1,...,n}$. Once the heights of these dendrograms are scaled to the range [0,1], a predefined parameter β is used to horizontally cut the dendrograms. Parameter β is choosen considering wheather we can accept the increasing of error and therefore decreasing the number of micro-temporalities, or we prefer getting more adjusted temporal constraints representatives (increasing the number of micro-temporalities) and therefore decreasing the number of micro-temporalities. These β-cuts provide three sets of clusters. The median of the values in each cluster defines the centroid of this cluster. Constraints which are the closest to centroids, are choosen as cluster representatives. These cluster representatives of different dendrograms are combined in the final micro-temporalities.

4.3 Incorporation of micro-temporalities in representation diagrams

Terms in temporal CAs can be extended with micro-temporalities with the help of the instances of treatment in the medical databases under the data model described in section 4.1.

As representation formalism for temporal CAs (representation of micro-temporality constraints) are choosen SDA* diagrams. Each encounter in the database represents the medical actions taken for a patient in a particular state. The terms in the encounter come related to micro-temporalities. Identifying these terms in the atemporal SDA is the first step of the process. Identifying the state of the patient S_E among all the states in the SDA is made with the operation of similarity $S_E \approx S_{SDA}$ defined in subsection 4.2. Identifying the medical action of the encounter A_E in the SDA is made with the operation $A_E \approx A$, where A is each one of the actions in $Actions(S_{SDA}, S_E)$, and $Actions(S_{SDA}, S_E)$ the set of alternative actions in the SDA that patients in condition S_E may follow after the SDA state S_{SDA}. For example in Fig. 2, $Actions(S_5, \{noD_3\}) = \{A_5, A_6\}$ because a patient in state S_5, which is not D_3, may be derived to action A_5 if he is not D_4 or to A_6 if he is D_4.
After this identification of the encounter in the states, decisions and actions of the SDA, the micro-temporality of the terms of the encounter are attached to the corresponding terms in the SDA states, decisions, and actions. This process is repeated for all the encounters in the database. At the end, all the micro-temporalities attached to each one of the terms in the SDA are combined with the procedure of clustering algorithm, described in subsection 4.2. The final SDA has several micro-temporalities attached to each one of its terms. If all the micro-temporalities of the terms are close (i.e., temporalities in similar cases are similar) then the terms in the SDA are related a single micro-temporality.

4.4 Case study

For two action terms (take thiazide-type diuretic and take beta-blocker) of the CA shown in Fig. 2 as a part of the action A4, we consider three sorts of constraints, s_t, e_t and f_t. We have to find clusters (and centroids) for each one of them. Micro-temporality $[s_t, e_t, f_t]$ of the applied action term is given for each patient. Assume we have different patients with the same action term but different micro-temporalities ($[-, 2w, 6h]$, $[-, 3w, 4h]$, $[-, 2w, 6h]$, $[-, 1w, 8h]$, $[-, 6d, 6h]$, $[-, 10d, 8h]$, $[-, 4w, 6h]$, $[-, 15d, 6h]$, $[-, 4d, 8h]$, $[-, 20d, 4h]$). We apply the clustering algorithm separately for all s_t, e_t and f_t. Finding the clusters for groups of s_t, e_t and f_t gives us the centroids of those clusters. The closest constraint to each centroid constructs the micro-temporality of a term. For example, if all e_t are divided into more than one cluster, the result is more than one centroid. The closest constraint to the centroid is taken as a time constraint on the end time in different micro-temporalities of the same action term (for above introduced example of patients' micro-temporalities, the result of the clustering are four clusters and therefore four constraints closest to the centroids for e_t ($6d$, $2w$, $3w$, $4w$) and two clusters and therefore two constraints closest to the centroids for f_t ($4h$, $6h$); which give as the result four micro-temporalities $[-, 6d, 6h]$, $[-, 2w, 6h]$, $[-, 3w, 4h]$ and $[-, 4w, 6h]$ for the action term 'take thiazide-type diuretic'). In this particular case, we would choose $[-, 2w, 6h]$ micro-temporality from the four possible, because this one is the representative of most micro-temporalities. However, choosing one representative is resulting in increasing the error and decreasing the confidence.

5. Conclusion

CAs derived from CPGs make explicit knowledge necessary to assist physicians in order to make appropriate decisions. They should give procedural and temporal indications. The first one are indications on what to do, and the second one are indications on what are the time restrictions. Still the most CAs are atemporal, offering indications on what to do but not on time restrictions. To deal with this problem, we have defined micro- and macro-temporality constraints and offered the methodologies for generalization of micro- and macro-temporalities. We are introducing temporal constraints from existing patients' temporal data. We have presented two possible aproaches to generation of macro-temporality constraints, using statistical methods or quantiles. Quantiles are less susceptible to long tailed distributions and outliers. We came to the conclusion that if the data we are analyzing are not distributed according to some assumed distribution or if we have other potential sources for outliers that are far removed from the mean, then quantiles may be more useful than other statistical models. Obtained macro-temporalities are attached to connectors of the CAs. We have also offered the methodology for micro-temporality constraints generation using a clustering algorithm. The obtained micro-temporalities are attached to a state, decision or action term of the CAs. We have presented different representation formalisms which can be used for representation of CAs, and have explained different situations in which STDs, TTDs and/or SDA*s are used. As CAs now include temporal constraints (time dimension), physicians are able to provide also indications on time restrictions considering medical procedures.

6. References

Combi, C.; Keravnou-Papailiou, E. & Shahar, Y. (2010). *Temporal Information Systems in Medicine*. Springer, 978-1-4419-6543-1, New York, 2010

Fox, J.; Johns, N. & Rahmanzadeh, A. (1998). Disseminating Medical Knowledge-The PROforma Approach. *Artificial Intelligence in Medicine*, 14(1-2): 157-182, 1998

Grabmeier, J. & Rudolph, A. (2002). Tehcniques of Cluster Algorithms in Data Mining. *Data Mining and Knowledge Discovery*, 6(4): 303-360, October 2002

Henzinger, T. A.; Manna, Z. & Pnueli A. (1992). Timed Transition Systems. *Real Time: Theory in Practice*, LNCS 600: 226-251, 3-540-55564-1, Springer Verlag 1992

Institute for Clinical Systems Improvement(2006). Health Care Guideline: Hypertension Diagnosis and Treatment, October 2006, `http://www.icsi.org/hypertension_4/hypertension_diagnosis_and_treatment_4.html`

Kamišalić, A.; Riaño D.; Real F. & Welzer T. (2007). Temporal Constraints Approximation from Data about Medical Procedures. *Machine Learning and Management of Health-Care Procedural Knowledge, 20th IEEE Int. Workshop on CBMS2007*, Maribor, Slovenia

Kamišalić, A.; Riaño D. & Welzer T. (2008). Generating Macro-Temporality in Timed Transition Diagrams. *'From Knowledge to Global Care' AIME2007 workshop K4CARE*, LNCS 4924: 62-74, 978-3-540-78623-8, Springer Verlag 2008

Kamišalić, A.; Riaño D. & Welzer T. (2009). First Approach to Micro-temporality Generation for Clinical Algorithms. *European-Japanese Conference EJC2009*, Maribor, Slovenia

Musen, M. A.; Tu, S.W.; Das, A.K. & Shahar, Y. (1996). EON: A component-based approach to automation of protocol-directed therapy. *Journal of the American Medical Information Association*, 3(6): 367-388, 1996

Riaño, D. (2007). The SDA Model: A Set Theory Approach. *Machine Learning and Management of Health-Care Procedural Knowledge, 20th IEEE Int. Workshop on CBMS 2007*, Maribor, Slovenia

Riaño, D.; Lopez-Vallverdu, J. A. & Tu, S. (2007). Mining Hospital Data to Learn SDA* Clinical Algorithms. *'From Knowledge to Global Care' AIME2007 workshop*, LNCS 4924: 46-61, 978-3-540-78623-8, Springer Verlag 2008

Seyfang, A.; Miksch, S. & Marcos M. (2002). Combining Diagnosis and Treatment using Asbru. *International Journal of Medical Informatics*, 68 (1-3): 49-57, December 2002
Sicherl, P. (2005). Time distance - a new generic approach for analysis and visualization of time related data, *Complex objects visualization - COV2005*, Ljubljana, Slovenia
Sneath, P. H. A. & Sokal, R. R. (1973). Numerical Taxonomy, *Freeman*, San Francisco, 1973

10

Predicting Pathology in Medical Decision Support Systems in Endoscopy of the Gastrointestinal Tract

Michael Liedlgruber and Andreas Uhl
Multimedia Signal Processing and Security Lab (WaveLab), Department of Computer Sciences, University of Salzburg Austria

1. Introduction

Since medical endoscopy is a minimally invasive and relatively painless procedure, allowing to inspect the inner cavities of the human body, endoscopes play an important role in modern medicine. In medical practice different organs such as the respiratory tract, the urinary tract, and the female reproductive system are regularly inspected by using an endoscope. Another important field in medical endoscopy, which this chapter focuses at, is the inspection of the gastrointestinal tract (GI tract).

Based on endoscopy of the GI tract, physicians are able to detect severe diseases already in early development stages and therefore the mortality rate for many diseases, especially different types of cancers, has been lowered drastically throughout the last years. Some examples of conditions which are known to be pre-malignant or to increase the risk of

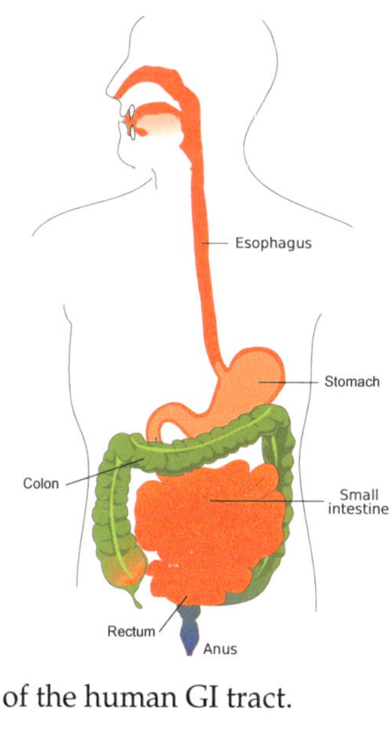

Fig. 1. A schematic illustration of the human GI tract.

cancer in the GI tract are adenomas, Barrett's esophagus, Crohn's disease, celiac disease, GI bleeding, and a Helicobacter pylori infection. The parts of the human GI tract, which are most commonly inspected with an endoscope, are shown in Figure 1.

In general the area of applications for endoscopes is wide. Besides medical procedures, endoscopes are also used to inspect airplane turbines, pipes in buildings or industrial machinery, car engines, tanks in ships, and for veterinary endoscopy. However, throughout this work the terms "endoscope" and "endoscopy" always denote the medical device and procedure, respectively.

1.1 Technological advances in endoscopy

The first time the term endoscope was used was in 1806, when Philipp Bozzini developed the first kind of endoscope which he called "Lichtleiter". By using this device he already made the first attempts to examine the inner cavities of the human body. But endoscopes as we know them today significantly differ from the one Bozzini developed. In the early days of endoscopy the devices were lit by external light sources (a candle in the case of by Bozzini's apparatus) and not flexible. Thus, these devices were somewhat limited in terms of their usability.

(a) Flexible endoscope (b) WCE capsule

Fig. 2. (a) A flexible endoscope (Image courtesy of Olympus) and (b) an example of a WCE capsule (Image courtesy of Given Imaging).

Endoscopy, as we know it today, is performed using a flexible endoscope (Figure 2(a)), sometimes also referred to as videoscope. This type of endoscope has been introduced in the mid 1960s. While the first endoscopes used fiber optics and an eyepiece lens to visualize the inner cavities of the human body, modern endoscopes are very compact devices, including a light source, and a CCD or CMOS chip for taking pictures. But the basic concept did not change very much since those days. In addition to the digital imaging chip, modern endoscopes contain a light source at the distal tip and are equipped with an accessory channel, which allows the entry of medical instruments for example to take tissue samples, perform cleansing of poorly prepared areas, perform polypectomies, and perform endoscopic resections without any invasive surgery involved.

More recent advances in endoscopy are zoom-endoscopy and chromoendoscopy. Zoom-endoscopy allows to zoom in at regions of interest, using a magnification factor of up to 150. Such devices offer a significant advance since smaller and finer details in the region to be examined get uncovered (Hurlstone et al., 2004). Another possibility to obtain images with a higher level of detail are high definition (HD) endoscopes, which also provide images of higher resolutions and therefore allow to detect subtle changes in the mucosa. Chromoendoscopy aims at enhancing superficial patterns on a mucosal layer by topically

applying color dyes. An alternative to this rather time-consuming procedure is to use Narrow Band Imaging (NBI), which allows to enhance the contrast of vascular patterns on the mucosal surface (Emura et al., 2008). Since NBI is based on a rotating filter in front of the light source (narrowing the spectrum of the visible light to bands of blue and green) this technique is not dependent on applying color dyes. Other systems similar to NBI, like FICE (Fujinon Intelligent Chromoendoscopy) or I-scan, use computer algorithms to post-process endoscopic images. Systems like NBI, FICE, or I-scan are referred to as "virtual chromoendoscopy".
Another recent advance in endoscopy is confocal laser endomicroscopy (CLE) (Kiesslich & Neurath, 2007). This procedure allows to inspect the mucosal surface in a highly detailed manner. This is achieved by a laser-based endomicroscope which scans the surface of the mucosa and even allows to inspect sub-surface features up to a depth of 250 microns by adjusting the focal point of the laser. The resulting images have a resolution corresponding to a magnification factor of 1000, making "smart" biopsies possible, thus avoiding random and possibly unnecessary biopsies. It has already been shown that the diagnostic accuracy of CLE is comparable to histology (Buchner et al., 2010).
Since the small intestine is very long and convoluted a traditional flexible endoscope is only of limited use. A recently developed technique to overcome this limitation and to make endoscopic procedures more safe, less invasive, and more comfortable for the patient, is wireless capsule endoscopy (WCE) (Coimbra et al., 2007). To perform WCE the patient swallows a small capsule (Figure 2(b)), containing a light source, lens, camera, radio transmitter, and batteries. Propelled by peristalsis, the capsule then travels through the digestive system for about eight hours and automatically takes more than 50 000 images. These are transmitted wirelessly to a recorder worn outside the body. Throughout the last years WCE has already proven to be valuable tool to detect the cause of gastrointestinal bleeding within the small bowel (Eliakim, 2004). Recently also other areas of interest for WCE within the GI tract have emerged, such as the colon (Fireman & Kopelman, 2007) or the esophagus (Eliakim et al., 2004). Although WCE currently lacks the ability to treat lesions, obtain biopsy samples, and clean poorly prepared areas, this new technique has already proven to be an effective diagnostic modality for detecting small bowel tumors and small bowel lesions (Cobrin et al., 2006), and may also become an important tool to detect other abnormalities in the GI tract (El-Matary, 2008).

1.2 Computer-aided pathology prediction

Due to the digital imaging chips used in modern endoscopes such devices are also regularly used to take digital pictures and record video sequences. These abilities created the whole new field of computer-aided decision support systems (CADSSs) in medical endoscopy. The aim of such systems is to predict pathologies and thus to assist a medical expert in improving the accuracy of medical diagnosis (Doi, 2007). Hence, the development of such systems is motivated by the following key aspects:

- **Saving time and reducing cost**
  CADSSs usually help to identify regions which may be of particular interest for a medical expert. Since, in general, such systems are designed to detect abnormal changes within the GI tract (e.g. neoplastic or metaplastic changes) they are also able to help avoiding possibly unnecessary biopsies, allowing to perform targeted biopsies. In the course of such targeted biopsies the time needed for an endoscopy procedure may be lowered drastically. As a consequence the procedure gets more comfortable for the patient. Furthermore, since

the number of necessary biopsies to be taken can be reduced, the time needed for the subsequent histopathologic examination can be reduced too.

Reducing the time needed for an endoscopy and the subsequent histopathologic examination also results in a reduction of costs associated with such procedures.

Considering the fact that re-investigating a video recorded during an endoscopy session may consume as much time as the endoscopic procedure itself, there is a potential to save time and costs if CADSSs are able to identify parts of such videos which might be of interest for a medical expert. Especially in case of WCE such systems are of particular use, since, due to the vast amount of images generated per WCE session, inspection of such videos is time consuming and therefore expensive in terms of the time raised by a medical expert (Swain, 2003).

- **Enhancing accuracy of diagnosis**
  Endoscopy is a tedious procedure, demanding a constantly high level of concentration by an endoscopist. This is mainly due to the fact that missing an abnormality during endoscopy may be hazardous. Especially lesions which are rather small or only noticeable for a short fraction of time may be missed easily. This particularly applies to WCE, where a lesion may show up in a single frame only (out of more than 50 000 frames in total!). This is due to the rather low frame rate of currently available capsules which usually is about two frames per second.

  The advantage of CADSSs is that computers always exhibit the same level of "concentration" – no matter how long an endoscopic procedure lasts or how many of such procedures a computer has to analyze in series. Also situations with bad light conditions, poor image quality, or poor contrast usually pose a problem for a medical expert, increasing the risk of missed lesions. If designed properly, a computer-based systems may be able to cope well with such circumstances. The constant level of "concentration" and the resistance against poor image conditions may help to avoid missing lesions, leading to an enhanced diagnostic accuracy of an endoscopic procedure.

  But, as indicated in (Church, 2008), sometimes there is a more simple reason for missed lesions: an abnormality may be simply get missed since it is misinterpreted and therefore not recognized as being abnormal. The likelihood of missing a lesion for this reason heavily depends on the expertise of the medical expert who performs the endoscopy, leading to a lowered inter-observer agreement level. CADSSs, on the other hand, do not suffer from this problem. If the detection of abnormalities is designed in a robust way and there is sufficient training data available, a CADSS is expected to always deliver roughly the same level of accuracy.

- **Training of experts to new endoscopic imaging modalities**
  As already pointed out in Section 1.1, there have been many advances in endoscopy within the past few years. While the new imaging modalities have the potential to greatly increase the efficiency of endoscopy, medical experts need to get trained on these new techniques. In order to assess the skills of a medical expert on new techniques, CADSSs can be used as an expert training tool to predict pathology, verify the detection or prediction performance of a medical expert, and serve as an educational resource.

To highlight the relevance of CADSSs we conducted an exhaustive search for publications dealing with this topic (on PubMed [1] and on ScienceDirect [2]), which yielded the search results

[1] PubMed located at `http://www.ncbi.nlm.nih.gov/pubmed`
[2] ScienceDirect located at `http://www.sciencedirect.com`

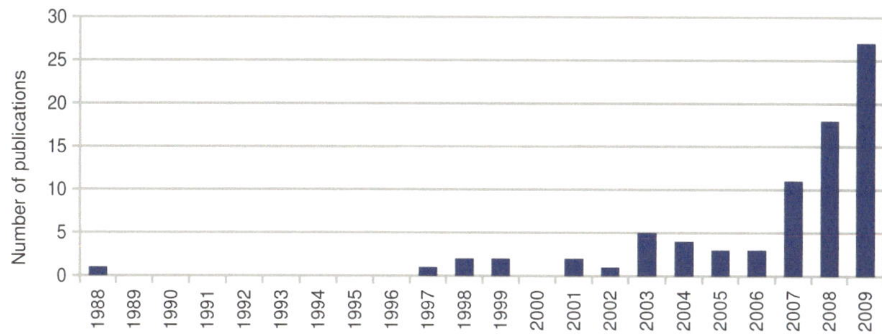

Fig. 3. Number of publications between 1988 and 2009 found on PubMed and ScienceDirect when searching for publications targeting at computer-aided decision support for medical endoscopy in the GI tract (search was conducted in 2010, hence, publication from 2010 are not considered).

presented in Figure 3. The results show that there is a rising interest in this research topic, starting about one decade ago.

2. Fundamentals of pathology prediction

Basically there exist two different approaches for CADSSs aiming at pathology prediction: medical image classification (MIC) and content-based image retrieval (CBIR) (Müller et al., 2004). While these two concepts share some basic building blocks, there are also fundamental differences. In the following section we therefore explain the parts each of these concepts consists of. In addition, we discuss the similarities as well as the differences between CBIR and MIC.

2.1 Building blocks of CBIR and MIC

CBIR systems as well as MIC systems both basically consist of two steps. The first step is to obtain training data along with ground truth information, which represents the knowledge of the respective system. Based on the training data, the prediction is carried out.

2.1.1 Obtaining training data

No matter, whether we are dealing with a MIC or CBIR system, in order to be able to perform a prediction of pathologies, in both cases the first step is the generation of training data along with known ground truth. The respective steps are illustrated in Figure 4.

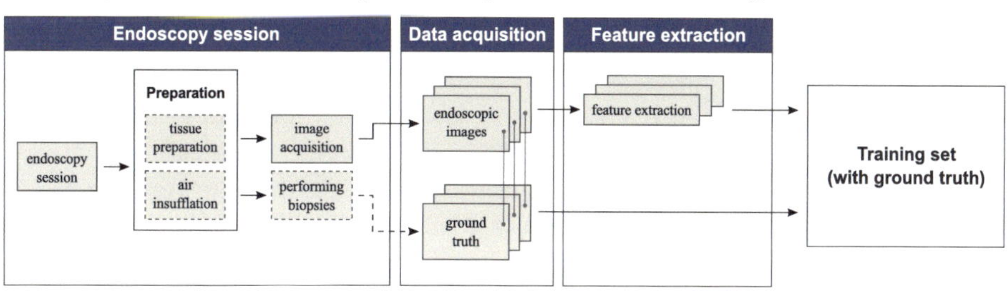

Fig. 4. Schematic illustration of creating training data with ground truth.

It must be noted however, that some of these steps are not possible in case of capsule endoscopy. Since these devices currently offer no possibility to obtain tissue samples, a histopathologic examination to establish a ground truth is not possible. Hence, in case of WCE, the ground truth is usually obtained by a visual inspection of the images recorded by a medical expert. Apart from that, air insufflation is not possible either. These steps are therefore denoted by dashed lines in Figure 4.

- **Preparation steps (not available in case of WCE)**
  Before actually being able to capture images and taking tissue samples, certain preparation steps may be necessary. One such step is air insufflation, which is performed to expand the wall of the part of the GI tract under inspection. This makes regions of the mucosal wall visible which otherwise would be hidden behind folds and therefore increase the probability of missed lesions. Another step, performed on a regular basis, is the preparation of the tissue under investigation. In order to cleanse poorly prepared areas water is used to flush away e.g. stool residuals inside the colon or undigested food.

  Another possibility for tissue preparation is the topical application of color dyes in order to enhance the superficial structure of the mucosa in the region under investigation (e.g. vascular patterns). If a NBI-enabled endoscope is used this step can be omitted since NBI allows to enable and disable the structural enhancement with a simple tip of a button, hence, no color dyes are needed.

- **Capturing images and obtaining ground truth information**
  Images are taken with the tip of a button on the endoscope or, in case of WCE, continuously. When performing endoscopy using a flexible endoscope, also a biopsy is taken in the region covered by the image just taken. After the endoscopy session, the resulting tissue sample is examined by a pathologist under a microscope. In the course of this examination the pathologist determines the histopathologic type for the respective biopsy (e.g. assessing whether there is a malignant potential or not). This classification by the medical expert serves as ground truth for the training data.

  Due to the limitations of WCE in terms of taking biopsies, the respective ground truth information is usually obtained by visual means.

- **Feature extraction**
  Since images represent rather high dimensional data, suitable features have to be used to reduce the amount of data to be stored in the training set.

  While there is a wide range of feature types used throughout CADSS-related work found in literature, these can be roughly grouped into two categories:

  - **Low-level features**
    Feature types falling into this category are based on the raw information contained within images. Examples for such features are histogram features (e.g. simple color histograms and co-occurrence matrices), features capturing the textural contained within images (e.g. Local Binary Patterns and Markov Random Fields), or statistical features (e.g. computed from histograms).

    But also features based on some sort of frequency-domain transform are used quite often throughout literature. Examples are the wavelet transform or the Fourier transform (e.g. features based on raw coefficients or statistics computed from the respective coefficients, e.g. Häfner et al. (2010)).

  - **High-level features**
    Approaches found throughout literature are also quite often based on features describing the content of images in an abstract way. Features belonging to this

category are for example shape-based features, describing shapes obtained by different edge-detection methods (e.g. Häfner et al. (2010)).

But the final choice on the types of features to be used usually depends on the type of pathologies the respective system should be able to deal with and eventual constraints posed to the system (e.g. time constraints). But also the endoscopic imaging modality (e.g. WCE, flexible endoscopy, CLE) the system is designed for plays an important role, as different imaging techniques may result in considerably different types of images. To emphasize on this, Figure 5 show examples taken with different types of endoscopes.

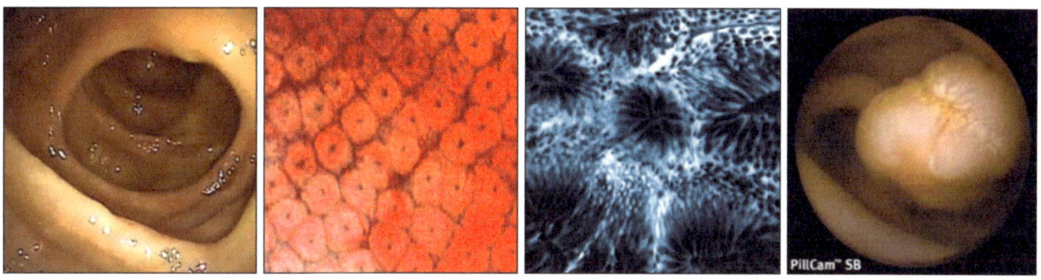

(a) (b) (c) (d)

Fig. 5. Images acquired by using different endoscopic techniques (a) endoscopy (Kelsey, 2005), (b) zoom-endoscopy, (c) confocal laser endomicroscopy (Kiesslich, 2007), and (d) WCE (Copyright © 2005-2010, Given Imaging. All Rights Reserved).

2.1.2 The pathology prediction

While obtaining training data with ground truth is identical, no matter whether a CADSS is based on CBIR or MIC, the actual prediction differs in some aspects. The different steps required for pathology prediction are outlined in Figure 6 (similar to Figure 4, the steps not available in case of WCE are denoted by dashed lines).

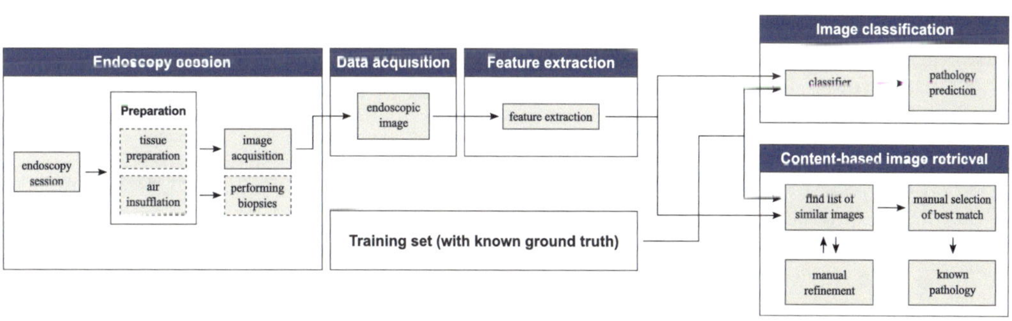

Fig. 6. Schematic illustration of performing pathology prediction for an image with unknown pathology (using either classification methods or image retrieval methods).

As we notice from this illustration, the steps to generate an image to be classified are very similar to the steps already outlined for obtaining training data. However, while biopsies will most likely be performed too, the histopathologic classification remains unknown to the

system (since the histopathologic examination takes place after the endoscopy session, the classification result is not available during the endoscopy session anyways).
After obtaining an image, the same type of features as used to generate the training set is extracted from the image. Then, along with the training set composed earlier, the pathology is predicted either using MIC or CBIR. The steps for the respective system types can be outlined as follows:

- **Classifier-based approaches**
  The basic idea behind classifier-based approaches is to provide a second opinion to a medical expert. Given an unknown image, this is achieved by predicting the pathology in a fully autonomous manner.

  In case of MIC the first step is to train a classifier using the training set available. Then the classifier is used to predict the pathology based on the features extracted from the image with unknown pathology.

  Throughout literature dealing with CADSSs targeted at medical endoscopy of the GI tract various different types of classifiers have been used for this task (e.g. k-nearest-neighbors classifier, Support Vector Machines, artificial neural networks, Bayesian classifier, Linear Discriminant Analysis classifiers, or simple clustering-based classifiers) (Duda et al., 2000; Fukunaga, 1990). The choice for the classifier to be used mostly depends on the features used (and the according feature dimensionality). While also time-constraints may play an important role in choosing the classifier (since some classifiers have a rather high complexity and, therefore, a high computational demand), each type of classifier has advantages and disadvantages which must be considered too.

  The classification outcome of the classifier then corresponds to the predicted pathology.

  Due to the fact that classifier-based approaches are operating without any intervention needed, such approaches also potentially suited for an online-diagnosis (i.e. predicting the pathology during endoscopy already).

- **Systems based on content-based image retrieval**
  CBIR can be regarded as the digital counterpart of current clinical practice, where medical experts compare cases with unknown pathology to cases with an already known and verified diagnosis. Since, however, searching through an existing database, containing a huge number of cases, is a time-consuming task. As a consequence, performing the search for similar cases or images in an automated fashion helps to save time and greatly simplifies the work of medical experts.

  For CBIR-based systems the first step is to choose a suitable metric which determines the similarity between two images (or the respective features). Based on such a metric the system returns a list of the images most similar to the image with unknown pathology, along with the respective similarity scores. The result can then be refined by a medical expert by choosing one or more images which seem to be relevant (commonly termed "relevance feedback"). Then a new query is started based on the images marked as being relevant.

  Once, the medical expert has found the image which, in his opinion, matches the unknown image best, the pathology of the best match can be used in order to determine the pathology for the image with unknown pathology.

  The fact that in case of CBIR-based systems an intervention by a medical expert is needed restricts such systems from being used to obtain a diagnosis during endoscopy already (i.e. online-diagnosis), making CBIR useful for offline-diagnosis only.

Despite the different prediction strategies in case of MIC and CBIR, in certain cases both methods are very similar. If a MIC-based system employs the k-nearest-neighbors classifier with $k > 1$ (the number of neighbors to consider for the prediction process) MIC is very similar to CBIR. This is because the neighbors determined by the classifier basically correspond to the most similar images compared to the incoming images. These k most similar images, however, can be considered to be the k best matches in context of CBIR. But while in case of MIC the classifier determines the final prediction (based on some sort of voting), in case of CBIR the prediction is based on a manual selection of the best matching image.

One of the main differences between MIC and CBIR is therefore the fact that, while MIC performs the prediction in a fully autonomous fashion, CBIR allows a medical expert to refine the prediction process. In case of CBIR, it is up to the medical expert to choose the final match (along with the respective known pathology) and therefore make a judgment on the pathology of the unknown image.

In addition both types – MIC and CBIR – significantly differ in terms of the possible application scenario. While MIC-based systems allow to perform a real-time diagnosis, CBIR-based systems are restricted to be used in offline-scenarios only. This restriction is imposed by the interactive nature of CBIR. As a consequence, interacting with a CBIR system during an endoscopy procedure would constrain the endoscopist (in particular if the expert needs to provide relevance feedback to the CBIR system).

2.2 Detection vs. classification

Despite the differences already highlighted, which exist between MIC-based system and CBIR-based systems, the goals of such CADSSs fall into two categories.

The first branch aims at the detection of abnormalities without making a prediction about the respective pathology. Such systems are for example used to detect polyps or adenomas within the GI tract. If such an abnormality has been detected it is up to the medical expert to decide upon determining the respective pathology. Another field of applications for such systems is to find abnormalities within endoscopy videos, usually containing a huge number of frames. The result is a subset of frames, showing abnormalities which might be of particular interest for a medical expert.

But the frames found might also be used as input for another system, which is specifically designed to assess the malignant potential of a potential abnormality found. Such systems fall into the second branch. In contrast to the detection systems the classification systems are usually not able to locate abnormal pathologies. Moreover, they rely on input which already contains the abnormality candidate to investigate (e.g. images showing polyps). Based on such abnormality candidates, these systems are designed to perform a classification according to some medical classification scheme (e.g. classifying the colonic mucosa as being normal, hyperplastic, neoplastic, or metaplastic). Hence, the outcome of such systems is the prediction of the pathology according to an input image.

Depending on the desired application area, a system performing either detection or classification is needed. For a fully automated pathology prediction for endoscopic imagery or videos, however, a combination of both system branches is needed.

2.3 Confidence in prediction systems

When it comes to computer-based systems, designed to assist a medical expert in the course of obtaining a diagnosis, an important question arises: how trustworthy are such systems from the perspective of medical experts?

Due to its interactive nature CBIR allows to roughly follow the steps from an input image to the final match. Since the medical expert interacts with such a system, the final outcome of the system is at least partially comprehensible. The expert is also able to steer the search into another direction, which probably seems to be more appropriate to the medical expert, based on his medical know-how.

In case of classifier-based systems, however, the actual process of pathology prediction is some sort of a black box. The system is given an image and returns a prediction on the pathology of the image (either a detection or a classification result). As a consequence there is no intermediary medical expert, who is able to complement the system in terms of his experience.

3. Pathology prediction issues

In order to be of practical use, the quality, reliability, accuracy, and usability of pathology prediction systems are important issues. The following section therefore contains a discussion of these issues.

3.1 Obtaining ground truth information

As already indicated in Section 2, there basically exist two different ways of obtaining ground truth information: either by visual means or through a histopathologic examination of biopsies.

Obtaining the ground truth for an image by visual inspection by a medical expert has the disadvantage that there is no profound knowledge about the real pathology for that image (i.e. the pathology is not verified histologically). Another disadvantage is the fact that in the course of visual pathology assessment the inter-observer agreement rate is likely to be lower, resulting in different diagnosis results. This is due to the fact that the judgment of different medical experts heavily depends on the respective level of experience.

If samples of suspicious tissue are taken the ground truth can be based on the outcome of a subsequent histopathologic examination. But the biopsy site does not need to perfectly correspond to the respective image taken. This may be due to peristaltic motion or slight movements of the endoscope tip (for example in the course of preparing a biopsy), which are especially noticeable in case of high-magnification endoscopy. Hence, while the histopathologic classification can be considered to be the gold standard, the respective pathology is not necessarily visible on the respective endoscopic image.

However, the choice on the way to obtain the ground truth often is not upon the medical expert. As already mentioned earlier, in case of WCE-based systems there is usually no other option than to rely on visual inspections by one or more medical experts, since taking biopsies is not possible with current capsule endoscopes. In case of flexible endoscopy the ground truth can be gathered histologically since taking biopsies is possible.

A special case is constituted by CLE since this technique allows in-vivo histologies due to the high level of magnification. As already mentioned in the introduction, it has already been shown that the diagnostic accuracy of CLE is comparable to histology. Hence, the inter-observer agreement is also expected to be similar to the agreement in case of histology.

Considering the CADSS approaches found throughout literature which are based on flexible endoscopy, about 12% of the methods base their experiments on a visually obtained ground truth, while the vast majority of the methods is based on histological findings (about 68%). The remaining approaches are not accompanied by the according information.

Making a recommendation concerning this issue is not easy, since the best way of obtaining the ground truth information very much depends on the endoscopic technique used. While in case of WCE a visual inspection is usually the only way a ground truth can be obtained, in case of CLE a visual ground truth gathering is likely to be sufficient due to its closeness to histology. In case of traditional flexible endoscopy a histological ground truth is highly desired due to its accuracy over visual inspection (in terms of the histopathologic classification).

3.2 Training and validation data

When developing a system aiming at pathology prediction, an important aspect is the quality of the imagery used to validate the overall effectiveness of the system.
To assess the accuracy and robustness of a CADSS some sort of image database is needed in order to be able train and validate the system. But the explanatory power of the quality assessment is directly dependent on the quality of the image database set used. The following factors are of particular importance in order to be able to compose a solid image database.

- **Size of training and validation sets**
  An important factor for the quality of an image database is the number of images available for training and validation. A low number of training images may limit the ability of the system to generalize to the prediction problem. As a consequence the probability of a wrong prediction result for new image samples is likely to be higher compared to an image database which contains a sufficiently high number of training samples.

  If the number of validation images is too low it does not matter how many training samples were used, the resulting validation accuracy computed from the data would be rather questionable (due to a rather low informative value).
- **Balance between different image classes**
  In general, image databases used in CADSSs consist of two or more image classes, each denoting a particular pathology. To avoid overfitting the system to a particular pathology the number of images used for the different classes should be balanced.

  In case of an imbalanced training set the CADSS used may have problems to adapt to the image database, resulting in a higher likelihood of assigning unknown images to the image class which contains the most images within the training set (which might result in a wrong prediction). If the validation image set is imbalanced the different accuracy estimations may vary significantly across the classes in terms of their significance. This applies to MIC systems as well as to CBIR systems.

  In case of classifier-based systems the overfitting to the dominant class (in terms of the number of images available) happens in the underlying classifier already. But the likelihood of running into this kind of problem also depends on the classifier used. While there exist classifiers which are more resistant against imbalanced training sets (e.g. the Support Vector Machines classifier), others are not able to cope well with this kind of problem (e.g. the k-NN classifier).

  Depending on the degree of imbalance and the number of results to be returned from the system, a CBIR-based system is also likely to return a list of wrong matches – in favor of the class containing the most training images. But since a CBIR system usually also returns a similarity score along with the retrieval result, wrong matches can be identified more easily.

Another problem is a rather high feature vector dimensionality compared to the number of training images available. In this case a problem called the "curse of dimensionality"

(Bellman, 1961) might arise. This problem is caused by the fact that high-dimensional feature vectors are more likely to be sparsely distributed in the feature space if the pool of training images is not sufficiently large. As a consequence the system might loose its ability to generalize to the prediction problem and overfitting might occur.
A possible solution to the "curse of dimensionality" are feature subset selection algorithms, which, based on some selection criterion, reduce a given feature set to a nearly optimal subset (Jain & Zongker, 1997). But, depending on the dimensionality of the original feature set, the desired target dimensionality, and the selection algorithm chosen, the computational burden imposed to the training process of the system might get considerably high (which, however, has no impact on the computational performance during prediction).

3.3 Pathology prediction accuracy

Before a CADSS can be used in clinical routine, it must be ensured that certain accuracy requirements are fulfilled.

3.3.1 Commonly used validation protocols

To measure the accuracy of a system usually different strategies can be employed. While the best choice is to use separate training and validation image sets to assess the accuracy of a pathology prediction system (as implicitly assumed in Section 3.2), this is sometimes not possible due to the limited number of images available in the image database used.
Anyhow, in such cases different possibilities exist to be able to assess the system accuracy of a pathology prediction system (Duda et al., 2000). In literature, dealing with CADSSs in medical endoscopy of the GI tract, the most commonly used approaches for system validation are Leave-One-Out cross-validation, Leave-One-Patient-Out cross-validation, and k-fold cross-validation. A schematic illustration of these validation methods is provided in Figure 7.

- **Leave-One-Out cross-validation (LOO-CV)**
  In case of LOO-CV one image out of the used image set is considered to be an unknown sample. The remaining images are used to train the classifier or, in case of CBIR, simply serve as the image database available for retrieval queries. Then the predication step is carried out for the image left out (the unknown sample). These steps are repeated for each image in the image database, resulting in an estimate of the prediction accuracy of the system.
- **Leave-One-Patient-Out cross-validation (LOPO-CV)**
  LOPO-CV is rather similar to LOO-CV. But in contrast to LOPO-CV a more tight restriction is posed to the training (or CBIR database composition) in the cross-validation process. In addition to the image left out for training, all images originating from the same patient are left out too. The prediction and final estimation of the prediction accuracy are then carried out the same way as in case of LOO-CV.

  Sometimes a slightly relaxed variation of LOPO-CV is employed. Instead of restricting the training to images originating from a different patient than the image to be classified originates from, only images from the same pathology (e.g. polyp) must not be used during the training phase. Hence, when training the system, images from the patient currently subject of classification may be included in the training set as well (as long as these do not show the same abnormality). In case of polyps, this is sometimes referred to as Leave-One-Polyp-Out cross-validation.

- **k-fold cross-validation (KF-CV)**
This type of cross-validation is basically a generalized version of LOO-CV. For KF-CV the set of available images is partitioned into k different subsets. Then, while the samples from one subset are used for the prediction, the samples from the remaining subsets are used to train the classifier in case of MIC-based systems (or compose the training image database for CBIR). This is repeated for each partition available. As a consequence, the training only considers images from other subsets than the one currently under classification. For k equals the number of images in the image database, KF-CV reduces to LOO-CV. If the partitions are chosen to be disjoint in terms of the patients, KF-CV equals LOPO-CV.

Fig. 7. Schematic illustration of the different cross-validation methods described in the text.

Despite the fact that cross-validation is a convenient way of dealing with a limited number of images available, these methods also have one common drawback, at least in case of classifier-based systems. Since the training set changes with each image, patient, or subset left out during cross-validation, the classifier used must be retrained. Depending on the classifier, this may result in a considerable increase of the computational demand. But at least in case of KF-CV this can be controlled by adjusting the number of partitions accordingly. However, while in case of KF-CV a higher number of partitions means a reduced loss of training data, this also increases the computational demand for training (since training has to be performed more often in this case).
Another problem, especially noticeable in case of LOPO-CV and KF-CV, is the reduced training data available under certain circumstances (this applies to MIC-based systems as well as to CBIR systems). For LOPO-CV this problem emerges in case of a high number of images per patient. As a consequence, leaving out one patient from training may result in a considerable drop in terms of the training images available. Since a rather low number of partitions used in case of KF-CV results in a high number of samples within each partition, the training set gets considerably smaller if one such partition is left out during training. As a consequence, the system might be unable to generalize to the prediction problem stated. The

partitions should also be chosen in such a way the the number of images available for each image class is well balanced throughout the partitions used for training.
For LOO-CV the training set reduction is usually not noticeable. However, when using this cross-validation protocol, the increase of the computational demand for training a classifier in MIC systems can get especially noticeable. In addition, the fact that the training set may contain images similar to the image for which the pathology should be predicted for, the accuracy outcome may have a substantially lowered informative value (since there is no restriction imposed on training images, neither in terms of the patient nor in terms of pathologies of single patients).
Considering the different properties of the cross-validation protocols just discussed, the best choice would be to use LOPO-CV. This way, compared to LOO-CV, the danger of overfitting reduced to a great extent. While KF-CV must also be favored compared to LOO-CV, the partition of the image set must be performed carefully in order to have roughly the same number of images from each image class within each partition. In addition the partitions should be chosen such that they are disjoint to a maximum possible extent in terms of patients (or pathologies of single patients).

3.3.2 Explanatory power of results

While it is important for a pathology prediction system to exhibit a certain level of accuracy to be of practical use, it is also important to be able to compare the accuracies of a system to accuracies reported for other approaches from literature.
The first issue to be addressed is therefore the choice of the right measures, which must have enough explanatory power in order to make the results reported useful. Throughout literature, dealing with automated pathology prediction in endoscopy of the GI tract, the use of different measures can be observed. In case of MIC-based systems usually one or more of the following measures are used:

- **Overall accuracy**
  The overall accuracy of a system is computed by dividing the total number of classified correctly by the total number of images available in the image database used. While the overall accuracy gives an overview of the overall performance of a system, there is no evidence about the classification performance for the different image classes.
- **Specificity and sensitivity**
  These measures are only applicable if the prediction should be carried out for two image classes only (e.g. is a polyp visible or not on a given image? shows a given image neoplastic tissue or not?). The specificity, also known as true negative rate, corresponds to the number of images taken from healthy patients, which have been predicted as belonging to the image class containing the images from healthy patients. The sensitivity, also known as true positive rate, on the other hand, denotes how many images, showing abnormal pathologies, have actually been classified as belonging to the class of sick patients.

  Usually both measures are given together, as providing only one of both measures may lead to a misinterpretation of the results. If for example a naive classifier is used (which classifies all images as belonging to the class of healthy patients) the respective specificity would equal 100%, but the sensitivity would equal 0%. Hence, in this case, providing the specificity only could lead to the conclusion that the classification performance is perfect. However, when providing both measures together it is obvious that the classifier performs rather poor.

- **Class accuracies**
  Computing accuracies for each image class is necessary in cases where the image databases consists of more than two classes (e.g. distinction between normal tissue, hyperplastic tissue, neoplasms, and metaplastic changes). Hence, the accuracy for a single class is determined by dividing the number of images correctly classified as belonging to the class by the total number of images contained in the class.
- **Area under curve of a ROC plot**
  In ROC plots (Receiver Operating Characteristics) the sensitivity of a system is plotted against the false positive rate (1-specificity). When computing the sensitivity and the specificity for different choices of parameters inherent to the respective system, the result is a plot. This plot is of particular interest, especially for medical experts, since an investigation of the plot allows to get an idea of the overall system performance. In addition, by computing the area under the curve (AUC) (Hanley & McNeil, 1982), the overall performance of a pathology prediction system can be expressed with a single value.

Compared to MIC-based systems, CBIR-based systems are usually judged by precision and recall (but sometimes also measures typically used in case of MIC-based systems are given). Precision is computed as the number of relevant images in the retrieved list of images divided by the total number of retrieved images, where relevant images are those which should be retrieved since they are of particular interest. Recall, on the other hand, is computed as the number of relevant images contained in the retrieval result divided by the total number of relevant images (in the context of a classifier the recall rate is equal to the sensitivity). Similar to ROC plots plotting precision against recall leads to the PR plot, which allows to get an idea of the overall retrieval performance of the prediction system.

To compare a pathology prediction system against others in terms of accuracy it is not sufficient to just compare the methods in terms of the different measures available. Even if two approaches deliver different values for some accuracy measure there is no evidence given that the observed differences are of any significance. Hence, to assess whether two different approaches differ significantly some sort of statistical test has to be employed.

An example for a tool to decide on statistical significance is McNemar's test statistic (Everitt, 1977). This statistic keeps track whether two different approaches classify an image correctly or not. Based on this information, McNemar's test allows to assess the statistical significance of differences observed between two methods. In addition, using McNemar's test, a p-value can be computed, which is used frequently in medical publications and, hence, of particular interest for medical experts.

3.4 Runtime performance

An important issue, which depends on the target application area, is the computational demand of the CADSS. If a pathology prediction system is to be used offline (i.e. the system is used after the endoscopy procedure) the requirements in terms of the runtime performance are not as tight as this is the case with systems to be used in a real-time environment. This issue is of special importance in case of MIC-based systems since CBIR-based systems are usually designed to be used offline anyways. Nevertheless, even in case of CBIR the system should be designed and optimized such that the prediction can be obtained in a reasonable amount of time. If a query of a CBIR system lasts for several minutes or even hours, the benefit of using the system would diminish or get lost completely.

But if we strive for a MIC system applicable in real-time environments certain time constraints must be met in order to be of practical use. If we assume an endoscopy video to be captured at a frame rate of 25 frames per second, the pathology prediction of the system must be feasible in less than 40 milliseconds for a single frame. If detection of potentially abnormal regions is carried out by the endoscopist, who already provides regions of interest to the MIC system (designed solely for classification, not the detection), the time constraints may be relaxed to a few seconds for a single image. However, if the time constraints are not fulfilled, similar to CBIR, the advantage of using such a system would get lost.

4. Examples from literature

In the following we compare some recent works found in literature dealing with CADSSs in medical endoscopy of the GI tract. For each prediction type – MIC and CBIR – we present and compare two approaches in terms of issues discussed in the previous sections.

4.1 Classifier-based prediction

In order to compare two classifier-based approaches found in literature we picked two recently published approaches (found in Tischendorf et al. (2010) and Häfner et al. (2010)). Some facts about these approaches are listed in Table 1.

	Tischendorf et al. (2010)	Häfner et al. (2010)
Endoscope type	Zoom-endoscopy (NBI)	Zoom-endoscopy (Color dyes)
GI tract part	Colon	Colon
Abnormality	Polyps	Polyps
# of classes	2	2
Prediction aim	Neoplastic (Yes/No)	Neoplastic (Yes/No)
Ground truth	Histology-based	Histology-based
Cross-validation	LOO-CV	LOO-CV
# of images available	209	627
# of patients	223	N/A
Overall accuracy	$\approx 85\%$	$\approx 93\%$

Table 1. Some facts about the two examples for MIC-based approaches recently proposed.

While both methods are similar in terms of the GI tract part under investigation, the pathology of interest, the prediction goal (hence, also the same number of classes), the cross-validation protocol used, and the way the ground truth has been obtained, we also notice some differences between these works.

- **Endoscope type**
  Although both methods rely on zoom-endoscopes, the way to highlight mucosal features differs between these works. While in (Tischendorf et al., 2010) NBI has been used, the approach presented in (Häfner et al., 2010) is based on the application of topical staining (using color dyes), which still is common practice in clinical routine.
- **Number of patients**
  While in (Tischendorf et al., 2010) the experiments are based on images originating from 223 patients, the work presented in (Häfner et al., 2010) makes no statements about this detail. Nevertheless, as already pointed out earlier, using too many images from one patient may lead to an overfitting. While we know that Tischendorf et al. on average use roughly one image per patient, we are not able to get a picture about the possible degree of overfitting in case of (Häfner et al., 2010). This is especially problematic since LOO-CV

is used to assess the prediction accuracy for the system. Hence, the experiments in (Häfner et al., 2010) might be overfitted if images from one distinct polyp are used for training and classification.

- **Number of images used**
  Comparing the total number of images between the two approaches clearly shows that the number of images used in (Häfner et al., 2010) is roughly three times higher compared to (Tischendorf et al., 2010). Since, as pointed out above, we have no figures about the number of patients in case of (Häfner et al., 2010), it is not possible to assess whether this is beneficial (since, in case of only a few patients, this would lead to overfitting).

Although, at a first glance, the approach presented in (Häfner et al., 2010) seems to perform better in terms of the overall prediction accuracy compared to (Tischendorf et al., 2010), a comparison of the overall system accuracies would be meaningless. This is mainly due to the fact that both approaches are based on quite different image databases. In addition, as already pointed out, we have no idea about the degree of possibly happened overfitting in case of (Häfner et al., 2010).

4.2 CBIR-based prediction

The number of CBIR-based prediction systems found in literature is very limited compared to MIC-based approaches. According to our literature review 4 out of 5 methods found in total, proposed for CBIR-based prediction in case of endoscopy of the GI tract, have been published by the research group around André et al. Nevertheless, we carry out a comparison of two exemplar approaches (found in André et al. (2009) and Münzenmayer et al. (2009)). Some details on these approaches are given in Table 2.

	André et al. (2009)	**Münzenmayer et al. (2009)**
Endoscope type	CLE	Traditional endoscope
GI tract part	Colon	Esophagus
Abnormality	Polyps	Barrett's esophagus
# of classes	2	3
Prediction aim	Neoplastic (Yes/No)	State of epithelium
Ground truth	Histology-based	Histology-based
Cross-validation	LOPO-CV	LOO-CV
# of images available	1036	390
# of patients	52	61
Overall accuracy	$\approx 80\%$	$\approx 81\%$

Table 2. Some facts about the two examples of CBIR-based approaches recently proposed.

While both systems base their experiments on a ground truth obtained by a histopathologic examination and the overall accuracies reported seem to be very similar, a direct comparison of the reported accuracies is not feasible due to some significant differences (different GI tract parts, different abnormalities of interest, and different prediction aims). We nevertheless discuss a few aspects of these approaches:

- **Endoscopy type**
  While both methods rely on flexible endoscopes, in case of (André et al., 2009) a CLE endoscope is used. In contrast to (Münzenmayer et al., 2009) this is an advantage since, as already pointed out in Section 1.1, this allows in-vivo histologies. Nevertheless, André et al. support their finding with a histopathologic examination.

- **Number of images used**
  While the number of patients contained in the underlying image databases is rather high in both approaches, we notice that in case of (André et al., 2009) the number of total images used is nearly four times higher compared to (Münzenmayer et al., 2009). The implies that the average number of images per patient is approximately 20 and 6 in case of (André et al., 2009) and (Münzenmayer et al., 2009), respectively.
- **Cross-validation used**
  A key difference between the methods compared is the type of cross-validation employed. While in (Münzenmayer et al., 2009) LOO-CV is used, André et al. use LOPO-CV (the images from the patient currently under prediction are left out). Hence, compared to the experiments in (André et al., 2009), the approach validated in (Münzenmayer et al., 2009) suffers from the fact that images from patients currently under prediction might well be contained in the training set too.

Although a comparison would not be meaningful we can at least deduce, that the validation accuracy reported in (Münzenmayer et al., 2009) must be taken with caution, since overfitting might have happened due to the validation-protocol used. André et al. bypassed this problem by employing LOPO-CV.

5. Conclusion and future outlook

In the previous sections we gave an overview of CADSSs targeted at pathology prediction in medical endoscopy in the GI tract. We showed that especially throughout the past two decades the is a rising interest in this research topic.

Since throughout literature concerned with this topic usually either MIC-based systems or CBIR-based systems are proposed, we highlighted the similarities and differences between such systems. We outlined the different different aspects of such systems and highlighted different issues inherent to the development of such systems. In addition, we also discussed common pitfalls which have to be considered to develop reliable and comparable prediction systems.

Especially for a potential use in clinical practice it is important that the accuracy of a prediction systems is above a certain level. But, as we also discussed in the previous section, with the danger of overfitting in mind, it is even more important that the accuracy of such systems is validated properly. While the best option is using different training and validation set this if often not possible due to a limited number of images. In such a case it is therefore even more important to choose a suitable validation protocol which limits the danger of overfitting.

We are currently not aware of systems used in daily routine. While the reasons for this are most probably manifold, it is apparent that stronger collaborations between developers of prediction systems and medical experts are needed, as this is the basis for real world testing of such systems. In addition, the feedback given by medical experts is valuable in order to develop more reliable and accurate systems. However, in order to allow meaningful collaborations with medical experts the explanatory power of the prediction results is important to allow the expert to quickly assess the quality of the system.

Considering recent technological advances in case of endoscopy devices and the new possibilities offered by these endoscopic modalities for a computer-assisted diagnosis, it is out of question that automated prediction will get more precise by fully taking advantage of these techniques. Especially, CLE is a prospective candidate to replace time-consuming biopsies and foster real-time diagnosis systems.

6. Acknowledgments

This work is partially funded by the Austrian Science Fund (FWF) under Project No. L366-N15 and by the Austrian National Bank "Jubiläumsfonds" Project No. 12514.

7. References

André, B., Vercauteren, T., Perchant, A., Buchner, A. M., Wallace, M. B. & Ayache, N. (2009). Endomicroscopic image retrieval and classification using invariant visual features, *In Proceedings of the 6th IEEE International Symposium on Biomedical Imaging: From Nano to Macro (ISBI'09)*, Boston, Massachusetts, USA, pp. 346–349.

Bellman, R. (1961). *Adaptive Control Processes: A Guided Tour*, Princeton University Press.

Buchner, A. M., Shahid, M. W., Heckman, M. G., Krishna, M., Ghabril, M., Hasan, M., Crook, J. E., Gomez, V., Raimondo, M., Woodward, T., Wolfsen, H. C. & Wallace, M. B. (2010). Comparison of probe-based confocal laser endomicroscopy with virtual chromoendoscopy for classification of colon polyps, *Gastroenterology* 138(3): 834–842.

Church, J. (2008). Adenoma detection rate and the quality of colonoscopy: the sword has two edges, *Diseases of the Colon & Rectum* 51(5): 520–523.

Cobrin, G. M., Pittman, R. H. & Lewis, B. S. (2006). Increased diagnostic yield of small bowel tumors with capsule endoscopy., *Cancer* 107(1): 22–27.

Coimbra, M., Mackiewicz, M., Fisher, M., Jamieson, C., Scares, J. & Cunha, J. P. S. (2007). Computer vision tools for capsule endoscopy exam analysis, *EURASIP Newsletter* 18(1): 1–19.

Doi, K. (2007). Computer-aided diagnosis in medical imaging: Historical review, current status and future potential, *Computerized Medical Imaging and Graphics* 31(4–5): 192–211.

Duda, R. O., Hart, P. E. & Stork, D. G. (2000). *Pattern Classification*, 2nd edn, Wiley & Sons.

El-Matary, W. (2008). Wireless capsule endoscopy: Indications, limitations, and future challenges, *Journal of Pediatric Gastroenterology and Nutrition* 46(1): 4–12.

Eliakim, R. (2004). Wireless capsule video endoscopy: three years of experience, *World Journal of Gastroenterology* 10(9): 1238–1239.

Eliakim, R., Yassin, K., Shlomi, I., Suissa, A. & Eisen, G. M. (2004). A novel diagnostic tool for detecting oesophageal pathology: the PillCam oesophageal video capsule, *Alimentary Pharmacology & Therapeutics* 20: 1083–1089.

Emura, F., Saito, Y. & Ikematsu, H. (2008). Narrow-band imaging optical chromocolonoscopy: advantages and limitations., *World Journal of Gastroenterology* 14(31): 4867–4872.

Everitt, B. (1977). *The Analysis of Contingency Tables*, Chapman and Hall.

Fireman, Z. & Kopelman, Y. (2007). The colon–the latest terrain for capsule endoscopy, *Digestive and Liver Disease* 39(10): 895–899.

Fukunaga, K. (1990). *Introduction to Statistical Pattern Recognition*, 2nd edn, Morgan Kaufmann.

Häfner, M., Brunauer, L., Payer, H., Resch, R., Gangl, A., Uhl, A., Vécsei, A. & Wrba, F. (2010). Computer-aided classification of zoom-endoscopical images using fourier filters, *IEEE Transactions on Information Technology in Biomedicine* 14(4): 958–970.

Häfner, M., Gangl, A., Liedlgruber, M., Uhl, A., Vécsei, A. & Wrba, F. (2010). Classification of endoscopic images using Delaunay triangulation-based edge features, *Proceedings of the International Conference on Image Analysis and Recognition (ICIAR'10)*, Vol. 6112 of *Springer LNCS*, Povoa de Varzim, Portugal, pp. 131–140.

Hanley, J. A. & McNeil, B. J. (1982). The meaning and use of the area under a receiver operating characteristic (ROC) curve, *Radiology* 143(1): 29–36.

Hurlstone, D. P., Cross, S. S., Adam, I., Shorthouse, A. J., Brown, S., Sanders, D. S. & Lobo, A. J. (2004). Efficacy of high magnification chromoscopic colonoscopy for the diagnosis of neoplasia in flat and depressed lesions of the colorectum: a prospective analysis, *Gut* 53(2): 284–290.

Jain, A. & Zongker, D. (1997). Feature selection: Evaluation, application, and small sample performance, *IEEE Transactions on Pattern Analysis and Machine Intelligence* 19: 153–158.

Kelsey, P. (2005). Colon - Normal Colon. The DAVE Project. Available at `http://daveproject.org/viewfilms.cfm?film_id=300`.

Kiesslich, R. (2007). Colon - Endomicroscopic Imaging of NSAID Associated Colitis. The DAVE Project. Available at `http://daveproject.org/viewfilms.cfm?film_id=561`.

Kiesslich, R. & Neurath, M. F. (2007). Endomicroscopy is born – do we still need the pathologist?, *Gastrointestinal Endoscopy* 66(1): 150–153.

Müller, H., Michoux, N., Bandon, D. & Geissbuhler, A. (2004). A review of content-based image retrieval systems in medical applications–clinical benefits and future directions, *International Journal of Medical Informatics* 73(1): 1–23.

Münzenmayer, C., Kage, A., Wittenberg, T. & Mühldorfer, S. (2009). Computer-assisted diagnosis for precancerous lesions in the esophagus, *Methods of Information in Medicine* 48: 324–330.

Swain, P. (2003). Wireless capsule endoscopy, *Gut* 52(4): 48–50.

Tischendorf, J. J. W., Gross, S., Winograd, R., Hecker, H., Auer, R., Behrens, A., Trautwein, C., Aach, T. & Stehle, T. (2010). Computer-aided classification of colorectal polyps based on vascular patterns: a pilot study, *Endoscopy* 42(3): 203–207.

11

Workflow and Clinical Decision Support for Radiation Oncology

Daniel L McShan
Department of Radiation Oncology, University of Michigan
USA

1. Introduction

Radiation oncology involves a complex set of processes and accompanying workflow to evaluate, plan, deliver, and monitor patient treatments. The workflow includes a mixture of process steps requiring clinical decisions at many points, quality assurance checks along the way, on-line and off-line evaluations, and careful patient monitoring. Computerized decision support is a vital component to a number of these processes, providing computational services and evaluation tools for decision alternatives.
In this chapter an overview of the current processes and decisions typically required for radiation oncology patient management will be presented. A description of recent "Lean Thinking" approaches to improve efficiencies in these processes with the primary goal to improve patient care and staff satisfaction will be presented. Finally we present future treatment scenarios that may lead to improved treatments and discuss resulting new requirements for the management and clinical decision support in radiation oncology.

2. Radiation oncology

Radiation oncology is one of the major treatment techniques for the management of malignant tumors (cancer). Radiation therapy is typically used to treat deep-seated, well-localized (focal) regions where high-energy radiation can be concentrated. The radiation used causes ionization within the tissue exposed and this ionization leads to DNA single and double strand breaks which can destroy a cell's ability to undergo mitosis (grow). Concentrating the radiation at target areas and reducing the volume irradiated outside of the target provides the therapeutic advantages that radiation oncology uses to treat cancer.
Decisions regarding treatment of a patient's cancer typically begins with a referral based on diagnostic evidence. Within larger institution, this decision is made within the context of a tumor review board (organized by disease site) at which the patient's case is presented, reviewed, and choices of treatment (including not only radiation but other treatment options including surgery and chemotherapy) are discussed. The various treatment options have their own advantages and disadvantages. It is not unusual for radiation treatments to be preceded by surgery to remove easily extracted parts of a tumor. Nor is it unusual for radiation therapy to be combined with chemotherapy that can treat regions where tumor cells are more disseminated (spread out). In the review board setting, a patient's case is usually screened for possible inclusion into a clinical trial if appropriate.

Patients who are referred to radiation oncology can expect an initial evaluation exam (consult) followed by general decisions about an appropriate treatment course with the possibility of accepting the option of participating in a clinical trial.

2.1 Simulation and contouring

Assuming the treatment decisions includes external beam radiation therapy, as is most often the case, the patient will be scheduled for "simulation" involving a series of steps including design of custom immobilization to insure stable and reproducible positioning of the patient (typically treated on a flat couch) followed by acquisition of volumetric imaging studies that are used to precisely define target volumes, to be treated, and critical neighboring anatomy, to be avoided.

Often a patient will have multiple imaging studies requested including computerized tomography (CT), magnetic resonance imaging (MRI), and/or positron emission tomography (PET - Nuclear Medicince (NM)) used to build the patient model (Fig. 1).(Kessler 2006)

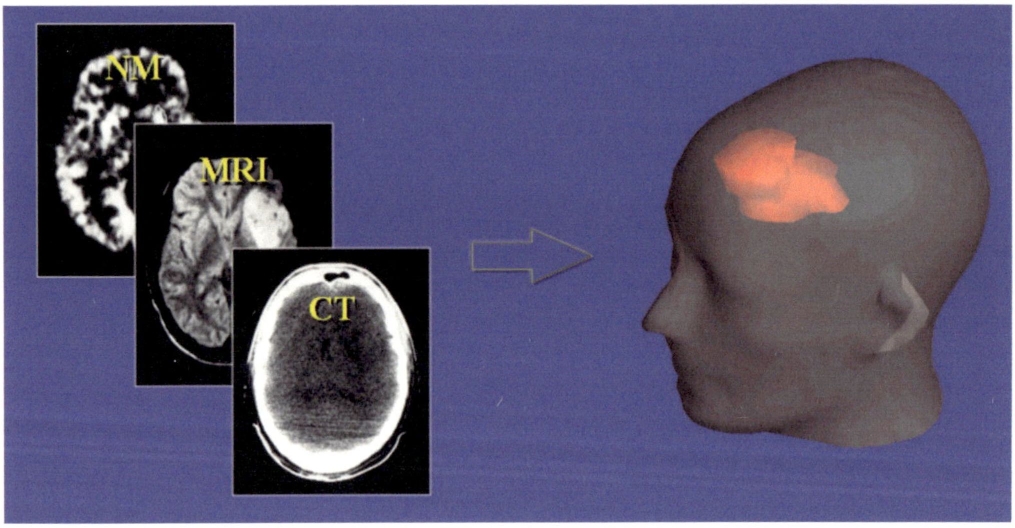

Fig. 1. Multiple modality volumetric images are often used to build a geometrical model of the patient

These studies often provide complementary information that can be useful for radiation treatment planning. The different imaging studies require different equipment, different personnel, different imaging procedures or protocols and have separate scheduling demands. Once imaging studies are completed, additional steps are needed for the cases with multiple imaging studies in that they need to be geometrically registered to each other so that the derived information can be consolidated into a self-consistent picture of the patient. Although the image registration process uses automated techniques, there is still a need to visually inspect the results to insure that they are consistent with expectations (i.e. registrations are not always perfect.)

Throughout these various workflow steps, there are variety of points where there are clinically-based decisions to be made and ultimately, it is the responsible physician who needs to approve the overall results prior to the next step of treatment planning (designing beam arrangements).

Following image acquisition and registration, the next steps are to generate volumetric definitions of the target and surrounding anatomical features. In some cases these regions can be generated via automated segmentation algorithms. Automated segmentation is often based on trying to identify connected edges which are closely matched to the underlying image data based on absolute image values and image value gradients. Difficulties with this approach occur when the neighboring tissues vary significantly around the periphery of the desired region. The use of standard anatomical models provides some promise for automating segmentation of more of the anatomical features; but a fundamental problem is that cancer by its nature tends to create abnormal distortions which are difficult to account for.

Some manually delineated drawing and editing is still the norm for completing the identification of key volumes. Part of the reason is the failure of even the most robust segmentation algorithms to achieve reasonable segmentation for many cases. In addition, manual volume segmentation is needed to define regions such as the clinical target volume (CTV) which includes not only the contrast enhanced regions visible on cross-sectional imaging (the gross target volume (GTV)) but also includes suspected tumor burden at a microscopic level (not detectable with current imaging techniques) at the periphery of the GTV. Once the CTV is defined, then this volume is typically further expanded to generate a planning target volume (PTV) which accounts for setup and motion uncertainties.

Efforts towards adding computer-assisted support to aid in the process of defining the CTV have been undertaken by a number of researchers. A recent effort by Kalet, et al. 2009(Kalet, Mejino et al. 2009), uses content from a large scale anatomy ontology (Foundational Model of Anatomy(FMA)) to look at identifying and mapping the lymphatic system close to the region of a given tumor. The lymphatic system is a preferred avenue for cancer cells to spread and the primary terminating lymph nodes closes to the tumor are candidates for inclusion in the volume to be treated. Unfortunately, from this study, the completeness and consistency of the FMA knowledge model was found to be an issue. Nevertheless, this study points to techniques that can be employed (in the future) to further assist clinicians.

2.2 Treatment planning

The most prevalent type of radiation therapy is the use of external beam treatments involving the design of a number of directed external beams of high-energy x-rays or particles. Typically a treatment involves radiation exposures delivered sequentially from a pre-defined set of directions all of which are aimed at the target but are otherwise separated to reduce radiation to non-involved tissue. Computer graphics play an important component in the treatment planning design. A beam's eye view (BEV) graphics is shown in Figure 2 showing the view of the anatomy from the perspective of the radiation source (in the head of the gantry). The BEV graphics assists in the shaping to the target and avoidance of normal critical structures. (McShan, Fraass et al. 1990)

Estimation of the expected radiation dose (absorbed energy) requires extensive computer calculations on a volumetric grid. The next step in planning is to then evaluate those results. Figure 3 and 4 provide examples of some of the graphical presentations used for dose evaluation. (Kessler, Ten Haken et al. 1994)

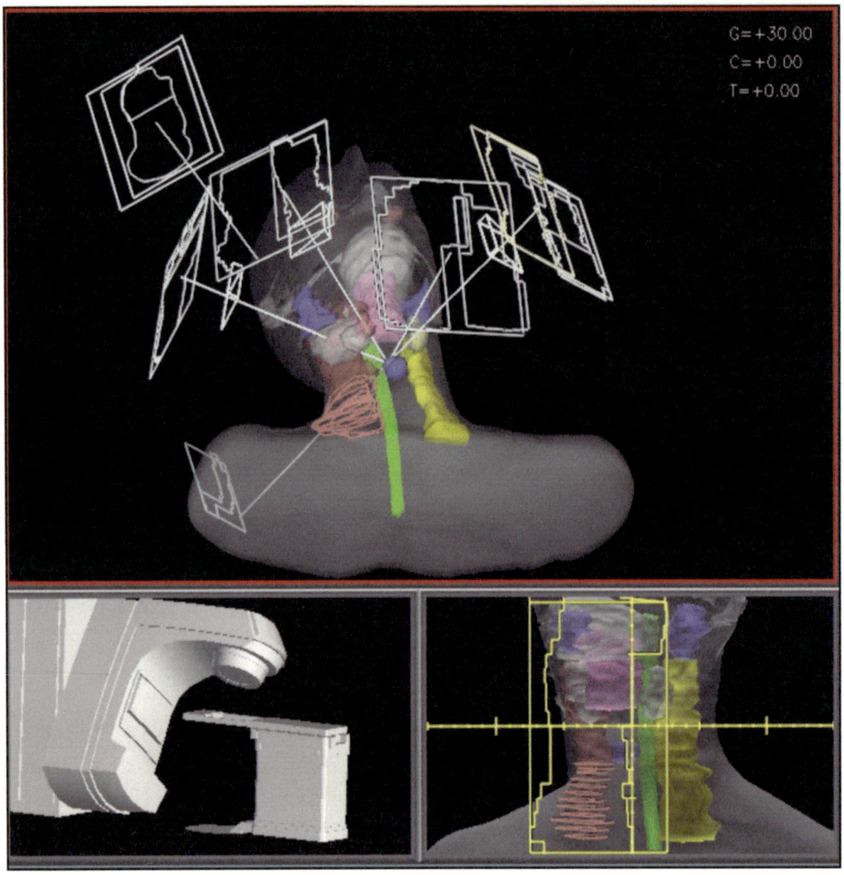

Fig. 2. External beam design for neck (parotid) treatment. Lower left is treatment machine model position for one of the treatment fields. Lower right shows the beam's eye view projection of target and field shaping.

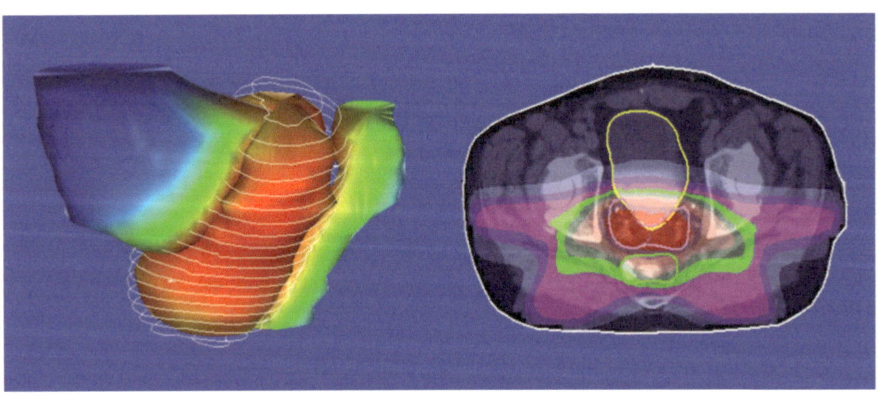

Fig. 3. Dose evaluation graphics for conformal prostate. Left image shows bladder and rectum with color wash representation of dose along with isodose contours surrounding the prostate target volume. Right image shows color wash dose overlaying a single axial slice.

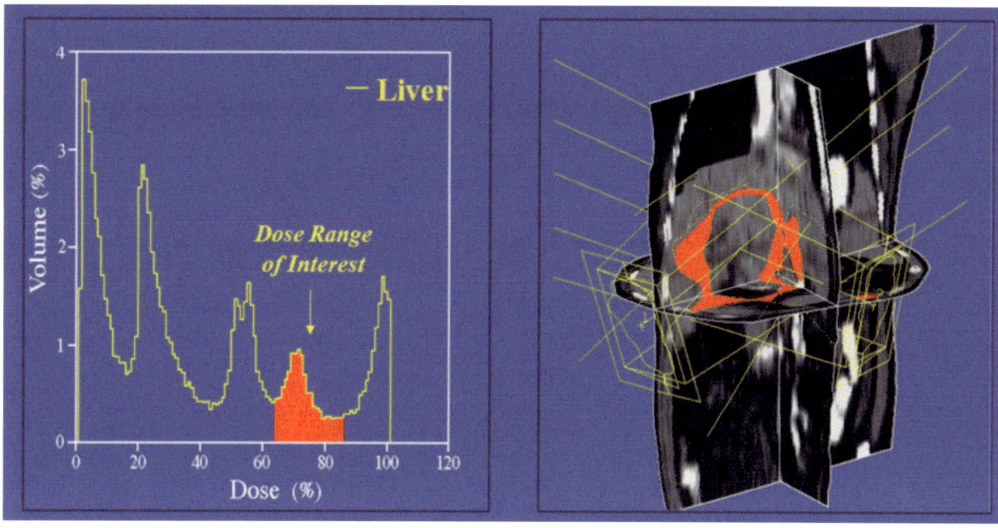

Fig. 4. Dose volume histogram analysis (with dose range highlighted)

Evaluating the achieved planned dose distribution is a key decision step resulting in physician approval prior to treatment. Despite upfront specification of various treatment planning goals, numerous factors and trade-offs are involved that are not easily quantified or assessed requiring the physician to use his or her judgment and experience by reviewing the dose distributions and the relative shapes of dose volume curves. Ideally, of course, this would not be the case since a decision rejecting the proposed plan can require significant rework based on new previously unstated "goals".

Computer assisted treatment planning is often an iterative process with the dosimetrist responsible for the treatment planning making changes interactively to the beam design to improve the resulting dose distribution. With modern intensity modulation delivery techniques, computerized optimization can be used to design "optimal" treatments based on analytical planning goals. In practice, though, the planning is not fully optimized and there are numerous steps and decisions involved in setting up beam arrangements and even iterating on priorities and goal requirements to achieve an acceptable treatment plan.

2.3 Treatment delivery

Once a treatment plan is approved, then the next steps in the process require that the data be transferred from the treatment planning system to the treatment machine. In some cases where new or particularly complicated treatments are being proposed, it is necessary to interject quality assurance steps where the treatment plan is delivered to a test phantom with dose measurement devices. The measured data then needs to be analyzed and compared to dose estimations from the treatment planning system (calculated using the same geometry) and the comparison approved prior to treatment.

Another step in treatment preparation can be treatment delivery simulation. As treatment machines become more sophisticated and treatment planning becomes more clever, it is possible to design a plan requiring complicated motions. There are issues of not having the machine collide with itself or worse with the patient (as shown in Figure 5). A delivery simulation step can facilitate the sequence of delivery and interject non-treatment "moves" as necessary for safety.(Kessler, McShan et al. 1995)

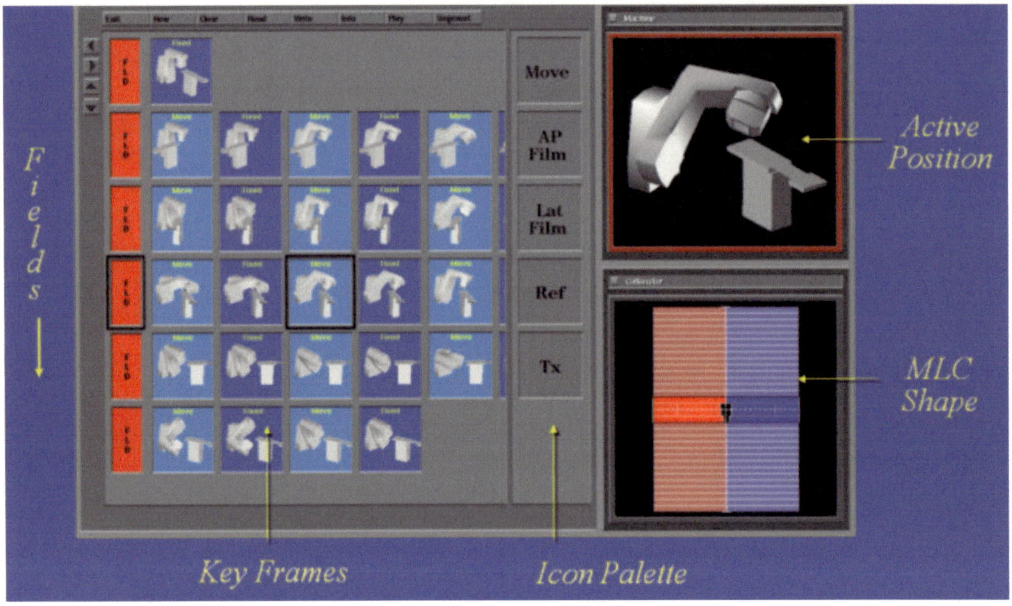

Fig. 5. Treatment delivery simulator

Individual radiation therapy treatments themselves also require several workflow steps. Radiation patients are frequently treated on an out-patient basis which means they need to show up on schedule and the radiation therapist needs to be notified to prep the patient. For the treatment, the patient is placed on the treatment table using the same immobilization device created during simulation. The patient is moved to the approximate treatment position using laser guided adjustments. Typically orthogonal portal images (diagnostic x-rays) or cone-beam CT volumes are taken to assess the patient position against a computer generated version using the planning CT volumes. Generally small adjustments to the patient position are made automatically. Alternatively, small markers implanted directly in the tumor can be used to provide more direct positioning information. (Often tumors themselves are not detectable from typical planar x-ray imaging.)

The actual treatments then involve moving the treatment machine (gantry) to the starting beam angle and then proceeding through the succeeding beams usually without manual interruption. Typical treatment times range from 5-10 minutes for simple cases to over 30 minutes for more complex treatments.

Typically radiation treatments are delivered in fractions (a fraction being one complete delivery of all beams) and fractions are repeated for 30 or more days, usually treated 5-6 times per week. Because of the repeated treatment sessions, there are number of factors which affect the quality of the treatment. Because the patient's setup is repeated for each fraction, there are unavoidable geometrical errors. These are usually inconsequential since the targeted PTV accounts for this possibility. Normal respiratory and cardiac motions also affect the actual dose delivered. For some patients, respiratory gating is used to reduce these effects.

While these issues can generally be managed, the patient can lose weight over the weeks of treatment, their tumor may progress or shrink, and any number of other changes may affect the treatment given. In these circumstances, the patient's situation needs to be reassessed and parts of the entire simulation, planning processes are repeated (as illustrated in Fig. 6) to define a new treatment design suitable for the balance of the desired treatment.

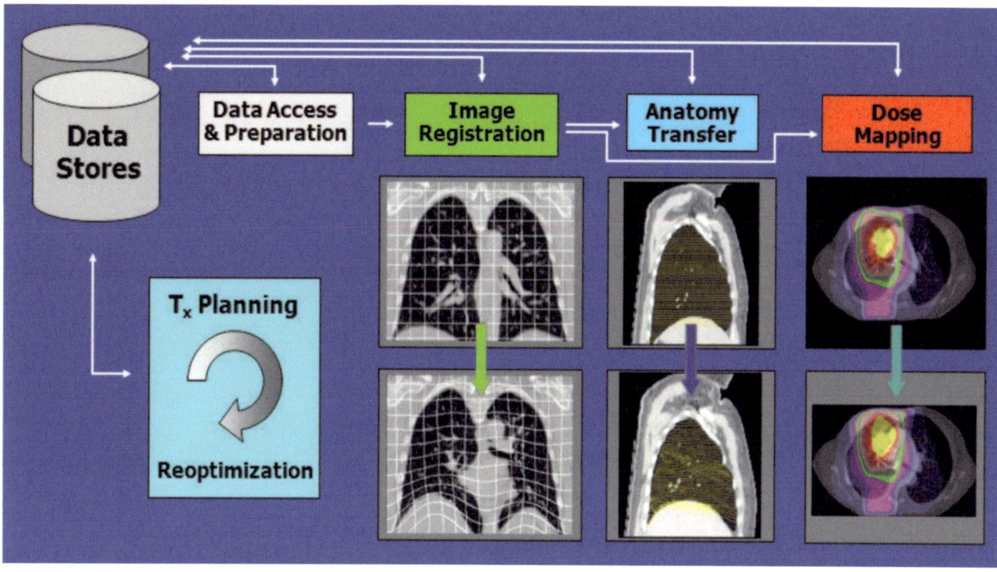

Fig. 6. Treatment modifications typically require new imaging, deformable registration, and propagation of dose which will be used in designing the balance of the treatment.

3. Lean thinking process improvements

The various processes involved in acquiring and preparing data needed for planning and the associated approvals prior to treatment involves a team of people including the attending physician, residents, nursing staff, clerical staff, dosimetrist who do the bulk of the treatment plan design work, physicist for expertise on radiation accuracy and safety, and radiation therapist who control the actual treatment delivery processes. For such a complex intertwining of personnel and processes, it is unavoidable to have inefficiencies that most often arise due to incomplete data or underspecified requirements leading to extra reworking steps. At the University of Michigan, our department has adopted "Lean Thinking" (Womack and Jones 2003) as a consistent approach to quality and process improvement. We have applied the principles and tools of Lean Thinking, especially value as defined by the customer, value stream mapping of our processes, and then with the desire to have one piece flow (i.e. no waiting) make improvements to the workflow processes associated with delivering care to our patients.

Using the lean approach, teams of representatives from our various personnel groups have been formed to first outline the current state value stream map (CS VSM) for selected parts of our processes. (Rother and Shick 2003)A CS VSM is a detailed flowchart that reveals all the actions and processes required to deliver a service to a customer (example in Figure 7).

The CS VSM allows the identification of points in our process where there are large wait times. This activity is then followed by the creation of a future state value stream map (FS VSM) based on the elimination (or minimization) of these no value wastes. Our use of lean techniques has resulted in demonstrable improvements in the management of our patients in our department improving the timeliness of treatments and improving staff efficiencies.(Kim, Hayman et al. 2007)

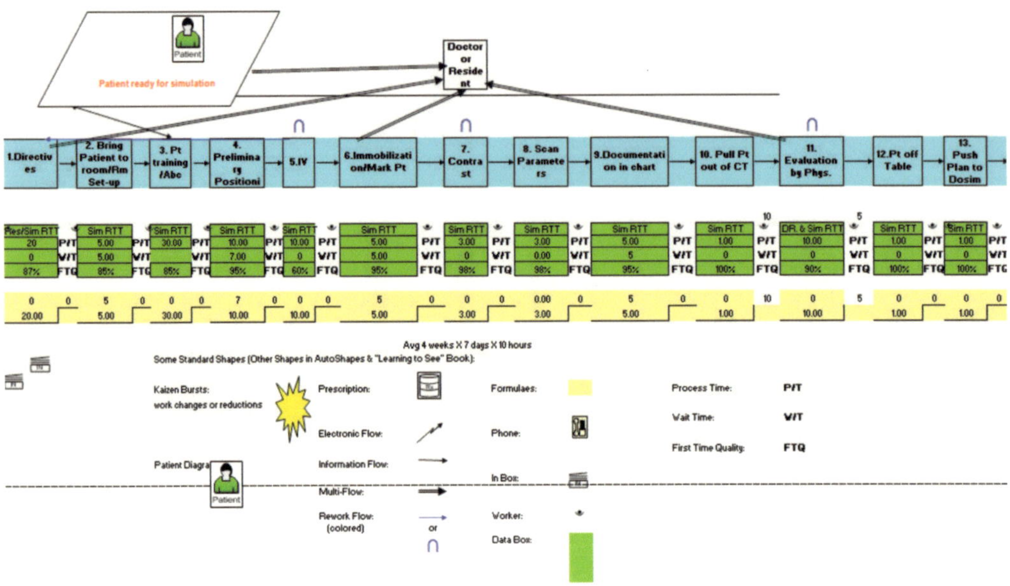

Fig. 7. Partial current State value stream map

Among the improvements in process efficiencies has been the development of planning directives where details about the data required for planning a patient's treatment are itemized. These directives are distinguished by body site, tumor type, and protocol. The directives specify what image acquisitions are needed and specify the subsequent use of this data to delineate anatomical and targeted regions. The directives also specify desired planning goals including treatment type and dose constraints for critical structures and desired target doses to be achieved. As these are generally competing requirements, a prioritization of these goals is also specified. An example directive is shown in Figure 8.

To date, these directives have been implemented on paper as a set of guidelines. The physician will make patient specific changes to these guidelines before signing off on a patient's directive. These treatment plan directives describe a standard path for each type of case in the belief that standard work leads to fewer quality problems, less rework, better attention to patient needs, more effective communication, and more efficient use of resources. The standard planning patterns represent a clinical consensus for each type of case. The directives lead to better-documented decisions and instructions, and more easily allow specification of non-standard instructions.

4. Future workflow

Surprisingly much of the Lean Thinking improvements have not, to date, required additional technology beyond a bit of paper (directives) and consensus building to understand the processes flow and when they don't. Nevertheless, it is expected that more technology will be introduced in a world that is already extensively technology based. Complex computerized machines are used for imaging, planning and delivery for radiation therapy. The information that is currently communicated is detailed but not necessarily complete in terms of understanding the overall picture of the process flow.

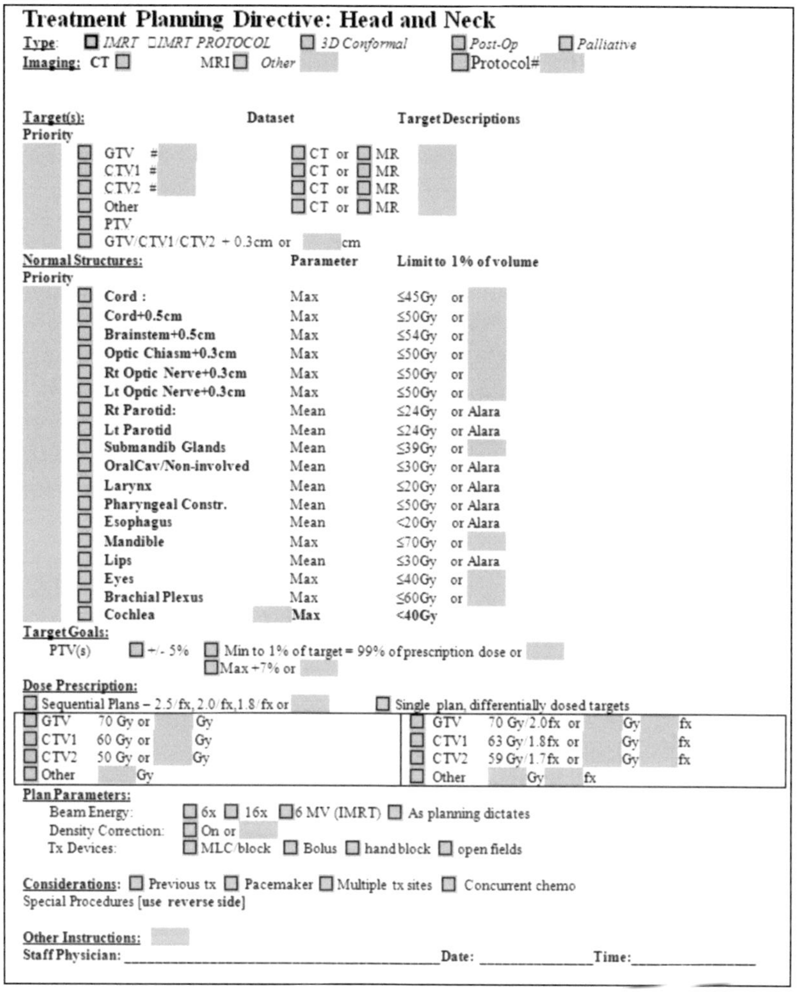

Treatment Planning Directive: Head and Neck

Type: ☐ *IMRT* ☐ *IMRT PROTOCOL* ☐ *3D Conformal* ☐ *Post-Op* ☐ *Palliative*

Imaging: CT ☐ MRI ☐ *Other* ☐ Protocol#

Target(s):

Priority		Dataset	Target Descriptions
	☐ GTV #	☐ CT or ☐ MR	
	☐ CTV1 #	☐ CT or ☐ MR	
	☐ CTV2 #	☐ CT or ☐ MR	
	☐ Other	☐ CT or ☐ MR	
	☐ PTV		
	☐ GTV/CTV1/CTV2 + 0.3cm or cm		

Normal Structures:

Priority		Parameter	Limit to 1% of volume
	☐ **Cord :**	Max	≤45Gy or
	☐ **Cord+0.5cm**	Max	≤50Gy or
	☐ **Brainstem+0.5cm**	Max	≤54Gy or
	☐ **Optic Chiasm+0.3cm**	Max	≤50Gy or
	☐ **Rt Optic Nerve+0.3cm**	Max	≤50Gy or
	☐ **Lt Optic Nerve+0.3cm**	Max	≤50Gy or
	☐ **Rt Parotid:**	Mean	≤24Gy or Alara
	☐ **Lt Parotid**	Mean	≤24Gy or Alara
	☐ **Submandib Glands**	Mean	≤39Gy or
	☐ **OralCav/Non-involved**	Mean	≤30Gy or Alara
	☐ **Larynx**	Mean	≤20Gy or Alara
	☐ **Pharyngeal Constr.**	Mean	≤50Gy or Alara
	☐ **Esophagus**	Mean	<20Gy or Alara
	☐ **Mandible**	Max	≤70Gy or
	☐ **Lips**	Mean	≤30Gy or Alara
	☐ **Eyes**	Max	≤40Gy or
	☐ **Brachial Plexus**	Max	≤60Gy or
	☐ **Cochlea**	**Max**	**<40Gy**

Target Goals:

PTV(s) ☐ +/- 5% ☐ Min to 1% of target = 99% of prescription dose or
☐ Max +7% or

Dose Prescription:

☐ Sequential Plans – 2.5/fx, 2.0/fx, 1.8/fx or	☐ Single plan, differentially dosed targets
☐ GTV 70 Gy or Gy	☐ GTV 70 Gy/2.0fx or Gy fx
☐ CTV1 60 Gy or Gy	☐ CTV1 63 Gy/1.8fx or Gy fx
☐ CTV2 50 Gy or Gy	☐ CTV2 59 Gy/1.7fx or Gy fx
☐ Other Gy	☐ Other Gy fx

Plan Parameters:

Beam Energy: ☐ 6x ☐ 16x ☐ 6 MV (IMRT) ☐ As planning dictates
Density Correction: ☐ On or
Tx Devices: ☐ MLC/block ☐ Bolus ☐ hand block ☐ open fields

Considerations: ☐ Previous tx ☐ Pacemaker ☐ Multiple tx sites ☐ Concurrent chemo
Special Procedures [**use reverse side**]

Other Instructions:
Staff Physician: ______________________ **Date:** ____________ **Time:** ____________

Fig. 8. Treatment planning directive for head and neck treatments

Eliminating paper is currently a big driver to reduce costs and improve process flow in most radiation oncology departments. Current vendor solutions to this problem is to provide databases with a mixture of digital data (images, treatment plan design, radiation dose results, treatment records) as well as document management (digitized images of paper documents). While useful, these do not directly help improve data flow needed to tie together the various processes needed for treatment planning and delivery. Despite the high level of technology used in radiation oncology, there are quite often different vendors for the various components of technology used. Communications from process to process are reduced to using DICOM[1] standards for images, radiotherapy plans, and treatment records communication. Unfortunately even with a standard, often vendors interpretation of the standard are not always consistent. The standards, however, do not include (or is not supported by one or the other vendor) related data needed to establish the context of the data communicated.

[1] Digital Imaging and Communications in Medicine division of NEMA http://medical.nema.org/

For example, from our treatment planning system, we can see that an imaging study is available for a particular patient but without other guidance we sometimes don't know the context of that imaging. A particularly thorny issue is that often multiple imaging series are acquired but one is preferred for any of a number of reasons. This leads to workflow issues when the wrong series is pulled and work is begun or even completed before the error is detected. Eliminating of the planning directive "paper" poses another issue. Simply digitizing the directive completed and signed by the physician does not necessarily lead to more efficient use. What is needed in this case is electronic communication of these directive directions to the various personnel and (electronically) to computerized processes involved in acquiring and preparing patient specific information needed for treatment planning. This also implies that the imaging systems and treatment planning system have defined ways to import the directive information. Unfortunately, standards for directives do not currently exist. However, there commonly are ways to "prime" these systems through specifications of default configuration or template files. The ability to create and invoke data translation services is a key requirement of a computerized workflow solution.

Without paper and charts, it is essential to have a method for reviewing a patient's status, assigning tasks, accepting tasks, completing task. The system needs to provide services for change notification, monitoring, and reporting from the various process tasks. Certainly solutions are being provided (or at least being worked on) by equipment vendors to manage the data and work relevant do the specific vendor equipment related tasks. Unfortunately, as has been mentioned there are variety of equipment being used and rarely is there a single vendor solution. Alternative solutions are, of course, in the works with hospitals gearing up to digitize all of the patient record keeping, scheduling, and task monitoring. It is not clear at this point, though, that the particular needs and quirks of individual radiation oncology departments will be readily addressed by vendor's "one size fits all" solutions.

Towards implementing a more flexible workflow environment, we have undertaken work on using an open-source light-weight workflow and Business Process Management (BPM) Platform (Activiti)[2] coupled with a number of in-house developed applications to build a workflow system. We are still at the exploration phase, but a small example of what can be anticipated follows.

The small example scenario presented here is that when a course of radiation treatments are completed, it is necessary to notify the physician who then needs to add summary notes for the patient's record. The treatment machine database system (in our case Varian's Aria system[3]) records the results of the final treatment day, there are, of course, notifications used to start billing processes but no active notification to the physician. The goal of this example project is to add an end of treatment trigger to the Aria database that would then send a message to a workflow engine listener which would (based on workflow model guidance) send a message to the attending physician. Figure 9 shows the graphical process modeling needed to implement this simple workflow. We are implementing a small app to run on a Android cell phone that will receive such messages and allow the physician to view the message and directly dictate notes over their phone.

---

[2] Activiti BPM Platform http://www.activiti.org/

[3] Varian Medical Systems, Inc. http://www.varian.com/

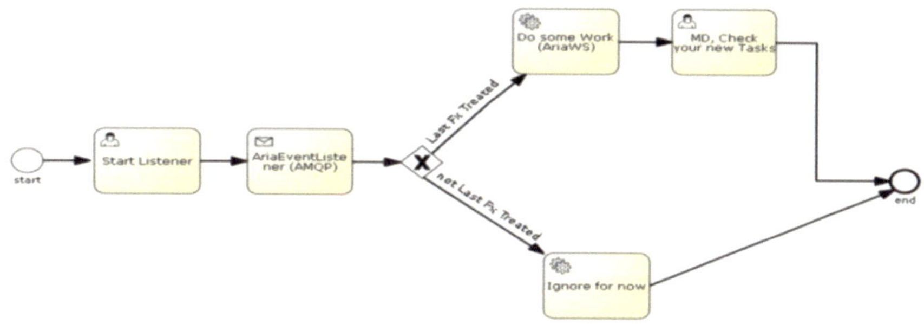

Fig. 9. BPM workflow modeling for signaling end of treatment

5. Future: Adaptive individualized treatments

The rapidly growing understanding of cancer biology and responses to radiation is dramatically impacting the future of cancer treatments. This understanding, for instance, has lead to the introduction of drugs that when combined with radiation can enhance tumor control or reduce normal tissue toxicities. Better understanding of cancer biology has also led to the identification of a number of measurable biomarkers that are indicative or predictive of tumor and normal tissue responses to radiation. The biomarkers may be in the form of lab results or may be from functional imaging techniques. The biomarker information can be used to select between possible sets of planning goals or may be utilized more directly to make patient specific alterations in treatment plans. Furthermore biomarkers, may even provide evidence during the course of treatment suggesting changes to the treatment plan to increase radiation dose to under-responding tumor regions or if well responding, decrease dose to reduce toxicity.

Such adaptive treatment approaches will add additional workflow steps to gather the new biomarker information and then to use that information for planning. In cases when updates of this information are received during a treatment course, then a decision is called for as to whether or not to use that new information to make alterations. That decision may need to be based on an assessment as to the potential gains based on a new treatment design, requiring possibly new imaging and contouring and requiring use of the dose to date propagation techniques illustrated in Figure 6. A decision would, of course, need action levels based on anticipated gains.

Clinical decisions associated with choosing to alter a treatment course, are complex with numerous factors affecting the choice. Evidence provided by biomarkers will have a certain degree of confidence that must be included in those decisions. Also because of the accumulative nature of radiation treatments (dose to date), there is a limit to the amount of alterations that can be effective and that factor also needs to be considered.

Adaptive individualized treatment management seems counter to our earlier described attempts at making the radiation oncology processes lean. It should not be forgotten though that the overall task of treatment plan preparation and design is already centered about conforming to individual patient geometry variations. So, what will be new is adding more biology motivated knowledge to those processes. Fortunately, many of the adaptive tasks can be automated. For instance, contours defined from the original planning scans can be propagated automatically to newer scans based on (deformable) registration and the accumulated doses can be similarly mapped and summed. Treatment beam placements for a new design are likely to follow the original design but will be "tweaked" to achieve the new treatment design. For this support, then the amount of new staff work will be reduce to mainly reviews of the results of the automated process results. It seems clear that computer assisted workflow and decision support will be even more critical in the future to insure that patient management steps are properly scheduled and completed in a timely fashion.

6. Conclusion

This chapter has presented an overview of the workflow and clinical decision needs for radiation oncology. A variety of tasks being carried out by a variety of professional workers are required to plan and manage a patient's course of radiation therapy. Many parts of these tasks require computer assistance for data management, graphical visualization, and calculation services. In terms of overall workflow, a "lean" approach to process mapping and process evaluation has proven valuable towards minimizing wait (waste) times thereby increasing the timeliness of care for the patient. The use of directive instructions has helped in achieving these results by providing physician approved guidelines for various tasks and planning goals needed to develop a proposed treatment. Future workflow and clinical decision support in radiation oncology will need to be robust and flexible to deal with a changing scenario of increasing knowledge about cancer biology and radiation effects and use of evidence-based biomarkers to aid in decision strategies for the management of patient care.

7. References

Kalet, I. J., J. L. Mejino, et al. (2009). "Content-specific auditing of a large scale anatomy ontology." *J Biomed Inform* 42(3): 540-549.

Kessler, M. L. (2006). "Image registration and data fusion in radiation therapy." *The British journal of radiology* 79 Spec No 1: S99-108.

Kessler, M. L., D. L. McShan, et al. (1995). "A computer-controlled conformal radiotherapy system. III: Graphical simulation and monitoring of treatment delivery." *International journal of radiation oncology, biology, physics* 33(5): 1173-1180.

Kessler, M. L., R. K. Ten Haken, et al. (1994). "Expanding the use and effectiveness of dose-volume histograms for 3-D treatment planning. I: Integration of 3-D dose-display." *International journal of radiation oncology, biology, physics* 29(5): 1125-1131.

Kim, C. S., J. A. Hayman, et al. (2007). "The application of lean thinking to the care of patients with bone and brain metastasis with radiation therapy." *Journal of oncology practice / American Society of Clinical Oncology* 3(4): 189-193.

McShan, D., B. Fraass, et al. (1990). "Full integration of the beam's eye view concept intoclinical treatment planning" *Int J Rad Oncol* 18: 1485-1494.

Rother, M. and J. Shick (2003). Learning to See, Value-Stream Mapping to Create Valueand Eliminate Muda. Brookline, MA, The Lean Enterprise Institue Inc.: 102.

Womack, J. P. and D. T. Jones (2003). Lean thinking : banish waste and create wealth in your corporation. New York, Free Press.

12

Computerized Decision Support Systems for Mechanical Ventilation

Fleur T. Tehrani
California State University, Fullerton
USA

1. Introduction

In the USA alone, there are between 44,000 and 98,000 injuries resulting from medical errors each year (Kohn et al., 2000). The financial costs associated with serious injuries and mortalities resulting from medical errors are between 17 and 29 billion USD per year in the USA alone (Kohn et al., 2000) while the human costs of such incidents cannot be measured in financial terms. Expecting too much from clinicians results in inevitable rises in medical errors. This is particularly true in chaotic environments such as the hospital ICU settings where large amounts of medical data needs to be processed in a relatively short time and medical decisions can often make the difference between life and death.

Computerized decision support and knowledge-based expert systems can be used as helpful tools to clinicians in healthcare in general, and to the ICU intensivists in particular. There can be no doubt that a clinician provided with an efficient decision support system is better equipped to make complex medical decisions in time than a physician who does not have access to such resources.

Among various treatments used in the ICU settings, mechanical ventilation is an essential technology to treat many different illnesses and is relatively costly. Without this treatment most major surgical operations could not be performed and many respiratory illnesses could not be treated successfully. This life saving treatment costs about 1500 USD per day in the ICU settings and it has been reported that the average hospital cost for an ICU patient on mechanical ventilation is more than twice the average cost for an ICU patient not requiring this treatment (Dasta et al., 2005). It has further been reported that about two thirds of hospital costs for treatment of patients on mechanical ventilation are spent on about one third of patients who receive this treatment for an extended period of time of more than 96 hours amounting to about 16 billion USD annually in the USA alone (Zilberberg et al., 2008).

These data demonstrate the fact that the high cost of mechanical ventilation is bound to increase significantly if patients are not provided with proper treatment, and as a result, the duration of the treatment is unduly increased. This analysis is beside the point that when mechanical ventilation is prolonged due to non-optimal or inappropriate treatment, many medical complications such as ventilator associated pneumonia may result, which can significantly increase the mortality and morbidity rates of patients on this medical treatment. Effective decision support systems for mechanical ventilation can improve the treatment and expedite weaning from the ventilator and thereby significantly and positively impact both the quality and the cost of healthcare for patients who need this kind of treatment.

This chapter provides an overview of different methodologies employed in the design of computerized decision support systems for mechanical ventilation. These will include model-based technologies, rule-based methods, some combinations of the two techniques, as well as some major variations that are applied within the two distinct methodologies. The chapter further provides a brief overview of various decision support systems that have been presented to date for mechanical ventilation and a brief discussion of future trends in this technology.

2. An overview of different methodologies used in decision support systems for mechanical ventilation

Intelligent decision support systems (IDSSs) for mechanical ventilation can be designed as expert advisory systems or can also be used for automatic control of ventilation or weaning (Tehrani & Roum, Nov. 2008). These systems are designed to take patient's ventilatory data, process the data, and determine appropriate treatment options for the patient by using different methodologies. The required input data to these systems can be provided automatically by monitors and sensors, or if the system is an open-loop advisory tool without any capability to control the ventilator automatically, some or all of the input data can be provided manually by the clinician. Figure 1 shows a schematic block diagram of an IDSS for mechanical ventilation.

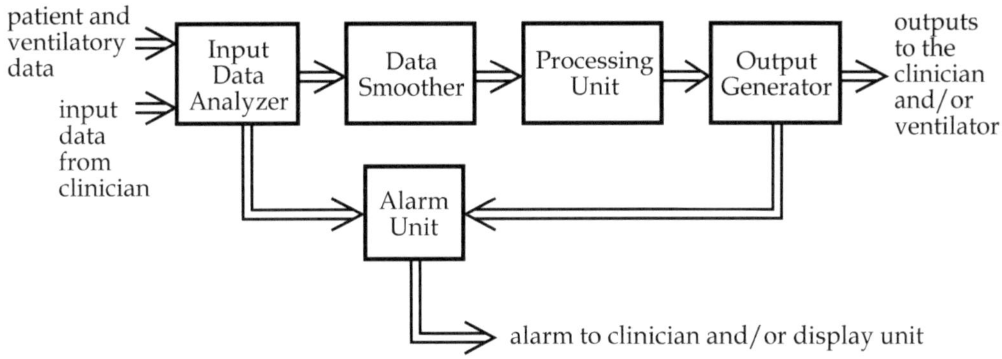

Fig. 1. A schematic diagram of an IDSS for mechanical ventilation.

As shown in this Figure, the input data from the clinician and the patient's physiological and ventilatory data are provided to an Input Data Analyzer that verifies the validity of the input data by comparing it to predefined acceptable ranges. This unit detects artifacts and corrects or discards erroneous data. It can also be used to remove noise from the ventilatory signals. The validated data is then transferred to a Data Smoother unit which is designed to prevent abrupt or inappropriate changes in the ventilatory parameters. The outputs of this unit are provided to a Processing Unit that determines the optimal treatment options for the patient. The outputs of this unit are communicated to the clinician by using a graphical display unit and if the system is designed to control the ventilator automatically, these outputs are applied to the ventilation system. In this process, if any of the patient's measured data or the computed parameters of the system fall outside predefined safe ranges, alarms are activated and communicated to the clinician by using an Alarm Unit.

The methods used by the Processing Unit differ greatly among various IDSSs and are based on the types of the inputs, the patient groups that the system is designed for, whether the system is based on established treatment protocols, physiological models, or a combination thereof, and also whether the system is an advisory tool or is for automatic control of the ventilator as well. An overview of various methodologies that are employed in the IDSSs for mechanical ventilation will be followed next.

2.1 An overview of different information processing and control techniques used in IDSSs for mechanical ventilation

An IDSS for mechanical ventilation receives various patient and ventilatory input data and processes that information by using many various techniques to determine the treatment options for the patient. A number of IDSSs developed to date use initial data validation and smoothing techniques to detect artifacts, validate the input data, and prepare data for further processing. These techniques include temporal abstraction techniques to select and process the input data in some of the more recent technologies.

The inputs required by IDSSs differ greatly based on the type of the system and the patient groups that the system is designed for. These inputs may include the following data types:

1. The patient's medical problems and data such as patient's gender, age, weight, height, ideal body weight, and body temperature
2. The patient's cardiovascular data such as heart rate, stroke volume, cardiac output, systolic and diastolic blood pressures
3. The patient's blood gas information and the rate of change of the data
4. The patient's respiratory mechanics data (e.g. respiratory resistance and compliance) and the rate of change of the data
5. The set and measured ventilatory parameters such as tidal volume, respiratory rate, minute ventilation, peak inspiratory pressure, fraction of inspired oxygen (F_{IO2}), the positive end-expiratory pressure (PEEP), the inspiratory to expiratory time ratio, the rate of change of these data, along with the set alarm levels on the ventilator for maximum and minimum pressure and volume
6. Additional patient parameters for use in a physiological model of the patient's respiratory system if such models are used in the structure of the IDSS

Table 1 shows different main categories of IDSSs for mechanical ventilation. As shown in this table, the structure of these systems can be divided in three basic categories: (a) rule-based, (b) model-based, (c) rule-based combined with model-based.

The systems that are rule-based use established clinical protocols and guidelines to determine the patient's ventilatory parameters. In model-based systems, the treatment options are decided based on simulation of a physiological model of the patient. However, there are some rule-based systems that determine the ventilatory treatment options based on statistical models and those are quite different from IDSSs whose structures are based on the patient's physiological models. Finally, there are systems in which clinical guidelines are used in combination with physiological models and the basic structure of those are referred to as rule-based + model-based in Table 1.

The IDSSs for mechanical ventilation use various mathematical and control procedures to determine and control their outputs. The techniques used in various IDSSs include classic as well as fuzzy control technologies. Many of these systems can be used in several ventilatory modes while some others are designed to be used in specific ventilation modes such as synchronized intermittent mandatory ventilation (SIMV) or pressure support ventilation (PS). Some systems are for use in the management phase of ventilation while several other systems are for use in the weaning phase of treatment only. Still, there are some IDSSs that can be used in a number of management and weaning modes of the treatment. Depending on their intended phases of ventilation treatments, IDSSs can be used for regulation of patient's blood gases, expediting weaning, or a combination of these factors. Furthermore, in addition to providing advisory guidance to clinicians, several systems can also be used to control the ventilator automatically in one or more ventilatory modes and treatment phases.

These systems also vary in their applications and patient groups that they are designed for. The patient groups served by different IDSSs can be based on patients' illnesses or on their age groups. There are systems that are designed for patients suffering of acute respiratory distress syndrome (ARDS) or chronic obstructive pulmonary disease (COPD) only, while others are to be used for a wider range of disease conditions. Some IDSSs are designed for adult and pediatric patients while several other systems are developed for neonate patients only. Still, there are a few systems that can be used for both adult and neonatal patient populations.

Main characteristics	Available variations		
Basic structure	Rule-based	Model-based	Rule-based + Model-based
Applicable ventilation mode	Single mode (e.g., PS)	Multiple modes	
Type of technology	Open-loop (advisory)	Open-loop (advisory) + Closed-loop (automatic)	
Patient group	Adults	Neonates	Adults + Neonates
Disease condition	ARDS	COPD	Various disease conditions

Table 1. Main categories of IDSSs for mechanical ventilation.

2.2 An overview of various IDSSs for mechanical ventilation

Table 2 lists the IDSSs developed to date for mechanical ventilation in a chronological order. The major features of these systems and the patient groups that they are intended for are listed in this table.

The early IDSSs for mechanical ventilation were developed in mid 1980s for adult patients. These systems were rule-based and used clinical guidelines and protocols to determine or critique ventilatory treatment options for patients (Fagan et al., 1985; Miller, 1985). Around the same time, another system was developed for treatment of neonates that was also based on set clinical guidelines (Carlo et al., 1986).

In late 1980s, another rule-based system for closed-loop adjustment of the length of mandatory breaths in the intermittent mandatory ventilation (IMV) mode was introduced that used the measured pressure in the patient's endotracheal tube to make its determinations (Hernandez et al., 1988). Later, another rule-based system for management of ventilation weaning was presented (Hernandez-Sande et al., 1989).

Around the same time, another computerized system for treatment of adult patients suffering of ARDS was introduced (Sittig et al., 1989). This system used clinical guidelines to treat ARDS patients in several ventilator modes including assist/control (AC), continuous positive airway pressure (CPAP), pressure-controlled-inverted ratio ventilation (PC-IRV), IMV, and positive pressure ventilation with extracorporeal carbon dioxide removal ($ECCO_2R$). This was followed by the introduction of another rule-based system that used statistical models of different patient groups to determine ventilatory settings (Rudowski et al., 1989).

Another rule-based system for weaning patients from mechanical ventilation was presented a few years later (Tong, 1991). At about the same time, another computerized system for ventilatory treatment of premature neonates was introduced (Arroe, 1991). This system was rule-based and was developed for use in the volume control mode of ventilation.

A computerized system for closed-loop control of weaning for adult patients was presented at about the same time (Strickland & Hassan, 1991). This rule-based system used the patient's measured oxygen saturation, respiratory rate, and minute ventilation data to control the rate of ventilation in the SIMV mode. If the rate could be sufficiently reduced while the measured patient data remained acceptable, the system then decreased the pressure support level until the patient was ready for extubation.

Soon afterwards, another rule-based system for closed-loop control of weaning for adult patients was introduced (Dojat et al., 1992). This system used the patient's measured respiratory rate, tidal volume, and the end-tidal pressure of carbon dioxide as inputs, and if these data remained in a predefined "comfort zone," the level of pressure support was automatically and incrementally reduced to wean the patient from the ventilator.

A computerized system for ventilation of adult patients was presented later (Rutledge et al., 1993). This system used a physiological model of the patient rather than clinical rules to determine ventilator parameters. No results were reported to show the performance of this model-based system.

Another computerized system for ventilator treatment of adult patients was presented a few years later (Shahsavar et al., 1995). This system was based on clinical rules and could be used as an expert system in the management and weaning phases of ventilation.

About one year later, another IDSS for ventilation treatment of neonates was presented (Miksch et al., 1996). This system was rule-based and used temporal abstraction techniques to prepare and process the input data. This system used arterial blood gas data, the interval of data, and the qualitative trends of data to process the inputs and determine ventilatory treatments. No results were presented to show the performance of this system.

Several years later, a closed-loop system for weaning patients from mechanical ventilation was introduced which used fuzzy logic control procedures (Nemoto et al., 1999). This rule-based system created fuzzy sets based on patient's measured heart rate, tidal volume, respiratory rate, and arterial oxygen saturation to determine the pressure support level provided by the ventilator during weaning.

Another IDSS that was based on a physiological model of the patient was presented several years later (Rees et al., 2006). A simplified model of respiratory mechanics and mathematical models of oxygen and carbon dioxide transport were used in this system to simulate the effects of changing some of the ventilatory parameters such as F_{IO2} on the patient's blood gases. This system could not simulate the effects of some other ventilatory parameters such as the PEEP level on patient's blood gases.

IDSS	Basic structure	Type of technology	Applicable ventilation modes	Patient group/disease condition
Fagan et al., 1985	Rule-based	Open-loop	Multiple modes	Adults
Miller, 1985	Rule-based	Open-loop	Multiple modes	Adults
Carlo et al., 1986	Rule-based	Open-loop	Volume control	Neonate RDS patients
Hernandez et al., 1988; Hernandez-Sande et al., 1989	Rule-based	Open-loop + Closed-loop	IMV, Weaning	Adults
Sittig et al., 1989	Rule-based	Open-loop	Multiple modes	Adult ARDS patients
Rudowski et al., 1989	Rule-based	Open-loop	Multiple modes	Adults
Tong, 1991	Rule-based	Open-loop	Weaning	Adults
Arroe, 1991	Rule-based	Open-loop	Volume control	Neonate RDS patients
Strickland & Hassan, 1991	Rule-based	Closed-loop	SIMV+PS, Weaning	Adults
Dojat et al., 1992	Rule-based	Closed-loop	PS, Weaning	Adults
Rutledge et al., 1993	Model-based	Open-loop	Multiple modes	Adults
Shahsavar et al., 1995	Rule-based	Open-loop	Multiple modes	Adults
Miksch et al., 1996	Rule-based	Open-loop	Multiple modes	Neonates
Nemoto et al., 1999	Rule-based	Closed-loop	PS, Weaning	Adult COPD patients
Rees et al., 2006	Model-based	Open-loop	Multiple modes	Adults
Tehrani, 2007; Tehrani & Roum, Apr. 2008; Tehrani & Abbasi, 2009	Rule-based + Model-based	Open-loop + Closed-loop	Multiple modes, PS, Weaning	Adults + Neonates
Tehrani, 2009; Tehrani & Abbasi, 2010	Model-based	Open-loop	Multiple modes	Adults + Neonates
Lozano-Zahonero et al., 2011	Rule-based	Open-loop + Closed-loop	Multiple modes	Adult ARDS patients

Table 2. A list of IDSSs for mechanical ventilation and their main features

About a year later, another computerized system for ventilation treatment was introduced (Tehrani, 2007). This system used clinical rules and guidelines, but many of its rules were adaptive and were derived on the basis of physiological models. Application of the system however did not require the simulation of physiological models of oxygen and carbon dioxide transport of the patient. This system incorporated the features of a closed loop ventilation technique known as Adaptive Support Ventilation (ASV) (Tehrani, 1991; Tehrani 2008), but augmented that system by adding many features including control of F_{IO2}, PEEP, and weaning. This system used patient's ventilatory and physiological data to control a wide range of ventilatory parameters including minute ventilation, tidal volume, respiratory rate, the inspiration to expiration time ratio, F_{IO2}, PEEP, and the pressure support level for spontaneously breathing patients. This system could be used as an open-loop advisory tool as well as a closed-loop system for automatic control of the ventilator in various ventilatory modes for both adult and neonate patient groups (Tehrani & Roum, April 2008; Tehrani & Abbasi, 2009).

At about the same time, a model-based IDSS for critiquing mechanical ventilation treatments was introduced (Tehrani, 2009). This system was based on physiological models of the human respiratory system for adults (Fincham & Tehrani, 1983), and neonates (Tehrani, 1993). The purpose of this model-based system was to provide a tool to the clinician to predict the effects of changing ventilatory parameters on the patient's blood gases. The system could simulate the effects of changing a wide range of ventilation parameters including minute ventilation, tidal volume, respiratory rate, F_{IO2}, PEEP, and pressure support level in different modes of ventilation on patient's blood gases. This system could be used for adults as well as neonate patients (Tehrani, 2009; Tehrani & Abbasi, 2010) for critiquing mechanical ventilation treatments. This open-loop advisory system could be used alone or with another computerized expert system. It could be used as a tool to assist the clinician to choose an appropriate ventilation treatment option for patients by predicting the outcomes of different treatment options at bedside.

Around the same time, another rule-based IDSS which employed fuzzy control procedures to adjust the respiratory rate of mechanically ventilated patients was presented (Lozano-Zahonero et al., 2011). In this system which was tested on adult patients suffering of ARDS, the arterial carbon dioxide partial pressure (P_{aCO2}) of the patient was used as the input parameter to the IDSS. Fuzzy rules derived from clinical experts' opinions and guidelines were used to determine the required respiratory rate of the patient based on his measured P_{aCO2} level.

The list of the systems provided in Table 2 represents a wide range of IDSSs for mechanical ventilation treatments. However, this list is not meant to be exhaustive and does not include some similar systems that have been developed to this date.

2.3 Summary comparison of IDSSs for mechanical ventilation

A comparison of the strengths and/or the main features of the systems listed in Table 2 is provided in Table 3. As can be seen, most of IDSSs developed to date for mechanical ventilation are rule-based, one is rule-based, but many of its adaptive rules are derived from physiological models, and several other systems are based on physiological models.

Some IDSSs use artifact rejection/correction techniques, smoothing processes, and data abstraction techniques to validate and smooth the input data. In addition to providing treatment advice to clinicians, several IDSSs can also be used for closed-loop control of ventilation and/or weaning, while others are strictly open-loop knowledge-based advisory systems.

System	Rule-based	Model-based	Adaptive rules	Use of data abstraction techniques	Appl. to multiple vent. modes	Open-loop	Closed-loop	Appl. to var. pat. groups/ dis. cond.
Fagan et al., 1985	√				√	√		√
Miller, 1985	√				√	√		√
Carlo et al., 1986	√					√		
Hernandez et al., 1988; Hernandez-Sande et al., 1989	√					√	√	√
Sittig et al., 1989	√				√	√		
Rudowski et al., 1989	√				√	√		√
Tong, 1991	√					√		√
Arroe, 1991	√					√		
Strickland & Hassan, 1991	√					√	√	√
Dojat et al., 1992	√			√		√	√	√
Rutledge et al., 1993		√	N/A		√	√		√
Shahsavar et al., 1995	√				√	√		√
Miksch et al., 1996	√			√	√	√		
Nemoto et al., 1999	√		√			√	√	
Rees et al., 2006		√	N/A		√	√		√
Tehrani, 2007; Tehrani & Roum, Apr. 2008; Tehrani & Abbasi, 2009	√	√	√	√	√	√	√	√
Tehrani, 2009; Tehrani & Abbasi, 2010		√	N/A		√	√		√
Lozano-Zahonero et al., 2011	√		√		√	√	√	

Table 3. Comparison of the key features of IDSSs for mechanical ventilation.

The number of ventilatory parameters that these systems can control or simulate, the modes of ventilation they can be used for, their control structures, and the patient groups or disease conditions that they can address, are also quite different for various IDSSs as discussed above.

3. Concluding remarks and future trends

In brief, if an IDSS for mechanical ventilation is easy to use and can provide helpful information to the clinician, it can be a useful aide to the intensivist for determining appropriate ventilation treatments for his patients. This is due to the fact that despite the application of a number of automatic control systems for mechanical ventilation (Tehrani, 2008), the majority of advanced ventilators are still open-loop controlled devices in which some or all of the main ventilatory parameters are manually set by an intensivist. Therefore, an expert IDSS can serve as a helpful advisory tool to the clinician to set the patient's ventilatory parameters.

The following features can be important in establishing the reliability and flexibility of an IDSS for mechanical ventilation (the first feature has a higher impact on a system's reliability while the other features mostly affect an IDSS's flexibility):

1. Having sufficient safeguards for data validation and artifact detection and correction
2. Applicability to a wide range of ventilatory modes
3. Capability to determine and/or simulate a wide range of ventilatory parameters
4. Applicability to various patient groups
5. Applicability to various disease conditions

Therefore, if a system has a high level of reliability and can be regarded as reasonably flexible, it can be concluded that it may be more easily and readily used by ICU clinicians.

Also, critiquing systems based on physiological models that can provide additional information to clinicians by predicting different treatment outcomes can provide more insight to clinicians and be helpful to them in choosing more appropriate treatment options for their patients. These systems can be used alone or in combination with other IDSSs to set ventilatory parameters for patients.

At the end, it may be noted that the trend of mechanical ventilation is towards more automation. Therefore, IDSSs that in addition to providing treatment recommendations in an advisory capacity can also be used for automatic control of ventilation or weaning, may be more desirable for use by clinicians and find more applications in the years to come.

4. References

Arroe, M. (1991). A computerized aid in ventilating neonates. *Computers in Biology and Medicine,* Vol. 21, No. 1-2, pp. (15-21), ISSN 0010-4825.

Carlo, W. A., Pacifico, L., Chatburn, R. L., & Fanaroff, A. A. (1986). Efficacy of computer-assisted management of respiratory failure in neonates. *Pediatrics,* Vol. 78, No. 1, (July 1986), pp. (139-143), ISSN 0031-4005.

Dasta, J. F., McLaughlin, T. P., & Mody, S. H. (2005). Daily cost of an intensive care unit day: the contribution of mechanical ventilation. *Critical Care Medicine,* Vol. 33, No. 6, (June 2005), pp. (1266-1271), ISSN 0090-3493.

Dojat, M., Brochard, L., Lemaire, F., & Harf, A. (1992). A knowledge-based system for assisted ventilation of patients in intensive care units. *International Journal of clinical Monitoring and Computing,* Vol. 9, No. 4, (December 1992), pp. (239-250), ISSN 0167-9945.

Fagan, L. M., Kunz, J. C., Feigenbaum, E. A., & Osborn, J. J. (1985). Extensions to the rule-based formalism for a monitoring task, In: *Rule-based expert systems; the MYCIN experiments of the Stanford heuristic programming project,* Buchanan, B. G., & Shortliffe E. H. (eds.), pp. (397-423), Addison-Wesley, Reading, MA.

Fincham, W. F., & Tehrani, F. T. (1983). A mathematical model of the human respiratory system. *Journal of Biomedical Engineering,* Vol. 5, No. 2, (April, 1983), pp. (125-133), ISSN 0141-5425.

Hernandez, C., Moret, V., Arcay, B., & Hermida, R. C. (1988). Weaning from mechanical ventilation using a prototype closed-loop system. *Microcomputer Applications,*Vol. 7, No. 3, pp. (128-130), ISSN 0143-3792.

Hernandez-Sande, C., Moret-Bonillo, V., & Alonso-Betanzos, A. (1989). ESTER: an expert system for management of respiratory weaning therapy. *IEEE Transactions on Biomedical Engineering,* Vol. 36, No. 5, (May 1989), pp. (559-564), ISSN 0018-9294.

Kohn, L. T., Corrigan, J. M., & Donaldson, M. S. (Eds.). (2000). *To err is human: building a safer health system,* Institute of Medicine, The National Academies Press, ISBN 0309068371, Washington DC.

Lozano-Zahonero, S., Gottlieb, D., Haberthur, C., Guttmann, J., & Moller, K. (2011). Automated mechanical ventilation: adapting decision making to different disease states. *Medical and Biological Engineering & Computing,* Vol. 49, No. 3, (March 2011), pp. (349-358), ISSN 0140-0118.

Miksch, S., Horn, W., Popow, C., & Paky, F. (1996). Utilizing temporal data abstraction for data validation and therapy planning for artificially ventilated newborn infants. *Artificial Intelligence in Medicine,* Vol. 8, No. 6, (November 1996), pp. (543-576), ISSN 0933-3657.

Miller, P. (1985). Goal-directed critiquing by computer: ventilator management. *Computers and Biomedical Research,* Vol. 18, No. 5, (October 1985), pp. (422-438), ISSN 0010-4809.

Nemoto, T., Hatzakis, G. E., Thorpe, C. W., Olivenstein, R., Dial, S., & Bates, J. H. T. (1999). Automatic control of pressure support mechanical ventilation using fuzzy logic. *American Journal of Respiratory and Critical Care Medicine,* Vol. 160, No. 2, (August 1999), pp. (550-556), ISSN 1073-449X.

Rees, S. E., Allerod, C., Murley, D., Zhao, Y., Smith, B. W., Kjargaard, S., Thorgaard, P., & Andreassen, S. (2006). Using physiological models and decision theory for selecting appropriate ventilator settings. *Journal of Clinical Monitoring and Computing,* Vol. 20, No. 6, (December 2006), pp. (421-429), ISSN 1387-1307.

Rudowski, R., Frostell, C., & Gill, H. (1989). A knowledge-based support system for mechanical ventilation of the lungs. The KUSIVAR concept and prototype. *Computer Methods and Programs in Biomedicine,* Vol. 30, No. 1, (September 1989), pp. (59-70), ISSN 0169-2607.

Rutledge, G. W., Thomsen, G. E., Farr, B. R., Tovar, M. A., Polaschek, J. X., Beinlich, I. A., Sheiner, L. B., & Fagan, L. M. (1993). The design and implementation of a ventilator-management advisor. *Artificial Intelligence in Medicine,* Vol. 5, No. 1, (February 1993), pp. (67-82), ISSN 0933-3657.

Shahsavar, N., Ludwigs, U., Blomqvist, H., Gill, H., Wigertz, O., & Matell, G. (1995). Evaluation of a knowledge-based decision-support system for ventilator therapy management. *Artificial Intelligence in Medicine,* Vol. 7, No. 1, (February 1995), pp. (37-52), ISSN 0933-3657.

Sittig, D. F., Pace, N. L., Gardner, R. M., Beck, E., & Morris, A. H. (1989). Implementation of a computerized patient advice system using the HELP clinical information system. *Computers and Biomedical Research,* Vol. 22, No. 5, (October 1989), pp. (474-487), ISSN 0010-4809.

Strickland, Jr., J., H., & Hassan, J., H. (1991). A computer-controlled ventilator weaning system. *Chest,* Vol. 100, No. 4, (October 1991), pp. (1096-1099), ISSN 0012-3692.

Tehrani, F. T. (1991). Automatic control of an artificial respirator. *Proceedings of the IEEE International Conference of Engineering in Medicine and Biology Society,* Vol. 13, pp. 1738-1739, ISBN 0-7803-0216-8, Orlando, Florida, November 1991.

Tehrani, F., T. (1993). Mathematical analysis and computer simulation of the respiratory system in the newborn infant. *IEEE Transactions on Biomedical Engineering,* Vol. 40, No. 5, (May 1993), pp. (475-481), ISSN 0018-9294.

Tehrani, F., T. (2007). A new decision support system for mechanical ventilation. *Proceedings of the IEEE International Conference of Engineering in Medicine and Biology Society,* Vol. 29, pp. 3569-3572, ISBN 1-4244-0788-5, Lyon, France, August 2007.

Tehrani, F., T., & Roum, J. H. (2008). FLEX: a new computerized system for mechanical ventilation. *Journal of Clinical Monitoring and Computing,* Vol. 22, No. 2, (April 2008), pp. (121-130), ISSN 1387-1307.

Tehrani, F., T., & Roum, J., H. (2008). Intelligent decision support systems for mechanical ventilation. *Artificial Intelligence in Medicine,* Vol. 44, No.3, (November 2008), pp. (171-182), ISSN 0933-3657.

Tehrani, F., T. (2008). Automatic control of mechanical ventilation. Part 2: The existing techniques and future trends. *Journal of Clinical Monitoring and Computing,* Vol. 22, No. 6, (December 2008), pp. (417-424), ISSN 1387-1307.

Tehrani, F., T., & Abbasi, S. (2009). Evaluation of a computerized system for mechanical ventilation of infants. *Journal of Clinical Monitoring and Computing,* Vol. 23, No. 2, (April 2009), pp. (93-104), ISSN 1387-1307.

Tehrani, F., T. (2009). Critiquing treatment and setting ventilatory parameters by using physiological modeling. *Proceedings of the IEEE International Conference of Engineering in Medicine and Biology Society,* Vol. 31, pp. 286-288, ISBN 978-1-4244-3296-7, Minneapolis, MN, September 2009.

Tehrani, F., T., & Abbasi, S. (2010). The role of physiological models in critiquing mechanical ventilation treatments. *Proceedings of the 21st Meeting of the European Society for Computing and Technology in Anesthesia and Intensive Care (ESCTAIC),* Amsterdam, October 2010, in press.

Tong, D., A. (1991). Weaning patients from mechanical ventilation. A knowledge-based system approach. *Computer Methods and Programs in Biomedicine,* Vol. 35, No. 4, (August 1991), pp. (267-278), ISSN 0169-2607.

Zilberberg, M., D., Luippold, R., S., Sulsky, S., & Shorr, A., F. (2008). Prolonged acute mechanical ventilation, hospital resource utilization, and mortality in the United States. *Critical Care Medicine,* Vol. 36, No. 3, (March 2008), pp. (724-730), ISSN 0090-3493.

13

Decision Support Systems in Anesthesia, Emergency Medicine and Intensive Care Medicine

Thomas M. Hemmerling
McGill University
Canada

1. Introduction

Decision support systems (DSS) in the context of anesthesia, critical care and intensive care medicine consist of several components: the 'brain', which integrates a variety of input parameters and delivers as output various informative data which can help the physicians to perform better. They might be considered as 'automated textbooks' which by the use of a digitalized infrastructure not only deliver immediately all the necessary health care knowledge to the clinician but also has the capability of intelligently monitoring the actual health status of any given patient - 'smart monitoring'. It is obvious that in the context of anesthesia, critical - emergency - care and intensive care medicine, such systems are a vital backbone of medical care of the 21st century with a growing number of parameters, growing number of diseases, diagnostic possibilities and treatment options. Decision support systems have the potential to bridge the gap between the theoretical performance of a well trained physicians -who has spent a decade acquiring knowledge and a multitude of manual skills - and his or her actual performance in daily practice. This latter performance can be influenced by any given contextual condition, be it emotional, intellectual or behavioral pattern. What we define as 'clinical error' is influenced by several mistakes, one of the most prominent the impossibility to recall all diagnostic and therapeutic options any time for any patient - 'prospective recall failure'. Computerized information tools have been investigated for more than 2 decades and have been proven to be highly effective in a research environment.

However, especially in the specialties which are the object of this chapter, they have not been widely introduced into practice.

One of the problems is the clustering of information in modern healthcare facilities between hospital administrators, several laboratory or investigative units and health care providers. The complexity of modern diagnostic and therapeutic options is such that only the most complete coverage of all available patient information can deliver a most complete decision support for the clinician. A lack of standardization, immediate delivery of patient data due to inherent lag times of different working systems, make some of these systems inefficient in reality. Another problem is the 'user-friendliness' of these systems - the significant additional time necessary to 'feed' the data into the system, as well as the gradual integration of these decision support systems into the daily work pattern: accessibility of the

information in a most efficient way for a variety of health care providers with different technological and intellectual background is another problem. The widespread introduction of simple anesthesia information management systems (AIMS) into the daily practice, especially in North America - has also been impaired by shrinking health care budgets and administrative ignorance.
This chapter will focus on painting an outline of possible DSSs in anesthesia, critical care and intensive care medicine with a special attention on presenting a vision of what is needed for the future.
It is beyond the scope of this chapter to present all the research which has been done in designing and testing DSSs in these three specialties. It is tried to present exemplary case studies of DSSs which are not merely theoretical constructs but close to clinical usability. The examples used shall spur the reader's curiosity and show what is feasible in the context of modern health care systems, presenting both present challenges and future directions. At the end of this chapter, some recent review articles on the topic are added to instigate further reading.

2. Decision support systems

Decision support systems have been used in research and clinical studies in the fields of anesthesia, emergency medicine and intensive care medicine. It is beyond the scope of this chapter to present all studies and clinical applications; instead, the author tried to outline the characteristics of DSSs in all three specialties with specific examples highlighting the advantages of these systems as well as specific challenges.

2.1 Decision support systems in anesthesia

Anesthesia is characterized by being a specialty where more than 100 parameters have to be monitored constantly and rapid and appropriate action often defines the difference between good or adverse outcome. Anesthesiologists are often compared with pilots, and described as 'pilots of the human biosphere' (Hemmerling, 2010). Similar to pilots, they need to coordinate their monitoring with direct supervision of surgical progress and interact with health care providers from different background, nurses, anesthesia technicians and surgical team. Organizational accidents can easily develop in this environment (Reason, 2005); an example of a schematic development of an organizational accident is described in figure 1.

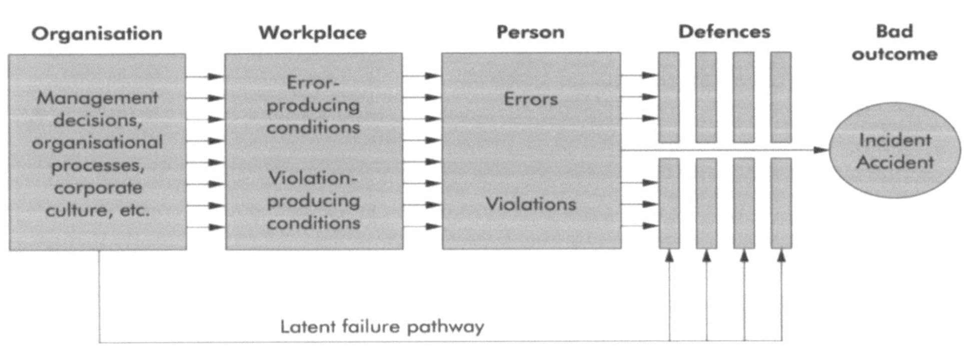

Fig. 1. Stages in the development of an organizational accident. (Reason, 2005)

Organizational deficits can be based on a specific culture, e.g. strictly hierarchical command structure, certain management decisions, e.g. organizational deficits in providing important drugs or devices or other forms of mistakes. The workplace can be faulted by lack of teamwork, communication issues, non-standardized or badly maintained equipment-or simply its absence - problems with proper drug labeling, delivery, OR scheduling or other planning deficits. All these deficits can lead to errors or violations of existing 'best evidence practice' with subsequent bad outcome.

As much as the various development stages of organizational accidents in anesthesia are common knowledge, as difficult is their analysis and efficient accident investigation. A possible model of efficient - in terms of avoiding subsequent bad outcome - accident investigation has long been presented (Eagle et al., 1992, Fig.2).

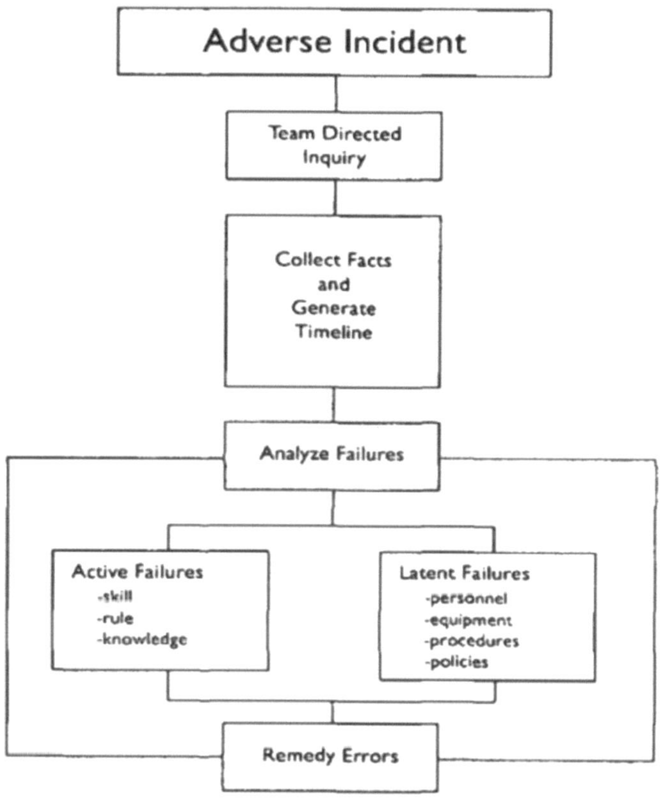

Fig. 2. A model of accident investigation. (Eagle et al., 1992)

Any adverse incident should therefore trigger a team-directed inquiry - any individualized search for mistakes will be doomed to fail. The correct establishment of both facts and timeline is the key for a successful analysis of the event. This will lead to the determination of both active failures, such as a lack of skill (e.g. intubation skill) and - more difficult to overcome - latent failures, such lack of equipment, wrongful procedures or policies. This can lead to better organizational DSS which allows to avoid bad outcome.

The influx of electronic data management systems - anesthesia information management systems (AIMS) - has helped to make this cascade of accident analysis readily available, reliable and easy to use. The fact that less than 10% of North American hospitals have AIMS available is still a major setback for proper management of accidents and adverse events. However, recently, DSSs have been developed to extract events from the AIMSs for an improvement of quality of care, compliance to established best evidence practices and documentation of outcome, be it good or bad. However, the performance of the DSS is influenced by the timeliness of the data entry, the incidence of missing data and any possible query interval. These latencies of data entry can be caused by the simple absence of data entry, retroactive data entry - with the risk of data omission, data management delay within the AIMS or between the AIMS and any other database or clock differences. Any such latencies can influence the implementation of clinical or management workflows for improved outcome. (Epstein et al., 2009, Fig. 3)

Latency source	Explanation
Absence of user entry	Providers may not document the event.
Delayed (tardy) user entry	Providers typically document after the fact.
Processing delay by AIMS on the workstation	AIMS may not process entered events immediately, but on a schedule.
Processing delay writing to AIMS database	It can take time to traverse the network and then write to the database.
Data extraction from production database	Queries may not run against the production database, but against a copy of the database, updated periodically.
Rounding of times	AIMS may round times to the nearest minute when users adjust the time.
Clock synchronization	Perceived latency between workstation timestamps and database timestamps on the server may be a result of the clocks being different.

AIMS = anesthesia information management systems.

Fig. 3. Potential Sources of Latency in Decision Support Systems. (Epstein et al., 2009)

Anesthesiologists constantly demand smart alarms. One of the few monitoring systems which have a good track record as 'smart alarms' are pulse oximeters. Any anesthesiologist of some experience will be able to follow the different tonality of the pulse oximetric signal to detect various degrees of oxygen desaturations. However, for the majority of monitoring alarms, smart decision support or monitoring systems need to be developed. One example of a simple but effective DSS for tow of the most common adverse events during anesthesia - unstable blood pressure and light anesthesia - was presented in 2000 (Krol & Reich, 2000). When computerized algorithms were compared with subjective assessment by anesthesiologists, it was found that a 12% change of mean arterial pressure in comparison to the median of the mean arterial pressure of the previous 10-min interval can be used as indicating light anesthesia. Best agreement between computer readings and human assessment was achieved when the absolute value of the fractional change of the mean arterial pressure in between 2-min periods was used. (Fig.4)

It is not the objective of this chapter to reason whether changes in mean arterial pressure are indicative of 'light anesthesia'; this study simply shows that very simple computerization can be helpful to readily indicate anesthesiologists - in this case anesthesiologists following the paradigm that hemodynamic ability indicates an insufficient degree of anesthesia - a decision support in daily routine.

How can knowledge- and rule-based DSS be designed so that a maximum number of clinicians adhere to them and use them to improve outcome?

Design considerations have recently been presented (Dunsmuir et al., 2008): rule structures should be easy to understand, the process of knowledge authoring tooling should be intuitive, all decisions visible to everybody, and the user interface easy to use for everybody. Such a user interface is presented in figure 5 by Dunsmuir et al. (Dunsmuir et al., 2008) as a smart monitoring tool for hemodynamic adverse events in children undergoing anesthesia.

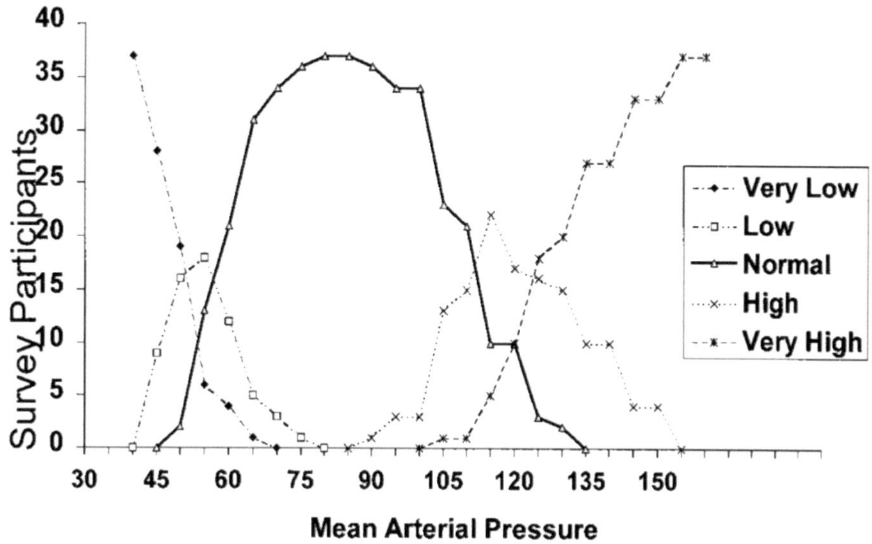

Fig. 4. Categorization of MAP by anesthesiologists. (Krol & Reich, 2000)

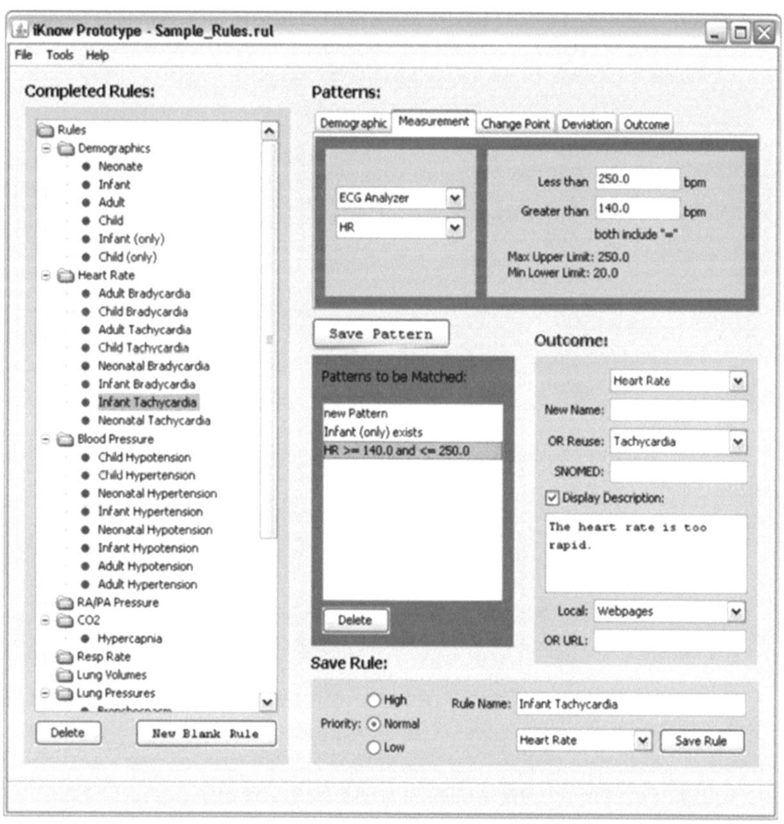

Fig. 5. The graphical user interface of the knowledge authoring tool. (Dunsmuir et al., 2008)

The importance of 'user feedback' is clearly demonstrated in this study. Some samples of results from a user questionnaire are presented and focus on 'user friendliness' of the interface more than a disagreement with the rules. (Fig. 6)

Statement	Median rating	Sample related comment
It was easy to learn to use this system	3.5	"Help sheet quite useful"
I believe I could become productive quickly using this system	2	"Quick learning curve"
The organization of the information on the system screens was clear	3	"The layout is nice but the boxes need to be labeled more intuitively"
Overall, I am satisfied with this system	3	"When using a system like this, I think when merging to be able to drag + drop rules into the new rule/outcome would be useful"

Fig. 6. Sample from PSSUQ results. (Dunsmuir et al., 2008)

The authors conclude that anesthesiologists can rapidly develop useful rules for use in a predefined clinical scenario (Dunsmuir et al., 2008). Using a fuzzy-logic evidence based expert diagnostic alarm system, similar success can be achieved for the diagnosis of intraoperative hypovolemia (Mirza et al., 2010). Its basic structure is depicted in Fig. 7.

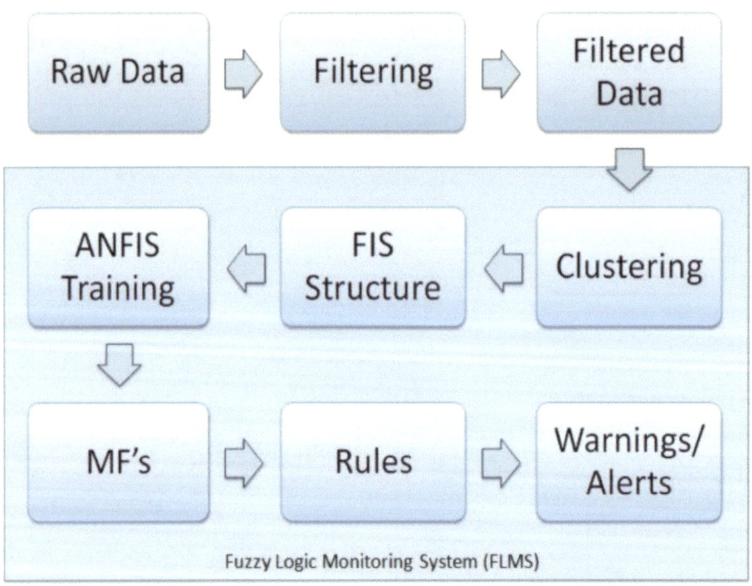

Fig. 7. Block diagram of the FLMS. ANFIS=Adaptive-Network-based Fuzzy Inference Systems ; FIS=fuzzy interference systems ; MF's=membership function. (Mirza et al., 2010)

An ideal scenario of anesthetic clinical practice almost implying the use of DSSs is the different PONV prevention strategies. The symbiosis of a clearly identified anesthetic problem - PONV - , clearly established guidelines - PONV guidelines - and the existence of several drug combinations make this an ideal work field for intelligent DSSs.
A recent study investigated the effect of such a DSS on guidelines adherence using an on-off design (Kooij et al., 2008). Fig. 8 presents the number of patients enrolled in this study.

	Control N (%)	Decision support N (%)	Post-DS N (%)	Significance
Prophylaxis indicated	373 (100)	871 (100)	321 (100)	
Prophylaxis prescribed?				$P < 0.001$
Yes	140 (38)	632 (73)	119 (37)	
No	233 (62)	239 (27)	202 (63)	
Total number of patients	1340 (100)	2715 (100)	1035 (100)	
Total prescribed	216 (16)	819 (30)	195 (19)	
Correctly	140 (10)	632 (23)	119 (12)	
Without indication	76 (6)	187 (7)	76 (7)	NS

NS = not significant.

Fig. 8. Scheduling Postoperative Nausea and Vomiting Prophylaxis. (Kooij et al., 2008)

However, this study shows as well that the use of DSS has no impact on 'changing the culture' of wrong-doing as an educational tool once it is withdrawn: although the DSS very significantly improved adherence to the PONV guidelines, guideline adherence decreased to the level before the DSS was used after its withdrawal. (Fig. 9)

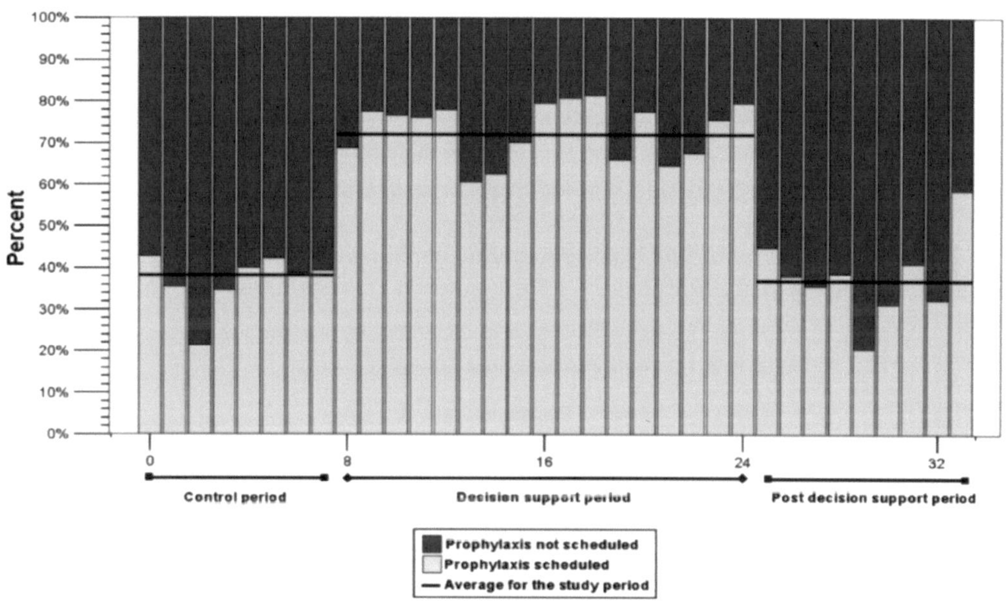

Fig. 9. Week by week analysis of all high risk patients. The bars show the percentage of high risk patients receiving postoperative nausea and vomiting prophylaxis prescribed. (Kooij et al., 2008)

Two studies have investigated the implementation of simple DSSs using an AIMS to improve adherence to proper antibiotic prophylaxis before surgery.

In one study (O'Reilly et al., 2006), a simple feedback system integrated in the AIMS was used to improve properly timed antibiotic prophylaxis provided by the anesthesiologist. (Fig.10)

Another group used the AIMS in combination with e-mail feedback of missed documentation, monthly summary reports and real-time electronic alerts to achieve a near 100% timely antibiotic prophylaxis; without filling out the antibiotic note, the AIMS anesthesia chart cannot be closed. (Nair et al., 2010)

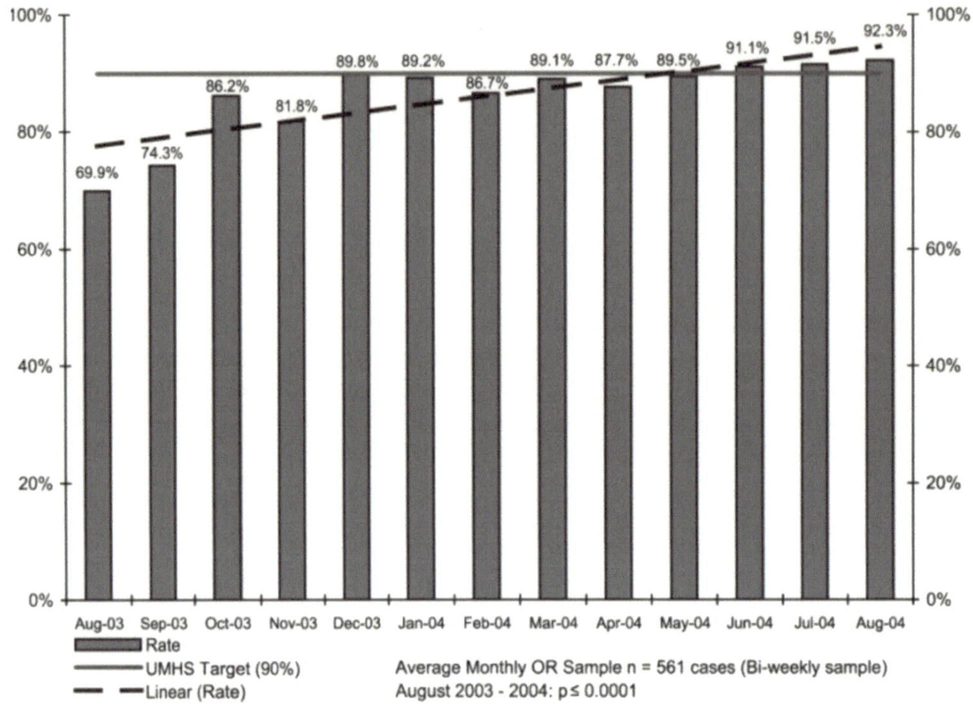

Fig. 10. Compliance with the timely administration of antibiotics gradually increased to about 92%. (O'Reilly et al., 2006)

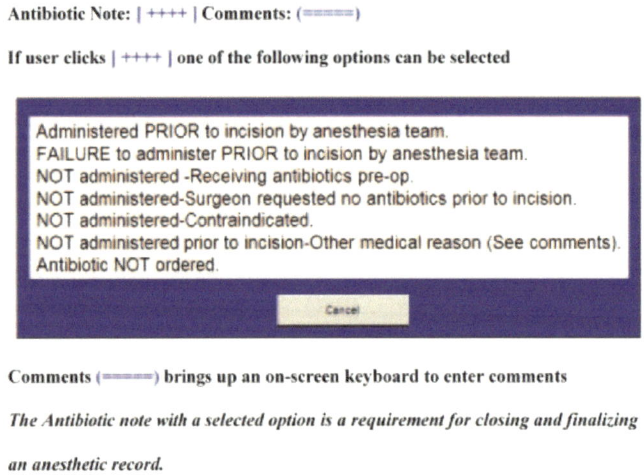

Fig. 11. Antibiotic compliance comment note options in AIMS (Anesthesia Information Management System). (Nair et al., 2010)

This was combined with 'smart messages". (Fig. 12) The user received messages which were displayed as a pop-up menu. These reminder messages are sent so that the users can see them before surgery starts and administer the antibiotic prophylaxis optimally timed for effect. Messages also appear when administration of antibiotics are not documented or incomplete.

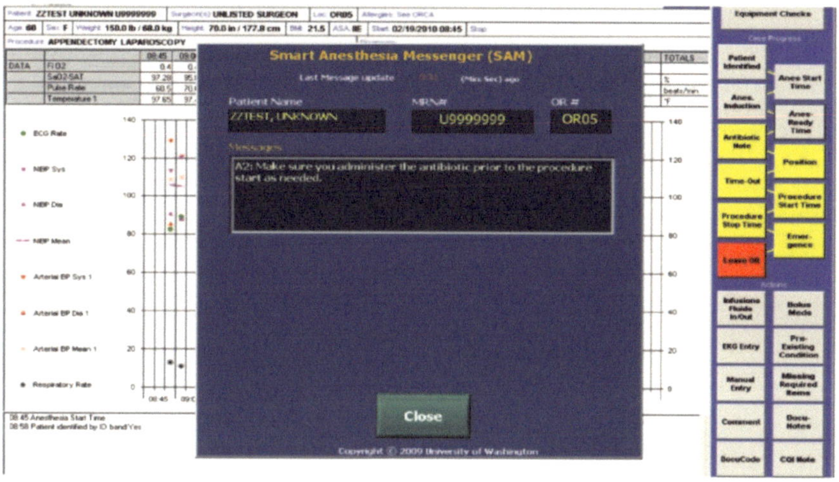

Fig. 12. Smart Anesthesia Messenger (SAM) alert screen overlaid on anesthesia information management system screen. (Nair et al., 2010)

In the course of the study period - june 2008 - jan 2010 - the weekly antibiotic compliance improved steadily, reaching a near 100% compliance at the end of step 4. (Fig. 13)

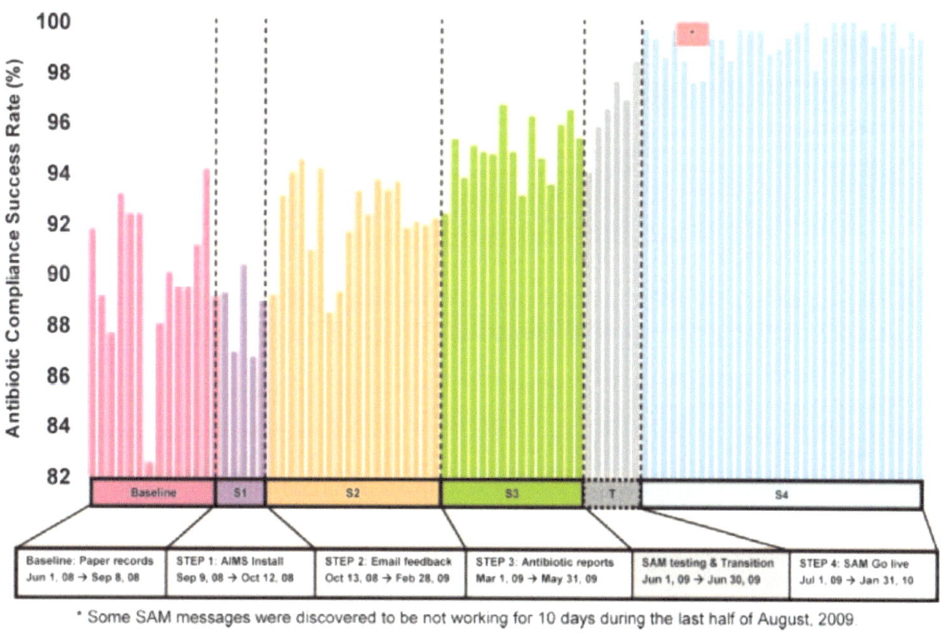

Fig. 13. Improvement in weekly antibiotic compliance success rate with each intervention. AIMS _ Anesthesia Information Management Systems; SAM _ Smart Anesthesia Messenger. (Nair et al., 2010)

Another example of an anesthetic DSS is the creation of an electronic algorithm for detecting insufficient depth of anesthesia based on computing different MAC values of volatile anesthetics with different intravenous sedative or hypnotic agents administered concomitantly. (Mashour et al, 2009).
The need for DSSs even for very simple anesthetic gestures, such as turning on the ventilator alarms after separation from cardiopulmonary bypass (which cardiac anesthesiologist has not forgotten this?), is demonstrated in a recent study (Eden et al., 2009). A simple electronic reminder as part of the AIMS (Fig. 14) improves significantly the incidence of alarm reactivation from 22% to 83%. (Fig. 15) At the end of the study period, there were significantly less electronic reminders and alarms were spontaneously reset after cardiopulmonary bypass.

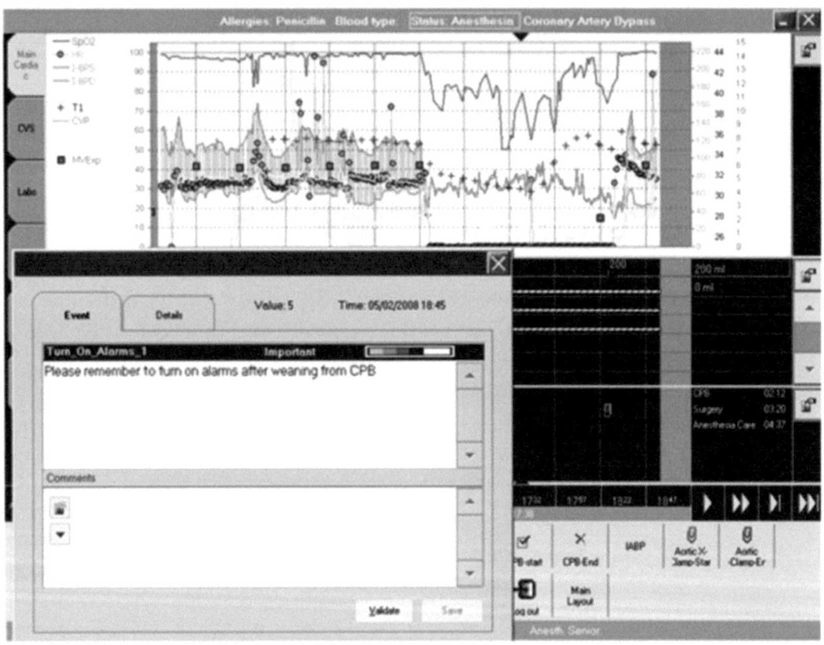

Fig. 14. The appearance of the electronic reminder on the anesthesia information management system main window. (Eden et al., 2009)

Characteristic	Stage I (*n* = 304)	Stage II (*n* = 256)	Stage III (*n* = 435)	*P* for trend
Alarm reactivation				
Yes	68 (22.4%)	160 (62.5%)	363 (83.4%)	*P*<0.001
No	236 (77.6%)	96 (37.5%)	72 (16.6%)	
No. of reminders per patient				
0	NA	60 (23.4%)	184 (42.3%)	*P*<0.001
1	NA	69 (27.0%)	162 (37.2%)	
2	NA	56 (21.9%)	62 (14.3%)	
3+	NA	71 (27.7%)	27 (6.2%)	

[a] Stage I = 5 mo before implementation.
Stage II = 5 mo after system introduction.
Stage III = Additional 8 mo follow-up, after the second educational meeting.
NA = not applicable.

Fig. 15. System Performance by Implementation Stage. (Eden et al., 2009)

However, these DSSs do not cover the actual administration of anesthetic agents, nor do they present different treatment options for adverse incidents. They mostly focus on the concept of smart monitoring, alarms for administering concomitant drugs, such as drugs for PONV prophylaxis or antibiotic prophylaxis, or alarms for insufficient depth of anesthesia or hemodynamic. They do not give several treatment options to the user - anesthesiologist. Recently, a hybrid system for conscious sedation with DSS was presented. (Hemmerling, STA abstract 2011). This system integrates closed loop sedation with a DSS, offering pop-up menus as smart alarms with several treatment advices for hemodynamic or respiratory adverse events, which need to be confirmed by the anesthetic team by clicking respective touch buttons on a touch screen. (Fig.16)

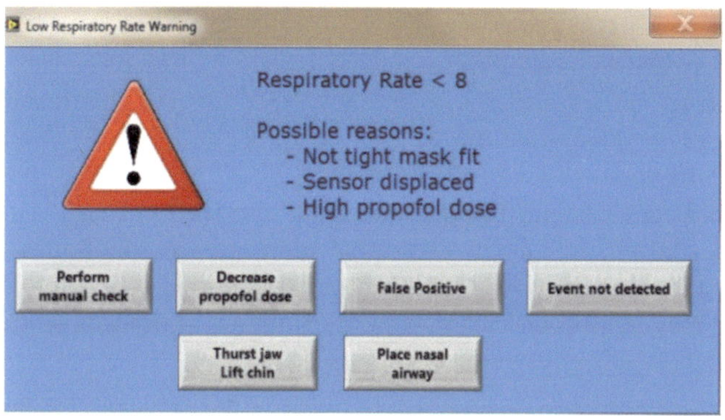

Fig. 16. Pop-up menu for respiratory rate critical event. (Hemmerling et al., 2011)

The DSS significantly improved the incidence of critical event detection as well as time between event occurrence and event recognition. (Fig. 17.)

	Protocol Group (N=50)	Control Group (N=50)	P
Events not detected (%)	0	25	***<0.0001 #<0.000**
AVG Delay (s)	7.4±4.0	32.6±21.7	**1**
Critical events/h	5.6±4.1	7.4±5.1	#0.05
MAP /h	3.2±3.1	3.7±3.6	N.S.
RR/h	4.3±3.6	3.8±4.1	N.S.
HR/h	0.9±0.5	0.7±0.3	N.S.
Sat/h	1.6±1.1	2.2±2.4	N.S.

Fig. 17. Performance of anesthesiologists in detecting critical events. (Hemmerling et al., 2010)

The above presented examples show that DSSs can be created for perioperative use in anesthesia; whereas most research has focused on designing DSS as smart monitoring and alert systems, future research has to focus on combining purely 'Monitoring-DSS' to alerting several treatment options for providing anesthesia or treating critical events thus integrating best evidence based treatment options in modern DSSs.

2.2 Decision support system in emergency medicine

Decision support systems have long played a significant role in the management of emergency patients. Emergency medicine is driven by a combination of out-of-hospital and in-hospital complex scenarios which pose logistical difficulties because of the following demands:

- rapid access to patients outside the hospital
- immediate care (both in diagnostics and treatment) by paramedical staff
- immediate link with logistical coordinators for transport organization
- acuteness of illness or trauma
- very often limited experience of health care providers as primary care
- resource management of both manpower and diagnostic tools
- single or mass casualties of primarily un-known trauma

The sheer combination of very often life-threatening illness or trauma with the need to rapidly diagnose and treat these pathologies is an ideal playing field for the implementation of computer-based decision support systems.

However, the studies are somewhat inconclusive: whereas DSSs have very successfully been implemented in the pre-hospital care system, making triage and organization far easier than without them, their implementation in the hospital based emergency care system is somewhat disappointing.

For the pre-hospital care system, the iRevive EMT application is a very good example of successful implementation of a DSS in a complex environment (Gaynor et al, 2005).

It is designed as a network of wireless, handheld computers, with wireless patient location and vital sign sensors, connected to an ambulance base station, and a central command center. (Fig. 18)

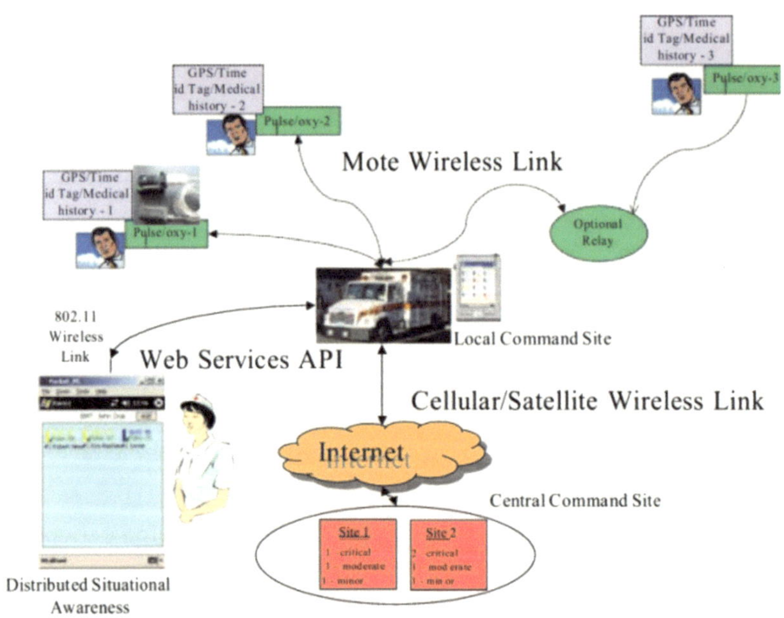

Fig. 18. iRevive System Architecture. (Gaynor et al, 2005).

It provides decision support at the site of the incident (pre-hospital), at local command centers, and at a central point of coordination. It is unique through its integration of vital sign parameters which are transmitted wirelessly. It is a key feature of emergency management in a pre-hospital setup to react not only to an initial patient conditions but adjust management and triage towards possible dynamic changes in the patient's status: both elements are provided successfully by the iRevive structure as illustrated in Figure 19 (left side: stable condition, right side: vital sign changes)

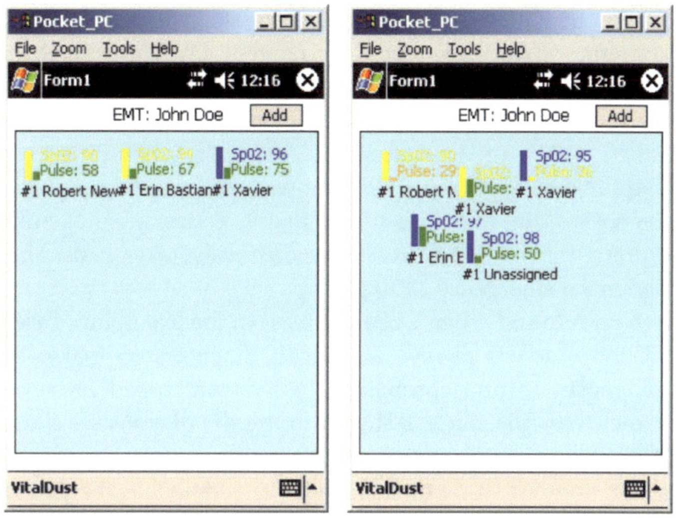

Fig. 19. Dynamic triage function in iRevive. (Gaynor et al, 2005).

A similar approach is presented by another Australian group for the in-hospital based emergency care management (Ceglowski et al, 2005). The task faced for the establishment of a DSS for the in-hospital based emergency department is illustrated in Fig. 20:

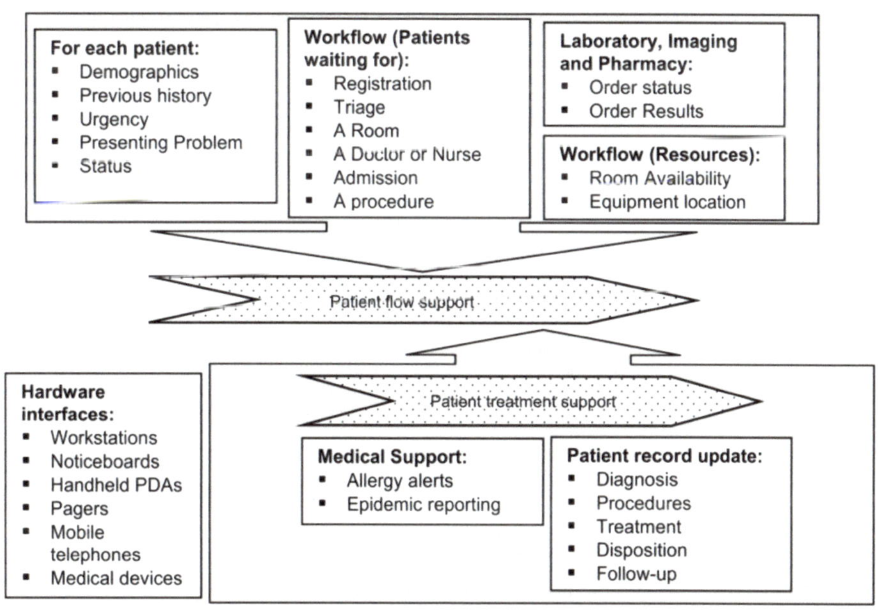

Fig. 20. EDIS support for emergency department patient flow (Ceglowski et al, 2005).

The combination of hardware interfaces, readily available through modern technologies, such as smart phones, and sophisticated software allow the modeling of a DSS, ready to help triage and improve the workflow of patients entering the emergency department.
However: how do these DSSs perform in a real-life setting?
Graber's study (Graber & VanScoy, 2003) has investigated the performance of a DSS in an emergency department. Whilst they could show that DSSs performed as well in this complex setup as in other medical fields, they also found a surprising under-performance of the DSS in comparison to the final human based emergency diagnosis: the final diagnosis was only found in 50 to 70% of the differential diagnosis, depending on which DSS was used, and only in approximately 30% of the time was the final diagnosis amongst the top 5 of the different diagnosis of the DSS. This means that its accuracy is not sufficient to allow to use it reliably at present. In addition, their use obviously takes considerable time, a key criticism when used in the emergency setting.
Similar results have been found when DSSs are used in the exemplary case of diagnosing a pulmonary embolism, which is always a difficult diagnosis to make: the characteristic element of this diagnostic setup - probability assessment based on several clinical and diagnostic tools rather than one single test confirming the diagnosis - should actually play in the hands of DSSs.
The study of Roy and another study of Drescher have looked at the performance of DSSs to diagnose pulmonary embolism. The first study (Roy et al, 2009) showed an improvement in the application of appropriate diagnostic strategies which was significantly better when a computer-based guidelines structure was used versus paper-based guidelines structure in a multi-centre study involving 20 centers and more than 1000 patients. (Fig. 21)
In the computer-based guidelines group, the same guidelines were used but on a handheld device into which the patients' parameters were entered: all clinical variables to derive a Geneva score, a probability score for pulmonary embolism are entered into the DSS. Then the DSS offers all necessary and available diagnostic tests to confirm or exclude the diagnosis of pulmonary embolism with probability thresholds. (Fig. 22)
This study clearly showed the superior performance of DSSs, which was confirmed for the same diagnostic setup by the second study (Drescher et al, 2010). However, the second study also showed one of the key problems of implementing DSSs in the context of in-hospital emergency departments: poor user (physician) acceptance. (Fig. 23)
The range of non-adherence to the DSS varied from 5% to 100% depending on the individual physician: only part of this non-adherence can be attributed to increased computer time in order to use the DSS. The authors state: 'emergency physicians attributed disbelief in its clinical utility and impatience with the time it required as the reasons for not following its recommendations or for opting out.'
Implementation of DSSs in the emergency medicine setting have been very successful for the preoperative environment; they can help make triage more efficient. Systems can help to provide better pre-hospital patient care.
In the in-hospital emergency medicine setting, the acceptance of DSSs is still limited: the significant amount of time necessary to enter all the data is one of the key aspects limiting their widespread use. However, the influence of human, emotional resentment towards the introduction of computer based decision-making cannot be excluded.

Appropriate Diagnostic Strategy Applied	Computer-Based Guidelines Group			Paper Guidelines Group			Adjusted Difference in Change (95% CI), *percentage points**†	*P* Value
	Preintervention Period, *n/n* (%)‡	Intervention Period, *n/n* (%)‡	Adjusted Absolute Change, %*§	Preintervention Period, *n/n* (%)‡	Intervention Period, *n/n* (%)‡	Adjusted Absolute Change, %*§		
By posttest probability‖								
All diagnoses	108/460 (23.5)	378/694 (54.5)	30.2	109/532 (20.5)	245/951 (25.8)	10.9	19.3 (2.9 to 35.6)	0.023
Pulmonary embolism ruled out	63/381 (16.5)	306/581 (52.7)	33.5	62/435 (14.3)	138/768 (18.0)	7.1	26.4 (10.1 to 42.7)	0.003
Pulmonary embolism ruled in	45/79 (57.0)	72/113 (63.7)	10.7	47/97 (48.5)	107/183 (58.5)	14.4	−3.7 (−31.7 to 24.3)	0.78
All diagnoses with data inputted in real time (per-protocol analysis)	66/190 (34.7)	345/557 (61.9)	26.0	71/186 (38.2)	169/369 (45.8)	12.3	13.7 (−6.5 to 33.9)	0.171
By strict application of recommendations¶	59/460 (12.8)	287/694 (41.4)	25.7	60/532 (11.3)	162/951 (17.0)	8.5	17.1 (1.9 to 32.4)	0.030

* Adjusted for age, known heart failure, chronic lung disease, current anticoagulant treatment, previous thromboembolism, sex, palpation pain, and lower limb edema (see Methods).

† Difference in absolute change of appropriateness between the computer-based and paper guidelines groups.

‡ Fractions represent number of patients for whom appropriate strategy was applied over the total number of patients who received that diagnosis.

§ Adjusted absolute change in the frequency of appropriate pulmonary embolism diagnostic strategies between the preintervention and intervention periods.

‖ We considered a diagnostic strategy appropriate when the diagnostic criteria (clinical probability and the results of diagnostic tests) resulted in a posttest probability <5% for exclusion or >85% for confirmation (**Table 1**). We estimated intraclass correlation for all diagnoses to be 0.10 according to the Murray formula for binary outcomes.

¶ Appropriate diagnostic strategy according to strict application of recommendations was defined by using a table that summarized the validated strategies according to clinical probability level and diagnostic test results and assuming that a diagnostic work-up was inadequate when the clinical probability was not assessed or when additional unnecessary tests were performed (see Secondary Outcomes in Methods).

Fig. 21. Improvements in Application of Appropriate Diagnostic Strategy for Pulmonary Embolism (Roy et al, 2009).

Test Result	Clinical Probability of PE		
	Low (5%–15%)	Intermediate (15%–50%)	High (50%–85%)
Exclusion of PE			
Normal pulmonary angiography	Stop	Stop	Stop
Normal lung scan	Stop	Stop	Continue
Low-probability VQ scan	Stop	Continue	Continue
Negative quantitative ELISA D-dimer test result	Stop	Stop	Continue
Negative moderate-sensitivity D-dimer test result	Stop	Continue	Continue
Negative CT angiography	Stop	Continue	Continue
Negative multidetector CT angiography	Stop	Continue†	Continue
Negative CT or multidetector CT and negative proximal leg vein US	Stop	Stop	Continue
Confirmation of PE			
Pulmonary angiography showing PE	Stop	Stop	Stop
High-probability VQ scan	Continue	Stop	Stop
Positive CT or multidetector CT showing segmental or supra PE	Continue	Stop	Stop
Positive leg vein US showing proximal DVT	Continue	Stop	Stop
Echocardiography showing right ventricular dilatation	Continue	Continue	Stop

CT = computed tomography; DVT = deep venous thrombosis; ELISA = enzyme-linked immunosorbent assay; PE = pulmonary embolism; US = ultrasonography; VQ = ventilation–perfusion.

* Stop: Appropriate diagnostic criteria—stop testing. No further testing is required to exclude or to confirm PE. Continue: Inappropriate diagnostic criteria—continue testing. Further testing is required to rule in or rule out PE with confidence.

† Data that were not yet available at the beginning of the study suggest that PE can safely be excluded by negative multidetector spiral CT when the pretest probability is not high.

Fig. 22. Recommendations for Exclusion or Confirmation of PE on the Basis of Test Results, by Clinical Probability (Roy et al, 2009).

Emergency Physician	CT Angiography Not Recommended*	CT Angiography Ordered	CT Angiography Recommended†	CT Angiography Not Ordered	Total Number of Recommendations	Not Adherent With CDSS	Percentage of Decisions Not Adherent With CDSS
1	0	0	1	0	1	0	0
2	0	0	2	0	2	0	0
3	0	0	2	0	2	0	0
4	0	0	2	0	2	0	0
5	1	0	2	0	3	0	0
6	2	0	4	0	6	0	0
7	1	1	0	0	1	1	100
8	4	0	8	1	12	1	8.3
9	8	0	13	1	21	1	4.8
10	4	1	17	0	21	1	4.8
11	5	1	7	2	12	3	25
12	8	0	17	4	25	4	16
13	12	2	10	3	22	5	22.7
14	16	2	23	4	39	6	15.4
15	9	3	15	3	24	6	25
16	14	4	9	2	23	6	26
17	14	0	25	7	39	7	17.9
18	13	1	19	7	32	8	25
19	2	0	27	9	29	9	31

CDSS, computerized decision support system.
*Low pretest probability: Low Wells score and negative D-dimer result.
†High pretest probability: Wells score or positive D-dimer result and low Wells score.

Fig. 23. Adherence of individual emergency physicians to the clinical decision support system algorithm (Drescher et al, 2010).

2.3 Decision support systems in intensive care medicine

One of the most complex environments for physicians: there is an overload of parameters to watch, access to the patients can be limited, there is often a combination of very complex pathologies and the amount of technologies whose management needs mastering is significant. The main focus of initial DSSs in this setup is the idea of making all relevant patient data readily available.

Two of these systems shall initially be discussed here: the ACUDES system and the Rhea.

The ACUDES system (Palma et al, 2002) makes all patient data, be it clinical, based on monitoring or laboratory/investigative results available within the temporal context of relation to other data, trying to explain disease evolution, relationship between different abnormalities. ACUDES uses three modules, a temporal behavior model (TBM), the causal and temporal knowledge acquisition tool (CTKAT) and the diagnosis agent (DA). (Fig.24)

This combination allows the physician to have access to a knowledge data base (TBM) in a causal network, relating each abnormality with both a temporal evolution and a causality. The physician can mange, build, construct the data within the TBM – as long as any changes fit within the basic ontological structure of the system, thus avoiding any inconclusive data entry. The DA gives an explanatory framework from which diagnostic reasoning can be deducted.

The Rhea system (Metais et al, 2006) integrates a similar set of data as the ACUDES with the focus on iatrogenic adverse effects and nosocomial infections. At the time of writing the publication, 30 French hospitals participated in this project with more than 3000 patients' data set entered. The assembly of data serves to perform knowledge discovery for research purposes. Some of the proprieties which Rhea can deliver are the establishing of disease course models, alert rules depending on the individual patient's data and establishing procedural guidelines in order to decrease nosocomial infections. (Fig. 25)

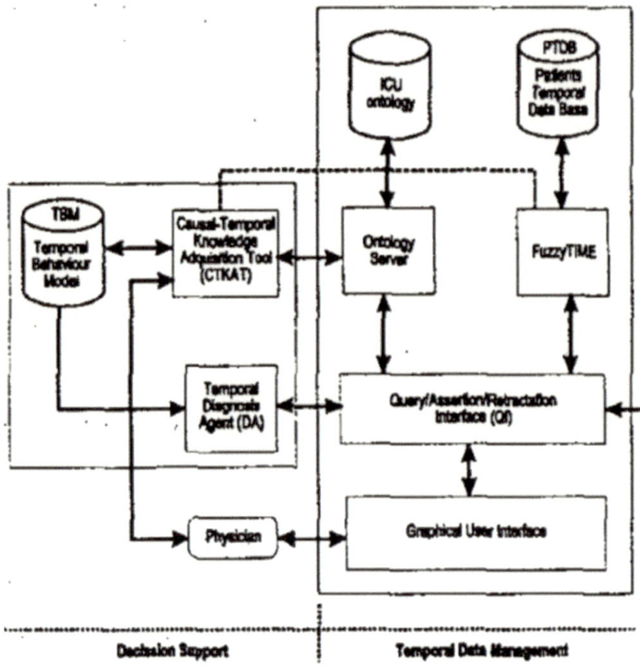

Fig. 24. ACUDES General Architecture (Palma et al, 2002)

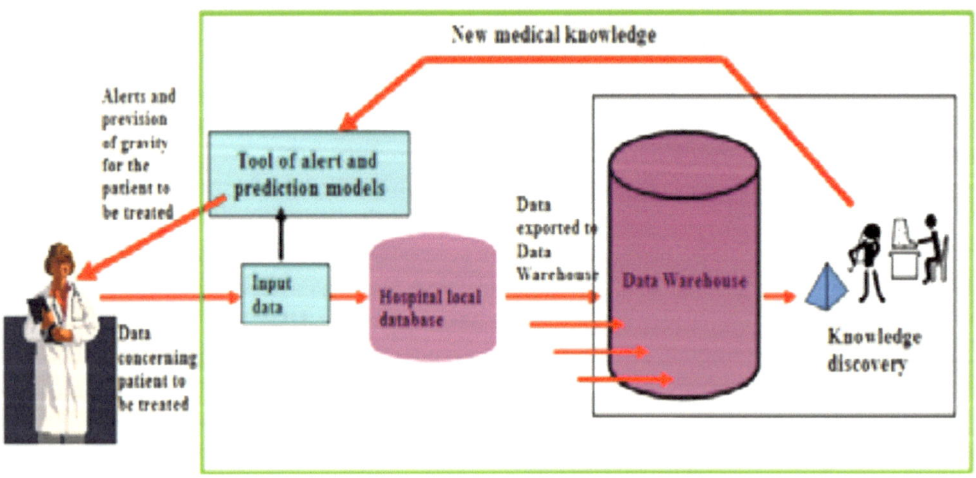

Fig. 25. General principle of Rhea project (Metais et al, 2006)

Each individual user can enter relevant data into the system at any time which renders the DSS 'dynamic' whilst making it available instantly to all users. (Fig. 26)
So far, Rhea has been solely used for biostatistical research; the increasing pressure on health care providers to audit safety and quality of their activities has led to the introduction

of these DSSs. However, these systems only provide actual 'decision support' with a significant lag time since they rely on studying data, auditing procedures and identifying possible shortcomings but do not provide an instantaneous help to the clinicians.

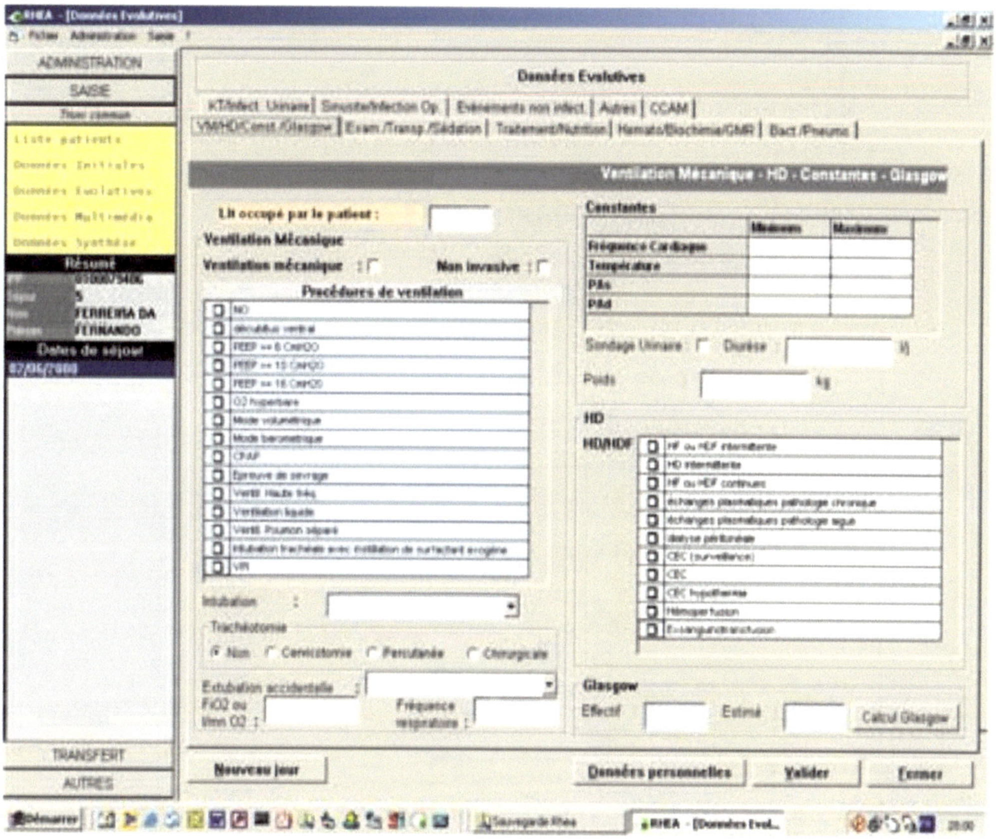

Fig. 26. Evolving data, tab "mechanical ventilation" (Metais et al, 2006)

The main area of DSSs in the field of intensive care medicine is a DSS for mechanical ventilation. Numerous systems have been developed and used for clinical trials. The fundamentals are outlines in a recent review of DSSs for mechanical ventilation (Tehrani & Roum, 2008, Fig. 27).

The efficacy of a DSS for mechanical ventilation is demonstrated in exemplary fashion by East's study (East et al, 1999) which was performed in 10 centers across the US. The use of DSS significantly reduced the overall morbidity in comparison to standard mechanical ventilation (Fig. 29) and a significant reduction in the incidence and degree of barotraumas. (Fig. 30)

In comparison to the poor efficacy of DSSs in in-hospital emergency medicine, the overall acceptance of these DSSs in this study was very good: 94% of the instructions were followed (out of 38546 instructions in total).

Might the high rate of DSS acceptance by the physician be a key to its success?

The main categories of DSSs for mechanical ventilation are outlined as follows (Fig. 28):

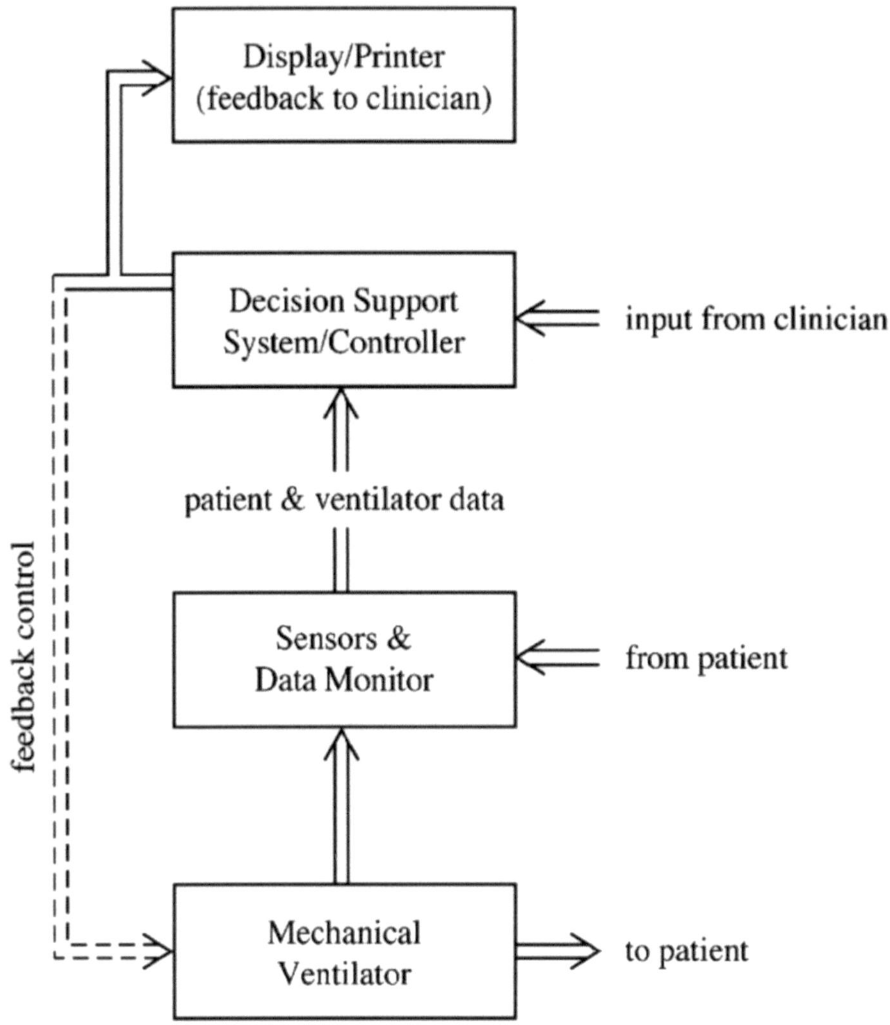

Fig. 27. Block diagram depiction of an IDSS for mechanical ventilation. The broken lines labeled as "feedback control" represent the automatic supply of control signals to the ventilator in case the system is used to control the ventilator in a closed-loop manner. (Tehrani & Roum, 2008).

Key characteristics	Available alternatives		
Basis structure	Rule-based	Model-based	Rule-based + model-based
Applicable ventilation modes	Pressure support (PS)	SIMV or IMV + PS	Multiple modes
Patient types	Adults	Neonates	ARDS patients
Optimized parameters	Blood gases	Weaning time	Blood gases and weaning time
Type of technology	Open-loop (advisory)	Closed-loop (automatic)	Open-loop + closed-loop

Fig. 28. Main categories of different IDSSs for mechanical ventilation (Tehrani & Roum, 2008).

Group	Survival	Age	MODS Score Mean	SEM	N
Control	died	<65	15.13	1.37	8
		≥65	16.59	0.70	22
	survived	<65	12.00	0.93	6
		≥65	11.58	0.44	57
Protocol	died	<65	14.88	1.63	8
		≥65	15.12	0.68	26
	survived	<65	11.42	1.30	12
		≥65	11.94	0.48	53

Fig. 29. The maximum daily MODS score in the protocol group and control group. (East et al, 1999)

Group	Baro	Barotrauma Score Mean	SEM	N
Control	non baro	0.73	0.20	59
	baro	3.56	0.36	32
Protocol	non baro	0.97	0.24	61
	baro	2.69	0.31	35

Fig. 30. Maximum daily barotraumas score of iatrogenic lung injury in the protocol group and control group. (East et al, 1999)

3. Conclusion

There are numerous examples of DSSs in the field of anesthesia, emergency medicine and intensive care medicine. The introduction of electronic anesthesia, ER or ICU management systems has been a key issue in these developments.

This chapter gives examples for design and smart alarm structure of DSSs in anesthesia. The introduction of DSSs in daily practice to assure following modern guidelines, as for PONV prophylaxis or proper antibiotic prophylaxis, is actually quite simple, and successful, depending on user compliance. Common areas of negligence and errors, such as turning on alarms after CPB, can be vastly improved by basic DSSs. Very few studies have looked at using DSSs in anesthesia delivery, but pop-up menus can be helpful to promote smart monitoring, alarms and help to treat critical events.

Emergency medicine is a particular arena where medical treatment needs to be coordinated between out-of-hospital and in-hospital treatment. Decision support systems provide the necessary logistical help in this complex environment. Their performance in a real life setting can be impaired by lack of compliance by physicians: however, this might be overcome with the more widespread introduction of these systems and the generational change of physicians, used to rely on technologies in their everyday life.

Decision support systems have long been introduced in intensive care medicine; complex ventilator settings are far easier to manage with DSSs than relying solely on human judgment.

Decision support systems have been studied for more than 2 decades in the fields of anesthesia, emergency medicine and intensive care medicine. They have an excellent track record for improving health care in the research setting; most of the studies have shown an

improvement in outcome, reduction of workload or better performance when DSSs assist health care providers. Before the widespread introduction of DSSs in these specialties, improvements in data entering and user interfaces need to be done.
There is no doubt that DSSs will in future healthcare systems be as common as computers in everyday life. All healthcare providers need to be ready for this.

4. Acknowledgement

The author wishes to thank Lingshan Tang, MD, for her invaluable support in editing this chapter. I am also grateful for all suggestions and comments provided by Shantale Cyr, PhD, during the writing process.

5. References

Ceglowski, R., Churilov, L. & Jeff, W. (2005). Facilitating Decision Support in Hospital Emergency Departments: A Process-Oriented Perspective. *Proceedings of the 13th European Conference on Information Systems*, Regensburg, Germany, 2005

Drescher, F. S., Chandrika, S. & Weir, I. D. (2010). Effectiveness and Acceptability of a Computerized Decision Support System Using Modified Wells Criteria for Evaluation of Suspected Pulmonary Embolism. *Annals of Emergency Medicine,* No. (November 2010), pp. 1097-6760, ISSN 0196-0644

Dunsmuir, D., Daniels, J. & Brouse, C. (2008). A knowledge authoring tool for clinical decision support. *Journal of Clinical Monitoring and Computing,* Vol.22, No. 3, (June 2008), pp. 189-198, ISSN 1573-2614

Eagle, C. J., Davies, J. M. & Reason, J. (1992). Accident analysis of large-scale technological disasters applied to an anesthetic complication. *Canadian Journal of Anesthesia,* Vol.39, No. 2, (February 1992), pp. 118-122, ISSN 0832-610X

East, T. D., Heermann, L. K. & Bradshaw, R. L. (1999). Efficacy of computerized decision support for mechanical ventilation: results of a prospective multi-center randomized trial. *Proceedings of AMIA Symposium,* pp. 251-255, ISBN 1531-605X, Washington D.C., USA, 1999

Eden, A., Pizov, R. & Toderis, L. (2009). The impact of an electronic reminder on the use of alarms after separation from cardiopulmonary bypass. *Anesthesia & Analgesia,* Vol.108, No. 4, (April 2009), pp. 1203-1208, ISSN 1526-7598

Epstein, R. H., Dexter, F. & Ehrenfeld, J. M. (2009). Implications of event entry latency on anesthesia information management decision support systems. *Anesthesia & Analgesia,* Vol.108, No. 3, (March 2009), pp. 941-947, ISSN 1526- 7598

Gaynor, M., Seltzer, M. & Moulton, S. (2005). A Dynamic, Data-Driven, Decision Support System for Emergency Medical Services. In: *Computational Science – ICCS 2005*. V. S. Sunderam, G. D. v. Albada, P. M. A. Sloot and J.J. Dongarra, pp. 61-100, Springer Berlin / Heidelberg, 2005

Graber, M. A. & VanScoy, D. (2003). How well does decision support software perform in the emergency department? *Emergency Medicine Journal,* Vol.20, No. 5, (Septembe 2003), pp. 426-428, ISSN 1472-0213

Hemmerling, T. M. (2009). Automated anesthesia. *Current Opinion in Anesthesiology,* Vol.22, No. 6, (December 2009), pp. 757-763, ISSN 1473-6500

Hemmerling, T. M., Arbeid, E., Tang, L. (2011). 'HSS'- A Novel Hybrid System for Conscious Sedation. *2011 Annual Conference of Society of Technology in Anesthesia,* Abstract 34, Las Vegas, January, 2011

Kooij, F. O., Klok, T. & Hollmann, M. W. (2008). Decision support increases guideline adherence for prescribing postoperative nausea and vomiting prophylaxis. *Anesthesia Analgesia,* Vol.106, No. 3, (March 2008), pp. 893-898, ISSN 1526-7598

Krol, M. & Reich, D. L. (2000). Development of a decision support system to assist anesthesiologists in operating room. *Journal of Medical Systems,* Vol.24, No. 3, (June 2000), pp. 141-146, ISSN 0148-5598

Mashour, G. A., Esaki, R. K., Vandervest, J. C. (2009). A novel electronic algorithm for detecting potentially insufficient anesthesia: implications for the prevention of intraoperative awareness. *Journal of Clinical Monitoring and Computing,* Vol.23, No. 5, (October 2009), pp. 273-277, ISSN 1573-2614

Metais, E., Nakache, D. & Timsit.Jean-François (2006). Rhea: A Decision Support System for Intensive Care Units. *4th International Multiconference on Computer Science and Information Technology,* 5-7 avril, 2006

Mirza, M., Gholamhosseini, H. & Harrison, M. J. (2010). A fuzzy logic-based system for anesthesia monitoring. *Proceedings of 32nd Annual International Conference of the IEEE Engineering in Medicine and Biology Society,* ISSN 1557-170X, Buenos Aires,Argentina, September, 2010

Nair, B. G., Newman, S. F., Peterson, G. N. (2010). Feedback mechanisms including real-time electronic alerts to achieve near 100% timely prophylactic antibiotic administration in surgical cases. *Anesthesia Analgesia,* Vol.111, No.5, (November 2010), pp. 1293-1300, ISSN 1526-7598

O'Reilly, M., Talsma, A., VanRiper, S. (2006). An anesthesia information system designed to provide physician-specific feedback improves timely administration of prophylactic antibiotics. *Anesthesia Analgesia,* Vol.103, No. 4, (October 2006), pp. 908-912, ISSN 1526-7598

Palma, J., Marin, R. & Campos, M. ACUDES: Arquitecture or Intensive Care Units Decision Support. *Proceedings of the Second Joint EMBSBMES Conference,* ISBN 0-7803-761 2-9/02, Houston, TX. USA, October, 2002

Reason, J. (2005). Safety in the operating theatre - Part 2: human error and organizational failure. *Quality & Safety in Health Care,* Vol.14, No. 1, (February 2005), pp. 56-60, ISSN 1475-3898

Roy, P. M., Durieux, P., Gillaizeau, F. (2009). A computerized handheld decision-support system to improve pulmonary embolism diagnosis: a randomized trial. *Annals of Internal Medicine,* Vol.151, No. 10, (November, 2009), pp. 677-686, ISSN 1539-3704

Tehrani, F. T. & Roum, J. H. (2008). Intelligent decision support systems for mechanical ventilation. *Artificial Intelligence in Medicine,* Vol.44, No. 3, (Nov 2008), pp. 171-182, ISSN 1873-2860

Zaouter, C., Tang, L., Charabati, S. (2010). McSleepy Light- A Novel Hybrid System for Controlled Sedation. *2010 Annual Conference of Canadian Anesthesiologists' Society*, Control ID: 803240, Montreal, June 2010

14

Decision Support by Visual Incidence Anamneses for Increased Patient Safety

Kerstin Ådahl and Rune Gustavsson
Blekinge Institute of Technology
Sweden

1. Introduction

1.1 How to get the right information?

Decision support in Health Care is based on proper collection and evaluation of relevant information related to the patient and her/his medical history. In the process of Anamnesis the patient will provide individual testimony regarding her/his status in a dialogue with the physician. The diagnosis will then be conducted by complementing this information with written information from (electronic) Health Records (EHR) followed by clinical examination, laboratory testing and imaging.

The quality and relevance of the information from Anamnesis is strongly dependant on the format and focus of the dialogue at hand. The dialogue itself is partly derived from analysing the patients EHR. As we know, the information found in EHRs is based on treatment of the patient by different hospital specialist departments. This structure of the EHR hampers the understanding of the treatment processes and their relevance in preparing the dialogue with the patient in the Anamnesis process.

We argue in this chapter that tools supporting the Anamnesis Process, such as the *Visual Incidence Anamneses* (VIA), have potential to improve decision support and process transparency in diagnosing patients and hence increasing patient safety. The following two figures capture our main ideas. Figure 1 illustrates information collected by the physician at two separate anamnesis events. Situation N is the present situation. Situation N-1 refers to

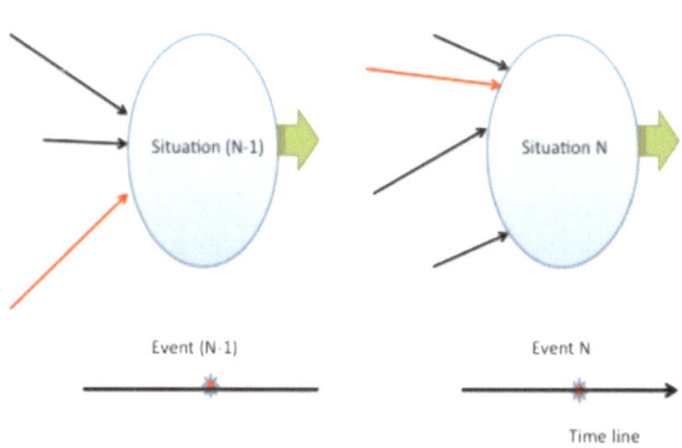

Fig. 1. Separate earlier events (N-1), randomly reported by the patient to the physician in the actual anamnesis phase (Situation N).

an earlier event (which could also be multiple earlier events). The inbound arrows denote different important aspects to consider in the anamnesis. The outbound arrow denotes the selected diagnosis and treatment.

In Figure 2 we illustrate a tool offering feedback to earlier anamneses allowing the physician to take these into account during the current anamnesis in Situation N. Specifically, it illustrates that the selected diagnosis and treatment might differ due to an enhanced *patient-centric greater context.*

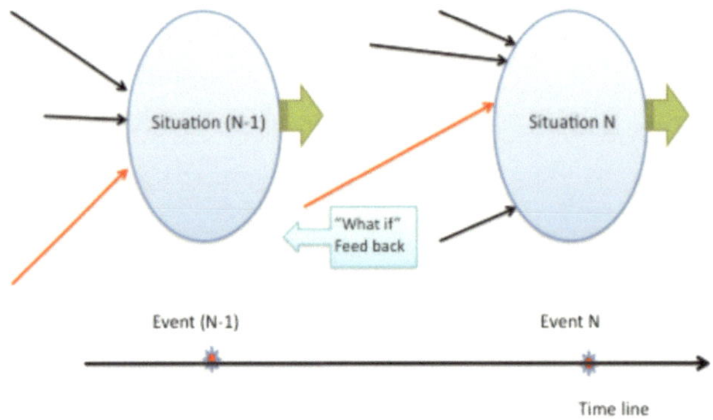

Fig. 2. Separate events (in situation/-s N-1) concatenated by automation of data; a visible historical feedback for the physician to consider, study and discuss with the patient in the actual anamnesis phase (Situation N).

In this chapter we will take a closer look at decision support tools and processes related to anamneses in the remaining part of this section. In *Section 1.2 Patient Safety* we shortly refer to the current alarming situation worldwide and the need for improved tools and methods (such as VIA) collecting and analysing patient information to improve Patient Safety. *Section 2 Artificial Intelligence in Medicine* gives a short overview of tools supporting decision making in medicine such as *2.1 Differential Diagnosing* and *2.2 Clinical Decision Support Systems (CDSS).* Issues related to decision making under incomplete and/or uncertain conditions are discussed in *Section 2.3 Safety Assessment.* The two complementary decision models "Find simplest cause" and "What if .." are discussed in *Section 3 Ockham's Razor vs. Hickham's Dictum.* In *Section 3.1 The rare cases and the probable* we stress that the concepts of "rare" and "probable" are *highly context dependant.* A "rare" cause can be highly propable due to more patient-process centric contexts such as enabled by, e.g., the VIA model and method. In *Section 4 Case studies* we motify exemplifies our VIA model as a mean to increase the quality of medical diagnosis. Our proposal is described in *Section 7 Visual Incidence Anamnesis (VIA).*The chapter ends with *Section 8 Conclusions* and *Section 9 References.*

Various types of Clinical Decision Support Systems (CDSS) have been developed to support the tasks to make the right diagnoses and decide on appropriate interventions such as treatments etc. However, a CDSS requires an *input* that is a critical point in the decision support process. In order to collect data for input to the system, the physician must initially perform an investigation of the situation and what might have lead up to it. The traditional action, even before any CDSS were available, is that the physician performs an interview with the patient and/or relatives to the patient, resulting in an anamnesis . Consequently, the anamnesis is a preliminary case history from the patients' perspective. In this step, the collection of patient specific data is vulnerable. Both the physician and the patient must cooperate towards a mutual understanding of what is important for the case or not. The patient (or relative) must be able to articulate information about the actual, or former, health status and the physician must be aware of which questions will sort out crucial information, valuable for further decision making.

The next step for the physician is to read relevant information in the (electronic) medical record. Grounded in information derived from the actual anamnesis, s/he decides what further information s/he might need to proceed with. Compared to earlier centuries, the information handling methods and the organization of Health Care are very different. In former times, the physician was reduced to use a complete medical history of the patients' experiences in order to make decisions. The modern society provides specialized Health Care, assisted by advanced medical technology, but the holistic view of the human body is mostly lost as the system is not process oriented and the patients report is marginalized. The current situation, dividing up Health Care (institutional care and primary care) into different clinical departments, is fragmenting. This jeopardizes a continuous information flow for each individual patient involving potential information breakdowns between the varying units of competence. A general lack of time for each patient will further increase the risk of mistakes.

The information elicitation process is delicate and the result depends on a variety of variables such as competence and observation of the physician, ability to communicate important experiences by the patient and time available for the anamnesis phase. Even if the prerequisites are perfect, there are still pitfalls resulting in missed, decisive, information. For example, varying symptoms of a disease might occur for a long period of time but earlier diagnoses could have been false. To concatenate symptoms from earlier events to more recent events might be crucial in order to find the true diagnosis. The anamnesis making process should therefore be supported by automation of data from the patients' medical history, instantly visible when the patient and the physician meet (Figure 2).

The difference between fragmented information flows, i.e. a number of disconnected and isolated information units on a time line, and a continuous information flow (of concatenated information units), where it is possible to observe and study earlier events due to *knowledge about their existence*, is vital. Figure 1 could be regarded as a model of a "hidden context", important for the physician to be aware of in the decision making process. Figure 2 is a model of visualization of such context.

It might be emphasized that it is not a simple task to collect data for input to a CDSS. The anamnesis is an important step in this information elicitation process as it provides the physician with patient specific information, but the method for this step is rather ad-hoc and insecure: The human brain is extraordinary in its ability to sort out apparently crucial information for conclusions, but simultaneously this ability is perilous as conclusions might occur prematurely and be false if vital information is missing. Consequently, in Health Care this defectiveness might affect Patient Safety despite any advanced and well-designed CDSS. The critical issue is collection of *relevant* data.

1.2 Patient safety

Due to alarming numbers of incidents, injuries and deaths in Health Care caused by deficiencies in the field of activities, Patient Safety has attracted considerable attention in the last decade. Declaring that every year in USA, approximately 44 000 to 98 000 deaths occur related to deficiencies in Patient Safety, the report "To Err is Human" (Kohn et al. 2000), is still frequently cited and regarded as significant in the western world. Therefore, it has caused far-reaching attention to the seriousness of the situation and constituted a starting point for appropriate actions. Furthermore, the findings in the report have been confirmed in other, more recent, reports in other western countries such as Sweden.

Consequently, for the last decade, in Sweden, as in the European Union, an increasing interest in Patient Safety is noticeable. Various efforts in order to manage the critical situation in Health Care are already in place and the efforts towards models and methods assuring improved Patient Safety have high priority.

In this *Section 1* and *Section 7* we propose Visual Incidence Anamneses (VIA) as a model and method to increase patient safety. Our proposal is underpinned by an analysis of two case studies illustrating some shortcoming of present methods and tools such as Differential Diagnosing (DD) and Clinical Decision Support Systems (CDSS).

However, first we must return to an outline of the present situation for Health Care, in relation to Patient Safety. In Sweden, a prevailing strategy to follow up and prevent faults in Health Care has been to "punish" registered individuals (such as registered nurses, physicians etc.). HSAN (Hälso- och Sjukvårdens AnsvarsNämnd; Eng. Medical Responsibility Board) has until 2010 received numerous cases each year to evaluate and take measures against. Today, the National Board of Health and Welfare has shouldered the responsibility for assignments related to Patient Safety cases. However, the perspective on action plans for a safer Health Care has radically changed towards the perspective of fault prevention in the transport sector, i.e. towards a "systemic perspective" on each situation. As a result, the tendency forward is to adopt a basic change of models and methods to address shortcomings in protocols, procedures and in information management in Health Care. For example, among other contributions, to the area, a new Patient Safety Law (SFS 2010:659) came into force January 1st 2011. Especially noticeable for this matter is that the law also embraces the encouragement of patients and their relatives to participate in the Patient Safety work. This is in line with the development of the *Patient Empowerment (PE) movement*, appearing more distinctly along with the strong attention to Patient Safety as a complementary approach. PE is contributing to Patient Safety as the empowered patient in Health Care is regarded as a co-operator and an important piece of the puzzle, contributing with experience in being the one who has the "inside information" of being ill and, to a certain extent, being capable of act as such instead of passively receive care (a former, more traditional, view of the patient). Patient Centered Medicine (PCM) is another related line of policy, where a holistic view on the patient is given priority over the earlier, most common, industrial inspired view of work flow in Health Care as comparable to an assembly production line. PCM aims to avoid fragmentation of Health Care and to find ways to coordinate the patient the whole way through the care process. A related perspective is "Lean Thinking", a management strategy for improvement of processes also applicable in Health Care. Accordingly, "Lean Health Care" is introduced at several hospitals in Sweden where Skåne Universitetssjukhus (SUS) (Eng. Skåne University Hospital), Lund, is one of those. These approaches are all connected to an aim of improving not only efficiency but also Patient Safety.

Returning to a very basic principle of Patient Safety, we must consider that Health Care is built on Information. Without information there will be neither conclusions nor decisions. Furthermore, the information in use must be *correct*. It must both be true and complete. Regarding the quality of knowledge used in Health Care, Evidence Based Medicine (EBM) is adopted as a guarantee of first rate quality of scientific information, used in clinical settings. As such, EBM is an important foundation for Clinical Decision Support Systems (CDSS), used for support in situations of diagnosing and treatment. Today, CDSS are used in different clinical settings, preferably at the point of care, by physicians as well as by nurses. However, referring to the areas of Patient Empowerment and Patient Centered Medicine, briefly described above, every medical case is unique as every patient is an individual carrying a unique set of historical events in his/her medical history. This medical history is both documented in medical records, such as Electronic Health Records (EHR) and in the consciousness of patients and their relatives. Every single event in a medical history is important as it might be a clue to, or affect, current or future events. Neither EBM nor EHR and traditional CDSS are completely or clearly covering such aspects on diagnosing or treatment for the patient. Nevertheless, these events are substantially important for Patient Safety as loss of such information might lead to wrong diagnoses and delayed treatment. For many diseases, the time aspect is highly important for the successfulness of treatment.

To be able to observe and identify appearances of critical information and information structures over time, a longitudinal case study, going on for ten years between 1999 and 2009, has been addressed. Moreover, a rather rare case occurring during a period of six months in 2010 added some more findings to the other and also questioned the widely adopted *Ockham´s Razor of Diagnostic Parsimony*. This seemed to be important with reference to the common use of CDSS. A qualitative methodology was chosen (including participatory observation, interviews and the study of medical records) which made it possible to more closely identify and study occurring, unpredictable, information breakdowns. Those breakdowns appeared to be critical for the outcome of the different cases, however not, or not clearly, visible in the EHR system for the physicians to observe. For each case, each new event was dependant on information from former events, sometimes carried by the patient or a relative, but not evident to be important at the time of the occurrence. To successfully use CDSS in order to find an accurate diagnosis or treatment requires patient data that is both true and complete. Figure 1 and 2 illustrates this aspect. In this chapter, we focus on incomplete causality models in Health Care. We suggest a feasible solution by utilizing graphical visualization of chronological information in EHR-systems. This information structure is suggested to complement the widely adopted rule-based Decision Support architectures. The rule bases can be regarded as isolated islands of knowledge while our graphical visualization ties together those patient specific events.

2. Artificial intelligence in medicine (AIM)

Health Care is basically built on Information. Without Information, *decisions* about investigations, diagnoses and treatment would be impossible to make. For example, patient specific data is important to collect. This is accomplished by the creation of an anamnesis, collection of body data by medical equipment and clinical medical examination of the body in different ways (palpation, percussion etc). Decisions also require general knowledge to connect to. To build such knowledge, scientific information of high quality is necessary. Patient data and general medical knowledge is the foundation for any decision about a disease; deciding to choose diagnosis and the best practise of treatment. The knowledge of physicians and nurses in Health Care (in this context referred to as "human agents") is evident to be part of the decision making process. However, the knowledge bases in human agents might differ from one agent to another as humans are individual; different levels or different directions in education and different former experiences, as well as more subtle tacit knowledge, build human knowledge. Artificial Intelligence (AI) has since decades been regarded as potentially useful in Medicine, forming a sub-area: "Artificial Intelligence in Medicine (AIM). An early apprehension of AIM was that it would offer possibilities to create "a doctor in a box" which even could surpass the competence of a human agent; a physician (Coiera 2003, p. 331). In more recent years, the ambitions have been more moderate. Instead, different applications of *Knowledge Management* have been addressed to complement the knowledge of human agents in this area. To support the decision making process in Health Care, Clinical Decision Support Systems (CDSS) are developed for clinical practise. However, the success of CDSS is conspicuous by its absence and the usage still not very often established as a part of work flow. Coiera (2003) refers to some reasons for reluctance to use CDSS:

"Reasons for the failure of many expert systems to be used clinically include dependence on an electronic medical record system to supply their data, poor human interface design, failure to fit naturally into the routine process of care, and reluctance or computer illiteracy of some healthcare workers."(Coiera 2003, p. 344)

Above a more user friendly and intuitive design, it seems to be necessary to more deeply consider work flow and the flow of information in Health Care, in order to develop and implement useful CDSS. Furthermore, additional tools for CDSS must be designed to repair shortcomings in protocols, procedures and information management in Health Care. However, to be able to do that, such shortcomings must be identified and analyzed. Patient Safety is an area where the results of such shortcomings are explicitly expressed. In this chapter, we will present a case study and some findings pointing at this need and we will also present a feasible solution for repair of information breakdowns which are jeopardizing Patient Safety. However, first we will deepen the reasoning about CDSS by presenting a logical method termed Differential Diagnosing.

2.1 Differential diagnosing

Symptoms might be caused by a great variety of causes. For example, fever is such a symptom. To pinpoint the true cause of occurring symptoms, i.e. the pathophysiologic explanation of the symptoms which is the actual disease, the decision making process embraces a method termed *Differential Diagnosing*. Referring to Merriam-Websters dictionary, the definition of Differential Diagnosis (ΔΔ or DD) is

"the distinguishing of a disease or condition from others presenting with similar signs and symptoms"

Accordingly, DD is, basically, a method used to systematically identify unknown variables; i.e. a "process of elimination". This is a logical tool by which a list of possible diagnoses is made by the physician, implicit in mind or explicit on paper, digital etc. The diagnoses are, at hand, narrowed down by excluding impossible diagnoses until only one diagnosis remains. This implies that for one patient only one diagnosis, representing the symptoms, is true any other false. The word *Diagnosis*[1] originates from the Greek word *Diagignoskein*, meaning to "discern, distinguish" which is the basic aim of diagnosing: to discern the right diagnosis from the wrong. Consequently, DD in Medicine are the process of eliminating alternative diagnoses that might have some common symptoms with the true diagnosis and which could mislead the physician. In this process, Diagnostic Algorithms are used as tools for elimination. However, in rare cases, two conditions might occur simultaneously, giving

---

[1] http://www.etymonline.com/index.php?term=diagnosis

rise to one similar symptom. For example, chest pain could arise both from cardiac infarction and gastroesophageal reflux disease. Normally, after process of elimination, at least one is excluded; but both *could* be true, resulting in one missed diagnosis. (Later in this chapter, "Hickam´s Dictum" in relation to "Ockhams Razor" will emphasize this phenomenon.) Consequently, a defective process of elimination could result in a wrong or incomplete diagnosis, especially if not every sign or symptom is available to notice. In this matter, the importance of a complete anamnesis should be stressed. Accordingly, it could be concluded that the process of elimination is delicate.

Another peril is the physicians' memory capabilities, necessary to be adequate, especially in situations characterized by high workload and stress. Therefore, IT-tools for DD are, along with the development of the Internet, available for physicians, for example *DiagnosisPro*[2], a free self-contained web service to be used as a memorandum aid in the diagnosing task, in order to increase the quality of care and patient safety. This is a tool, not a Clinical Decision Support System (CDSS); however many CDSS are typically designed for DD as they basically provide Diagnosing Decision Support. To more closely be able to explain how CDSS can be beneficial to DD and Patient Safety, CDSS will more closely be described in the next section.

2.2 Clinical Decision Support Systems (CDSS)

Clinical Decision Support Systems (CDSS) are computer systems dedicated to the decision making task, i.e. to support clinicians in practice. Typically, CDSS are of two main types: Knowledge-Based and non-Knowledge-Based. The most frequently used type in Health Care settings today is the Knowledge-Based CDSS, also known as "Expert Systems" [Coiera 2003]. However, the metaphorical designation "Expert" might be unfortunate as it could provoke opposition about the sometimes assumed intention of the implementation of such systems; to take over the role of the physician. To avoid such interpretations and emphasize its true role, Expert Systems are today most often referred to simply as CDSS. Their use is more and more commonly accepted as they also provide opportunity to pursue Evidence Based Medicine (EBM), to improve Patient Safety. More infrequently occurring in Health Care settings are non-Knowledge Based CDSS. They could also be regarded as Learning Systems as they belong to a sub-area of Artificial Intelligence called Machine Learning.

In this chapter, we will focus only the Knowledge-Based CDSS as it is the most common system for physicians to use in the decision making process (Coiera 2003). Furthermore, we will only focus decisions about Diagnosing as this action actually forms the basis for any further decision about interventions, such as treatment etc. However, the diagnostic types of CDSS (sometimes referred to as Diagnostic Decision Support Systems, DDSS) are considered not as successful in clinical practice as Prescribing Decision Support Systems or other much smaller systems. In the Cases, later presented in this chapter, the diagnosing phase of the decision process turned out to be deficient and threatening to Patient Safety and provided an indication of a need for additional decision supporting tools. However, in this section we will now continue with a brief description of the typical CDSS.

Human agents possess knowledge. Knowledge-Based CDSS also possess knowledge. Without presenting any in-depth analyzes, we will stress that there is a basic difference between human knowledge and the types of knowledge referred to in the area of AI. The

[2] http://www.diagnosispro.com/

knowledge in a Knowledge-Based CDSS is typically represented by a set of rules (i.e. Rule-Based systems). Furthermore, such CDSS also consists of an *inference engine* and a *communicating mechanism*. A *working memory* is necessary to store data and conclusions. Patient specific data will be combined with the knowledge in the rule-base by the inference engine while the communicating mechanism allows both input of such data and provides output of the results, from the CDSS. This architecture offers extended possibilities to store large amounts of scientific information, supporting Evidence Based Medicine (EBM). Nevertheless, a CDSS, despite the metaphor of an expert system, is not to compare with a human expert. Human agents are capable of reaching a different, and far more complex, level of thinking that is not possible to implement by AI. Instead, it is necessary for the human agent to interact with the CDSS in a way that will optimize the functions available. For example, it is necessary to provide the CDSS with patient data that is crucial for the task and to interpret and assess output from the system. Some parts of this task can be automated, but not entirely. In the next section we will further explain this and point at difficulties and perils of information management for CDSS.

2.3 Safety assessment

There is always uncertainty in the knowledge that underlies a decision. With reference to the assessment of risks to human health posed by chemicals, an uncertainty factor is used to compensate for a deficiency in knowledge and create margins-of-safety. On the other hand, in differential diagnosing, the uncertainty is handled by the "method of elimination". Nevertheless, wrong diagnoses occasionally occur. It might be concluded that there are no margins-of-safety to use as an imagined diagnostic value has only two states; true or false. Consequently, in the diagnosing process, the uncertainty is delicate. How can it be assured that the pathophysiologic explanation of the symptoms is true? If it turns out to be false, the consequences might be lethal. Due to clinical data that is imperfect and treatment that is not a guarantee for remedy, human agents in Health Care must deal with decision making under uncertainty. *Probabilistic Medical Reasoning* is an approach to this problem (Shortliffe 2006). Instead of expressing that diagnoses are either true or false, the human agents might express the assessment of diagnoses in terms of "probable" or "highly likely" (Ibid). In medical decisions requires strategies and one is to employ an iterative process for data collection and interpretation referred to as the *hypothetico deductive approach* (Shortliffe 2006, Elstein et al. 1978, Kassirer and Gorry 1978). The method comprises data collection and selection of a hypothesis of the most probable diagnosis, iteratively repeated (refinements of hypotheses by means of additional data) until there is a hypothesis that either is considered true or the uncertainty is reduced to lowest possible level (Shortliffe 2006). The set of active hypotheses are the differential diagnoses.

Human agents tend to use heuristic methods to collect data. This is perilous in medicine and a critical point for Patient Safety. In the process, the method of elimination is used to exclude hypotheses that are not probable to be true. This method is related to the use of a philosophical principle named *"Ockham´s Razor"* i.e. "The law of parsimony". A clinical application of this principle in medicine might be jeopardizing to Patient Safety if the interpretation is close to the well-known adage: *"when you hear hoof beats, think horses, not zebras"*, a rule-of-thumb for selection of diagnosis. Safety assessment in Health Care, concerning the diagnosing task, should be a process that results in an "acceptable diagnosis" chosen on the strength of highest possible amount of relevant patient specific information and scientifically assessed medical information (with reference to EBM). With a Socio-

Technical approach to development of usable information management systems for Health Care, CDSS could support such a process. Systems, supporting workflow, are more likely to be used and to be usable for the task. Moreover, to adopt a PCM approach in the field of activities, as well as taking PE into consideration in the design of CDSS, or additional tools for information acquirement for CDSS, would probably be favourable for Patient Safety. CDSS requires input of patient specific data and to elicit relevant data concerning the patient is both challenging and decisive. Referring to figure 2 in Section 1, it might be of vital importance to gain a comprehensive picture of earlier events. The next section will further relate to this angle of reflection as events occurring over time might oppose rules-of-thumbs such as Ockham´s Razor.

3. Ockham´s (Occam´s) razor vs. Hickam´s dictum

In the area of Medicine, "the Zebra" is most often familiar to everybody. More closely described, this refers to the adage: *"When you hear hoof beats, think horses, not zebras"*. For example, a patient consulting Health Care for fever, with no further distinct symptoms, the most probable diagnosis might be urinary infection or "a virus", not septicaemia. In this case, septicaemia is regarded as "the Zebra". The adage is simply a clinical "rule-of-thumb" in some stage of the differential diagnosing process. This aims at reducing efforts and costs in unnecessary examinations and tests, but at the same time, patients affected with "Zebra-diagnoses" evidently exist. Accordingly, a rule-of-thumb should not completely override other possible alternatives. To further explain and strengthen this point-of-view, we will continue with a closer description of Ockham´s Razor as a principle of simplicity.

As concluded, "The Zebra" is an interpretation of the philosophical principle "Ockham´s Razor" i.e. "The law of parsimony". In Health Care, this principle is also referred to as "Ockham´s Razor of Diagnostic Parsimony". The principle is derived from the philosophical apprehension of *simplicity*, which have been expressed in different ways for different fields over the centuries. Basically, the idea is that simplicity is a theoretical virtue; that simpler theories should be regarded as preferable (Baker 2010). In Health Care, this implies that in the diagnosing process, the physician must try to look for a minimum of hypotheses to explain all of the symptoms the patient have, i.e. Diagnostic Parsimony. In order to achieve this aim, only the most probable hypotheses will be tested. What is probable to be true in this perspective is what is probable for the patient as belonging to a large group of homogeneous "patients". However, if the view is that patient *is not* a member of a homogeneous group of earlier patients, but instead a unique individual with a unique set of patient-specific data, the perspective will change. Harvey et al. (1979) expresses this as follows:

"In making the diagnosis of the cause of illness in an individual case, calculations of probability have no meaning. The pertinent question is whether the disease is present or not. Whether it is rare or common does not change the odds in a single patient. ... If the diagnosis can be made on the basis of specific criteria, then these criteria are either fulfilled or not fulfilled" (Harvey et al. 1979, p.15).

Accordingly, Ockham´s Razor of Diagnostic Parsimony has been frequently questioned. Even if the approach towards simplicity has advantages, it also has serious disadvantages. One counterargument is Hickam´s Dictum. Referring to the hypothetico deductive approach in the diagnosing process, the principle of Hickam's dictum insists upon that, at no stage of the process, should a particular hypothesis be rejected because it does not seem to fit the principle of Ockham's razor. If the "Zebra" is a popular adage based on the

principle of Ockham´s Razor, Hickam´s Dictum is sometimes expressed as simple as “"Patients can have as many diseases as they damn well please". This text en clair could be exemplified by *Saint's triad* (of hiatus hernia, gallbladder disease, and diverticulosis), affirming Hickam´s Dictum, and simultaneously questioning Ockham´s Razor. Another counterargument to Ockham´s Razor is Walter Chattons “Anti-Razor” or the “Chatton Principle”, however not further described in this chapter.
Rules-of-thumb might be useful for most cases, and the “Zebra” should be successful for most patients as the most probable diagnosis is diagnoses that statistically is most common to have in relation to the symptoms occurring. We must conclude that this is not a problem. On the other hand, there is a rather serious problem closely connected to Patient Safety and the chances to increase Patient Safety. The problem is the “Zebra”, or, even, the “Fascinomas” (slang). Even more problematic are multi illness and systemic diseases. It seems to be momentous to develop protocols and tools to handle atypical and complex situations, in order to prevent mistakes, information misses, injuries and deaths.

3.1 The rare cases and the probable

Traditionally, Clinical Decision Support Systems (CDSS) are guiding tools, often grounded in probabilistic reasoning and/or knowledge based rules. The different reasoning mechanisms are implemented as differential diagnosing algorithms, i.e. methods of elimination. In a statistical view, where the patient is regarded as belonging to a large group of earlier patients, this notion will cover the majority of every possible cause of a symptom. Most diagnoses based on this view will probably be true. For example, the symptom “Headache” is most probably caused by muscular tension (in turn caused by nervous tension/stress) or it might be caused by migraine processes. Such more common diagnoses seem to be the first hand choices, which might *end the hypothetico deductive process prematurely*. Headache *could* be a symptom of encephaloma (brain tumor) or Stroke; which might be considered as “Zebras” at a glance. Furthermore, it should be noticed that more than one diagnosis might be true: referring to the example above, the cause of a headache could be multiple.
Consequently, the problematic cases are when the rule-of-thumb fails. For those reasons, “Occams Razor” is fairly questioned. Probabilistic thinking might limit the domain of possibilities in which a physician ventures to reason. To override such directions, preventing prematurely abruption of the diagnosing process, more relevant data is needed. The next section presents two cases where this need for more data is identified as crucial for the outcome. Data collection is not a simple task which also is observable. Context of a patient is complex, not periodically limited, and not entirely coverable by a traditional anamnesis and medical history available for the physician to make vital decisions on. The cases pinpoint a need for a more concrete time-line of events, alerting for “Zebras” if needed.

4. Case study I and II

These studies, Case study I and Case study II, comprise two different cases of which the first case describes a fatal “Zebra-case” and the second describes a life-threatening “Zebra-case” and simultaneously a typical “Fascionoma” where the diagnosis is preposterous in relation to probability. In addition, obviously in both cases, prematurely abrupt hypothetico deductive processes were noticeable. It might be presumed, that a potential cause of the abruption was heuristic thinking and an apprehension of probability in relation to certain, in these cases misleading, variables: data about immediate circumstances and data about the patient, such as age etc. Simultaneously, crucial data was missing.

In Case I, the crucial point is invisibility of earlier events and also the potential importance of earlier events. In Case II, initial invisibility of evidently important earlier events, in a time critical point of the care process, was directly jeopardizing Patient Safety. Interestingly, the roles of patients and the relatives were essential for both cases. They were the keys to whether the cases would prove fatal or not. However, even if patients and relatives always are important in the care process and always must carry patient specific information (Ådahl 2007), this must not be a single-handed task of the kind that the patients survival is directly dependant on if, or what, the patient or relatives report of the former medical history. Such tasks should also be automated, as a safety foundation for further interactive discussions with the patient/relatives.

4.1 Case study I: A retrospective longitudinal case study

This case is a retrospective longitudinal qualitative study, in progress for a period of ten years (1999-2009) and grounded in *observations, interviews* with the patient and relatives and *analyses of medical records*. This case presents situations in which hypothesis testing, in retrospect, seems to have failed. It demonstrates that patient specific information, collected for a long time, might be crucial for the Differential Diagnosing task.

Situation 1 (CISIT1): Transitory hemiplegia

In 1999, a 74 year old woman suddenly experienced an evident weakness in the right part of her body. The relatives, present at the time for the incident, called an ambulance whereupon the woman was transported to the Emergency Ward at the local hospital. After some days of hospital treatment, the physicians diagnosed the woman with Migraine. The hemiplegia was transitory and as she had suffered from frequent occurrences of flittering scotomas during the period of hospital treatment, in addition to a long term history (since childhood) of migraine, revealed in the anamnesis, and since she had experienced some months of increasing social stress factors, this was the exclusive focus for the physicians. One CAT scan was performed, revealing nothing suspicious in the brain. The diagnosis Migraine was established despite the absence of the usual migraine headache and, to the patient, the newly occurring neurological symptoms of scotomas and hemiplegia. As migraine is considered rather harmless, following up visits to Primary Health Care providers was not planned or recommended. The woman was, as many in her generation, reluctant to bother health care with more visits, even though the flittering scotomas continued to occur in the years to come. However, she was seriously bothered by this; in addition to the fact that she did not experience the usual symptoms of migraine by which she was spared after her menopause at the age of 58-60. Furthermore, she was since many years suffering from high blood pressure, but when she visited her physician for a routine blood pressure check, the information about the transitory hemiplegia was not accessible for the physician and the patient did not mention it either as she trusted the diagnosis "migraine" despite some skepticism.

Situation 2 (CISIT2): Weakness after syncope

A few years later, in 2002, the woman (now age 77) was found lying over her kitchen table with bilaterally very weak muscular tonus, nearly unconscious. She was able to answer when spoken to but not to move her body or keep her eyes open. She said that she had suddenly fainted, sitting on the chair, and after that not being able to move and still very close to fainting again. An ambulance was called and she was transported to the Emergency Ward at the local hospital.

After a few days, she was sent back home with no follow-up directions for the Primary Health Care. As she, when she arrived to the ward, had some unclear fever, and earlier that day, when she experienced the syncope and general weakness, had visited the local care center for the annual vaccination against the influenza, the diagnosis this time was "Reaction against the vaccination", after excluding Septicaemia by receiving repeated negative blood cultures. Furthermore, the general weakness disappeared within the first 24 hours. As she, after the Emergency Ward, this time was transferred to the Specialist Ward for Infectious Diseases, the physicians did not study the medical record from the Medical Ward and were not aware of the former situation (SIT1) with transitory hemiplegia. Furthermore, this time the weakness was general, occurring after the syncope, so the patient believed that these symptoms were dependant on the reaction of the vaccination. She also trusted the physicians' decision about the symptoms being dependant on a reaction of the immune defense.

Situation 3 (CISIT3): Hip bone fracture

The following situation occurred in 2008, when the woman, now 83, suddenly felt faintly weak and fell in her staircase, resulting in a fracture of the hip bone. For a year, she had problems with weakness, feebleness and dizziness which she thought was natural decrepitude. Not even her district medical officer thought of any other reason. She went by ambulance to the emergency ward where the physicians were puzzled by her, at this time, frequently intermittent unconsciousness: off and on she went unconscious, with a snoring breath. Furthermore, she felt very sick, by nausea and frequent vomiting.

However, they noticed that she did faint in spite of lying down in bed and having a slow pulse of 30 when it happened. She also had too low levels of oxygen (SaO2 90 at most) and therefore required oxygen supply. The ECG revealed a momentary asystolia and attacks of atrioventricular block (AV block III)*, not compatible with her medication: metoprololtartrat*[3] *(beta-blocker) which immediately was removed. Furthermore, obviously by notes in her EHR, she already was diagnosed by AV-block I which was unknown by the woman herself. Accordingly, she was not in an operable condition, so she was directed to the intensive care unit for cardiology until her heart was considered stable enough.*

Two days after the accident, she was transferred to the orthopedic clinic for surgical operation (hip replacement) which was a success. However, the day after she was, again, medicated by metoprololtartrat (Selokén), which obviously did not fit to her AV-block history stated at the emergency ward and the cardiology unit. In the subsequent rehabilitation at the orthopedic clinic, she fainted at least three times when trying to walk (one time in the arms of a physician) and probably, not recognized, some times lying down in bed. She felt very weak, but despite these indications, no one seemed to understand the connection between Selokén and her AV-Block and did not check her blood pressure, nor her pulse, at the moments of fainting. Instead, the dosage of metoprololtartrat was increased as the presumption was fall in blood pressure due to the operation, and her inconveniences of palpitations. The woman did not reach her habitual state, but instead she was very weak and faintly, seeming much "older" and more fragile than the last year before the accident.

Nevertheless, after a week, the orthopedic treatment programme was finished and she was about to be sent home. The daughter, being a nurse by profession, attended the care planning meeting at the ward, now gaining information about the current treatment, and according to this raised sharp protests against the decision to move her out of hospital. She claimed that her mother was not analyzed due to the cardiac failure and that the medication was lethal, at least a considerable risk factor for further accidents. The attending nurse did not seem aware of this situation but did after all pause the meeting and informed one of the physicians of the orthopedic ward who, in turn, consulted physicians at the intensive care unit for cardiology for a new standpoint on this "new" information.

---

[3] Contraindication for metoprololtartrat: AV-block II and III. (http://www.fass.se/)

However, the intensive care unit for cardiology was also unaware of the registered attacks of AV-block III at the emergency ward, solely focusing on cardiac stability for the orthopedic surgery! As a result, Selokén was still prescribed but due to the uncertainty of the situation and special arrangements in the woman's home, she was allowed to stay for some days more. Two days later, Selokén was suddenly removed and she was allowed to stay until she might be stable enough for short-time housing or home. An anemia was also discovered the day after the planning meeting and she was ordered a blood transfusion and iron tablets. After 2 months of recovery, partly on a rehabilitation clinic, she was able to go home and now the symptoms of fainting, faintness and decrepitude were also completely gone.

Situation 4 (CISIT4): Stroke

Seven months after the Hip Bone Fracture, in 2009, the woman, now almost 84, went to bed after a day feeling tired and feeble. In contrast to her usual active life style, she only wanted to sit in a chair, resting that last day. Some of her relatives, visiting her in the afternoon, did notice this change for the worse and her adult granddaughter decided to stay for the night as a result of a premonition of danger. After just about three hours of sleep; her granddaughter heard her calling for help and rushed into the bedroom. This time the woman, again, experienced the general weakness, difficulties in opening her eyes and felt very sick, vomiting and close to fainting. The granddaughter called an ambulance and the woman was, again, transported to the Emergency Ward at the local hospital. This time the physicians had no immediate explanation to present. They discussed if the symptoms could be caused by a stroke, but the general weakness did not clearly answered to that. The relatives was present at the ward and the daughter, being a nurse herself, asked for a CAT scan which was rejected as it was in the middle of the night.

After one hour, the woman suddenly experienced an approaching faint and called for help. She had an ECG, monitoring her heart rate, and a moment later the electric waves became straight as a result of a cardiac arrest. The daughter sounded the alarm and the personnel managed to revive her. After this occasion, the woman was transferred to the intensive care unit for cardiology for monitoring and acute treatment. The attending physician at the Emergency Ward, after consultation with the senior physician on standby duty, who did not want to order a CAT scan in the night, excluded stroke as the diagnosis, purely on clinical basis, despite suspicious signs. The patient herself, at this moment still being able to talk, pose the risk of a stroke, but got the answer it could not be. The relatives knew about new treatment methods for strokes caused by blood clots, but also that such methods must be initiated within hours after the stroke began. This made them feel very frustrated. However, the condition seemed to stabilize and the physicians were determined about it not being a stroke, so the relatives were sent home as the patient did want them to do so, to sleep and to being able to go to work in the morning.

However, in the morning, when a CAT-scan eventually was performed, it revealed escalation of thrombosis (blood clot) in the brain and brain oedema in progress. Two older infarctions were also revealed, not diagnosed before. A short while after that, the condition went worse. It was at this time too late to use any method to treat the clot (thrombolysis) and stop the stroke from proceeding. Accordingly, the woman rather quickly got an explicit paralysis in her right side (hemiplegia) and lost her ability to speak understandable (expressive aphasia). The following hours, she went worse, in the afternoon also unconscious and finally she died late in the afternoon, 17 hours after the first symptoms.

This case embraces four apparently different situations, with four different pathophysiological explanations of the symptoms occurring, and, as a consequence, treated with reference to four different diagnoses. In CISIT1, the DD process resulted in the diagnosis *Migraine*. The patient herself did find this strange, as she did not suffer from migraine since her menopause at the age of 58-60, approximately 15 years earlier. However, the CAT-scan did not reveal any pathological alterations in the brain and the inevitably most common cause of such symptoms is *Migraine*. Consequently, *Migraine* was the most probable diagnosis. However, in retrospect, we might question this by asking if CAT-scans are quite reliable or if MRI-Scanning (Magnetic Resonance Imaging) would have revealed something else. This imaging tool provides physicians with more detailed information, especially of the brain as it can "see through" bone (the skull). However, prescribing MRI is costly and must be done only if negative results from other tests require more testing. We know, with reference to CISIT4, that older blood clots in the brain at that time were identifiable by CAT-scan which must raise questions about *when* (during 1999 and 2009) those were originating. CISIT1 *could* have Stroke as the true cause of the symptoms. However, the hypothesis of Migraine as the most probable cause of the symptoms was chosen and the iterative process of a hypothetico deductive approach (Shortliffe 2006, Elstein et al. 1978, Kassirer and Gorry 1978) to the problem was decided to be stopped. No further tests were prescribed.

Analyzing this, both heuristic thinking in the DD-process and ambitions of cost-reduction might be influential to the decision. An elderly patient, with high blood pressure and migraine in the anamnesis, are at increased risk for Stroke. The occurring symptoms should have alerted for this. Furthermore unfortunately, critical information of CISIT1 was lost in the coming visits to the care center as an outpatient. Limitations of (electronic) information management at that time (1999), and deficient routines and protocols in Health Care for such information flow, was a probable cause of information breakdown. The patient herself was the only link to the earlier CISIT1.

Next episode (CISIT2), in retrospect now pointing at Stroke as a reasonable hypothesis to be tested more closely, the symptom Fever and the fact that she had a vaccination against Influenza earlier that day did override the symptoms of general neurological weakness and syncope. Furthermore, information from CISIT1 was not visible or easily accessible in CISIT2. Therefore, the actual (considered most probable) hypotheses this time were *Reaction* against the vaccination or *Septicaemia* (due to the vaccination). Septicaemia was excluded as the blood tests were negative and other symptoms of Septicaemia did not occur. Lacking crucial information from earlier alarming and critical events, the other symptoms were explained with reference to a rather unusual immune defense reaction on a vaccination. The patient was discharged with no further follow-up. Already in this phase of the study, we must consider other strategies for anamnesis creation, as information, potentially crucial for the differential diagnosing process, was obviously lost between CISIT1 and CISIT2.

Moving the attention for our analysis to CISIT3, we will absolutely agree about the diagnosis. There is no doubt about this. Diagnostic radiography ("X-ray") revealed a hipbone fracture (neck of the femur) in addition to inability to move the leg due to pain, the fracture and tissue lesions in the area. However, in this situation, we might inevitably bring Ockham´s Razor of Diagnostic Parsimony to mind. Furthermore, as in the preceding situations, the "Zebra" is probably basically adopted. We will also emphasize that information about CISIT1 and CISIT2, occurring about nine and six years earlier, was not available or presented in a way that the symptoms of these preceding situations could be related to this event. Information about the patients frequent occurring flittering scotomas, evident since CISIT1, was not either visible. Accordingly, in this situation (CISIT3) the patient fell and broke the neck of the femur. The main focus was on the fracture and towards a decision about treatment (surgery), the occurring heart problems of the patient were, at least temporarily, also in focus. A more comprehensive perspective would have been to question *why the patient fell* and try to identify this in relation to how she normally acts and related incidents in her anamnesis. As the focus was on the fracture and its treatment and the occurring cardiac arrhythmia identified at the emergency ward, this perspective was not entirely investigated. In retrospect of CISIT1 and CISIT2, and with knowledge about the woman in everyday life, we could create a new hypothesis of another diagnosis, as the *main cause of the others*. It is conceivable that Stroke was the main pathophysiologic explanation of the other diagnoses; Hipbone Fracture and Cardiac Arrhythmia as she might have fallen in the stairs due to a thrombosis in the brain and the heart was affected both by the thrombosis and the physical trauma. This would have been impossible to hypothesize without instant visualization about earlier events and their symptoms.

However, an even more serious conclusion, immediately jeopardizing Patient Safety in the situation, is that life critical information was lost within CISIT3, simply due to commonplace transfers of patients between wards. The EHR-system in use at this hospital was Systeam Cross providing access to medical records of other clinical departments, at least for physicians. Moreover, more traditional protocols for oral reporting in transfer situations are also, since many years, put into practise. An even newer protocol is adopted at the emergency ward; SBAR (**S**ituation, **B**ackground, **A**ctual condition and **R**ecommended actions), a model for structured communication in Health Care. But still, the information flow was broken, probably because the system did not actively visualize important events in patient transferring situations which became evident in this situation where a relative had to act as information carrier for the patient. Human agents as well as Information Systems in Health Care such as EHR must have access to relevant patient-specific data. The identification, collection, management and presentation of such data seem to be crucial.

The last situation in this case, CISIT4, occurred only a few months after the patient was discharged from the rehabilitation clinic, and also for this situation a lack of former information is evident which also became decisive for the result. The symptoms were vague and because of that, and an occurring situation of cardiac arrhythmia and cardiac arrest, the focus was on the heart. Now both the relatives and the patient realized that this, in relation to CISIT1, CISIT2 and CISIT3, could be caused by a stroke, trying to convince the physician on duty that night to prescribe a CAT-scan to find out if there were cerebral causes to the symptoms. But as the symptoms were undefined (as in CISIT1, CISIT2 and CISIT3) and the patient also has mentioned mushrooms (chanterelles) that she earlier that day had eaten, the nausea and attack of vomiting was primarily explained as a probable result from food poisoning, or even gastric influenza (the most probable cause of nausea statistically viewed). A decision was made about waiting to prescribe a CAT-scan, based on cost-reduction ambitions in Health Care and the lower probability of a serious cause of the symptoms, which delayed treatment *in case of a more rare and serious diagnosis* (stroke by thrombosis).

For many rarer diagnoses, the time aspect is decisive and a delay might even be life threatening. Stroke is one of these diagnoses. Heuristic thinking in the form of rules-of-thumbs is common for human agents, but in Health Care, other strategies may be needed to compensate for mistakes and misses dependant on hidden information. Health Care personnel are often working under pressure. For example, in the night, only one physician is at duty at the clinical department s/he is connected to (in addition to the emergency ward and the intensive care unit in cases related to the department) and usually must handle parallel multiple cases at the different wards. Even in the daytime, the pressure is severe and physicians often experience a lack of time to spend on each patient. A solution for insufficient routines and protocols in this matter must not be time consuming in itself. Instead, it must release time at the same time as it increases Patient Safety by providing a more holistic view of the patient and his/her entire medical history.

4.2 Case study II: A rare case

This study, in progress for a period of ten months (2010-2011), grounded in *observations*, *interviews* with the patient and relatives and *analyses of medical records*. The case study provides an example of a very rare case, where an initial impulse to follow "the Zebra" obviously was too firm, overriding every sign of something else being in progress resulting in a fatal situation. The time aspect was also in this case, as in Case study I, very decisive to the forthcoming events after the first misleading diagnosis. In addition to "the Zebra", the philosophy of simplicity in Ockham´s Razor was initially noticeable in the decision making process. Furthermore, this case exemplifies a causality dilemma ("Chicken or the Egg") for which an acceptable solution might have been decisive for prevention of any recurrences.

Situation 1 (CIISIT1)

"A young woman, 24 years old, diagnosed at birth with a complicated congenital heart condition with repeated open heart surgeries since then, falls suddenly to the ground with low blood pressure (syncope). At the emergency ward the body temperature rises quickly to 40 degrees (Celcius). No other symptoms are present. The physicians are not able to find any sign of a bacterial infection so she is permitted the following day to go home, despite a rising Bilirubin in serum, however not communicated to her or the relatives. Diagnosis is "virus infection – influenza" despite no other clinical influenza signs than the syncope and high fever. Her mother, being a nurse by profession, did raise a protest against the influenza diagnosis as she found it strange to have an "influenza" with no other symptoms occurring. She was under apprehensions about septicaemia, but the physician rejected this as it is a rather rare diagnosis and not probable at all for the young woman to have; "she would have been in a much worse condition if so", the physician reasoned. Accordingly, and as the fainting tendency has disappeared, the patient and her mother now were open to any other symptoms coming, pointing at "influenza".

The next day the young woman experiences nausea and frequent vomiting in addition to pain in the stomach and a mild nose bleed when she vomits. As those symptoms might be signs of influenza (such as gastric influenza), and intense vomiting might result in nose bleed, she and her relatives do not find this very suspicious with reference to the first apparently certain diagnosis. However, in the evening she starts to feel very weak and the pulse rises to the frequency of 120/min. At this point in time, two days and nights have passed since the first signs of illness. The mother did find this alarming, either as a symptom of heart failure or as a symptom of shock. After some advice from the Swedish medical advice telephone service "Sjukvårdsrådgivningen 1177", as the young woman was reluctant to see a doctor again after the first diagnosis, she was transported to the Emergency Ward. At the Emergency Ward, the examination, the blood sample, blood pressure and pulse shows that she most likely has developed severe Sepsis with a Septic Shock reaction, multiple organ failure and, basically, she was suffering from a Cholecystitis probably causing the Sepsis or vice versa.

Immediately, intra venous antibiotics are ordered, and the patient is transferred to the Intensive Care Unit for continuous supervision and treatment. However, after 12 hours at the ward, the patient is considered stable, and therefore transferred to a Surgery Ward for treatment of the Cholecystitis, a rare condition designated Acalcuolous Cholecystitis[4]*. The physician at the Intensive Ward was told,*

[4] A biliary infection, without stones. (http://emedicine.medscape.com/article/187645-overview)

by the mother, that the patient has a complicated congenital heart condition and that the cardiologists, both at the local hospital and at the University Hospital, where the patient has her attending cardiologist, must be consulted as she has inserted biological material inserted by operative surgery in her heart. As a result, the risk that she develops an Endocarditis, as a complication to the Sepsis, is rather high. Furthermore, her mother tells the Intensive Care Unit physician that the Cardiologist at the University Hospital has asked for information about changed health status as she also waits for a new surgery. She finds the answer she gets as "non sequitur" and "patronizing" and despite this information from the relative, the young woman is suddenly transferred to the Surgery Ward without further discussions and without any further supervision of the heart function. The time at the Intensive Care Unit is also questionably short. The mother, being a nurse by profession, and the supervising nurses at the Intensive Care Unit, find this odd and is worried about the situation. The mother immediately, by her own initiative, in person, contacts the Cardiology Unit at the hospital and, by e-mail and telephone, gets in contact with the cardiologists at the University Hospital. This causes an upset reaction, where the chief physician at the Cardiology Unit visits the young woman at the Surgery ward and informs her and her relatives that she now will be transferred to the Cardiology Unit for further treatment and supervision of the heart. He says, rather upset, that "he has been present at the hospital since nine a.m. and now it is six p.m. without anyone informing him about the patients' arrival and condition". Further on, the status of the heart is carefully examined, to avoid Endocarditis and heart failure caused by the bacteria in the blood and the substantial strain caused by the current disease."

Situation 2 (CIISIT2)

The patient survived the serious illness but recovered very slowly, taking several months. The heart condition seemed to affect her more after the disease than before, increasing the heart failure. Five months later, she suddenly experienced fatigue, diarrhea and nausea, later in the day also vomiting. As she started to feel something in the area of the liver, she contacted Sjukvårdsrådgivningen 1177 where she was directed to the "emergency care center", a care center open until 9 p.m, receiving an appointment time. She and her mother, helping her in this situation by driving, thought the choice of health care center was completely wrong, but because she was directed there they went there first. However, the mother started communication with the nurse at the care center with the assumption that the patient most likely was suffering from a recurrence of the acalculous cholecystitis five months earlier, which hastened the appointment time with the attending physician to occur one hour earlier. The physician immediately redirected the patient to the emergency ward, with a letter of referral with a question at issue: "Acute Cholecystitis?". At the emergency ward, the patient was examined by a surgeon which immediately questioned both the assumed diagnosis and diagnosis five months earlier based on that the symptoms (again) was atypical and that he could not find the information in the EHR at a glance. He strongly doubted the relatives repeated assurance of that this young woman actually had suffered from acalculous cholecystitis (the diagnosis is rare and the woman "too young") until the laboratory report arrives: Rising s-Bilirubin again, just as the relative said was missed at the earlier event. Now the surgeon did read the entire EHR report for the medical history of the last occasion and quickly ordered anthibiotics intra venously. However, an ultrasound of the biliary passage and the gall bladder should have been prescribed immediately to collect patient data for future events. The patient was transferred to the Specialist Ward for Infectious Diseases, and when arriving to the ward, the day after, some physicians again questioned the rare diagnosis, suggesting a more probable explanation to the symptoms: "gastric influenza". A physician decided to change the treatment, in the weekend, as she found it very unlikely to contract a rare disease such as acalculous cholecystitis more than once. However, the mother, being a nurse and medically trained, this time objected very firmly to this point of view, this time. She had found out that, despite the rare condition not likely at all to affect a young woman, of normal weight, even slightly underweight, a state of severe heart failure might cause ischemia in the gall bladder and this is one of the causes to acalculous cholecystitis. The mother had to be very firm, both in discussions with the physician and by leaving a written report of this hypothesis. Finally, she gained a hearing. The young woman did rather quickly recover from the symptoms, and also from the soreness and swelling over the liver, by treatment for the true diagnosis in a very early stage of the disease. When she later on made another visit to the clinic to control how she had recovered, she also met the doctor at the ward that treated her earlier that year, when the acalculous cholecystitis first appeared. He made a note in the medical record about paying attention to the fact that she might have this rare condition if she develops symptoms like the ones she already had twice. In cases of such symptoms occurring, a ultrasound of the gall bladder must immediately be performed, to be able to collect unquestionable data for proof. Early treatment is crucial in cases like this.

Situation 3 (CIISIT3)

Two months after the recurrence of the acalculous cholecystitis, she had to undergo another open heart surgery for her heart condition as her heart failure now was severe and might have been directly life threatening. It was discovered that her aortic valve (a biological xenograft) had an ejection fraction of only 37 percent. The surgeon deemed the valve as "destructed". Most probably were the initial missed diagnoses Septicaemia and acalculous cholecystitis, with the delayed treatment, a direct cause of the accelerating degeneration of the valve. Consequently, it was crucial to her survival that she received early treatment when the cholecystitis reoccurred.

This case study, divided in three situations, is pointing at several alarming deficiencies in both information handling routines and the decision making process. The first situation points at abruption of the differential diagnosing process prematurely, i.e. the hypothetico deductive process. In the continuation this situation, there are also (as in Case study 1) occurrences of information loss: when the patient is transferred between wards. Both crucial information of the current period of care and potentially crucial information about the previous medical history were lost, probably as information in the EHR is noted down by human agents, with individual apprehensions of the value of patient specific data, and that important data is not clearly visualized for the physician at the point of care.

A causality dilemma was also arising when the true diagnoses were decided (CIICIT1). It could not be concluded if the acalculous cholecystitis was the cause of the sepsis or vice versa. The most probable hypothesis was the first assumption. However, the strain of bacteria found in the blood test (culture) was not bacterias normally expected to be found in the biliary passage. Therefore, the probability of this was low. Instead the strain of bacteria was a rather common bacteria normally found the respiratory passages; Haemophilus Parainfluenzae. Even more intriguing was that acalculous cholecystitis is a very rare condition and the patient was not at all the typical patient in danger of such a condition. Most patients affected with this infection are elderly, seriously ill patients or trauma patients at the intensive care unit. This patient was a young woman; hastily and totally unexpectedly falling ill at work with no preceding warnings. Beyond her heart condition, with some inconvenience with a heart failure, she was completely healthy. It should sometimes be of importance to also identify the cause of the diagnosis, not only the diagnosis as a cause of the symptoms. In this case, it seems to be crucial. Acalculous cholecystitis is a life-threatening condition with a high mortality rate. Severe septicaemia with multiple organ failure is also extremely serious. For both conditions, the time aspect is critical for the possibility to survive. Consequently, causation is very important for the development of further events such as recurrences. The following could be hypothesized:

1. The Septicaemia is a result of the Acalculous cholecystitis.
2. The Acalculous cholecystitis is a result of the strain of the Septicaemia.
3. The Septicaemia and the Acalculous cholecystitis are separate, independent, conditions, randomly appearing simultaneously.
4. Due to the strain of a heart failure, the Septicaemia is a result of some undetected infection in the throat or respiratory passages.
5. The Acalculous cholecystitis is caused both by the strain of the Septicaemia and a potential ischemia in the gall bladder due to a heart failure.
6. The Acalculous cholecystitis in CIICIT2 is caused by an increasing heart failure.

Lack of time and high workload, unfortunately often evident in Swedish Health Care, prevent physicians from hypothesis testing aimed at finding a causal explanation for the *origin of the diagnosis itself.* Nevertheless, such testing might decrease the number of recurrences or further illness. In this case, the most probable hypotheses for this particular patient, with reference to hidden patient data, should be no. (2), 4, 5 and 6. However no. 1 and even 3 were the hypothesis in focus, but only occasionally. The different perspectives are dependant on presence or absence of critical patient data. Visualization of such information might change the perspective and provide possibilities of treatment to prevent recurrences.

Returning to the initial situation (CIICIT1), the physicians deciding on a very common, and therefore also most probable, diagnosis (Influenza due to a virus), were using the principle of Ockham´s Razor interpreted in the shape of the "Zebra". The actual disease started with a syncope and sudden high fever (ague) that declined until the next day. Interviews with the patient afterwards reveal a sense of confusion during the night at the hospital and an inability to communicate this experience clearly to the personnel. The patient was also exhausted when she was discharged the day after and despite notes in the EHR of being in good condition, she was not capable of walking and had to borrow a wheel chair to be able to make it to her mothers' car: This information had unfortunately been lost and the physicians were not aware of it. The time aspect was crucial for a true diagnosis to be found in this case. The blood tests were performed too early in the process and not repeated the next day. Therefore, the CRP-test (C-Reactive Protein) was rather low, pointing at a virus infection, and also the level of white blood cells was not alarmingly high. With reference to this, neglecting a rising Bilirubin in serum, and with a (false) apprehension of the patients apparently good condition, the hypothetico deductive process was ended and a simple and common virus diagnosis chosen. However, with a continued process, with repeated tests before a decision, a fast rising CRP and level of white blood cells, in addition to Thrombocytopenia (decreased number of platelets in the blood) and increasing stomach pains would have lead the physicians to another conclusion. Furthermore, more attention to patient specific data reported from the patient and the relatives would probably have diverted the physicians' from attending to the "Zebra-rule", instead trying to extend the hypothetico deductive process a little more until there was certainty.

Even more problematic was situation 2 (CIISIT2). In the EHR, the information from the first situation about four months earlier was not immediately visible at all for the physician at the emergency ward. Instead, the patient herself and her mother had to inform the physician about their apprehension of the current symptoms and how they related to the symptoms occurring in situation 1. This physician trusted this information and started to search for more information in the EHR, resulting in early treatment of the illness as the blood tests, with an increased Bilirubin in serum, also was evidently the same this time. Furthermore, the area of the liver was swollen and sore. However, again this information was incomplete and not clearly visible after transfer from the emergency ward to the Specialist Ward for Infectious Diseases. Some crucial information about the choice of treatment was lost, and therefore questioned which might have been jeopardizing for patient safety. Again the principle of "Zebra" was adopted and the physician at the new ward insisted on gastric influenza as the most probable cause of illness for a young woman. The burden of proof was on the patient and the relatives which is not a preferable or safe situation in Health Care.

5. Visual incidence anamneses (VIA)

Patient Empowerment (PE) is the underlying approach to VIA. Patients are providing Health Care with valuable information in many ways, generally being capable of cooperating for their own recovery. Participatory Medicine (PM) is a concept, developing from PE and related to Patient Centered Medicine (PCM). *Empowerment Systems*, suggested in the licentiate thesis "*Transparency of Critical Information for Patient Empowerment in eHealth*" (Ådahl 2007), are systems supporting these approaches. In the thesis (Ibid), architecture and design of Empowerment Systems, specifically supporting teams, were in focus. The following Figure 3 captures a comprehensive design context of such systems. It might be worthwhile to survey in order to grasp the idea of Empowerment Systems.

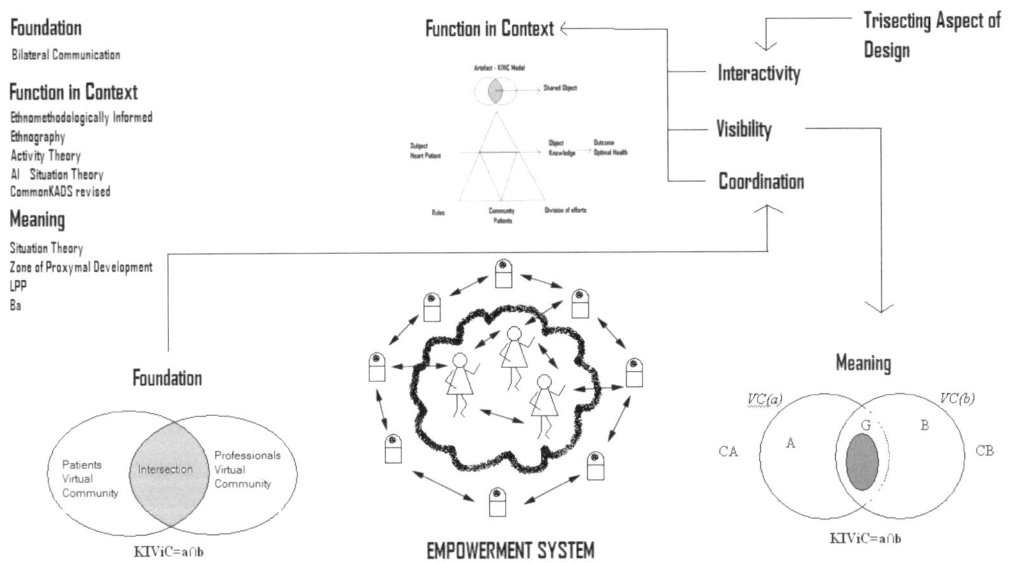

Fig. 3. Design context of Empowerment Systems. The main supporting components are Foundations and Functions in context. The latter includes Activity theory based on ethnographic studies while Foundations focus on issues related to interaction and semantics.

The picture captures some concepts, important for the design of an Empowerment System. Furthermore, it involves some design aspects, considered important for the functionality in such a system (Ådahl 2007). From this perspective, the VIA is developed. The Empowerment systems of Figure 3 are exemplified as prototypes in the Licentiate thesis (Ibid). The portals (interfaces) investigated were server-oriented allowing users to access network based tools and information. A classical CDSS can be seen as an Empowerment System of Figure 3. However, a VIA Empowerment System need a more refined architecture and design. Figure 4 outlines the basic idea of a VIA tool in diagnosing decision processes:

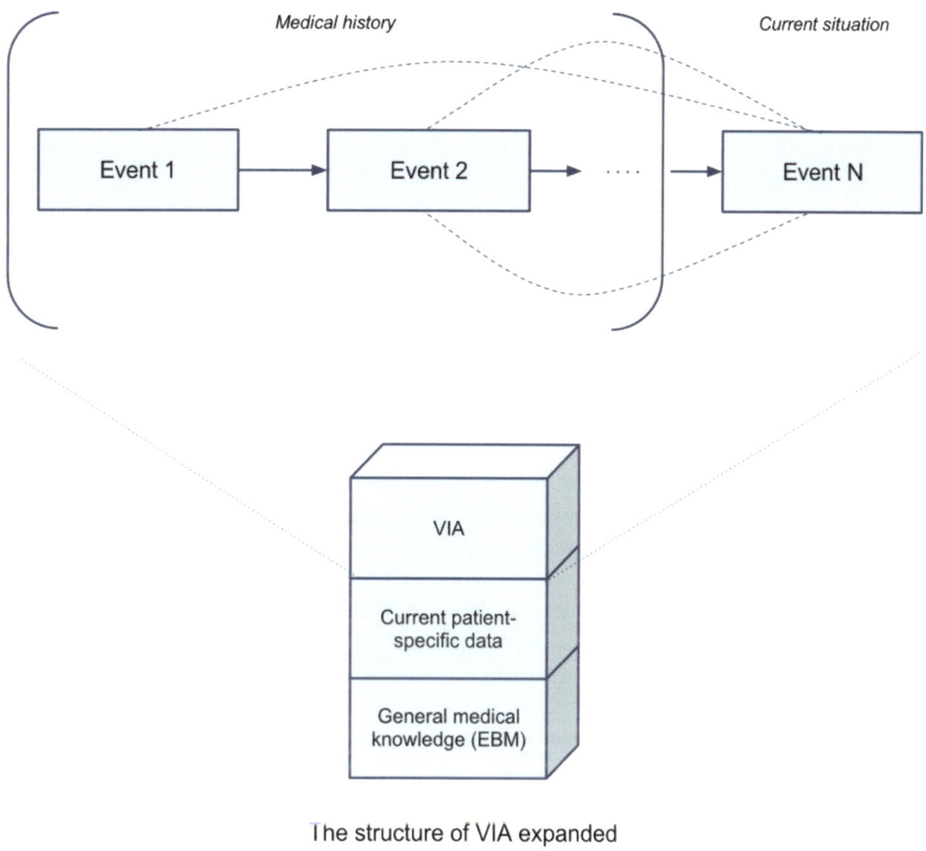

Fig. 4. Evidence Based Medicine for the application of general medical knowledge should be the foundation for any decision. In addition, Patient Specific Data is decisive. The VIA tool supports the collection of such data, viewed in a visual chronological perspective, independent of fragmenting specialist knowledge divisions in Health Care.

Consequently, considering the counter arguments to the use of Ockhams Razor, we argue that the patient should be viewed as the unique individual s/he is, which means that the probability of a certain diagnosis should not only depend on what diagnoses earlier patients as a group statistically had, but also on what kind of critical individual information *the unique patient holds as a result of his/her earlier medical history.* The sum of the symptoms experienced by a patient during the entire medical history must be considered as potentially reciprocal, caused by a common disease. Regarding atypical occurrences of symptoms, rare, or complex medical states such as systemic diseases where vague symptoms occur over a (longer) period, we have found that CDSS as such, based on probabilistic algorithms, i.e., *average values in a population, might not be sufficient, or even inappropriate in diagnosing an individual.*

To remedy some of those shortcomings, we propose an additional tool, a *Visual Incidence Anamnesis* (VIA), to help Health Care professionals use available CDSS towards individualized care and increased patient safety. The VIA collects the actual medical history of a patient, that enables reassessments of earlier diagnosis towards a more reliable patient-centric grounded health care (Figure 2). The VIA should be available as a *patient (individual) centered workflow*, quickly visualizing vital information such as symptoms, incidents and diagnoses, occurring earlier in the medical history, at different times, to make further vital decisions patient and context centric.

In effect this entails that the VIA enabled Empowerment system should be *configurable* from *selected components and tools* rather than a fixed client - server system. For example, the users could use *IPads with selected Apps* configured using *Memory Sticks* to ensure *flexibility and information security*. An example of such *experimental environment* is given in (Stahl et al. 2010). Furthermore, some of the input information to the entire VIA system could be provided by proper *sensor networks* (Lundberg & Gustavsson 2011). However, the VIA is basically an information visualizing tool, presenting valuable data graphically, in chronological order, for the physician and the patient to discuss in cooperation.

5.1 Core principles

The VIA is grounded in three main principles:

1. Clinical decisions in health care must be grounded in a sufficient amount of relevant and (potentially) important patient specific information.
2. Information of importance for decisions must be easy to comprehend; visualized in the anamnesis processes.
3. Clinical Decision Support Systems and additional tools to support diagnosis complement (such as the VIA) must be tailored to empower stakeholders of the work flow and not regarded as time-consuming and of doubtful value for the task.

Concerning the first principle, a sufficient amount of relevant information is information that will provide individual medical histories in such way that no vital information is missing or can be missed. The information must be presented in chronological order, with relations between important events along the time-line. Patient-specific information in this perspective is counterbalance to unfettered use of Ockham´s Razor in Health Care. It should be emphasized that Patient Empowerment and the development of this movement, Participatory Medicine, must be adopted in order to collect and classify relevant and important information. For example, in the anamnesis phase of the medical examination, certain input to the VIA-system can be performed interactively with the patient and/or relatives.

The second principle is the principle of Visualization. Information is considered more visible if it is graphically expressed. Large amounts of information are hard to survey and grasp, especially in a glance. The time aspect in the Anamnesis phase must not be neglected as this might be decisive for many cases of information misses. The physician must mentally construct an internal model of the information available, to decide which information is relevant to use in the hypothetico deductive process. Under the impact of stress and high work load this might fail. Visualization of information from earlier events, easily accessible in the EHR, will offer more input for the creation of such mental models.

The third principle concerns usability. A tool must be valuable for the task to motivate its usage. It must facilitate the work and the work load, as well as it must enhance the work flow in the activity. As already mentioned, the time aspect in Health Care is crucial and therefore it must not be time consuming or complicated to use. Above all, it must not jeopardize patient safety by being so.

5.2 Methodology

Our current work with VIA is entirely conceptual. The basic idea is, as described, outlined by the result of ethnomethodological studies, pointing at an evident need for additional decision support tools to avoid devastating or lethal information breakdowns. Decisions in Health Care must be supported, not only with existing CDSS but also with tools for elicitation and coordination of information. Consequently, VIA is not yet implemented in any setting. We are at this moment approaching the design phase, aiming at implementation and testing of a prototype within the next year. We have experienced positive feedback from Health Care personnel such as physicians. Furthermore, patients seem to be positive towards such a direction. A deep frustration about information misses and bad coordination of tasks exists, resulting in a situation of jeopardized Patient Safety. Accordingly, we believe and hope that VIA would be regarded as a missing link for an unbroken flow of information in future testing situations.

5.3 Pros and cons of VIA

Our proposal for VIA is grounded in our conclusions from in-depth analyses of actual cases in Health Care, where Patient Safety has been jeopardized due to identifiable information handling deficiencies and information breakdowns in the care process. In Section 4, we have presented two such cases. VIA should be an additional tool to the EHR, viewed as a decision support tool, and to traditional CDSS. The advantages of using VIA are visualization of otherwise hidden information (not visible or known to the physician). VIA also visualizes not easily accessed information, crucial for a *correct* diagnosis to be made or the correct diagnosis to be made *in time*. If VIA are designed in participation with the user, the use should be a part of work-flow, reminding the decision maker of information that should be considered before decision. Fewer information misses and mistakes based on lack of decisive information increases Patient Safety as the opportunity of correct diagnoses early in the decision process increases by correct information.

However, if not developed and implemented to fit requirements of Sociotechnical systems such as Information processing systems for Health Care, and with lack of understanding of which type of information that must be brought to focus, there is a risk of having a system not fit for purpose. This would not encourage the use of the system. Furthermore, with bad design, there is a risk that VIA visualizes too much information, resulting in information overload that paradoxically could make relevant information invisible. Therefore, system development based on the VIA model must comprise the users of the system (participatory design) and preferably also be grounded in close studies of the activity in which the VIA is intended to be implemented.

Furthermore, a VIA system is never completed. It must be continuously maintained during its lifetime to have the intended usefulness.

6. Conclusions

To be able to screen out unnecessary alternatives and decide on the cause of illness, a sufficient amount of significant patient-specific information is needed. This is the basic principle of the VIA. The patient specific information is unique to the individual patient and that point is necessary in dissociating the patient from overly firm expectations of hypotheses that are the statistically most probable.

7. References

Baker, Alan (2010) *Simplicity* The Stanford Encyclopedia of Philosophy (Spring 2010 Edition), Edward N. Zalta (ed.), Available from http://plato.stanford.edu/archives/spr2010/entries/simplicity/

Coiera, E. (2003). *Guide to Health Informatics*, ARNOLD, Oxford University Press, New York

Elstein A S., Shulman L S., Sprafka S A (1978). *Medical Problem Solving : An analysis of Clinical Reasoning*. Cambridge, MA : Harvard University Press

Harvey, A. M., et al (1979). *Differential Diagnosis (3rd ed.)*. Philadelphia: W.B. Saunders.

Kassirer J P., Gorry G A (1978) Clinical Problem Solving : A Behavioral Analysis. Annals of Internal Medicine, 89(2) :245-255.

Kohn, LT; Corrigan, JM. & Donaldsson, MS. Editors. (2000). *To Err is Human: Building a Safer Health System,* Institute of Medicine (IOM), National Academy Press, Washington D.C. ISBN-10: 0-309-06837-1 ISBN-13: 978-0-309-06837-6, 26.10.2010 Available from http://www.nap.edu/openbook.php?isbn=0309068371

Lundberg Jenny, Gustavsson Rune (2011) Challenges and opportunities of sensor based user empowerment. In *Proceedings of* 8th IEEE International Conference on Networking, Sensing and Control (ICNSC 2011).

Shortliffe E H., Cimino J J. (2006) *Biomedical Informatics: Computer Applications in Health Care and Biomedicine* Springer-Verlag New York Inc.

Stahl, B., Luang Le Thah, Caire R., and Gustavsson, R. (2010) Experimenting with Infrastructures. In Proceedings of *5th International Conference on Critical Infrastructures (CRIS 2010)*. IEEE Xplore, Object id: 10.1109/CRIS.2010.5617542.

Ådahl Kerstin (2007) *Transparency of Critical Information for Patient Empowerment in eHealth* Blekinge Institute of Technology, Licentiate Dissertation Series No. 2007:03

Part 5

Miscellaneous Case Studies

15

Pharmacoepidemiological Studies Using the Veterans Affairs Decision Support System

Benjamin Wolozin[1,2], Austin Lee[3,4], Nien-Chen Li[3,4] and Lewis E. Kazis[3,4]

[1,2]Depts. of Pharmacology and Neurology
Boston University School of Medicine, Boston, MA
[3]Center for the Assessment of Pharmaceutical Practices and Pharmaceutical Assessment Management and Policy Program, Department of Health Policy and Management BostonUniversity School of Public Health
[4]Center for Health Quality Outcomes and Economic Research
Veteran Affairs Medical Center, Bedford, MA
USA

1. Introduction

Over the past decade, we have utilized the Veterans Affairs (VA) Decision Support System (DSS) database to identify medications that are associated with a reduced incidence and progression of dementia. Our studies identify two general classes of medications that are associated with reductions in the incidence of dementia, compared to a group of patients with similar cardiovascular risk profiles (Li et al., 2010; Wolozin et al., 2000; Wolozin et al., 2007). We have shown that simvastatin, a medication that blocks synthesis of cholesterol, is associated with a significant reduction in the hazard ratio for incident dementia (HR 0.46, CI 0.44 - 0.48 $p<0.0001$) (Wolozin et al., 2007). Simvastatin has two primary effects. One effect is to lower cholesterol and a second effect, which is observed only at higher doses of simvastatin, is to reduce inflammation (Wolozin et al., 2006). The second major class of medications that are associated with reduced progression of dementia fall in the general category of angiotensin receptor blocking medications, which includes lisinopril, candesartan and valsartan (Li et al., 2010). In this work, the reduction in dementia incidence (HR, 0.81, C.I., 0.68 - 0.96, $p=0.016$) was not as striking as for statins, but we also examined nursing home admissions, where we observed a strong effect (HR, 0.51, CI 0.36 - 0.72, $p=0.0001$). In addition, we observed additive effects when angiotensin receptor blockers (ARBs) were used in addition to Angiotensin Converting Enzyme (ACE) inhibitors (Li et al., 2010). Finally, we have also examined the influence of coronary artery bypass on the incidence of dementia (Lee et al., 2005). This work was recently expanded upon to include an examination of the putative role of gaseous anesthetics on the incidence of dementia (no evidence supporting such a hypothesis was observed) (Vanderweyde et al., 2010).

This work derives from the immense size and richness of the DSS database, which is one of the largest integrated electronic health records in the world. The DSS began capturing data in October 2001 (fiscal year 2002), although some parts of the database go back to 1996 (Smith and Joseph, 2003). The database captures information on approximately 5 million subjects per year, with over 100 million medication prescriptions per year. The DSS database offers researchers a tool that is distinctly different than the classic cohorts developed at academic centers. Cohorts developed at academic centers tend to be smaller by a factor of 500 - 5000, often being in the range of 1000 - 5000 patients. These cohorts offer rigorous, uniform evaluations of well-characterized and carefully selected subjects using evaluators who are following rigidly defined protocols (Hayden et al., 2006; Launer et al., 2000; Seshadri et al., 2006). These types of cohorts are ideal for studying medications or other factors that are prevalent in the cohort (with a rate > 10%). However, such cohorts are unable to study most medications in a formulary because the prevalence of use is too low. The large size of the DSS database presents an outstanding resource for pharmaco-epidemiological studies where rates of use for many medications are 1% or less. We have used the DSS database for such studies, and have observed high concurrence with our studies upon investigation by other epidemiologists using other databases or cohorts.

The material in this chapter will explain the design and execution of pharmaco-epidemiological databases using the DSS database. We will define the elements available in the DSS database, the strengths and the weaknesses of dataset. The DSS dataset is particularly suited for studies meeting criteria that will be defined. An important preliminary point is that the size and security concerns related to using the DSS database create a unique set of requirements that must be considered and adhered to carefully. We will describe the elements that should be considered in defining optimal cohorts for the study, and the types of factors that should be considered in characterizing the demographic profiles of these cohorts. Cohorts, selection criteria and exclusion criteria all vary depending on the type of study, and the factors that should be considered in each of these decisions will be described. Studies can be performed with a focus on incidence or progression, and the considerations required for each such study will be described. Multiple models should be used for a particular study. The models can be varied based on the choice of covariates, exclusion criteria, comorbid illnesses allowed, concurrent medications allowed, as well as other elements. The considerations related to each of these choices will be discussed. The size of the DSS database offers the option for types of studies that are not feasible in smaller datasets. Medications can be compared by pharmacological properties, duration of exposure and medication switching. End points can include files in the DSS database, but increasingly can also include datasets not directly part of the DSS. For instance, the DSS data can be cross-referenced to Medicare, which can capture some off-plan elements such as nursing home utilization and use of health systems outside the system. After acquisition of the data, statistical models that can be applied include logistic regression, hazard rates and tests for sensitivity. Statistical models can also inform choice of subjects for cohorts, for instance by applying propensity analysis. Considerations for each of these choices will be examined.

The DSS database is also being continually upgraded and expanded. In the future, we can expect that computer based language algorithms will allow capture and quantification of written reports by the health care providers. Genetics will also become increasingly accessible. The VA is currently embarking on a plan to genotype DNA for 1 million subjects. Although this dataset will cover only a fraction of the subjects in the VA system, the large number of subjects analyzed will create a unique resource.

2. Experimental design: General considerations

The introduction above describes many of the inherent strengths of the DSS system. However, despite the apparent strengths, the DSS system also has some important weaknesses. The design of pharmaco-epidemiological studies of the VA DSS database must take into account these weaknesses. The VA pharmacy increasingly limits the medications that are used, trying to strongly encourage use of generic medications. This leads to two important considerations.

The first issue is that some medications commonly used outside the system, are not used inside the system. For instance, among statin users, atorvastatin and rosuvastatin are used by many patients not in the VA system, but most patients in the system use simvastatin (Wolozin et al., 2007). This limits the breadth of medications that can be analyzed using the DSS system. Formulation considerations also impact in other manners that are subtler. Changes in the types of medications on the formulary lead to changes in medication utilization by patients. Such changes alter the duration of time that patients might take a medication, which can lead to altered rates of disease. For instance, if entire groups of patients switch medications, the resulting studies could make it seem as if a particular disease is less prevalent among patients taking that medication, although the real reason is that the duration of exposure might be less than for other medications that were used throughout the analytic period. These types of biases can be adjusted for using careful analytic designs, but such analyses must be incorporated. Another large problem is that the clinical records have not been validated and are not uniform. The VA system comprises 23 VISNs, and multiple hospitals within each VISN. The size of the VA system leads to treatment diversity; physicians are trained differently. Diagnostic and/or treatment protocols can differ by VISN, as well as among physician within a VISN. Such variations can be particularly important when evaluating outcomes such as dementia, for which no widely utilized, definitive biomarker exists.

Other considerations include the demographics and health status of the patient population. The VA population is about 95% male, which means that most of the data will be represent a male cohort unless gender the study is designed to stratify by gender. VA patients tend to have more comorbid diagnoses than patients in other databases, such as medicare or Kaiser Permanente Database (Whitmer et al., 2009). Finally, a significant fraction of patients also utilize health care providers outside of the VA system to supplement their health plans. Such "out-of-network" services are not captured by the DSS database, and must be considered. Utilization of services out of the network can lead to disparities among patient populations, since wealthier patients are more likely to use "out-of-network" providers. In addition, use of providers out of the network can cause patients to be lost to follow-up.

The analytic approaches that we have designed attempt to take these considerations into account. The first two approaches can be implemented using only the DSS system. The third approach requires utilization of an additional database to validate the observations from the DSS system.

2.1 Analysis using two parallel strategies

One strategy is to match cohorts using a propensity analysis in which subjects are selected and matched based on risk factors for cardiovascular disease, dementia and the number of concurrent medication utilized. Regression analyses is then performed to determine the appropriate weighting co-efficient for each matching variable. A second strategy is to analyze cohorts based on descriptive or multivariate regressions using logistic and hazard rate models. For the descriptive analysis, one selects matched cohorts and characterizes the outcomes by odds ratios. For the multivariate cohort analysis one identifies a cohort based on age, diagnosis and medication use, and follows the cohort prospectively employing a multivariate regression analysis that includes comorbid diagnoses and other medications (to control for poly-pharmacy).

2.2 Using physiological responses to assess medication action

Epidemiological studies are supposed to derive from hypotheses that rely on a biological basis of action for medications in question. However, patients differ in their response to medications due to genetic factors (e.g., polymorphisms in metabolic genes), usage patterns (medication compliance) and environmental factors (e.g., other chemicals modifying drug metabolism). The medication response for each patient can be assessed by examining biomarkers that are directly linked to the mode of action of the medication. For instance, in the case of antihypertensive medications, such as angiotensin receptor blockers, one can analyze patients by degree of biomarker response, using blood pressure lowering to assess anti-hypertensive use. The physiological response is then be employed as a covariate in the analyses, to insure that the outcome is tethered to the physiological activity of the medication.

3. Establishing the cohorts: Propensity analysis

3.1 Definition of cohorts

Medications to be analyzed are grouped by action and compared as a group to determine whether the group is associated with differential outcomes. For instance, in the study of angiotensin receptor blockers, ideal comparison cohorts are those corresponding to subjects with similar health problems taking medications that exert similar effects but through a different mechanism of action. Beta-blockers provide a good example of a comparison cohort because beta-blockers are anti-hypertensive agents that act by a different set of receptors than angiotensin receptor blockers. ACE inhibitors provide another comparison cohort because they act on a different molecular target than angiotensin receptor blockers, however ACE inhibitors have the weakness that their ability to reduce angiotensin II levels would also reduce action at the angiotensin AT1 receptor (much like angiotensin receptor blockers). A more general cohort would be subjects taking cardiovascular medications other than angiotensin receptor blockers. If the group shows an effect, then it is possible to code the data in a manner that allows stratification of the data within each group by individual medications, and then quantify outcomes for each medication within each group. Comparing individual medications can be important because medications can differ in many important properties, such as brain penetration and off-target effects.

Regardless of the particular choice of medication cohort, it is important to consider poly-pharmacy. Subjects frequently take multiple medications. Poly-pharmacy can be taken into account by considering other medications as a covariate, or by excluding particular medications from each cohorts. The latter approach, though conceptually appealing, has the weakness that it frequently reduces the cohort size and therefore power of the study.

3.2 Medication utilization

A critical issue in studying pharmaceutical action, is to make sure that any subjects being studied actually use the medication as prescribed. Medication utilization can be assessed by requiring several criteria for inclusion of subjects in a cohort:

3.2.1 Subjects must exhibit utilization of the medication as demonstrated by 80% medication coverage over the first 6 months upon entry into the study, and for the 6 months preceding any event.

3.2.2 Subjects must be on each medication for at least 6 months prior to any outcome event.

3.2.3 Subjects must use the health care system at least once in the 6 months preceding an event or the end of the study; those who do not fulfill this requirement are considered lost to follow-up and removed from the study.

3.3 Components for propensity analysis: Co-variates and matching variables

Setting up a cohort requires assessment of key variables. In the case of our studies of angiotensin receptor blockers, and of statins, used the following criteria:

3.3.1 Age: A clear risk factor for dementia.

3.3.2 Co-morbidities: Major diseases that are known risk factors for AD. Subjects will receive an additional point for each ICD9 diagnosis: cardiovascular disease (ICD9 277.7, 429.2, 410-414, 428-429, 440, 444, 445), stroke (430-438) and diabetes (ICD9 250). Retinopathy (ICD9 362), neuropathy (ICD9 249.6, 250.6) and nephropathy (ICD9 249.4, 250.4) will also be included in the scoring because these are manifestations of microvascular disease. Note: hypertension (ICD9 401-405 and 459.3) are not used in the propensity scoring because it is present in all subjects taking anti-hypertensive medications and does not affect the outcome.

3.3.3 Number of prescription medications: Patients receive a point for each medication for which they have a prescription.

3.3.4 Cholesterol/blood pressure/HbA1C/GFR/BMI: For each laboratory value subjects are categorized into one of three groups for the propensity analysis: Normal (<1 Std. Dev. from Mean), High (1-2 Std. Dev. from Mean) and Very High (>2 Std. Dev. from Mean). Mean values for each subject will be determined based on values obtained during the first year in the study: HDL, LDL, triglyceride values, blood pressure values (diastolic and systolic as independent variables), HbA1C, BMI and estimated glomerular filtration rates (GFR, calculated as a measure of renal function based on the modification of diet in renal disease, MDRD, equation).

3.3.5 Smoking status: Smoking status is captured from VA/KP screening tools.

3.3.6 Prior healthcare utilization: Health utilization is determined for the year preceding entry into the study. For subjects who were already on anti-hypertensive medications prior to 2002 (the earliest year of the DSS database), health care utilization is assessed based on fiscal year 2002.

3.4 Scoring method

Propensity scores are used to reduce selection-to-treatment bias. A matched-propensity score approach reduces the dimension of the confounding variables by providing an estimate of the probability of receiving treatment, essentially reducing the number of variables to one.

The distribution of propensity scores is examined in the comparison samples to check for sufficient overlap and balance in the strongest predictors. If the balance is not sufficient, the samples may be further stratified, interactions and transformation of variables considered; if there is no overlap in some part of the distributions of propensity scores, patients with the non-overlapping propensity scores will be removed from the analyses (after noting why they are different in their likelihood to receive a particular treatment). A propensity score is the conditional probability that a patient receives a treatment. It is estimated from a logistic regression model: Expected(log-odds of treatment A compared to B) = b0 + bX where X is a vector of patient characteristics and conditions at the time of treatment assignment. If there are more than two treatments, three propensity scores and comparisons are made, A to B, A to C, and C to B. A greedy-match algorithm (http://www2.sas.com/proceedings/sugi26/p214-26.pdf) is used to match patients by propensity scores. Once matched, one obtains estimates of effects using either conditional regression models or paired comparison of outcomes.

4. Outcomes: Incident dementia, nursing home admission and death

Each cohort is matched based on propensity to develop dementia, as described in the section above. The risk of dementia is compared among each cohort using a Cox proportional hazards model for the outcomes listed below. The hazard rates are adjusted using the covariates listed below. The risk of AD or dementia, nursing home admission and death among the general population is studied excluding subjects who have a pre-existing diagnosis of AD or dementia (based on analysis of medical records in the year preceding entry into the study). We will also study the risk of nursing home admission and death specifically among subjects with an existing diagnosis of AD or dementia.

4.1 Outcomes

Outcomes for each of the cohorts also are plotted with a log(-log(time)) vs. log(time) graph. Curves parallel for each of the groups, validate the application of the Cox proportional hazards model approach. Others models such as the Weibull model can be tested for purposes of sensitivity analysis, to determine if results are corroborated.
End of follow-up is defined as a particular date (for example, December 31, 2009), disenrollment from the health care system, nursing home admission, initiation of dialysis or death. Membership in the health care system can be determined from administrative databases. AD (ICD9 331.0) or dementia (ICD9 290, 294, 331.0) is ascertained based on ICD9 diagnoses. Nursing home admission is ascertained through the DSS and Medicare records. Note: the VA system recently established an agreement to allow purchasing of Medicare records and harmonization with the VA, this agreement is to being finalized between the VA and the Center for Medicare and Medicaid Services (CMS). Records are obtained to insure that we are capturing all nursing home admissions. Death is ascertained from linkage to the VA mortality files (to be obtained through the VA HERC which has the most complete records of VA mortality combining mortality records from multiple sources that include the VA BIRLS files and have been previously validated).

4.2 Co-variates

Establishing covariates increases the power of a study by identifying factors that could bias the outcomes, and then incorporating them into the model.

4.2.1 Age: Age is of course the major risk factor for any disease and must always be included as a covariate.

4.2.2 Health Index/Co-morbidities: The major disease risk factors that we will characterize are cardiovascular disease (ICD9 277.7, 429.2, 410-414, 428-429, 440, 444, 445), stroke (430-438) and diabetes (ICD9 250); hypertension (ICD9 401-405 and 459.3) will not be analyzed as a covariate because our preliminary studies indicate that it is present in all subjects taking anti-hypertensive medications and does not affect the outcome.

4.2.3 Microvascular disease: Retinopathy (ICD9 362), neuropathy (ICD9 249.6, 250.6) and nephropathy (ICD9 249.4, 250.4) are manifestations of microvascular disease.

4.2.4 Hospital utilization:Hospital utilization rates are calculated for subjects and include these as co-variates.

4.2.5 Cholesterol/blood pressure/HbA1C/GFR/BMI (all are co-variates): Captured variables include: HDL, LDL, triglyceride values, blood pressure values (diastolic and systolic as independent variables), HbA1C and BMI. Estimated glomerular filtration rates (GFR) are also captured and calculated as a measure of renal function based on the modification of diet in renal disease (MDRD) equation.

4.2.6 Duration of Insulin use: Insulin use is commonly associated with late stage Type II diabetes, which is strongly associated with dementia.

4.2.7 Diuretic use: Anti-hypertensive medications are frequently used in conjunction with diuretics. We include diuretic use as a co-variate a binary measure for diuretic use as one group (± diuretic).

4.2.8 Location: VA centers (VISN groups) where treatment occurred are identified, and these regions are used as co-variates. In the event that a subject utilized multiple centers, the first center identified in the record is the designated center for the analyses.

4.2.9 Gender: The gender ratio is determined (by counting the number of male and female subjects), and used as a co-variate.

4.3.0 Smoking status: This is captured from VA screening tools on the basis of the CDC BRFSS items previously administered in the VA.

4.3.1 Medications: Other cardiovascular medications on the VA formulary are analyzed as covariates to control for poly-pharmacy.

4.3.2 Ethnicity: Ethnicities can differ in medication responsiveness. Between 5 - 20% of subjects in the DSS database have defined ethnicities other than Caucasian. Categories of defined ethnicity (e.g., Caucasian,Asian, African-American and Hispanic.

4.3.3 Prior healthcare utilization: Health utilization is determined for the year preceding entry into the study. For subjects who were already on anti-hypertensive medications prior to 2002 (the earliest year of the DSS database), health care utilization is assessed based on fiscal year 2002.

4.4 Outcomes: Secondary analyses

Should one observe differences among the medication groups, one can examine the specific groups using the secondary analyses described below:

4.4.1 Dose-response: The mean daily exposure for each medication is derived for each subject by dividing the total use of each medication (cumulative dose based on prescription records for each medication) by the cumulative the days of use. Subjects will be stratified into a high dose and low dose groups around the median daily exposure. A Cox proportional hazard model is used to determine HRs for each medication with a model utilizing multivariate regression involving co-variates.

4.4.2 Medication switching: One approach to validating effects is to examine medication switching. In such a study, one identifies subjects who are using only one class of anti-hypertensive medications (concurrent use of diuretics will be allowed and will be analyzed as a covariate), and show stable use of the medication over the first 6 months following entry into the study. Subjects are followed and the type of medication used at the end of the study will be determined. Subjects using one particular anti-hypertensive medication, and who showed stable use of the medication over the 6 months preceding the end of the study will be selected for further analysis. The data are analyzed using a Cox proportional hazard model to determine whether switching from one group of anti-hypertensive medications to another group is associated with a change in the HR.

4.4.3 Ethnicity: Each cohort can also be stratified by ethnicity. Ethnicities to be examined will include the major ethnicities (to allow sufficient power for the analysis): Caucasian, African American, Hispanic, Asian (see section E.4., Power Analysis, for a quantification of ethnic distributions).

4.4.4 Gender: Gender can be included as a co-variate. However, because the DSS database is predominantly male, a study using gender stratification will be restricted to the KP database.

5. Interpretations

5.1 Incidence and progression

The approaches outlined above enable us to make assessments of the association of particular medications with measures of dementia, including incidence and progression. Population based epidemiological studies typically examine incidence of a disease, but employing outcomes that are commonly associated only with more severe forms of dementia allows us to also gain insight into progression. A key element in assessing progression is to use outcomes that are unequivocally associated with progression. These considerations led us to restrict out markers of progression to two very extreme outcomes, nursing home admission and death. Studies of incidence provide utility from the public health perspective, but do not necessarily help those who already suffer from disease symptoms (cognitive decline). Subjects typically present to the neurologist only when they are already experiencing cognitive decline. Hence, one would like to be able to gain insight into medications that specifically address this group of patients.

5.2 Pharmacological properties

The large size of the DSS database allows a depth of analysis that is typically not possible with smaller datasets. We have used this size to query whether the epidemiological results are consistent with known pharmacological properties of particular medications. For instance, classic studies of pharmacology employ dose response profiles. We tested the strength of the ARB findings by examining whether differences in ARB exposure was associated with corresponding differential outcomes (Li et al., 2010). These studies focused on dementia because the larger number of incident dementia cases allowed for sufficient statistical power to enable further stratification of the groups. The mean daily exposure to for each ARB was determined for each subject by dividing the total use of ARBs (cumulative dose based on prescription records for each medication) by the cumulative number of days of use. Subjects were then stratified into a high dose and low dose groups around the median daily exposure. A Cox proportional hazard model was used to determine HRs for each ARB. The model included age, stroke, diabetes and cardiovascular disease as covariates. Each of the major ARBs used by the VA system, candesartan, irbesartan, losartan and valsartan showed clear dose-response relationships, and exhibited lower rates of incident dementia with higher doses of medication.

We also examined whether subjects who switched from ACE inhibitors to ARBs, or vice-versa, adopted the dementia risk value for the subsequent medication (Li et al., 2010). We identified subjects without a prior diagnosis of dementia who were prescribed either ARBs or ACE inhibitors (but not both), and showed stable use of the medication over the first 6 months following entry into the study. The "ACE inhibitor" group included all of the ACE inhibitors on the VA formulary. Subjects were followed and the type of medication (ACE inhibitor or ARB) used at the end of the study (dementia or censoring) was determined. Subjects using either ARBs or ACE inhibitors (but not both), and who showed stable use of the medication over the 6 months preceding the end of the study were selected for further analysis. The data were analyzed using a Cox proportional hazard model adjusting for age, stroke, diabetes and cardiovascular disease. Subjects who were on ARBs throughout the study or who started on ACE inhibitors and switched to ARBs showed a significantly lower HR (protective) for incident dementia compared to the reference group (Li et al., 2010). These data show that the association between ARB use and risk of incident dementia is sensitive to dose of medication and medication switching.

Another pharmacological characteristic that we examined was correlation between effect and expected brain penetration of the medications based on the published literature. Our study of statins, in 2007, produced striking results in this respect (Wolozin et al., 2007). The statins differ in their order of lipophilicity, which leads to the observation that some statins cross the blood brain barrier well, while others don't (Reinoso et al., 2002). Lovastatin, and (to some extent) simvastatin are lipophilic, which allows them to cross the blood brain barrier, while pravastatin and atorvastatin are hydrophilic and do not cross the blood brain barrier; despite these traits, both lipophilic and lipophobic statins appear to modulate cholesterol metabolism in the CNS (Reinoso et al., 2002; Vega et al., 2003). In the 2007 study, we observed that simvastatin was associated with an effect size for incident dementia that was significantly stronger than that for atorvastatin or lovastatin HR, 0.46, CI 0.44-0.48, $p < 0.0001$, for simvastatin, HR 0.91, CI 0.80-1.02, $p = 0.11$ for atorvastatin and HR 0.95, CI 0.86-1.05 for lovastatin (Wolozin et al., 2007). Our study of ARBs also showed evidence that medications with greater brain penetration appear to be associated with better outcomes (Li et al., 2010). The rank order of effect size for the different ARBs was candesartan>irbesartan>losartan>valsartan (HRs. 0.73, 0.84, 0.82, 0.91 respectively), which corresponds strongly with brain penetration for each medication (Li et al., 2010).

6. Conclusion

The approaches and results presented above show a range of data-mining strategies that can be applied to the DSS database. Much of the strength of the DSS database comes from its large size and the availability of multiple types of data. The power of the database increases as the duration of time from the inception of the DSS database increases. The positive attributes of this database must be balanced against weaknesses that are inherent to any population based data source derived from dispersed centers. Despite these weaknesses, the studies performed by our group have shown good reproducibility in subsequent literature. Epidemiologists throughout the world have reproduced our observation of a reduction in incident dementia associated with statin. Work on ARBs by other groups is only beginning, however in collaboration with Rachel Whitmer (Kaiser Foundation), we have already reproduced major elements of this story and have presented this replication at major meetings (AAICAD, 2010, Whitmer et al).

What lies in the future? One of the most exciting prospects is that of pharmaco-genomics. The VA is collecting DNA from 1 million subjects, for use in genetic studies. As this genetic information becomes available, it will be possible to cross-reference it with the DSS database and investigate potential interactions between genetic polymorphisms and health care outcomes.

7. Acknowledgments

This work was supported by a grant award to BW from the Retirement Research Foundation.

8. References

Hayden, K. M., Zandi, P. P., Lyketsos, C. G., Khachaturian, A. S., Bastian, L. A., Charoonruk, G., Tschanz, J. T., Norton, M. C., Pieper, C. F., Munger, R. G., *et al.* (2006). Vascular risk factors for incident Alzheimer disease and vascular dementia: the Cache County study. Alzheimer Dis Assoc Disord *20*, 93-100.

Launer, L. J., Ross, G. W., Petrovitch, H., Masaki, K., Foley, D., White, L. R., and Havlik, R. J. (2000). Midlife blood pressure and dementia: the Honolulu-Asia aging study. Neurobiol Aging *21*, 49-55.

Lee, T. A., Wolozin, B., Weiss, K. B., and Bednar, M. M. (2005). Assessment of the emergence of Alzheimer's disease following coronary artery bypass graft surgery or percutaneous transluminal coronary angioplasty. J Alzheimers Dis *7*, 319-324.

Li, N. C., Lee, A., Whitmer, R. A., Kivipelto, M., Lawler, E., Kazis, L. E., and Wolozin, B. (2010). Use of angiotensin receptor blockers and risk of dementia in a predominantly male population: prospective cohort analysis. Bmj *340*, b5465.

Reinoso, R. F., Sanchez Navarro, A., Garcia, M. J., and Prous, J. R. (2002). Preclinical pharmacokinetics of statins. Methods Find Exp Clin Pharmacol *24*, 593-613.

Seshadri, S., Beiser, A., Kelly-Hayes, M., Kase, C. S., Au, R., Kannel, W. B., and Wolf, P. A. (2006). The lifetime risk of stroke: estimates from the Framingham Study. Stroke *37*, 345-350.

Smith, M. W., and Joseph, G. J. (2003). Pharmacy data in the VA health care system. Med Care Res Rev *60*, 92S-123S.

Vanderweyde, T., Bednar, M. M., Forman, S. A., and Wolozin, B. (2010). Iatrogenic risk factors for Alzheimer's disease: surgery and anesthesia. J Alzheimers Dis *22 Suppl 3*, 91-104.

Vega, G. L., Weiner, M. F., Lipton, A. M., Von Bergmann, K., Lutjohann, D., Moore, C., and Svetlik, D. (2003). Reduction in levels of 24S-hydroxycholesterol by statin treatment in patients with Alzheimer disease. Arch Neurol *60*, 510-515.

Whitmer, R. A., Karter, A. J., Yaffe, K., Quesenberry, C. P., Jr., and Selby, J. V. (2009). Hypoglycemic episodes and risk of dementia in older patients with type 2 diabetes mellitus. Jama *301*, 1565-1572.

Wolozin, B., Kellman, W., Ruosseau, P., Celesia, G. G., and Siegel, G. (2000). Decreased prevalence of Alzheimer disease associated with 3-hydroxy-3- methyglutaryl coenzyme A reductase inhibitors. Arch Neurol *57*, 1439-1443.

Wolozin, B., Manger, J., Bryant, R., Cordy, J., Green, R. C., and McKee, A. (2006). Re-assessing the relationship between cholesterol, statins and Alzheimer's disease. Acta Neurol Scand Suppl *185*, 63-70.

Wolozin, B., Wang, S. W., Li, N. C., Lee, A., Lee, T. A., and Kazis, L. E. (2007). Simvastatin is associated with a reduced incidence of dementia and Parkinson's disease. BMC Med *5*, 20.

16

Decision Support Systems in Animal Health

Nguyen Van Long, Mark Stevenson and Bryan O'Leary
EpiCentre, Institute of Veterinary, Animal and Biomdedical Sciences
Massey University, Palmerston North
New Zealand

1. Introduction

The safety of food derived from animals has received significant public media attention in recent times and it is likely that this trend will continue in the short to medium term future. Examples of diseases in humans arising from the consumption of animals or animal products at the centre of recent food safety scares include variant Creutzfeld-Jakob disease (Anonymous, 2000), *Salmonella Typhimurium* DT104 (Threlfall et al., 1994), *Salmonella Enteritidis* (Anderson, 1996) and *Escherichia coli* O157 (Rangel et al., 2005). Of additional concern to the general public are infectious diseases of livestock, particularly those that have required large numbers of animals to be pre-emptively slaughtered or culled as part of control and eradication measures. Since 2000 there have been a number of large outbreaks of infectious disease in farmed animal populations that have been managed using pre-emptive slaughter or culling. This approach to disease management has raised questions about the legitimacy, ethics and long term future of intensive farming practices. Examples include the outbreak of classical swine fever (CSF) in The Netherlands in 2000 and foot-and-mouth disease (FMD) in the United Kingdom in 2001. Infectious disease has impacted heavily on the health and productivity of livestock populations in Southeast Asian countries in recent times. Highly pathogenic avian influenza (HPAI) H5N1 has emerged as a disease of international concern not only because of its ability to cause illness and death in poultry and humans, but also by its capacity to disrupt poultry trade and to threaten food security in resource-poor countries. To deal with infectious disease outbreaks in domestic livestock populations quickly and efficiently it is essential that animal health authorities have access to appropriate information to guide decision making. Animal health information includes (but should not be restricted to) details of the population at risk and details of incident cases of disease conditions of interest. This information allows the distribution of disease to be described in terms of the established epidemiological triad of individual, place and time. Individual animal-level analyses include estimates of the number of cases per head of population and for various subsections of the population (e.g. animals of a given age, sex, breed or type). Spatial analyses provide insight into geographical factors influencing the distribution of disease (e.g. proximity to pollutants, farming practices characteristic of a given area). Temporal analyses provide insight into short and long term variations in disease frequency. All three categories of analysis are useful in that firstly they provide an objectively measured point of comparison once control measures have been implemented and secondly, they provide information that can be used for hypothesis generation about factors associated with, or causing disease. Collection of additional information about the environment in which animals are located and events they

are exposed to over their lifetime allows these hypotheses to be tested which in turn allow authorities to identify risk factors for disease. Concentrating surveillance and control activities on animals or farm premises with identified risk factors then allows (often scarce) resources to be more effectively targeted at the sector of the animal population in greatest need of attention.
In this chapter we provide an overview of the infrastructure required to carry out the analytical procedures outlined above using an animal health decision support system (DSS). The chapter is divided into three main sections. In the first we provide a description of an animal health DSS and review DSSs currently in operation in various countries throughout the world. In the second we provide a description of how these systems are implemented in developing countries. The third and final section looks to the future, briefly outlining the planning that should be done by developing countries to ensure that current animal health DSSs continue to meet their needs well into the future. We conclude by proposing that a standardised format for recording and storing animal demographic, productivity and health data needs to be agreed on. Widespread adoption of this format will help to make animal health DSS components more readily transferable from one jurisdiction to another, ultimately reducing their cost and in doing so helping alleviate one of the important obstacles to more widespread uptake of this technology.

2. Animal health decision support systems currently in use

A DSS is an interactive, flexible and adaptable system (including, but not limited to, computer-based systems) comprised of relevant databases, technologies and appropriate analytical techniques to identify problems, predict consequences and provide solutions for improved decision making (Turban, 1995). An animal health DSS should have two main goals. The first is to provide authorities with the ability to trace animals from 'farm to fork', an essential requirement for food safety and documenting health status for domestic and international trading partners. The second is to provide a means to detect the emergence and re-emergence of diseases, allowing appropriate deployment of field operations and resources to deal with identified problems if and when they occur. Such a system promotes transparency in the state of animal health, allowing animal health policies to be based on the best available evidence.
A key component of an animal health DSS is a so-called 'data warehouse' which provides the facilities to capture, store and link all relevant information about an animal population of interest (Figure 1). Relevant information in this context includes demographic details of the population at risk, details of where that population resides, disease events, and the results of laboratory and residue analyses. We acknowledge that most (if not all) countries producing food from animals already have established facilities to record some, or even all, of this information. The key feature that distinguishes a DSS is that the various tables listed in Figure 1 are linked using unique individual animal and/or farm identifiers to form a coherent relational database design. This allows the analyst to easily extract details of (for example) diseased animals, their location of origin and the identities of farm locations they might have visited throughout their lifetime. At the population level, the burden of disease in an animal population can be quantified in terms of incidence and prevalence. Maps of the distribution of diseased animals can be produced and interpreting in context of the distribution of the population at risk. An additional requirement of a DSS is that it needs to be both flexible and user friendly for those interrogating the system and those interpreting the information it produces.

EpiMAN (Sanson, 1993) is an early example of an animal health DSS with a data architecture similar to that shown in Figure 1. The system combines a database management system, a geographic information system, a graphic user interface to allow the user to conduct descriptive analyses of infectious disease outbreak data, manage resources (e.g. scheduling of patrol visits) and run a simulation model to evaluate the effect of alternative control measures. EpiMAN was originally developed to manage data that would be generated during the course of an outbreak of FMD. The motivation for doing this was that timely analysis of outbreak event details would allow control and eradication activities to be fine-tuned as the epidemic progressed, as individual circumstances dictate (Sanson et al., 1999).

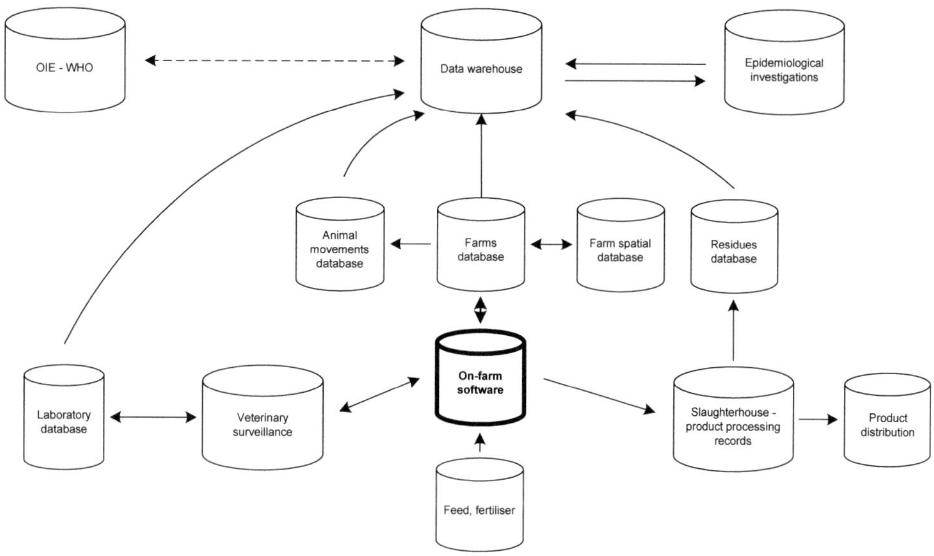

Fig. 1. Schematic diagram showing how on-farm data, veterinary practice records, diagnostic laboratory data, slaughterhouse processing records, details of residue assessments and animal movements might be integrated within an animal health decision support system (Morris, 1997; Stevenson et al., 2007). OIE – Office International des Epizooties; WHO = World Health Organization. Reproduced with permission from the New Zealand Veterinary Journal.

Another, more recently developed animal health DSS is the Rapid Analysis and Detection of Animal-Related Risks (RADAR)[1] system which has been in operation in the United Kingdom (UK) since 2003 (DEFRA, 2011; Lysons et al., 2007; Paiba et al., 2007; Scudamore, 2003; Smith et al., 2006). RADAR brings animal health and demographic data together in a standardised format to support research and the reporting requirements of a wide group of stakeholders. RADAR integrates data sets from existing systems and transforms them into a common coding system called the extraction, transformation and loading process. The system derives additional information from raw source data automatically using a variety of calculations and algorithms with metadata fully adherent to the UK government's e-Government Metadata Standards (Roberts, 2004).

[1] URL: `http://www.defra.gov.uk/foodfarm/farmanimal/diseases/vetsurveillance/radar/index.htm`

Before RADAR animal health information in the UK was collected and stored by different authorities using different nomenclatures, collection standards and coding systems. This meant that collation of information was slow and integration of different data sources difficult (Morris et al., 2002). The RADAR project has been conducted in three phases. The first (2003-2005) focused on the establishment of the data warehouse managing details of the cattle population, details of salmonella and exotic disease cases and analytical tools. The second phase (2005-2006) enhanced data cataloguing and reporting tools and extended the scope of data collection to other species (sheep, pigs, goats, and deer) and other diseases. This information has been used for the investigation and control of a range of animal health issues such as surveillance for salmonella in dairy cattle and poultry (Evans & Jordan, 2003), cattle movement patterns (Vernon & Keeling, 2009), bovine tuberculosis (Green et al., 2008), bluetongue (Wood et al., 2008), avian influenza (Knight-Jones et al., 2010) and FMD (Paiba et al., 2007). The third and final phase (2006-2013) expanded species coverage to include horses, companion animals and wildlife (Smith et al., 2006). An example report from RADAR is shown in Figure 2. Figure 2 shows the density of poultry premises (expressed as the number of premises per 100 km^2) throughout Great Britain. By simply identifying the location of the poultry population at risk animal health authorities are better placed to carry out a range of activities to maintain poultry health: identify high risk areas for disease transmission, target surveillance activities and monitor poultry movement.

In 2002 the Swiss government funded development of a system titled KODAVET (*Koordiniertes Datenverwaltungs und Analysesystem des Veterinärdienstes Schweiz*), subsequently renamed ISVET (Presi & Heim, 2010). The purpose of the system is to manage information related to both food producing and companion animals (Schaller, 2006; Stärk et al., 2006). Unique, individual animal identifiers and mandatory reporting of livestock movement events mean that animals can be tracked through the system throughout their lifetime. A feature of ISVET is that it provides a standardised facility for generating and storing health certificates for producers as well as scheduling routine inspection visits by Swiss Federal Veterinary Office staff. The system links a number of databases, including those from local veterinary offices in the cantons, the National Animal Movement Database and the National Database of the Federal Office of Agriculture. This project is on-going and has provided information useful for decision making and efficient use of resources (Swiss Federal Veterinary Office, 2009).

Partial animal health DSS systems exist in a number of countries such as Australia (The National Livestock Identification System)[2] (DAFF, 2006), Argentina (The Sanitary Management System database, maintained by the National Service for Agrifood Health and Quality, SENASA), and New Zealand (AgriBase[3] Sanson & Pearson, 1997). In Brazil the *Serviço de Rastreabilidade da Cadeia Produtiva de Bovinos e Bubalinos* (SISBOV)[4] provides the facility to register all cattle and buffalo born in Brazil or imported into the country since July 2002 (Bowling et al., 2008; Cardoso & Cardellino, 2004). The primary purpose of SISBOV is to allow tracing of registered individuals to meet international market requirements. The system provides the government with information to enhance the control of cattle herds, particularly management of FMD free zones and high risk areas.

The examples cited here are by no means exhaustive and the reader is referred to Stevenson et al. (2007) for a more detailed review and critique of systems in place within individual countries. A key point is that while most countries producing food derived from animals

---

[2] URL: `https://www.nlis.mla.com.au/`

[3] URL: `http://www.asurequality.com/geospatial-services/agribase.cfm`

[4] URL: `http://extranet.agricultura.gov.br/primeira_pagina/extranet/SISBOV.htm`

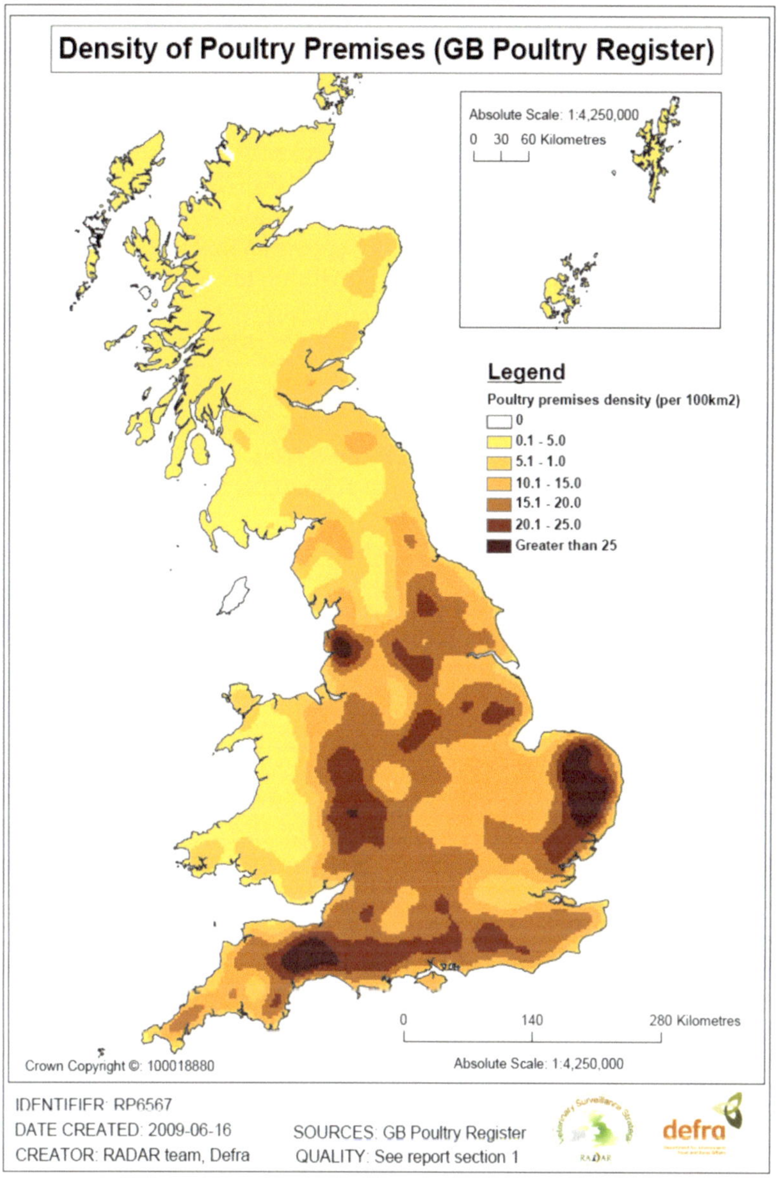

Fig. 2. Map of Great Britain showing the density of poultry premises (expressed as numbers per 100 km^2).

for export have components of a DSS in place few, if any, are capturing and using all of the data elements shown in Figure 1. The reason for this is that individual system components are expensive and time consuming to implement, requiring substantial changes in infrastructure and behaviour of users of the system. For example, implementation of an animal movement database means that livestock producers are no longer able to freely move animals from one location to another. Systems need to be established to issue movement permits as well as a mechanism to police the system to ensure that all movement events are recorded and appropriate penalties are applied to those that ignore system directives. Substantial information technology infrastructure needs to be built to record and store collected information and finally, facilities need to be put in place to retrieve and analyse data that is actually recorded. Given the time and expense required to set up workable system components we predict that it will take a number of years before 'full' DSSs become commonplace. A powerful facilitator of progress has, in the recent past, been exotic infectious disease outbreaks and the emergence of novel disease conditions such as bovine spongiform encephalopathy and HPAI H5N1. It is likely that progress in this area will be driven by a need to deal with these types of hazards in the short to medium term future.

3. Animal health decision support systems in developing countries

The key difference between developed and developing countries in terms of recording of animal health information is that developing countries often lack a system for identifying and recording the location of individual farm enterprises. A second point of difference is that recording of disease event information in developing countries is generally restricted to diseases classified as List A by the OIE.

Because sampling frames listing the identity of individual farm enterprises are not available in developing countries it is common for animal health details to be aggregated at the tertiary administrative unit level. In the case of Vietnam (for example) this is the commune. In the outbreaks of HPAI H5N1 that have occurred in Vietnam since December 2003 the commune has been the official unit of interest to define outbreak locations (MARD, 2005; Pfeiffer et al., 2007; Phan et al., 2009).

Similar area-based systems are in use in other Asian countries. For example, in the recent outbreaks of HPAI H5N1 in Thailand the location of affected flocks was assigned at the village level using codes managed by the Thai Department of Livestock Development. These details were then aggregated to provide summaries at the sub-district level, as shown in Figure 3 (see also Tiensin et al. 2007 and Tiensin et al. 2009 for examples). In the early days of the epidemic of HPAI H5N1 in Indonesia outbreak details were recorded at the district (secondary administrative unit) level (Gilbert et al., 2008; Pfeiffer, 2006). Modifications to the Participatory Disease Surveillance and Response (PDSR) database now allow disease event information to be recorded at the individual *desa* (village) level (Perry et al., 2009).

A number of factors work against animal health authorities in developing countries in terms of the amount and level of detail of animal health information able to be routinely recorded. The first is that the majority of production units are small-scale and managed at the individual household level. For example, backyard poultry are ubiquitous in many Southeast Asian countries such as Cambodia, Lao PDR, Thailand, Vietnam and Indonesia. In addition, the distribution of backyard herds and poultry flocks (in particular) are under a constant state of change as stock are frequently moved and sold. Rural areas, where animal disease problems tend to be greater, are characterised by poor communication networks and transport infrastructure (Baldock et al., 1999). Livestock owners are therefore often unable to contact veterinary staff and it is difficult for veterinary staff to access livestock, which means that provision of services and collection of the necessary information related to outbreak events is either delayed or non-existent.

The Transboundary Animal Disease Information System (TADinfo),[5] developed by the Food and Agriculture Organization of the United Nations, provides an off-the-shelf and flexible

[5] URL: `http://www.fao.org/ag/againfo/programmes/en/empres/tadinfo/about.html`

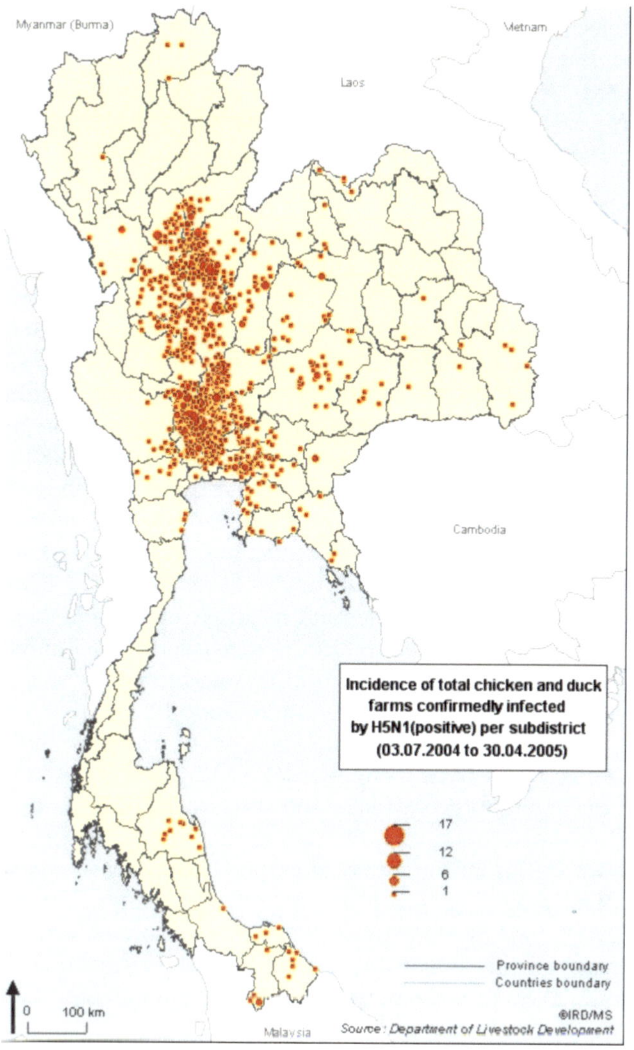

Fig. 3. Map of Thailand showing the incidence of chicken and duck farms confirmed with HPAI H5N1, by sub-district (Souris et al., 2010). Reproduced with permission from the International Journal of Health Geographics.

solution for recording many of the items listed in Figure 1 (Kamata et al., 2006; 2009). The system is fully customisable, combining a relational database with a mapping system that allows users to record details of disease observations, abattoir surveillance, livestock census details and vaccination records. The smallest unit of interest within the system is user defined with typical choices being either the individual farm or small area (such as the village).

Choice of an appropriate unit of interest at the time TADinfo is deployed is important. If, for example, a country initially uses the small area (e.g. village) as the unit of interest and then, at some later date decides to change over to a system based on individual farms data incompatability issues will arise: inference about disease risk at the individual farm level cannot be made using aggregated data. On the other hand, switching from an individual farm-based system to one based on small areas (while uncommon) presents little problems since it is straightforward to aggregate farm details to the small area level. These issues need to be thought through carefully by animal health authorities at the time these systems are first implemented. In particular, consideration needs to be given to the likely animal health information needs of the country 10-15 years into the future as well as immediate requirements.

4. The future

In developed countries a major focus of animal health is to maintain food safety and provide transparent evidence of a country's disease status for the purpose of international trade. In developing countries, on the other hand, animal health activities tend to mainly concentrate on the control and management of infectious diseases such as FMD, CSF and HPAI H5N1. Some countries, such as Thailand, are at a crossroad exporting food of animal origin (chicken meat) to other countries (Bowles et al., 2005) while at the same time having to deal with infectious disease outbreaks affecting predominantly backyard livestock enterprises. It is likely that many developing Asian countries will follow in the footsteps of Thailand, moving away from predominantly subsistence farming to becoming exporters of animal product. For this development to progress smoothly it is essential that a credible track record in food safety is developed and maintained so these issues do not become a future trade barrier. On-farm use of pesticides, anthelmintics, antibiotics and fertilisers are details that could be recorded within a DSS, providing a means for monitoring usage trends which might then allow steps to be taken to avoid unacceptable chemical residue concentrations being held up as a future trade barrier (Theresa Bernardo, personal communication). Developing countries therefore need to develop a planned approach to data management, recognising that over time there will be a need to move away from using animal health data to control infectious disease outbreaks towards documentation of disease and chemical residue status to trading partners and consumers.

Given the expense of designing and implementing DSS components we propose that a standardised format for recording and storing animal demographic, productivity and health data needs to be agreed on. Widespread adoption of this standard will help to make animal health DSS components more readily transferable from one jurisdiction to another, ultimately reducing their cost and in doing so helping to alleviate one of the important obstacles to more widespread uptake of this technology.

Just as, if not more important, than the development of the technology and infrastructure for data collection, it is vital to provide veterinary staff (particularly those in developing countries) with the appropriate analytical skills so that maximum value is derived from data that are actually collected. As an example, extremely large numbers of records are collected by animal movement databases, even in countries of moderate size. One of the skills required when analysing this data is the ability to summarise movements at the national level and then to 'drill down' on specific areas of interest identified from summary analyses (Aznar et al., 2011; Martínez-López et al., 2009). Extracting the maximum value out of animal movement data sets requires a range of analytical skills including epidemiology, social network analysis, and spatial statistics. Other analytical procedures, for example the design of disease surveillance strategies, rely on a different skill set including knowledge of sampling theory and economics.

Issues related to system sensitivity and specificity arise when DSSs are used to detect emerging diseases in an animal population. If the analyst is too sensitive in terms of declaring a pattern of disease events as indicative of an emerging syndrome investigative resources will be wasted. If, on the other hand, the system is too specific then it is possible that emerging syndromes that should have been identified and acted upon will be missed. In order to 'get the balance right' it is essential that those involved in the analysis of DSS data are given the opportunity to become familiar with the natural pattern of disease within a given country, particularly its temporal (e.g. seasonal) and spatial features. Our only suggestion here is that these skills take many years to develop and part of the costing of implementing a DSS should include a component to select, train and appropriately renumerate skilled system analysts. Regular and ongoing collaboration with relevant stakeholders is important to maintain consistent data quality and to refine outputs so that literally, numbers can be turned into knowledge.

5. Conclusions

A decision support system of the type described in this chapter provides authorities with a valuable resource for recording, validating, storing and analysing animal health data. Outputs from such systems can be used to manage and control outbreaks of infectious disease in animals, identify factors associated with the presence of disease, provide an objectively measured point of comparison once control measures have been implemented and provide an additional means to detect emerging disease syndromes.

As we have shown, a DSS is comprised of a number of components, some of which are expensive and time consuming to implement. For this reason, the current situation is that many food producing countries throughout the world have individual components of a full system in place and fully operational systems are the exception rather than the rule.

Unlike the situation in developed countries, developing countries tend to use DSSs for the management and control of infectious disease outbreaks with data typically aggregated at the small area level. Animal health managers in developing countries should be aware that, over time, focus will shift away from management and control of infectious diseases towards food safety and transparent documentation of animal disease status. A planned approach to animal health data management is therefore required, inevitably meaning that the unit of interest of DSSs need to shift away from the small area level to that of the individual producer.

Given the expense of designing and implementing DSS components we propose that a standardised format for recording and storing animal demographic, productivity and health data needs to be agreed on. Widespread adoption of this format will help to make animal health DSS components more readily transferable from one jurisdiction to another, ultimately reducing their cost. Just as important is the need to provide veterinary staff with the appropriate analytical skills so that maximum value is derived from the data actually collected.

6. References

Anderson, A. (1996). Outbreak of salmonella food poisoning at Junior World Rowing Championships, *British Journal of Sports Medicine* 30(4): 347–348.

Anonymous (2000). The BSE inquiry. The Phillips Inquiry into BSE and variant CJD in the United Kingdom, *Technical report*, HMSO.

Aznar, N., Stevenson, M. & León, E. (2011). Analysis of cattle movements in Argentina, 2005, *Preventive Veterinary Medicine* 98: 119 – 127.

Baldock, C., Forman, A., Geering, W. & Taylor, W. (1999). New Technologies in the Fight Against Transboundary Animal Diseases. FAO Animal Production and Health

Paper, *Technical report*, Food and Agriculture Organization of the United Nations. Available as: http://www.fao.org/docs/eims/upload/138251/newtech.pdf. Accessed 10 February 2011.

Bowles, D., Paskin, R., Gutiérrez, M. & Kasterine, A. (2005). Animal welfare and developing countries: opportunities for trade in high-welfare products from developing countries, *Revue Scientifique et Technique de l'Office International des Epizooties* 24: 783 – 790.

Bowling, M., Pendell, D., Morris, D., Yoon, Y., Katoh, K., Belk, K. & Smith, G. (2008). Identification and traceability of cattle in selected countries outside of North America, *Professional Animal Scientist* 24: 287 – 294.

Cardoso, F. & Cardellino, R. (2004). Brazilian and Mercosur experiences in development and implementation of animal identification and recording systems, *International Committee for Animal Recording Technical Series* 9: 121 – 132.

DAFF (2006). Report of Findings from a Review of the Operation of the National Livestock Identification System, *Technical report*, Department of Agriculture, Fisheries and Forestry, Canberra, Australia. Available as: http://www.daff.gov.au/__data/assets/pdf_file/0019/117325/nlis-report.pdf. Accessed 10 February 2011.

DEFRA (2011). A Review of the Implementation of the Veterinary Surveillance Strategy (VSS), *Technical report*, Department for Environment, Food and Rural Affairs (DEFRA), London, UK. Available as: http://www.defra.gov.uk/foodfarm/farmanimal/diseases/vetsurveillance/documents/vss-review-feb2011.pdf. Accessed 10 February 2011.

Evans, S. & Jordan, L. (2003). An integrated surveillance system for salmonella in livestock in Great Britain, *Proceedings of the 10th International Symposium on Veterinary Epidemiology and Economics*, Viña del Mar, Chile.

Gilbert, M., Xiao, X., Pfeiffer, D., Epprecht, M., Boles, S., Czarnecki, C., Chaitaweesub, P., Kalpravidh, W., Minh, P., Otte, M., Martin, V. & Slingenbergh, J. (2008). Mapping H5N1 highly pathogenic avian influenza risk in Southeast Asia, *Proceedings of the National Academy of Sciences of the United States of America* 105: 4769 – 4774.

Green, D., Kiss, I., Mitchell, A. & Kao, R. (2008). Estimates for local and movement-based transmission of bovine tuberculosis in British cattle, *Proceedings of the Royal Society B: Biological Sciences* 275: 1001 – 1005.

Kamata, A., Martin, V., Lubroth, J., Morteo, K. & Domenech, J. (2006). The second generation of TADinfo — Java-based disease incidence recording software equipped with GIS mapping, *Proceedings of the 11th International Symposium on Veterinary Epidemiology and Economics*, Cairns, Australia.

Kamata, A., Morteo, K., Menach, A., Pinto, J., Martin, V. & Lubroth, J. (2009). TADinfo for a national database system, *Proceedings of the 12th International Symposium on Veterinary Epidemiology and Economics*, Durban, South Africa.

Knight-Jones, T., Gibbens, J., Wooldridge, M. & St
"ark, K. (2010). Assessment of farm-level biosecurity measures after an outbreak of avian influenza in the United Kingdom, *Transboundary and Emerging Diseases* 58: 69 – 75.

Lysons, R., Gibbens, J. & Smith, L. (2007). Progress with enhancing veterinary surveillance in the United Kingdom, *Veterinary Record* 160: 105 – 112.

MARD (2005). Circular for Implementing Urgent Strategies for the Prevention and Control of HPAI/H5N1 in Vietnam, *Technical Report 69/2005/TT-BNN*, Ministry of Agriculture and Rural Development, Hanoi, Vietnam.

Martínez-López, B., Perez, A. & Sánchez-Vizcaíno, J. (2009). Social network analysis. Review of general concepts and use in preventive veterinary medicine, *Transboundary and Emerging Diseases* 56(4): 109 – 120.

Morris, R. (1997). Proposed design of a 'stable to table' information system for food safety, *Proceedings of the 8th International Symposium on Veterinary Epidemiology and Economics*, Paris, France.

Morris, R., Sanson, R., Stern, M., Stevenson, M. & Wilesmith, J. (2002). Decision-support tools for foot-and-mouth disease control, *Revue Scientifique et Technique de l'Office International des Epizooties* 21(3): 557 – 567.

Paiba, G., Roberts, S., Houston, C., Williams, E., Smith, L., Gibbens, J., Holdship, S. & Lysons, R. (2007). UK surveillance: Provision of quality assured information from combined datasets, *Preventive Veterinary Medicine* 81: 117 – 134.

Perry, B., Isa, K. & Tarazona, C. (2009). Independent Evaluation of FAO's Participatory Disease Surveillance and Response Programme in Indonesia, *Technical report*, Food and Agriculture Organization of the United Nations. Available as: `http://www.fao.org/docs/eims/upload/262940/PDSR%20evaluation%20report%2030%20July%20final.pdf`. Accessed 10 February 2011.

Pfeiffer, D. (2006). Assistance in the Geospatial Analysis of HPAI Outbreaks in Indonesia, *Technical report*, Food and Agriculture Organization of the United Nations. Available as: `http://www.fao.org/docs/eims/upload/199669/Pfeiffer_Report_Indonesia_2005.pdf`. Accessed 10 February 2011.

Pfeiffer, D., Minh, P., Martin, V., Epprecht, M. & Otte, M. (2007). An analysis of the spatial and temporal patterns of highly pathogenic avian influenza occurrence in Vietnam using national surveillance data, *Veterinary Journal* 174: 302 – 309.

Phan, Q., Morris, R., Schauer, B., Stevenson, M., Benschop, J., Hoang, V. & Jackson, R. (2009). Spatial-temporal epidemiology of highly pathogenic avian influenza outbreaks in the two deltas of Vietnam during 2003-2007, *Preventive Veterinary Medicine* 89: 16 – 24.

Presi, P. & Heim, D. (2010). BVD eradication in Switzerland — A new approach, *Veterinary Microbiology* 142: 137 – 142.

Rangel, J., Sparling, P., Crowe, C., Griffin, P. & Swerdlow, D. (2005). Epidemiology of *Escherichia coli* O157:H7 outbreaks, United States, 1982-2002, *Emerging Infectious Diseases* 11(4): 603 – 609.

Roberts, S. (2004). Metadata standards for RADAR reports, *Technical report*, Department for Environment, Food and Rural Affairs (DEFRA), London, UK.

Sanson, R. (1993). *The Development of a Decision Support System for an Animal Disease Emergency*, PhD thesis, Massey University.

Sanson, R., Morris, R. & Stern, M. (1999). EpiMAN-FMD a decision support system for managing epidemics of vesicular disease, *Revue Scientifique et Technique de l'Office International des Epizooties* 18: 593 – 605.

Sanson, R. & Pearson, A. (1997). AgriBase — a national spatial farm database, *Proceedings of the 8th International Symposium on Veterinary Epidemiology and Economics*, Paris, France.

Schaller, P. (2006). KODAVET — Annual Report of the Swiss Federal Veterinary Office, *Technical report*, Swiss Federal Veterinary Offie, Berne, Switzerland.

Scudamore, J. (2003). Partnership, Priorities and Professionalism. A Strategy for Enhancing Veterinary surveillance in the UK, *Technical report*, Veterinary Surveillance Division, Department of Environment Food and Rural Affairs, London, UK.

Smith, L., Paiba, G., Holdship, S., Lysons, R., Lawton, S., Hicks, J. & Roberts, S. (2006). UK surveillance: Adding value to data by conforming domains and deriving additional attributes, *Proceedings of the 11th International Symposium on Veterinary Epidemiology and Economics*, Cairns Convention Centre, Cairns, Australia.

Souris, M., Gonzalez, J.-P., Shanmugasundaram, J., Corvest, V. & Kittayapong, P. (2010). Retrospective space-time analysis of H5N1 avian influenza emergence in Thailand, *International Journal of Health Geographics* 9(3).

Stärk, K., Tempelman, Y., Rüfenacht, J., Stern, M. & Morris, R. (2006). Development of a system for the standardized recording of epidemiological data within Swiss Veterinary Services, *Proceedings of the 10th International Symposium on Veterinary Epidemiology and Economics*, Viña del Mar, Chile.

Stevenson, M., Sanson, R., Miranda, A., Lawrence, K. & Morris, R. (2007). Decision support systems for monitoring and maintaining health in food animal populations, *New Zealand Veterinary Journal* 55: 264–272.

Swiss Federal Veterinary Office (2009). Evaluation of the Swiss Veterinary Service, *Technical report*, Swiss Federal Veterinary Office, Berne, Switzerland.

Threlfall, E., Frost, J., Ward, L. & Rowe, B. (1994). Epidemic in cattle and humans of *Salmonella Typhimurium* DT104 with chromosomally integrated multiple drug resistance, *Veterinary Record* 134: 577.

Tiensin, T., Ahmed, S., Rojanasthien, S., Songserm, T., Ratanakorn, P., Chaichoun, K., Kalpravidh, W., Wongkasemjit, S., Patchimasiri, T., Chanachai, K., Thanapongtham, W., Chotinan, S., Stegeman, A. & Nielen, M. (2009). Ecologic risk factor investigation of clusters of avian influenza A (H5N1) virus infection in Thailand, *Journal of Infectious Diseases* 199: 1735 – 1743.

Tiensin, T., Nielen, M., Songserm, T., Kalpravidh, W., Chaitaweesub, P., Amonsin, A., Chotiprasatintara, S., Chaisingh, A., Damrongwatanapokin, S., Wongkasemjit, S., Antarasena, C., Songkitti, V., Chanachai, K., Thanapongtham, W. & Stegeman, J. (2007). Geographic and temporal distribution of highly pathogenic avian influenza A virus (H5N1) in Thailand, 2004-2005: An overview, *Avian Diseases* 51: 182 – 188.

Turban, E. (1995). *Decision Support and Expert Systems: Management Support Systems*, Prentice Hall International, London, UK.

Vernon, M. & Keeling, M. (2009). Representing the UK's cattle herd as static and dynamic networks, *Proceedings of the Royal Society B: Biological Sciences* 276: 469 – 476.

Wood, J., Webb, C. & Oura, C. (2008). Scientific study of bluetongue vaccine uptake and efficacy, *The Veterinary Record* 162: 831.

17

Development of an Image Retrieval Model for Biomedical Image Databases

Achimugu Philip[1], Babajide Afolabi[2],
Adeniran Oluwaranti[2] and Oluwagbemi Oluwatolani[1]
[1]*Department of Computer Science, Lead City University, Ibadan*
[2]*Department of Computer Science and Engineering, Obafemi Awolowo University, Ile-Ife*
Nigeria

1. Introduction

Image processing is the field of signal processing where both the input and output signals are images. Images can be thought of as two-dimensional signals via a matrix representation. Image processing a is very important subject, and finds itself in such fields as photography, satellite imaging, medical imaging, and image compression, to name but a few. In the past, image processing was largely done using analog devices (Cheng et al., 2006). However, as computers became more powerful, processing shifted toward the digital domain. Like one-dimensional digital signal processing, digital image processing overcomes traditional analog "problems" such as noise, distortion during processing, inflexibility of system to change, and difficulty of implementation.

Image retrieval, popularly referred to as content-based image retrieval is an emerging technology that allows a user to retrieve relevant images in an effective and efficient manner. Digital imaging has extensive applications in our daily lives and it is being used for several applications. Examples of imaging applications are in museums for archiving important images and manuscripts from art gallery and museum management. Many useful applications of imaging are found in security for tracking an intruder, crime prevention, law enforcement and object recognition in digital forensic.

In particular, image retrieval is potentially useful in discovering brain activation patterns, in classifications and in diagnoses by comparing observed patterns with those of known diseases, leading to clinical applications. In biomedicine, content-based image retrieval is critically important in patient digital libraries, clinical diagnosis, clinical trials, searching for 2-D electrophoresis gels, and pathological slides. Most existing content-based image retrieval systems (Flickner et al., 1995; Gupta and Jain, 1997; Ma and Manjunath, 1997; Rubner, 1999 and Wang et al., 1998) are designed for general purpose picture libraries such as photos and graph.

The storage, manipulation and analysis of the contents of digital images are essential requirements for the next generation of healthcare information infrastructure. The aim of this infrastructure is to bring timely health information to support communication among healthcare decision makers and communities at large. Among several healthcare services that can be provided with the aid of the emerging grid technology for ubiquitous access, image classification and diagnosis services are important. The ubiquitous access and retrieval services enable the storage, retrieval, analysis, management, manipulation and sharing of all kinds of healthcare specific digital images. The healthcare community is currently exploring collaborative approaches for managing image data and exchanging useful knowledge. It also eases distributed management of clinical data and scenarios for integration of image retrieval access methods into picture archiving and communication systems as well as healthcare information infrastructure. However, retrieval results of the existing image retrieval systems are generally not satisfactory due to the weak connection between low level image features and high level image semantics. Moreover, traditional text-based description requires images to be manually annotated. This can be a very time-consuming task that is cumbersome, error prone and prohibitively expensive. Additionally, images can have contents that texts alone cannot adequately convey. Thus, due to the rich content of images, traditional text-based retrieval methods can be complemented with efficient and effective image retrieval algorithms and techniques to enhance medical diagnosis and therapy planning.

2. What is digital image processing?

An ***image*** as defined in the "real world" is considered to be a function of two real variables, for example, a(x, y) with **a** as the amplitude (e.g. brightness) of the image at the real coordinate position (x, y). Furthermore, an image may be considered to contain sub-images sometimes referred to as regions-of-interest, ROIs, or simply regions. This concept reflects the fact that images frequently contain collections of objects each of which can be the basis for a region.

Therefore, *Digital image processing* is the use of computer algorithms to perform image processing on digital images. As a subfield of digital signal processing, digital image processing has many advantages over analog image processing; it allows a much wider range of algorithms to be applied to the input data, and can avoid problems such as the build-up of noise and signal distortion during processing.

2.1 What can be done by image processing?

a. Geometric transformations such as enlargement, reduction, and rotation.
b. Color corrections such as brightness and contrast adjustments, quantization, or conversion to a different color space.
c. Registration (or alignment) of two or more images.
d. Combination of two or more images, e.g. into an average, blend, difference, or image composite.
e. Interpolation and recovery of a full image from a RAW image format.
f. Segmentation of the image into regions.
g. Image editing and Digital retouching.
h. Extending dynamic range by combining differently exposed images.

2.2 Applications of image processing

Image Processing finds applications in the following areas:

a. Photography and Printing
b. Satellite Image Processing
c. Medical Image Processing

d. Face detection, Feature detection, Face identification
e. Microscope image processing

3. Digital image basics

When using digital equipment to capture, store, modify and view photographic images, they must first be converted to a set of numbers in a process called digitization or scanning. Computers are very good at storing and manipulating numbers, so once your image has been digitized you can use your computer to archive, examine, alter, display, transmit, or print your photographs in an incredible variety of ways.

Digital images are composed of *pixels* (short for picture elements). Each pixel represents the color (or gray level for black and white photos) at a single point in the image, so a pixel is like a tiny dot of a particular color. By measuring the color of an image at a large number of points, we can create a digital approximation of the image from which a copy of the original can be reconstructed. Pixels are a little like grain particles in a conventional photographic image, but arranged in a regular pattern of rows and columns and store information somewhat differently. A digital image is a rectangular array of pixels sometimes called a *bitmap*.

For photographic purposes, there are two important types of digital images; color and black and white. Color images are made up of colored pixels while black and white images are made of pixels in different shades of gray.

A black and white image is made up of pixels each of which holds a single number corresponding to the gray level of the image at a particular location. These gray levels span the full range from black to white in a series of very fine steps, normally 256 different grays. While a color image is made up of pixels each of which holds three numbers corresponding to the red, green, and blue levels of the image at a particular location. Red, green, and blue (sometimes referred to as RGB) are the primary colors for mixing light; these so-called additive primary colors are different from the subtractive primary colors used for mixing paints (cyan, magenta, and yellow). Any color can be created by mixing the correct amounts of red, green, and blue light. Assuming 256 levels for each primary, each color pixel can be stored in three bytes (24 bits) of memory. This corresponds to roughly 16.7 million different possible colors. Note that for images of the same size, a black and white version will use three times less memory than a color version.

3.1 Binary or Bi-level Images

Binary images use only a single bit to represent each pixel. Since a bit can only exist in two states; on or off, every pixel in a binary image must be one of two colors, usually black or white. This inability to represent intermediate shades of gray is what limits their usefulness in dealing with photographic images.

3.2 Indexed color images

Some color images are created using a limited palette of colors, typically 256 different colors. These images are referred to as indexed color images because the data for each pixel consists of a palette index indicating which of the colors in the palette applies to that pixel. There are several problems with using indexed color to represent photographic images. First, if the image contains more different colors than are in the palette, techniques such as dithering must be applied to represent the missing colors and this degrades the image. Second, combining two indexed color images that use different palettes or even retouching part of a single indexed color image creates problems because of the limited number of available colors.

3.3 Resolution

The more points at which we sample the image by measuring its color, the more detail we can capture. The density of pixels in an image is referred to as its *resolution*. The higher the resolution, the more information the image contains. If we keep the image size the same and increase the resolution, the image gets sharper and more detailed. Alternatively, with a higher resolution image, we can produce a larger image with the same amount of detail and the resolution of an image is reduced no matter the size; the pixels get larger and larger and there is less and less detail in the image.

4. Image digitalization

The process of converting an image to pixels is called *digitizing* or *scanning* and this function can be performed in many different ways as described below:

4.1 Film scanners

This type of scanner is sometimes called a slide or transparency scanner. They are specifically designed for scanning film, usually 35mm slides or negatives, but some of the more expensive ones can also scan medium and large format film. These scanners work by passing a narrowly focused beam of light through the film and reading the intensity and color of the light that emerges.

4.2 Flatbed scanners

This type of scanner is sometimes called a reflective scanner. They are designed for scanning prints or other flat, opaque materials. These scanners work by shining white light onto the object and reading the intensity and color of the light that is reflected from it, usually a line at a time. Some flatbed scanners have available transparency adapters, but for a number of reasons, in most cases these are not very well suited to scanning film. On the other hand, flatbed scanners can be used as a sort of lensless camera to directly digitize flat objects like leaves.

4.3 Digital cameras

One of the most direct ways to capture an image is a digital camera which uses a special semiconductor chip called a CCD (charge coupled device) to convert light to electrical signals right at the image plane. The quality of the images created in this manner is closely related to the number of pixels the CCD can capture. Affordable digital cameras suffer from relatively low resolution, limited dynamic range, and low ISO film speed equivalent, and consequently do not always produce high quality digital images. To get images with quality comparable to film photography currently requires very expensive digital cameras.

4.4 Video frame grabbers

This type of scanner uses a video camera to capture a scene or object and then converts the video signal that comes out of the camera to a digital image in your computer memory. A video camera can be used to digitize scenes containing 3- dimensional objects, but they usually have much lower image quality than film or flatbed scanners.

4.5 Scanning services

Photo CD is a service started by Kodak a number of years ago whereby your film can be scanned using a high quality scanner and written to a compact disk your computer can access. Using Photo CD service is an inexpensive way to get high quality scans of your images without purchasing a scanner. Many other scanning services are available which can scan prints or film to floppy disks or removable disk cartridges. These vary from low resolution snapshot quality images to professional drum scans at very high resolution.

5. Image compression

Image compression is the application of data compression on digital images. In effect, the objective is to reduce redundancy of the image data in order to be able to store or transmit data in an efficient form. Image compression can be lossy or lossless. Lossless compression is sometimes preferred for artificial images such as technical drawings, icons or comics. This is because lossy compression methods, especially when used at low bit rates, introduce compression artifacts. Lossless compression methods may also be preferred for high value content, such as medical imagery or image scans made for archival purposes. Lossy methods are especially suitable for natural images such as photos in applications where minor (sometimes imperceptible) loss of fidelity is acceptable to achieve a substantial reduction in bit rate. Compressing an image is significantly different than compressing raw binary data. Of course, general purpose compression programs can be used to compress images, but the result is less than optimal. This is because images have certain statistical properties which can be exploited by encoders specifically designed for them. Also, some of the finer details in the image can be sacrificed for the sake of saving a little more bandwidth or storage space. This also means that lossy compression techniques can be used in this area. The image compression technique that is most often used is transformed coding. A typical image's energy often varies significantly throughout the image, which makes compressing it in the spatial domain difficult; however, images tend to have a compact representation in the frequency domain packed around the low frequencies, which makes compression in the frequency domain more efficient and effective. Transform coding is an image compression technique that first switches to the frequency domain, then does it's compressing. The transform coefficients should be de-correlated to reduce redundancy and to have a maximum amount of information stored in the smallest space. These coefficients are then coded as accurately as possible to not lose information.

6. Statement of problem

The retrieval results of the existing image retrieval systems are generally not satisfactory due to the weak connection between low-level features and the semantics of images. This problem is generally referred to as the semantic gap problem. Image retrieval approaches based on low level concepts naturally have some inherited problems for human perceptual recognition. Humans recognize images based on high-level concepts such as texts and they typically query images by their semantics. Alternatively, high level concepts alone are not sufficient for image retrieval, because images can contain important information that texts cannot reveal. Another very important problem in image retrieval is the need for suitable similarity measures and image representations that can lead to an improved retrieval result. In particular, variations can occur among semantically similar objects in medical images such as MRI, x-ray, ultrasound, digital radiography, etc; which have direct reliance on medical diagnosis and intervention. These variations can cause serious problems for an image representation method, making it difficult to conceive a measure for similarity in image retrieval (Olugbara, 2008). Therefore, it would be pertinent to develop a database processing models or schemes for improving retrieval results in healthcare applications; hence this study.

7. Related works

A lot of opinions and methods have been developed in solving problems that relates image processing and computer graphics. This has led to extensive research that resulted, in less than a decade, into numerous commercial and research based system, including QBIC (Niblack, et al., 1993), Virage (Bach, et al., 1996), Photobook (Pentland, et al., 1996), Excalibur (Feder, 1996), Chabot (OVE and Chabot, 1995), and Visual SEEK (Smith, 1997). These systems allow users to formulate queries using combinations of low-level image features such as colour, texture and shape. The queries are specified explicitly by providing the desired feature values or implicitly by specifying an example image. Some system also uses the spatial organization of the image features, so that similarity is determined not only by the existence of certain features but also by their absolute or relative location in the image (Hou, et al., 1992; Bach, et al., 1996; Stricker and Dimai, 1996; Smith, 1997; Das, et al., 1997; Cohen, 1999).

Early systems focused on the search engine (given a query, find the best matches) and did not use precious queries to understand better what the user was looking for. Recent system allows the user to redefine the search by indicating the relevance (or irrelevance) of images in the returned set. This is known as relevance feedback (Rui, et al., 1997; Minka and Picard, 1997; Smith, 1997).

In (Idris and Panchanathan, 1997), the authors provide an in-depth review of content-based image retrieval systems. They also identify a number of unanswered key research questions, including the development of more robust and compact image content feature and dissimilarity measures that model perceptual similarity more accurately.

(Michalski, 1972; 1973) examined how symbolic AQ rule learning could be used for discrimination between textures or between simple structures. These seminal papers presented the Multi-Level Logical Template (MLT) methodology in which windowing operators scanned an image and extracted local features. These features were used to learn rules describing textures (or simple structures); the rules were then used for texture (or simple structure) recognition.

(Shepherd, 1983), encoded examples as feature vectors, learned decision trees for an industrial inspection task especially, classification of the shapes of chocolates. Comparisons of classification accuracy were made between decision tree, *k*-nearest neighbor (*k*-nn), and minimum distance classifiers. Experimental results for these classifiers were similar, with the minimum distance classifier producing the highest accuracy, 82%.

(Channic, 1989) extended the MLT methodology in (Michalski, 1972; 1973) by using convolution operators in conjunction with the original set of windowing operators for feature extraction. Using the AQ learning system, Channic investigated incremental learning and iterative learning from sequences of images using ultrasound images of laminated objects.

Instead of representing examples using feature vectors, (Connell and Brady, 1987) learned generalized semantic networks from images of classes of hammers and of overhead views of commercial aircraft. Training examples were generated by a vision system that took gray scale images as input and produced semantic networks for the objects; a learning system, which was a modified version of (Winston, 1984) ANALOGY program, learned by generalizing the training examples. The learning system was extended to learn disjunctive concepts and to learn from only positive examples. These generalized representations were used to classify unknown objects.

(Cromwell and Kak, 1991) proceeded as Shepherd did, using feature vectors to characterize shapes. Electrical component shapes were learned using a symbolic induction methodology based on that developed by Michalski. They reported that their method achieved 72% on testing data, but no comparisons were made with other learning methods.

(Pachowicz and Bala, 1991) also used the MLT methodology, following (Michalski, 1972; 1973) and (Channic, 1989), but added a modified set of Laws' masks for texture feature extraction. They also applied techniques for handling noise in symbolic data. These techniques included optimizing learned symbolic descriptions by truncating rules, as well as removing training examples covered by weak rules and relearning. The PRAX method for learning a large number of classes was introduced by Bala, Michalski, and Wnek in 1992 and 1993.

(Segen, 1994) used a hybrid shape representation consisting of a hierarchical graph that takes into account local features of high curvature, and the angles and distances between these local features. This representation is invariant to both planar rotation and translation. Shapes were silhouettes of hand gestures. Segen's system runs in real time and has been applied to airplane simulator control as well as to control of a graphics editor program. Error rates were between 5% and 10%, but most errors were unknowns rather than misclassifications.

(Cho and Dunn, 1994) described a new learning algorithm for learning shape. This algorithm memorizes property lists and updates associated weights as training proceeds. Forgetting mechanisms remove useless property lists. Shapes are modeled by a series of line segments. Using the orientations of these segments, local spatial measures are computed and form a property list for a shape. The system was used to classify tools and hand gestures and achieved predictive accuracies of 92% and 96% on these problems.

(Dutta and Bhanu, 1994) presented a 3D CAD-based recognition system in which genetic algorithms are used to optimize segmentation parameters. Qualitative experimental results were presented for indoor and outdoor motion sequences in which the system recognized images of wedges (traffic cones) and cans from gray scale and depth map images. Sung and (Poggio, 1994) worked on automatic human face detection. An example-based learning approach was tested for locating un-occluded frontal views of human faces in complex scenes. The space of human faces was represented by a few \face" and \non-face" pattern prototypes. At each image location, a two-valued distance measure was computed between the local image pattern and each prototype. A trained classifier was used to determine whether a human face is present. The authors showed that their distance metric is critical for the success of their system.

(Zheng and Bhanu, 1996) examined how Hebbian learning mechanisms could be used to improve the performance of an image thresholding algorithm for automatic target detection

and recognition. Qualitative results were presented in which the adaptive thresholding algorithm was shown to be superior to the classical thresholding algorithm for both SAR and FLIR images.
(Rowley, et al., 1996) built a neural network-based face detection system by using a retinally connected neural network to examine small windows of an image and decide on the existence of a face. A bootstrap algorithm was implemented during training so as to add false detection into the training set and as a consequence, eliminate the difficult task of manually selecting non-face training examples. Experimental results showed better performance in terms of detection and false-positive rates.
(Romano, et al., 1996) built a real-time system for face verification. Experiments showed that simple correlation strategies on template-based models are sufficient for many applications in which the identity of a face in a novel image must be verified quickly and reliably from a single reference image. The authors suggested that this automatic real-time face verification technique could be put to use in such human-machine interface applications as automated security systems. The technique has been integrated into a screen locking application which permits access to workstations by performing face verification in lieu of password authentication.
The MLT methodology developed by Michalski in 1973 and 1973 has recently been extended into the Multi-Level Image Sampling and Transformation (MIST) methodology. MIST has been applied to a variety of problems including natural scene segmentation and identification of blasting caps in x-ray images. For classifying natural scenes, three learning techniques were compared: AQ15c, a back propagation neural network, and AQ-NN.
AQ-NN is a multi-strategy learning technique in that it uses two different representations and two different learning strategies. Specifically, the AQ learning algorithm is used to learn attributional decision rules from training examples. These decision rules are then used to structure a neural network architecture. A back propagation algorithm is then used as a learning step to further optimize the AQ induced descriptions. In such a system, learning times and recognition rates are often significantly decreased, while predictive accuracy is improved, with respect to conventional neural network learning. To learn classes such as ground, grass, trees and sky, hue, intensity, and convolution operators are used to extract features from a user-designated training area. These examples are then presented to the learning system, which induces a class description.
AQ15c, used alone, achieved a predictive accuracy of 94%, while AQ-NN and a standard neural network achieved predictive accuracies near 100%. The training time of AQ-NN was approximately two orders of magnitude shorter than the training time of the standard NN.

8. Our approach

An environment has been developed and implemented which support the interactive processing, classification and browsing of medical images. Such an environment can be used over an existing Image DataBase (IDB) system for the purpose of assisting the interaction between the user and the IDB. An "Image DataBase" (IDB) is a "system in which a large amount of image data and their related information are integratedly stored". Important considerations in the design and implementation of IDB systems are: image feature extraction, image content representation, organization of stored information, search and retrieval strategies, as well as user interface design. In particular, the following were taking into consideration when designing the system:

8.1 Processing and segmentation of medical images

Before any required image descriptions are extracted and used (e.g., stored or matched with others stored in the IDB), images must first be segmented into disjoint regions or objects (Petrakis and Orphanoudakis, 1992). Segmentation refers to the process of partitioning a digital image into multiple segments (sets of pixels). The goal of segmentation is to simplify and/or change the representation of an image into something that is more meaningful and easier to analyze. Image segmentation is typically used to locate objects and boundaries (lines, curves, etc.) in images. More precisely, image segmentation is the process of assigning a label to every pixel in an image such that pixels with the same label share certain visual characteristics. The result of image segmentation is a set of segments that collectively cover the entire image, or a set of contours extracted from the image (edge detection). Each of the pixels in a region is similar with respect to some characteristic or computed property, such as color, intensity, or texture. Adjacent regions are significantly different with respect to the same characteristic(s). Furthermore, image segmentation help compute a variety of image features specific to a particular image representation. Therefore, the active contours method was used for segmenting images in this research because of its protrusious ability and specific topological effect.

8.2 Classification of medical images

In the classification procedure, each test image is represented using the local features selected. To approximate the posterior probability that a certain local features image belongs to an image in a given class, the *k-nearest* neighbour algorithm was used. This posterior probability is then used to obtain a combined decision for the set of local features. Therefore, images were pre-classified into high level semantic categories like graph or photograph, texture or non-texture, which are relatively simple to classify. After this classification, the retrieval system returns only the images belonging to the same semantic categories.

8.3 Efficient Image Database (IDB) organization

A fast, simple and low complexity technique for image database organization is what is required. The basic idea is to reveal the connectivity relations of the database in order to obtain information of the database structure and facilitate the clustering processes. This will mean partitioning the image database into segments that reduces the search space thereby enhancing faster retrieval since a query addresses only a specific database segment as depicted in Figure 1. It was achieved by randomly selecting a certain number of prototype data and using appropriately the membership values of the rest data points to the selected prototypes. The clustering was easily performed in the final step by using graph theory methodology.

8.4 Retrieval of medical images

Content-based image retrieval (CBIR), a technique that uses visual contents to search images from large scale image databases according to users' interests, has been an active and fast advancing research area since the 1990s. During the past decade, remarkable progress has been made in both theoretical research and system development. Figure 2 shows the general model used in CBIR.

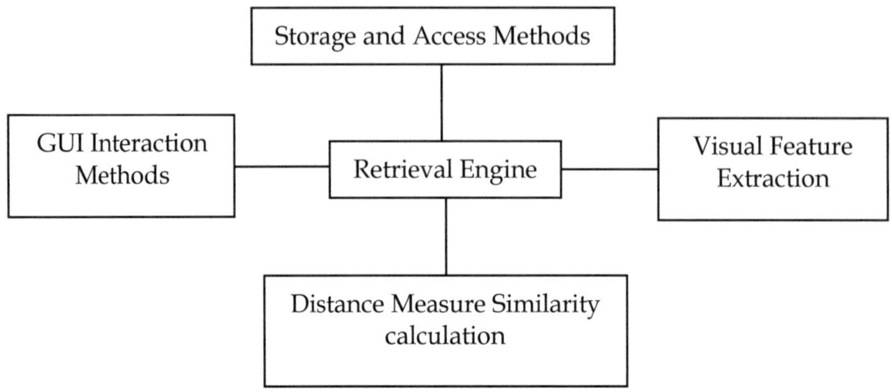

Fig. 1. Principal components of a CBIR system

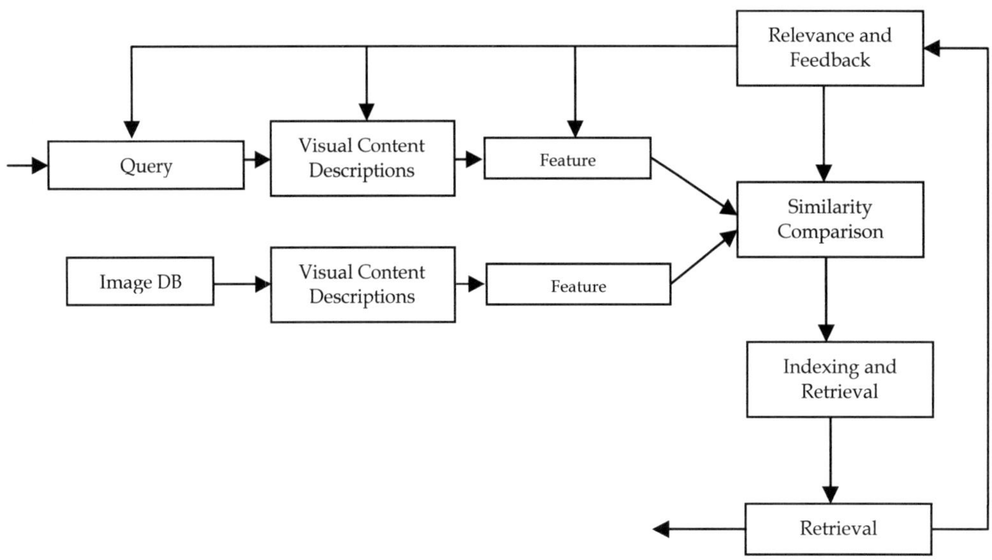

Fig. 2. Diagram of content based image retrieval system

Before the emergence of content-based retrieval, medical images were annotated with text, allowing the images to be accessed by text-based searching. Through textual description, medical images can be managed based on the classification of imaging modalities, regions, and orientation. This hierarchical structure allows users to easily navigate and browse the database. Searching is mainly carried out through standard Boolean queries. However, with the emergence of massive image databases, the traditional text based search suffers from the following limitations:

a. Manual annotations require too much time and are expensive to implement. As the number of images in a database grows, the difficulty in finding desired images increases.

b. Manual annotations fail to deal with the discrepancy of subjective perception. The phrase, "an image says more than a thousand words," implies that the textual description is not sufficient for depicting subjective perception. Typically, a medical image usually contains several objects, which convey specific information. Nevertheless, different interpretations for a pathological area can be made by different radiologists. To capture all knowledge, concepts, thoughts, and feelings for the content of any images is almost impossible.
c. The contents of medical images are difficult to be concretely described in words. For example, irregular organic shapes cannot easily be expressed in textual form, but people may expect to search for images with similar contents based on the examples they provide.
d. Low resolution and strong noise are two common characteristics in most medical images. With these characteristics, medical images cannot be precisely segmented and extracted for the visual content of their features.

For the purpose of this research however, queries can be specified either by a conditional statement indicating various attributes or by specifying an example image (grey level image or sketch). Therefore, a user may point or specify the actual database segment to be searched for and all images satisfying the query criteria will be retrieved. A user is then allowed to make a final selection by browsing the retrieved images in order to determine the correctness (precision) of the retrieved image.

8.5 Browsing the IDB

The main goal of healthcare information infrastructures is to provide the needed information on time, at the right place and to the right persons so as to improve the quality and efficiency of care processes. (Olugbara, 2008). Therefore, in order to achieve this goal, the user interface is loaded with friendly graphical tools and mechanisms, called the "image browser" for both displaying and selecting image classes as well as class their respective properties and schemas.

9. Image representation, indexing, storage and retrieval

Quantized images are commonly represented as sets of pixels encoding color or brightness information in matrix form. An alternative model is based on contour lines. A contour representation enhances easy retrieval of images in a bitmap form. It is primarily used for data compression of an image. The idea is to encode, for each level, the boundaries of connected regions of pixels and to reconstruct an original image from those boundaries. One problem is how to store such representations in a compact manner. In practice, one rarely needs the entire contour representation. An image subset is considered to be the basic entity in the proposed indexing scheme. On the other hand, images are indexed based on representations of the set of all the derived subsets. The objects contained in each group are first ordered. Ordering must be based on criteria that clearly differentiate the objects among them. Position is such a criterion, since objects are usually scattered in the image. Size or shape does not necessarily provide good ordering criteria, since images may contain similar objects. Each of these ordered subsets is then represented by a set of attribute strings corresponding to the set of properties involved in a particular image representation. An individual image subset is indexed by treating each of its corresponding attribute strings as a separate key.

Furthermore, representing image contents is indeed the first problem to face when defining an automatic annotation system. There are different strategies to extract features from images depending on which is considered the most relevant information to capture. As the x-ray images do not contain any color information, edge, shape and global texture features play an important role in this task and were used by several groups (Bo et al., 2005; Deselaers et al., 2005; Liu et al., 2006). Various methods used the pixel values directly and accounted for possible deformation of the images (Image Distortion Model, IDM) (G¨uld et al., 2005; Deselaers et al., 2005). Approaches coming from the object recognition field mostly followed the currently widely adopted assumption that an object in images consists of parts that can be modeled independently. Thus these methods considered local features extracted around interest points and used a wide variety of bag-of-features approaches (Mar´ee et al., 2005; Liu et al., 2006; Tommasi et al., 2007; Avni et al., 2008). Generally the ordering of the visual words is not taken into account and only the frequency of the individual visual word is used to form the feature vectors. However, some groups added the spatial information to patches extracted from images (Deselaers et al., 2006; Avni et al., 2008) after observing that radiographs of a certain body part are typically taken in the same spatial arrangement. Another widely adopted strategy consists of combining different local and global descriptors into a unique feature representation (Bo et al., 2005; Liu et al., 2006; Tommasi et al., 2008a).

9.1 Indexing biomedical images

The purpose of content-based indexing and searching for biomedical image database is now an important subject in the field of image processing. This is because; users of a biomedical image database are often interested in images with similar objects at the finest scale. Therefore, various indexing techniques were reviewed and analyzed for suitable use. This has to do with selecting the rules that form the basis of the annotation process. Many different indexing strategies were applied and while in the earlier years nearest neighbour-based approaches were most common and most successful; for example, (Deselaers et al., 2005; G¨uld et al., 2005), in 2006 and later, discriminative approaches such as log-linear models (Deselaers et al, 2006), and decision trees (Setia et al, 2008), as well as Support Vector Machines (Setia et al, 2008; Tommasi et al, 2008a; Avni et al, 2008) became more and more common and outperformed the nearest neighbor-based approaches. The training images are used as the image database and the test images are used to query it. For each query, the training images are ranked according to their similarity and the nearest neighbor decision rule is applied, that is, the class of the most similar training image is chosen for every test image.

In this research however, our aim is to propose a system that will be able to link an image or image region with a semantic label that combines the Unified Medical Language Systems (UMLS) concepts and visual percepts using statistical learning. In this way, we have a common language for both images and the associated text. Two complementary indexing schemes were used within this learning framework; that is, a global indexing to access image modality and a local indexing to access semantic local features that are related to modality, anatomy, and pathology concepts.

In our model, a set of disjoint UMLS-based concepts that do -not share common visual instances with visual appearance in medical images is first selected to define a Visual and Medical vocabulary. Secondly, low-level features are extracted from image region instances

z to represent each Visual and Medical terms using color, texture and shape. Thirdly, these low-level features are used as training examples to build hierarchical semantic classifiers according to the Visual Medical vocabulary. The classifier for the Visual Medical vocabulary is designed using Support Vector Machine (SVM) classifiers. The conditional probability that an example z belong to a class c given that the class belongs to its super class C is computed using the softmax function as follows:

$$P(c \mid z, C) = \frac{\exp D_c(z)}{\sum_{j \in C} \exp D_j(z)} \qquad \text{i}$$

Where, Dc is the signed distance to the SVM hyper plane that separates class c from the other classes in C. The probability of a Visual Medical term VMTi for z is:

$$P(VMT_i \mid z) = \prod_{l=1}^{L} P(C^l(VMT_i) \mid z, C^{l-1}(VMT_i)) \qquad \text{ii}$$

Where, L is the number of levels, $Cl-1$(VMTi) is the super class of Cl(VMTi), $C0$(VMTi) is the class for all Visual Medical terms, and $P(Cl$(VMT$i) \mid z$, $Cl-1$(VMTi)) is given by Equation (Lim et al., 2007).

9.2 Image storage

Biomedical images are crucial asset for biomedical research and medical practice. There are multitude of devices for biomedical image acquisition that range from simple; for example, a digital camera coupled with a conventional optical microscope, to complex; for example, specialized equipment for Positron Emission Tomography (PET). These devices are routinely used in the daily medical practice and biomedical research, generating a continuous stream of images. The great majority of these images are digital and a good amount of them are permanently stored in digital image repositories. These image collections are a potential source of information and knowledge. However, the realization of this potential requires effective mechanisms for image storage and retrieval, image analysis, image-collection analysis and image-collection exploration.
Image data can be distinguished into "physical" and "logical" (Chang, 2006). Original (grey level) images, segmented images, and image miniatures are physical images. On the other hand, image related data (information extracted from images, attributes, text etc.) are logical images. Physical and logical images are stored separately in a physical and a logical database respectively (Petrakis and Orphanoudakis, 1992). Pointers are implemented from the logical to the physical database. To reduce storage requirements, physical images are compressed prior to storage and conversely decompressed upon retrievals. Therefore, images are stored in clusters based on the likelihood of being retrieved together in response to a particular query (for example, the set of all images corresponding to a patient's examination may be stored close together on disc). The logical database consists of a set (H_2 …, H_{Kmax}) of relational tables, where K_{max} is the maximum size of image subsets under consideration. The specification of value K_{max} depends on the application. The purpose of each H_k table is to resolve queries which specify k objects. Therefore, K_{max} can be set equal to the maximum number of objects allowed in queries, if such a value can be specified in advance. In general, K_{max} may take any value greater than or equal to 2. Typically, the number of objects specified in image queries is not greater than 6. Therefore, we set $K_{max} = 6$.

The image subsets of size k, $2 \leq k \leq K_{max}$, together with their representations are all stored in table H_k. Each image subset is represented by a tuple of one dimensional strings of the form: (p, r, w, ...) where p is the ordered sequence of object indices, r is its corresponding rank string representing the "left/right" and "below/above" relationships between objects, w is the inclusion string, and the remaining strings correspond to properties of individual objects (Petrakis and Orphanoudakis, 1992). Two such strings have been used, s to encode the size property and c to encode the roundness property of those objects whose indices are in p. Therefore, the representation of an image subset is given a tuple of the form (r, w, s, c). Indexing is performed by creating a secondary index for each attribute string. In general, the logical database may be considered as consisting of a set (H, H_1, H_2 ... H_{Kmax}) of relational tables. Table H stores information about each image as a whole and has attributes such as: image file name, dates, names, text descriptions, image header information etc. Table H_1 on the other hand, can be used to store representations of the shape of objects such as those proposed in (Tsai and Yu, 1985; Stien and Madioni, 1990).
Figure 3 demonstrate how medical images are stored, compressed and retrieved; which means that, the application has to provide access to multi-resolution of sub-region views of images. This requires that the system be able to efficiently extract the views from the stored compressed data. The system typically provides query facilities such as content based retrieval methods that allow the users to search for images in the database.

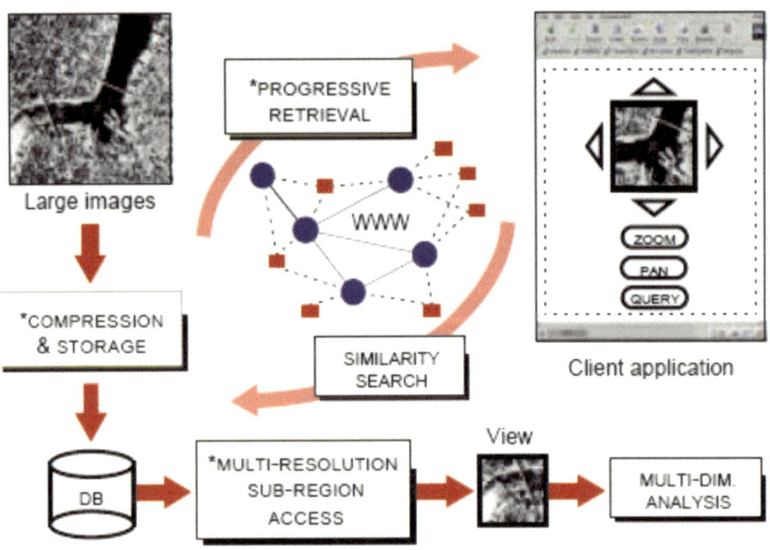

Source: (Smith et al., 1999)

Fig. 3. Large Image Storage and Retrieval Environment

9.3 Image retrieval

Image Database Management Systems (IDBMS) aim to store large collections of image data, and to support efficient content-based retrieval of these data. Like any other Database Management Systems (DBMS), an IDBMS has a storage facility and the data are arranged according to some type of data model. It also has a query facility where images are retrieved according to the queries. All queries address the logical database rather than the raw image data stored in the physical database. Generally the selection queries are used. For example, selecting a few images from the database, based on their content. Imagine a query facility that loads all the images from the database and checks each image to see if it fits the selection criterion. In all but extreme cases this query facility would be inefficient. The only other option is to have more information about the images stored in the database so it can be used for evaluating the selection criterion. This is known as indexing, discussed from the previous section. When an image data is stored in the database, an index is constructed and stored as well for that data. Queries are executed using only the information in the indexes. Images are retrieved only after confirming that the index conforms to the selection criterion. This means that any content information queried must be in the index. Therefore, the type of information in the index limits the expressiveness of any IDBMS query language. Efficient processing of queries in a database requires sophisticated indexing techniques. Content-based querying of medical image databases requires development of indexing techniques that are significantly different than traditional DBMSs. In general, two types of indexes occur: text indexes to facilitate queries of the type "Find all the images that are labeled as 'ear' and content similarity indexes that facilitate queries of the type "Find all the images that are similar, in color, to this sample image". When an IDMBS is to be developed, some extra data types (arrays, images, etc.) are required that are not in the standard relational data model. Therefore, what is needed is an object relational data model with the capacity to store large uninterrupted images.

10. Results

Evaluations have been carried out based on a number of test queries addressing a prototype IDB storing 30 medical images. Queries are distinguished based on the number m of objects they specify. To obtain average performance measures, for each value of m ranging from 2 to 6, 5 image queries have been used and the average performance to queries specifying an equal number of objects has been computed. Measurements of both the answer set (percentage of images returned with respect to the total number of images stored) and of the retrieval response times have been taken and shown in Figure 4. Queries become more specific and the size of an answer set decreases as the number of objects contained in queries increases. Therefore, response time decreases with the number of query objects since search space and thus the amount of information to be processed decreases too.

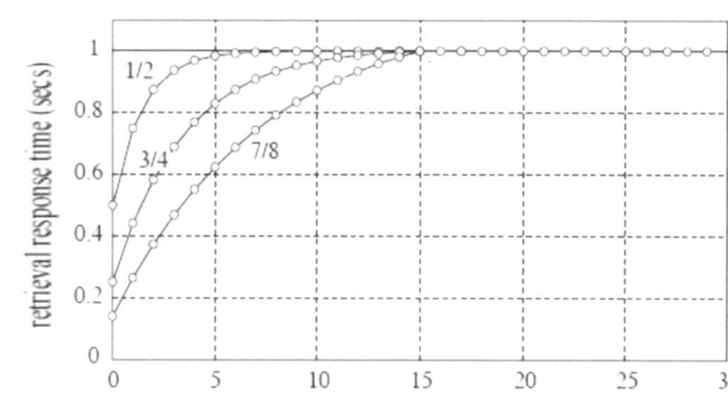

Fig. 4. Number of query objects Vs response time

11. Discussion

An IDB system has been described which supports the efficient processing, archiving, and retrieval of medical images by content. The system consists of an interactive IDB environment, which supports the communication between the user and the various system components, and a methodology which supports the automated indexing and retrieval of images. Such tools and methodologies will be integrated into a prototype IDB system which is currently under development. The system can be easily extended with additional features and mechanisms facilitating the processing and accessing of image data. For instance, the user interface may be extended with additional tools and mechanisms for image registration and image processing, as well as a powerful query language supporting various types of image queries, in addition to queries by example (e.g., queries by specifying an identifier, a class, a hierarchy, range queries etc.), such as those proposed in (Petros and Stelios, 1992). Furthermore, the proposed methodology for image indexing can be easily extended to include the indexing of image sequences in three or four dimensions, where the fourth dimension is time. In developing an IDB system which supports the efficient management of various kinds of image data, is extensible and easy to use, we have to choose an appropriate data model and a database management system (DBMS) which provides persistent storage of both the model and the data, as well as mechanisms for defining, creating, modifying and accessing the model and the data. Furthermore, it must provide a query language, transaction management, concurrency control and authorization for a multiuser environment, as well as performance features such as secondary indexing and clustering.

Such features and mechanisms are inherent within a relational DBMS. Besides, a relational DBMS offers the most direct way of implementing the logical database proposed in this work. However, in order for a DBMS to be appropriate for IDB work it must be augmented with semantic data modeling concepts (e.g., class definition and hierarchies) to assist application modeling. In particular, in developing an IDB system which satisfies the need for a hierarchical database organization, takes advantage of the property of inheritance, and is extensible, the object-oriented approach seems to be more appropriate. All database entities (e.g., various types of data) will be defined as either primitive or complex objects, while system functions (e.g., image processing and retrieval functions) will be defined as methods encapsulated within the same representation with the above database entities. Extensions of relational data models and DBMS's with object-oriented characteristics do exist and can be used to develop an IDB system which satisfies our needs.

However, the main challenge of this system is scalability. Therefore, further research work can focus on developing a system that can accommodate more images.

12. Conclusion

In this research, we have described a method for storage, retrieval and manipulation of digital medical images by content. The system consists of an interactive IDB environment, which supports the communication between the user and the various system components which supports the automated indexing and retrieval of images. Our analytical and empirical results have shown the effectiveness of the image retrieval system. The work also presented a possible direction for further future research.

13. References

Avni, U., Goldberger, J., Greenspan, H., (2008) TAU MIPLAB at ImageClef 2008. In: Working Notesof CLEF 2008, Aarhus, Denmark

Bach, J., Fuller, C., Gupta, A., Hampapur, B., Horowitz, B., Humphrey, R., Jain, R., and Shu, C., (1996). Virage Images Search Engine: An Open Framework for Image Management. *In SPIE Conference on Storage and Retrieval Management for Image Database IV,* vol 2670, pp76-87.

Bo, Q., Wei, X., Qi, T., Chang, S., (2005) Report for annotation task in ImageCLEFmed 2005. In: Working Notes of CLEF 2005, Vienna, Austria

Cohen, S., (1999). Finding Colours and Shape Pattern in Images. PhD, Stanford University.

Cheng, H., Zhicong, H., & Mark, K., (2006). Final Project Proposal-Image Processing Techniques. UCLA Electrical Engineering, EE 113D, Spring.

Dana, H., Ballard, B., and Christopher, M., (1982). *Computer Vision,* chapter 4, pages 119–149. Prentice Hall.

Das, M., Riseman, E., and Draper, B., (1997). FOCUS: Searching for Multi-Coloured Object in a Diverse Image Database. *In; Processing of IEEE Conference on Computer Vision and Pattern Recognition.* Pp756-761.

Deselaers, T., Weyand, T., Keysers, D., Macherey, W., Ney, H., (2005) FIRE in Image CLEF: Combining content-based image retrieval with textual information retrieval. In: CLEF 2005 Proceedings, Springer, Lecture Notes in Computer Science (LNCS), vol 4022, pp 652–661

Deselaers, T.,Weyand, T., and Ney, H., (2006) Image retrieval and annotation using maximum entropy. In: CLEF 2006 Proceedings, Springer, Lecture Notes in Computer Science (LNCS), vol 4730, pp 725–734

Feder, J., (1996). Image Recognition and Content-Based Image Retrieval for the World Wide Web. *Advance Imaging* 11(1):26-28.

Flicker, M.., Sawhney, H., Nibleck, W., Ashley, J., Huang, Q., Dom, B., Gorkani, M., Hafner, J., Lee, D., Petkovic, D., Steele, D. & Yanker, P. (1995). Query by Image and Video Content: The QBIC system. *IEEE Computer.* 28(9), 23-32.

Fridtjof, S., and Gerard, M., (1990). Efficient Two Dimensional Object Recognition. *In Proceedings of 10th International Conference on Pattern Recognition,* pages 13–17, Atlantic City, New Jersey.

Gianni, L., Vernazza, S., Serpico, B., and Silvana G., (1987). A Knowledge-Based System for Biomedical Image Processing and Recognition. *IEEE Transactions on Circuits and Systems,* Cas-34(11):1399–1416.

G¨uld, M., Christian, B., Lehmann, T., (2005) Combining global features for content-based retrieval of medical images. In: Working Notes of CLEF 2005, Vienna, Austria

Gupta, A., and Jain, R., (1997). Visual Information Retrieval. *Comm. Assoc. Comp. Mach.,* vol. 40, no. 5, pp. 70-79.

Hou, T., Hsu, A., Liu, P., and Chiu, M., (1992). A Content-based Indexing Technique Using Relative Geometric Feature. *SPIE Conference on Storage and Retrieval Management for Image Database IV,* vol 1662, pp59-68.

Idris, H., and Panchanathan, R., (1997). Review of Image and Video Indexing Techniques. *Journal of Visual Communication and Image Representation.* 8(2):146-166.

Ioannis, K., (1990). Segmentation and Feature Extraction for Magnetic Resonance Brain Image Analysis. In *Proceedings of 10th International Conference on Pattern Recognition,* pages 583–590, Atlantic City, New Jersey, June 1990.

Lim, J., Chevallet, J., Thi, D., Le, H., and Goh, H., (2007). Bi-modal Conceptual Indexing forMedical Image Retrieval. Satoh, S., Nack, F., and Etoh, M., (Eds.): MMM 2008, LNCS 4903, pp. 456–465,c_Springer-Verlag Berlin Heidelberg.

John, S., Vittorio, C., and Chung-Sheng L., (1999). Adaptive Storage and Retrieval of Large Compressed Images. IS&T/SPIE Symposium on Electronic Imaging: Science and Technology-Storage and Retrieval of Images Database VII. Pp 2.

Ma, W., and Manjunath, B., (1997). NaTra: A Toolbox for Navigating Large Image Databases. *Proc. IEEE Int. Conf. Image Processing*, pp. 568-71.

Minka, T., and Picard, R., (1997). Interactive Learning with a Society of Models. Pattern Recognition 30(4):565-581.

Muller, H., Michoux, N., Bandon, D. & Geissbuhler, A. (2004). A Review of Content-based Image Retrieval Systems in Medical Application-clinical Benefits and Future Directions. *International Journal of Medical Informatics*. 73(1), 1-23.

Niblack, W., Barber, R., Equitz, W., Flickner, M., Glassman, E., Petkovic, D., Yanker, P., Faloutsos, C., Taubin, G., and Height, W., (1993). Querying Image by Content using Color, Texture and Shape. *SPIE Conference on Storage and Retrieval Management for Image Database IV*, vol 1908, pp173-187.

Lehmann, T., Guld, M., Thies, C., Fischer, B., Spitzer, K., Keysers, D., Ney, H., Kohnen, M., Schubert, H., & Wein, B. (2003). The IRMA Project: A State of the Art Report on Content-based Image Retrieval in Medical Applications. *Proceedings of Korea-Germany Joint Workshop on Advanced Medical Image Processing*. 161-171.

Liu, J., Hu, Y., Li, M., Ma, S., Ying, M., (2006). Medical image annotation and retrieval using visual features. In: CLEF 2006 Proceedings, Springer, Lecture Notes in Computer Science (LNCS), vol 4730, pp 678–685

Olugbara, O. (2008). Content-based image retrieval in Healthcare information infrastructure for Classification and diagnosis. PhD Thesis, University of Zululand, South Africa.

OVE, and Chabot, S., (1995). Retrieval from a Relational Database of Images. *Computer*. Pp 40-48.

Petros, K., and Stelios, C., (1991). Graphical Tools and Retrieval Strategies for Image Indexing by Content. In *Proceedings of Computer Assisted Radiology, CAR91*, pages 519–524, Berlin, July 1991.

Pentland, A., Picard, R., and Sclaroff (1996). Photobook: Content-based Manipulation Image Databases. *International Journal of Computer Vision*, 18(3):233-254.

Rubner, Y., (1999). Perceptual Metrics for Image Database Navigation, PhD Dissertation, Computer Science Department, Stanford University.

Setia, L., Teynor, A., Halawani, A., Burkhardt, H., (2008) Grayscale medical image annotation using local relational features. Pattern Recognition Letters 29(15):2039–2045

Smeulders, A., Worring, M., Santini, S., Gupta, A. & Jain, R. (2000). Content-based Image Retrieval at the End of the Early Years. *IEEE Transactions on Pattern Analysis and Machine Intelligence*. 22(12), 1349-1380.

Smith, J., (1997). Integrated Spatial and Feature Image Systems: Retrieval, Analysis and Compression. PhD Thesis, University of Columbia.

Shi-Kuo, C., (1989). *Principles of Pictorial Information Systems Design*, chapter 8, pages 172–211. Prentice Hall International Editions, Englewood Cliffs, New Jersey 07632.

Tommasi, T., Orabona, F., Caputo, B., (2008a). CLEF2008 Image Annotation Task: an SVM Confidence–Based Approach. In: Working Notes of CLEF 2008, Aarhus, Denmark

Tsai, W., and Shiaw-Shian., Y., (1985). Attributed String Matching with Merging for Shape Recognition. *IEEE Trans. on Patt. Anal. and Mach. Intel.*, 7(4):453–462.